RENDEZVOUS WITH DESTINY

The 101st Airborne Division, which was activated on August 16, 1942, at Camp Claiborne, Louisiana, has no history, but it has a rendezvous with destiny . . .

MAJ. GEN. WILLIAM C. LEE IN GENERAL
ORDERS No. 5, HEADQUARTERS 101ST
AIRBORNE DIVISION, AUGUST 19, 1942

Rendezvous With Destiny

A History of
The 101st Airborne Division

•

By
LEONARD RAPPORT
AND
ARTHUR NORTHWOOD, Jr.

KONECKY&KONECKY

Konecky & Konecky
72 Ayers Point Rd.
Old Saybrook, CT. 06475

Copyright © 1948 by 101st Airborne Division Association

ISBN: 1-56852-376-2

The Publishers gratefully acknowledge the assistance of
Captain Vincent Vicari for help in the preparation of this edition.

Printed in the United States of America

101ST AIRBORNE DIVISION ASSOCIATION

7698 State Route 41
P.O. Box 101
Bentonville, OH 45105

July 6, 2001

Sean Konecky
W. S. Konecky Associates, Inc.
72 Ryers Point Road
Old Saybrook, CT 06475

Dear Mr. Konecky:

The 101st Airborne Division Association is proud to endorse the publishing of this edition of *Rendezvous with Destiny*.

Our sincere appreciation goes to authors Leonard Rapport and Arthur Norwood, Jr., and to historian S.L.A. Marshall for his contributions to this outstanding story and its glorious history of the Screaming Eagles.

This book is more than a tribute to the gallantry of this great Division. It is a needed voice for every freedom-loving person. The publisher has our appreciation for extending its life.

James H. Patton, Jr.
Executive Secretary/Treasurer

THE 101ST AIRBORNE DIVISION ASSOCIATION, under President Murray L. Cohen, is proud to publish this second edition of Rendezvous with Destiny.

The 101st Airborne Division Association was founded in Southern Germany in June, 1945, at the conclusion of hostilities in Europe by combat veterans of the 101st Airborne Division who had served in Normandy, Holland, Bastogne, Belgium, Alsace, the Ruhr Pocket, and Southern Germany. Its purpose as, and is, "to preserve in patriotic reverence the memory of the fame and glory of the 101st Airborne Division, to maintain and strengthen the bonds of comradeship that distinguished the men of that Division, and to provide for the gathering and dissemination of information concerning these men and for their periodic assembly in local and national reunions." To this purpose, the 101st Airborne Division Association has been pleased to include the men of the current 101st Airborne Division who have served their country in peace and war in carrying on the traditions of the great 101st Airborne Division.

Since 1946, an annual Reunion has been held and thirteen local chapters formed to carry out the purpose cited above. A periodical named, "The Screaming Eagle," is published regularly and distributed to all members. Membership is open to any individual who served honorably with the 101st Airborne Division. The 101st Airborne Division Association has supported the active Division by awards to outstanding individuals and units.

The 101st Airborne Division is proud to publish this outstanding story which included pages of glorious American history in accord with its motto of, "Keep That Eagle Screaming".

101st AIRBORNE DIVISION ASSOCIATION
NAT.-SEC (1962-1972)

Walter L. Miller, Jr.
Secretary-Treasurer
Lt. Col., USA-RET.

Contents

Maps

PREFACE BY:
GENERAL DWIGHT D. EISENHOWER

DDE

Palm Desert, California
April 1, 1965

101ST AIRBORNE DIVISION

Learning that a history of the 101st Airborne Division
is soon to be published, I not only send best wishes to
the success of the project but, responding to the invitation
of the editors, I wish to express something of the sense
of obligation I feel to all members of the Allied Forces
who fought so valiantly and brilliantly in conquering Hitler
and his minions.

I sent the 101st Division on many important missions;
never once did its fighting men fail to add new luster to
their reputation as one of the finest units in the Allied
Forces. To every alumnus of the Division I send warm
greetings along with my gratitude and the hope that each
will enjoy a long life of health and happiness.

Dwight D. Eisenhower

PREFACE BY:
GENERAL MAXWELL D. TAYLOR

EMBASSY
OF THE
UNITED STATES OF AMERICA

American Embassy,
Saigon, Viet-Nam,
March 8, 1965.

On the occasion of the publication of the new edition
of "Rendezvous with Destiny", I should like to salute anew
the 101st Airborne Division, both as I knew it in World
War II and as it is today. The original history of the Division
recorded its deeds along the road which led from Normandy
through Holland, Bastogne and Alsace to Berchtesgaden. Its
exploits attested the quality of the officers and men who
composed it, and the white crosses along its route are evidence of their gallantry and unstinted devotion to duty.
The records made by the members of the Division in later
years in military and civil life are impressive proof of the
fact that this was an unusual Division filled with unusual
men.

The present Division with its great past record in war
typifies in peace the potential mobile strength of the U.S.
Army to cope with the military requirements of a new age.
It is one of the elite Divisions held in strategic reserve
for employment worldwide in any military contingency which
may arise. It must be ready to reinforce U.S. troops already
deployed in Europe or in the Pacific or to enter new and un-
developed areas where military strength is to be applied.
It must be prepared for nuclear conflict, for conventional
combat, similar to that of World War II, or for defense
against the new and favored technique of Communism, "The War
of Liberation", such as we know in South Viet-Nam. Thus,
our Division has a new and expanded role which makes virtually
every country in the world a possible field for its employment. Armed with improved weapons, provided with extended
mobility and ever animated by the intrepid spirit which has
always characterized its officers and men, the new Division,
like its forbear of World War II, is a mighty force for peace
and for the security of our nation.

To all Screaming Eagles, old and young, past and present,
an affectionate greeting from its World War II Commander.

Maxwell D. Taylor
Maxwell D. Taylor

PREFACE BY:
GENERAL A. C. McAULIFFE

WASHINGTON, D.C.

The sage of the 101st Airborne Division is pretty well known to the American public because of the reporting by press, radio and subsequent books of the great fighting qualities of the airborne troopers and because of the continued brilliant record of public service to the division commander, General Maxwell D. Taylor, now Ambassador to South Viet Nam.

Initially "Rendezvous with Destiny" was written by two platoon leaders of the Screaming Eagles, Lieutenants Leonard Rapport and Arthur Norwood, Jr. Much of their source material comes from the writings of the military expert, Brigadier General S.L.A. Marshall, historian of the European Theatre during World War II. General Marshall became fascinated by the exploits of the 101st airborne invasion of Normandy and covered in detail the later operations in the airborne invasion of Holland and the siege of Bastogne. This new edition has been brought up to date with a chapter on the present active division stationed at Fort Campbell, Kentucky.

There were no official textbooks to guide us in the tactical employment of airborne troops. We had only the limited data available from our own small operation in Sicily and the German experiences at Eben Emael and Crete.

But our lack of knowledge of this new form of warfare was balanced by the courage, toughness, vitality and aggressiveness of the individual airborne soldier. He had no equal as a fighting man. This history conveys something of the severe discipline, the rigors of weather, the rugged combat and the usually unpleasant living conditions which this great soldier accepted in order to accomplish the mission.

Today a new generation of troopers is making the same sort of sacrifices as their pioneer forebearers did in the 1940's. It seems to be the consensus of war veterans, serving with the present division, that these new troopers are superior in almost every way to their predecessors of World War II. What mighty fellows they must be. And how comforting it is to know that our country can still depend upon such a worthy bulwark for the preservation of peace.

acme auliff

A.C. McAuliffe
General, U.S.A. (ret)
Washington, D.C.
March 22, 1965

PREFACE BY:
GENERAL B. E. POWELL

The history of the 101st Airborne Division was not to end, finally, with the triumph of American arms on the battlefields of World War II. To meet the rising challenge of communist imperialism, its colors were uncased and the best of a new generation of soldiers was chosen to fill its ranks again. Today, ever ready to keep its "Rendezvous With Destiny," the Division of that new generation does credit to the great heritage of Bastogne.

The place of the 101st is secure in the annals of military history; its exploits in combat will be remembered for as long as men honor the memory of valor.

But events of historical significance in the life of a military unit are not limited to the battlefield. In this cold war era new history is being made by the Screaming Eagles. It is being made over the drop zones, on the firing ranges, in the logistical installations, at the headquarters. It is being made wherever troopers of this Division practice their art and perfect their skills.

The professional accomplishments of the succeeding members of the 101st Airborne Division merit a permanent record. It is to this purpose that the continuation of the Division's published history is dedicated.

B. E. POWELL
Major General, US Army
Division Commander 1965

Introduction

RENDEZVOUS WITH DESTINY began in the fall of 1945 when the job of writing a history of the 101st Airborne Division was assigned to Lieutenant Arthur Northwood, Jr., a platoon leader in the 501st Parachute Infantry Regiment. Northwood asked for and obtained as co-author a friend he had known at the Parachute School at Fort Benning, Georgia, a platoon leader in the 502d Parachute Infantry Regiment, Lieutenant Leonard Rapport. Work began at St. Germain-en-Laye, France, where Colonel S. L. A. Marshall, ETO Historian, offered the two officers the facilities of his Historical Section. After two months of research and writing work stopped when the 101st was inactivated, and the authors, as members of the 82d Airborne Division, were redeployed to the United States. Work began again in early 1946 at the offices of the publishers of the history, the Infantry Journal Press of Washington, D. C. That summer, Lieutenant Northwood, who had a wife and a home in New York City, returned to civilian life, leaving his bachelor co-author to finish the assignment. However, as a civilian Northwood continued to contribute his time and effort toward the completion of the book.

Lieutenant Northwood wrote the U. S. and Holland chapters. For the first eight days of the Bastogne battle, Colonel Marshall's book, *Bastogne*, has been reprinted, with a few omissions and additions. Lieutenant Rapport is responsible for the balance of the history.

Airborne operations, because of their nature, are likely to be conducted with few written records. Work on this history began when most of the outstanding participants of the 101st Airborne Division's major campaigns were dead, hospitalized, or had returned home. It very soon became apparent to the two historians that the biggest break they were to have, had a beginning in the spring of 1944.

That spring, just before Normandy, Colonel Marshall decided to cover personally the airborne phase of the invasion. Almost as soon as the fighting was over Colonel Marshall was interviewing officers and men, companies and battalions, of the 101st Airborne Division, to reconstruct significant actions. From these combat interviews came a series of detailed regimental, battalion, and small-unit studies: *Cassidy's Battalion, The Fight at the Lock, 506 Parachute Infantry Regiment in Normandy Drop,* and *The Carentan Causeway Fight.* A similar series was also written on the actions of the 82d Airborne Division.

Normandy confirmed Colonel Marshall's interest in the airborne. When the 101st went into Holland, Marshall and his assistant, Captain John G. Westover, followed, and from this campaign came *Parachute Battalion in Holland* and *502d Regiment at Best.*

When the encirclement at Bastogne was broken, Colonel Marshall,

Captain Westover, Lieutenant A. Joseph Webber, and Artist Olin Dows came into the town to begin a study of the battle—a study made while Bastogne was still nearly surrounded and the fiercest fighting was going on. The result was. *Bastogne: The Story of the First Eight Days,* published in 1945 by the Infantry Journal Press.

All of this material prepared by Colonel Marshall and his assistants was made available by the Historical Section of the War Department, and extensive use has been made of it in this history. Some of it had to be omitted or shortened because of length; parts have been rewritten or paraphrased to fit the requirements of this history; much of it has been used in its original form.

Besides Colonel Marshall and his assistants, literally hundreds of persons had a part in the writing of this history. After they had built up the framework of their story, the historians found that there remained many gaps. So for about a year mimeographed questionnaires were distributed monthly to over three thousand members of the 101st Airborne Division Association. Each month scores of answers were received. The historians entered into extensive correspondence with some of these veterans. Sometimes these correspondents were able to furnish names and addresses of other men who in turn were able to fill in the gaps. To all these men, whose names are too numerous to be listed here, the historians and this history are indebted.

The ideal way to have reconstructed the action of the 101st Airborne Division would have been to have followed Colonel Marshall's method: to gather together as soon as possible the participants on the scene of action and with their help decide what happened. Since this was impossible the historians adopted the following method: First, from all available records and sources they constructed the skeleton of their narrative. This skeleton they fleshed with material obtained from interviews with available participants, from the questionnaires, and from additional material gathered from such sources as German Army records, histories and records of other units, diaries, correspondence, and the like. When the chapters were thought to be substantially complete they were taken or sent to several Army posts where there were stationed the largest remaining groups of 101st veterans. At those places these groups would gather and discuss with the authors or pass around to read the chapters, making additions and corrections, and offering criticisms and suggestions.

This method proved very effective. These men, with maps and records to jog their memories, were able to be of great assistance. Almost always there was someone with first-hand knowledge to throw light on vague or disputed points. Whenever anything questionable arose—details of actions, names of persons, dates, and so on—a question in the monthly questionnaire usually brought in at least one response from someone with first-hand knowledge.

When the history was completed there was an obvious lack of balance in the space given to the various actions. Some unit actions, such as the 502d's fight on the Carentan Causeway which had been recorded in such effective detail by Colonel Marshall, received .much more space than other actions of almost equal importance but of which no such record was made at the time and for which such a detailed account could no longer be reconstructed. Rather than balance the history by cutting, the authors are leaving in this material which otherwise might never be available to the men who fought in these actions; and they express their regret that the less detailed accounts could not have been made equally as complete even at the cost of lengthening an already long book.

Of the many veterans of the 101st Airborne Division to whom this history is indebted there were some who, because of their assignments as Division staff or command officers, were best able to get an overall picture of what happened during the 101st's campaigns. It was to these men, at Washington, West Point, Fort Bragg, Fort Benning and Fort Monroe, that the authors turned most frequently. Of the many who gave so generously of their time in reading the manuscript and discussing personally or by letter parts of this history, the authors wish to list those on whom they most often called:

Generals William C. Lee (who sometimes talked or wrote from inside an oxygen tent), Maxwell D. Taylor, Anthony C. McAuliffe, and Gerald J. Higgins; Colonels Robert F. Sink, Ned D. Moore, Harry W. O. Kinnard, Joseph H. Harper, Allen W. Ginder, Charles H. Chase, Ray C. Allen, John H. Michaelis, Steve A. Chappuis, Thomas L. Sherburne, Jr., and Julian J. Ewell; Majors Larry Legere, Walter L. Miller, Jr., and Elvie B. Roberts; and Captains Lincoln Stevenson, Frank L. Lillyman, and Lawrence Critchell. In an effort·to achieve accuracy some of these officers, at the request of the historians, read the manuscript completely through several times.

Some of the outstanding writing in this history are excerpts from an as-yet unpublished manuscript by a former soldier of the 506th Parachute Infantry Regiment, David Kenyon Webster. A number of wartime diaries and narratives were loaned by former members of the 101st: extensive use was made of those of George E. Koskimaki, Thomas B. Bruff, and Glen A. Derber. A valuable contribution was received from Melton H. McMorries. Al Brodell collected a large amount of data for the historians during the first months of research. Credit is given throughout the text to a number of other persons whose contributions are used.

The publication of this history was made possible by the 101st Airborne Division Association which underwrote the cost of publication. The Secretary-Treasurer of the Association, Carl E. Trimble, worked constantly with the historians. No call was ever made on him on which he did not come through. This former Arizona cowboy who lost a leg at Carentan rode herd on his two historians until they finally produced a book.

Thanks are due the following: Colonel Joseph I. Greene and the staff of the Infantry Journal Press for their never-failing cooperation; the Historical Division, War Department Special Staff, for permission to use material from their publications and for reproduction rights to a number of maps; to Gordon A. Harrison, Roland G. Ruppenthal, and Mrs. Cecilia G. Markey and other members of the Historical Division; to Charles Wahrman, who contributed work on a number of maps used in this history; to the members of the Departmental Records Branch of the Adjutant General's Office and especially to Miss Thelma K. Yarborough, Miss Margaret Emerson and Royce Thompson; to Harcourt, Brace & Company for permission to quote from Ralph Ingersoll's *Top Secret;* to the Ziff-Davis Publishing Company for permission to quote from Robert E. Merriam's *Dark December;* to the *Military Surgeon* for permission to quote the material beginning on page 469; to H. I. Phillips for permission to reprint his poem, "Tony McAuliffe's Answer;" to Bill Mauldin and United Features Syndicate for permission to reproduce the cartoon on page 714; to Press Association for permission to reproduce the photographs on pages 5, 6 and 742; to the editors of *Life* for their courtesy in allowing the historians to go through their picture files and to use "The Incredible Patrol" by Corporal Russ Engel, the map which accompanies the article and which was the basis of the map reproduced on page 404; and the photographs by *Life* photographers Robert Capa on page 592 and William Vandivert on pages 746 and 748, all this material being reprinted from *Life* and copyrighted by Time, Inc., 1945; and to the U. S. Army Signal Corps for the majority of the remaining photographs in this book.

There is one last personal acknowledgment. Only the authors know how indebted they are to Major Leo H. Schweiter, last G-2 of the 101st. If anybody can be called the father of this history, Hank Schweiter is that man.

. . . I saw men crying that day . . .

. . ..I knew him in basic at Wheeler. He was real quiet there. Then
the Army changed him, did something to him. He began hollering
at guys in other companies. When everybody was tired and could
hardly make it he'd go right along with his machine gun; he was a
machine-gunner even back then. In the 'troops he was always kidding
the officers. He'd even kid the colonel—not disrespectful, you understand. Everybody in the battalion, in the regiment, knew him . . .

. . . He was a real soldier. He wouldn't take a commission. We wanted
to make him a staff but Pfc was as high as he wanted to go. On the
range you'd see him fire, pull a patch out of his pocket and run it
through the bore. It wasn't that he bucked—he was just a good soldier.

. . . Sir, he was the best soldier I've ever known. He was good in
garrison and a good field soldier. He was an expert machine-gunner.
Sir, he was the best soldier an officer could have . . .

. . . If every machine gun in the battalion quit firing and there was one
still going it would be his . . .

. . . He got the Silver Star in Normandy. I don't remember what for;
he was just a good soldier . . .

. . . He and Kelly and Jantosik were going in business together; they
were always talking about it. Now he and Jantosik are dead and Kelly's
gone home wounded . . .

. . . He saved his candy to throw to the kids.. Things like that. He was
lots of fun . . .

. . . He got shot in the head—never knew what hit him. I'm glad he
got it the way he did. Captain Cody wouldn't leave him out there—
had his body brought back to the CP . . .

. . . He kept telling me, "Kid, I'm going to get you home" . . .

Neither of the authors of this history knew the man about whom
these things were said, but one of us was for a time leader of the platoon
of which he had been a member, heard many men speak of him, and
recorded some of the things they said. His name was William F.
Haddick, Private First Class. He was one of approximately 2,043 men
of the 101st—from private to general—who died in the war. And
because most of their names, like his, never have occasion to appear
in this history, because their deaths, like his, are generally recorded
in words such as those which head this page, and because each of them
left a similar legacy, greater or less, in the memory of his comrades,
we dedicate this history to Bill Haddick as representative of all the men
of the 101st Airborne Division who didn't come back.

RENDEZVOUS WITH DESTINY

The U.S.

August 16, 1942 . . . eight months after Pearl Harbor . . . nine days after the Guadalcanal landing . . . twelve weeks before the North African invasion. An American people still unaware of the beating they were taking, and equally unaware of the immensity of the forces they had set in motion to avenge that beating. An American Army, still untried, but expanding with increasing speed, strenuously training to qualify for its coming job. Three years, less one day, before that Army and that people won complete victory.

August 16, 1942. Activation Day for the 101st Airborne Division at Camp Claiborne, Louisiana. It was a strange form of activation for it meant the amoeba-like breaking-in-two of one of the most promising divisions in the United States Army, the 82nd.

The 82nd Infantry Division was not among the best accidentally. It had only recently been taken through basic training by Maj. Gen. Omar Nelson Bradley who had just left it to go on to higher assignments. It was this outfit which the War Department, in the early summer of 1942, decided to split into two new airborne divisions.

Nothing could happen in Washington without a parallel flock of rumors arising in Claiborne, and in late July one of the most fascinating reports of all started to fly across company streets, through latrines and orderly rooms: "We're going airborne!" No one knew if it were true, and certainly no one knew what it meant. Privates and sergeants together hoped that any future training would be easier than the weeks of basic they had just been through. Surely, they felt, long hikes were out. And it was such an exciting rumor that even staid first sergeants were seen to lose their dignity and with spinning arms outflung, come circling into their orderly rooms shouting "Airborne!"

Rumors crystallized into knowledge in early August when Brig. Gen. Matthew B. Ridgway, who had succeeded General Bradley as commander, announced that the Division had been selected for airborne training. A few days later, word of the split was also confirmed.

With these developments for a background, the first and last review of the 82nd (still being referred to in Washington as a motorized division) was held on August 15, with Maj. Gen. Oscar W. Griswold, commander of the IV Corps, participating as guest of honor. General Bradley was also present. As the Alexandria *Town Talk* described it, "Fifteen thousand sun-bronzed American men from all of the forty-eight United States marched together for the first and last time at Camp Claiborne as the 82nd All-American Infantry Division." But to many of the men that Saturday afternoon, the heat and glare of the

1

Major General William C. Lee, father of U. S. Airborne

midsummer Louisiana sun suddenly became more important than the news or the guests or their newly acquired military discipline. They quietly fainted in their tracks.

The next day was Sunday, ever a significant day of the week for the 101st. It was on a Sunday in June that Colonel Cole was to order the bayonet charge on the causeway at Carentan. It was on a Sunday in September that the 101st was to hurtle into Holland. It was on a Sunday in December that General McAuliffe was to call his staff together and say: "All I know of the situation is that there has been a breakthrough and we have got to get up there." And it was on this Sunday in August that Col. Don F. Pratt, Acting Division Commander, issued General Order No. 1:

The 101st Airborne Division is activated at 0001 this date, and will be composed of the following units:

Headquarters, 101st Airborne Division
Headquarters Company, 101st Airborne Division
327th Glider Infantry
401st Glider Infantry
502nd Parachute Infantry, Fort Benning, Ga.
(without change of station)
Headquarters and Headquarters Battery, 101st Airborne Division Artillery
377th Parachute Field Artillery Battalion
321st Glider Field Artillery Battalion
907th Glider Field Artillery Battalion
101st Airborne Signal Company
326th Airborne Engineer Battalion
426th Airborne Quartermaster Company
326th Airborne Medical Company

The next day Brig. Gen. William C. Lee arrived and, taking charge, gave the Division its mission in a prophetic message.

The 101st . . . has no history, but it has a rendezvous with destiny. Like the early American pioneers whose invincible courage was the foundation stone of this Nation, we have broken with the past and its traditions to establish our claim to the future. Due to the nature of our armament and the tactics in which we shall perfect ourselves, we shall be called upon to carry out operations of far-reaching military importance, and we shall habitually go into action when the need is immediate and extreme.

The men did not then know what he meant. They learned later.

The First Leader

The selection of General Lee to head one of the two new divisions was peculiarly appropriate, for he more than any other man had worked to develop an airborne arm for the United States Army. Even if he had never commanded the 101st Airborne Division, as the "Father of American Airborne Troops" he would still be a part of this story.

General Lee was a North Carolinian and remained closely identified with his state. Ruggedly built, he walked with the gait of the outdoorsman. Born in Dunn, North Carolina, he had always maintained his residence there. He went to Wake Forest and North Carolina State College where he played on the football and baseball teams. When World War I began he was twenty-two. He entered the service with a reserve commission as a second lieutenant in the Infantry. Going to France, he saw combat duty as a platoon leader and later a company commander.

Having received his Regular Army commission in 1920, he spent the next decade doing the rounds of the army schools, and teaching military science at North Carolina State College. Always forward-looking, he gradually emerged as an expert on tank warfare with a reputation for knowing more about foreign armor than any other American. During one of his two extended trips to Europe in the thirties he spent a full year as an officer in a French armored unit. Returning to this country he taught at the Tank and Infantry School, won a B.S. in Education at the University of North Carolina, attended the Command and General Staff School, and saw further troop duty. He was then ordered to the Office of the Chief of Infantry in Washington. It was there that the airborne story really begins.

It was there that Major Lee became the leading member of that small group of men who, by their combined vision, persuasiveness, stubbornness and daring, were to bring about the creation of airborne divisions by the time the U. S. Army had to have them.

U.S. Airborne History

It was an American who first sensed the possibilities of vertical envelopment. Almost two centuries ago Benjamin Franklin said: "Five thousand balloons capable of raising two men each could not cost more than five ships of the line; and where is the prince who could afford so to cover his country with troops for its defense as that ten thousand men descending from the clouds might not in many places do an infinite deal of mischief before a force could be brought together to repel them."

During World War I, Brig. Gen. William Mitchell had conceived the idea of using parachute troops to break the stalemate of trench warfare on the Western Front. He received provisional approval of the idea and tentatively planned for November, 1918, in the Metz sector a drop of something less than a division. It was to be a build-up drop and was to be reinforced and resupplied by a breakthrough in the sector. The 1st Division was picked as the unit which would furnish the personnel, and a few men, mostly from the Regular Army, volunteered to jump experimentally. To investigate the possibilities of

Three U. S. Army planes drop parachutists during
maneuvers near San Antonio, Texas, 5 November 1928.

the operation, General Mitchell assigned his A-3, Lt. Col. Lewis H. Brereton. Colonel Brereton found that although enough bombers could be got together from all Allied sources to transport such a force there would not be enough parachutes available (and these were of the rip-cord type) nor were there any weapons other than the standard ground types. Before anything except paper planning was done the break-through by the Allies occurred and the war ended. Colonel Brereton was to wait twenty-six years before another war placed him in command of the world's first airborne army.

During the twenties and thirties the American Army showed very little interest in airborne troops.

In 1928 and 1929 small-scale experiments in dropping parachutists and weapons were conducted at Kelly and Brooks Fields, Texas. But during the 1930s both the Russians and the Germans carried out extensive experiments, and peacetime paratrooping probably reached a climax with the reported Russian use of five thousand paratroopers in their maneuvers at Kiev in 1936.

It was not until war was again upon the world that the U.S. Army

The parachutists set up the machine gun dropped with them, 5 November 1928.

began to think seriously in airborne terms. Late in 1939 Capt. (later Maj. Gen.) Laurence S. Kuter of the War Department General Staff wrote the original memorandum which indicated the practicality of transporting troops by air. The memorandum was sent to the Chief of Infantry's Office and was routed to Major Lee. Long discussions followed and preliminary plans were made. The question of where to put the new troops quickly arose. It is not precisely true, as some detractors have said, that the Infantry and the Air Corps fought over who was to have the airborne troops, and the Infantry lost. For there were three sides to the argument; the Engineers also claimed them on the ground that they would be primarily saboteurs. And the Air Corps really wanted its "Marines," planning to call them Air Corps Grenadiers. But Maj. Gen. George A. Lynch, Chief of Infantry, made the point, remade many times since then, that once these troops got on the ground they would be ground fighters. Infantry won the argument. In the Office of the Chief of Infantry it was Major Lee who had primary responsibility for developing this new kind of fighting unit.

First thought was given to parachutists. Correspondence was initiated with the Infantry Board and the Infantry School which was to lead to placing the experimental work at Benning. Even while this correspondence was being processed the Germans gave a clear illustration of what paratroopers could accomplish by their masterful use of them in the Holland invasion. Suddenly seizing and holding bridges far out beyond their national borders, the German paratroopers made it possible for an armored column to do in hours and days what the Dutch had thought would require weeks. And Holland was quickly overrun. Little did Major Lee realize, as he speeded the paper work there in Washington, that one day his own division would land by air and help the Allies fight their way back over these same Dutch roads and bridges.

6

There was much to be done. After extensive inquiries, Major Lee found that the U.S. Forest Service in the West knew more about dropping men and equipment on a precise spot than any other group in America, and he went out there to learn how they did it. He also studied the meager reports on what few experiments there had been in the U. S. Army in transporting troops by air at Kelly Field, Texas, and in Panama.

Reports went in. Decisions came back. And on the 25th of June, 1940, the War Department directed the formation of a parachute test platoon at Benning, with personnel to be obtained from volunteers in the 29th Infantry on that post.

Test Platoon

The wording of the platoon's mission gives an insight into the tactical use of paratroopers as originally planned, and provides a reminder of the American Army's thinking back in 1940.

" . . . the employment of parachute troops in Hemisphere Defense to seize landing areas where only light opposition is expected, and to secure the areas for short periods until reinforced by air infantry."

Arrangements were made to secure for this platoon the planes and parachutes it needed. With Lts. William T. Ryder and James T. Bassett in charge, it embarked on an experimental eight-week training program that was in many ways to set the pattern for all future jump training in this country. The instructor in the technique of jumping was Warrant Officer Harry M. "Tug" Wilson, who had worked with the 1929 Kelly Field group.

Because of the hazardous nature of their work, the members of the group were authorized flight pay as long as they met flight-pay standards.

Though stationed in Washington, Lee, now a lieutenant colonel, was responsible for over-all direction, and made at least one spectacular alteration in the training program.

Studying the parachute towers at the New York World's Fair, he became convinced that they would help his men master the art of jumping. So on July 29 the Test Platoon was moved to Hightstown, New Jersey, for a week on the tower company's home grounds. Later, four modified towers were installed at Benning.

Back at Benning the Test Platoon made its first jump on August 16, 1940. Each jumper used a standard Air Corps T-3, free-type, human escape parachute; and, in addition, an emergency test-type parachute. The jumps were made from B-18 bombers. A few days later, on

August 21, the War Department issued the following instructions for the training of parachutists: "The initial jump of each individual will be at not less than 1,500 feet; thereafter, the altitude to be determined by the officer conducting training, but at not less than 750 feet without further authority."

On August 29 the first mass jump took place, before a number of high-ranking officers.

So successful was the jump, and so successful was the work of the platoon that in mid-September the War Department authorized the establishment of the 501st Parachute Battalion. Maj. William M. Miley, former Master of the Sword at West Point, was chosen as its commander. Working under him were many of the men who were to become the combat leaders of airborne battalions, regiments and divisions—Higgins, Haugen, Coutts, Sink, Jones, Michaelis, Strayer, Howell, Ewell, Lindquist, Cole and Cassidy.

Provisional Parachute Group

With further expansion already planned, the need for a control group on the spot became increasingly apparent. On March 10, 1941 the War Department set up, again under the Chief of Infantry, the Provisional Parachute Group, with Headquarters at Fort Benning. Lieutenant Colonel Lee was placed in command. The roster of this group contained the names of many combat leaders—Howell, Gavin, Lindquist, Yarborough, Ekman, Ewell. Together they worked on the missions that had been given the Group, developing cadres for future parachute battalions, studying parachute tables of organization and tactical doctrine and preparing training literature. The jump wings and the paratrooper hat patch came out of this period.

Shortly after the establishment of this Group, airborne thinking was modified by the spectacular German success in Crete. The parachute units in the Holland campaign had been small, auxiliary to the main effort. Crete showed that large airborne units operating independently could handle an entire campaign. To the Americans this meant that the independent battalions and small groups of saboteurs which they had been planning might be useful, but larger groups also were necessary. Crete also showed more clearly than Holland the importance of gliders as a means of getting large numbers of men and large amounts of equipment into combat. The Army, through the Air Forces, also started to experiment with them.

Expansion at Benning proceeded. On July 1 the 502d Parachute Battalion was activated. That fall it helped make airborne history by jumping twice in the First Army Carolina maneuvers, and obviously impressing the visiting brass with what a parachute battalion could do. Meanwhile, the establishment on July 10 of the Parachute School as a part of the Infantry School helped to assure a more steady flow of new men. This influx was shortly to make possible the activation of the 503d and 504th Battalions.

Soon the Alabama area of Fort Benning was procured and prepared for airborne use. A vigorous training program on the squad, company and battalion level was initiated.

Finally responding to such opinions as Lt. Colonel Lee's, "I think it would be dull of us to say that parachute troops will seldom be employed in units larger than a battalion," the War Department, on January 30, 1942, directed that four parachute regiments be constituted. The 502d and 503d were soon activated, though the former, because it was used constantly as a source of replacement of both individuals and units for the other airborne outfits, remained badly under strength.

Airborne Command

The establishment of these regiments served further to emphasize the necessity for increased unity of command at some level below that of GHQ. On March 21, 1942, the Airborne Command was set up, with Lee, now a colonel, in charge. Into it was incorporated the 88th Infantry Airborne Battalion, the forerunner of glider troops—a hitherto independent operation under Col. Elbridge G. Chapman. The new group moved from Fort Benning to Fort Bragg.

For his strenuous labors during the next few months General Lee, just before his retirement in 1944 from division leadership, was awarded the Distinguished Service Medal with this citation:

Maj. Gen. William C. Lee, United States Army. For exceptionally meritorious and distinguished service rendered in a duty of great responsibility while organizing and establishing the Airborne Command, Fort Bragg, North Carolina, for the training of airborne units. Through his creative genius he inaugurated and supervised the training of the original parachute groups in the Army of the United States from which the airborne units were developed. As the result of his efforts, the airborne program which exists at the present time was instituted. Major General Lee was instrumental in the establishment of the Parachute School, Fort Benning, Georgia, 15 May 1942. With meager facilities, a few partially trained instructors, and by exceptional ability, force of character and the will to get the job done, he built the framework for a powerful striking force. The creation of the Airborne Command was the first effort of the United States to train airborne units on a major scale.

The Parachute School, now under the control of the Airborne Com-

Field Marshal Sir John Dill, General Lee, and General George C. Marshall inspect paratroopers at Fort Bragg in the spring of 1942.

mand, was expanded still further. The increased flow of recruits made possible the quick activation of the 504th Parachute Infantry, the completion of the 503d and the subsequent activation of the 505th, the 506th and the 507th. Training progressed to such a point that by summer unit night jumps were being undertaken. An artillery test battery was set up with Maj. John B. Shinberger in charge. Personnel and pay problems were thrashed out. Plans were laid to give all infantry divisions some airborne or air transport training. It was still thought that the Army would not have any regular units larger than a regiment specializing in airborne techniques.

The Airborne Division

After two months engrossed in these problems, General Lee (he had been awarded his first star on April 19, 1942) was suddenly and secretly ordered to England in company with Generals Eisenhower, Arnold and Somervell. His mission was to find out what was expected of airborne troops in the invasion of Europe. He also was to study British airborne organization and technique as a possible model for our own. His conversations upon his return led to the inevitable recommendation —the United States needed airborne forces organized as divisions.

He indicated that the old idea of offensive employment of troops was now impractical.

In recent conferences abroad with British airborne commanders, the fixed opinion was held that enemy airfields and landing areas which will permit landing transport airplanes are generally so fortified as to make their capture a costly if not impossible operation. It is the experience of the British that it is highly wasteful to attempt to carry ordinary troops in gliders, as thirty per cent must be eliminated due to air sickness. It has been found that the selection, physical standards and special training for glider troops must approximate that prescribed for parachute troops.

Gen. Lesley J. McNair, Commanding General of Army Ground Forces, who, up to that time had been opposed to the creation of practically all types of special-purpose divisions, reacted favorably to General Lee's analysis. "Consequently," said General McNair in a memo to his chief of staff, "we should inaugurate studies without delay looking to the organization of whatever airborne divisions can be formed from one triangular infantry division, plus the available parachute regiments." He went on to set down the original over-all ratio for an airborne division—two glider units to one parachute unit. He evidently felt that General Lee agreed with him on this ratio, but General Lee, who believed very strongly in just the opposite ratio, thought subsequently that he must have been misunderstood. General McNair's memo made it apparent that he was still thinking in terms of the two-phase landing—a small group (paratroopers) to seize the field and a larger glider group to use it.

General McNair outlined the division set-up, saying in conclusion: "An airborne division should be evolved with a stinginess in overhead and in transportation which has absolutely no counterpart thus far in our military organization."

Thus was the groundwork laid. The Training Division of AGF commented a few days later on the proposed ratio between glider and parachute troops. It indicated that the current British ratio of two parachute for one glider seemed to have been the temporary and accidental result of the fact that at that moment the British had many more parachute troops available. The British also wanted to be prepared for the likely possibility that some of the parachute units might be detached at any moment for smaller independent operations. Its report made the statement that more than once saved the day for the airborne divisions: "The essential point is to provide in the TO that the number of parachute regiments and the number of glider regiments may be varied to meet the training situation or to fit the specific combat operation."

On July 6, 1942, in a memo, General McNair gathered the loose threads together and proposed that the 82d Motorized Division, which had been reactivated March 25, be reorganized into two separate airborne divisions. Each division was to have a strength of 8,321 (contrasting with the regular division's 14,000) and was to consist of two glider regiments, a parachute regiment, division artillery and service units. In this way two airborne divisions could be set up without the basic plans for army expansion in 1942 being altered. The proposal was referred to the Operations Division of the War Department, and by them to General Eisenhower. Both approved.

On July 30 the activation of two airborne divisions was ordered by Army Ground Forces to be effective August 15. This activation was to be accomplished by Third Army, with both divisions assigned to Second Army for supply and administration and to the Airborne Command for training. General Order 86, Headquarters Third Army, dated August 8, did the job. As has already been indicated, General Lee, named for a second star on August 10, arrived at Claiborne on the 17th to take charge of the 101st.

It is significant that these two airborne divisions were planned as small striking forces rather than as regular divisions. Not only was their over-all size much smaller than that of a triangular division— their units were smaller. *The History of the Airborne Command* records that "the parachute and glider infantry regiments had a strength of 1,958 and 1,605 respectively, in contrast to the 3,000 of the standard infantry regiment. All service units were smaller than those of the standard infantry division. Weapons were much the same as in the infantry division with a predominance of the lighter types; the artillery consisted of thirty-six 75mm pack howitzers. Vehicles numbered 408 motors and 239 trailers, a total of 647 in contrast with some 2,000 in the standard infantry division, with a preponderance of jeeps and their trailers."

These figures show a division stripped down to emergency strength from the moment of activation. In the States and in England this was not so bad, even though it meant that at times a regiment would have only six jeeps with which to transact all its business. But even in a quick campaign like Normandy shortages were keenly felt. And when an airborne division was expected to hold a section of the line for a matter of weeks as in Holland or Alsace, these shortages made it extraordinarily difficult to do an effective job.

It was always easy for the casual observer to believe that an airborne division, simply because it was airborne, was more capable in every way than an ordinary division. Such misunderstanding dates from the very first announcements, as when the Alexandria *Town Talk* said in the previously quoted article, "The new divisions will have about 8,000 officers and men. The fire power, relatively speaking, will be far greater than it is of the infantry type [*sic*]."

The net result of the tables of organization was to make the airborne divisions inveterate violators of the TO. By the time the war ended they had come a long way from the standards originally laid down by General McNair.

In the matter of the two-to-one glider-paratroop ratio, there had also been reversal, at first by subterfuge, and later by regulation.

But such changes as these were well beyond the horizon as General Lee arrived in Claiborne to take over his new division.

ORGANIZING THE 101st

General Lee's first job was to supervise the latter stages of the reshuffling necessary to fit the men and units he received from the 82d Division into the strange new TO and get them operating as a division. Some of his organizations had been integral parts of the 82d, with a

World War I record to boast about. Others were new, just established by General Order 24 of the 82d Airborne Division, dated August 15, 1942. Two were still to be constituted. This order of August 15, issued by command of Brigadier General Ridgway, was over the name of Maxwell D. Taylor, Colonel, GSC, Chief of Staff. The battle leader was present at the birth.

The older outfits were the 327th Glider Infantry, the 321st Glider Field Artillery and the 907th Glider Field Artillery. The groups activated on August 15 were the 401st Glider Infantry, the 326th Airborne Engineer Battalion, 377th Parachute Field Artillery, the Division Headquarters and Headquarters Company, the Division Artillery Headquarters Battery, the 101st Airborne Signal Company, the 426th Airborne Quartermaster Company and the 326th Airborne Medical Company. Activated later were the 81st Airborne Antiaircraft Battalion and the 801st Airborne Ordnance Company.

The 502d Parachute Infantry also was part of the Division. It was not brought over from Benning, but waited until the Division moved to Bragg before joining it. More will be said about that later, as well as about the other two parachute regiments—the 506th and the 501st—that fought with the Division.

After its World War I experience, the 327th in 1921 had been constituted as an Organized Reserve unit, assigned to the State of South Carolina. It had been reactivated at Claiborne the preceding March along with the rest of the 82d. Filled up with men fresh from civilian life it had, under the leadership of Col. George S. Wear, just taken them through their basic training.

Since the new TO gave glider regiments only two battalions, it had many more men than it needed. Its extra personnel was used to fill out many of the other units of the Division. It was a complicated process, typified by the following paragraph of the August 15 order:

The 327th less Companies D, H, M and Antitank, is redesignated the 327th Glider Infantry and transferred to the 101st Airborne Division. Companies D, H, M and Antitank are disbanded. The personnel of the 1st Battalion, 327th Infantry, less personnel of Company B, is transferred to the 401st Glider Infantry, 101st Airborne Division. The personnel of Companies H, M and Antitank are transferred to the 327th Glider Infantry, 101st Airborne Division.

The second glider regiment, newly created for its present role, was the 401st. To command it Lt. Col. Joseph H. Harper, a former battalion CO of the 326th, was chosen. Colonel Harper's Army career had the usual varieties of peacetime service—Alaska, Hawaii, Fort Benjamin

Harrison, platoon leader, company commander, aide-de-camp, post adjutant, Benning and Leavenworth. He had graduated from the University of Delaware in 1922, and taken a reserve commission. A cool man, he was destined to inherit some of the worst headaches of the division, and to deal with them in completely successful fashion. He was with the 101st until the end.

His men came from the 327th in the manner just described and from the two infantry regiments remaining in the 82d, the 325th and the 326th.

Some of the 327th personnel were subsequently sent on to fill out the 326th Airborne Engineer Battalion. This also was a newly activated group made up primarily of men from the 82d's 307th Battalion. In accordance with the basic ratio of the Division, it was to have two glider companies and one parachute company. There were as yet no jumpers to put in such a company. So on September 4, the first group of forty-five volunteers was sent to the Parachute School at Fort Benning. The man who was to command this Battalion in Normandy, John C. Pappas, was at this time a captain in charge of Headquarters and Service Company.

Turning to the artillery battalions, the 321st Glider Field Artillery Battalion, like the 327th Glider Infantry Regiment, had been reactivated in March and taken a new group of men through basic training. It boasted that in the subsequent tests it made the best score in the Division. However, all its work during basic had been with 155s and 105s. The change to airborne status meant that it had to start all over again with the pack 75. Lt. Col. Edward L. Carmichael, who commanded it at the time of the split, was to continue as CO throughout combat.

In World War I the 907th was known as the 307th Ammunition Train. Made an Organized Reserve unit in 1921 it changed its designation in January of 1942 and was activated again in March. For it, as well, as for the 321st, going airborne meant the loss of C Battery and Service Battery (or the AA-AT Battery). Among the extra men those who were willing to volunteer for the Parachute School later served with the 377th Parachute Field Artillery Battalion. Lt. Col. C. F. Nelson assumed command of the 907th and led the battalion until inactivation after the war.

The 377th started off as a parachute battalion without any jumpers —and it was in for a rough period of training that fall. All the new artillerymen it received had to be sent to jump school. To add to the confusion, most of the parachute replacements sent to fill out its roster were infantrymen rather than artillerymen, and had to be retrained.

With this personnel situation, the 377th had to take up where the Airborne Command had left off in developing one of the most difficult small-scale operations of the war—getting a battalion of artillery into combat by parachute.

Experiments by the Airborne Group and the Airborne Command had shown that the pack 75mm howitzer and its ammunition could be broken down into nine loads that the 24-foot cargo chute could carry. "The problems of assembly," says the unit historian, "establishment of a complete communications net (both wire and radio), occupation and organization of position, organization of fire direction, employment of survey, and ammunition supply and resupply — all these remained to be worked out." Lt. Col. Benjamin Weisberg, who was to command the battalion on through Normandy, took charge in October.

Division Headquarters Company, Signal Company, Medical Company and Quartermaster Company were activated in the original order, each being composed of about half the officers and men of the similar unit in the 82d.

The Signal Company was made up of four small platoons whose names serve to describe the company duties—Radio, Wire, Message Center, and Headquarters. The growth of this company illustrates what has already been said about General McNair's "stinginess" (his own word) in cutting the Division down too far, and its subsequent regrowth. Here are the dates of the three TOs under which the company operated, and the number of officers and men which each allowed:

5 September 1942: 4 officers, 81 enlisted men
10 August 1943:   4 officers, 1 warrant officer, 95 enlisted men
16 December 1944: 10 officers, 4 warrant officers, 271 enlisted men

Division Headquarters originally included Headquarters Company, the Reconnaissance Platoon, Transportation Platoon, MP Platoon, and the personnel of Division Headquarters. The Division had two bands at the time, but neither was in Headquarters, one being with Division Artillery and the other belonging to the 502d. The Reconnaissance Platoon was transferred to the 401st in mid-1943, but was sent back in a 1945 reorganization. At the latter time, the Division Artillery band was also put in Division Headquarters Company.

The 326th Medical Company was set up with ten officers and 215 enlisted men. Its commanding officer, Maj. William E. Barfield, was to become Division Surgeon at Bastogne.

The Quartermaster Company received all its members from the 407th

Quartermaster Battalion of the old 82d. It started with five officers and eighty-six enlisted men.

The 801st Ordnance Company was not activated until the 2d of October, 1942. It was then made up of four officers and sixty-eight enlisted men, more than half of whom had come from the old Quartermaster Battalion, and had to be retrained.

Also activated after the mid-August date was the 81st Airborne Antiaircraft Battalion filled primarily with men from the old 327th, who came either directly from or via the 401st. It was set up to include six 71-man batteries. Batteries A, B, and C were antitank, armed with the 37mm AT gun. Batteries D, E and F were antiaircraft, armed with .50 caliber machine guns. Its first commander was Lt. Col. William C. Scoggins. When discovery of his night-blindness during maneuvers in England led to his transfer, he was replaced by his Executive Officer at the time of activation, Capt. X. B. Cox.

Such were the units that were to operate under General Lee. To assist him in running them as a division he received a group of executives the first of whom was the Assistant Division Commander, Brig. Gen. Don Forrester Pratt. Like General Lee, General Pratt had entered the Army during World War I, but unlike him had not been sent overseas. His military experience between the wars was typical, culminating in his becoming Assistant Division Commander of the 82d. With the split, he came over to the 101st. His general rank dates from August 1 although he issued the activation order as a colonel. Well liked by both officers and men, he played a vital role in the development of the Division until his death in Normandy.

The third general officer was Anthony C. McAuliffe, the Division Artillery Commander. Unlike the other two, he was a West Pointer of the class of 1918. His additional schooling in the Army included the Field Artillery Basic School, the Command and General Staff School and the Army War College. Upon finishing at the latter in 1940, he worked for two years with the War Department General Staff, and then in the Services of Supply. He was developing weapons, clothing and equipment for the Army Ground Forces when appointed to the Division. His general rank dates from August 8, 1942. An easy-going, jovial man he could come quickly to a hard decision when one was necessary.

As Chief of Staff, General Lee had Col. Charles L. Keerans, Jr. A West Pointer (1919), Keerans had served under General Lee at Bragg as G-4 of the Airborne Command. With the 101st, he handled the key job in a masterful way, at the same time gaining a certain amount of notoriety for the equally masterful way he handled a motorcycle over the roads of Claiborne. He left the 101st the following January to become Assistant Division Commander of the 82d. As a brigadier general, he was killed in the attack on Sicily. To Colonel Keerans must go the credit for the smooth working of the Division staff. Unlike other AGF divisions the top five men did not have a quiet month together at Leavenworth to learn their new jobs. Colonel Keerans trained them at their posts.

There was hard work still to be done at Claiborne, but it was made easier by the almost universal round of promotions and mutual congratulations which the staffing of a new division had made possible. In this atmosphere strangers familiarized themselves with each other, and with their new duties. Among the less significant changes, officers' insignia of rank were ordered on the left side of their caps, and the jump patch, unit by unit, moved over to the right, the 502nd officers being the last to go along.

The reviews continued, as did ceremonies for the presentation of colors to new units. It was still possible to cover the eighteen miles to Alexandria, which offered all the mushroomed attractions of a typical Army town, and many a man spent his evenings there.

The serious work of being airborne had to wait for the move to Bragg. But that move was not long in coming. Warning orders began to appear about the middle of September, and advance parties started to leave for "somewhere."

Finally, the Division itself, unit by unit, was on the move. In the words of the historian of the 321st, "The trip was made without incident, and we arrived at the famous Fort Bragg. It wasn't at all the lovely spot that we had been led to believe by the cadremen." Here training started in earnest. And here also the Division picked up its parachute regiment, the Five Oh Deuce or Five Oh Duck.

The 502d Parachute Infantry had been activated March 2, 1942, with Lt. Col. George P. Howell in command and with practically the same personnel it had when set up as a battalion back in July, 1941. Colonel Howell, leaving to take command of the Parachute School, was succeeded by his executive officer, Lt. Col. George Van Horn Moseley, Jr. A third-generation Army man, and a West Pointer, Colonel Moseley quickly began to put his unique stamp on the entire regiment. A remarkable combination of intellect and will power, he made enormous demands, both of himself and of those under him. Men of the 502d, justly proud of the record their regiment made in combat, insisted that much of the credit was due "Old Moe" and his training even though he was their combat leader for only a few hours. His training stayed with them.

The men of the 502d did not fit easily into the life of the Division, for they felt in a class by themselves. They had met the high parachute standards when they were at their highest. They had participated in the Carolina maneuvers, and were not slow in pointing out these facts.

Two other factors served to set them off from the rest of the Division —they were all volunteers and they were drawing extra pay.

It will be noted that no one at Claiborne was asked whether or not he wanted to ride a glider. The powers-that-be in the Army assumed that a man could be ordered into a glider as readily as he could be ordered into a truck. Only actual experience on maneuvers and in combat was to show how hazardous a glider flight might be. Even accidents and death did not work to put glider flying on the same volunteer basis as paratrooping, perhaps because the same amount of training and the same degree of skill on the part of the participants were never necessary, perhaps because it never took the same kind of act of will to step into a glider that it took to step out of a plane. Other compensations were found later; but at this time there was plenty of basis for inter-organizational jealousy, even aside from the best basis of all, the extra pay for the paratroopers.

When the Test Platoon was set up, its members were authorized to draw not parachute pay, but flight pay. This was the roundabout way adopted to compensate them for the extra hazard involved in their work. As the number of paratroopers increased, this stratagem was continued, except that enlisted men could draw such pay only if they were rated specialists first class, and the number of such ratings was limited. There was a somewhat similar limitation on the number of officers who could get the extra money. This was discrimination, and it led to hard feelings. The Pay Readjustment Act of 1942 finally straightened matters out by providing for real parachute pay, a hundred dollars a month for officers and fifty dollars for enlisted men.

This solved the problem until the creation of airborne divisions, when glidermen began to discover that they were doing things just as dangerous as anyone else and not drawing one cent extra. As early as October 1942, General Lee, along with General Ridgway, recommended that something be done to remedy this injustice, but no action was taken. The famous "Join the Glider Troops!" with its photographs of wrecked gliders and inscriptions "No Flight Pay, No Jump Pay, But Never a Dull Moment" had made its appearance during the Laurinburg-Maxton training.

This poster was designed by glidermen in the U. S. before glidermen began receiving extra pay.

The dangers of gliding into combat were highlighted by an accident which injured General Lee during the Tennessee maneuvers. But it was not until April 1944 that the War Department made it possible for glidermen to draw extra money—it said they might become paratroopers and draw jump pay. Later the same year Congress solved the problem by making glidermen eligible for flight pay, with a top of one hundred dollars a month for officers and fifty dollars for enlisted men. Long before this new arrangement the commanders of all airborne units were working hard to abolish the distinction between glidermen and jumpers, and to make "airborne" the criterion. One step had been the adoption, in the spring of 1943, of an Airborne hat patch combining the parachute and glider. The glidermen liked it but the paratroopers screamed. Parachutist replacements were later sent to the glider units and in the course of time a number of glidermen became jumpers.

Pay was not the only problem bothering the new division as it squared off for its new training at Bragg. There was the matter of getting more officers and men; the 101st was not yet filled up to the limited TO that it had received, and there was the related problem of getting rid of some of the officers and men whom the division already had—those obviously incapable of measuring up to the high standards which an airborne division had to set for itself. This problem became especially acute in the case of the men, for personnel figures revealed that the average age in the new division was high, with 2,486 men over thirty-three years old. They also showed that the division had almost twice as many men in the lowest Army intelligence bracket as would ordinarily be expected. This was serious in a unit where high casualty rates and frequent small-unit actions might make almost any man a leader at any time.

Accordingly, Army Ground Forces was asked to give complete discretion to the new division in weeding out old and incoming personnel. This was refused. But in an order of September 18, 1942, General McNair gave to the commanding generals of the two airborne divisions such sweeping powers to transfer officers and enlisted men on various grounds that by indirection they could come close to getting precisely what they wanted.

At the same time the commanding generals of all procurement agencies in the Army were informed of the need for outstanding officers of all arms and branches willing to volunteer for airborne duty and to fill places in the new divisions. Many good men responded. Ultimately, most officers in the 101st were volunteers.

Through the fall and winter months, while intensive training was in progress, the process of weeding out and taking on continued, until a definite airborne type began to emerge. As the whole Division began to feel something of the superiority that at first had characterized only the parachute regiments there came the beginning of a battle morale. It wasn't only that they believed they were better than ordinary soldiers. They knew what training the man next to them had been through and believed he too was better. As a result they had more confidence in him and less inclination to run when the going became rough. It was largely as a result of this basic feeling of mutual confidence that the Division became famous for its dash and spirit.

During October came the first CG4A glider ride within the new Division. To understand this ride and the report about it in the Division newspaper it must only be remembered that the glidermen had not volunteered to travel in the flimsy craft. They were going to be ordered in. The flight of the six officers was part of an effort to make them think it could not be as dangerous as it looked. Let the Division newspaper take over.

Six high-ranking officers of the 101st Airborne Division recently inspected and traveled in a transport glider in order to become familiar with the craft that are scheduled to become the prime mover of the streamlined "Eagle Division."

Upon completion of the trip which took the officers a distance of more than 100 miles, the entire group had become enthusiastic and completely sold on this •newest mode of transportation.

Brig. Gen. Don F. Pratt said after his trip: "I believe every man of the Division will be enthusiastic about them after one ride."

Brig. Gen. Anthony C. McAuliffe, who rode as co-pilot of the glider on the trip commented: "I have every confidence in the safety of the glider as a mode of transportation. It was said to be a 'rough air day' when we took the ride, but I was pleasantly surprised with the smoothness and maneuverability of the glider."

Lt. Col. Joseph H. Harper described his experience this way. "Riding in the glider while being towed was very much like being in a transport plane. I believe I really felt safer. I was tremendously impressed with the ease with which the pilot handled the ship and he assured me it was almost impossible to crash. I couldn't help thinking that if a glider should crash there was no possibility of a fire following the crash. No ignition and no gasoline, consequently, no fire. I believe they are perfectly safe and that my men will be enthusiastic about them after their first ride."

Though this account does not say so, the 82d Airborne Division also was represented on the trip—by two officers, one of whom was its Chief of Staff, Col. Maxwell D. Taylor.

November brought news of the invasion of North Africa. Division leaders read the papers closely, knowing the special way in which the fate of the 101st was staked on airborne performances there. They were elated at first reports of the success of Lt. Col. Edson Raff and his 509th Parachute Infantry Battalion. As fuller accounts came through tacticians took to heart their meaning.

Young Abe

The early stay at Bragg was also made notable by the induction of Young Abe as the official mascot of the 101st Airborne Division. A relationship was started that should have proved glorious for both the Division and Young Abe. But it was destined to end anti-climactically with his death the following spring.

Young Abe was a Wisconsin eagle—but before his story must come the story of the Division itself.

The 101st, when it was set up, had an appropriate shoulder insignia but very little else in the way of tradition. There was ample justification for the opening part of the first sentence of General Lee's statement, "This Division has no history . . ." The first reference to a 101st Division came on July 23, 1918, when the War Department took initial steps to constitute one. As a part of the new Division the 201st Infantry

Members of the 506th doing rope climbs during training at Camp Toccoa.

Brigade was to be organized in France from white pioneer troops, as soon as Negro pioneer troops could be found to replace them. Meanwhile, a cadre for the new Division slowly collected at Camp Shelby, Mississippi. At one time it numbered more than 750 officers and noncommissioned officers. On September 30, Brig. Gen. Roy Hoffman reported to Shelby to take command of the 201st Brigade. But the organization was not to proceed any farther—the Armistice intervened. On the 24th of November, General Hoffman was relieved and on the 30th the War Department wired instructions to demobilize such organizations as had been set up. There was no rendezvous with destiny in World War I.

The 101st Infantry Division was next heard of when it was constituted in the Organized Reserves in 1921. It was this division which later secured the eagle as its shoulder insignia, in accordance with the following order of May 23, 1923:

1. The Secretary of War approves the following shoulder sleeve insignia for the 101st Division, Organized Reserves:

23

SHIELD: 2½ inches in height, sable the head of a bald eagle erased proper. The design is based on one of the Civil War traditions of the State of Wisconsin, this State being the territory of this Division. The black shield recalls the old "Iron Brigade" one of whose regiments possessed "Old Abe" the famous war eagle.

Thus was approved the basic patch which the men of the 101st Airborne were to make famous in Normandy, Holland and Bastogne. The references to the "Iron Brigade" and "Old Abe" were explained in an article in the June 1912 issue of the *American Historical Magazine* quoting a veteran of the Brigade, Robert J. Burdette:

My regiment was one of the four which, with the Second Iowa Battery, composed what is known as the Eagle Brigade. It got its name from the fact that the Eighth Wisconsin Regiment of that Brigade carried a young American eagle all through the war.

Old Abe had the post of honor at the center of the regiment, his perch being constructed of the American shield, and he was carried by a sergeant between the two flags, the Stars and Stripes and the regimental standard of blue emblazoned in gold with the State coat of arms.

All the brigade adored him, and secured chickens for him—he was fonder of chicken than the chaplain and not half so particular about the cookery. To see him during a battle fly up into the air to the length of his long tether, hovering above the flags in the cloud of smoke, screaming like the bird which bore the thunderbolts of Jove, was to raise such a mighty shout from the Brigade as would have blown Jericho off the map. Other regiments had dogs, bears, coons, goats. There was only one eagle in the Army.

He was an eaglet when the war broke out, and enlisted young, like many of the boys who loved him and fought beside him. He was captured on the Flambeau River, Wisconsin, in 1861, by a Chippewa Indian, Chief Sky, who sold him for a bushel of corn. Subsequently a Mr. Mills paid $5.00 for him and presented him to C Company of the Eighth Wisconsin Regiment, known as the Eau Claire Eagles. The soldiers at once adopted him as one of their standards, made him a member of the color guard, named him in honor of the greatest of Presidents, and he never disgraced his name.

Through thirty-six battles he screamed among the trumpets, smelling the battle afar off, fluttering among the thunder of the captains and shouting. Never once did he flinch. He was wounded in the assault on Vicksburg and in the battle of Corinth. At this battle it is said that a reward was offered by the Confederate General Price for the capture or killing of the eagle.

Old Abe can still be seen in the "Cyclorama" in Atlanta's Grant Park. The Division shoulder insignia was developed to its present form by the addition of the word "Airborne" on a tab above it. General McAuliffe arranged for this before he left Washington to join the Division at Claiborne.

The idea of the eagle gained further prominence as the result of a contest to select an appropriate nickname for the Division which General Lee arranged shortly after his arrival at Claiborne. The winning suggestion was "Eagle Division" submitted by Pvt. Jesse M. Willis, an ex-newspaperman who later became public relations sergeant in the G-2 Section. For the record, the Adjutant General's Office stated that there was no connection between the 101st Division and the 101st Airborne Division. The former was disbanded August 15, 1942. The latter was constituted on the inactive list on August 15, 1942, and activated August 16, 1942.

This background made it inevitable that the 101st should acquire an eagle for a mascot. It did. And the bald eagle that it secured was a peculiarly appropriate eagle for whom the claim could be made without fear of successful contradiction that he was a descendant of Old Abe. Inevitably he was named Young Abe.

Captured in the backwoods of Wisconsin in July 1939, he had been turned over to the State game farm. By the State he had been presented to Major Carmichael and the men of the 321st Glider Field Artillery, many of whom came from Wisconsin. They, in turn, gave him to the Division. The ceremony of acceptance, broadcast over MBS, was stiffly formal with an order read by Lt. Col. Edward Schmitt, the Adjutant General, and a speech of acceptance by General Lee.

Young Abe seemed destined for great things. But he never rode the skies with his men. The promise of November turned into the tragedy of July. Perhaps he had been inducted too late in life, and found it impossible to adapt himself to the rugged conditions of training in an airborne division. Without apparent cause he died July 6 at Fort Bragg. It was a lonely death, for the Division was far away on the Tennessee maneuvers.

One episode remains to be told. When Abe was ailing fresh meat was prescribed for him. The only thing available, a live hen, was put in his cage one evening. The next morning when his attendant came around to clean the chicken feathers from the cage he found Abe and the hen snuggled side by side, and the hen had laid an egg.

Training

By such expedients General Lee endeavored to keep his men interested and alert through the period when the drudgery of training was at its worst. That fall and winter the units of the 101st were going through not one arduous training program, but several of them simultaneously. The training situation was especially unusual in that Generals Lee and Ridgway, both now wearing two stars, had been made responsible to General Lee's successor in the Airborne Command,

It was on this 34-foot tower at Camp Toccoa that paratroopers had their first experience of stepping out into space.

Brigadier General Chapman. But the three generals knew each other well and got along with no more than minimum difficulties.

Training plans were laid down in an Airborne Command order of November 4, 1942. Excerpts from it are quoted at length because, whether they were aware of it or not, it was at that time probably the most important document in the lives of the men in the 101st.

> *b.* Training will be conducted in three phases, as follows:
>> (1) Individual Training . . . . 13 weeks
>> (2) Unit Training . . . . 13 weeks
>> (3) Combined Training . . . . 11 weeks
>
> *c.* All units will follow applicable parts of this directive except as indicated below:
>
> (1) Individuals taking special parachute, riggers, communications, and demolitions courses at the Parachute Schools will be brought to the training level of their organization, by special courses of instruction if necessary by the end of the unit training phase.
>
> (2) The 82d and 101st Airborne Divisions (less Parachute Infantry Regiment) will begin the 6th week of unit training on November 9, 1942, and follow this directive, as applicable, thereafter.
>
> (3) The 502d and 504th Infantry Parachute Regiments will continue their

26

present training programs until their parent divisions enter the combined training phase, when each will follow this directive.

(4) Parachute artillery battalions will continue jumping of personnel so that each parachutist jumps at least once a month.

III. TRAINING PHASES:

a. Individual training:

During the 13 weeks of individual training all troops will be hardened physically and mentally to withstand modern combat requirements. All individuals will be conditioned to withstand extreme fatigue, loss of sleep, limited rations and existence in the field with only the equipment that can be carried by parachute, glider, or transport aircraft. An indication of individual proficiency and a basis of test is considered the ability to make a continuous foot march of twenty-five miles in eight hours, a five mile march in one hour and a nine mile march in two hours, with full equipment.

Men will be mentally and physically conditioned for battle field environment by obstacle courses that overtax endurance as well as muscular and mental reactions, by passage of wire obstacles so situated as to permit overhead fire, by a night fighting course with sound only as an indication of danger, and a street fighting course with booby traps and sudden-appearing targets. Live ammunition will be employed in all three tests.

b. Unit training:

By the end of the 9th week of unit training Infantry battalions will be able to function efficiently, by day or night, independently or reinforced.

The unit training phase of infantry battalions will include tactical exercises in which the battalion is supported by a battery of field artillery.

During unit training, combat firing exercises, emphasizing infiltration tactics, rapid advance, and continuous fire support will be planned to conclude each phase.

d. Combined training:

Regimental combat team and divisional tactical exercises will be held during this period. Tactical situations which require the complete staff planning of an airborne attack will be the background of each problem, but the paramount importance of the ground operation will be impressed on staffs and troops, all problems to be solved will envision, or will actually require, the presence of appropriate troop carrier and air support units.

IV. MISCELLANEOUS:

a. Airborne Training:

The Airborne Command will furnish instructional teams to teach basic airborne operational procedure. Thereafter, divisions will continue training in transport aircraft and gliders which will be furnished on request to this headquarters. Flying command post exercises and divisional airborne problems will be conducted by divisions during the combined training phase in keeping with availability of aircraft.

Such was the order. There was a great deal of confusion in working it out. New men were arriving constantly, some with basic training already under their belts, others still needing it. Old men were leaving

Free falls from the 225-foot tower at Fort Benning, Georgia.

for Benning and jump school. Others were returning from Benning to take up training where they had left it off six weeks before. Equipment shortages were a headache every step of the way. In spite of all this the unit training phase was completed January 3, 1943, and the Division embarked on combined training January 18. In the sense of the schedule laid down by ABC, this was never completed.

Here is how it went according to the historian of the 377th Parachute Field Artillery Battalion:

Training at first consisted, not by choice, of physical training, long marches and judo, together with a review of infantry tactics, carbine instruction, gas precautions, and other subjects from basic training cycle. Material necessary for field artillery training just wasn't available. Four pack howitzers were finally secured on loan from the test battalion of Airborne Command, on which batteries of the battalion rotated with other batteries of Division Artillery in the training of gun crews. It was not until December that the battalion was issued its own howitzers. The training received on the borrowed guns, however, was so effective that a successful service practice was carried out the same month.

By February this battalion was considered capable of carrying on its own program and was released from ABC supervision. In March it started its combat team relationship with the 502d, a working arrangement that was to hold good through the war. By April its airborne training had progressed so far that it was making battery jumps with full equipment. And in May it brought off the first artillery battalion jump in the history of the American Army.

Much of this training did not take place at Bragg at all. Beginning about December 8, all the glider units spent two months apiece at the Laurinburg-Maxton Army Air Base in Maxton, North Carolina, learning the secrets of the glider rider, and making first flights. As the 321st describes that training:

At two o'clock in the morning you were just as apt to be found loading gliders as sleeping. Naturally, this was all done with full field equipment on top of an overcoat, including arms and steel helmets. The operation usually took place in complete blackout and strict silence.

It was only five miles to the airport, so we invariably walked. If it happened that you couldn't go to the airport, you simply had to figure those Centers of Gravity again. They could only be done at night. Did anyone ever hear of the 321st doing its figuring in the daytime? There was too much training to be done. Cannoneers Hop, the vital factor in winning the war, along with pulling those wooden-wheeled 75s across plowed fields with drag ropes, had to be done in the light of day.

How did you know that in the years to come you would always have light to load your glider? Also that you would have two or three days instead of the twenty minutes then allowed?

Such absentee training was especially hard on the Quartermaster Company which had a day-to-day supply job to do at Bragg. But its men did learn both ground and aerial supply, including the packaging of materials for dropping. And they learned how to fight.

The engineers' training was different from ordinary instruction because their equipment would always be limited to what was transportable by parachute, glider or plane. The emphasis was on demolitions, construction of roadblocks and tank traps, mine-field clearance, and, finally, fighting. Few division engineers were to have as much chance to fight as those of the 101st.

The training of the Engineer Parachute Company culminated March 9th in the attack on the Chapel Hill airport. This was the first time the men had jumped with demolitions. No one exploded.

The 502d made several battalion jumps on the field at Spout Springs.

The antiaircraft batteries of the 81st went to Camp Davis and Fort Fisher on the North Carolina coast for their range work. Along with the antitank batteries they subsequently learned combat team work with the infantry regiments.

The Signal Company worked to teach everybody to do everything. Emphasis at this time was on radio, for it was not until after the Tennessee maneuvers that the division realized that wire was to be the mainstay of its communications.

The Medical Company received normal training, except that it had to learn how to get along without the ambulances such a company would ordinarily have. Techniques were developed to convert jeeps and captured vehicles to the litter-bearing job.

The Division's first Christmas provided a welcome break—celebrated with all the services and parties that could be crowded in. The Airborne Area had its own Christmas-carol sing. Most of the companies provided appropriate gifts for the men and in many mess halls open house was declared for the personnel and their visitors. The Christmas dinners were complete with turkey and all the trimmings. The holiday was climaxed with an egg-nog party at the Service Club beginning at five o'clock Christmas afternoon. This party was made possible by the cooperation of both divisions—eighty gallons of egg-nog —two thousand soldiers and their guests—and the big crowd was orderly and happy. Bastogne was two years away.

MANEUVERS

The first trip from Fort Bragg involving the entire division was a ten-day affair taking place the latter part of March in the Southern Pines area. Here the 101st used its parachute elements to the full for the first time. That not all parachutists landed where they were supposed to is obvious from the following receipt:

I, J. D. McLeod, of Hoffman, North Carolina, for and in consideration of one (1) bag of cement, value ninety cents ($.90), thirty-five (35) bricks, value one dollar and seventy-five cents ($1.75) and three (3) bundles of shingles, value three dollars and fifty cents ($3.50), total value six dollars and fifteen cents ($6.15), receipt of which is hereby acknowledged, do hereby forever release Pvt. Earl F. McGrath, Headquarters Company, Third Battalion, the 506th Parachute Infantry, The United States government, and any and all agencies thereof from any and all claims and damages to my property arising out of Pvt. Earl F. McGrath landing on my roof March 31, 1943, and kicking aforementioned chimney therefrom.

On May 23-28 came the Camden maneuver, a small rehearsal for the big-time Tennessee affair that was to follow. Transport to Camden was by air, with gliders cutting loose and parachutists jumping

Camp Toccoa, where the 506th and 501st were formed and trained. The tents at left were "W" Company where recruits lived.

over the target area. The very day the Camden maneuver ended the advance detail took off by plane for Tennessee. The 101st was about to enter the big league.

This South Carolina maneuver was of course plagued by the shortages that afflicted all the Army at that time. Jeeps with orange cloths on them were tanks. Flour sacks served as bazooka shells. But with all these disadvantages, many an officer and enlisted man from this exercise got his first real idea of what this airborne fighting was about. And they took Kershaw.

What is remembered about all such training was that it was "rough." "We cheered when they told us we were going airborne, because we didn't know any better" was the way one man put it. "We thought that hikes were over, but they gave us runs instead."

This last was not precisely true. Hiking was then regarded by the training masters as one of the best possible conditioners, and the men of the 101st got more than their share. Division news columns are full of accounts of hikes:

. . . The 401st Glider Infantry, commanded by Col. Joseph H. Harper, took a twenty-mile march with full field equipment and weapons without the loss of a single man. The distance was covered in seven and one-half hours.

The men of the 101st Airborne Division Artillery resorted to infantry tactics this past week when every unit of the big guns took a typical twenty-five mile infantry march ... Marching honors for the artillerymen go to Headquarters and Headquarters Battery which completed the twenty-five miles in the remarkable time for that distance of six hours and thirty-five minutes.

Demonstrating to the complete satisfaction of Maj. W. E. Barfield, unit commander, and other officers of the company that they are as rugged as any other airborne troopers, the men of the 326th Airborne Medical Company of the "Eagle Division" completed a twenty-mile march recently in four hours and twenty minutes.

TEN MILES IN TWO HOURS IS MARCHING RECORD OF
81st BATTALION

Company H of the 502nd Parachute Infantry completed a total of 145½ miles in 57¼ hours marching time . . . The first thirty-three miles was covered in eleven hours, cross-country and over back roads at night.

THE 506TH JOINS THE DIVISION

Members of the 506th Parachute Infantry regard June 10, the day of the attachment of their regiment to the Division, as the greatest day the Division ever had. There were many who would dispute this claim. Some detractors from the 502d insist to this day that the 506th was a "rout-step" outfit. But none would deny that the words "colorful, rugged, unusual" could be applied to it. It was the men of the 506th who took their reviews on the double, wearing blue trunks. It was the men of the 506th who made those widely publicized marches from Toccoa to Atlanta, and from Atlanta to Benning.

Like the 502d, the 506th was modeled in the image of its commanding officer, Col. Robert F. Sink. Colonel Sink had run his regiment from the moment of its activation and was to continue to handle it all through its fighting days. More important, his men came to him direct from the reception centers. Most of them had only one commanding officer in the Army, "Bob" Sink.

Colonel Sink was a West Pointer, but no one would have guessed it from the unorthodox way in which he ran his regiment. The book went out the window when he undertook a job, and direct methods, intuition, and the individual ability of subordinates all had their chance.

With the 506th in tow, the Division left for Springfield, Tennessee, in early June. The two parachute regiments stationed at Camp Campbell, Kentucky, and Evansville, Indiana, swung into action immediately. Attached to the Blue forces they dropped behind the lines of the retreating Reds to establish roadblocks, destroy bridges and generally snarl Red communications. They were eventually captured, but not before they had given an awakening country some idea of the meaning of vertical envelopment. Commenting at a press conference on the paratroopers, General McNair said: "They, like the Rangers, are our problem children. They make a lot of money and they know they're good. This makes them a little temperamental but they're real soldiers."

The entire Division participated in the last phases of Maneuver No. 1, and in several phases of Maneuver No. 2. It came out a fighting team. This was the country's and the Army's first chance to see gliders used en masse. They measured up beautifully—this in spite of the fact that one of them gave General Lee a good shaking-up and several fractured ribs. The inferiority-complexioned glidermen were inclined to yell "I told you so" when they learned that his first remark had been "Next time I'll take a parachute."

The maneuvers were not all work. Mention of Lake Wartrace brings back to many a man memories of a quiet, if not a clean swim. Passes to Nashville were frequent.

With the feeling of a job well done, the Division entrained for Bragg again on July 19.

Acts of bravery during the maneuver had brought the division its second and third Soldier's Medal. Lt. Robert G. Goodall of the Medical Company won one for rescuing a trooper who had dropped into a pond and was unable to extricate himself from the harness and equipment he was carrying. The other went to Sgt. George R. Puflett of the 506th for a similar rescue of a drowning fellow-soldier.

The Division's first Soldier's Medal had been awarded posthumously under more tragic circumstances. Near Fort Bragg glider infantrymen of the 401st were crossing the Middle River on a tarpaulin raft. One fell overboard. Lt. Thomas E. Parlaman dived in after him. In the icy water Parlaman drowned. The man drifted to safety.

The latter half of the Bragg training and the maneuvers had been under somewhat different direction. The January departure of Colonel Keerans to join the 82d Division left the post of Chief of Staff vacant. Lt. Col. Edward G. Herb of the Engineers filled the job temporarily, until it could be turned over to the former G-3, Lt. Col. Gerald J. Higgins. Colonel Higgins was destined to hold this key spot during all the crucial days of training in the United States and England handling problems which normally never developed in an infantry outfit. His rise was about as rapid as a rise in the infantry can be and finally resulted in his becoming a general on the 1st of August, 1944, at the age of thirty-four, the youngest general officer in the Army Ground Forces. He was a West Pointer, 1934, appointed from the ranks of the Army. His desire for action drew him to the paratroopers in the very beginning, and he served as a company commander in the 501st Parachute Battalion. Reference has already been made to his part in the work of the Airborne Command.

Colonel Higgins' old G-3 position was taken in January by Lt. Col. Raymond D. Millener, who was later to follow him as Chief of Staff.

While at Bragg the Division lost its first G-4, Lt. Col. W. F. Kernan, who had already acquired a national reputation as the author of the popular studies of strategy, *Defense Will Not Win the War* and *We Can Win This War*. He was replaced by Lt. Col. Carl W. Kohls, at that time Division Quartermaster. Colonel Kohls was a West Pointer, 1931, who had been in the Infantry until his transfer to the Quartermaster Corps in 1939. He was destined to hold the G-4 position through the rest of the training and all of the fighting.

For all the training and traveling there was still time for the soldier's own special events at Bragg. January saw the inauguration of a six-team basketball league. Unit boxing had already started. The "Screaming Eagle" team of the 502d, coached by Lieutenant Mc-Kearney and managed by Captain Danahy, not only became the local champions but won the district Golden Gloves contest at Greensboro and the regional fights at Charlotte. Three men—Plemons, Tippins, and McIntosh—were sent to the New York Golden Gloves meet.

The title "Screaming Eagle," eventually to belong to the entire Division, seems to have been used for the first time in connection with this team. The 502d used it again in England for the football team. The Division boxing team that fought at Rainbow Corners took it up. Some *Stars and Stripes* correspondents applied it to the Division itself, and other correspondents copied. Thus did the Eagle Division of Fort Bragg become the Screaming Eagles of battle fame.

"Priming the Pump" at Fayetteville was one of the major evening sports of all soldiers at Bragg, or of all soldiers who could get into the not-so-large drinking house of that name. Enough has already been said to indicate that there was a basis for brawls between paratroopers and glidermen. An even stronger rivalry existed between the 82d and 101st Divisions. There was also the question of relations between airborne troops and the regular units on the post. In other words, no matter who was there on a particular night there might be a good fight, and generally there was. All that could unite such separated elements was a mutual dislike for the MPs, a feeling that the MPs, as they too took their casualties at the Pump, reciprocated. Even the use of tear gas had only a slightly quieting effect on proceedings.

Fayetteville had not only the Town Pump, and other drinking places, but also some motion-picture houses, recreational centers and a swimming pool. Married officers obtained living quarters either at Fayetteville or at nearby Southern Pines and Pinehurst. For all there was the chance of a week-end at Charlotte, Raleigh, or Wilmington, or some small spot on the coast of North Carolina.

REVIEWS

Interspersed throughout the months at Bragg were the formal reviews which were part of the life of every division training in this country. The first such inspection in ranks and review, on October 10, was in honor of Col. J. W. Harrelson, Dean of Administration at North Carolina State College. Colonel Harrelson had been General Lee's 1917 mathematics teacher, and an intimate friend thereafter.

Three weeks later the Eagles acknowledged their debt to the Airborne Command when their guest of honor was Brigadier General Chapman. February saw the next such formal occasion when Lt. Gen. Lesley J. McNair, Commanding General of Army Ground Forces, was welcomed to Bragg and to the airborne division at whose birth he had played such a major role.

A demonstration rather than a review was presented during the March 22-24 visit of Foreign Minister Anthony Eden of England and his party, which included Field Marshal Sir John Greer Dill and Gen. George C. Marshall. Organized by General Chapman, it showed the two parachute regiments, the 502d and the 504th, attacking under the protection of artillery fire furnished by the guns of the two divisions plus those of a separate brigade from the post. Lieutenant Colonel Higgins gave the running commentary. It was an impressive demonstration, winning for Colonel Moseley and his men the warmly expressed admiration of Mr. Eden. A re-supply flight coming directly after the attack provided a colorful ending to the afternoon.

The occasion was entirely different on April 10 when the guest was film star Dick Powell. A week later came the farewell review for the 82d, a heartbreaking day for the fire-eaters of the 101st. The other division was to go overseas and get in the fight first. General Lee wished them good hunting.

The following Saturday the 101st stood an inspection and review in honor of Lt. Gen. Ben Lear, Commanding General of Second Army. Late July brought Lt. Gen. Lloyd R. Fredendall, new Commanding

General of Second Army, to Bragg to see the 101st put on a glider demonstration. J. Melville Broughton, Governor of North Carolina and long-time friend of General Lee, was the guest on August 11.

Even before this review was held, seventy-six officers and men of the Division had left Bragg on the most secret, the most exciting mission of all—advance party to England. Most units sent their executive officers, and division sections sent their assistants. Lt. Col. Curtis D. Renfro, Executive Officer of the 327th, was in charge.

As day followed day in the mid-August heat of Bragg, no one in the 101st had to be told that his stay in the States was drawing to a close. Five to ten day furloughs gave some a chance to go home and say goodbye. Inspection followed inspection. Officers and noncoms got to know the *Preparation for Overseas Movement* manual by heart. Whatever time was left from inspections was taken up with fatigue work as the Division prepared to sign out of Bragg.

The movement started August 22. By the first of September the last of the twenty trainloads had closed in at Camp Shanks, thirty miles up the Hudson River from New York.

Shanks was the same for everybody, a succession of inspections, inoculations, and repackings, the frustrated or successful effort to get to New York, the anger at not being allowed to wear jump boots.

The Crossing

The crossing was made in two ships. The experience of the group which travelled aboard the *SS Samaria* may be summed up in a letter written by Pfc. David Kenyon Webster, Company F, 506th, to his young nephew:

Dear Cam,

If you ever sail on a troopship—and I pray God you won't—I suggest that you buy yourself several cakes of salt-water soap, a dozen sets of underwear, a solid aluminum mess kit, and several interesting books. You will then be in a position to enjoy the trip and to live in relative comfort.

Because there were so many of us on the *Samaria,* our sooty, dishevelled Cunard Line transport, there was not enough fresh water to go around. This is a standard phenomenon of army voyages. Indeed, fresh water could be used for drinking only at stipulated 15-minute intervals for a grand total of an hour and a half a day. If you think that was bad, consider the beards of my fellow passengers, who were allowed fresh water for shaving only from 7:15 to 8 in the morning and from 6:45 to 7:30 at night. Thus, to remain even tolerably clean, we had to resort to salt water, which was always on tap in the showers. This required special salt-water soap. It might not smell sweet or give us a schoolgirl complexion, but at least it lathered a little. I rubbed ordinary landlubber soap on my hands for five minutes at a time and produced nothing but wet slime. No lather. Salt water left us sticky, but we were clean, we kept telling ourselves, and that's what counted.

We needed a dozen sets of underwear, because we were sleeping with our clothes on and wanted to change as often as possible; my undershirt, to take a rank example, grew black and moldy in just three days' time. On account of the submarine menace all ranks had to wear their life jackets, two little pillows fastened together with strings and their cartridge belts with canteens attached and had to sleep in their clothes. People who had been raised in pajamas found this both disturbing and uncomfortable. It was also rough and dirty on underwear. Incidentally, it would have been a smart idea, though discouraged by our officers, to have bought an extra pair of fatigues, so that we could have varied our wardrobe a little. Our outer garments got dirty from sleeping in corridors and on the crummy deck.

We found ourselves wiser and happier soldiers if we could beg, borrow, or steal a solid aluminum mess kit, for we were washing our utensils in salt water. Salt water, as we discovered to our sorrow, corrodes and rusts; after three days my spoon was so rusty I cut my lips when I ate with it. We ate twice a day —in the morning and at night—in a dark brown, crowded, unventilated mess hall on a lower deck where the soldiers fetched the food in tin buckets and cleaned the tables with dank black dishrags, the same tables we so blithely laid our bread on to spread our butter. Our diet, which consisted of typically British stewed tomatoes, baked fish, delicious hot ship's bread, and excellent tea, was on the whole not exactly appetizing. The coffee was horrible. Etiquette was abandoned and the grabbing at the table became so unbelievably ferocious that the *Samaria* took on the air of a floating madhouse. An aluminum mess kit, however, might have helped a little by preventing rust and saving our cups from the corrosion inherent in English coffee.

The salt-water mess-kit dip was set out in three pans. If you were on the end of the line, you felt you might as well wash your mess kit in a garbage pail, the water was so full of floating débris—bread, fish, corn flakes, etc.

Above all, a man with a good mess kit had to be watchful, for we were living together so intimately that anything left loose would be stolen. I lost two blankets and a shelter half. A sleeping man was robbed of his life jacket and first-aid packet. But on that voyage an aluminum mess kit was the most coveted possession.

As for the interesting books, they were a Godsend to people like us with so much time on our hands. The only fire breaks in our daily forest of idleness were breakfast and supper, lifeboat drill (at noon), and rifle inspection (at one). The rest of the time we leaned on the rail and watched the convoy, which stretched as far as we could see, or walked the deck, tourist fashion, or shot craps or played blackjack. Starting with five dollars, Haney in the second platoon worked up to twenty-two hundred, lost that trying to get twenty-eight more dollars, and came out with two hundred. If you didn't gamble, however, you read. We were so bored we read candy wrappers, newspaper scraps, antique magazines, anything printed. I even read a comic book. If we had been smart or had been forewarned, we would have brought several interesting books along in our barracks bags.

In some ways that trip was rough, but I enjoyed it, for it was a new, illuminating experience, a peek at the convoy system and the army at sea. We were so crowded we slept two men to a bunk, a day outside on deck, a day inside. On wet nights we hunted out a warm corridor or a spot down below, or we slept in the aisle next to our bunk. The decks were so overrun that there was little time for calisthenics. At night we had to stake out a sleeping place early, if we wanted to lie in a sheltered spot away from the rain and fog. Still, for most of us this voyage was an interesting and novel undertaking and we took it by and large with a jovial spirit. People talk about morale, but all we asked of the army was good food, a warm bed, and fair treatment.

The weather, thank God, was smooth all the way. Once the ocean was so unruly I clung to the rail in utter misery and missed both meals, but that lasted only a day. The Atlantic failed to live up to its reputation that trip, and we arrived without incident or injury off Liverpool ten days after leaving New York. Now we are preparing to disembark. Goodbye.

Your loving uncle,

KEN

Another group, including the 502d, the 377th, the 907th, the Engineers and the Quartermaster, Signal and Ordnance Companies sailed on the S.S. *Strathnaver*. Though their daily shipboard life did not differ much from that of the *Samaria* as described by Webster their overall trip was to turn out somewhat differently. Excerpts from a daily report of the voyage on this vessel follows:

September 4. The last elements closed on the *Strathnaver* at 2140. The *Strathnaver,* a British ship designed for coastal waters on a semitropical run, did not appear to be a suitable troop ship for the number of troops involved and the heavy Atlantic waters of the approaching winter season. Under British standards she was set up to transport about 4,300 troops, which would be overcrowding under American regulations. As it was there were approximately 5,800 troops aboard including a WAC detachment and an RCAF detachment. Accommodations down to include "E" deck were satisfactory. "F" deck was unsatisfactory due to unsanitary garbage disposal bins and low decks open to the sea. "G" and "H" decks were unsatisfactory due to lack of light and air. A rotation was worked out so that while troops were exercising on "A" deck troops in the hold could come out on deck for fresh air. *September 5.* Under way at 0906. *September 6.* The convoy closed up in both interval and distance and there was very little outside activity other than the usual changes in course. *September 9.* Boat drill went off smoothly. *September 11.* Ship arrived in St. Johns [Newfoundland] harbor and anchored for repairs at 0800. *September 12.* Harbor town announced as off limits to all troop personnel. Red Cross arranged for movies in warehouse adjoining docks. Negotiations for use of Fort Pepperrell were in progress. *September 13.* Approximately 1,400 men marched to Fort Pepperrell to spend the night; the remainder of troops marched 8½ miles through the rugged country side bordering the fort. *September 14.* Troops rotated at Fort Pepperrell. Time at post spent in cleaning and recreation. Many soldiers washed their clothing and took lengthy turns at the hot showers. Troops were allowed to visit the post exchange. Picture shows, beer gardens and dances were made possible under supervision of officers. *September 17–18.* Road marches and trips to camp continued. Inspections of barracks have become routine. *September 20.* Obtained clearances on sanitary condition and Quartermaster property at fort in company of Assistant Post Executive Officer. Units at camp returned to ship in passenger list order. *September 21–22–23–24.* False alarm. Road marches continued. Passenger list checked and rechecked by marching men off and on boat. *September 25.* Activity indicates boat about to move out. Boat drill at 1230 hours. *September 26.* Ship headed out to sea. Returned for "lack of air support" and another inspection by divers after striking rock on side of harbor while heading out. *September 27.* Ship headed out to sea again and returned after taking on twenty-eight inches of water due to shifting of ship's weight under live load. *September 28–29–30.* Road marches and trips to Fort Pepperrell again. *October 1.* Have word that an American ship is due to relieve the *Strathnaver*. *October 2.* Began inspections for clearances of troops from Fort Pepperrell. Completed rounds at 2230 and packed for movement to new ship on following day. *October 3.* Cleared remaining two buildings by 0745. Remainder of day and night spent aboard SS *John Ericsson,* a German-built, Swedish ship purchased by the United States Lines. Many German-made items have been replaced by American machines of great efficiency, less volume and requiring less supervision. After the experience with the British ship and seamanship the soldiers cheered when the *Ericsson* skidded into the harbor and sidled up to the dock virtually in one movement. The *Ericsson* was well converted to troop transport work and quarters were much more adequate for the enlisted men. Except for 94 men, bunks were available, and mattresses were procured from the Fort Quartermaster for them. *October 4.* Charted violations of guard orders. Consolidated totals of personnel aboard by compartment. Moved out for Halifax [Nova Scotia] to reprovision and refuel ship for trip over. *October 5.* Reached Halifax. Troops remained aboard. *October 6.* Pulled out late at night for rendezvous with outbound convoy from States. *October 7.* Joined convoy in late afternoon and noted that it exceeded in size the one which we started with. *October 8 to 17.* At sea. Usual convoy tactics. Troops in much better spirits. Administration continues. Troops issued rations for trip to camp after landing. *October 18.* Docked at Liverpool.

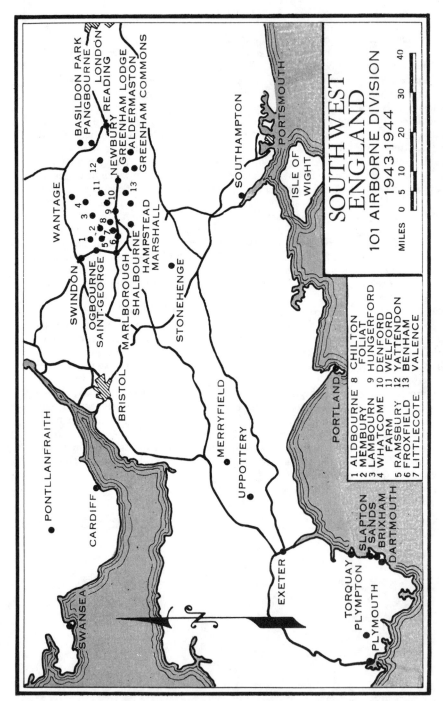

SOUTHWEST ENGLAND
101 AIRBORNE DIVISION
1943-1944

MILES 0 5 10 20 30 40

1 ALDBOURNE   8 CHILTON
2 MEMBURY   FOLIAT
3 LAMBOURN   9 HUNGERFORD
4 WHATCOME   10 DENFORD
   FARM   11 WELFORD
5 RAMSBURY   12 YATTENDON
6 FROXFIELD   13 BENHAM
7 LITTLECOTE   VALENCE

Map 2.

England

"Burdened with barracks bags and looking curiously at the bomb holes in the dock's roof, we staggered down the gang planks, across the pier, and, after the inevitable army wait, on to a quaint, cozy English train. We had arrived.

"As we shuttled rapidly southward, we settled back in our compartments and admired the scenery. The rolling green hills, the endless succession of depressing manufacturing and coal-mining towns, the people waving and giving us the V sign, the little greystone, picture-postcard houses: England. Late that night, just as we were falling asleep, the train stopped at a tiny station called Ogbourne Saint-George. We unloaded in a daze, like men walking in their sleep. All around us were big gentle hills. The air smelled sweet and crisp. Although we were supposed to be in a combat zone, everything was so quiet and orderly I found it hard to believe we weren't just on maneuvers in Connecticut. Then a column of dimmed-out GI trucks rolled down to the station and took us away to what was to be our home for the next nine months.

"When I woke up the next morning, I thought I'd passed out on a Hollywood movie set. All around the area were fairy-book cottages with thatched roofs and rose vines on their sides. Vast horses shaking long manes stomped down narrow winding cobblestone lanes. A soft village green, soon to be plowed by GI vehicles, set off a weathered old grey church whose clock's bell chimed the hours just like Big Ben, and five ancient public houses, their signboards swinging in the breeze, bade us welcome to the land of mild and bitter. I asked the name of the place and was told it was Aldbourne, in Wiltshire County. We were located eighty miles due west of London and nine miles south of Swindon, a 100,000-population railroad town on the Great Western Railway.

"Aldbourne became, as I said before, our home. If the boys wanted to raise hell, they went to Swindon or London; around Aldbourne they acted with restraint, sipping their beer quietly in The Bell or The Cross Keys or the other pubs. Naturally, everybody got a little raucous, especially on the nights the beer and liquor rations came in, but on the whole there were very few fights and not many breakages. We got settled enough in town to become steady customers of the three bakers, who slipped us a lardy cake now and then, and to know most of the local inhabitants by sight, if not by name. Gradually the people thawed out and began to speak to us. A few men in the battalion even married Aldbourne girls. Since our messhall was on the other side of town from our barracks, we had to march through the village on our way to and from meals. The reassuring sight of civilian houses and civilian people made life seem more normal and homelike than it had been in a vast, barren army camp like Bragg.

"Our own physical setup wasn't too bad. F and Headquarters Companies lived in Nissen huts, while D and E Companies savored the comparative luxury of regular one-story wooden barracks. The Nissen huts were dark and gloomy and very dusty, but we improved them as much as possible by painting the interiors with gaudy blue, white, and red enamel and installing radios, which we purchased at outrageous prices in Swindon. (Our first-squad noise box, a triumphant cabinet affair for which we paid 33 pounds, or $132, received only the BBC and the German propaganda station.) The floors of those Nissen huts were made of a tarlike compound so soft our double-deck bunks sank into it and formed cavities all over the surface. We fixed that by putting boards under the bunks, but, clean as we would, we could never get rid of the dust which collected in the holes left behind. Small Victorian coal stoves provided a semblance of heat during the winter.

"Sanitary facilities left much to be desired, however. Our toilet, an unimposing wooden shanty, housed a pair of stone troughs and two rows of wooden seats on honey buckets. The toilet paper, when it was present for duty, was coarse brown, very wartime English stuff. That latrine was no place to linger on a cold night.

"The shower room and wash room were adequate, if somewhat primitive. Despite coal rationing, we managed to have enough hot water, provided, of course, the latrine orderly didn't goldbrick and let the fire go out. Once in a while a clogged drain would flood the place. There were five showers for our two companies of about 250 men, but this was enough, because nobody was very shower-conscious in the cold climate. We washed our hands and faces and shaved in helmets filled with ice water in a building across the street. We looked back on our life in camps in the States as a period of great luxury.

"Living conditions weren't the only things which had changed since we left Fort Bragg. Our diet, hitherto so rich in such accepted staples as fresh milk, fried eggs, and oranges and apples, suddenly dried up on us, and powdered milk, powdered eggs, dehydrated apricots, and dehydrated potatoes became the order of the day. Once or twice a month we got fresh eggs, but we were never given fresh milk while we were overseas. Although it seemed to me that we got more steak in England than we had in the States, the rest of our food, poured from cans, suffered a serious decline in quality. We were not subjected to a constant diet of Spam however. As a matter of fact, I could never see the point of all those jokes about Spam, because as far as the 506th, which missed the pre-Africa, or Spam, period in England, was concerned, we ate the dish only as a variety item, never as a regular. I personally found the powdered eggs hardest to take; even though the cooks converted them into omelette pancakes, they could never disguise their indefinable dry, dull flavor to taste like real eggs.

"Since our PX goods were now rationed, chow hounds accustomed to completing an inadequate meal at Toccoa by stuffing themselves with candy, crackers, Coke, and beer at the PX found themselves cut off without relief in Aldbourne, where our weekly ration consisted of seven packs of cigarettes, three candy bars, one pack of gum, one cake of soap, one box of matches, one package of razor blades, and, sporadically, washrags, towels, combs, crackers, coat hangers, etc."

Thus did David Kenyon Webster of the 506th first view England.

Home in England

The 101st Division's move to England had been spearheaded by an advance detail of 34 officers, 3 warrant officers, and 39 enlisted men who came ashore from the SS *Louis Pasteur* at Liverpool on August 21, 1943. The detail had gone by train to Ogbourne St. George, a village in Wiltshire, one of the two counties—or shires—in which the 101st was to be quartered. Wiltshire and neighboring Berkshire were in the south of England. They were among the English counties nearest to the Cherbourg Peninsula where, months later, the 101st was for the first time to drop into battle.

These two shires, Wilts and Berks, were to be home for the Division for almost a year. To them the Division returned for the few weeks between Normandy and Holland, and it was only in December 1944 that the rear-echelon troops finally closed and moved to the Division's next home, Mourmelon, France (arriving there a few hours after the Division had left for Bastogne). In fact, the Provisional Division Parachute Maintenance Company remained at Chilton Foliat until February 9, 1945. It was to the familiar Wiltshire or Berkshire villages that many of the men of the Division later returned on leaves and furloughs from France, Germany, and Austria, and some of the passengers on the postwar brideships were 101st wives from these towns and villages.

These shires, where most of the men were for the first time to become acquainted with the ways of people of another country, were mostly agricultural and pastoral; a country of plains (Salisbury Plain and the historic Stonehenge were in Wiltshire); of large flocks of sheep, herds of cattle and droves of hogs, one breed of which got its name from Berkshire; and of neat villages. The only large towns were Reading, thirty-five miles from London, whose prison was the scene of Oscar Wilde's *Ballad of Reading Gaol,* and Salisbury with its 700-year-old cathedral, the 404-foot spire of which is still the tallest structure in England.

On the afternoon of September 15, the SS *Samaria* docked in Liverpool, England. The next day that half of the Division which was aboard was on its way to its new billets. All the units except the 506th went to Berkshire.

The 506th was settled in Wiltshire with the regimental CP at Littlecote. At Littlecote also were regimental Headquarters Company, 1st Battalion Headquarters Company, and the regimental staff. The rest of the regiment moved into the nearby villages. The 2d Battalion and Companies A and B were installed in Nissen huts and tarpaper shacks in the little five-pub village of Aldbourne, a two-pound taxi ride from the nearest sizable town, Swindon. The 3d Battalion and Company C were at Ramsbury. Service Company moved into the village of Froxfield and the rigger section moved near the newly established packing sheds at Chilton Foliat.

Of the other units aboard the *Samaria* who settled in Berkshire, the 327th Glider Regiment went to Camp Ranikhet near Reading; the 81st Airborne AA Battalion to Basildon Park, three miles from the town of Pangbourne; the 321st Glider Field Artillery Battalion to Whatcombe Farm, six miles from the town of Wantage where Alfred the Great was born; and the 326th Airborne Medical Company to Donnington Castle at Newbury (later, on December 16 moving to Templeton House in Hungerford).

The SS *Ericsson,* with the rest of the division, reached Liverpool more than a month later, docking on October 18. The Division CP had been set up at Greenham Lodge, just outside Newbury, a town of about 15,000. Division Headquarters and Headquarters Company settled at Greenham Lodge. Just out of Newbury the local racetrack stables were thrown open to the Division Signal Company (which stayed there until January, then replaced the Division medics at Donnington Castle). Two of the artillery battalions, the 907th Glider and the 377th Parachute, moved into Benham Valence near Newbury.

The 502d Parachute Infantry Regiment was quartered in Chilton Foliat just on the Wilts side of the Wiltshire–Berkshire boundary, and in Denford, both sites being near Hungerford, Berkshire. The 426th

Airborne Quartermaster Company and the 801st Airborne Ordnance Company joined the 327th glidermen at Camp Ranikhet, near Reading, and the 326th Airborne Engineer Battalion joined the 81st AA Battalion at Basildon Park. Here the engineers had their headquarters in a 91-room, 232-year-old manor house. The 401st Glider Infantry Regiment moved in near the 327th, at Brock Barracks, Reading, the home of the Royal Berkshire Regiment.

THE 501ST JOINS THE DIVISION

On the 30th of January, 1944 the last unit to make the ocean crossing, the 501st Parachute Regiment, arrived in the United Kingdom. Though long before the fighting was over the status of this regiment became, in the minds of the men of the 101st, a purely academic point, the 501st, due to the tables of organization of airborne divisions, was never an organic part of the 101st Division. Nor, for that matter, was the 506th until the spring of 1945, when a new TO went into effect; until that time the Division, on paper, was composed of two glider regiments, the 327th and the 401st, and one parachute regiment, the 502d, with the other two regiments attached. The new TO authorized two assigned parachute regiments, the 502d and 506th, and one glider regiment, the 327th; the 501st remained attached.

Just as the 506th and the 502d had been marked by the colorful personalities of "Colonel Bob" and "Old Moe" so did the 501st take on something of the personality of its CO, Jumpy Johnson. A large part of the men of the 501st had been volunteers who had gone directly from reception stations to the 501st and there had come under the influence of the Regiment's first and, until his death in Holland, only commanding officer, Col. Howard R. Johnson. A vigorous leader who had attended the Naval Academy but had taken a commission in the Infantry, he was one of the few officers or men who had made more than a hundred parachute jumps. Johnson, then a lieutenant colonel, had become commanding officer of the 501st Regiment upon its activation on November 15, 1942. The place of activation was Camp Toccoa, Georgia, which had just been cleared by the 506th's departure for jump training at Fort Benning. There, beneath Currahee Mountain, Colonel Johnson began to build one of the toughest and most spirited regiments in the United States Army. The period at Toccoa was spent in basic training and in March and April 1943, the regiment moved, a battalion at the time, to the Frying Pan area of Fort Benning for jump training. As the battalions qualified they moved on to Camp Mackall, North Carolina, the regiment closing at that camp on May Day, 1943. In

September the regiment went to Tennessee and there participated in the Second Army maneuvers, returning to Camp Mackall during the first week in November. It was then alerted for overseas shipment, left Mackall on New Year's Day, 1944, for Camp Myles Standish, near Boston, and on January 19, 1944 sailed from Boston aboard the SS *George W. Goethals* in convoy. The 501st landed at Glasgow, Scotland, and moved by train to England. The 1st and 3d Battalions were settled in Lambourn, Berkshire, being quartered in houses, stables and Nissen huts; the rest of the regiment moved to Hampstead Marshall, about fifteen miles away. At Hampstead the parachutists were almost entirely under canvas except for a few headquarters occupying Nissen huts.

The 501st brought with them one of the Regiment's proudest possessions, the original "prop blast" cup. The origin of this cup has been described by Major Larry Legere of the 502d.

In the latter part of October 1940 a group of about ten officers executed a mass jump—I think the first such jump of the 501st. Miley, Howell, Haugen and Yarborough are the only names of which I am certain. To commemorate the day a loving cup was made. A 75mm shell case was partially wrapped with suspension line, which was glazed or bronzed right to the surface of the shell. Two ripcord grips were welded on to serve as handles, and a plaque was also welded on. On the plaque was engraved an inscription noting the execution of the first mass jump, the date, and the names of the officers who had participated. Finally, at the bottom of the plaque, appeared a code message. When decoded with one of the Signal Corps drum-like affairs, it proved to be the formula for the famous "prop blast" a secret concoction drunk by every newly qualified officer while the assemblage chanted (slowly, of course) "1000, 2000, 3000." The 501st threw several prop blast parties for its newly qualified officer-parachutists. When the first group of 502d officers had qualified in August of '41, I was given the task of decoding the message and preparing the punch. (Bill Yarborough, I understand, claims credit for the original recipe.) It consists of two quarts of champagne for every one quart of vodka, with lemon juice and sugar added in proportions which I cannot recall. When we of the 502d wished to make a cup of our own, Chuck Billingslea donated his doorstop—the shell case of an old British 4-inch shell (leave it to the 502d). This was taken to England. The 506th also had one—a very pretty affair and not at all as crude as the 502d version.

TRAINING

The Division was scattered along an east-west line with the glider units in the Reading area, the area nearest London, to the east; Division headquarters, artillery, and special troops about midway, in the Newbury area; and the parachute units in the Hungerford area along the Berks–Wilts boundary and in Wilts, to the west. However, though the Screaming Eagle patches became a familiar sight throughout the area and even throughout England, it was not until January 26, 1944, that the presence of American airborne troops in the ETO was publicly acknowledged, and even then the 101st Division was not identified.

The first days and weeks were spent in getting accustomed to the new surroundings—the little villages, the makeshift barracks, the powdered eggs, the fog, the warm mild and bitters, the pence, shillings and pounds, the "You cawn't miss it, old chap." Orientation talks and films on how to get along with the British were given a high priority on the program. After the troops were settled and oriented in Anglo-American relations, training for the invasion was begun.

Specific training for the missions which were still to be assigned could not begin for several months, but a program of physical conditioning, airborne training, small-unit tactical training, and general subjects was put into effect. A six-day week with forty-eight hours per week of actual training was adopted; and, remarkably, the weather stayed good for days on end. The average program of a parachute infantry unit of the 101st for the month of October 1943 called for 15-, 18-, 21- and 25-mile hikes, eight hours a week of night operations, an hour daily of close combat, and other scheduled subjects such as street-fighting technique, combat-team field exercises, map reading, first aid, and chemical warfare training. Instruction was given in the use and firing of German weapons.

Test marches for all personnel were conducted in late November and early December, bringing back memories of the early Toccoa–Atlanta and Fort Bragg–Chapel Hill hiking days. All troops were required to make a 25-mile hike with full field equipment in twenty-four hours, and a 25-mile hike with combat pack in twelve hours. Service and administrative troops were required to do fifteen miles in five hours with a combat pack.

Parachute regiments made company- and battalion-size jumps during these months. During one of these jumps, on November 26, there occurred a dramatic example of quick thinking which saved a man's life. Technician Corporal—later Lieutenant—Francis Fleming of Headquarters Company, 1st Battalion, 506th, was coming down when another trooper with a streamer hit his chute. Corporal Fleming was able to grab the collapsed canopy as it went by and held on until the man, Corp. Robert S. Brochard, was able to open his reserve chute and save himself from fatal, though not from serious, injury. Corporal Fleming received the Soldier's Medal.

The glidermen began learning about the big British Horsa gliders; how to load and lash aboard equipment such as jeeps, trailers, and antitank guns; and personnel flights familiarized them with the feel of riding in the new type of motorless craft. The artillerymen and anti-aircraft and antitank batteries went out on the artillery ranges, often to Wales, for combat-firing practice. In December and January anti-aircraft firing was held on the almost treeless downs of Penhale Anti-aircraft Range in Cornwall at the southwestern tip of England; more than four hundred soldiers from the Division participated, including everybody assigned to a .50-caliber machine gun or to any other auto-matic antiaircraft weapon.

A number of schools and training courses were organized during the fall and winter months. Officers' and noncommissioned officers' schools operated throughout the Division. Specialized courses such as those run by the Division engineers on booby traps and removal of mines drew quotas from all the 101st units. Other officers and men left for schools and training centers throughout England. Courses ranged from cooking and baking to military intelligence, from combat swimming (four days in London) to servicing servicycles (two days at the 801st Ordnance Company's third-echelon shop).

Another type of schooling was tried somewhat later, in February and March 1944, when several hundred officers and enlisted men from all of the Division organizations exchanged places for two weeks with an equal number from the British 6th Airborne Division. As nearly as possible the exchange was made to corresponding units and indi-vidual assignments—personnel from the 326th Airborne Engineer Battalion, for example, went to units of the Royal Engineers (Air-borne), a lieutenant from the 81st AA Battalion acted as a section leader in an Airlanding Antiaircraft Battery, a sergeant from the 506th took over his British counterpart's position in a parachute battalion. The exchange was profitable for both divisions, for those concerned gained new ideas of weapons, procedures, and tactics and arrived at a better understanding of the men beside whom they were to fight in Normandy and Holland.

On October 21st the 101st Parachute Jumping School was activated in the 502d Headquarters area at Chilton Foliat in order to qualify as parachutists certain key personnel in non-parachute units of the Divi-sion. Col. Robert F. Sink of the 506th was named commandant, and the first classes began on November 7. By invasion time Colonel Sink, assisted by Capt. Herbert M. Sobel, Lts. David Herber and James Pothier, and an enlisted cadre, had trained and put through their five qualifying jumps more than four hundred officers and men, not only from the Division but from all over the ETO.

During the winter officers and men from various units were sent to a Pathfinder School conducted by the Troop Carrier Command. These men were then set up as a provisional Pathfinder company under the command of Capt. Frank Lillyman.

With the winter coming on the training of the Division intensified and began to be integrated into a pattern in which exercises and operations on a battalion, regimental and, finally, a Division scale became possible. Already battalion jumps had been made. Now the first exercise involving all units of the Division, a command post exercise, was held on December 10-11 in the vicinity of Yattendon, northeast of Newbury and toward Reading. Only command staff communication elements down to and including battalions participated, so the mass of the Division was not involved. The exercise was directed and controlled by General McAuliffe.

Following the CPX and until the end of the month regimental combat team field exercises for both the parachute and glider regiments were held. The parachutists operated in the vicinity of Shalbourne, south of Hungerford, and the glidermen maneuvered near Ramsbury, west of Hungerford. The parachute operations were directed by General McAuliffe, assisted by Lt. Col. Charles H. Chase of the 506th. The glider operations were under General Pratt, with Lt. Col. Curtis D. Renfro of the 327th Glider Regiment as his deputy. Due to the tight situation in planes and gliders only one regiment at a time, parachute or glider, plus its attached units, was able to undertake an actual airborne exercise.

A second Division CPX was held in the Ramsbury–Hungerford area on December 28-29 with all personnel participating. However, only command-post personnel were flown; all other personnel ran through the problem from simulated landings after being hauled to their drop or landing zones by truck. On January 7 an experimental resupply mission was flown, with two serials totalling 80 planes and 80 gliders dropping or landing 225 tons of supplies.

During the winter the Division adopted unit code names which it used during the rest of its existence. Division itself became Kangaroo; Division Headquarters and Headquarters Company was Klaxon; the 501st was Klondike; 502d, Kickoff; 506th, Kidnap; 327th, Keepsake; 326th Engineers, Kiwi; 81st AA, Kentucky; Division Artillery, King-fish; 321st FA, Kansas; 377th FA, Kite; 907th FA, Kilogram; 326th Medical Company, Kindergarten; 426th Quartermaster Company, Kitchen; 801st Ordnance Company, Kildare; Division Signal Company, Kilowatt; and the Division Reconnaissance Platoon, King. The 463d

Parachute Field Artillery, when it was attached to the Division just before Bastogne, took the code name Keynote. The usual military designations for battalions and companies or batteries were used—Red, White and Blue for 1st, 2d and 3d battalions of a regiment and Able, Baker, Charlie, Dog, Easy, Fox, George, How, Item, King, Love and Mike for the alphabetical companies. Thus, Company E of the 327th Glider Infantry Regiment became Keepsake Easy and was part of White Battalion. Easily recognizable emblems were also adopted and stencilled on the sides of the helmets. The regimental emblems were the suits of playing cards; the 501st had diamonds, the 502d hearts, the 506th spades, and the 327th clubs. Division Artillery was identified by a circle, the engineers by the letter E, the 81st AA Battalion by a triangle, and Division Headquarters by a square. Battalions within a regiment and other component units were designated by marks: a mark on the right side of an emblem indicated first battalion; at the bottom, second; at the left, third; and at the top, headquarters.

Genesis of Operation Overlord

As the 101st went into its second winter its destiny was still a matter of conjecture to its members. That the Division would participate in the expected invasion of Europe almost nobody doubted; but where and when was a popular subject during night sessions in the barracks and huts and tents. However, the plans which were to send the 101st into Normandy on the morning of June 6, 1944, had already had their conception months, even years before. Soon after Pearl Harbor—before there was even an airborne division in the United States Army—the first cross-Channel invasion plans were put down on paper.

The first of these U.S.-British plans, drawn up in the early months of 1942, was Operation Roundup. Roundup contemplated an invasion date of April 1, 1943, with an emergency date of September 15, 1942. The emergency plan, known as Operation Sledgehammer, was to be put into effect only if the Russian situation became desperate or in the event that the Germans themselves should become critically weakened. Sledgehammer assumed that there would be available in England for the operation four United States parachute battalions and one British parachute brigade. For the 1943 Roundup version it was estimated that there would be available one United States airborne division and eleven parachute battalions, all American, and one British parachute brigade. Airborne troops were to be employed in these operations "in assisting the ground forces to establish beachheads and to prevent rapid movements of German reinforcements."

It was in connection with Roundup that General Lee in June 1942 made his hurried trip to England with General Eisenhower. General Lee, after studying Roundup, especially the airborne phase, warned the planners that the available airborne troops would be inadequate to carry out the airborne mission; and he reported this finding to Gen. Mark W. Clark, then Chief of Staff of Army Ground Forces. His recommendation, that an American airborne division and an American parachute brigade be organized, equipped and trained as soon as possible for the Roundup operation, was approved by General Clark.

Meanwhile, another plan was in the making and though it turned out that neither Roundup nor Sledgehammer was attempted this new operation was successfully carried out. It was Torch, the November 1942 invasion of North Africa. Thus it happened that when General Lee's recommendation was forwarded by General Clark to Lt. Gen. Lesley J. McNair, Commanding General of Army Ground Forces, General McNair, to provide an additional division for use in the Mediterranean area, approved the activation of not one, but two airborne divisions. Thus were born the 82d and 101st Airborne Divisions.

Actually, only one U.S. parachute battalion, the 2d of the 503d Parachute Regiment (later the 509th Parachute Battalion), was used in Operation Torch, jumping to seize North African airports. But in July 1943, the 82d Airborne Division went into action as part of the first large-scale use of airborne troops by the Allies. This was in Operation Husky, the American–British invasion of Sicily. Here parachutists and glidermen of the U.S. 82d and the British 1st Airborne Divisions were dropped on the island. In September, while the 101st was making the move from the U.S. to England, Operation Avalanche, the joint American–British invasion of the Italian mainland, was launched. Units of the 82d still in Sicily were used in this assault, chiefly to reinforce the threatened Italian beachheads.

While these operations were getting under way in the Mediterranean, planning for a 1944 cross-Channel invasion had begun. The final decision that an invasion of France would be mounted during 1944 was made in May 1943, at a Washington meeting of President Roosevelt, Prime Minister Churchill, and the combined Chiefs of Staff.

Two months before the invasion plan was accepted by the President and the Prime Minister, General Lee made another trip to England, this time accompanied by Maj. George M. Griswold, Assistant G-4; Maj. Lewis M. Gable, Assistant G-3; his aide, Lt. Evans Thornton; and an Air Corps officer, Lt. Col. Silas R. Richards. There in London, during March 1943, General Lee was briefed on the new operation. He held long talks with the planning staff and with the top officers of the British and American armies, going over the plans in detail with these men. As the operation stood in March 1943, use of only one American airborne division, the 101st, was contemplated, for the 82d had already been ordered to Africa, was earmarked for the Mediterranean, and, assumedly, would not be available for a cross-Channel invasion. General Lee again recommended that the number of American airborne troops for the operation be upped; and by the time the plan was presented to the President, Prime Minister and Combined Chiefs of Staff, it provided for additional parachute units.

The first draft of the cross-Channel invasion plan emerged in July 1943 with the operation name of Overlord. In August, at the Quebec Conference in Canada, Operation Overlord was approved by the President, the Prime Minister, and the Combined Chiefs of Staff.

This first draft, as of July 15, 1943, envisioned a landing to be made on the coast of France somewhere between Le Havre at the mouth of the Seine and the Cherbourg Peninsula. Actually, except for the 1944 addition of Utah Beach, this original concept of two main invasion areas, a British beach near Caen and an American beach (later called Omaha) a few miles west, remained unchanged.

This first draft estimated that on May 1, 1944, there would be available for the invasion one U.S. airborne division, five parachute regiments, and one airborne tank battalion; the British would have available one airborne division. However, it was estimated that only the equivalent of two-thirds of an airborne division, approximately one-third of the total airborne forces available, could be put into action simultaneously, due to an expected shortage of planes. Six hundred thirty-two aircraft were assigned to the mission, 594 being C-47s and 38 being converted British bombers. First priority missions were to be the capture of the city of Caen and the crossings of the Orne River between Caen and the Channel, both missions in the British zone of operations, and the destruction of a battery of 155mm coastal guns at the western edge of Omaha Beach. The Caen area missions were to be carried out by the British airborne division and the coastal guns were to be taken care of by a U.S. parachute battalion. These missions would initially take all the available aircraft. In addition there were certain secondary missions to be carried out if additional aircraft were available or if those used on the first wave were able to fly a second mission.

These secondary missions called for six U.S. parachute battalions to drop inland from Omaha to seize and hold crossings over the Aure River and to block crossings over the Vire River. It was also hoped that aircraft might be available to make an airborne assault on Carentan on the Douve River, well to the west of Omaha Beach, and to attempt the capture of the Vire River bridge at Isigny.

Further details of Operation Overlord were worked out during the Cairo and Teheran Conferences of November and December, 1943. Meanwhile, the men, weapons, and materials which were to make possible the operation were moving across the ocean from the United States to England.

In April, General Lee had returned from England to the United States, leaving Major Gable in London with the planners. In August, as the Division was preparing to leave Fort Bragg for England, General Lee was again ordered to fly to England. He arrived in London on August 21 with Lt. Col. William Stewart, 101st Division Air Officer; Lt. Col. R. D. Millener, G-3; and Lt. Jack Robbins, his aide. There he set up an airborne planning agency under Lt. Gen. Jacob L. Devers, commander of the European Theater of Operations. General Lee and his staff were brought up to date on Operation Overlord, and began intensive work on the airborne phase. About the 1st of September, General Lee made a trip to the Mediterranean to observe the airborne operations there and returned in the middle of the month to find only part of his Division had reached England, the rest having been delayed in Newfoundland by ship trouble. Six members of his staff were flown by plane from Newfoundland to England.

All that summer and fall General Lee and his staff attended an almost constant series of conferences on Overlord and certain other tentative emergency, alternate, and deceptive operations. One of these last, Cockade-Wadham, was among the amazing deceptions of the war.

OPERATIONS WADHAM AND RANKIN

On July 1, 1943, the Commanding General of ETO issued two Wadham directives: the first, revealed to only a few officers in higher headquarters, explained that it was an elaborate deceptive invasion plan, not to be actually mounted; the second, to all appearances genuine, made no reference to the deception features. Planning proceeded on the basis of the second directive.

Wadham ostensibly called for the invasion of the Brest Peninsula of France at the end of September 1943 by a task force of the U.S. V and VII Corps. V Corps, the assault corps, was to consist of the 28th and 29th Infantry and the 101st Airborne Divisions. Once Wadham got under way it took on every indication of a *bona fide* operation. Real activities were phased to create the illusion of an invasion.

General Lee and his G-3, Colonel Millener, after their arrival in England on August 23, were briefed on both the real and deceptive plans, and Colonel Millener worked out the 101st's part of the Wadham plans. Shortly thereafter the 101st began to arrive and immediately a Berlin English language broadcast announced the arrival, the location of Division Headquarters at Newbury, and assured the General that he and his command were welcome to Europe and would receive a warmer welcome if and when they ever came to the Continent. How this information leaked to the Germans was never learned; however, it resulted in a good deal of security instruction being given to the troops.

Another operation, details or even the existence of which were known to only a very few officers, was worked out down to battalion and company levels, and the plans were held in a standby condition. This operation was Rankin, which was to be carried out in case of a German surrender before the Normandy invasion, a possibility due to a military disaster on the Russian front, a German internal collapse, or both. As the only airborne division available in England in February 1944, the 101st figured prominently in Rankin.

Maturing of Operation Overlord

In December, Gen. Dwight D. Eisenhower was appointed Supreme Commander of the Allied Expeditionary Force with the mission of crossing the Channel and destroying the German armies in Western Europe. At the time of General Eisenhower's appointment Operation Overlord had not been essentially altered since the original version. There was still the one landing beach and the target date remained May 1, 1944.

General Eisenhower, once he had familiarized himself with the operation, was concerned about the size of the invasion force and the width of the invasion beaches; he felt both should be increased. In January, to allow for these increases another beach, Utah, fifteen miles north of Omaha and the nearest beachhead to Cherbourg, was added. Utah Beach presented certain disadvantages; it was separated from Omaha by the Carentan Estuary with the Vire and Douve Rivers to be crossed in order to link-up the beaches. Behind the beach itself was a flooded area which would present an obstacle to the advance of the troops from the beach inland. This latter terrain factor was one of

the things which made Utah Beach a textbook setup for the employment of airborne troops.

During December and January the detailed planning with both U.S.
and British officers participating continued. In London the United
States First Army, which was the main force in Neptune (the code
name for the assault phase of Overlord), had set up a headquarters
under its new commander, Lt. Gen. Omar N. Bradley who held many
conferences with his commanders, and to these he asked the ranking
U.S. airborne commander in England, General Lee. To General Lee's
advice on the airborne phase of the operations he listened attentively. It
had been decided during the fall to bring Maj. Gen. Matthew Ridgway's
division, the 82d, up from the Mediterranean for Operation Overlord.
The 82d had landed in North Ireland on December 9, 1943, and had
moved to Braunstone Parke, Leicester, England, on February 14; after
his arrival in Ireland General Ridgway frequently came to England to
join the conferences.

On January 21 in London, General Eisenhower presented the revised
plan of Operation Overlord to a meeting of the highest British and
American officers. Under the revised plan the new beach, Utah, was
added, the target date was set back a month, to May 31, and an enlarged
use of airborne forces was called for. This last step was made possible
by an increase in the estimated number of aircraft which would be
available. Instead of the 632 troop-carrying or towing aircraft originally provided for, Overlord now called for almost twice that number.

Estimated as being available for D-day were 1,234 planes, 1,022 being
C-47s and 218 being converted British bombers. There would also be
available 3,300 gliders. This lift would be sufficient for one complete
airborne division and approximately two airborne brigades, followed
approximately twenty-four hours later by a second complete airborne
division. The original idea of assigning the city of Caen to an airborne
division was discarded and instead two British airborne brigades were
to land east of the Orne River to cover the left flank of the British
beach. The destruction of the Omaha Beach coastal battery was transferred from the airborne to the Rangers.

Of the two U.S. airborne divisions one, under the command of the
U.S. First Army, was to drop behind Utah Beach with the main objective of assisting the seaborne landing on that beach. It is probable that
from the beginning General Bradley had in mind the 101st for this
assignment. The other U.S. airborne division, the battle-tested 82d, was
to drop approximately twenty-four hours later in either the U.S. First
Army area or in the British area.

The location of the airborne zone fulfilled exactly General Lee's prediction of August, 1942, when he had pointed out to General Ridgway on a map of France where he believed their two newly activated divisions would be employed if a cross-Channel invasion were attempted. The location of the zones, both American and British, also coincided very closely with a prophetic book, *Paratroops,* published in early 1943 and written by Maj. F. O. Miksche, a Czech then with the Fighting French Forces in England. A map in *Paratroops* illustrating the employment of three airborne divisions in support of a hypothetical seaborne invasion of Normandy showed the divisions landing in three zones, two of which were almost overlays of the actual D-day zones and the third only a few miles off. (After the war Gen. Maxwell Taylor, who succeeded General Lee, confessed that on the eve of D-day one of his two worries stemmed from having discovered the book, with its map, being sold on the bookstalls of London and, presumably, in the hands of the German General Staff. His other chief source of concern was a series of aerial photographs made just before the invasion showing a sudden studding of stakes and poles on possible parachute and glider landing fields in the invasion area.)

The strongest objection to the revised use of the airborne troops was raised by the Deputy Chief Commander, Air Chief Marshal Sir Trafford Leigh-Mallory, Commander in Chief of the Allied Air Expeditionary Force. The Air Marshal was dubious about the new beach and particularly, knowing the strong antiaircraft defenses in the area, of the chances of a successful airborne drop. General Eisenhower finally had to proceed with the operation over the strong objections of his Air Commander in Chief; and even in the last days before the invasion the Air Marshal believed that the airborne losses would run seventy-five per cent or higher. (On D-day, after the drop, Leigh-Mallory wrote Eisenhower, congratulating him on the wisdom of his decision. Nothing, he wrote, had ever given him greater pleasure than to admit he was wrong.) Almost four years later, on February 7, 1948, when he retired as Chief of Staff of the United States Army, General Eisenhower was asked by a reporter what he considered the high point of his thirty-three years of military service. "Pondering a moment, he replied that he supposed 'the natural thing would be to say it was when the surrender agreement was signed.' This occasion, however, had been anticipated and 'discounted' somewhat in advance, Eisenhower added. 'I think the greatest moment was when I got the word that the 82d and 101st Airborne Divisions had landed and gone into action on the Cherbourg Peninsula . . .' Had it failed, he went on, he would have gone to his grave haunted by the thought that he had killed 20,000 young Americans stupidly."

The same group of American officers who had worked together with their British counterparts in producing the Initial Joint Plan now went to work to prepare the plan which would cover the first twenty days of the American phase of the operation. On February 25 the plan was completed. Now, for the first time, divisions knew their assignment and could begin specific training.

THE NEPTUNE PHASE

Neptune, the assault phase of Overlord, called for simultaneous D-day landings to be made on the American and British beaches. The assault on the American beaches was to be made by the United States First Army. On Omaha the V Corps, with the 1st and 29th Infantry Divisions, was to attack; on Utah VII Corps was to send the 4th Infantry Division in by sea.

The 101st was to come in by parachute and glider at about H minus 4 hours with the principal mission of knocking out the defense along the causeways which crossed the inundated areas back of Utah Beach and the margin of land beyond the inundations. The Division had the additional missions of taking the battery of guns just back of the beach, of capturing St. Mère-Église, six miles inland, and of seizing certain crossings both of the Merderet River which bounded the beachhead area on the west and of the Douve River which bounded the area to the south. Later the Division was to attack and seize Carentan and was, in general, to be responsible for the security of the southern flank of the beachhead as the VII Corps pushed north to capture Cherbourg.

The 82d was to land in the vicinity of St. Sauveur-le-Vicomte, more than half way across the base of the Peninsula, and was to prevent the enemy from moving reinforcements up the western side of the Peninsula from the south. The two divisions were eventually to effect a juncture, thereby cutting the Peninsula at its base.

On February 5 General Lee had a heart attack and was hospitalized; General Pratt, the Assistant Division Commander, took temporary command. On March 4 General Lee got the heart-breaking news that he would not return to active duty with the Division which he had activated, trained, and carried to the edge of combat. On April 9 he began the trip back to the United States where, after eight months of hospitalization and convalescence, he was retired with the rank of major general.

Brig. Gen. Maxwell D. Taylor, former artillery commander of the
82d, took over the 101st Division on March 14th. The 43-year-old general had been considered one of the promising officers of the Army since
his West Point days, when, the second youngest man in his class, he
had graduated fourth from the top. While in Sicily he had made a
dangerous trip by boat and plane into enemy-held Rome to arrange
with Marshal Badoglio for a drop by the 82d paratroopers to seize the
Rome airfields—a mission which had to be cancelled because of the
German forces in the area. To General Taylor and his staff went the
job of breaking down the mission assigned to the Division under Overlord, of figuring out who was to do what, and of seeing that the Division on D-day was as prepared for its job as it was possible to be.

A big question always in the background during this winter and
spring of planning and preparation was lift; how many planes, gliders,
and ships would be available to the airborne? The question of lift for
the 82d was settled during the spring when enough planes were made
available to enable the parachute elements of that division along with
those of the 101st to drop before H-hour instead of the following night
or next day, as called for in the first plan. One of the results of this
simultaneous drop was a drastic reduction in the number of gliders for
the 101st due to the assignment to the 82d of the planes which would
have been used as tugs. Whereas in March 1944 sufficient gliders were
allotted to bring in 2,353 troops of the 101st, including the two battalions of glider artillery, 1st Battalion of the 401st Glider Infantry, the
antitank batteries of the 81st AA Battalion and the antitank platoons of
the 321st and 401st Regiments, the Medical Company, most of Division
Headquarters, Signal Company, Quartermaster Company, the Reconnaissance Platoon, and a number of vehicles, the predawn glider serials
on June 6 brought in only 148 personnel, followed by 165 more that
evening. This reduction required careful readjustment of assignments
of the remaining gliders, necessitated a larger seaborne echelon, and
was a deciding factor in setting back the timing of the attack on Carentan until the seaborne glider battalions could be brought up.

As the winter and spring months passed more and more officers and
men in the Division were "bigoted." (A bigoted person was one who
had been told when and where the invasion was to come.) The process continued down through the ranks until about a week before D-day
battalion staffs were bigoted; and then, a few days later in the marshalling area, the information was given to every man who was to take part
in the invasion. Division officers taking part in the planning read
through and studied pounds of documents—plans, annexes, overlays,

intelligence reports, maps, aerial photographs. From many sources came a constant stream of information; a German defense battalion had been shifted, a new gun emplacement was being built, antilanding poles had been installed in a certain field, a pillbox had been put in at a certain crossroads. Available information ranging from who owned the milk-plant in Carentan, to which houses were to be put off-limits in Cherbourg were in the Overlord-Neptune documents. And as the information came in and was analyzed, certain changes had to be made. The intelligence responsible for the most drastic of these changes came less than a week before D-day. It had to do with the carefully plotted enemy strength in the Utah Beach area.

It was known to the planners of Overlord that the 101st and 82d Divisions would be greeted, at least at first, by two German divisions, the 709th and the 243d. The 709th, with an estimated strength of 14,000, had the job of manning most of the coastal defenses along Utah Beach. Between a quarter and a third of the 709th was believed non-German, including many Russians who for one reason or another had chosen or had been forced to fight in the German Army. These non-German units were commanded mostly by German officers and noncoms. The 243d, whose estimated strength was 6,000-7,000, was located on the western part of the peninsula opposite Utah Beach and was assigned the defense of the western shore; this division would be readily available for the defense of the eastern shore and had many units in the sector in which the 82d was to drop. Both divisions had been classified as "static" troops, troops not considered fit for arduous field duty, but as the invasion became more imminent both had been upgraded to "limited employment" or "low establishment"; the 243d was supposed to have a number of veterans from the Russian front.

In addition to these divisions there were smaller units in the area. It was believed that elements of the 716th Division might be met; part of the 17th Machine-Gun Battalion was believed to be in Carentan; and many field, coastal, naval, and antiaircraft batteries were known to be scattered throughout the sector. No panzer battalions were believed to be near the beach area.

But less than ten days before the invasion, it was learned that the 91st Division had moved into the Carentan–St. Sauveur-le-Vicomte–Valognes area, between the 82d and 101st drop zones. Though there was nothing to indicate that this movement was based on a leak in the Neptune plan it necessarily caused far-reaching changes in the Utah Beach operation plans. The new strength represented by the 91st Division meant that the three enemy divisions might be able to launch an early counterattack in force against Utah Beach. On May 27 the ambitious original plan of cutting the Cherbourg Peninsula by dropping the 82d on the western side was discarded and the 82d drop zone was moved well to the east. The 82d was now to drop astride the Merderet River, in the area where the main strength of the 501st had been scheduled to drop. Two regiments would land west and one east of the river to establish bridgeheads west of Ste. Mère-Église; and the capture of that town was also assigned to the 82d.

The effect of the arrival of German 91st Division was less radical in the case of the 101st. Most of the missions remained unchanged. The 501st, less the 3d Battalion, had its drop zone moved from the Merderet–Ste. Mère-Église sector where the 82d now was to drop, to the southern sector along the Douve. There it was to jump with the 3d Battalion of the 506th and take over the job of destroying the railway and highway bridges across the Douve just north of Carentan, and the seizure and operation of the nearby Douve River locks. The additional strength along the Douve now allowed General Taylor to plan an earlier drive south across the Douve with the objective of taking Carentan and joining up with the Omaha Beach forces. It was decided, therefore, that the two wooden bridges between Carentan and the sea which had been scheduled for demolition by the 3d Battalion of the 506th would be prepared for destruction with the decision whether or not to blow them left up to the commanding officer of the 506th. Part of the 3d Battalion would cross to the far side of the bridges and hold the two bridgeheads for the Division's drive south. Before the 82d's last-minute change the 101st's mission, once it had been relieved back of the beach by the 4th Division, had been to "make contact with V Corps in vicinity of Carentan." Now the new and final plan made the 101st's D-day-plus mission more specific: "As soon as practicable after its elements in the 4th Division sector have been relieved by the 4th Division Carentan will be seized and contact with the V Corps in the vicinity of Carentan established and secured."

EXERCISE BEAVER

While the Neptune phase of Overlord was taking its final shape during the late winter and spring of 1944, a series of coordinated preparatory exercises was being conducted in England by the assault forces which were scheduled to invade Hitler's Fortress Europe. These exercises, each involving more men, vessels, and materials than the one preceding, were conducted on certain parts of the English coast from which all inhabitants had been cleared. These great amphibious operations not only allowed the commanders and the men to gain experience but they also had the effect of confusing the enemy. His aerial reconnaissance and intelligence would report each massing of invasion-size armadas and cause the German defenses to be alerted, only to have nothing happen. The confusion was not restricted to the enemy; to those participating each operation seemed more snafued than the last; yet it was the experience gained, the strayed platoons, the snarled communications, the stalled tanks, the uncoordinated artillery, which eventually made possible the D-day payoff. The 101st took part in three of these exercises.

The first in which the 101st joined was Exercise Beaver, held during a five-day period from March 27 through March 31. Beaver was held on a stretch of coast near the port of Torquay in Devonshire, down in the very southwest corner of England and not far from the Cornwall downs where the Division's artillery and antiaircraft practices had been fired. The 101st's sector, at Slapton Sands, ten miles south of Torquay, was in as many ways as possible a tactical reproduction of Utah Beach in Normandy. Slapton Sands was a long, narrow beach separated from the mainland by an elongated shallow fresh-water lake and adjoining swampland, both a few hundred feet wide, and crossed by two bridges. The lakes corresponded to the inundated areas back of Utah Beach, and the bridges to the Utah Beach causeways.

The VII Corps' part of the exercise, carried out under the direction of the corps commander, Maj. Gen. J. Lawton Collins, was the same operation which, in June, was to succeed in Normandy. Spearheading the VII Corps attack in the exercise was the 4th Infantry Division, which came ashore from landing craft at H-hour of D-day, 0900, March 26, to seize the beachhead and cover the landing and advance inland of the VII Corps toward an imaginary Cherbourg. Preceding the 4th Division at H-hour minus 5—0400—the paratroopers of the 101st "jumped" behind the beach to clear the way.

Actually, this was a GMC "jump" out of the back of a truck. The units participating—Division Headquarters, the 502d, the staff of the 506th, Company C of the 326th Engineers, and the 377th Parachute Field Artillery Battalion—left Wiltshire and Berkshire by truck and train on the 26th and 27th of March. On the 28th the troops were briefed on the operation and at dusk on the 29th were marched or trucked to their drop zones and scattered as they would have been on a normal drop.

During the night and the following day, the 502d, as in the Neptune plan, proceeded to capture the causeway bridges leading inland from the beaches and a simulated 155mm gun position, and secured the north flank of the beachhead; the 506th established the southern flank. Actual aerial and naval bombardment of areas from which all personnel had been cleared preceded the 4th Division's landing, and the infantrymen used live ammunition against simulated beach defenders.

Exercise Beaver, like the exercises which were to follow and like the real thing, Neptune, was complete with field orders, annexes, maps, overlays, and all the other paraphernalia of a large-scale operation. And, as all such operations seem to the participants, Beaver was mostly confusion to the paratroopers of the 101st. Coordination between units of the 101st and other organizations and communications were frequently snarled. Once, a group of artillery observers found out just in time that they were in the 502d's machine-gun and mortar impact zone. But lessons were being learned and when on the 31st the Division entrained for its home stations, General Taylor and his staff were aware of the kinks which would have to be straightened out before the real D-day.

EXERCISE TIGER

Less than a month later and at the same place the second large-scale exercise, and the first in which all units of the Division engaged, was held. This exercise, Tiger, was staged during the week of April 23-30. Like Beaver, Tiger was a rehearsal of the opening phase of the Utah Beach landings. Also like Beaver, Tiger was a VII Corps affair directed by the corps commander, General Collins; and the seaborne division for which the 101st was to open the way inland was the 4th Division.

Air landings were again simulated, the paratroopers and glider-riders being brought up ahead of time to their drop zones. This time a CPX group from the 501st joined the 502d and the 506th Parachute Regiments. There were now three 101st echelons; parachute, glider, and seaborne. In the parachute echelon were the 502d, 506th, and 501st Regiments, the 377th Parachute Field Artillery Battalion, and Company C of the 326th Engineers; and elements of Division Headquarters, Division Artillery Headquarters, the Division Signal Company, and the 326th Medical Company. The glider echelon which, like the parachute, simulated landings, was composed of the 321st and 907th Glider Field Artillery Battalions, the 326th Medical Company, the Division Signal Company, the 426th Airborne Quartermaster Company, and elements of Division Headquarters and Division Artillery Headquarters. The seaborne echelon consisted of the 327th Glider Regiment and the 1st Battalion of the 401st Glider Regiment.

Movement by train and truck from the Wilts–Berks area took place

Prime Minister Winston Churchill and General Taylor review the 327th Glider Infantry Regiment at Newbury.

The demonstration drop on 23 March 1944 at Newbury, before General Eisenhower and Prime Minister Churchill.

between April 23 and 25. Confusion began early. Some of the units reached their marshalling areas to find they were not expected. The 327th was bivouacked in sixteen different camps spread out over forty miles and the regimental commander had no transportation to contact his units. When this regiment loaded at Dartmouth and Plympton onto sixteen different LSTs and LSIs and no notice of the order of loading or unloading was given to Division or regiment, the confusion was compounded. Embarkation for the short sea voyage was completed by the morning of the 26th. During the sea voyage, German torpedo boats slipped in among the assault craft and sank two LSTs, killing 442 and wounding 41 U.S. troops, in addition to naval losses. None of the vessels carrying Division personnel was touched, however.

In Tiger, Neptune plans, formations, and conditions were adhered to as closely as the limitations of equipment and facilities would permit. The handling of the troops through the concentration and marshalling areas, the embarkation of the seaborne units, the control by the Navy of the seaborne phase, the carrying out of prearranged naval fire on and aerial bombardment of cleared areas, the establishment, maintenance and testing of all means and channels of communications, the testing of the supply and evacuation arrangements—all these and other phases of what was to be the greatest, toughest, and most complicated invasion ever staged were given a semi-final dry run. Elaborate secrecy and security precautions were taken. To prevent identification of the units taking part in the exercise through German interception of radio messages all units were redesignated and such words as "parachute," "glider," "airborne" and the like were carefully avoided. The 101st Division became for the duration of the exercise the First Tank Destroyer Group, the 327th Glider Regiment became the 899th Tank Destroyer Battalion, the 907th Glider Field Artillery Battalion became the 951st Field Artillery Battalion, and so on throughout the Division units.

The missions of the 502d and 506th remained about the same as in Beaver; the 502d with the 377th Parachute Field Artillery Battalion attached, seized the northern sites across the inundations back of the Slapton Sands beach, captured the simulated gun position and protected the north flank of the beachhead. The 506th less the 3d Battalion seized the southern exits and the 3d Battalion protected the south flank. The 506th took two points on the left flank which corresponded to the wooden bridges across the Douve River below Carentan in Normandy.

The 501st less the 3d Battalion simulated a landing farther inland and took a road junction and two crossings of the Avon River, corresponding to the 501st's Neptune mission which at that time was the capture of Ste. Mère-Église and two nearby crossings of the Merderet. The 3d Battalion of the 501st marked and protected the glider and assembly areas. The 327th and 401st were at first in Division reserve.

Early in the exercise the 65th Armored Field Artillery Battalion, armed with self-propelled 105mm howitzers, was attached to the Division, an attachment which was to pay off in Normandy where the battalion's guns were to be a steady source of help.

The exercise began on the morning of April 27 when the parachute echelon's simulated drop was reported completed before 0300 and the glider echelon simulated landing between 0645 and 0700. The first-phase missions were completed by 1400 that afternoon and the second phase, clearing the enemy from the area between the Avon and Erme Rivers (an area corresponding roughly to the Douve–Vire area—the Carentan Estuary—between Utah and Omaha Beaches in Normandy), began. The next day the 327th Glider Regiment, the first elements of which had come ashore late on D-day, joined in the attack, the area between the rivers was declared clear, and the 82d Airborne Division, which had simulated a drop farther inland, was contacted. This completed the airborne phase of Tiger, and the troops began the return trip to Wiltshire and Berkshire.

EXERCISE EAGLE

The 101st's dress rehearsal was Exercise Eagle held on May 9-12. A month before enough aircraft to enable the Division to carry out such an exercise had been promised by the Air Forces; and shortly thereafter General Taylor had submitted the outline of an exercise to which he gave the name Eagle. Both the outline and the name were approved and the Division staff began implementing the outline.

General Taylor's objective was to set up a situation which would resemble as closely as possible the Division's part of Neptune. The airborne troops were to move to the same airports from which they would later take off for France. Personnel and equipment were, as far as possible, to be loaded onto the same aircraft which would take them to Normandy. The takeoff, drop, and assembly were to follow the Neptune plan. Only the parachute and glider echelons were to take part, which allowed the exercise to be held inland in the nearby Wilts area north of Hungerford and Newbury.

As in Beaver and Tiger the Division's mission was to take the causeways leading inland from a simulated Utah Beach, to secure flank objectives, and to knock out an enemy gun battery covering the beach.

Landing by parachute were the Division Pathfinders, the 501st, 502d, and 506th Parachute Infantry Regiments, the 377th Parachute Field Artillery Battalion, Company C of the 326th Airborne Engineer Battalion, and elements of Division Headquarters, Division Artillery Headquarters, the Division Airborne Signal Company, and the 326th Airborne Medical Company. Batteries A and B of the 81st Airborne Antiaircraft Battalion and elements of Division Headquarters, Division Artillery Headquarters, and of the Signal and Medical Companies were to come in by glider.

The first units of the Division began leaving their home stations for the airports on the morning of May 9 and by the following day all participating elements had closed in on the airfields. On the night of May 10-11 an enemy detail from the 28th Infantry Division moved into the exercise area and dispersed according to a prearranged plan.

In almost every case the airfields used as departure points were the same fields from which the units were to depart for Normandy: Greenham Commons, Membury, North Witham, Uppottery, Welford, Merryfield, Exeter and Aldermaston. At some of these airfields the inevitable confusion arose when the troops arrived to find that Service of Supply had failed to make sufficient advance preparations to receive them. There was further confusion when the Division's effort to maintain total security by the sealing of the airport areas ran into the local Air Force and Service of Supply units' persistence in continuing to issue passes to their own personnel at the fields. Despite the latter relaxation the pre-exercise realism was enough to build up in the minds of many men the feeling that though they knew this was an exercise it just might turn out to be the real thing.

May 10 and 11 were given over to briefing the paratroopers and glidermen on the operation. The first paratroopers were airborne just before midnight of the 11th. The jumps began just after midnight and three hours later seventy-five per cent of the parachute personnel and ninety per cent of the landed equipment were effective. However, due largely to pilot error, 28 planes brought back 529 parachutists to the departure airfields. Through error eight of the nine planes carrying Company H of the 502d dropped their parachutists on the village of Ramsbury, nine miles from the DZ. (The pilot of the Company's lead plane had asked his radio operator to check the Aldis lamp. The operator understood him to say to flash the lamp, the signal to the following pilots to give their jump-masters the green "Go" light. Thus only the lead plane carried its stick on to the DZ.) During the exercise 436 men passed through the clearing station for broken bones, sprains, and other jump injuries in addition to many who were treated without passing through the clearing station.

The gliders arrived at dawn, 44 of the 55 landing in the correct landing zone, Welford Airdrome, at the correct time. Seven landed on other fields and four returned to their takeoff airfield.

The problem, once the troops were dropped or landed, went satisfactorily and when the exercise ended that night all the D-day objectives were considered taken. The next day the Division returned to its home stations.

OTHER TRAINING

During the spring months in which Beaver, Tiger, and Eagle were held a continuous training program was going on for those units of the Division which were not engaged in the larger exercises and, in between the three exercises, for all the units. During April reinforced assault companies from each infantry battalion in the Division underwent training at an assault training center. Infantry units worked on problems in conjunction with the Division artillerymen and fired joint demonstrations. The parachute battalions worked on their particular problems of attacking gun positions, bridges, causeways, or other objectives, sometimes attacking after a real jump, sometimes simulating the air flight. A participant of the 506th describes one of the latter:

The jump was simulated—as usual. The field DZ X-ray was thirty miles by foot, halfway between Newbury and Reading. This you made half-swimming, half-wading through the torrential rain that plagued you constantly. You arrived near dusk and were aroused somewhat by the cooks and their inevitably scalding coffee. At ten you scattered onto the jump field and at the sound of whistles denoting the jump you headed for the dit-da-dit-dah of the bugles, the shouts of the officers, and the red, white, and blue lights, deciding as you raced along that this must be the assembly area and arriving at the designated point in time to take off on the problem — to knock out simulated coastal defenses and strongpoints. After traipsing across great expanses of English countryside, encountering untold hundreds of barbed-wire fences, and stumbling deviously through mud holes, you became hopelessly lost. Then everything went against you, the compass refused to point north, the maps got wet and obliterated, and still the rain came down! It seemed as though the devil himself was riding your foot prints! But you persisted and eventually you knocked out something, set up a haphazard and hasty line of defense, and bedded down, each person finding his own choice mud hole in which to lie. Then at long last came the dawn. The enemy to your front turned out to be regimental Headquarters Company. The problem being over you returned to camp the same way you came down, "by foot." Glancing down the line you were of the opinion that everyone had that combat expression, an unshaven face showing extreme weariness and disgust, caked mud from head to foot, and every jump suit looking as though it had come out second best in the ordeal of the fences. You finally dragged your weary body those last few tortuous kilometers, and throwing yourself across the bunk you said — combat can't be that rough. You thought!

Distinguished Visitors

Some of the exercises attracted visits from the ranking political and military people in England, and the Division, as the first and for a time the only American airborne division in England, became used to looking at and being looked at by personages. The first of these visits came in early October, 1943, when Lt. Gens. Jacob L. Devers and Omar N. Bradley and Maj. Gen. Leonard T. Gerow visited the Division and watched a demonstration jump by Company B of the 506th. In January the Duke of Gloucester inspected the Division and a week later Gen. Sir Bernard L. Montgomery arrived. For the Duke's visit Company G of the 506th made a demonstration jump which was marred by the death of one man due to a parachute failure. In February Jimmy Cagney put on a show for the 401st in Reading. On March 23 came the "big" inspection; that day Prime Minister Winston Churchill, Generals Eisenhower, Bradley and Lewis H. Brereton and a trainload of correspondents, photographers and newsreel men visited the 101st. An impressive and carefully rehearsed jump demonstration was put on by Regimental Headquarters Company and 2d and 3d Battalions of the 506th, and the 377th Parachute Field Artillery Battalion. The last visit of a notable before General Eisenhower came down to see the parachutists off on D minus 1 was that of Under Secretary of State Edward R. Stettinius and a party, who visited the Division in April.

Social Life and Athletics

Along with the continuous military preparation there was a social life in England. Some of the efforts along this line were official and some were made by the individual according to his own desires, opportunities, and conscience. London wasn't too far away and there were few men who hadn't heard of Piccadilly Circus even before they landed in England. However, efforts were made to develop the local resources and most of the organizations sponsored their own series of dances and parties. Some of the unit dance bands such as the Airborne Cavaliers of Division Artillery and the Swing Eagles of the 502d were well known and occasionally played for dances outside their own area. Whenever there were WRENs, WAAFs, or other British female auxiliary groups stationed near a 101st installation, the dance-partner situation was solved.

Athletics had also thrived. The Division got settled too late to have a very extensive 1943 football season. The standout contest was a tough game played in Reading between the 502d Screaming Eagles and the 506th Sky Train which ended in a 6-6 tie. A year later the game was scheduled for Christmas Day in Rheims, France; Bastogne intervened. The playoff finally came almost two years later.

Another game, played on November 1st, was witnessed by Pfc. David Kenyon Webster.

Three cheers for our team. A motley, colorful crew, led by a Pfc. and composed of privates, sergeants, lieutenants and the colonel of the 3d Battalion, they beat the Air Corps' "E.T.O. Champs" to quote *Stars and Stripes* sports page, 40 to 0. The 506th team had to practice on their own time while our highly publicized friends in the Air Corps lived on detached service and white bread.

The game started at 2:30, Sunday, at Reading, a metropolis halfway between us and London. We traveled there by truck and train and walked a mile and a half through the city, where we paused for a glass of stout, an apple, and a look at an Iron Cross which a British sergeant had acquired in the last war.

When we reached the stadium, we found an atmosphere resembling that of a football crowd at home. Most of the spectators, of course, were dressed in olive drab, not coonskin, and the Mustangs, Spitfires, and reconnaissance Cubs flying overhead were not skywriting "I. J. Fox, Fifth Avenue" or "Come to the Hotel Commander After the Game," but the spirit was the same as in the Ivy League. Great indeed was the cheering, and many the wisecracks and catcalls, and there was much stamping of feet. One solid part of the stands, filled with paratroopers, was especially raucous. Our team knew they had the Regiment behind them.

The Air Corps was so confident of victory that one of their coaches started the game by asking for bets. He gave 4 to 1 odds. After a few minutes of play, however, he changed his tune, when a 506th man got the ball and ran 80 yards for a touchdown. All our runs in training began to pay off, for a little later it happened again. The umpire ruled it out, because our team was off sides.

Nothing daunted, our men kept plugging, making one lovely touchdown after another. Cries of "Nothing can stop the Air Corps! Yeh! Yeh!" came from the stands. Although the glamor boys fought hard, they were no match for our regimental dark horses, who even surprised some of us who had bet against them, and the game ended in a drizzle, the score 40 to 0. Some wise guy put the finishing touch to the game by saying, "There are only two things that can stop the Air Corps: The weather and the 506th," but this may have been an exaggeration.

The most successful sports were basketball and boxing. In the first sport, teams were organized on all levels from company to Division and contests were held all during the winter. On the boxing front the 101st, with its outstanding record in the U.S., was considered quite a threat to other division teams in England. The boxers were able to maintain their excellent match record although their string of thirteen straight victories was broken by the 29th Division, ETO champions, who, in January, at Rainbow Corner in London, set the 101st back five bouts to three. A tournament was held within the Division at Newbury in March; the 502d won four weight championships, the 501st two, and the 506th and the 327th one each.

To the Marshalling Areas

In mid-May, like the parts of a giant jig-saw puzzle being separated, the units of the 101st began moving out to the airdromes and marshalling areas. Once in the areas the units were not to see each other until they met in France. On D-day the parts of the puzzle would move by airplane, parachute, glider, or boat and, starting at different times and from separated places would come together in a closely fitted and integrated pattern on a strange and hostile shore. Many of the pieces would have to be fitted into place in a matter of minutes or hours; the lives of the parachutists and glidermen, the lives of men on landing craft still many miles away, the success of the whole invasion, might depend on how completely the parts of the jig-saw picture were reassembled at daylight on D-day. The key to the puzzle was in the reams of mimeographed pages marked TOP SECRET-BIGOT-NEPTUNE which told each unit when, how and where it was to go to await the jumping-off signal and what it was to do between that time—the time it climbed into its C-47s, Waco or Horsa gliders, or boats—and the hour its mission or missions would be completely accomplished.

The parachute echelons went to the same airfields from which a few days before they had emplaned for Exercise Eagle. These airports were in the now familiar Newbury–Exeter area. The "chauffeurs" were to be the same IX Troop Carrier command pilots with whom the Division had worked during the past seven or eight months. Groups of the 50th and 53d Troop Carrier Wings of the IX Troop Carrier Command were to furnish the pilots, planes, and gliders.

The marshalling area to which his company of the 3d Battalion of the 506th went is described by David Kenyon Webster:

We traveled by train to Honiton, Devonshire, in southwestern England, about ten miles from the coast, transferred to trucks, and climbed uphill to a sprawling transport field still undergoing construction. Here we were put in the same closely guarded area we had occupied a couple of weeks previously, before taking off on a night jump. Only this time there was no roaming around.

Our marshalling area was a series of fields bounded by high hedges. Lining the hedges in each of these fields was a row of pyramidal tents headed by a wall tent which served as a mess hall sufficient to hold a company. Slit-trench latrines were off to one side. The officers', of course, was screened; ours was in the open. We were forbidden to cut across the open fields, lest a profusion of trails be noted by German observation planes as a sign of occupancy and we be bombed. To keep us from leaving the company area, guards were posted at every opening in the hedgerows; people with business elsewhere had to show a pass to that effect written by their company commander.

Our standard of living went up considerably in the marshalling area. Since a unit of rear-echelon aviation engineers pulled all KP and other details, we were blissfully free to do nothing but sunbathe, play poker and blackjack, shoot crap, and eat and sleep. Here, eating was a pleasure, we had ice cream (our first overseas) and we stuffed ourselves at the hospitable mess hall ("Want some more, boys? Just help yourselves—take all you want") on such luxuries as fried chicken, fruit cocktail, an item usually monopolized by the officers' mess, and, also for the first time overseas, white bread with lots of butter. The realization that we were being fattened for the slaughter didn't stop us from going back for seconds. After supper we formed by companies and went to the movies.

But we didn't just lie around and eat all the time, delightful though that would have been. As the days passed, we found ourselves increasingly occupied. We were briefed and were given our chutes and our ammunition. Briefing, indeed, was our most time-consuming occupation. Each battalion S-2 (Intelligence Section) had decorated two wall tents with maps and sand tables for the intimate instruction of the companies, a platoon at a time, in their mission ("to jump behind the enemy lines on the peninsula of Normandy"), their landing zone, their method of assembly, and their expected opposition.

A week before D-day the commanding officers of the Division learned where their places would be in the great skytrain which would run between England and France during the hours before H-hour. First would be the Pathfinders, six serials of three planes each, the first of which would take off just before midnight and was scheduled to arrive over the drop zone at forty-nine minutes after midnight. The first three serials—nine planes—were the 101st Pathfinders, followed about an hour later by the three serials of 82d Pathfinders. These planes would follow the course which all the paratroop-carrying planes would follow that night. The planes, taking off from North Witham, would leave England across the peninsula of land of Portland Bill, fly a little west of south for fifty-seven miles to a marker boat, there make a 90-degree turn to the left and fly south of east for fifty-four more miles, passing over the Channel Islands a little north of Guernsey and Jersey, and hitting the French coast on the west side of the Cherbourg Peninsula. From that point it was about twenty-five miles due east to the 101st's drop zones, a little less to the 82d's. The entire distance, from the tip of England to the center of the 101st drop zone, was 136 miles; the elapsed time allowed the Pathfinder planes was fifty-four minutes, the paratroopers' planes, fifty-eight minutes, and the gliders, seventy-one minutes.

At twenty-one minutes after midnight the first of twenty serials which were to follow the Pathfinders was to cross Portland Bill; and then for more than two hours the train of C-47s would thunder overhead along a ten-mile-wide corridor to France. The planes were to cross the Channel in Vs of three 3-plane Vs at five hundred feet altitude, climb to 1,500 feet as they crossed the French coast, and then slope down to seven hundred feet for the parachute drop. The 150-mile-an-hour speed of the flight was to be slowed down to not more than 110 miles an hour for the parachute drops; the pilots were given strict orders to that effect. The pilots were also instructed that evasive action would not be tolerated; that steady formations were to be held; and that if a drop zone or landing zone were missed on the run-in the plane would turn at the coast and drop its troops on Drop Zone D, the drop zone nearest the Douve bridges.

The twenty serials which were to follow the Pathfinders each averaged forty planes. The first ten of these serials were those of the 101st parachutists. A six-minute interval between the heads of the serials was to be maintained. Serials 7 and 8 (1 through 6 being the Pathfinders) totalling eighty-one planes, were to take off from Greenham Commons with the 502d less the 1st Battalion; 1st Battalion of the 502d, the 377th Parachute Field Artillery Battalion, a plane of medics from the 326th Medical Company, and five supply planes, all taking off from Membury, made up serials 9 and 10. There were 1,400 men in serials 7 and 8 and 1,157 in 9 and 10, a total of 2,557 paratroopers who were scheduled to land on Drop Zone A, the northern Drop Zone, near St. Martin-de-Varreville.

Serials 11 and 12, leaving from Uppottery airfield aboard eighty-one C-47s, were made up of the 506th less its 3d Battalion. Serial 13, leaving from Welford aboard forty-five planes, carried the 3d Battalion of the 501st, six planes of Division Headquarters, Division Signal Company, and Division Artillery personnel, and three planes of supplies. These three serials—11, 12 and 13, totalling 1,995 paratroopers—were to land on Drop Zone C, the central drop zone nearest the Utah Beach Causeways 1 and 2.

The 501st less the 3d Battalion, part of Company C of the 326th Engineers, a plane of medics, and four supply planes, a total of ninety planes, were to take off from Merryfield in serials 14 and 15. Serial 16, made up of the 3d Battalion of the 506th, two platoons of the 326th Engineers, and three supply planes, a total of forty-five planes, was to take off from

Exeter. These last three serials were to place 2,118 men on DZ D. Altogether, 6,670 101st men were scheduled to hit the silk on D-day.

The 438th Group of the 50th Troop Carrier Wing was to fly serials 7 and 8; the 436th, serials 9 and 10; the 439th, serials 11 and 12; the 435th, serial 13; the 441st, serials 14 and 15; and the 440th, serial 16.

Two serials of CG4 (Waco) gliders, one for each airborne division, were to come in just before dawn. These smaller gliders had been substituted for the Horsa gliders just two days before D-day in order to bring in antitank guns and command personnel as early as possible when the glider mission was changed from a daylight to a pre-dawn landing. Fifty-two of the CG4As, taking off from Aldermaston and towed by C-47s of the 434th Group, were to carry personnel from Division Headquarters, Signal Company, 326th Engineers, 326th Medical Company, and Batteries A and B, antitank batteries of the 81st AA Battalion. At 2100 that evening, several hours before dark, a 101st serial of thirty-two of the larger Horsa gliders was to bring in additional personnel of Division Headquarters and Signal Company and jeeps for the parachute regiments.

The gliders were to approach Normandy from a direction opposite to that followed by the troop-carrying planes. The glider lift was to leave England by the route followed by the planes, but about thirty miles past Portland Bill the lift was to make a left turn, go east up the Channel until past the Cherbourg Peninsula, then swing right and come in over Utah Beach from the east. This approach was also the return route of all serials, parachute and glider, once their loads had been dropped.

While the parachute and glider echelons waited for D-day at the airdromes a large part of the Division was in marshalling areas along the coast of England and Wales, near the ports from which they were to sail. Scheduled to embark at Plymouth, the historic southwest English port from which the Pilgrims had sailed to the New World more than three centuries before, was the 1st Battalion of the 401st Glider Infantry,[1]* the 326th Airborne Medical Company, and part of Division Headquarters. Waiting in the Dartmouth–Brixham area, just south of the Slapton Sands area where the Division had run through Exercises Beaver and Tiger, were the 327th Glider Infantry, part of the 426th Quartermaster Company, and 148 of the Division's vehicles and their drivers. In Wales, along the Usk and Ebbur Rivers about the port of Cardiff, were the 321st and 907th Glider Field Artillery Battalions, Division Artillery Headquarters and Headquarters Company, part of

---

* Notes are at the end of each chapter.

Brigadier General Don F. Pratt, standing in the doorway
of the glider in which he rode to his death on D-day.

*Some of the Division's seaborne echelon departed
from the Dartmouth area of the Dart River, shown here.
(Painting by Charles Baskerville)*

Division Headquarters, the 326th Engineers, the 81st AA Battalion, and part of the 426th Quartermaster Company. Through another Welsh port, Swansea, a large part of the Division's trucks, along with the attached 3808th Quartermaster Truck Company, was scheduled to embark. The 801st Airborne Ordnance Company was to shuttle over from the English port of Portland.

By the third week in May most of the seaborne echelon had left for the marshalling areas. There they waterproofed their guns, vehicles and radios. The last week in May saw the parachute and glider echelons in the airdromes from which they were to leave only by air and then on a one-way ride to France. By May 30 part of the seaborne echelon was already aboard the invasion craft; two days before, in the theater in Pontllanfraith, Wales, General Taylor, visiting every marshalling area, had personally disclosed to the men who would come in by sea that France was their destination. Now for the first time every man knew where he was to go. Gathered around the maps and sand-tables the men saw the familiar theoretical contours, causeways, bridges, and streams pinned down to actual locations in France.

In the airdrome areas life was pretty much the same from field to field. The days of preparation were over and, though there were bursts of activity (as when the first glider echelon two days before D-day had to change from Horsas to the smaller CG4As with the attendant revision of loads), and some personnel had duties which forced them to work steadily and overtime, for most of the men who would, in a matter of days, be fighting along the Normandy hedgerows it was a time of waiting. Movies, baseball, reading, letter-writing, cutting each other's hair Indian scalp-lock style, putting the last touches on personal equipment, or just resting took up the time. The men slept crowded in hangars, tents, and huts often served by the English-type bucket latrines and helmet bathtubs. Finally, each man received a week's free PX rations and a partial payment of French invasion francs, a tangible clincher that France was to be the target.

Sunday night, June 4, was to be the takeoff date; but early that morning 21st Army Group sent the code word indicating a 24-hour postponement. The delay was caused by bad weather. The next morning, June 5, all units were notified that June 6 was to be D-day. The first seaborne waves were already under way. During the day at the airdromes final checks of equipment, final fittings of parachute harnesses, final issues of ammunition were made. A meal of steak and ice cream was served in the afternoon. By 2130 of June 5 all parachutists were alongside their parked planes.

The mounting tension of the days and hours before H-hour has been recorded by three parachutists of the Division. One of the three, T/5, later T/3, George E. Koskimaki, jumped in General Taylor's stick as his radio operator. Sergeant Koskimaki managed to keep a diary covering every day of his stay in the army, in combat making his entries on the transparent sheets found in the back of Signal Corps message books and later transcribing them into his diary. ("When the ultimatum came to surrender to the Germans at Bastogne I was all set to begin chewing up my little bits of info.") Excerpts from his diary follow:

May 13: The invasion time is drawing very near. The boys think we shall leave for the marshalling area this week. *May 15:* We should be leaving for the marshalling area this week. Part of the Division has moved out already. Have to memorize Division Signal Operating Instructions for operations. *May 16:* Our duffel bags were sent ahead today. We have to sew our stripes and Division insignia on both of our jump suits. We're really hot now! *May 17:* Tonight I am guarding the war room where all the Division invasion plans are being made. *May 22:* The seaborne echelon boys leave at 5 o'clock in the morning. We had to move out of our barracks because our extra stuff is gonna be stored there. *May 23:* Sergeant Labare was shot in the side accidentally

Lieutenant Alex Bobuck looks over part of his platoon of the 506th just before boarding the plane for Normandy.

when one of the boys was showing him how to work the Thompson sub-machine gun in the barracks. *May 24:* Went out on a night problem again to practice assembling. It was very satisfactory this time. The real McCoy should come sometime next week. *May 26:* We packed our combat parachute equipment bundles today. We put in five sub-machine guns, so we are armed to the teeth. *May 27:* Got our combat parachutes as well as equipment chutes. It shouldn't be too long now. *May 29:* Packed all our equipment today ready for shipment. Adjusted our chutes. Leave for marshalling area today sometime. Turning diary over to Hanneman until return. *May 30:* I learned today our exact location and mission when I helped Lieutenant Brierce work on some maps. I hope we make a good show of it. *May 31:* The entire Division Headquarters parachute echelon was briefed for the first time today. All the boys were greatly surprised when they learned where we would jump. *June 1:* I typed up the plane loads and scrambled all secret codes. *June 2:* Each man sketched the road network of the area in which we land from memory. We get a good two hours' briefing each day. *June 3:* Each man was given his ammo and grenades. Today we had hot showers and some extra cigarettes and candy rations. *June 4:* We were equipped and packed ready to leave today. Bad weather is said to have caused postponement of the invasion until tomorrow or the next day. *June 5:* Tonight we ring the bell on the greatest invasion show in the world.

Pfc. David Kenyon Webster of the 506th describes the pre-jump time:

As one long, quiet summer day followed another and we became more and more familiar with our mission each man gradually built up a stockpile of equipment. We were issued $10 worth of crisp new French money just minted in Washington for the invasion. Every man had three yard-square maps, which, when pieced together, represented the entire peninsula of Normandy, a special, distorted photomap of the jump field which nobody could figure out, and one or two diagrams and overlays of the village or strong point his platoon or company was assigned to take. Small brass pocket compasses were issued, so we might orient ourselves on the ground, and dime-store metal crickets for identification purposes: one squeeze (*click-clack*) to be answered by two (*click-clack . . . click-clack*). We drew American flags about five inches by three and fastened them to the right sleeves of our jump jackets. We shaved our heads. Boxes of machine-gun and mortar ammunition were rolled in equipment bundles and attached to the bottoms of the planes. We wove strips of green and brown burlap into our helmet nets for camouflage. Then we drew Mae West life jackets. We went down to the hangars, adjusted our chutes, put our rifles in their cases, checked our ammunition (as an ammunition bearer, I carried two hand grenades and two bandoleers of M1 clips), broke down our K rations, and arranged our chutes in kit bags by companies. Then we waited.

The night of June 4 we had an outstanding meal: steak, green peas, mashed potatoes, white bread, ice cream, coffee—all a soldier could ask for. A terrific wind was blowing, but we all felt that our day had come. Some officer told us to go to bed, however; we weren't leaving tonight.

By the late afternoon of June 5 the wind had died down. We were going. Cans of green paint circulated among the companies as the men daubed their faces in fierce Indian camouflage. Some of them took charcoal and blackened the skin under their eyes and drew streaks down their noses and foreheads. I wanted to say goodbye to my old squad in F Company, but I couldn't leave the area. We ate a hurried meal of stew and left for the airport. Nobody sang, nobody cheered. It was like a death march.

After we had found our kit bags, we boarded trucks and drove to our planes, where we climaxed our equipment issue by receiving seasick pills and round cardboard ice-cream containers, in case the pills didn't work. We put on our gear and waited.

The summer days are long in England. In June the sun doesn't go down until nine o'clock. You can sit for hours and watch the big, soft hills change color and wonder what it's like back in the States now. Trapped in your harness and your solitude, you look south to the winding valley to the sea. And what are the Germans thinking now? Of home, perhaps, and better days? When will it get dark? Why do I go on doing this? What chance does a para-trooper have? Stay, light, stay on forever, and we'll never get to Normandy.

Small quiet groups sit under the plane wings and watch the sun go down. *Eight o'clock.* "It won't be long now," says Porter the medic. Porter the medic who was machine-gunned the next day and will never leave the cemetery in Ste. Mère Église. *Nine o'clock.* A few planes started to roar. Checking their motors. Jesus Christ, I hate that sound! *Ten o'clock.* Their nervousness increasing, the men get up and relieve themselves continuously. *Ten-thirty.* We clamber aboard the plane and sit down, each in his silence. This is the end of our training, this is the one-way road. I try to sleep, but I can't. Now the whole field is shaking with the roar of motors—the final warmup. *Ten forty-five.* "There they go!" the crew chief shouts. "They're off!"

Eleven o'clock. Our tail swings around. We wheel about and head up the runway. Dead silence. I swallow my seasick pills and try to act nonchalant, but it's no go. My legs are weak and my throat is dry and I can only talk in a stuttering whisper. Some of the boys are chain-smoking their cigarettes. A few are asleep. With a soft rush, we leave the ground; we are airborne. There is no going back.

At another field Sgt. (later Lt.) Thomas B. Buff of Division Head-quarters Company was spending his last hours in England:

I had eaten lunch and was taking a nap in my tent when in burst S/Sgt. Nick Calabrese with the news that at last we were going within the hour. We met at Division Headquarters. Every one of our friends whom Fate had placed in the rear echelon was there to tell us goodbye. Just before we got into our trucks, the boys who had come to see us off took rolls and rolls of photographs of us. How those guys wanted to go too. Even though I had a compass, Ser-geant Bill Urquia of our Photograph Interpreter Team, gave me his, saying: "Tom, this is a lucky compass; it has been through North Africa, Sicily and part of Italy. Take it to France for me. Dammit, I am not going." Everyone shook hands, and then we drove off. We later learned that all of those fellows just roamed around, killing time until far into the night so they could count our planes as we flew over, wave to us and bid us Godspeed.

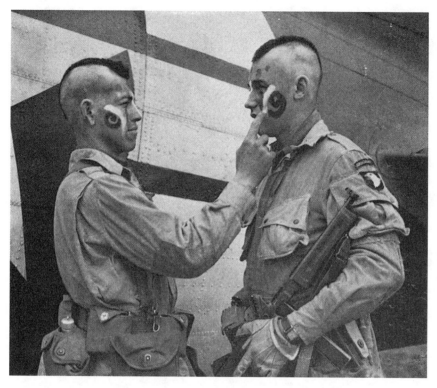

Private Clarence C. Ware gives a last-minute touch-up to Private Charles R. Plaudo before the take-off.

The route to the airdrome was through the heart of "Ourtown," [Newbury]. We waved and spoke to the civilians just as we had done on other occasions while en route to the same airdrome for the purpose of making training jumps. There was nothing changed about the town's atmosphere. It seemed incredible to me that the next morning the papers would be filled with announcements of history's most masterful military undertaking and yet these people of Ourtown were now totally ignorant of it. The complete absence of Joe Jumps on the streets aroused no suspicion; such restrictions were not unusual—they had been placed in effect many times before.

After riding for an hour or so, we reached the airdrome and hunted up our outfit. Only at a time similar to this can one fully appreciate the size of our Division. There were Joe Jumps everywhere.

We met our friends of the Division Headquarters Parachute Echelon and it was nice to see them. John Cooper, Andy Fisher of G-4, our Military Police jumpers, Romano, Butler, Columbus, Milbrath, Taylor, Smith, Hamilton and many others. Others of our friends would take off from other airdromes. We would not see them again until we landed in Normandy. To these we had said goodbye before they went into confinement at their respective departure airfields. Still others of our friends, the division seaborne echelon, were already aboard their landing craft, afloat somewhere off the coast of Southern England.

81

General Eisenhower talks to Lt. Wallace C. Strobel, 502d, just before the take-off for Normandy.

We had gotten to our airdrome around three or four o'clock on the afternoon of June 5. Briefing was over; everyone having been briefed and briefed again. Now, everyone was on hand. All officers were there with the men of their particular section, casually going over plans and alternate plans, checking maps, technical equipment, etc. Last-minute preparations for an early morning "vertical invasion" of Fortress Europe went forward in exactly the same manner as had been done for our many problems or field exercises. There was no visible sign of nervousness, tenseness, brooding, doubt, and certainly not fear. Time and time again we had gone through this very same procedure in our training to equip ourselves for the moment so near at hand; at least we hoped it was near at hand and that this would not develop into the well known dry run.

While we were blackening our faces and hands, Butler, Bill Smith and Phil Romano, who had already completed their make-up, combined forces to put on an *ad-lib* minstrel act for us. We laughed until our sides hurt at their mad antics, their exaggerated Southern drawl.

General Taylor had already spoken to the officers and men. Unfortunately for us, this occurred before we reached the airdrome. It was he who, as a tribute to his predecessor, Maj. Gen. William C. Lee, asked each of us to yell "Bill Lee!" as we left the door of our plane over France. All of my friends, and all of the line company boys with whom I later talked, bellowed: "Bill Lee!" when making their exit.

Somewhere around ten o'clock we prepared to go to our planes. To reach them called for another truck ride, the airdrome being of monstrous proportions.

As we marched from our billets one of our bands played marches familiar to all of us.

Prior to boarding the trucks, the officer in command of Division Headquarters Parachute Echelon, Maj. Paul A. Danahy, talked to us briefly, informally. He ended by saying, in effect: "Men, for God's sake be careful. We all know the German soldier for what he is. He is full of tricks. Be cautious; fight fairly; give no quarter—expect none. Even though most of you are technicians, you are American paratroopers—we think the world's finest military men. Give them hell, boys. *Give them hell!* Good luck, and may God bless you. That's all . . . I'll see you in France." We broke away for the trucks and at that moment I rather think our little group could have manhandled an SS panzer division.

Reaching our planes, we tried on our chutes again, made any adjustments necessary, and then removed them. Our stick was briefed again on various subjects, time of departure, time of flight, course to be flown, what to do in emergencies of any kind. This had all the aspects of the real thing; but some of us just could not help believing, however vaguely, that the show might be called off.

Around eleven o'clock we were visited by General Eisenhower and other high-ranking officers of his staff. I feel reasonably sure that General Eisenhower was proud—just as we are—of the 101st. He was not a stranger to our Division, nor was it to him. This was his second or third visit to the 101st. This time, though, there was no Division review, no bands, no speeches. Yet there was no grimness; everyone was cheerful, inconceivably lighthearted. For as long as time permitted the General went from plane to plane, his hands in his pockets, chatting pleasantly with almost every member of each plane's stick of jumpers. We were told that General Eisenhower remained at our drome and saluted the waves of planes as they circled and left.

A chill was in the air, so we climbed aboard our plane, No. 5, where we would be more comfortable. Some of the boys almost immediately went to sleep, others smoked, others made light conversation, were content to dwell upon their own mental meanderings, while others of us indulged in a bit of everything. My little friend, Dave Bernay, fell asleep as soon as he was seated and continued so almost all the way from there on out.

Finally, the crew of our plane came aboard and shortly thereafter we lumbered out onto the runway. I thought: "Well, if this is a dry run, we'll soon find out about it and maybe I can carry through with my plans for Saturday after all." Down the runway we sped, and in a few moments we were airborne. As we circled, drawing into formation, it was possible to see the airport below. I wouldn't even hazard a guess as to the number of troop-carrier planes, all laden with paratroopers and their equipment, lined up awaiting their turn to join us.

Looking at the compass Urquia had given me, I could see that we were headed generally south. The shades of the plane's passenger compartment were drawn, there were no lights burning inside, and the only way to tell now just what was happening outside was to stand in the door. I have never derived too much pleasure from standing in the door of a troop-carrier plane under any circumstances, but I did want to get a peak at this vast armada of aerial GI trucks and their escorts, so I worked my way back and looked out. You have

A bazookaman and his buddy bound for Normandy.

read how the line of planes was nine abreast, two hundred miles long. Then, it seemed to me that the pattern was no less than two hundred miles square. I could hardly see the sky for planes—there just was not room for more. It was cold standing there, so I went on forward to my No. 13 seat and sat down, to begin waiting, with about the same degree of composure as one has while waiting in the reception room of a dentist's office—waiting for the time when I'd get nervous, jittery, even afraid. I think all of us might have had the feeling that sooner or later we'd give way to nerves, fear, or *something*. Just what, I don't know, but whatever it was, I was waiting for it. Surely thus far I hadn't been upset or worried in any wise. But, I knew very well I'd not be able to react calmly to what was coming. So, I just waited, saying to myself: "I'm lucky as hell to be mixed up in this affair. I am glad to be along; honored to be a member of the Division which will be the first to land in France." How much truth is contained in that statement is open to question.

There was no talking now. We just sat there and dozed or smoked. For some inexplicable reason, I recalled the joke about the paratrooper making his first jump. As he stood there in the door, prepared to jump, he said: "I wish the boys at the office could see me now—*at the office.*"

Capt. Leo Schweiter, our jumpmaster, who almost continuously was crouching in the door peering out, yelled: "Say goodbye to England." We had just left the southern coast. Bernay, sitting next to me, said: "Well, we know damned well this ain't no dry run." He then went back to sleep.

I stood in the door only once while crossing the Channel. The crossing was made without incident. Inwardly, without really knowing it, I was fighting to remain unruffled, and unconsciously I guess I was waiting to see which would win out, the civilian part of me, or the military part. After all, I had been a civilian considerably longer than I had been a soldier. Of one thing I was sure: it was hard to realize fully that there I was, approaching the coast of Normandy, just above the very terrain, with its landmarks, civilians, enemy soldiers and installations, about which we had tried to learn so much, and in connection with which we had worked such long, wearying hours for months on end.

It seemed to me that at the moment we crossed the Coast (Captain Schweiter, had shouted to us: "Say hello to France") we went into a gradual dive. I am not sure as to this. However, I feel reasonably confident that the throttles of all planes were wide open, and that on no previous occasion had troop-carrier planes been driven harder. Our hosts on the ground soon started throwing everything they had at us but hand grenades, old shoes and the family album. Our plane bounced and bobbed like a ball on a water-spout. We were vibrating from stem to stern and the roar of our motors was deafening. The old boat was straining every nerve, but bearing up under it like the gallant lady we all know the troop-carrier plane to be. Through it all, with the plane's crew doing its stuff dodging the "fireworks" and staying out of other people's way, our jumpmaster remained crouching at the plane's door, observing, following the course, keeping all of us informed of our progress. We encountered fog, but Captain Schweiter stayed right there at the door, sometimes crouching, sometimes lying flat on the floor, watching, keeping track of our course. We knew what time we would pass over the French coast and exactly how many minutes should elapse before we were over our target area. Eventually, after what seemed like an eon plus six, the red light flashed on. At the jumpmaster's command, we stood up and hooked up. The jumpmaster and his assistant, Lt. Cecil Wilson, got the door bundles in readiness, as we checked our own and each other's equipment. The jumpmaster came back and rechecked it. All this time we were speeding along like a runaway armored division, but with several times the racket.

For the first time in my life I really wanted to jump, to get the hell out. To jump out. Not once have I ever hesitated to make a jump, but no one, under normal conditions, is exactly exuberant over the prospect of making a jump just prior thereto. As for me, I always feel as though it really isn't I who is doing the jumping—that when making a jump I actually leave the real me in the plane. But now, conditions weren't normal, and neither was I. *I wanted to jump and to take the real me with me!*

It became more and more difficult to stand upright in the plane. I wondered why the green light had not come on. All of us were swung from side to side, then flung backwards and forward. Eyes were fixed, glued, to the red light. Looking down, Captain Schweiter saw that we were over an expanse of water. We had passed completely over the Peninsula and had emerged over the Channel on the other side. He dashed headlong to the pilot's cabin. We made a 180-degree turn and roared back, this time like *two* armored divisions. As he returned to his post at the door, the jumpmaster bawled out: "Is everybody happy?" "Hell Yes!" came the reply. We were careening from side to side and going like nobody's business when the green light flashed on.

In less time than it takes to write (or read) this, the door bundles were pushed out; Captain Schweiter slapped the switch controlling the parapacks (belly bundles), bellowed: "Follow me" and jumped. Planes might have been cleared faster than we cleared ours; they might have been cleared in a more orderly fashion, but no plane has ever been cleared more *willingly*. And, to be entirely honest, I seriously doubt that any plane was ever vacated more quickly or orderly than ours. There wasn't a hitch, no hesitations, no bad exits. I was No. 13, as I have said (No, I didn't like it), and almost before I knew it, I was approaching the door.

It has always been a source of amazement to me how, at this stage of a jump, my thoughts become accelerated. I seem to think in pictures, not individual, separate, considered thoughts. Complete thoughts seem to pass through my mind—whole scenes. I came up to the door and, while turning to go through it, a turn which I know I made without pausing, I murmured a prayer: "Dear God, bless the men of this Division and let them all land safely." Just before I jumped, which I did without so much as touching the door (and I'll bet I cleared it by twenty feet—straight out), I yelled "Bill Lee!"

Up until now, on previous jumps, I had never failed to count after making my exit. I always figured that, in jumping, all safety precautions should be adhered to. That, although I hoped never to have to use it, should I ever have to pull the rip-cord of my reserve I certainly wanted to do so in plenty of time for it to open. So, heretofore, I always counted, thus, in a sense, doing *my* part, and hoping the chute would follow through with its—and open. However, I was surprised when, in place of counting, I cursed at my chute: "Open, you b . . . .!"

If there was any opening shock I do not remember it, probably not having noticed it in my temporary state of desperation to leave the plane (doubtless the same emotion which prompted me to call my chute an illegitimate child). Floating downward, I could see none of the fellows who had jumped with me. But, I couldn't squander time in the air looking for my pals—I'd do that on the ground. I'll eat my tin hat if I was in the air more than twenty-five seconds. The passage of time, it seems to me, is controlled in large measure by the events and surroundings during the period involved. Of course, a minute has only sixty seconds in it, but some seconds pass more slowly than others. At no time in my life have seconds passed, lagged, more excruciatingly slow, I felt like climbing right up inside my canopy and hiding there.

At one and the same time, I was preparing to land; looking to see if I was being fired upon; waiting to be fired upon; hoping I'd drift away from the small-arms and machine-gun fire on the ground; trying to judge where I would land. In the distance other troop-carrier planes roared over, unquestionably having already discharged their cargoes of paratroopers. They were skimming the treetops and each was drawing machine-gun fire from the ground. I saw no enemy fighter planes, but tracers from the ground streaked across the sky in all directions. There was a hell of a bombardment, aerial and naval (all ours) on the coast, and high in the sky to the south flak bursts (enemy) were plainly visible.

It was as bright as day during my descent, and I wondered why I was not being fired at. One redeeming feature of landing via parachute is that in the process no noise is made. Of this I was glad as I had drifted directly across enemy ground fire. Seeing that I would clear by a goodly margin the activity below me, I slipped to hasten my descent. I quick-slipped when it appeared I'd land in some tall trees. I wanted to avoid those babies. I have never made a tree-landing, but I understand they aren't so bad—on maneuvers. But this was no maneuver and to end up suspended in a tree, until I got myself down, or waited for someone else to assist me wasn't just then an attractive prospect. I felt that while in the plane I'd already been a defenseless target quite long enough—I never got around to cultivating much of a taste for being a target— so I was more than casually interested in staying out of those trees. Well, I missed them, but barely so. I overlooked mentioning that during my descent I saw cows placidly standing around in the fields below me. This was a welcome sight as presence of those "milk dispensaries" meant but one thing to me—at least my landing would not be made in a mined area. Nor did I see evidences of other obstacles in the fields. It wasn't a bad landing at all, save for coming in backward and coming down right smack in the latrine for every cow in France. I must have been an awesome apparition when I finally reached cover, and how I *smelled!* What a stench. I had cow dung all over me. But, at any rate, I had landed, and I was still very much alive.

NOTE

[1] The 401st Glider Regiment, like the 327th, was a two-battalion regiment. In March 1944 the 2d Battalion of the 401st had been sent to the 82d Airborne Division and never rejoined the 101st. The 1st Battalion, though it officially remained the 1st Battalion of the 401st Regiment during the first months of combat actually functioned as the 3d Battalion of the 327th and is hereafter referred to by that designation. This was made official in the reorganization of the 327th in the spring of 1945, just before the end of the war in Europe. Until the reorganization the Battalion's companies retained their A, B, C, D designations, giving the 327th two sets of companies with these letters.

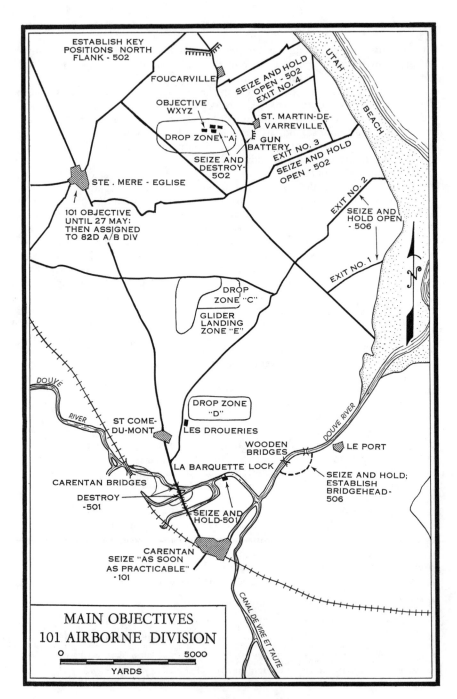

ESTABLISH KEY
POSITIONS NORTH
FLANK - 502

FOUCARVILLE

SEIZE AND HOLD
OPEN - 502
EXIT NO. 4

UTAH

BEACH

OBJECTIVE
WXYZ

ST. MARTIN-DE-
VARREVILLE

DROP ZONE "A"

GUN
BATTERY
EXIT NO. 3

SEIZE AND
DESTROY-
502

SEIZE AND HOLD
OPEN - 502

STE . MERE - EGLISE

EXIT NO. 2

101 OBJECTIVE
UNTIL 27 MAY;
THEN ASSIGNED
TO 82D A/B DIV

SEIZE AND
HOLD OPEN
- 506

EXIT NO. 1

DROP
ZONE "C"

N

GLIDER
LANDING
ZONE "E"

DOUVE

RIVER

DROP ZONE
"D"

ST COME-
DU-MONT

LES DROUERIES

DOUVE RIVER

WOODEN
BRIDGES

LE PORT

LA BARQUETTE LOCK

SEIZE AND HOLD;
ESTABLISH
BRIDGEHEAD-
506

CARENTAN BRIDGES

DESTROY
-501

SEIZE AND
HOLD-501

CARENTAN
SEIZE "AS SOON
AS PRACTICABLE"
-101

CANAL DE VIRE ET TAUTE

MAIN OBJECTIVES
101 AIRBORNE DIVISION

0   5000

YARDS

Map 3.

Normandy

The light changed from red to green; the lieutenant colonel stepped out into the night. It seemed to him that three of the Roman-candle antiaircraft guns below were hunting him personally, with their fire converging just above his head. He thought: they must have been concentrating on the lead plane—mine.

The fire followed three-fourths of the way down; then other planes came over and the tracers lifted back toward them. The colonel's feet hit pavement.

He realized, lying in the road, that his canopy was hung in a tree. As he tried to get clear of the chute a machine gun opened fire toward him. They see my chute, he thought; they've singled me out as a personal target. (Later he decided the gun must have been ranged in on the crossroads where he had landed.) After some effort he got a grenade loose; by that time the gun was again searching skyward for the planes still coming over.

He worked out of his chute. From the line of flight of the planes he thought he knew his east-west line. He began crawling; before he got ten yards the gun again fired his way. He lay still, waiting for more overhead targets to draw the gun's attention. When that relief came he again started crawling, hugging hedges and ditches, in the direction in which he had seen some other paratroopers coming down. A horseman galloped through the crossroads where he had been. Mortar fire bracketed him, about four rounds. More planes came over. The mortars quit. It was an opening; he moved along.

On the other side of a hedgerow something moved. He found a hole in the embankment and looked through. About ten yards away, hugging the hedge, were two men. Even in the darkness he could tell that their backs were turned toward him. He snapped his cricket once. The two men went flat and did not reply. In that second he wondered what to do next. Then from close at hand a third man whom he hadn't seen snapped a cricket.

"Where are you going?"

"We're looking for the colonel," one of the men answered.

So, at about 0130 o'clock, some five hours before H-hour, Lt. Col. Patrick J. Cassidy began assembling the 1st Battalion of the 502d Parachute Infantry Regiment. At the same time and from such lonely, groping beginnings in the neighboring hedgerowed fields, woods and marshes of the Cherbourg Peninsula of moonlit Normandy other officers and men of the 101st were gathering.

The Cherbourg Peninsula is a thumb of Normandy extending up toward southwest England. At the tip is the city of Cherbourg. This port was an objective of great importance under Operation Neptune since the invasion area included no other port capable of sustaining the operation. Neptune called for VII Corps, spearheaded by the 4th Infantry Division, to land on Utah Beach, the beachhead nearest Cherbourg, on D-day at H-hour—0630—and move on to capture the city.

The three-mile-wide Utah Beach, on the eastern side of the Cherbourg thumb just before it curves into the hand of France, was the extreme right—facing inland—of the five beachheads to be established on D-day. Thirteen miles around the bend of the hand to the southeast was Omaha Beach. Water set up the major tactical problems at Utah Beach. To the rear of the beach, starting anywhere from 150 to 1,000 yards from the ocean's edge and extending inland one to two miles, was an area whose surface varied from complete saturation to shallow flooding. The dominant terrain feature of the country back of this flooded area was the Douve River which, with its tributary, the Merderet, drains the major part of the Cherbourg Peninsula. The Douve and Merderet flow in a southeasterly direction, merge ten miles inland from Utah Beach, and continue southeast another seven miles to the vicinity of Carentan, the largest town of the lower Peninsula. At Carentan the Douve makes a rounded L turn to the northeast and empties into the English Channel a mile below Utah Beach and between that beach and Omaha Beach. Much of the lower course is through swamps and water meadows similar to the inundations just back of Utah Beach. The river itself is tidal up to the Merderet juncture; it is narrow— twenty to forty feet—but deep. Additional areas along the lower course of the river which are below sea-level at high tide can be flooded by the manipulation of a set of locks at the bend of the Douve, locks built about a hundred years ago to hold back the sea at high tide from the below-sea-level bottom lands above the locks.

Crossing the flooded area immediately back of Utah Beach are four parallel roads or built-up causeways running from the dry dunes of the beaches to the solid ground inland. Crossing the lower Douve bottomlands is a highway running north out of Carentan to Valognes, half way up the Peninsula, and on from there to Cherbourg. Paralleling this road is a railroad.

This watery terrain and its traversing and controlling elements— causeways, bridges and locks—dictated most of the 101st missions. There were the four causeways, easily obstructed, in from the beach; across them would have to come most of the traffic from the sea, and an assault

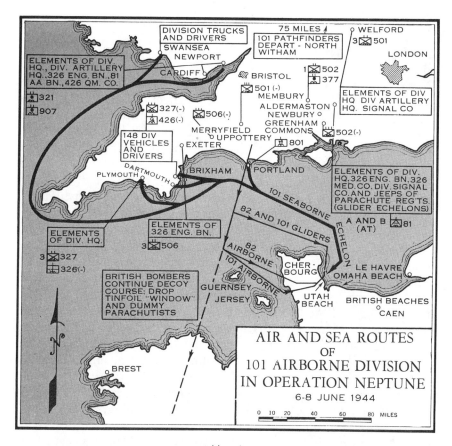

Map 4.

in daylight by the seaborne troops against alerted and reinforced defenders along these channeled routes might result in a shambles. Their capture was assigned to the 1st and 2d Battalions of the 506th, which would take causeways 1 and 2, the two southern exits, and to the 3d Battalion of the 502d, which would take causeways 3 and 4, the northern exits.

The Douve River, with its marshes, water meadows, and lock-controlled inundated areas, was an important water barrier: control by the Germans of its crossings would aid an armored counterattack from the south against the Utah Beachhead; these crossings destroyed or in American hands would augment the defense characteristics offered by the inundated areas against such a counterattack. From the junction of the Douve and Merderet to the sea there were just five crossings of the river itself. One was the railroad. The railroad ran out of Carentan to the northwest and crossed the Douve two and a half miles from town.

The Valognes highway, running roughly parallel, crossed the Douve about a mile to the west of the railroad. A small tributary joins the Douve here and the river splits and rejoins itself so that the highway crosses four bridges within a mile and a half of Carentan. The other crossings of the Douve were two wooden bridges three miles down the river, about halfway from Carentan to the sea and—between the highway bridges and the wooden bridges—the locks at La Barquette, which could be crossed on foot.

To the 1st and 2d Battalions of the 501st was assigned the mission of destroying one of the railroad bridges and two of the four highway bridges. The two wooden bridges downstream were to be seized, prepared for destruction, and held by the 3d Battalion of the 506th. Company C of the 326th Airborne Engineers had the job of preparing these bridges for destruction and the personnel of the company was divided among the three battalions assigned to the bridges. Seizure of the La Barquette locks, which controlled the tidal flow up the Douve and therefore some of the flooded lands along the river, was an additional assignment of the 1st and 2d Battalions of the 501st. The locks at the time of the invasion were being operated by the Germans in such a way as to flood the area upstream, creating a barrier against a breakout from the beachhead area to the south. Control of these locks by the invaders would put them in position to keep the area flooded against a German counterattack from the south or, by draining, aid the American drive south through the lowlands.

These water-dictated assignments employed six of the nine parachute battalions. Of the remaining three, 1st and 2d Battalions of the 502d along with the 377th Parachute Field Artillery Battalion had the job of knocking out a battery of four 122mm howitzers and installations near St. Martin-de-Varreville, just back of the northern sector of the beach, and of securing the Division's northern flank. The last battalion, the 3d of the 501st, was to jump as Division reserve and be prepared to mark and protect the glider landing zone. Other units were to come in glider- or sea-borne.

The nature and location of the missions dictated that the 101st would be dropped just inside the boundaries of an eighteen- or twenty-mile half-circle, the ends of which were secured inland north and south of Utah Beach, and which curved eastward along the beach. The 101st would strike outward to the north, east, and south on a perimeter starting with the 502d's mission along the northern flank, circling around down the beach where the 502d and 506th were to seize the causeways, and curving back inland along the Douve, for whose cross-

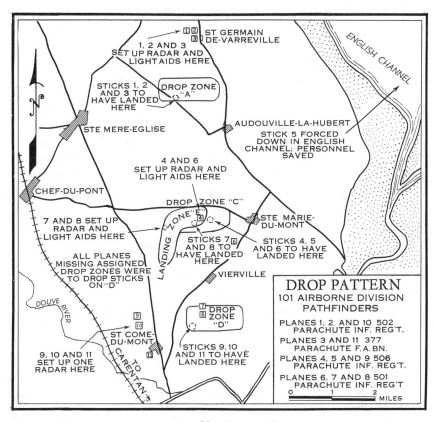

Map 5.

ings and controlling locks the 506th and 501st were to strike. The direction of these strikes—north and south to the flanks and east toward the sea and the oncoming seaborne troops—indicated the Division's two primary missions: the clearing of the way inland for the 4th Division and the securing of its flanks. Of special importance was the protection of the southern flank along the Douve, for, as VII Corps swung north and drove on Cherbourg, the 101st was to be responsible for the overall security of the corps' southern flank.

The Pathfinders Take Off

Starting at 2150, June 5, the 101st's pathfinders had begun taking off from North Witham Airdrome in the Midlands. The lead aircraft, piloted by Lt. Col. Joel M. Crouch of the IX Troop Carrier Pathfinder Group, carried the leader of the 101st pathfinders, Capt. Frank L. Lillyman, his stick of pathfinder personnel, a small security detachment from the 502d, and three men from the 502d S-2 section. By 2330 all of the 6,600 parachutists of the 101st were airborne in 490 C-47s. In the Channel five thousand ships were moving toward the French coast. Shortly after midnight Colonel Crouch was notified by his radar operator, Major William Culp, that the time and distance pips on the radar scanning screen had merged; and simultaneously the copilot, Maj. Vito Pedone, verified the village of St. Germain-de-Varreville below them. The green light to the right of the door was flashed and Captain Lillyman went out, followed by his No. 2 man, Lt. Samuel Mc-Carter, and the rest of the parachute personnel. In the plane Major Culp and Major Pedone recorded the time—0015, June 6, 1944. Five minutes later over the British beachhead the leader of the British path-finders, Capt. Ian Andrew Tait, led his stick out. The invasion was on.

Eleven sticks of pathfinders marked out with lights and radar three drop zones and one landing zone. None of these pathfinder teams was dropped exactly at the predestined points but in all cases teams came close enough to carry out their assignment at least in part. Drop Zone A was marked with both lights and radar at a point approximately one mile north of the intended DZ. On C a radar and a single light were put in operation approximately a quarter mile southeast of the planned spot. On DZ D the pathfinders met their roughest going and lost almost half the force assigned there; one radar was put into action about a mile west of the DZ (and, strangely enough, in spite of the absence of lights, received the most accurate drop of any DZ). On glider landing zone E both radar and lights were set up at the previously designated points.

H Minus 5

At first the timing and formations of the main body were remarkably accurate. Following an hour behind the pathfinders the formation flew through clear weather with good visibility from a full moon. Once over the coast fog was encountered. The planes took additional interval. Then flak began coming up, increasing in intensity as the DZs were approached. Most of the pilots were as new to combat as the parachutists they carried. Some held their formation, others took evasive action, violating their orders to hold a rigid formation. Later, reactions of the parachutists were governed by the performance of the planes in which they rode. Jumpmaster reports varied from requests for the same air crew to "I suggest that we fly the planes and let the Air Corps jump." The Troop Carrier Command's losses were relatively light, amounting to 46 planes or 2.8% of the 1,656 night and day sorties flown on D-day and on D plus 1. At 1700 of June 6 the IX Troop Carrier Command totalled its D-day losses to that hour and listed (exclusive of glider pilots) 6 air-crew personnel killed, 79 missing, and 10 wounded. By the time "stand in the door" was given the airfleet was so widely dispersed that anything closely approaching the planned drop was out of the question.

The Division's drop could be inclosed (disregarding a few stray sticks) by a rectangle twenty-five by fifteen miles. Three hundred planes, 70 per cent of the lift, unloaded in an area eight miles square outlined by Ravenoville, Ste. Mère-Eglise, the Carentan–Cherbourg railroad, and the Douve River. Of the fifteen hundred paratroopers who were to land outside this area most were to be killed or captured without contributing directly to the accomplishment of the D-day mission.

The hours between landing and daylight were hours of loneliness, confusion, danger and death. The planes had roared over, parachutes lay scattered over the ground, parachutists were crawling toward the ditches and hedgerows. From out of the moon-shadows came the sharp, sudden sound of snapping crickets and occasional answering cricks. Each man carried what he had once thought of only as a child's toy: now in the darkness his life depended on whether he could answer the snapping challenge with one of his own. Thus men in strange fields were trying to find their buddies, locate a familiar landmark, get on toward memorized missions. The 101st was working against time; daylight and the approaching invasion craft were moving toward an H-hour junction.

Pouppeville and the Lower Causeways

Division Headquarters and the Division reserve, 3d Battalion of the 501st, were to drop on DZ C. This DZ, about as close to the western approaches of Causeways 1 and 2 as was tactically possible, was also the DZ of 1st and 2d Battalions of the 506th whose mission it was to take these causeways.

Maxwell D. Taylor, commander of 14,000 men, found himself on a battlefield without a single one of those men within sight or hearing; any order he might have given would have been received only by a circle of curious Normandy cows. After ten minutes of struggling and with the aid of a jump knife he got out of his parachute harness and started, pistol in hand, to find his division. Twenty minutes later, at the corner of a hedgerow, in a somewhat irregular general officer-enlisted man relationship, he and a bareheaded 501st rifleman warmly hugged each other. After this meeting other parachutists, chiefly 501st men, began turning up. Then General Taylor found his artillery com-

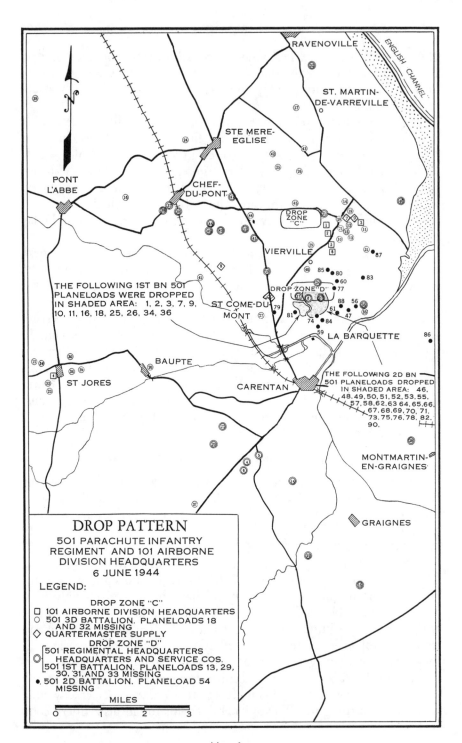

RAVENOVILLE

ENGLISH CHANNEL

ST. MARTIN-
DE-VARREVILLE

STE MERE-
EGLISE

PONT
L'ABBE

CHEF-
DU-PONT

DROP
ZONE
"C"

VIERVILLE

THE FOLLOWING 1ST BN 501
PLANELOADS WERE DROPPED
IN SHADED AREA: 1, 2, 3, 7, 9,
10, 11, 16, 18, 25, 26, 34, 36

DROP ZONE "D"

ST COME-DU-
MONT

LA BARQUETTE

BAUPTE

THE FOLLOWING 2D BN
501 PLANELOADS DROPPED
IN SHADED AREA: 46,
48,49,50, 51,52,53,55,
57,58,62,63 64,65,66,
67,68,69,70, 71,
73,75,76,78, 82,
90.

ST JORES

CARENTAN

MONTMARTIN-
EN-GRAIGNES

GRAIGNES

DROP PATTERN

501 PARACHUTE INFANTRY
REGIMENT AND 101 AIRBORNE
DIVISION HEADQUARTERS
6 JUNE 1944

LEGEND:

DROP ZONE "C"
□ 101 AIRBORNE DIVISION HEADQUARTERS
○ 501 3D BATTALION. PLANELOADS 18
    AND 32 MISSING
◇ QUARTERMASTER SUPPLY
    DROP ZONE "D"
⊙ ⎡501 REGIMENTAL HEADQUARTERS
   ⎢ HEADQUARTERS AND SERVICE COS.
   ⎣501 1ST BATTALION. PLANELOADS 13, 29,
      30, 31, AND 33 MISSING
• 501 2D BATTALION. PLANELOAD 54
   MISSING

MILES
0   1   2   3

Map 6.

mander, General McAuliffe, with a group of artillerymen. Merging the two forces they began moving eastward. Though they were never able to locate themselves during the period of darkness they were about halfway between Ste. Marie-du-Mont, the largest village in the vicinity of the lower causeways, and Vierville, and west of the highway connecting those villages.

As the night went on more and more key officers began to find their way to the growing group. Lt. Col. Julian J. Ewell, whose 3d Battalion of the 501st was the Division reserve, reported to General Taylor and a little later Colonel Higgins, Chief of Staff, and Lt. Col. John C. Pappas, the Division Engineer (killed on June 15), reported in together. Col. Thomas L. Sherburne, the Division Artillery executive officer, was dispatched with Capt. Cecil Wilson, also an artilleryman, and ten men from Colonel Ewell's battalion to collect men from the gliders which were beginning to come over. At noon they arrived at Hiesville with 115 men and 35 prisoners.

Contact had already been made with the Germans. A group of the enemy had mistaken Maj. Larry Legere of the G-3 section and Capt. Thomas White, General Taylor's aide, for Frenchmen, and had asked what they were doing. "I come from visiting my cousin," answered Major Legere in French; and as he spoke he pulled the pin of a hand grenade and tossed it among them.

At first light a sight of the church tower of Ste. Marie-du-Mont—familiar from long study of air photographs—told them where they were.

Uppermost in General Taylor's mind were the causeways leading inland from the beaches. Of the two battalions of the 506th which had the missions of securing these causeways and should therefore be in the vicinity he had not seen a man; so he knew the regiment must have been dropped far out of position. There was only one thing to do—take whoever was available and strike out for the causeways. Because of the small size of his force General Taylor decided it would be unreasonable to try for more than one of the exits, and he chose Number 1, the southernmost. He gave command of the group to Colonel Ewell.

Colonel Ewell's battalion had been badly scattered on the drop and three of the 3d Battalion planes had been shot down with 36 fatalities. About 90 men had managed to land on or near the DZ. These had assembled just south of Ste. Marie-du-Mont. During the night another 150 men from the battalion had assembled, according to plan, near Hiesville, two miles west of Ste. Marie-du-Mont. This second group had been assigned to set up and maintain the Division command post,

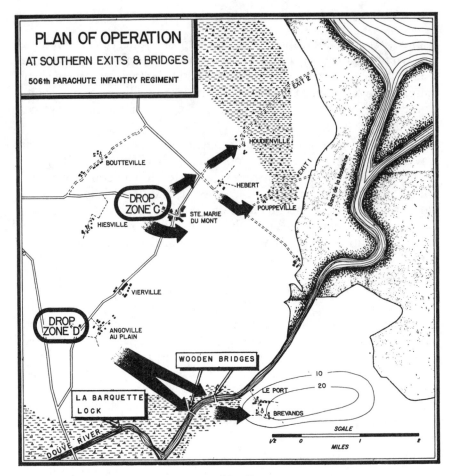

Map 7.

dúties which were to keep them on that ground for most of the day.

It was a strange conglomeration that moved out just after dawn. Ewell had about 60 of his infantrymen plus about 25 assorted Division Headquarters men—clerks, MPs, artillerymen, both generals, staff officers, even a correspondent for Reuters, the British news agency. Major Legere led a squad, lieutenants served as scouts. The abundance of brass caused General Taylor to remark, "Never were so few led by so many."

The force moved across country, meeting no resistance, and came to the main road leading into Pouppeville. Moving down the road, a column on each side with flankers out, they picked up a few additional men—Colonel Ewell's executive officer, the assistant S-3, the adjutant, and some troopers who had come down atop houses in Ste. Marie-du-

Mont. In that town several parachutists had been badly beaten and two were alleged to have been stood up against a wall to be shot, being saved only by the arrival of other paratroopers.

First contact with the enemy came near Ste. Marie-du-Mont. A German sentry yelled and seven men came running out of a dugout. Corp. Vergil E. Danforth, a scout, got four of the men with single shots through the head; another scout got two; the remaining two Germans got away. For most of the men it was their first sight of German dead.

Stopping at a farmhouse General Taylor, who spoke fluent French, asked about the nearest town and found it to be Pouppeville. As he thanked the peasant the old man handed him a clip of ammunition and asked that it be used on the Germans.

By the time the column got to Pouppeville the original force of 85 or 90 men had grown to about 150. A scattering of fire from the outlying buildings of that village brought the column to a halt. General Taylor, impressed by the business-like way in which Colonel Ewell had led the force down to Pouppeville, left the clearing of the town to him and his line-company paratroopers.

Major Legere was shot and the force had its first man killed when an aid man from the 501st disregarded the exposed position, ran out and went to work on the major; the aid man was shot through the head. Legere was never able to learn his name. During this engagement the first prisoner, a young Pole, came running to give himself up.

The 506th Assembles

Meanwhile, what of 1st and 2d Battalions of the 506th, the battalions whose missions it had been to secure Causeways 1 and 2?

Drop Zone C was to be the starting point of the 506th's attack on the two lower causeways. But so bad were the scattering and confusion of the air armada that only ten of the 81 planes scheduled to drop their men on the DZ found the mark. The 2d Battalion, which was actually supposed to attack the causeways, came to earth with the battalion center about four miles from the drop zone. The 1st Battalion, which was to divert the German forces in the vicinity, prevent them from taking 2d Battalion from the rear, and serve as a regimental reserve, had a comparatively good drop pattern and not too far from the DZ; nevertheless it was scattered enough that an additional four hours were required to collect and get the battalion going toward its objectives. Regimental headquarters, which was supporting the two battalions, came closest to the DZ; in fact, most of the ten planes hitting the DZ

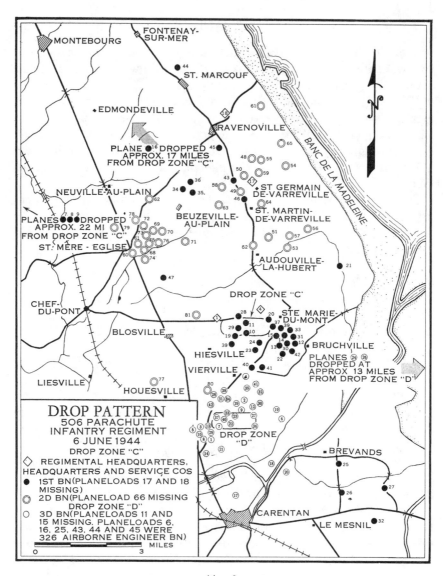

Map 8.

carried headquarters men. However, the regimental commander, Col. Robert F. Sink, found himself handicapped by a lack of communications men, including the commander of the communications platoon, the communications section and all of the operators. Days later the capture of Cherbourg revealed some of these men wounded in the hospitals there; and marked graves revealed what had happened to others. Three of their planes had missed the DZ by twenty miles.

On DZ C Colonel Sink began collecting his staff. He had landed only a short distance from the rendezvous and soon began picking up men. From a startled French farmer who was awakened and informed that there was an invasion going on the colonel learned his exact location; he moved to his jump-field command post, arriving there just before 0200, and within two hours had collected forty regimental headquarters personnel. At once he began trying to contact his 2d Battalion which should have been nearby; but there was no word. Lacking a radio he had no word of 3d Battalion. He did know where his 1st Battalion was for at 0230 he had contacted Lt. Col. William L. Turner, the commanding officer, who was collecting the battalion nearby.

At 0315, as the men quit trickling in, Colonel Sink decided to move his regimental group and Colonel Turner's battalion to the nearby small village of Coulaville which was the designated regimental command post. Arriving there an hour later Sink continued to send out scouts in search of some trace of his 2d Battalion. Though he had no contact with General Taylor the colonel too was worrying about the mission at the causeways, and just before dawn, as General Taylor was deciding to commit his reserves to the capture of the lower causeways, Colonel Sink likewise decided he would have to send his reserve, the 1st Battalion, to these causeways. At dawn 1st Battalion started out— about fifty men. In view of the size of this force, he decided, just as General Taylor had decided, to try at first only for Causeway 1 and the village of Pouppeville astride it. The battalion marched on through to its objective, fighting a few minor skirmishes, to find Colonel Ewell's force in control of both the town and the causeway. So Colonel Turner returned with his battalion to Coulaville.

Meanwhile, 2d Battalion, the battalion assigned to the lower causeways and for which Colonel Sink had searched without success, though far from its assigned drop area was having a comparatively good assembly—in fact, the most rapid and complete of any of the regiment. The troopers had had the experience of watching their DZ pass beneath them; they had seen the lighted Ts set up by the pathfinders but apparently their pilots didn't, and minutes later when they got the jump light in the planes they knew they would land in the wrong location.

In a little more than an hour the battalion S-3, Capt. Clarence Hester, and the S-2, Lt. Lewis Nixon, had collected approximately eighty men from Battlion Headquarters Company, ninety men from D, six from F, and eight from E. Lieutenant Nixon routed out a Frenchman and found they were near Foucarville, up the coast and pretty well in DZ A, the 502d's drop zone. At about 0330 Lt. Col. Robert L. Strayer, the

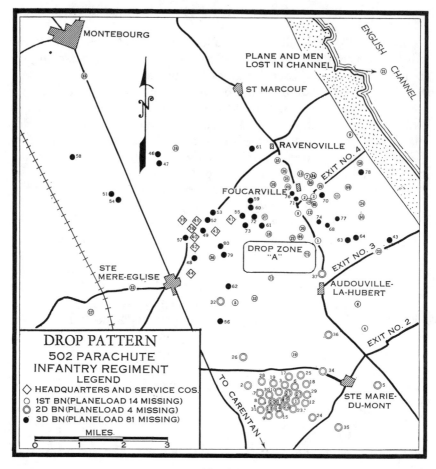

Map 9.

battalion commander, with fifteen more 506th men came along and took over. Twenty men from the 508th Regiment of the 82d Division, dropped far out of their zone, also joined up.

Just before dawn the group, more than two hundred strong, moved southward with their objective the lower or southern causeways. Almost at once they ran into resistance, so that at 1100, six hours later, they were still north of Causeway 4, the northernmost of the four exits from the beach, held up at the village of St. Germain-de-Varreville by the accurate fire of a German artillery battery. They had in the meantime killed twenty-five Germans, captured as many more, and had knocked out four machine-gun positions. Still out of contact with Regiment and not knowing that both Regiment and Division had each separately sent its reserves to carry out his battalion's mission and that

102

both reserve battalions were much closer to the objective than was his battalion Colonel Strayer felt obliged to continue his drive toward the lower causeways. So part of Company D passed around the troublesome battery and continued south past Causeways 4 and 3 to Number 2, reaching it at 1330 and bringing it under control almost without fighting. The rest of Colonel Strayer's force kept the German battery busy until Capt. R. D. Winters of Company E slipped down to the beach and brought back a group of tanks from the 70th Tank Battalion. The tanks brought the battery under fire and destroyed it. The force then joined Company D at Causeway 2, and by 1800 Colonel Strayer, with about three hundred men on hand including strays from other units, had his battalion well organized there.

THE 502D COMES THROUGH

The capture of the northern Causeways, 3 and 4, had been assigned to the 502d. Within the regiment the task was detailed to 3d Battalion. However, the other regimental objectives were so situated that their capture was closely tied in with the opening of the causeways to the 4th Division troops. The coastal battery of four 122mm guns dominated both causeways as well as the beach and the area offshore; although these guns had been worked over intensively by the Air Corps during the preceding days the extent of the damage wasn't definitely known and if only partially operative they could have made it costly for the vessels offshore and the troops on the beach and causeways. The job of destroying this battery was assigned to 2d Battalion. So important was the assured destruction of this battery that 3d Battalion was to back up 2d Battalion, if any help was necessary in its attack on the guns; before moving on to the capture of the causeways.

The guns were located just west of St. Martin-de-Varreville; a few hundred yards west of the guns was a group of barracks housing the artillery garrison. Causeway 4 ran through the barracks area. Causeway 3 was about seven hundred yards to the south. Mopping up of the barracks area—a position identified in the American plan as WXYZ —was assigned to 1st Battalion. Attached to and jumping with the regiment was the 377th Parachute Field Artillery Battalion.

The 502d's drop zone was DZ A, the closest serviceable field to its missions and just inland from the gun battery and Objective WXYZ. The regiment had a scattering drop, with 1st Battalion landing nearest the intended zone and 3d Battalion and the field artillery being the worst scattered. The 2d Battalion had a fairly compact drop, but on DZ C instead of DZ A. The regiment suffered an initial setback when

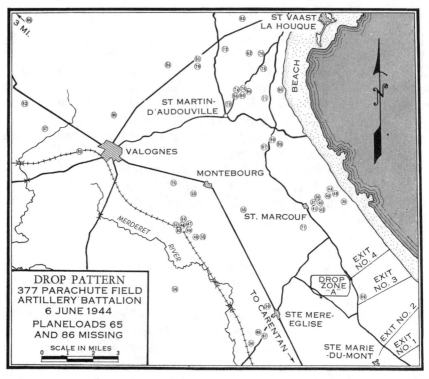

Map 10.

its commanding officer, Col. George Van Horn Moseley, Jr., broke his leg on the jump.

Another leg injury, less serious, was suffered by Lt. Col. Steve A. Chappuis of the 2d Battalion. Colonel Chappuis' battalion, which had carefully rehearsed for one of the most important single missions of the Division, the destruction of the gun battery, was mostly on DZ C instead of DZ A. Chappuis managed to collect a dozen men and, in spite of his injury, moved directly to the battalion objective. There he found a welcome sight—a blasted and unmanned site. Though there were powder and shells in the magazines there was no trace of any guns; the Germans had moved them from the position which was still partly under construction. (The battery had consisted of captured Russian 122mm guns and had been manned by the 1st Battalion, 1261st Artillery Regiment of the Army Coastal Artillery.) The air arm had done a thorough bombing job of what was left. This unexpectedly easy cancelling of one of the chief threats to the beachheads and one about which General Bradley had been particularly concerned was a real break. Colonel Chappuis remained at the position to collect his bat-

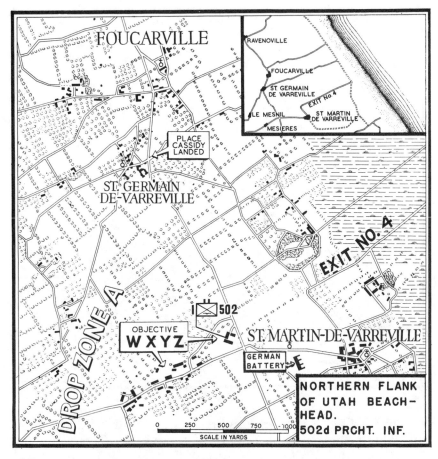

Map 11.

talion and went into regimental reserve. At dawn the next morning, D plus 1, 2d Battalion took over outposting the northern front from 1st Battalion.

The battalion responsible for the actual seizure of the northern causeways, 3d Battalion under Lt. Col. Robert G. Cole, after an unpromising start also moved toward the accomplishment of its mission with unexpected speed. Colonel Cole, after landing, wandered, trying to get his bearings, and picked up four men. Moving along a hedgerow he found the regimental S-4, Maj. J. W. Vaughn, and Capt. George A. Buker, regimental S-2, with two men, also lost. The party moved out and picked up a few more men, chiefly from the 506th, and the 505th and 508th Regiments of the 82d. After about an hour they came to the edge of a town. Colonel Cole beat on the door of a house until a woman answered. She refused to open the door. While the colonel continued

105

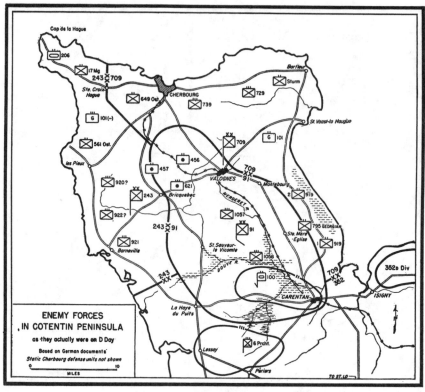

Map 12.

to pound a French-speaking private from the 505th tried some soft-talk, with the desired result (and thereupon probably became the first American soldier of the war to successfully *"parlez"* with the French mademoiselle). From her they found they were at Ste. Mère-Église, the main target of the 82d Division. Backing out Colonel Cole led his men toward one of the 502d goals, the St. Martin-de-Varreville coastal battery, picking up officers and men as they went until they numbered about seventy-five or eighty.

After about an hour of walking they ran into an enemy convoy of five carts hauling mines and other equipment. Here 3d Battalion had its first skirmish, killing several Germans and capturing ten; but in this action Major Vaughn was killed. Taking along the wagons the party continued toward the coastal battery. Just before getting there they got word that the gun position was bombed out and deserted. Now that this primary mission was out of the way Colonel Cole could turn his attention to the causeways. He divided his group into three parties. One, under Lt. Robert G. Burns of Company I, he sent south to contact the 506th. Another, under Capt. Robert L. Clements of Company

106

G, moved to exit 4, the northernmost causeway, cleaning out St. Martin-de-Varreville on the way. Colonel Cole accompanied the third party which moved toward Causeway 3. By 0730 the party was in position at Number 3, and by 0930 German troops pushed back by Americans landing on the beach began retreating inland across the causeway. The well concealed paratroopers killed about 75 Germans without loss to themselves. At 1300 they contacted troops of the 4th Division, Colonel Cole meeting the commanding officer of the 1st Battalion, 8th Infantry, at a rendezvous which they had agreed upon some days before leaving England.

By nightfall Colonel Cole had collected 250 men. He was then ordered to join the regiment the following day to go into regimental reserve near Blosville.

The remaining battalion of the 502d—1st Battalion—had the job of mopping up position WXYZ, the artillery garrison barracks, and of establishing the airborne north flank. Since Causeway 4 ran through the WXYZ area the clean-up of this position was an important part of clearing the causeways.

Lieutenant Colonel Cassidy found two of the three men he ran into on his drop to be his runner and radio operator. Then he found Colonel Strayer of 2d Battalion, 506th, with some 506th men; the group had been dropped far out of their own area and on the 502d DZ. In the same field was Colonel Cassidy's machine-gun officer, Lt. Jack Williams, who had rounded up some paratroopers and had retrieved two machine guns. Cassidy sent him out to get information as to their whereabouts. Williams soon returned, bringing Capt. Fred Hancock with some of his Company C men, and a number of strays, about thirty men in all. Captain Hancock had passed a road marker which indicated the battalion was only a short distance from WXYZ. During this time Lt. Samuel B. Nickels joined the growing battalion with some Company A men. Unknown to anyone at the time Company A's commanding officer, Capt. R. L. Davidson, and his entire stick had been dropped in the Channel and drowned.

Marching down the road to save time the battalion, halfway to St. Martin-de-Varreville, met Capt. Frank Lillyman of the pathfinders. Captain Lillyman had already scouted out the enemy battery and reported that it had been demolished by Air Force bombing. This cleared the colonel's mind on this very important regimental objective. Colonel Cassidy gave Lillyman a few men and sent him to establish a roadblock to the north, thus starting to accomplish the battalion mission of securing the northern flank.

At daybreak the column reached the first house west of the German gun position—the first slice of Objective WXYZ. From the house came a single wild shot. A detail rushed the house but no enemy was found. (All day, while the house was being used as the 1st Battalion command post, two Germans lay concealed in the building. The landlady, who connived, explained that the Germans had been kind to her.)

Colonel Cassidy, after much effort, at about 0815 got radio communication through to the 4th Division and gave them the news that the gun position at St. Martin-de-Varreville was in American hands. He also sent a patrol under Sgt. H. J. Snyder of Company B to see what was happening along Causeway 4. At about that time wounded began coming in from the fighting at the barracks, and a first-aid station was set up in the command post. A dentist's assistant, Pvt. Patrick J. Callery, took over a horse and wagon and for the rest of the day, exposed many times to enemy fire, drove up and down the Normandy roads bringing in the wounded and jump-injured paratroopers.

Sergeant Snyder got back from St. Martin-de-Varreville and reported that his patrol had cleaned out a German position in the church there and had killed a number of the enemy. Another sergeant was then sent to take the patrol back into the village, set up roadblocks, and cover the causeway. On the basis of his actions Colonel Cassidy then radioed the 4th Division that Causeway 4 was now open to their advance.

During this time fighting was going on to take the houses which constituted the barracks area WXYZ. Led by S/Sgt. Harrison Summers of Company B a group of about fifteen men moved down the road toward the houses. The patrol was a mixed group which had never worked together before; Sergeant Summers didn't know a single man by name. So he figured it would be easier to start the assault single-handed than to attempt to give orders. At the first house he walked up and kicked open the door. Inside the first room the Germans were firing through ports and looked up only as the sergeant, firing a tommy gun from the shoulder, burst in. Four of them dropped from the fire; the others escaped to the third house. The second house was taken without difficulty, the occupants having fled. Pvt. William A. Burt set up a machine gun to fire on the third house. His fire on the gun ports made the Germans keep their heads down and Sergeant Summers and Lt. Elmer F. Brandenberger of Company C sprinted for the door. As they closed in next to the wall an explosion knocked the lieutenant down and shredded his arm; Sergeant Summers smashed the door in and entered firing. There were six Germans inside; he got them all with one sweep of his gun. Then Summers started for the next house. A captain from the 82d Division joined him but was plugged by a sniper before he got twenty yards. Through the next five houses Sergeant Summers went, one man aiding him—Pvt. John F. Camien, Jr., armed with a carbine. The two men switched weapons from house to house, one covering with the carbine while the other rushed the door with the tommy gun. They killed thirty Germans in the five buildings, said nothing to one another, took no prisoners.

Beyond the last house was a larger building. The two men rushed it and kicked open the door. It was the troop messhall. There at mess and apparently oblivious of the fighting and racket sat what must have been the fifteen biggest chowhounds in the German or any other army. Summers cut them down as they started to rise. (Later, when asked why he did what he did that day, he answered: "I have no idea why. I know now that it was a crazy thing to do and I wouldn't do it again in the same circumstances. But once started I felt that I had to finish. The other men were hanging back. They didn't seem to want to fight." Sergeant Summers received the Distinguished Service Cross and a battlefield commission, and has been recommended for the Medal of Honor.)

Past the messhall was a two-story barracks. Summers, Camien and the others tried an attack; it resulted in four dead and four wounded paratroopers and the building still stood. Private Burt then fired tracers into a haystack next to the building and started a fire which spread to a nearby ammunition shed. As the stuff began to explode Germans came pouring out of the shed. They were shot down—about thirty of them—as they tried to dash across the open space to the barracks or the field beyond. Just then S/Sgt. Roy Nickrent of Headquarters Company, 1st Battalion, arrived with a bazooka. He put seven rounds into the building, the last one setting fire to the upper story. The remaining Germans—about a hundred—made a dash from the building. They picked a poor time. In addition to the troopers lying in the hedgerows the first elements of the 4th Division were just arriving over the causeway from the east, and coming up from the west was a regimental group under the regimental executive officer, Lt. Col. John H. Michaelis. Those whom the original besieging group didn't kill or capture fell into the hands of the newcomers.

It was then about 1600. Summers and his group sat down in the last house and had a smoke.

And so the four beach exits were secured by the 101st Division's parachutists in ample time to prevent the seaborne troops having to

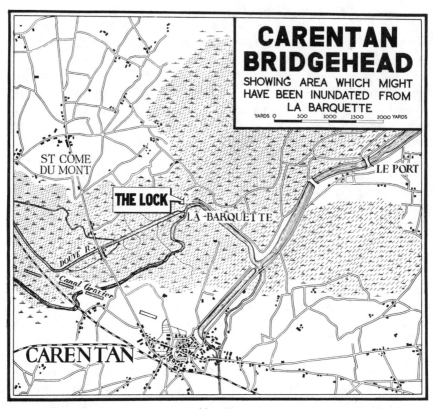

Map 13.

pay a high toll in blood for their use. As a matter of fact the two airborne divisions at Utah Beach made D-day a relatively easy one for the 4th Division. The 4th Division's spearheading 8th and 22d Infantry Regiments which landed before noon of D-day suffered a total of twelve fatalities that day; the entire Division suffered 197 casualties, of whom 60 were men from an artillery battery missing through loss at sea. And over Utah Beach that day came more than 20,000 men and 1,700 vehicles.

The Fight at La Barquette Locks

While the successful fight for the causeways was in progress other and more bitter fights were going on for the various crossings of the Douve. There were five crossings, counting the locks at La Barquette. Capture of the locks and the destruction of the railroad and main highway bridges northwest of Carentan were 501st missions; seizing the two wooden bridges on the lower Douve near Le Port was a 506th mission.

110

Except for Colonel Ewell's 3d Battalion which was Division reserve and subsequently used to capture Causeway 1 the entire 501st Regiment was assigned to the Douve missions. The beginning of the task was anything but auspicious. The 1st Battalion and regimental headquarters were in the leading serial of the regiment on the flight; this serial was badly scattered, some of the sticks landing south of Carentan, much deeper in enemy territory than the Allied attack was supposed to encompass. It is easy to see why this could happen, since the drop zone of the 501st was on the peninsula of relatively high ground extending inside the bend of the L formed by the Douve at Carentan, and there was saturated and flooded land on both sides. The 1st Battalion was so badly scattered—only 18 out of 45 planes unloaded on or near the DZ—that during the first stage of the operation it could not function as a tactical unit. In addition the battalion's commanding officer, Lt. Col. Robert C. Carroll, was killed, there was no sign of the battalion staff (though the S-1 and S-4 finally found their way back to the regiment), the executive officer, Maj. Philip S. Gage, Jr., was wounded and captured, and all of the company commanders were missing. The battalion mission was taken over by a pickup force under the regimental commander, Col. Howard R. Johnson.

Colonel Johnson and his stick accidentally landed in the drop zone; they had actually got the green light some thirty seconds previously but a bundle became jammed in the doorway and no one could get out. That delay was their salvation and enabled the stick to make a bull's eye on the DZ. Colonel Johnson figured afterward that many of the men in other planes who jumped on the signal and never rejoined the regiment probably came down in the marshes near Carentan and drowned before they could come free of their chutes.

Colonel Johnson, after a narrow escape from an enemy rifleman who fired on him at twenty-five yards as he landed, and, later, after almost walking into a German command post, ran into a party of fifteen men, some his, some from the 506th. They kept moving along ditches and through streams, picking up men as they went, until at dawn they numbered 150 and were only a few hundred yards from the locks. As day broke he sent fifty of his men on a dash for the lock. The group made it in one rush. There was a scattering of rifle fire as they raced across the flat but no one was hit. The lock and the ground immediately around it were unguarded, and it wasn't until the men got to the far bank, moving across the top of the dam and lock, that they saw some fire pits and hutments about fifty yards beyond the lock.

The La Barquette lock looking northwest toward St. Come-du-Mont. Most of the action of Colonel Johnson's group took place across the river.

The lock itself they found in working condition; it was a pretty simple affair, about thirty feet wide and hand-operated.[1]

The Americans dug in and when the Germans finally came to life and began to shell the lock area the men were well sheltered. The ease with which the objective had been attained encouraged the colonel and he felt that with a little additional strength he could move on up the river and proceed with his other mission, the blowing of the Douve bridges. There was little that morning to indicate that the map name of the lock, La Barquette, was to be replaced by another by which men of the 501st were to remember it always—Hell's Corners.

The highway bridges were only a mile upstream, but small patrols sent to feel out the area drew fire all the way and reported the bridges well guarded. The colonel decided that a stronger force than he had would be necessary to attempt the mission. Meanwhile he had got word that his S-3, Maj. R. J. Allen, had a force at Bse Addeville, a hamlet a thousand yards to the northwest. Colonel Johnson decided to join forces, so he started for Bse Addeville with about fifty men, leaving the rest to hold the lock. They reached Bse Addeville at 0900. There they found Major Allen with about one hundred men, including some of the regiment's key personnel. Also there was a Lieutenant Farrell

A close-up view of the locks.

from First Army who had taken special training with the Navy in directing supporting naval fire. Major Allen's force was made up of men from practically every unit dropped between the Merderet River and the coast. The major had rounded up a number of carts and draft animals from the farmhouses and had sent them out under protection of patrols to the drop zone to collect arms and ammunition. They returned at noon, well loaded. Meanwhile, an aid station which the major had set up in the village began filling up as jump casualties and the wounded began trickling in.

At the lock the situation remained fairly in balance. From runners who kept moving back and forth between the lock and the village Colonel Johnson learned there was no increase in enemy pressure against the lock but that enemy fire was beginning to take toll of the men dug in along the embankment. Of the general D-day situation he knew nothing. He had not heard from Division. He had no idea whether other American forces had succeeded in forming or whether the beach landings were successful. A few minutes before 1200 a medic got a small radio in action in time to catch the noon newscast from London. It said that the invasion was proceeding according to plan and that the operations of the American airborne divisions were going strongly.

Colonel Johnson turned to Major Allen. "I have decided," he said, "if things are going well elsewhere, the thing to do is make ourselves as strong as is necessary at the lock and then get to the bridges as quickly as we can." It was decided to leave a small force there at Addeville; the bulk of the men would go back to La Barquette, then move on the bridges.

113

Just as they were ready to move out word came that Lt. Col. Robert A. Ballard of 2d Battalion was about a thousand yards to the northwest in the vicinity of a large farming establishment called Les Droueries. Colonel Ballard had with him about 250 of his men and was being heavily engaged by enemy forces. Colonel Johnson contacted Colonel Ballard on the radio and ordered his force to join him for the mission at the bridges. The enemy was between them however; Colonel Ballard's forces couldn't move. Colonel Johnson left word for him to disengage and join up at the earliest possible moment. At about 1330 Colonel Johnson moved out toward the lock, leaving fifty men with Major Allen. Accompanying him was most of the demolitions platoon, which had collected at Addeville, with a sufficient supply of explosives retrieved from the drop zone to destroy the highway and railway bridges.

At first all went well; but just as the column reached a road inter-section near the lock all hell broke loose. The Germans had apparently observed the column's progress but had held their fire. Their weapons were ranged in on the intersection. Rifle, machine-gun, mortar, and 88mm fire simultaneously enveloped the group. Flat on the ground, with his men in the ditches, the colonel felt that he was between the devil and the sea. He had nothing with which to counter the mortar and 88 batteries; if he stayed his force would eventually be destroyed. But if he moved he felt that the enemy observation was such that the attempt would be no less fatal. Then he remembered one card he still held. He crawled back to the rear of the column where Lieutenant Farrell was. Following the drop that morning Farrell had been lucky enough to have retrieved his SCR-609. At Colonel Johnson's request he raised the U.S. cruiser *Quincy* maneuvering not far off the coast. Five minutes later a salvo of eight-inch shells whistled over the locks toward the German positions. Despite the range and the difficulties of adjustment the work of the *Quincy's* batteries was uncannily accurate; the German fire slackened at once. The naval fire was then turned in support of Colonel Ballard's position. The adjusting was done in roundabout fashion; Colonel Ballard radioed his sensings to Major Allen who radioed them on to Lieutenant Farrell who in turn relayed them over his 609 to the *Quincy*.

When things had quieted down a bit Colonel Johnson resumed his plans for the bridges. But a patrol which he had sent out earlier reported in with word that progress toward the bridges would be impossible due to the heavy enemy fire. Reluctantly Colonel Johnson gave up his idea of immediately pushing on toward the bridges. He then disposed his forces on both sides of the lock and told them to dig in deep. There was no food or water supply on hand and not more than a basic load of ammunition; and the position was isolated beyond prospect of getting easy resupply. But the colonel noted that his men were calm and unconcerned and took the show like veterans.

Meanwhile Lieutenant Farrell had been having ship fire put on the Carentan area. Colonel Johnson thought he might be able to destroy the bridges that way and save a possibly costly attack; naval fire bracketed the roadway but failed to damage any of the spans. While the firing was going on Captain Shettle of the 3d Battalion, 506th, who had captured the two wooden bridges downstream from the lock, came in and, reporting that he was hard pressed, asked for some men. These the colonel couldn't spare; but he did promise help in case of an emergency, and he put out a contact patrol toward Captain Shettle's position. Captain Shettle also requested some naval gunfire support and the word was passed along to Lieutenant Farrell.

That night Colonel Johnson could count some 250 officers and men with him at the locks. The rest of his regiment was in three different groups. The 3d Battalion under Colonel Ewell was in Division reserve. Divided between Colonel Ballard at Les Droueries and Major Allen at Addeville were what personnel of 1st and 2d Battalions each had been able to assemble.

The Fight at Les Droueries

The 2d Battalion of the 501st, whose mission was the destruction of the highway and railway bridges, had made a promising start. The battalion commander, Lt. Col. Robert A. Ballard, had had a good drop, landing on the right DZ; his experience was unique among the battalion commanders of the 101st Division in that he knew from the beginning that he was in the right spot. He was about a third of a mile southeast of Les Droueries. He quickly picked up two sergeants and then found Maj. Raymond V. Bottomly, his executive officer, with an ankle badly twisted from the jump. Major Bottomly couldn't walk but said that he could do "a damn good job of crawling." Colonel Ballard and the two noncoms split up and set out to gather other parachutists. Some men they found had had to get rid of all their equipment to get out of the Carentan swamps. When Colonel Ballard returned to the assembly area at 0330 he found that Major Bottomly had been organizing the men sent in and had checked their weapons. There were four machine guns, 125 rifles, one bazooka, and one 60mm

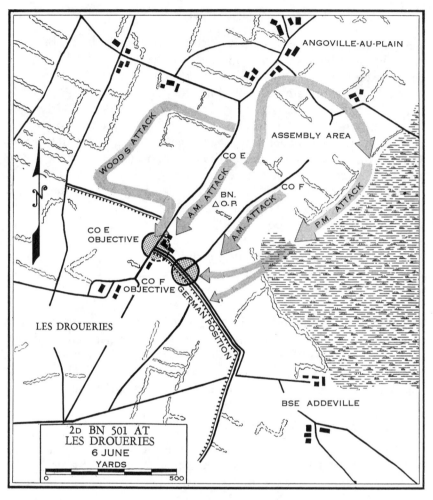

ANGOVILLE-AU-PLAIN

ASSEMBLY AREA

WOODS ATTACK

CO E

A.M. ATTACK

BN.
△ O.P.

CO F

A.M. ATTACK

P.M. ATTACK

CO E
OBJECTIVE

CO F
OBJECTIVE

GERMAN POSITION

LES DROUERIES

N

BSE ADDEVILLE

2D BN 501 AT
LES DROUERIES
6 JUNE
YARDS

0   500

Map 14.

mortar. There was also an SCR-536 with which Colonel Ballard had jumped.

The colonel's intention was to move on St. Come-du-Mont, about three miles northwest of Carentan; all the highway bridges were on the section of the highway between Carentan and St. Come-du-Mont. Meanwhile a scout reported seeing a German go into a building at Les Droueries. This Colonel Ballard took as an indication of enemy strength there and he decided that an attack on this settlement was called for before going on to St. Come-du-Mont. At 0430 the attack order was issued; at 0530 the force moved out. Company E on the right, thirty men strong, was to go after the farm buildings and the

116

road crossing on that side while Company F with thirty men was to attack toward the crossroads on the left. Company D was to follow Company F.

During the wait before the attack Colonel Ballard noticed that many of his men appeared to be in a dazed condition. The men who had fallen in the swamp were still wet and shivering and they walked or crawled around for warmth. But those who had landed dry dropped in their tracks and were asleep any time the movement stopped and some even slept standing. Many were suffering from sprains or fractures. Only two of the sixteen members of the battalion medical unit had assembled with the battalion; they were doing a superior job, having begun to collect the wounded and injured as soon as they landed.

As the light grew Colonel Ballard noticed a lift in the spirits and energies of his men. They seemed filled with a sudden, false sense of well-being as if, now that daylight had found them, their major trials were over and victory was assured. But after advancing two hundred yards unopposed a sudden burst of intense fire from small arms and mortars restored their sense of proportion.

The enemy fire continued heavy and the battalion was pinned down by it. By 0700 both forward companies had seven or eight casualties apiece, mostly from mortar fire. Both companies tried at different times to organize rushes but were thrown back with losses. By 0800 Colonel Ballard realized that he was up against a position which his force was not strong enough to take; yet he could not go on and attack St. Come-du-Mont for to do so would mean that he would leave an enemy force of unknown size in position to take him from the rear. On the other hand the Les Droueries position also blocked his way to the lock at La Barquette where the larger elements of the regiment were supposed to be concentrating.

While the colonel was considering what to do Lt. Walter W. Wood of 1st Battalion of the 501st came up with twenty 506th men he had collected. Colonel Ballard decided to commit this fresh unit in a wide swing around to the right. Lieutenant Wood started out, ran into strong opposition, swung back again to a road that ran alongside Company E, and, by a bold attack up this road, captured a house at the far crossroad. Company E took advantage of the situation to infiltrate into the house at the nearer intersection though at the cost of losing its acting company commander. A German counterattack was repulsed by Lieutenant Wood's men. The first group of houses at Les Droueries had been taken and held.

It was in the midst of these actions that Colonel Johnson's radio message came, telling Colonel Ballard to move down to Bse Addeville, pick up Major Allen's force, and then reinforce the La Barquette position. Colonel Ballard couldn't withdraw at the moment, but after the houses had been taken he did begin a withdrawal. Lt. Denver R. Bennett of Company D was sent with fifteen Company D men to Angoville-au-Plain about a mile northeast; from that point they were to reconnoiter a route across the marshes to Bse Addeville. The rest of the force pulled out gradually, moving in the same general direction. The worst problem was getting the casualties out; it took almost half an hour to clear the ground. Meanwhile half of each of the two forward companies was left in place to act as a covering force.

At Angoville-au-Plain a fight had been going on all morning between an enemy group and some men of the 326th Airborne Engineers for control of the village and it had changed ownership three times. That morning Colonel Ballard had sent his adjutant, Lt. Edward A. Allworth, to the village to set up a temporary aid station in the church. Lieutenant Allworth had managed to stay more or less on the job of caring for the wounded by running from the place whenever the Germans came in. His aid men stayed on with the wounded in the church. The Germans came in, noticed that a few German wounded were also being attended, and left the Americans unmolested.

Lieutenant Bennett's patrol ran into considerable difficulty. No suitable route could be found. Colonel Ballard's group was tight against the edge of the marsh and the enemy covered it with a parallel line of defense. There was only one route of approach to join Major Allen's group at Addeville—along the marsh's edge. Colonel Ballard therefore decided he would have to try to force this route, knocking out the enemy's forward defenses. Just as he started moving he was joined by Capt. D. A. Brown of Company E with forty-five men from various units. Company F skirmished ahead of the column and soon met a wall of German fire. The company was now fighting for the same crossroads it had occupied earlier after Lieutenant Wood's maneuver, though this time coming at it from a different direction. The whole battalion was stopped and went into position. The plan hadn't worked. At 2200 a message came from Major Allen, who had joined with Colonel Johnson, saying that he had quit Addeville, so a junction with him there was no longer a possibility. The battalion, in close contact with the enemy, settled for the night.

CAPTURE OF THE DOWNSTREAM BRIDGES

Just as the 501st battalion, scheduled to take the upper bridges, had

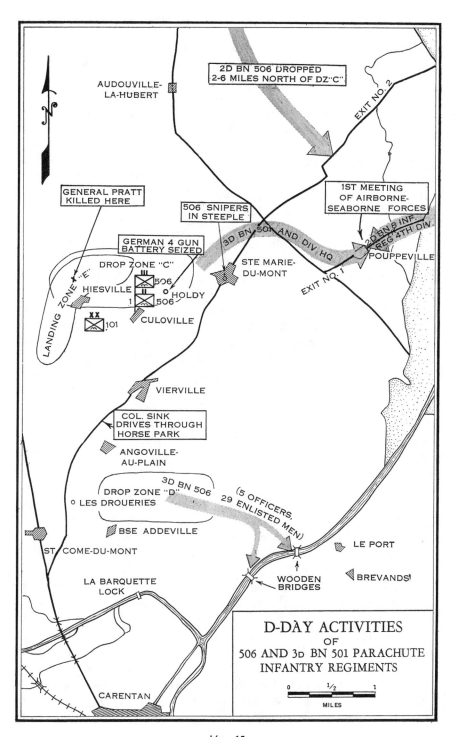

AUDOUVILLE-LA-HUBERT

2D BN 506 DROPPED
2-6 MILES NORTH OF DZ"C"

EXIT NO. 2

GENERAL PRATT
KILLED HERE

506 SNIPERS
IN STEEPLE

1ST MEETING
OF AIRBORNE-
SEABORNE FORCES

2D BN 8 INF.
REG 4TH DIV.

3D BN 501 AND DIV HQ

GERMAN 4 GUN
BATTERY SEIZED

DROP ZONE "C"

STE MARIE-
DU-MONT

POUPPEVILLE

LANDING ZONE "E"

HIESVILLE

506

HOLDY

1   506

EXIT NO. 1

101

CULOVILLE

VIERVILLE

COL. SINK
DRIVES THROUGH
HORSE PARK

ANGOVILLE-
AU-PLAIN

3D BN 506

DROP ZONE "D"

LES DROUERIES

(5 OFFICERS,
29 ENLISTED MEN)

BSE ADDEVILLE

LE PORT

ST. COME-DU-MONT

BREVANDS

LA BARQUETTE
LOCK

WOODEN
BRIDGES

CARENTAN

D-DAY ACTIVITIES
OF
506 AND 3D BN 501 PARACHUTE
INFANTRY REGIMENTS

0   1/2   1

MILES

Map 15.

a relatively good beginning only to have the situation develop unfavorably, so the 506th Battalion whose mission it was to take the two wooden bridges downstream had, after an unfavorable beginning, found itself with a handful of men quickly achieving its objective. The 3d Battalion of the 506th dropped on DZ D, that night one of the hottest spots in Normandy. The Germans had figured that the area might be used for just such a purpose and were waiting with machine guns and mortars ringed about the field. An oil-soaked house was purposely touched off as the first planes approached and the giant flare lit the surrounding countryside. Twenty men were lost from enemy action before the first American groups could collect. However, the Germans were unwilling to close in for the hand-to-hand fighting that might have wiped out the scattered paratroopers. Among the dead were the battalion commander, Lt. Col. Robert L. Wolverton, and the battalion executive, Maj. George S. Grant. By D plus 3 only one of the four company commanders, Capt. Robert F. Harwick, had been found. Captain Harwick later took over command of the battalion.

The battalion S-3, Capt. Charles G. Shettle, picked up two other officers and thirteen men. After talking things over the group decided to strike out for the 3d Battalion objective, the wooden bridges. En route they picked up sixteen more men and two officers, one of them an engineer officer who cut the Carentan power line when they came to it. Thus the "battalion" numbered five officers and twenty-nine men when it reached the bridges at 0430. The group succeeded in closing in on the western approaches to the bridges and bringing the eastern approaches under fire. Five more officers and fifteen enlisted men joined them. It was decided to try to force a crossing of one of the bridges and establish a bridgehead.

A volunteer, Pfc. Donald E. Zahn of Company H (later awarded the DSC and a battlefield commission), crossed the bridge under machine-gun fire and scouted out the opposite shore. After half an hour he was joined by Pfc. George Montilio, also of Company H. (Montilio was promoted to sergeant and also received the DSC. Due to a mixup his was awarded several months before Zahn's; he refused to wear the decoration pinned on him by General Bradley until Zahn received his. Montilio was killed in Germany on April 19, 1945, one of the Division's last battle fatalities.) Later, Lt. Kenneth H. Christianson and Lt. Rudolph E. Bolte of Company H each led five-man patrols to the far bank, crossing on the girders under the bridge flooring. Lt. Richard P. Meason of Company H followed with more men. The united force redeployed against the enemy positions, killing thirteen

Germans and knocking out three machine-gun emplacements. After
two hours, however, faced by a constantly reinforced German force
and lacking ammunition, the troopers had to pull back to the west
bank. That evening forty men who had dropped in the Carentan area
joined them. After dark the seven engineers and the two demolitions
men with the group prepared the bridges for destruction in case they
could not be held.

So D-day ended along the Douve River front. Captain Shettle and
his little battalion held steady, not knowing what the situation was
elsewhere but controlling their two bridges which might be so important in the linking of the Utah and Omaha Beaches. That night the
Germans tried a sortie across one of the bridges but were driven back
by fire. Upstream the 501st had partially completed its missions. At the
La Barquette locks Colonel Johnson's force still held firm, but the
upstream bridges were still in German hands and available for use in
a German counterattack. During the night Johnson sent out a fifty-
man patrol to try for these bridges. They ran into a wall of fire, took
losses, and returned. From his position near Les Droueries Colonel
Ballard also sent out a patrol; its mission was to get supplies, for the
battalion was down to its last belts of machine-gun ammunition. On
the drop zone they found enough ammunition to see the battalion
through another day of battle.

The groups fighting for the Douve crossings were also the airborne
outposts to the south and the Douve was beginning to shape up as
the southern front. At the same time another force, 1st Battalion of
the 502d, was establishing a northern front.

502d's Fight in the North

The missions of the 1st Battalion, 502d, included not only the establishment of a northern front but also the wiping out of the WXYZ
artillery barracks positions. This had been accomplished by Sergeant
Summers' group. But even before reaching the artillery barracks
Colonel Cassidy had given thought to the mission of establishing a
northern front, for when he met Captain Lillyman on the way to the
barracks he had given Lillyman a few men and had sent him north
to establish a roadblock south of Foucarville. Foucarville, a village
about two miles inland from the northern boundary of Utah Beach,
was a key point in the northern defense line plan. However, before
Captain Lillyman and his group approached, an entry into the village
had been made. At about 0200 eleven paratroopers led by Capt. Cleve-
land R. Fitzgerald of Company B, and Lt. Harold Hoggard of Com-

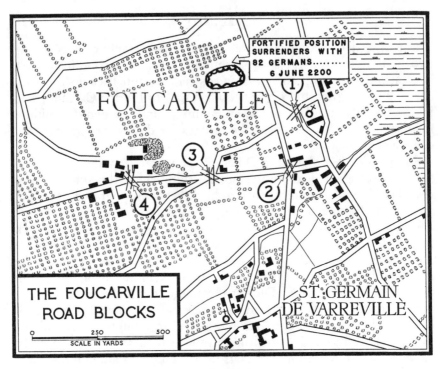

Map 16.

pany A entered Foucarville and became probably the first American unit to close with the enemy in the invasion of Europe. In the darkness they blundered into the German command post. A startled sentry shot Captain Fitzgerald, who, as he fell, killed the German with his submachine gun. (The captain, believed dying, lay there all night. He survived, however, later became the battalion's commanding officer, and was killed in a jeep accident in France after the war was over.) The group pulled back about seven hundred yards and waited for daylight. Then, reinforced to twenty-five men, they tried again but after penetrating into the village were driven out. Lieutenant Hoggard sent a request back to 1st Battalion for reinforcements. At about 1030 Lt. Wallace A. Swanson, who was to command Company A during the rest of the war, with forty men had already pushed into and through the village and ran into Lieutenant Hoggard's party. Lieutenant Swanson and Lieutenant Hoggard set up two blocks in the village and sent Sgt. Cecil Thelan with a party to establish Block 3. These forces took off at 1230 and by 1400 the last of the blocks was in. These blocks came under continuous fire as the troops landing on Utah Beach forced the Germans to fall back inland and toward the

122

village. There was also an annoying sniper fire from the village church tower and attacks from German strongpoints located outside of the town. At one time during the afternoon just after an attack had been turned back at Sergeant Thelan's block an antitank gun began ranging in uncomfortably close. On his own initiative Pvt. John T. Lyell of Company A crawled toward the gun, located it, and got within a few yards. There were two dugouts next to the gun; Lyell called for the Germans to come out and surrender. Three came out; a fourth threw a grenade as he left the dugout entrance. Lyell heaved a grenade as he saw the German's arm go back to throw. The Germans were killed by Lyell's grenade and by rifle fire from behind him. A grenade fragment hit Lyell in the shoulder. Pfc. James Goodyear with Pvt. Richard Feeney and S/Sgt. Thomas Wright covering him, made it to Lyell and attempted to save him, but he died two hours later from loss of blood.

The afternoon wore on with such individual actions. Three men, Sgt. Willis Zwiebel, Sgt. Charles Assay, and Pvt. Leroy Nicolai, all of Company A, late that afternoon cleaned out the church, ending the sniping point. Around 1630 Lieutenant Swanson went on beyond Roadblock 3 to a road intersection and set up a fourth roadblock, the strongest of all, with two machine guns, two bazookas, and fifteen pounds of explosives. It proved to be one of the happiest moves of the day. For not long afterward a German artillery convoy was spotted balling down the road toward the block. The paratroopers got out the explosives, lit the fuze, and sent the lead vehicle skyward. There were four trucks behind, all loaded with artillerymen. The bazookas threw four rounds into them before the Germans could pile out and the machine guns blazed away at the broad targets. The remaining Germans scrambled out to seek cover where they could.

Back at the battalion command post at WXYZ Colonel Cassidy received word that Lieutenant Swanson's men at Foucarville were doing all right. During the afternoon, Colonel Michaelis, the regimental executive officer, who had taken command after Colonel Moseley's leg was broken, came up with two hundred men. Colonel Michaelis directed Colonel Cassidy to move his CP and Company C, which he had been holding about the command post to protect the center position, on to the village of Beuzeville-au-Plain, about two more miles inland from Foucarville on the northern defense line, and set up Blocks 5, 6, 7 and 8. This would round out the line of barricades covering the northeast portion of the beachhead and complete the battalion's mission. Company C moved out late in the afternoon.

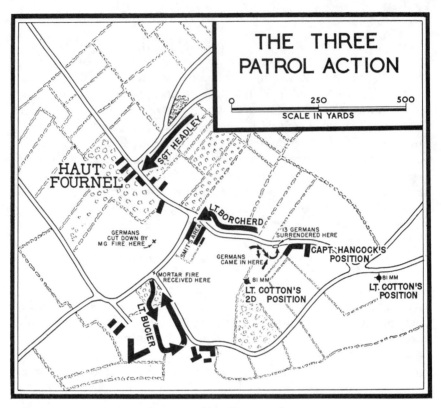

Map 17.

Preceding the main body was a point of twenty-three men under Lt. Morton J. Smit. As the point approached the village of Haut Fornel Lieutenant Smit mistook it for the target, Beuzeville. In the village Lieutenant Smit and Pvt. Harold F. Boone began searching a large barracks-like building. While loading up a bag with German loot Lieutenant Smit heard shots fired and running feet. Two trucks pulled up and more than a squad of Germans unloaded. Lieutenant Smit let them have a tommy gun load; about ten fell. The two men pulled back into the building where, temporarily, they were safe. They could hear sounds of fighting going on around the village. After about thirty minutes grenades drove them to seek an exit. They went through a courtyard and over a wall; before them was a muddy hog wallow. Into it they dived and there they stayed for an hour, only their noses and mouths out, while the Germans hunted them. At last they heard American voices; Lieutenant Smit's men had drawn back from the village, re-formed, and come forward again. Pfc. John Leviski almost bayonetted the mud-covered lieutenant before he recognized his voice. Lieutenant Smit, Boone, and Leviski started out together, only to again run into a squad of Germans; back into the hog wallow they went. The Germans searched for them in vain. After dark the three muddy paratroopers escaped.

Meanwhile the main force of Company C under Captain Hancock could hear the firing of the action in Haut Fornel but had very little idea of what was actually going on. Just as the firing got well started Captain Hancock saw a German battery—two 88s on halftracks—come down the road through the village and halt just in front of him. The capture of the guns became his overriding consideration.

Captain Hancock split his force into two groups. Seventeen men under Lt. Bernard Bucior he sent on a wide sweep to the left while another seventeen under Lt. Jack Borcherd were to come in from the right. He himself with a few remaining men took up a defensive position.

Lieutenant Borcherd swung in from the right as planned. He had meanwhile split his group, sending part of it under Sergeant Harold Headley on a wider sweep to come in at the far end of the village. Borcherd's group spotted some enemy vehicles and opened up on them, setting a truck on fire; another truck towing an artillery piece came along and was stopped by their fire. (This truck was the tail end of the convoy which ran into Lieutenant Swanson's trap at Blockade 4 at Foucarville.) Both Borcherd's and Headley's groups dashed for the village. They searched it in spite of rifle and machine-pistol fire from the houses. Shortly thereafter, however, Lieutenant Borcherd saw an enemy platoon coming down the road and ordered his men out of the town. The part of the patrol under Sergeant Headley at the other side of the village continued searching houses, unaware of the approaching enemy. Pvt. William Kelley of Sergeant Headley's group disabled one of the 88s with two bazooka rounds (the other 88 had disappeared). The enemy fire had built up so much that the group had to withdraw after losing some dead and wounded. Sergeant Headley and Kelley were trapped in a vegetable garden; they sat back to back, one with a carbine, the other with an M-1, among the cabbages until dark, when they got away. (While sitting there Sergeant Headley watched a cabbage leaf shaking back and forth and wondered what was wrong with it until he discovered that it was next to his knee.)

Lieutenant Bucior's group ran into strong opposition as they attempted to approach the village from the left. The lieutenant was shot in the shoulder but remained in the action. A line of twenty Germans made the mistake of advancing across the field toward the group. Pfc. Donald L. Mathews, who was carrying a light machine gun without tripod, stood in full view with the gun in his arms and hosed lead at the Germans. Standing beside him was an 82d Division paratrooper working a Schmeisser. About sixteen of the Germans went down and lay where they fell.

Enemy rifle fire and mortars continued to take toll of the patrol; Lieutenant Bucior was hit again and, with only two men in the group unhurt, he ordered his group back to Captain Hancock's position. The captain pulled back somewhat from Haut Fornel and established a front facing northwest. The Germans made an attempt to break this front and twenty-five enemy troops, unobserved, moved almost up to the Company command post before running into Lt. Rance Cotton, leader of the mortar platoon of 1st Battalion Headquarters Company, who had been supporting Company C with an 81mm mortar. Lieutenant Cotton ran toward the Germans yelling at the top of his voice and throwing hand grenades as he ran; the Germans scattered like quail. He shot four of them. Then he and Captain Hancock went forward and brought in thirteen as prisoners.

Colonel Cassidy during this time could get no estimate of the over-all effect of the varied and almost unrelated actions of the units of his command. He realized that there was a large tactical gap between Company A confronting Foucarville and Company C at Haut Fornel. The amount of 88 fire in the area between his companies made him suspect that a counterattack was coming; he could gauge the rise in pressure on his companies by the casualty reports he was receiving.

Actually, however, the situation was working out very favorably for the battalion. Just after 2200 from the enemy strongpoint facing Foucarville a white flag went up and eighty-two Germans and a French woman (married to a German soldier) surrendered. This surrender came as a welcome surprise to Company A; another surprise followed. As these people started moving toward the Americans there was a sudden commotion behind them and much firing; more Germans were seen running in the opposite direction. Then in the center of the German position appeared a small group of paratroopers who had been held prisoners by the Germans. What was happening is told by one of the prisoners, S/Sgt. Charles R. Ryan:

I hit inside a barbed-wire entanglement [the Foucarville strongpoint]. Before I unharnessed my chute I heard a low groan which was T/5 Howard Baker of the same company. He had hurt his knee, so I assisted him to a ditch where four or five Germans came on top of us.

We were taken about thirty yards up a gentle slope to a dugout. Once inside we were surprised to see about seven more men of the Regiment . . . I looked at my watch and it was then about 0120. In the dugout were T/5 Baker, Pfc. [Hewett C.] Tippens and Corporal Gromack from A Company. A man from C Company was hit bad in the hand and chest with a wooden bullet. There was also a Pfc. Harland Danks.

The day passed until about three in the afternoon. A few bazooka shells had been hitting overhead plus an occasional burst of machine-gun fire . . . I started talking to Baker and Gromack. Then I got my steel helmet which we were permitted to keep. I kept glancing at my watch and looking worried, talking to the rest of the men and telling them of a 2230 barrage that the 377th FA was to begin firing at this point. During the day it was seen that the guards could understand a little American and I found out we were in Foucarville which I knew was our [A Company] H plus 9 objective. When the hour passed I thought something had gone wrong with our attack. A German sergeant in the dugout kept playing a harmonica and we thought he was playing our funeral march so we were plenty nervous. Dusk was coming fast so we put it on a little more about the 2230 barrage. I had managed to get a bayonet down from the wall for the worst, figuring that they would kill us off and make an attempt to retreat.

Pfc. Tippens, close to the entrance, was taken to the opening and was told to wave a white sheet or cloth. He did so, yelling, "Hey, Yanks, come on in!" After a while my Company, A, rushed across the field. A squad of Company A, of the 22d Regiment, 4th Division, was on their left flank. . . .

The strongpoint was commanded by a German major. He was not taken in the initial surrender. I later killed him with his own pistol which I now have. He was hiding in a dugout and started to run so I went after him. . . .

A minority of the Germans had made a break to escape and as they ran the paratroopers picked up the arms dropped by the surrender party and started shooting. The Company A men joined in and about fifty of the running men were killed.

On Company C's front also the critical period had passed, for the Germans withdrew entirely from Haut Fornel. By 2300 the battalion front was completely quiet. At 0500 the next morning, June 7, 1st Battalion was relieved by 2d Battalion.

Colonel Cassidy received the Distinguished Service Cross for D-day. Of his battalion's performance the Historian of the ETO, Col. S. L. A. Marshall, had this to say: "An examination of the record and accomplishment of Cassidy's battalion, weighed critically against all others in the American Army, warrants the estimate that on D-Day, in point of fighting effectiveness and tactical scope, this was probably the outstanding battalion of the Normandy operation."

COLONEL SINK TAKES A RIDE

As had been expected the D-day fighting had developed into outward thrusts north, east, and south toward the semi-circular line of objectives

—to the northern border from Beuzeville-au-Plain through Foucarville; east, to the coastal causeways and the artillery battery and barracks; south, to the crossings of the Douve. Most of the fighting at the north was being carried by the 502d; at the south by the 501st; along the beaches all three regiments had organized elements fighting. Inland there were scattered, unplanned fights going on. In the midst of these fights and somewhere near the center of the whole Division area was Colonel Sink of the 506th.

Colonel Sink's central position was dictated by circumstances which separated his command, assigning two of his battalions to the beach causeways and one to the crossings of the Douve. His command post was at Coulaville, a village about equidistant from the Douve bridges and Pouppeville astride Causeway 1. The command post was set up in a group of farm buildings around a central court. During the day the courtyard became a center of activity. Maj. Louis R. Kent, the regimental surgeon, set up an aid station which became almost a task-force aid station as casualties began coming in from the fights at the beach exits and at a battery of German 105mm guns. By noon there were forty or fifty wounded there. A nearby field became the collecting point for strays of all units and from this force a reserve of sorts was maintained. In the courtyard and in the field men slept, waked and went out on outpost duty. Patrols were organized, moved out, and returned with bits of information. Two captured German vehicles were brought in and a number of horses and carts and wagons, and these were sent out to haul the bundles dropped on the jump fields. What was left of the radio and wire sections worked steadily trying to establish communications with higher and lower echelons. A French family stood around weeping while Major Kent and a surgeon from the Division Medical Company operated on their little boy, hit by a bullet. The people who lived in the farmhouse went about the milking and care of their cows and watched with interest all the goings-on.

As the day went by the major concentration of 101st strength had tended to build up about Colonel Sink; but the colonel had been curiously detached from the larger operations. Having lost most of his communications personnel, he had almost complete radio isolation. During the night hours he had been unable to locate his 2d Battalion and finally at dawn had had to send his 1st to the lower causeways. Shortly thereafter he contacted his 2d Battalion but he was still unable to get any word of his 3d Battalion, a fraction of which under Captain Shettle had already captured its objective, the wooden bridges across the Douve. Throughout the day he sent out patrols searching unsuccessfully for the lost battalion and seeking information. Later in the morning, after three officer-led patrols had failed to contact 3d Battalion Colonel Sink himself started out, travelling with his S-3, Maj. H. W. Hannah, in a jeep driven by Pvt. George D. Rhodes of Battery A, 81st Airborne Antiaircraft Battalion. Also in the jeep were Amory S. Roper and Salvadore G. Ceniceros (both later to be killed at Bastogne). About a mile southwest of the village of Vierville the five Americans suddenly found themselves speeding through a large enemy horse park. There was a sentry standing at the gate; Major Hannah shot him with his frontier model .38 Colt revolver and kept going. Rhodes stepped on the gas; ahead and alongside Germans started rising out of the roadside ditches—the jeep was going down the center of a German column that had just fallen out. In Wild West fashion the four passengers fired their rifles and pistols while Rhodes hell-drove. The Germans, taken by surprise, ran or dove for the ditches. But down the road ahead more and more "hostile boys" (as Colonel Sink called them) were rising and the colonel realized that such luck couldn't last. After running past troops for over half a mile they saw a crossroads where twenty-five Germans were congregated; the colonel yelled for Rhodes to whip the jeep around. They came back down the line, still firing. A machine gun fired a burst, but missed them. On the road back to the CP they met a platoon from the 501st and sent them on to clean out the "hostiles." Only after the jeep got back to the CP did it occur to anyone how effective it might have been if they had tossed out a few of the hand grenades they all carried.

THE 506TH USES ARTILLERY

At the 506th command post that morning were an additional seventy-five men from 1st Battalion. At daylight Lt. John Reeder, leader of the regimental Headquarters Company's communications platoon, had come in with word that a mixed group, including some 506th men, were engaging the enemy at Holdy about a mile and a half to the northeast, where the enemy had a battery of 105s (the only battery encountered which had not been plotted on the pre-invasion intelligence overlays). Colonel Sink sent the seventy-five men from 1st Battalion under command of Capt. Knut H. Raudstein and Capt. Lloyd E. Patch to support the attack. A few minutes later thirty or forty more men under a lieutenant from the 502d had arrived at the command post; this group was sent to support the Raudstein-Patch force. By the time these last reinforcements got there the gun position was wiped out. It was a bloody sight; besides the fifty or sixty German artillerymen who had made their last stand there, there were the remains of several sticks of parachutists who had landed in the middle of the alerted Germans and had been chewed up by automatic fire. Eight were still in their chutes.

Captain Patch was ordered to take the force on against Ste. Marie-du-Mont where the enemy was still resisting. He left the 502d men to guard the four 105s. After penetrating a little way into the village Captain Patch drew back, determined to do something about the accurate mortar fire that was following him. Deciding the fire was being regulated from an observation post in the tower of the village church, he returned to the Holdy guns, obtained permission to fire on Ste. Marie from Lt. Col. Charles H. Chase, the Regimental Executive Officer, and bore-sighted one on the steeple.

Though Captain Patch didn't know it, the church at the time was in the hands of a group of 506th troopers who had moved in during the night. By morning they had collected sixteen or eighteen men and were engaging in sniping and fighting small engagements in the village. The first round from Captain Patch's artillery missed the church but hit a barn in which a paratrooper was hiding. Another round hit the church steeple and caused the troopers to pile down; however, four scared Germans who had hidden all night under the steeple steps stayed until they were found later in the day.

After firing on the steeple Captains Patch and Raudstein advanced into the village. They were held up by machine-gun fire coming from behind a stone wall on the south side of the church. While Captain Raudstein's men laid down a base of fire Captain Patch and a machine-gun crew worked their way out to a flank, got into a favorable position and opened up on the enemy gun. The Germans returned the fire, got Patch's machine-gunner in the cheek, and Patch himself operated the gun for a while. Unable to budge the Germans, the Americans continued to fire and waited for the 4th Division troops approaching the village. The ground infantrymen joined the parachute infantrymen shortly thereafter in the village and most of the German defenders fled.

Colonel Sink, hearing about the four guns at Holdy, sent a detail to tow them back to his command post. However, the lieutenant who had been left to guard them had become nervous about a German counterattack, and by the time Colonel Sink's detail got there he had blown three of them. The one gun left was turned over to the 377th Parachute Artillery Battalion. (This gun was one of twelve 105s located near Ste. Marie-du-Mont and manned by batteries of the 191st Artillery

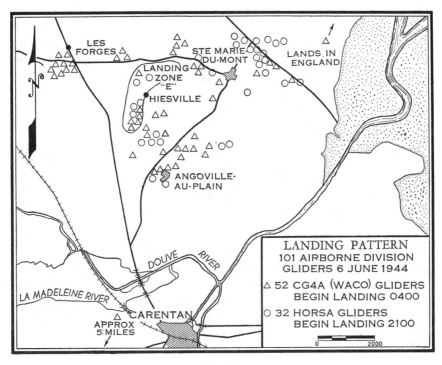

Map 18.

Regiment. Besides those captured or destroyed by the 101st, four were taken by the 4th Division and four got away.)

D-Day Summary

When D-day dawned and H-hour arrived about 1,100 of the 6,600 parachutists had been on or near the Division's objectives. Of these 1,100 many had been at objectives not their own, having picked up with the nearest available group. All during the day there was a slow buildup of strength and as darkness came and D-day ended, the organized parachute strength had doubled to about 2,500 men. The 506th had the largest concentration; with the exception of the still-uncontacted group of about one hundred with which Captain Shettle was holding the wooden bridges most of these men were with Colonel Sink in the vicinity of Culoville.

Other parachute elements of the Division were fighting alongside the three regiments. There was the Division Headquarters group made up of parachutists from Division Headquarters and Headquarters Company, the Military Police Platoon, Division Artillery Headquarters and Headquarters Battery, and the Division Signal Company. These units were concentrated at the Division Headquarters at Hiesville; earlier in the day many of them had participated in the attack with the 3d Battalion of the 501st on Causeway 1 at Pouppeville. By evening there had assembled in the Foucarville area to the north about eighty-five artillerymen of the 377th Parachute Field Artillery who had jumped with the 502d. They had with them only one 75mm howitzer. Five other howitzers had been recovered but at such a distance that they could not be used and had to be abandoned. Due to a bad scattering most of the artillerymen had fought during the day as infantrymen with various pick-up groups. Company C of the 326th Airborne Engineers had jumped with the 506th and 501st and was fighting alongside the infantrymen.

There were two 101st glider landings on D-day, one by night and one by daylight. The first glider landing, the night landing, took place at 0400. The decision to try a night landing in order to bring in antitank guns and certain command personnel considered essential was made just before D-day. A tactical night landing had never been attempted in training by the IX Troop Carrier Command; in view of what might prove to be a dangerous mission it was decided to use the smaller American CG4A (Waco) gliders and to limit the serial to fifty-two gliders and the personnel riding them to 148. Forty-four of these gliders had been assigned to Batteries A and B of the 81st Airborne Antiaircraft Battalion and the two batteries brought in a total of sixteen 6-pounder (57mm) antitank guns. The 326th Engineers had two gliders and brought in a small bulldozer.

Personnel of the 326th Airborne Medical Company were in the first serial; they had been preceded by other members of the company who had parachuted in and set up aid stations in the vicinity of the landing fields. During the day the Medical Company had established its command post under Maj. Albert J. Crandall, senior surgical officer, in the Château Colombières, near Hiesville.

We were in a typical U-shaped farmhouse with stables connected to the living quarters. We told the family we were going to start a hospital there, and they moved everything out for us, keeping only one bedroom. They took us as a matter of course. We set up the operating room in the milkhouse, which had concrete floors, windows and a pump with spring water. We set up a litter on two boxes and used that as an operating table, and set up sterilizers and arranged drugs around us on shelves. We treated casualties in the milkhouse. We also used the living room for the casualties, who were put on the floor. We wrapped them in parachutes, which were collected by two of our men. The parachutes were very warm, and were excellent for this purpose.

Three days later, just before midnight of D plus 3, German planes dropped three bombs on this makeshift hospital, killing eleven, including six of the Medical Company, and wounding fifteen. The hospital had to be moved.

Three noncoms of the 101st Airborne Signal Company brought in a large 499 radio; with it they established what is believed to be the first radio contact of any unit on the Continent with England. The signalmen almost missed their rendezvous. Their first glider landed them just four miles from where they had taken off—in England. They unloaded, hurried back to the field, reloaded on another glider, and took off in the next serial. In France they landed under fire, hailed a jeep which hauled them to the Division CP, and there they set up their radio which for several days was widely used by other organizations in Normandy.

The landing zone, LZ E, near Hiesville, had been marked as planned by the pathfinders. The platoon from the Division reserve, 3d Battalion of 501st, and the Division artillerymen, under the overall command of Colonel Sherburne, had arrived at the LZ to meet the incoming gliders. In spite of the ground fire and the inexperience of the pilots in night landings there were surprisingly small losses both of personnel and matériel, although many of the gliders were badly wrecked. Five men were killed, 17 were injured, and 7 were missing or captured. One of the dead, however, was Brigadier General Pratt, Assistant Division Commander, who was killed when his glider overshot the field and crash-landed. General Pratt was the first American general to lose his life in the invasion. A young officer who, in England, had worked very closely with General Pratt remembered him thus: "From a first impression of General Pratt—that he was a well meaning but dated officer—my respect for him grew continually. He was a sound tactician, sincere and loyal, definitely close to the junior officers and troops with whom he worked. . . . Originally designated to command the water lift into Normandy, he was as tickled as a schoolboy when it was decided to permit him to enter the combat area by glider."

Just before dark on the evening of D-day a second glider landing was made. At 2100, thirty-two of the large Horsa gliders carrying 165 command, communication, and medical personnel and matériel arrived. The size of the gliders and the smallness of the fields resulted in considerable loss as gliders crashed into trees and hedges, and some landed south of the lines in the presence of the enemy. About a third of the personnel was lost, fourteen being killed, thirty injured or wounded, and ten missing or captured. The most disastrous crash in the 101st

This Horsa glider crashed near Holdy in the 506th's sector at dawn of 7 June. Eighteen members of the 82d Airborne Division were killed and fourteen seriously injured. Eight of the dead are shown.

area was that of a Horsa glider of the 82d Airborne Division which wrecked about two hundred yards from the 1st Battalion, 506th, aid station; 18 dead and 14 badly injured men were taken from the wreckage. Little damage was done to the equipment carried in the 101st gliders in spite of the crash-landings. (The successful recovery of glider-borne equipment contrasted with about a sixty per cent loss of bundle equipment dropped with the parachutists, due to the dispersed drop which resulted in many bundles landing in swamps or water areas or in areas covered by enemy fire. Especially felt by the parachutists was the loss of many radios and mortars, handicapping the D-day action.)

That evening Generals Taylor and McAuliffe and their headquarters party arrived at Colonel Sink's command post at Culoville. Culoville was not the safest place in Normandy; twice that afternoon Colonel Sink had had to rally his headquarters force and even the walking wounded to drive back German infiltrating attacks on the command post. It was here though that the greatest strength of the 101st had tended to center and it was to Colonel Sink that General Taylor assigned the execution of the Division's most important D plus 1 mission.

As he outlined the mission General Taylor could look back upon a day of action whose main courses were just beginning to reveal themselves, though in some cases they were still obscure or blank. He felt, however, that the prearranged plans which each commander had were ample to meet any development of their individual situations and he had no great concern during the first twenty-four hours of redirecting the efforts of these commanders. It had been a day of small-unit actions;

134

sometimes of single men, of small, squad-size groups, of companies of platoon size, of battalions of company size. Lack of communications minimized the effectiveness of the regimental and divisional organizations. That lack had resulted in three different battalions, each unsure of the others, heading for Causeway 1. In the north General Taylor had the feeling that things were going pretty well and that the 502d had the situation under control; and he knew that along the beaches the primary mission of capturing the causeways had been successfully accomplished. The situation of the 82d Airborne around Ste. Mère-Église was vague, though having seen the parachute planes and gliders and hearing the sounds of battle from that direction, he knew the Division was putting up a strong fight. The 82d's chief of staff, Col. Ralph P. Eaton, badly shaken up in a glider landing, had been treated at Colonel Sink's aid station and General Taylor had talked with him there; but the colonel had known little about his Division's situation.

In the south, though, the enemy seemed everywhere. The wooden bridges were still held by Shettle's men but a bridgehead had had to be abandoned and the small force holding there faced an uncertain night. Of this force General Taylor had received no word. Colonel Johnson's hold at the lock was also uncertain. The situation along the southern front seemed, to the Division Commander, fluid, even disturbing, a state that was not aided by the lack of news of other units. The securing of this front was now the main objective of the Division. The danger points were the Douve highway and railway bridges which had not been blown as planned; presumably as long as they remained passable and in the hands of the enemy there was nothing to keep him from throwing his armor across them and at the American flank. So he ordered Colonel Sink to move out with what forces he had toward these bridges at dawn of D plus 1.

Thus ended the 101st's first day of battle. It had been a confusing day to the leaders of the airborne units; but it had also been confusing to their counterparts waiting to repel the invasion. The unplanned dispersion and scattering of the airborne troops upset many preconceived plans of the airborne commanders; but in the big picture the effect on the enemy of having troops landing all over the Peninsula and his resultant bewilderment and strategical miscalculations probably more than made up for the mishap. Jitters-producing reports came in from all sides to the High Command of the German Seventh Army, the army defending the invaded area. "Parachutists have been dropped since 0105 hours in the area east and northwest of Caen, St. Marcouf,

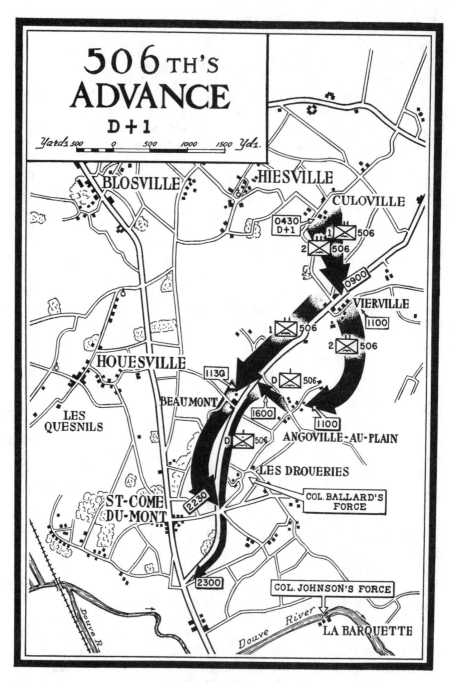

Map 19.

and Montebourg, both sides of the Vire, and on the east coast of Cotentin" is the first entry in the war diary of the Seventh Army High
Command. Some of these points are far out of the invasion sector and
apparently represented chance drops from lost planes. Others were
dummy parachutists which the RAF scattered. RAF Stirlings had also
dropped silver paper, "window," to confuse the German radar. But as
a consequence the High Command had had to mark time for several
hours trying to figure out what the various thrusts meant. At 0250
the report was received of "Cargo-glider landings in open field south
of Carentan. Ten machines. Twelve machines southwest of Marais
de Gorges." Actually, of course, no gliders were to land until more
than an hour later. At 0200 there were reports that the airborne landing embraced Montebourg, almost fifteen miles north of Carentan, and
"there is fighting by Le Ham." Debate went on among the German
generals as to whether they were facing a major or a diversionary action. By 0400 an army corps commander concluded in a report to
the Seventh Army High Command that "the general plan seems to be
to tie off the Cotentin [Cherbourg] Peninsula at its narrowest point."
By evening more landings and a terrain feature which the Americans
may have believed troublesome to themselves exclusively appeared in
the reports: "2240 . . . On Cotentin new airborne landings from Madeleine to Quinéville. It is difficult to clear out some of them because of
the hedgerow country."

D Plus 1: Advance on St. Come-du-Mont

On D-day night Colonel Sink published his order for the movement
which was to get under way at 0430 the next morning. He had, for
the advance, about 225 men from his 1st Battalion under Lieutenant
Colonel Turner and about 300 men from his 2d Battalion under Lieutenant Colonel Strayer; these two battalions had fought at the causeways and were now at Sink's command post. No definite word from
3d Battalion, or that part of it under Captain Shettle at the wooden
bridges, was to reach Sink until a report came the next evening through
the 501st. It remained for two days, as far as the regimental commander was concerned, a lost battalion. There were also available at
the command post about forty men from the 82d Airborne Division,
some of the 326th Engineers who had jumped with the regiment, about
a hundred miscellaneous men from all units, and Battery A of the 81st
Airborne AAA Battalion with eight six-pounder antitank guns. (This
battery was usually attached to the 506th for combat missions all during
the war; Batteries B and D generally made up part of the 501st Regi-

mental Combat Team, C and F were usually with the 502d RCT, and E with the 327th.) The 3d Battalion, 327th Glider Infantry, which had come ashore just after noon, and had bivouacked near the beach that night, was also attached to the 506th for the movement.

The advance was to pass through the village of Vierville and on to St. Come-du-Mont, which was on the Carentan–Cherbourg highway and less than a mile from the first of the highway bridges into Carentan. The leading element was to be the 3d Battalion of the 327th, followed in order by 1st and 2d Battalions of the 506th, Regimental Headquarters, and the antitank guns and engineers.

At 0430 the glider battalion had not appeared so 1st Battalion stepped off as the leading element. From the very first the column was harassed by small-arms fire from behind hedges, trees, and farm buildings flanking the line of advance. By 0900 1st Battalion had reached Vierville. At Vierville the advance was halted temporarily until the houses were cleared of enemy riflemen. While in the town, General Taylor and Colonel Sink saw at a distance of about two thousand yards to the southeast several hundred men moving about in the open. Whether they were Germans or Americans could not be detemined even with glasses. A patrol was sent out which determined they were enemy; but by that time they were out of range and sight. It seems likely that this was a German parachute battalion which later bounced off Colonel Ballard's battalion at Les Droueries and was finally captured by Colonel Johnson's force at La Barquette.

The advance became slower and slower as 1st Battalion met fire from both sides of the road; in two hours it had advanced only a thousand yards. Reaching a crossroads below Vierville the battalion paused for reorganization. There it was joined by six Sherman tanks from Company A of the 746th Tank Battalion. Moving behind the tanks but still under heavy fire all the way the battalion fought its way into the village of Beaumont, about halfway to St. Come-du-Mont. There it reorganized, but before it could resume the march the Germans drove in again. Company B met and turned this thrust, driving the enemy back a quarter of a mile and killing fifteen. Again the battalion took to the road toward St. Come-du-Mont, driving forward about six hundred yards where it was counterattacked and had to retreat back into the village. Lieutenant Colonel Turner, 1st Battalion CO, who had been up forward directing artillery and machine-gun fire from the lead tank, started out to try to neutralize the German machine-gun fire with tank artillery. His tank had moved out only a little way when he raised his head from the tank turret and was shot dead. Maj. Franklin E. Foster,

This picture of Dead Man's Corner, looking north, was taken after the war. The left road is to St. Come-du-Mont; the right road is to Vierville.

the Executive Officer, took over. At 1600 Company B, supported by two Shermans, assaulted with grenade and bayonet some fortified farm buildings on the flank, but was unable to budge the enemy.

Meanwhile Colonel Sink had detached Company D and a platoon of light tanks from 2d Battalion and this force joined 1st Battalion at Beaumont. Company D numbered ninety-four men, possibly as large an assembly as any parachute company in Normandy. This company under its commanding officer, Capt. Joe F. MacMillan, proceeded to drive the enemy skirmishers back beyond rifle shot of Beaumont. At 1830 the company, paced by a light tank, moved out on the Carentan road The body of the 1st Battalion was strung out behind them, A, C, Head-quarters, and B. Major Foster had been wounded in the late afternoon and the battalion command had passed to the CO of 1st Battalion Head-quarters Company, Captain Patch. The men moved as fast as they could down the ditches and along the hedgerows following the tank. In the first thousand yards only one man was hit. As the column passed a crossroads a quarter mile east of St. Come-du-Mont one of the light tanks accompanying the main body of the battalion was knocked out by a rocket, and machine-gun fire again became intense. This tended to split the column, for the rear half was delayed by the necessity of searching out the enemy guns. However, Company D and a platoon from each of Company A and Headquarters Company were already south of the crossroads when this incident occurred, and this force continued toward the objective. The two platoons became pinned down by enemy fire a little farther down the road, and Company D continued the advance alone. Company D came at last to the crossroads south of St. Come-du-Mont, the far objective given the company when it re-

139

ceived the attack order in Beaumont. There the company halted and waited for its support to come up. At that moment the luck which the company had been pushing all day changed. The tank which had led the advance all the way was struck by a German rocket; several members of the crew were killed. (For days the hull remained at the intersection, a dead man inside, and the place became known as "Dead Man's Corner.")

The company took this loss in stride; the mission had been accomplished and the men figured they could hold what they had gained. Too, the company received some unexpected reinforcements. At the crossroad as the company came up was a convoy of eight American trucks loaded with quartermaster supplies. By accident the convoy had become lost, and by some miracle it had driven right through enemy-held St. Come-du-Mont without receiving a bullet. The lead driver, unaware that his truck was the spearpoint of the American invasion, was studying a map when the company came up. Captain MacMillan told the Negro truckers they had better stick with the company if they wanted to stay alive, and remarked to some of the other officers: "It looks just like a field problem—trucks waiting here to carry us home."

At about 2330, having failed to receive support at the far crossroads, Captain MacMillan had his men and the truck convoy fall back a few hundred yards to join Captain Patch's force east of St. Come-du-Mont. Meanwhile, at midnight Colonel Sink, though sorely tempted to leave it there, decided that the small force was too extended and ordered it back to Beaumont. By 0130 the force was back in Beaumont. Ironically, Company D, after its excellent performance, hadn't quite run its course for the day. When the retirement order had come most of the company had taken it that they were relieved and would return to 2d Battalion. So they marched all the way to Angoville-au-Plain and didn't learn until they reached there that they were to attack next morning from a line of departure just beyond Beaumont. They doubled back to Beaumont and wound up with less than an hour's rest before forming for the morning's fight.

The 2d Battalion of the 506th which had followed 1st Battalion toward St. Come-du-Mont ran into trouble almost at once in spite of its position in the advance. Colonel Sink had shaken them out to the left of the main road with the general mission of clearing the enemy from the vicinity of Angoville-au-Plain. However, after 1st Battalion had cleared through Vierville, the enemy filtered back around the flanks of the advancing line, again took up fire positions behind hedges and in the houses, and opened up on 2d Battalion as it entered the village. The men took to the ditches and stayed there until four of six Sherman tanks which had been assisting the column up forward doubled back and threatened the Germans from the rear. After several hours of skirmishing Vierville was cleared a second time. The 2d Battalion then moved on to Angoville-au-Plain; and it was there that Company D rejoined them that night only to find they should have stopped in Beaumont.

501st's 1st Battalion

Meanwhile, on the left edge of the line of advance of Colonel Sink's force was a battalion whose efforts were gradually to be coordinated with the main drive of the 506th force. This battalion was the 1st of the 501st under Colonel Ballard. D plus 1 had dawned with this battalion still pressed against the edge of the marsh near Les Droueries. At 0430 Lieutenant Colonel Ballard had roused all hands and during the early hours they repulsed small groups of attackers. At 0630 the colonel ordered the battalion to resume its own attack but this withered almost at once. The battalion was tightly pinned.

In the early afternoon Colonel Ballard made radio contact with Lt. Col. Harry W. O. Kinnard, the 501st Regiment's Executive Officer, who was then with Colonel Sink along the line of the 506th advance at Angoville-au-Plain, and arranged for artillery fire. After forty-five minutes of attempting to get satisfactory adjustment Colonel Ballard, who was observing and adjusting, ordered the first concentration on the target, a house believed to be the German command post. The first concentration fell squarely on the house. It was the most heartening sight for a long time and the colonel thought the artillery might be able to pull his men out of the spot they were in. The next concentration, twelve rounds, was supposed to fall back one hundred yards. Instead it came back 350 yards, falling directly on Company F. Five men were killed and eight hard hit. This was a tense moment; but only three men left their positions and when Lieutenant Colonel Ballard ordered them back they returned without hesitation. He yelled to his officers to tell the men that there would be no more shorts and that he was again calling for the same concentration and making the necessary adjustments. They told him to fire away. The shelling continued.

That afternoon Colonel Johnson, the regimental commander, again sent word to Colonel Ballard to bring his force to the locks and join him there. Colonel Johnson still had in mind the collecting of a force of sufficient size to break through and accomplish the regimental mission at the Carentan–St. Come-du-Mont bridges. Ballard, by radio, got in touch with Colonel Kinnard at Angoville-au-Plain and told him of the order. Kinnard in turn informed General McAuliffe of Colonel Johnson's order; General McAuliffe immediately told Colonel Ballard to stick where he was for the time being; another plan was in the making in which his battalion was to figure. Five minutes later a message came for the colonel to come to Angoville-au-Plain, about a mile away, to talk things over.

About the time Colonel Ballard started for Angoville-au-Plain the German battalion which General Taylor and Colonel Sink had seen earlier near Vierville began to cross the swamp to the east of 2d Battalion. Maj. Raymond V. Bottomly, Jr., the Battalion Executive Officer, saw it first and pointed it out to the fifteen men of the command post group whom he had with him at the edge of the swamp. This strong enemy force, had it turned on the battalion, would have been a serious threat, but the main body passed out of range across the marsh toward the La Barquette locks. About twenty Germans came down to the edge near where the command-post group was. Of the twenty, twelve were killed by the Americans and the other eight came in with their hands up.

In Angoville-au-Plain Colonel Ballard found that his battalion was to join in the 506th drive toward the battalion's original objectives, the causeway bridges into Carentan. He got the order to continue to attack southward, the intention being that his battalion would eventually come abreast of Colonel Sink's two battalions which were advancing down the road to the right from Vierville through Beaumont toward St. Come-du-Mont. Colonel Ballard asked for and got six medium tanks. After a reconnaissance with the tank commander Colonel Ballard outlined his plan. The tanks and infantry were to move out together, the tanks gunning the enemy's automatic-weapons positions. Two tanks were to move on column in the road in Company E's sector, and two on the left were to move abreast directly across the fields and through the hedges. The plan worked very effectively. The tanks moved out boldly, turrets open, and their example gave the paratroopers confidence. They sprayed the hedgerows with machine guns and fired their 75s against buildings and other suspected strongpoints.

Half of the enemy force fled. The other half attempted to hold their ground. A few tried to surrender but the fight had gone on too long for that. Too, the conditions of the combat were such—with active fighting elsewhere along the line and the enemy so distributed that the surrender of one group did not lessen the menace from another—

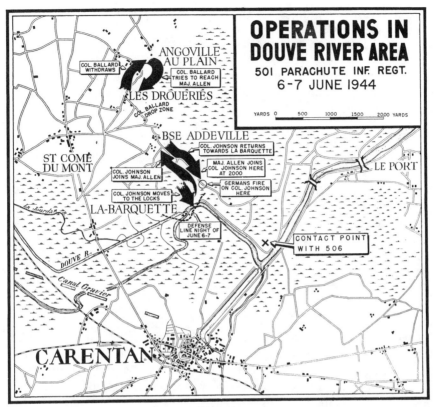

OPERATIONS IN DOUVE RIVER AREA
501 PARACHUTE INF. REGT.
6-7 JUNE 1944

YARDS 0   500   1000   1500   2000 YARDS

ANGOVILLE AU PLAIN

COL. BALLARD WITHDRAWS

COL. BALLARD TRIES TO REACH MAJ. ALLEN

LES DROUERIES

COL. BALLARD DROP ZONE

BSE ADDEVILLE

COL. JOHNSON RETURNS TOWARDS LA BARQUETTE

ST COME DU MONT

COL. JOHNSON JOINS MAJ. ALLEN

MAJ. ALLEN JOINS COL. JOHNSON HERE AT 2000

GERMANS FIRE ON COL. JOHNSON HERE

LE PORT

COL. JOHNSON MOVES TO THE LOCKS

LA-BARQUETTE

DEFENSE LINE NIGHT OF JUNE 6-7

CONTACT POINT WITH 506

DOUVE R.

Canal Gravier

le Jourdan

CARENTAN

Map 20.

that the Americans had to take extreme chances with their own lives to take individual prisoners. So most of those who had stayed were killed. Throughout the combat the action of the tanks dominated the offensive; they refreshed the men, in Colonel Ballard's words, "like rainfall on a desert."

Company E, on the right, once more took the road junction at which there had been so much hard fighting the day before, and then came under fire from the same house which it had captured the previous day. On the left Company F, which had been hard hit that day by the American artillery concentration which fell short, was replaced by Lieutenant Wood's group of 506th paratroopers and fifteen men from Company D under Lt. Richard Snodgrass. This mixed group was under Major Bottomly. In the closest fighting of the day, they used a tank as a shield to move up to within ranges of only two and three yards of the machine-gun and fire positions deeply dug in the hedgerows. The Germans in the foxholes and at the machine guns were shot to death with carbines and rifles, or grenaded, at five- or six-foot ranges; bayonets

143

were not used. The troopers stayed right with the tank until it had delivered them into the position. Then they ducked out from behind it and in a few minutes had eliminated the German force to the last man. Major Bottomly's group had captured eight of the Germans' fifteen machine guns at a cost to themselves of four killed and six wounded.

The battalion had not yet made contact with the 506th but the men could hear the firing of Colonel Sink's men about a thousand yards to the right rear as they came down from Beaumont. Colonel Sink ordered Colonel Ballard to hold where he was for the night. The tanks were released, and water, rations, and ammunition came up. Thirty men under Lt. Bill Morgan were sent to reinforce Colonel Johnson at La Barquette. Then 2d Battalion reorganized and prepared to defend for the night. Though not in close contact with the main body the battalion was holding down the left flank of Colonel Sink's general position as D plus 1 ended.

The Continuing Fight at the Locks

Colonel Johnson, regimental commander of the 501st, though he had personally led a force which, early on D-day had captured one of his regiment's objectives, the Le Barquette locks, had continued to fret all that day and night at his force's inability to spare enough men to accomplish another regimental mission, the destruction of the Douve highway and railway bridges. As D plus 1 began Colonel Johnson, holding the locks—or Hell's Corners, as it was beginning to be called—with his 250 men, began worrying about his ammunition supply. About 0630 a resupply mission was flown by the Air Corps; but the nearest bundles landed in the swamps almost a mile away and were so covered by enemy fire that there was no chance of recovery. The morning wore on with the men at the locks constantly plagued by 88 fire and harassed by snipers who, after pulling back that night, now began to crowd in from all sides.

About 1500 a large body of troops was seen approaching the position from the north. Colonel Johnson did not know that the group had been seen at a distance that morning by General Taylor and Colonel Sink, and had later passed near his own 2d Battalion at Les Droueries where twenty of them had been killed or captured by the Americans. At first the scattered and irregular formation advancing through the swamps couldn't be identified as friendly or enemy even with glasses. But at last Colonel Johnson decided they were enemy and began preparing a reception. He sent his officers to notify the men, one by

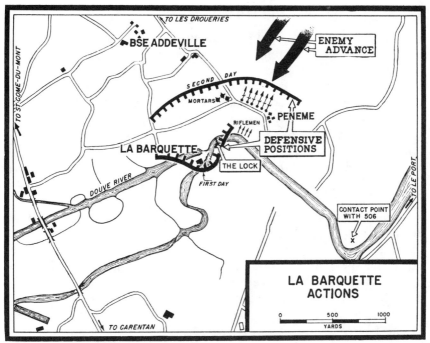

Map 21.

one, to keep quiet and remain under cover. All fire was to be held until one machine gun on the position's flank opened up; that would be the signal for everything to cut loose. Every man who could be spared and six of the eight available machine guns were shifted to this part of the perimeter; what had been the rear now became the front. The mortars were already well set up in the exact center of the position. The men waited.

The Germans came on across the swamp slowly and laboriously, putting out no security and apparently feeling certain there were no Americans in the vicinity. At 1600 the forward groups of enemy were within 350 yards of the paratroopers. This was the interval Colonel Johnson wanted—a point where the first volley would sweep with one killing blast yet not permit the Germans to rush on in and overwhelm his position by sheer weight of numbers. He said to the man on the forward gun, "OK, now! Let 'em have it!" Before the gun had gotten away more than two rounds every weapon along the perimeter front was in action. Within thirty seconds not a German could be seen. Many were hit; the marsh and the canals gave good cover to the others. They answered the Americans with small-arms fire and sent up a rocket signal which brought a renewal of mortar fire from St. Come-du-Mont and artillery fire from Carentan upon the Americans.

145

After the fight had gone on half an hour Colonel Johnson began worrying about his ammunition supply, but there seemed no way to get his men to ease their expenditure. S/Sgt. Lester A. Patty, a wire sergeant turned rifle grenadier, kept up a continuous and effective fire with his weapon and prisoners later attributed more of their casualties to rifle grenades than to any other weapon. A few weak cries of *"Kamerad!"* came from the direction of the swamp. That gave Colonel Johnson the idea that a way might be found to produce a total surrender of the force. His men didn't want that and told him so. They wanted to fight it out until every German was dead. But the colonel was doubtful that his ammunition supply would last.

Colonel Johnson asked for a couple of volunteers to accompany him, one to carry a flag and the other to interpret. Pvt. Leo F. Runge volunteered for one job and T/5 William F. Lenz for the other. Word went down the line for the troopers to cease fire. The three started toward the German lines, Runge carrying an orange flag lofted on his rifle. The German fire stopped except for the shells coming over from Carentan and St. Come-du-Mont. But as the party advanced Colonel Johnson heard fire coming from his own lines. So he stopped and had the orange flag shifted from the rifle to a long pole. Still there was a spattering of rifle fire from behind him. He didn't know whether his men hadn't heard the order or just had itchy trigger fingers, but it made him apprehensive that the Germans would answer back. Runge and Lenz showed no sign of fear, neither flinching nor opening their mouths; Colonel Johnson said later that their bearing helped his own courage more than anything else. The party went on about a hundred yards. By then all fire had ceased. A few Germans were standing up and moving toward the American lines. They advanced another twenty-five yards. In an instant, the people who were standing up on the German side suddenly hit the ground and small-arms fire broke out all along the German line. The three Americans went flat, and from behind them the men at Hell's Corners returned the German fire. The three crawled or rolled back to their own lines. Runge had been hit in the arm and Colonel Johnson in the hand.

The fire fight went on for another half hour. There came a lull in the German fire and Colonel Johnson decided to try again. He told his men to hold their fire and he and Runge and Lenz walked once more toward the swamp. The front became quiet. They went about a hundred yards and saw two men coming from the German side. They said that most of the men wanted to surrender but the officers and non-commissioned officers had already shot several for talking about it.

Colonel Johnson sent one of the Germans back to tell his commander that he had thirty minutes to surrender. "Otherwise," said the Colonel, "our superior force will annihilate you—to the last man." The soldier went back into the swamp and Colonel Johnson's party returned to Hell's Corners, bringing the other German along.

Firing resumed, but from the German side it started sporadically and broke down gradually as if the enemy had lost heart. The colonel passed around word about the parley and told his men not to fire if the Germans began to stand up. In just thirty minutes he saw a few men rise from the swamp and start to line up one behind the other. As they did so there was a rifle shot from behind Colonel Johnson. He whipped around and saw one of his lieutenants getting ready to fire again. The colonel jumped for him and kicked him in the rear with all of his might. "Goddam it!" he yelled, "What are you doing?" "Goddam it, Colonel," the lieutenant answered, "those bastards have been killing my men all day and now you won't let me shoot them." He broke down and cried like a child. Colonel Johnson turned him around and said, "Get your———in the CP and stay there for the rest of the day."

However, the shot had no ill effect, the Germans paying no heed to it. Their procession—only a little group at first—came on toward Hell's Corners, reaching the perimeter at 1800. They turned out to be the 1st Battalion of the 6th Parachute Regiment. Groups filtered in until after dark. At the end came the battalion commander, an arrogant lieutenant colonel who wanted to "talk over" his surrender; he found it was too late in the game for that. Altogether there were 350 prisoners. About 150 had been killed or badly wounded. All through the night German casualties dragged themselves from the swamps and into the American perimeter. American patrols searched out and brought in others. The aid station soon ran out of bandages, and sulfa and blood plasma ran low.

The American losses for the afternoon fight had been about ten killed and thirty wounded. However, as the victory round-up proceeded, one more blow fell on Hell's Corners. The prisoners had been lined up and were being shaken down by Capt. Altus F. McReynolds, the regimental adjutant, who had been detailed to the job, when an 88 round from Carentan landed squarely in the group, killing Captain McReynolds and twenty of the Germans and wounding many more. Another 88 round hit the command post, killing one man and narrowly missing Major Allen. Maj. Francis E. Carrel, the regimental surgeon, was hit in the knee but dressed his own wound and continued to labor all night among the wounded.

Colonel Johnson had not abandoned the plan to reach the Douve bridges. But that evening he was informed via radio by his executive officer, Lieutenant Colonel Kinnard, that Lieutenant Colonel Ballard's battalion was to be used elsewhere and wouldn't be able to get to him. Colonel Johnson's force therefore remained in position at Hell's Corners that night and all the following day, D plus 2.

Downstream from the locks the little group of men from 3d Battalion, 506th, which had got control of the wooden bridges continued its solitary battle during D plus 1, wholly out of touch with the regiment, and without information as to how things were going elsewhere. After the one unsuccessful sortie during the night the enemy had confined his efforts during the morning of D plus 1 to shelling the area with artillery and mortars. About noon Captain Shettle was able to contact by panels a flight of P-47s appearing overhead, asking them to bomb the enemy on the opposite bank. At 1430 the fighter-bombers returned and dropped a dozen bombs, three of them landing in the American position, killing one and injuring three, the remainder destroying the two bridges. One plane came in to strafe the American positions; it was diverted just in time by Chaplain Tilden S. McGee of the 506th and S/Sgt. Edward D. Shames of 506th 3d Battalion Headquarters, who waved orange flags in its path. A few hours later about two hundred Germans were seen approaching the position from the rear. The Americans quickly built up a defensive line in that direction and sent out patrols to observe the enemy's movements. The patrols contacted the Germans as they began to deploy into a woods about three hundred yards to the American rear and went into a brisk fire fight. The enemy, apparently under the impression that they were dealing with superior forces, began surrendering in groups of twenty-five or thirty. By the end of the day the American force had taken 255 prisoners and had killed thirty-five or forty Germans. The night of D plus 1 passed quietly except for an unsuccessful attempt by an enemy group to complete the destruction of the bridges. At 2200 regiment finally got word, through Colonel Johnson of the 501st, that the battalion had reached the bridges and was, presumably, still holding them.

The 502d Has a Quiet Day

For the 502d in the north D plus 1 was a relatively quiet day. Unlike the 101st troops in the south, they found more 4th Division soldiers around them than Germans. During the day the commanding general of the 4th Division was contacted and all elements of the 502d and their artillery jumpmates, the 377th Field Artillery Battalion, were released from their mission of securing the northern flank. They were then ordered to proceed to and bivouac in the vicinity of Haute Folie, two and one-half miles north of St. Come-du-Mont and near the Carentan–St. Come-du-Mont–Cherbourg highway. This move took the 502d from the northern edges of the Division perimeter to the western borders. The regiment, by then numbering about nine hundred men, reached the bivouac area about 1500. At 1800 the regiment received orders to establish a roadblock near La Croix Pan on the main highway, south of Haute Folie. This was to prevent any enemy movement up the highway from the direction of St. Come-du-Mont. On approaching Le Croix Pan that night the troops found the vicinity strongly defended, and established the roadblock on the highway about a thousand yards to the north. The 502d also received a mission for the next day: to tie in with Colonel Sink's continued drive toward St. Come-du-Mont.

On the march to La Croix Pan the regiment had picked up Capt. Adolph Blatt, a 3d Battalion surgeon, who had gone up to a crossroads to wait for the troops. In a letter he described the line of march:

Just after noon the first of the regiment came along and then in quick succession Mike Altoff [another 3d Battalion surgeon] came up from the south and the 3d Battalion came in from the east. It was perfectly wonderful to see the boys march by. We scanned the ranks of every company seeing who was present and who was absent. Each company had a French horse and cart to carry its heavy equipment and besides that there were at least half a dozen men in each company riding horses. There were a few captured German jeeps. . . . The line of march was right down the road to the west, passing about one-half mile to the south of the aid station I was running. In about ten minutes we were in an area that was enemy-infested only four hours before, but no one shot at the column. At the next main road we turned south and along that road there were a lot of dead Germans and paratroopers both. All in all the column moved about seven miles to its inland bivouac area and we had no sooner gotten into the fields assigned to us when our scouts started to exchange shots with the enemy.

The 3d Battalion of the 501st, under Colonel Ewell, which on D-day had captured Pouppeville and Causeway 1 and had then reverted to its original assignment of Division reserve, continued in that capacity on D plus 1. During the day it was engaged with the close-in protection of the Division command post at Hiesville.

The D Plus 1 Buildup

As D plus 1 ended the scattered and meager forces, which had vindicated the principle of airborne surprise by the results of their actions during the first two days, were now concentrating and forming up into a considerable task force. Those units of the Division which had not been committed by air were now coming over the beaches. The 1st and 2d Battalions of the 327th Glider Regiment had begun landing on Utah Beach on D-day and by the night of D plus 1 were completely assembled near Ste. Marie-du-Mont. Also ashore was the 3d Battalion which had landed about noon of D-day and moved that night from an initial assembly area near the beach into a final assembly area southeast of Ste. Marie-du-Mont. On D plus 1, 3d Battalion fought several engagements in an effort to join Colonel Sink's march on St. Come-du-Mont, but was unable to penetrate the German forces between it and the scene of the day's main effort. Just before midnight the battalion contacted Colonel Sink's force near Angoville-au-Plain.

The glider infantrymen of the 327th were the welcome answer to the Division's most urgent need—combat personnel for the protection of the southern front which was taking shape along the Douve. Another much-needed buildup, that of artillery, was also taking place.

THE ARTILLERY

The 377th Parachute Field Artillery Battalion, under Lt. Col. Benjamin Weisberg, which jumped with the 502d, was the first artillery in. Due to the loss of eleven of their twelve 75mm pack howitzers and the wide scattering of the sticks they were at first a negligible factor in the artillery picture, though of great aid as impromptu infantrymen. On D plus 1 a seaborne echelon of four officers and thirty men came ashore with nine jeeps, some trailers, but no guns. The following day the captured German 105mm howitzer which Colonel Sink had given them blew up on the second round, killing an infantryman and injuring two other infantrymen and two artillerymen. On D plus 2 the 377th got two 7.62 howitzers captured by the 327th glidermen and on D plus 4 they salvaged an American 105mm howitzer from a glider, thus becoming a four-gun battalion—one original 75 pack howitzer, two 7.62s and a 105. A second seaborne echelon of the battalion came in on D plus 6. By that time the German 7.62s had used up all the captured ammunition on hand and the 105mm howitzer was out of commission. This resulted in a battalion of 218 men and one gun, the little 75mm pack howitzer which had come in by parachute with the first jumpers and which had now fired 1,061 rounds. So, on D plus 8, the 377th was temporarily split up among the other artillery units of the Division and was brought back together a week later when eleven additional 75mm pack howitzers came in over the beach.

The 321st Glider Field Artillery Battalion landed most of its personnel on Utah Beach on D-day, but was unable to go into action for several days. The battalion had been divided into two groups; the smaller group consisting of drivers, chiefs of sections, and two men from each section had crossed the Channel on the *John S. Mosby,* a Liberty ship, which also carried the battalion matériel. The larger part of the battalion personnel crossed on a converted passenger ship, the *Susan B. Anthony.* The *Susan B. Anthony* struck a mine and sank off Omaha Beach. The artillery personnel was transferred to other vessels without loss of life and went ashore on Utah Beach on D-Day. There they waited until June 9, D plus 3, for the guns and vehicles and key personnel on the *Mosby.* Meanwhile, that ship was sitting uncomfortably out in the Channel off the beach, sweating out German air marauders. Finally, on June 9, after some prompting by Division Artillery officers on the beach, a naval officer who had been hunting the battalion for two days pulled alongside; that evening men and equipment went ashore to join the rest of the battalion. During this time the only part of the battalion in action was a forward observer team which had jumped into action with the 506th to direct naval and self-propelled 105 fire. The 907th Glider Field Artillery Battalion also sent in a parachute echelon of an officer and three enlisted men, but the body of the battalion came in seaborne. Part of the battalion was aboard the *Susan B. Anthony;* they however managed to transfer to other vessels when the *Susan B. Anthony* sank and were all ashore by 2100 of D Day. The remainder of the 907th landed on the afternoon of D plus 3 and reported in to Division Artillery with ten 75mm pack howitzers.

On D plus 2 ten officers and seventy-five enlisted men from Division Artillery Headquarters came in over the beaches to join General McAuliffe and the four officers and fifteen enlisted men who had parachuted in with him. On D plus 1, during the morning two Cub artillery liaison planes had come in and landed near Ste. Marie-du-Mont.

The main artillery support of the Division during the first days of the Normandy fighting was provided by the 65th Armored Field Artillery Battalion, veterans of the Mediterranean Theater, who had come ashore at H plus 3 hours and had soon thereafter been released from the 8th Combat Team and attached to the 101st. The battalion was armed with self-propelled 105s—"Priests"—and did an excellent job during the three weeks they were attached to the Division. Another armored field artillery battalion, the 87th, was attached on June 8 and supported the Division during the next week of fighting.

The three antiaircraft batteries of the 81st Airborne Antiaircraft Battalion—D, E, and F—landed on Utah Beach at H plus 15 minutes and an hour later had sixteen .50-caliber antiaircraft machine guns set up and protecting the landing. By 1300 the batteries were manning a total of thirty guns on the beach and by the end of the next day were credited with knocking down a Focke-Wulf 190 and a Messerschmitt 110. Of the three antitank batteries—A, B, and C—A and B had arrived in the first glider serial before H-hour, and Battery C came in over the beach at 1600 of D-day with the 3d Battalion, 327th. Battery C was held in Division reserve until June 9 when it rejoined the battalion. On the evening of the 9th battalion headquarters came in over Utah Beach.

Other Units

Aboard the *Susan B. Anthony* when she struck a mine were Headquarters and Service Company and Companies A and B of the 326th Airborne Engineer Battalion. The engineers succeeded in transferring to an escort vessel, HM Frigate *Narbrough,* and were landed on Utah Beach at 1430. All engineer and personal equipment was lost, however, and the men waded ashore with little more than the clothes they wore. Bothered by strafing planes the weaponless engineers moved inland about a mile to their bivouac.

The seaborne echelon of the 101st Airborne Signal Company came across the beach at 1800 of D plus 1 and went directly to the CP at Hiesville. By 2200 that night all echelons of the Company, parachute, glider and seaborne, were assembled; they totaled 77 enlisted men, 7 officers, and a warrant officer. During the first week ashore the wire section of the company laid six hundred miles of wire.

An advance detail of the 426th Airborne Quartermaster Company consisting of two officers and twenty enlisted men came ashore at 2300 on D plus 1 and before daylight reported in at the Division CP to the Division Quartermaster, Lt. Col. Charles J. Rich. Lieutenant Colonel Rich had come in on D-day by glider. On D plus 2 the 3807th Quartermaster Truck Company, hauling Division supplies, reported in and the 426th began establishing supply depots. On D plus 3 a second detachment of 2 officers and 64 enlisted men came over the beach and aided the advance detail in making deliveries to the fighting units and supplying the units of the Division who had lost their equipment in the Channel.

A small detail from the 801st Airborne Ordnance Maintenance Company consisting of an officer and seven enlisted men came ashore on D plus 1 to join the Division Ordnance Officer, who had landed on D-day with one ordnance enlisted man, and the Division Ammunition

Officer, who had come in on D-day by glider. On D plus 3 the Adjutant-General, Postal and Civil Affairs sections came ashore and joined the Division Headquarters group.

On D plus 3 there also arrived two welcome men, Joe Blankenship and Gilbert Doster, Red Cross Field Directors attached to the Division. On the following day their 2½-ton truck, loaded with Red Cross supplies, came in and the two men were kept busy trying to meet the needs of troopers who had lost their personal articles on the *Susan B. Anthony,* on the jump, while filtering through enemy lines, or from normal battle losses. Within two days they had distributed more than 2,500 razor blades and more than 300 razors, shaving cream, toothbrushes and paste, towels and soap, cigarettes, smoking and chewing tobacco, matches, and candy, and were trying to get more. Often eight to ten men were sharing a razor or towel. It was several weeks before adequate supplies finally reached the field directors.

D Plus 2: Attack on St. Come-du-Mont

By 1800 of D plus 1 it was apparent to the Division Commander that the German resistance in the area north and east of the Douve was pretty well broken with the exception of the section around St. Come-du-Mont. However, as long as the Germans held that sizable bridgehead, the Carentan highway, and the railroad crossing, there would remain the possibility of strong counterattacks against Utah Beach from the south. The clearing of the St. Come-du-Mont area would also allow a penetration into the nearby La Barquette locks area and contact with and relief of whatever troops Colonel Johnson had managed to get together in that sector. The capture of the village and the crossings became increasingly urgent and assumed top priority among the Division's missions.

That night Colonel Sink made his plans for an attack the next morning on St. Come-du-Mont. It was scheduled for 0445 and was to be preceded by preparatory artillery fire, after which the infantry would move out behind a rolling barrage by the 65th Armored FA Battalion. For the attack Colonel Sink had five 101st battalions: his own 1st and 2d Battalions, 3d Battalion of the 327th, and 2d and 3d Battalions of the 501st. Attached were eight light tanks, five six-pounder antitank guns manned by 81st's antitankers, and five 37mm antitank guns manned by 327th Glider Regiment gunners. Beside the 65th's self-propelled 105s there were some 377th Parachute Field Artillery Battalion personnel with the one 75 mm howitzer salvaged from the D-day jump and the remaining 105 howitzer captured by the 506th on D-day.

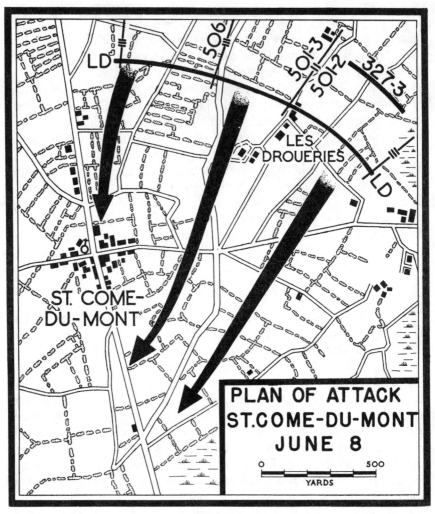

Map 22.

The glider battalion was put behind Lieutenant Colonel Ballard's 2d Battalion of the 501st with orders to attack through the 2d Battalion's position at 0445. The 2d Battalion was pretty well worn from its two days of combat around Les Droueries and was not to be used except for a general reserve. This put 3d Battalion of the 327th on the left flank of the attacking force. The glidermen, commanded by Lt. Col. Ray C. Allen, were to slant off to the leftward of St. Come-du-Mont, advance to the main road beyond the town, get to the Carentan causeway, and blow the bridges—the mission assigned initially to the 501st. Next in line to the right of the glider battalion and just north of Les

154

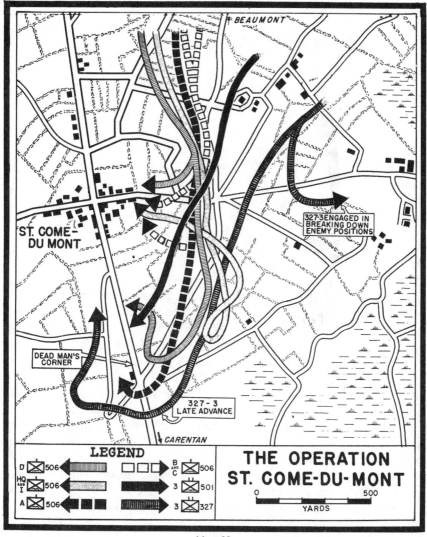

BEAUMONT

327-3 ENGAGED IN
BREAKING DOWN
ENEMY POSITIONS

ST. COME-
DU MONT

DEAD MAN'S
CORNER

327-3
LATE ADVANCE

CARENTAN

LEGEND

D ⊠ 506
HQ AND I ⊠ 506
A ⊠ 506
B AND C ⊠ 506
3 ⊠ 501
3 ⊠ 327

THE OPERATION
ST. COME-DU-MONT

0   500
YARDS

Map 23.

Droueries was the 3d Battalion of the 501st under Colonel Ewell. This battalion was to attack straight through, aiming at the main highway just below St. Come-du-Mont. On the right flank, at Beaumont, were 1st and 2d Battalions of the 506th, in column. They were to drive directly on St. Come-du-Mont.

The artillery planning and preparation were as elaborate as the time and circumstances permitted. The guns had registered in on fifteen targets, mainly enemy strongpoints and road intersections around St. Come-du-Mont and Les Droueries, and the artillerymen were given

155

their orders. They were to put preparatory fire on these targets, then pull the fire back toward the American lines, and then move forward again, with the infantry timing its advance to follow this rolling barrage. The fire would jump forward one hundred yards every four minutes.

The attack started, preceded by effective fire on the registered targets. At 0445 the moving barrage began, the first screen continuing for several minutes so that the infantry could adjust their positions before moving out behind it. By 0605 the 65th had fired approximately 2,500 rounds of 105mm. Colonel Ewell's battalion, two companies in line and platoons in column, seemed to run into the strongest enemy positions. They first encountered the enemy at Les Droueries. The shelling had already had its effect on the Germans, and when they saw the Americans they began to fall back. Colonel Ewell's men chased them through Les Droueries, firing at a closing range and killing about thirty-five.

But as the day progressed the fighting became scrambled. On the previous night, Company D of 2d Battalion, 506th, had moved from Dead Man's Corner which it had reached during that day, all the way back to 2d Battalion at Angoville, was ordered back to Beaumont, and arrived there only an hour before time to prepare for the attack. The other parachute units had also reached the line of departure only a short time before they had to jump off, and the troops in general were near exhaustion. Both officers and men in many cases started the attack that morning travelling on their nerve. Men were so tired that they often could not understand orders given clearly; just as often officers were so near sleep-walking that they could not give clear orders. Much of what happened on D plus 2 made only vague impressions on the exhausted participants; later, trying to remember verbal orders, messages, and objectives, officers and men found many blanked-out periods.

Company D, probably the weariest of all the units, either misunderstood or had only a vague idea of its mission. Some of the men apparently had the idea they were to go to the same intersection as the day before and therefore most of the company moved down the Vierville road to the place to which they had previously fought, Dead Man's Corner, with its still-smouldering tank and dead tanker. From there they swung north along the main road toward St. Come-du-Mont, took up a favorable position, and remained, receiving some scattered rifle fire from the direction of the Carentan marshes to the south. Company A of the 506th followed Company D in the advance, though some of the men of Company A failed to get the attack order and simply held

Dead 101st paratroopers near St. Come-du-Mont.

their ground. Thus, a good part of the force that was supposed to move directly onto St. Come-du-Mont took an oblique shift to the left, throwing the movement out of balance. The operation began to stall. The whole force seemed to be converging on Dead Man's Corner. South of Les Droueries Colonel Ewell's force began to brush the right flank of the 327th Battalion; ahead of him he could see Company D moving down the main road with other elements of the two battalions of the 506th strung out behind it. The glider battalion, which had come through Colonel Ballard's lines, was held on its own left flank by the swamp and on its front by the German positions along the high ground southeast of Les Droueries. This situation called for a reorganization for it threatened to pinch out Colonel Ewell's force.

Colonel Ewell contacted 1st Battalion of 506th and asked to have troops of that battalion pulled out of his sector. Capt. Eli H. Howell, S-3 of that battalion, called Colonel Sink for direction and was told to move his battalion to the right (west) and take up defensive positions to keep the Germans from attacking from that direction. But the battalion could hardly execute this movement as a battalion because Company A and most of Company D were already out of reach at the road junction and the rest of D and C had become immobilized by engaging in hedgerow fighting in the fields east of St. Come-du-Mont. During this stalemate Company D lost its commanding officer, Capt. Jerre S. Gross, killed by German artillery fire from Carentan. Companies A and D were engaged south of Companies B and C after looping north from the junction at Dead Man's Corner. Part of Company H of 506th, which was back on the left of the road, was pulled out

157

and, alone, made what was to have been the battalion advance onto the village from the east. They penetrated the first line of houses on the eastern edge of St. Come-du-Mont, but were forced back by German patrols pushing in from the north.

After the reorganization, about 0800, Colonel Ewell pushed ahead. His force reached the main highway just above the junction of the Vierville road—Dead Man's Corner—south of St. Come-du-Mont. It was about 0800 and Colonel Ewell thought he saw signs of the enemy's withdrawal westward from St. Come-du-Mont. So he decided to go south along the highway to seize the causeway and bridges. But as his men got on the road they were met by heavy machine-gun fire from the buildings at the first bridge at Pont-du-Douve, supplemented by 88 fire from Carentan. Unable to contact his supporting artillery Colonel Ewell pulled his battalion back to the east of the Carentan–St. Come-du-Mont road.

While his men were deploying the Germans hit them from the north in counterattack, seemingly coming down both sides of the road from St. Come-du-Mont. The battalion, which had just been fighting toward the south, turned to meet this threat from the north. Six times the Germans came, from 0930 until 1600, each attack a little better organized than the preceding one, and each time closing to within one hedgerow of the battalion's forward line. Curiously, the left flank of Company D of the 506th, which earlier had come to Dead Man's Corner, had swung up the road toward St. Come-du-Mont and was now in the fields east of the road and northeast of Ewell's position, felt very little of this pressure.

Across the road from the 3d Battalion of the 501st the Germans had occupied a small hill which dominated the road. Colonel Ewell realized the value of this terrain and when the enemy faded back the first time Colonel Ewell sent twenty-five men across; they stormed the hill and killed the defenders. Possession gave the paratroopers an east-west line straddling the road and facing north; from this position they beat back each German thrust.

The critical moment for the battalion came about 1430 when the fire became so hot that the troopers on the right (east) of the road began to bend and fell back one hedgerow. For a moment it looked like the whole position was on the verge of collapse. Colonel Ewell made a quick decision. He ran to the men on the hill to the west of the road, shouted "Follow me!" and led them in a quick maneuver across the road and around the rear of the hedgerow along which the men on the right were fighting. This caught the Germans on their left flank. At the same time three light tanks appeared, moved in frontally, and the paratroopers from the right flank fell in behind the tanks in line of skirmishers. Under this pressure the Germans faded back, leaving their dead and wounded.

Colonel Ewell's force had suffered rather heavy losses, and since there was no sign of support for his position other than the three tanks he went to the rear to see what was happening. While he was away the costliest counterattack of the day cost the battalion three officers and twenty men, including the tank commander, but no ground was yielded. (Altogether during the day 40 of the 160 men had started out with Colonel Ewell were killed or wounded.) Ewell found the glider battalion still at the rear where he had left it that morning. At his request Colonel Sink ordered this unit to go in on Colonel Ewell's right. By the time this reinforcement was effected the enemy withdrawal had started. The two battalions started west, but contact with the enemy was not regained. German files could be seen moving down the railway embankment. About forty loaded wagons hauling most of the equipment of the 6th Parachute Regiment were captured. Soon after 1600 a patrol from 1st Battalion, 506th, entered St. Come-du-Mont and found it empty.

At 1400 some aid men had heard and reported an explosion to the south. The Germans had blown one of the highway bridges along the causeway to Carentan, a job which Colonel Johnson, Colonel Ewell, Colonel Ballard and so many others had been trying to accomplish.

The 502d Takes Houesville

The 502d's mission for D plus 2, to tie in with Colonel Sink's attack on St. Come-du-Mont from the east, was a drive from the north down the Cherbourg–Carentan highway toward St. Come-du-Mont. The immediate objective was the village of Houesville, a half-mile to the west of the highway and two miles south of the regiment's jump-off position just north of La Croix Pan. Two battalions were available for the attack, 2d Battalion having been ordered to Division for protection of the Division CP. The attack started at 0530 against La Croix Pan with 1st Battalion attacking to the right of 3d. Lack of communication and difficulty of observing the supporting artillery slowed down the attack, but at 1225 3d Battalion entered Houesville.

During the fighting General McAuliffe had come down the highway to observe the progress of the regiment. At the front, within range and sight of the retreating Germans, he found Col. George Van Horn Moseley, Jr., the regimental CO, his broken ankle in a cast, directing the battalions from a wheelbarrow. In spite of his pleas, General McAuliffe ordered him to the rear and appointed Lt. Col. John H. Michaelis, the regimental executive officer, regimental commander. Reluctantly, Colonel Moseley went back to Division where he argued, unavailingly, with General Taylor to be allowed to continue in action. Like Sink and Johnson, Moseley had commanded his parachute regiment almost since activation; for two years he had trained and prepared it for combat. Now after two days of combat he was leaving, not to return; quickly the word got around to the men, most of whom had never had another regimental commander, that "Old Moe" had been evacuated.

After taking Houesville the regiment took up defensive positions and spent the rest of the day and the next clearing out occasional spots of resistance in its zone of responsibility, which extended from the confluence of the Douve and Merderet Rivers where it was in contact with the 508th Parachute Regiment of the 82d Airborne Division down the Douve to where the 506th took over.

ALONG THE DOUVE

For the more or less isolated groups holding the southern flank— Colonel Johnson's at the La Barquette locks and Captain Shettle's at the downstream wooden bridges—D plus 2 brought contact with their larger organizations and relief. Colonel Johnson during the day was able to establish satisfactory radio communications with his 2d and 3d Battalions and, through them, with Division. He reported that the situation at Hell's Corners was becoming critical. Ammunition was dangerously low. His wounded were slowly dying from lack of adequate aid facilities, and he wanted to dispose of his battalion of captured German parachutists whose number had become greater than that of his own force. That morning a small relief party with a jeep broke through to take care of their most pressing needs. The following day the 501st was relieved at Hell's Corners by the 506th, and moved to the vicinity of Vierville where it was joined by 2d and 3d Battalions. D plus 4 was spent in resting and reorganizing. The 1st Battalion was reorganized as a tactical unit and Colonel Kinnard, the regimental executive officer, was designated as battalion CO.

On the morning of D plus 2 Captain Shettle, in command of the 506th force downstream from the locks holding the now-bombed-out wooden bridges, decided to try to get through to regiment and Division. At 0800 he sent Lts. Linton A. Barling and Charles J. Santasiero, each with two riflemen, to contact the larger units. Meanwhile, Colonel Sink, in the midst of directing the attack on St. Come-du-Mont, was anxious for just such a contact. Early that morning the colonel requested Division to send an observation plane over the bridges to see if his battalion was still holding out there. Soon after, regiment received encouraging word from S/Sgt. Isaac Cole of Company E, 506th who had been fighting with the 501st; he had talked with Chaplain McGee who was at the bridges and had been told that Captain Shettle was holding the position with 150 men. Thereupon the battalion S-4, Lt. John King, was sent in a captured vehicle with water and rations and ammunition enough for 550 men. He reached the battalion at 1100.

During this time Lieutenants Barling and Santasiero had been running into stray groups of Germans withdrawing from the beach. In several skirmishes they killed six and took three prisoners. Finally they got through to Division and at 1400 returned with the welcome word that the little battalion would be relieved at 1900 by the 327th Glider Infantry. At 2000 units of the 327th marched up and took over. Captain Shettle took the 3rd Battalion back to the bivouac area near Hiesville. With them they brought 258 German prisoners; sixty to seventy more enemy were believed casualties. During the three days of fighting the battalion had totaled 19 officers and 117 enlisted men of whom 7 had been killed and 21 wounded. In the bivouac area approximately 4 officers and 100 men, who had fought with other units, rejoined the battalion. The next day, D plus 3, Capt. Robert F. Harwick, of Company H, rejoined the battalion and assumed command.

The Far Flung

Each day the 101st grew as the scattered paratroopers began to report in. Sometimes they came in in company or platoon-size groups, each group with its own story to tell. One such group had been led in by Lt. Col. R. D. Millener, the 101st G-3, for whom the jump into Normandy had been his first from an airplane. With about twenty officers and men from Division Headquarters and Signal Companies he had landed across the Douve, about 9 miles west of Carentan. Under his command and with the help of some French volunteer guides the men began making their way east, fighting as they went. During the first day they came upon two tanks guarded by a single German. They killed him and destroyed the tanks. That day the group doubled in size when it picked up an officer and twenty-two men from regimental headquarters Company of the 501st.

Near the village of Le Port on the Douve they hid out, and during two nights a Frenchman managed to ferry them across the river. On

Two 101st sergeants who dropped far behind the German lines return to their unit.

June 8 the group set up a block at a crossroads and knocked out a German *Volkswagen,* a motorcycle, and an ammunition wagon. Having disclosed its presence the group moved on toward the village of Picauville. Near Picauville the troops ran into an 82d Division scout who told them of the presence of Germans there; so they dug in south of the village. That night they fought a sharp engagement with Germans retreating from Picauville, killing many of them and knocking out two halftracks with rifle grenades. The next morning the group was relieved by advance units of the 90th Infantry Division and returned to the 101st.

Another such group assembled in the village of Graignes (not to be confused with Montmartin-en-Graignes) about six miles south of Carentan. Made up of both 101st and 82d men and including paratroopers, glider infantrymen, and pilots the force held Graignes, unmolested by the Germans, fed by the French inhabitants, and sending out patrols to blow bridges and sabotage, until June 10, when a three-motorcycle patrol approached the village. Four Germans were killed but one cycle got away to report the news and the next day the Germans attacked, using mortars and artillery. Forced out of the town that night they scattered, leaving nine dead Americans. A group of sixty men, aided by Frenchmen with boats, stuck together and moved through the surrounding swamps by night, hiding during the day. This group made contact with a patrol of the 2d Armored Division on the 14th and was brought into the American lines. Other segments of the Graignes force infiltrated the German lines at other points to reach safety. Meanwhile, in Graignes, the Germans killed two priests, apparently in revenge, and the mayor escaped execution by hiding.

On the northern flank a group of 377th Parachute Field Artillery jumpers landed near Ravenoville, about four miles north of their drop zone. Lt. Thomas B. Swirczynski of Battery A, 377th, began gathering men and equipment. By noon of D Plus 1 he had thirty-three men under his command, armed with carbines, hand grenades, a light machine gun, and a bazooka. That afternoon Lieutenant Swirczynski led his force down to the coastal village of Gd Hau-des-Dunes which was being bombarded by naval vessels. By 2000 that evening the parachute artillerymen had received the surrender of the 130 Germans in the village. An hour later a battalion of the 22d Infantry Regiment of the 4th Division came up and the prisoners were turned over to them. Since the 4th Division did not know the exact whereabouts of the 101st the parachute artillerymen remained with the infantry battalion until the 10th, serving as a flanking force as the 4th Division continued its attack up the coast toward Cherbourg.

Other groups, varying in size from a single man to good-sized platoons wandered through German-held territory killing, destroying, and sabotaging, until they themselves were killed, captured, or managed to make their way back to the American lines. A typical small group was one which landed east of Carentan, almost at the Vire River. Originally numbering eighteen men the group fought a series of sharp actions on D-day. The next day it was trapped by the Germans and nine paratroopers were killed. Two wounded members of the party gave covering fire to allow the escape of the seven unhurt survivors. These seven fought their way west for several days, finally making contact with the 3d Battalion of the 327th. It was estimated that the eighteen men had killed or wounded ninety Germans. The similar experiences of hundreds of men and their tales of adventure and daring were accepted by the airborne troops as the normal accompaniment of a badly dispersed drop over enemy territory.

The Carentan Causeway Fight

Though at the end of D plus 2 none of the airborne battalions had got through to the bridges between St. Come-du-Mont and Carentan their approach had forced the Germans to destroy one of

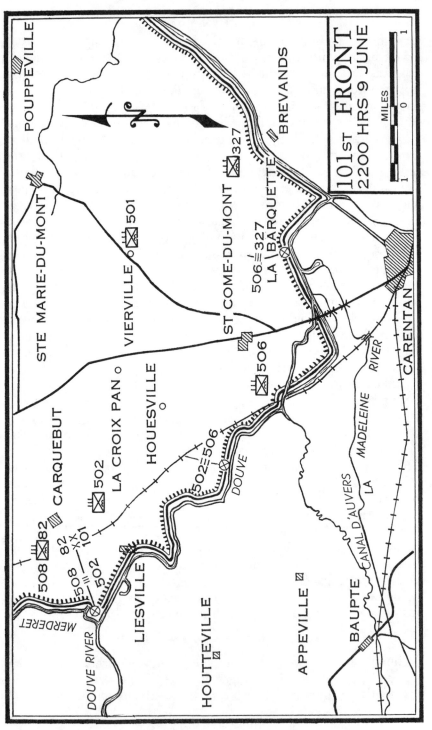

Map 24.

the spans. Except for the blowing of the remaining highway and railway bridges (tasks no longer necessary or desirable in view of the possibility of their use in an American attack toward Carentan) the 101st had completed its assigned D-day missions. It had also freed St. Come-du-Mont. It occupied on the western and southern flanks of VII Corps a defensive arc extending from the juncture of the Merderet and Douve Rivers along the northern bank of the Douve to the sea. The 502d held the upstream sector from the Merderet juncture to a point along the river southeast of Houesville. From this point the 506th held the river on around to the La Barquette locks (where it relieved the 501st on D plus 3). The 327th, which had relieved Captain Shettle's force at the wooden bridges, held the river bank from below the locks to the mouth of the Douve. The 501st on D plus 3 assembled in the vicinity of Vierville as Division reserve.

Now the Division could turn its undivided attention southward. Southward meant Carentan.

Among the various tasks assigned the units in VII Corps the capture of Carentan now enjoyed the highest priority. Since the mission of the corps was the capture of Cherbourg, all its actions were subservient to the attainment of this objective. However, on D plus 3 (June 9), Lt. Gen. Omar N. Bradley, commanding the First Army, visited the corps commander, Maj. Gen. J. Lawton Collins, at Gen. Collins' CP at Audouville and altered the corps' mission to give first priority to the joining of the two beachheads. This was the result of the unexpected resistance which both V Corps on Omaha Beach and VII Corps on Utah Beach had met and the consequent difficulty in achieving their D-day objectives. General Eisenhower had made this the top-priority mission when he came ashore on Omaha Beach on D plus 1. General Bradley even suggested the reinforcement of the 101st if the Division could not accomplish this in conjunction with the 29th Division.

The importance of the juncture of the forces from Utah and Omaha Beaches was not lost on the Germans. Even as the 101st was driving into St. Come-du-Mont, Field Marshal Erwin Rommel knew by June 8 not only the intentions of the Allies but also the number of divisions involved; for early that morning an operational order had been fished out of the Channel. Rommel was conferring in the area with the commanding general, the chief of staff, and the G-3 of the German Seventh Army. After the chief of staff gave a résumé of the situation on the Peninsula it was decided, according to the captured Seventh Army war diary, that: 'The main factor is that the enemy, attacking to the west from Isigny [seven miles due east of Carentan and in the Omaha Beach area], had not yet established contact with the Carentan bridgehead. The 6th Parachute Regiment, which had been fighting far better than expected, has been ordered to defend Carentan to the last man."

General Collins was a corps commander who believed in giving his division commanders a mission and then letting them work out a solution without interference. Thus, when General Taylor reported to him that St. Come-du-Mont and the north bank of the Douve had been secured by the 101st he said, "All right. Now take Carentan."

The tactics to be used in attacking Carentan had been decided on in England and General Collins had been informed of them at the time. A map study of the terrain had convinced General Taylor that a crossing of the Douve might be made in the vicinity of Brevands near where Captain Shettle's force had seized the wooden bridges with a holding attack to be carried out along the Carentan causeway which might draw off the Brevands defenders. This fitted in very well with additional missions which General Collins had assigned the Division: to join with V Corps troops about five miles east of Carentan in the vicinity of the highway bridge over the Vire, a river which empties into the Channel a mile east of the mouth of the Douve; and to secure the area between the Vire and Douve rivers north of the railroad, which runs somewhat south of the Carentan–Isigny highway and crosses the Vire a mile and a half south of the highway bridge, and also the area between Carentan and the Prairies Maracageuses-de-Gorges, a large swampy area west of Carentan.

Carentan, located between Utah and Omaha Beaches, is the largest town of the lower Cherbourg Peninsula. It is not a large town in the American sense; the population is about four thousand. However, it is astride the main highway from Cherbourg to Caen and St. Lô and the double-tracked Paris–Cherbourg railroad passes through it. Small ships can come up to the town by a canal which connects with the Douve.

On the afternoon of June 8 an engineer reconnaissance party looked over the ground and reported to General Taylor that an advance from along the highway from St. Come-du-Mont toward Carentan might be possible. This was the beginning of the operation against Carentan. The chief obstacle to an attack in that direction was that the highway crossed a wide stretch of marsh just before it entered Carentan. For more than one-half mile the route was a coverless defile. After pushing the enemy out of St. Come-du-Mont, the 506th had outposted the eastern abutment, a collection of houses called Pont-du-Douve, and the first two of the four bridges of this causeway. On the afternoon of June 9, Colonel Sink with nine men went up to look things over. At first they drew no fire. At the second bridge, which had been demolished by the Germans as they retreated the day before, they found an old boat and rowed across the stream. Just beyond the third bridge they drew machine-gun fire which sounded to Colonel Sink like the fire of American machine guns. He put up orange smoke but continued to draw fire. Colonel Sink then withdrew the patrol, leaving several men and a machine gun—a "protective association" Colonel Sink called it —to cover the bridges and prevent the Germans from destroying them (a real reversal, for the destruction of the bridges had been the 101st's own mission on D-day and following). He reported to Division what had happened; the report, by the time it got to the 502d, was so twisted that it gave the impression Carentan was lightly held. That same afternoon, Lt. Ralph B. Gehauf, S-2 of 502d's 3d Battalion, made a route reconnaissance past Carentan in an L-4 plane. He obtained no positive information about enemy dispositions around Carentan and there was thus nothing to offset the G-2 estimate that Carentan was held by less than one battalion.

The CP of the 502d was near La Croix Pan, about four and a half miles from Carentan on the Cherbourg highway north of St. Come-du-Mont. At about 2100 on June 9, Division ordered 3d Battalion of the 502d to attack toward Carentan, moving on such a schedule that it would reach Bridge 2—the ruined bridge—at around 0300.

THE GROUND

The asphalt highway from La Croix Pan to Carentan was quite straight, about forty feet wide and with a strong dirt shoulder. It had the same solid character where it became a causeway crossing the marshes at the confluence of the Douve and Jourdan Rivers. The road ran along levelly for the entire distance with its crown about six to nine feet above the surface of the water, depending on whether the salt marsh was full or draining. The marsh extended both ways from the road for more than rifle-shot distance. Reeds and marsh grasses covered the water surface but the growth was not thick enough to provide more than the scantiest screening cover for men moving along the causeway embankment. Out in the swamp to the westward, between the causeway and the railroad, there were a few large hummocks of fairly solid ground which might have accommodated a machine gun or a few riflemen who would have had fair concealment. On this side the causeway embankment fell away sharply to the edge of the water. A

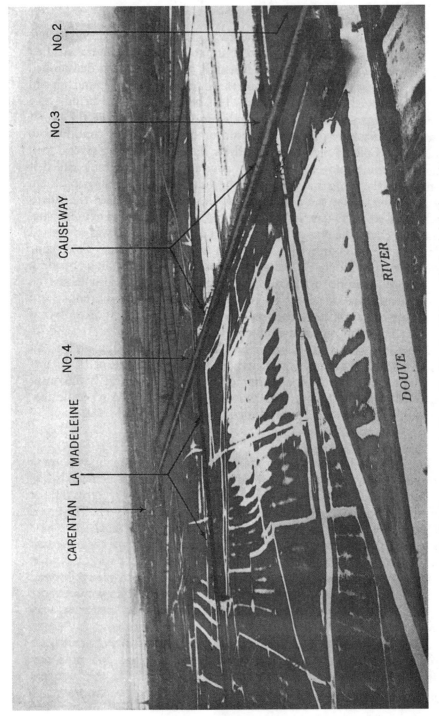

NO.2

NO.3

CAUSEWAY

NO. 4

CARENTAN   LA MADELEINE

RIVER

DOUVE

The Carentan causeway looking south. Clearly visible are the flooded fields, canals and drainage ditches which restricted the 502d's attack to the causeway proper.

rifleman might walk along this bank, perhaps stumbling and slipping into the water occasionally, but he could do no more than that. There was not enough dirt on the right embankment to permit troops to dig in. The embankment of the left was wider and did not fall away as steeply. A man might burrow in there with a spade, or even cut a two-man foxhole running back into the bank. Even so, the foxholes would have been open to flanking fire. There was no concealment along the road itself; it was naked to fire from any direction. The drainage ditches which ran along the embankment were only a few inches deep.

The four bridges along the causeway were simple, single-span affairs. The Douve and the canals all ran with fair swiftness and were deep-to-drowning. But all were narrow streams. The Germans had put up roadblocks at Bridges 2 and 4, heavy concrete posts about four feet by four feet. Iron gates of heavy design and great weight had been fixed to the posts with steel cables. The demolition of Bridge 2 had eliminated one of these blocks but on Bridge 4 the barrier still blocked the right of way. Why the Germans had not blown up all the bridges was a mystery, though an appreciated mystery, to the Division; after all, they themselves for three days had fought a bloody way toward these bridges with the mission of destroying them to prevent their use in a German counterattack. Now the Division was interested in maintaining them as intact as possible for their own attack on Carentan.

What most threatened an approach was the complete exposure of the causeway. Running straight as a die and standing boldly above the marsh it was a nearly perfect target to the enemy from three directions. Snipers might hide in the reeds on either side. Artillery could put it under fire for its entire length. From the solid ground beyond the marshes, automatic weapons could be disposed along the crests and hedgerows where they would be twenty feet above the level of the causeway and in line to rake either embankment.

These were the risks which had to be accepted. The stunted poplars along the causeway banks were hardly leafed at all and were too thin to provide any cover. Bridge 2 was still down, and before the infantry could move up a way had to be found to cross the water.

THE RECONNAISSANCE

The mission of 3d Battalion, 502d, was to seize and occupy Hill 30 near La Billonnerie half a mile southeast of Carentan and so cut off the enemy line of withdrawal from the town. (It was for the purpose of finding a suitable route to Hill 30 that Lieutenant Gehauf had made his reconnaissance flight.) En route to this objective, the battalion was to by-pass Carentan to the west. The over-all plan envisaged that Carentan would be taken by the 327th which would cross near the mouth of the Douve on the night of June 9, that elements of the 29th Division, coming up from Omaha Beach, would be moving toward La Billonnerie at about the same time, and that the 3d Battalion of the 502d might meet them in that vicinity. Such were the prospects as the 502d moved toward its assignment.

About one-half hour before dark on June 9 Capt. Henry G. Plitt, the regimental S-3, was told that an alternate route might be required for the advance and that it would have to be specified by 0300. He took a Piper Cub from Houesville and scouted the railway which paralleled the highway north. The hour was 2130 and there was just enough light left for his purpose. Flying at 1500 feet, he could see the railroad bridge over the Jourdan–Douve confluence and he noted that the bridge looked passable for foot troops. However, upon circling from southwest to east and coming back along the railway line, he saw that a ten-yard section of the railroad causeway and track had been blown out. The plane flew back and forth above Carentan for about thirty minutes, but received no fire. On returning to the regiment Captain Plitt reported that the railway line was not a feasible route of advance and that Carentan had been evacuated. In consequence, it was decided that the whole regiment would go forward, with the other two battalions following the 3d.

The regiment reached its assembly area at St. Come-du-Mont about 0530 on June 10. The 3d Battalion was already going forward when Captain Plitt got back. Moreover, the battalion quickly established that he was wrong about the German withdrawal. The infantry had been told that the 326th Airborne Engineer Battalion would repair the twelve-foot gap in Bridge 2 at around midnight and the structure would be solid when time came for the infantry to go forward. Colonel Cole moved his men out at 0145. One and one half hours previous, Lieutenant Gehauf, having completed his air reconnaissance, had taken off on a road reconnaissance. The night was fair but a thin mist partly obscured the full moon. With Lieutenant Gehauf were ten men under Sgt. Robert P. O'Reilly—six from the regular reconnaissance section and four others from Headquarters Company. They were armed with pistols and rifles.

The party reached the ruined bridge at 0130. There were no engineers at work but there were bridge beams, ropes and other matériel piled along the bank. Several engineers were under cover near the bridge.

They told Lieutenant Gehauf's men that an 88mm gun had found their range and compelled them to quit work. Finding a small boat along the embankment the party crossed the stream three men at a time. As they crossed the 88 opened fire again. From the far bank, they proceeded past the third bridge and on to Bridge 4 where the iron gate stopped them. They could budge one end of it about eighteen inches and they managed to wriggle through, one man at a time. Pfcs. James Roach and James R. Pace led the others through, and went on about fifty yards beyond the gate. Lieutenant Gehauf then got up to Roach and told him to hold it and give the Battalion a chance to catch up. Just then a mortar shell landed within a few yards of them and everyone went flat along the embankments. Flares went up from the solid ground beyond them. As if that were a signal, machine guns and mortars, forward of them and on their right, put their end of the causeway under steady fire. Lieutenant Gehauf sent a private back to tell the lead company to get its mortars forward to deal with the enemy machine guns. On the other side of Bridge 2 the messenger met Colonel Cole and reported: "Lieutenant Gehauf says don't bring the battalion through because the fire is too heavy," a message almost exactly opposite the one intended. In the sum total of things, however, his error didn't count, for the movement had already been called off for the night due to the failure of the engineers to repair Bridge 2. Battalion had called regiment and from there Colonel Michaelis had called Division, telling them that his men were blocked due to the engineer failure. At 0400 the attack order was cancelled. The 3d Battalion marched back to Les Quesnils and slept a couple of hours in a field.

Back at the causeway Lieutenant Gehauf waited; nobody had notified him of the withdrawal. At 0500 he sent back Pfc. Allen W. Bryant to learn the battalion's intentions. Bryant failed to find the battalion and returned, walking down the middle of the road, drawing no fire. This gave the patrol new confidence. Meanwhile, Private First Class Roach had checked the fourth bridge, the one nearest Carentan, found it wired for demolition, and had cut the wire. The patrol returned to Les Quesnils without drawing fire. There they found Colonel Cole just preparing to send an officer out to bring them back.

THE 327TH PREPARES TO CROSS THE DOUVE

While the 502d was making these preliminary probings of the Carentan defenses in an effort to find a way across the Douve and its adjacent inundations the 327th Glider Regiment began its part of the drive on the town. The 3d Battalion, which had taken part in the capture of St. Come-du-Mont, was relieved at 0830 on the 9th by the 506th, which was also in the town. The battalion started back to Hiesville to go into what the men thought was a rest area. During the march they were ordered to change their course for Le Groseillier, a village closer to the river than Hiesville. The battalion reached Le Groseillier at noon and was there attached to the 327th. They found the regiment planning a crossing of the Douve, to be made that night. In the woods nearby seaborne engineer units had brought up and hidden rubber boats and treadway bridge equipment. Officers of the 327th reconnoitered the area about the wrecked wooden bridges captured on D-day by Captain Shettle's force, in anticipation of a crossing that night.

During the day patrols from the 327th managed to cross the Douve. About noon Lt. Carlton Werner (killed on another patrol later in the week), Pfc. Gordon Hatchel (killed at Bastogne), Pfc. George Groh (severely wounded at Bastogne), and Pvt. William Webb (captured at Bastogne) of Company A, swam the stream and salvaged a ferry grounded on the far side. A combat patrol from the 2d Platoon of Company A and led by Lt. Kenneth Vyn, crossed on this ferry. Only a short distance from the river the patrol ran into German small-arms fire and lost one man, Cpl. Harry O. Maynor, killed and five wounded. (Lieutenant Vyn, one of the wounded, returned from the hospital two days before Holland. His glider missed Holland and landed in Germany in the midst of a panzer outfit. He and his men fought it out and four lived to be captured. Vyn was among the dead.) Carrying its wounded the patrol returned to the river to find the ferry out of commission. Mortars of the 327th laid down a protective barrage and under it the non-swimmers were brought back on a raft made of two signboards. Others, including two of the wounded, swam back. Two swimmers who got in trouble, Pfc. Roy Goodnight and Pvt. Marvin D. Taxman, were saved from drowning by Pvt. Arthur Mayer. Mayer was shot in the arm and leg during the rescue and later received the Distinguished Service Cross for gallantry under fire. Among the other members of the patrol were S/Sgt. William Southers, Sgt. Joseph Mitcavish, Pfc. Richard A. Lorrello, and Pvts. Clyde Stephenson and Harrison Spencer, the last, a BAR man, doing some remarkable shooting and credited with wiping out two machine-gun nests.

After dark, glidermen of the 327th brought the rubber boats by hand from where they were hidden, almost a mile down to the river. Under cover of a barrage furnished by the 321st Glider Field Artillery Battalion, the 65th Armored Field Artillery Battalion, a company of chemical mortars, 81mm mortars and machine guns of the 327th's 2d Battalion, and .50-caliber machine guns manned by two companies of the 237th Engineer Battalion. Company C of the 1st Battalion, 327th, crossed the Douve at 0145 that night (June 9-10). Casualties from enemy fire were very light but several dozen casualties occurred just after the crossing due to explosions. Regimental officers attributed these losses to short rounds from the chemical mortars; General McAuliffe, who was present coordinating the artillery fire plan, identified the explosions as German mines.

The rest of the 1st Battalion ferried across and immediately the 49th Engineer Battalion began construction of a bridge. By 0600 the entire 327th was across. Meanwhile, the 3d Battalion had left Le Groseillier at 0300 and moved down to the river. The tide was out and most of the men were able to wade across, the entire battalion reaching the other side by 0700. By that time, against light resistance, the 327th had occupied the village of Brevands across the river three miles below Carentan. The combined force then began its two-day fight up the south bank of the Douve toward Carentan.

First Blood on the Causeway

About 0930, 3d Battalion of the 502d, waiting at Les Quesnils, was told that it would advance again some time that afternoon, June 10. Division said that it would be supported by substantial artillery fire. Detailed to that purpose were the 377th Field Artillery Battalion, which had lost all but one of its original 75mms during the jump and had since captured two artillery pieces from the Germans; the 907th, which had come by sea with twelve pack howitzer 75s; and the 65th Armored Field Artillery Battalion with its eighteen self-propelled 105mms. The fire positions were in the general vicinity of St. Come-du-Mont. The mass of the shells was delivered against the enemy left, in and around Pommeranque, a settlement past the fourth bridge where the battalion might meet resistance as it swung southeast of the town to get to Hill 30. About noon, Colonel Cole and Lieutenant Gehauf went on down to the causeway to see if the road were again solid. Nothing had been done, so Colonel Cole grabbed hold of a rope and told Capt. Robert L. Clements of Company G and two of the enlisted men to get planking from the stores which the engineers had left. Working together, the four men jury-rigged a foot bridge. By 1400, the bridge was complete, though a bit wobbly. A heavy iron fence which had been part of the enemy roadblock had been torn

loose and was used as a flooring. At about 1500, Lieutenant Gehauf
and Private First Class Bryant crossed Bridge 2 ahead of Company G's
1st Platoon. The battalion thus began its move into the causeway defile.
The men had to proceed single file when they came to the bridge. It
could not accommodate more than a single line of men, and if they
jammed up at all an 88mm gun whiz-banged away at them from up
around Carentan.

This intermittent pot-shotting by the 88mm gun, which had flushed
the engineers the night before, harassed the infantry without stamped-
ing them. The first portion of the advance along the causeway was
relatively uneventful. Several hundred yards off to the right of Bridge 2
there was a patch of solid ground in the marsh, and across the front
of it stretched a hedgerow. From behind the hedge, a sniper cracked
down on the mortar squad of Company G. He missed. Corporal N. F.
Ellis sent Pvt. Claude A. Williams out after him. Williams crawled
along a ditch until he was close enough to arch a grenade over the
hedge. Then he waited a few minutes, but he drew no return fire.
Staff Sgt. A. L. Zeroske had crawled along behind Williams. Both
men saw the German move behind the hedge, both fired, and when
he went down with a scream, both felt that they had hit him. That
was the first casualty on either side. Only one man was knocked out
by the 88 fire on Bridge 2; the blast toppled him over, but his head
was clear again in a few minutes. Realizing what concentrated artillery
fire would do if it struck the battalion while they were still on the
causeway Colonel Cole moved up and down swearing and pleading
with his men not to bunch. But they kept herding together, and as
rapidly as he broke them up, they came back together. However the
enemy seemed to be paying no attention to the advance; the men of
the battalion began to believe that the operation could be carried off
almost without cost. In the first three hours all of the battalion except
the last half of Company H crossed the narrow planking to the far
side of Bridge 2.

Lieutenant Gehauf and the Intelligence Section and five men of
Company G's 1st Platoon were on the far side of Bridge 4, the other
men of the platoon were between Bridges 3 and 4 and the remainder
of the battalion was strung out all the distance back along the causeway
to the solid ground at Pont-du-Douve when the enemy opened fire.
It was small-arms and automatic fire. Most of it seemed to be coming
from the high ground forward and on the right, ahead of Bridge 4.
On this bearing and only about three hundred yards in front of the
head of the column a grassy bank rose sharply out of the marsh. In

the center of this high ground was a capacious farmhouse whose landscape, screened all around by hedgerows, gave the enemy ideal cover.
The first burst of fire broke all around the leading platoon and the
bullets zinged ·off the pavement. The men who were in the point
went flat in the embankment ditches and in a few minutes resumed
the crawl forward on hands and knees.

There was a thirty-yard gap in the reeds and in the sparse embankment foliage just forward of Bridge 2. This gap became the target of
snipers hidden in the marshes. Other snipers had deployed to the left
of the column ahead of Bridge 4. The point crawled on along the
slippery embankment until further advance seemed impossible. Cpl.
Martin Washko could see a machine gun spitting at him from a
hundred yards away. Pvt. Tony Diaz De Leon, who was the fourth man
of the point, looked back and saw there was no one coming up behind
him. He yelled to the men ahead of him, "Let's hold it." Pvt. Carl
Deyak and Pvt. James E. White, the two scouts, were on ahead about
fifteen yards along the right embankment. White sat up in the ditch.
Deyak continued to lie in it. A burst—probably from a mortar—came
in close to them. White hugged the bank. Then a second burst got
Deyak in the face and a bullet creased White through the hair. De
Leon, five yards back of Washko, took a bullet through the arm. He
yelled to Washko, "Hurry! I'm hit. I'm going to bleed to death."
Washko crawled back and put a tourniquet on the arm. He saw then
that he and the three others had crawled just a little too far. The
enemy machine gun at the hedgerow could search the ditch and get
all of them, whereas a little behind De Leon there was a bulge in the
embankment which provided them with defilade. So he told the others
to turn about, and they crawled rearward for a few yards. The enemy
must have seen this movement, for a German came worming along
the ditch behind them, occasionally firing with a machine pistol. So
far as Washko knew, this German turned back before hitting anyone,
though two more men of the point were hit by machine-gun bullets
during the withdrawal. The point had seen enough to make its reconnaissance worthwhile.

The gate at Bridge 4 which had caused Lieutenant Gehauf's detail
to defile the night before was still jammed and unmovable. Only one
man could rush it at a time. Sgt. Delwin J. McKinney, the noncom
in charge of the point, had been going through this gate when the
enemy opened fire. He had saved himself by jumping into an old
enemy foxhole which was on the embankment, right next to the gate.
He had an idea that the German guns were zeroed in on the roadblock.

Also, Lieutenant Gehauf had taken another good look at the enemy fire as well as at our own. He came back to Sergeant McKinney with the message that the American shells were dropping far beyond the German fire positions along the hedgerows and that the artillery should lower its fire about two hundred yards. Sergeant McKinney yelled the message back to Lt. David Irvin of Company G, who was still on the nigh side of the bridge. Lieutenant Irvin put it on the radio. But it was 2200 before this message finally reached the artillery. By that time the 3d Battalion had been held in check for somewhat more than four hours. The head of its column had felt out the enemy fire positions forward. The right side of the column had become badly seared by fire from the flank. The few men who had made the passage of Bridge 4 could not go forward. Every man who had run this gantlet had done so under a hail of bullets. Telephone and electric wires were down in a tangle over the gate and as a man would make his run diagonally through the breach those watching from the rear could see a fireworks of sparks fly as the bullets hit the gate and bridge iron and the electric wires. The shattered Bridge 2 restricted any withdrawal. On both sides the battalion was held by the marshes. In this manner the battalion became largely immobilized through the remainder of the daylight hours, except as it trickled forward painfully a man or a squad at a time, extending the advance toward Bridge 4.

The limited protective measures which were taken during the daylight hours proved largely unavailing and the infantry companies suffered quite heavily. The bullet fire from the farmhouse area continued to build up steadily and to strike deeper into the column. In Company G, the 2d and 3d Platoons had followed the 1st Platoon across the first three bridges. When it reached Bridge 3 the 2d Platoon deployed leftward. A thick dyke about eight feet high confined the canal to the left of the third bridge. Riflemen and machine gunners dug in along this dyke so as to build up a fire position facing forward. A little behind this line one machine gun was set up on the right side of the road to fire into the enemy positions around the farmhouse. The weapons on the canal line opened fire. Company G then began its move through the narrow opening in the roadblock at Bridge 4. Six men got through. The seventh man, Sgt. Joe L. Clements, was hit by a bullet while trying to squeeze through the gate. Captain Clements, the company CO, ordered the rest of the company to hold up. The men got ropes and levers and tried to force the gate, but it would not budge. So the body of Company G stayed behind Bridge 4 and more of the men deployed out to the left where a steady fire from the enemy automatic weapons peppered the muddy ridge along which the 2d Platoon had dug in. It did not seem to the men that this fire was well aimed but there was enough of it that they crawled around on their bellies in extending the line along the dyke. They kept their guns working and within less than two hours they had run out of machine-gun ammunition and had to send back for more. The riflemen also maintained a fire. They could see little or nothing of the enemy but the tracers from the guns around the farmhouse gave them a line to the fire positions. The two 60mm mortars were put up along the dyke and trained on the hedges in front of the farmhouse. Pvt. Allen Emery of Headquarters Company, lugging an 81mm mortar, pushed up to within thirty yards of Bridge 4 and put eighteen rounds on the enemy ground within the hedgerows around the farmhouse. He opened fire at 400 yards' range, moved up to 350 yards and then back to 400 again. He was almost out of ammunition when a German mortar shell burst within seven yards of him. The blast was muffled in a small defilade just down the embankment. So he moved back a hundred yards, set up again, and fired another half dozen rounds into the hedgerows.

At about 1800, Colonel Cole left the situation at Bridge 2 in charge of his executive, Maj. John Stopka, and worked his way forward through the column to the head of Company G. As he moved along he found the men of Company I hugging the low spots along the grassy embankment on the right side of the road and trying to keep their heads below the level of the reeds. They were doing nothing. He told them, "Goddam it, start firing and keep firing." He felt that any action would give them confidence and build their morale and that inaction might prove fatal. The men were well dug in, yet the enemy bullet fire took steady toll of them, mainly because of ricochets. Some of these bullets bounced off the pavement and into the fire line along the dyke but more of them caromed off the metal gate and into the foxholes. Colonel Cole stayed up with the forward company for about four hours watching this phenomenon. He did not see how he would be able to get his men across Bridge 4 if the enemy continued his fire. So he proposed to Captain Clements that he make ready to swim his Company G across the last canal and that he reconnoiter off to the left to find a suitable place for the crossing. Colonel Cole figured that if he could get one company across the canal he could throw some ropes to them and pass the rest of the battalion over the water, hand over hand.

Company I held the most exposed ground in the column—on the

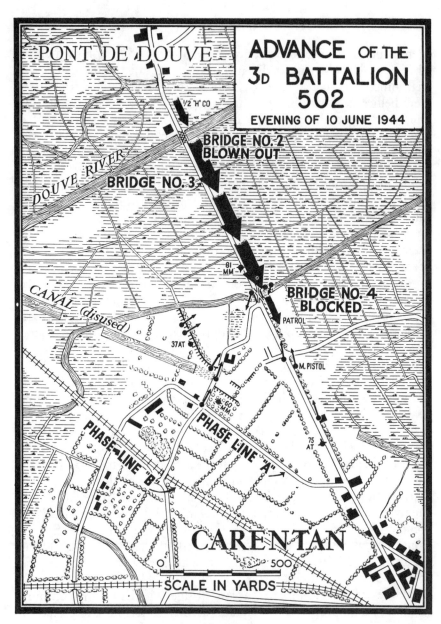

Map 25.

right side embankment to the south of Bridge 3. There was not enough dirt in this embankment for troops to dig in; it was without any cover except the slight screening afforded by the reeds. They got a steady fire from somewhere way out in the marsh. The barren spot had become an alley of death and anyone who approached it became the choice target for the fire of the enemy. After fifteen of their number got hit, the men of Company I grew weary of running this gantlet and weary of the day. An aid man, Pfc. Stanley W. Tkaczyk ("an excellent aid man and a credit to his organization"), was hit in the head and died almost instantly. Lieutenant George A. Larish, leader of the 1st Platoon, was shot through the heart. Lt. John P. Painschab was mortally wounded. Cpl. Earl Butz was killed. The curious part was that the rest of the column had a kind of insulation from the shock of these losses. The battalion was so spread out that it felt almost nothing as a whole. Juniors knew that their superiors had become casualties only when someone passed the word along the line for them to take over. The men on the right embankment had a general idea that the men on the left embankment were faring a little better than themselves and they would have crossed over to the other side had that passage not become suicide. Bullets were scratching the asphalt of the road in two directions. The men moved forward, crawling. Those who were hit got it while lying down. Those who remained untouched could see very little of what was going on except the heels of the men in front of them.

Cpl. Lloyd King, Pvt. Wesley Jackson and Pvt. Thomas A. Pinon, from Headquarters Company worked their way up to Bridge 3, carrying a machine gun. They then crawled under the bridge and made their way to the far bank by passing along the struts. Pinon's ammunition carrier was hit during this passage and dropped into the water. Pinon got the gun set up in a foxhole right beside the bridge and began firing rightward at an angle of ninety degrees from the road. The time was about 1800. There was no more sniper fire from that direction during the evening. Bridge 3 began to cool off, although Pinon's action was the only thing done to counter the bullet fire at this point. The men of Company I had been under steady fire for about two hours.

Capt. Cecil L. Simmons got Company H up to Bridge 2 about 1630. Half of the lead platoon crossed Bridge 3 before the general movement of the column was halted by the coming of dark. Five rounds of enemy mortar fire struck around the bridge coincident with their arrival and two men of the company were hit. Also wounded by the mortar fire was Lt. Robert L. McLauchlin of Headquarters Company. A patrol was sent out through the reeds to the right of the causeway. It waded for about sixty yards but saw no enemy and drew no fire. Several of Company H's men were nicked by stray rifle bullets while trying to hug the ditch on the right embankment. But on the whole Company H stood the evening better than the others. Colonel Cole figured that if he had to swim any men across the Madeleine that night he would move Company H up through Company G and let Captain Simmons' men take the beating for a while.

With the coming of dusk the situation quieted a little because the enemy could not see the live targets wriggling along the causeway banks. Company G was still drawing heavy bullet fire up front and was taking losses as some of the men tried to crawl across the road to get the better protection on the left side. The time was about 2330. Pvt. Hans K. Brandt had moved up to Bridge 4. He noted that the men were badly bunched at that point, seven or eight of them crowding into a ten-yard space. From somewhere off in the reeds to the right— he thought it about seventy-five yards—a German machine gun suddenly opened fire and the bullets began to bounce off the bridge. Brandt figured that with the men bunched as they were, the fire would get some of them. He took a grenade and started out through the reeds. At about this moment the men farther back along the causeway, being not so closely engaged, saw and heard a plane coming toward them from the direction of Carentan. The men saw that the plane's wheels were down and they recognized it as a dive bomber. It came steadily along, flying the line of the road and about 150 yards up. No one yelled. Those who had seen the plane still scarcely realized what it signified. Above Company I the plane unloaded six or eight small personnel bombs which hit along the flank of the road, dead on the ground where Company I's men had been trying to hide from the snipers. Private Brandt had moved only a few yards when he heard a heavy explosion close to him. He looked up and saw the dive bomber. In the same instant that he went flat next to a stunted tree, there was another explosion and he felt a jar against his left leg. Brandt went out cold for a few seconds, then got up and went on to his objective. He waded as far as he could and then heaved his grenade in the general direction of where he thought the enemy gun lay. He didn't know whether he hit anything but the company got no more fire from there. Coming back, he found a man who had been knocked out by the concussion of the bombing and had slipped down into the water. Brandt carried him to the embankment. He noted that the men who had been only lightly wounded by the bombing had now properly spaced themselves. Those who couldn't move were still bunched together. He got some of them spaced out, then started back for first aid. There were so many wounded along the embankment that he was blocked that way. He then walked right down the middle of the road. There was no fire. After dropping its bombs—or so the men along the causeway thought—the enemy plane went right on down the position, blistering the column with machine-gun bullets. Between bombs and bullets, Company I lost another thirty men in those few seconds, the strafing taking the greater part of them. About eight of the thirty were either dead or badly hit. Curiously, the men who were strung out along the causeway thought without exception that only one plane attacked them. Others, who had watched the attack from behind Bridge 1, saw clearly that two German planes had crossed above the column at right angles to one another in a split second. The plane which had dropped the bombs had flown across the marshes while the plane which attacked with its machine guns had come right along the road from Carentan. They had seen the tracers "bouncing like ping-pong balls off the pavement."

The air attack practically eliminated Company I from the reckoning for the time being. Having gone flat when the bombs fell, the men of the company did not rise again save for the few whose first thought was to evacuate the badly wounded. One of these men, Pvt. Glenn A. Moe, had started digging a foxhole on the left embankment and was about three feet down when the bombs hit. Two shell fragments struck him in the left hand and shoulder. Two men who were lying within ten feet of him were also hit. He completed digging the foxhole. Then he walked on back to Pont-du-Douve, carrying one of the wounded. After getting his wounds dressed, he returned and brought the other man back with the aid of a stretcher bearer, this work taking him until 0400. The others fell victim to the deadly drowsiness to which infantrymen are especially susceptible after they have experienced heavy shock losses. According to their officers later, they had almost no interest in what had happened to them and no curiosity about who had been hit. Lt. Robert G. Burns found that he could not keep his men awake no matter how he tried. Some were asleep within two or three minutes of the bombing. This confused Burns because he could not tell which were the sleepers and which were the wounded men. He saw men who had tumbled down the embankment and lay still with their bodies half in the marsh. He went to them, figuring they had been hit, and then discovered that they were sleepers who had rolled down the bank and had not been awakened when they slipped into the water. Others lay there in their ODs and jump suits, wet through and through, yet sleeping the torpid sleep of utter spiritual exhaustion. The officers had to yield any attempt to rouse these men and for the next four hours Company I remained a cipher in the column.

But there were signs that the enemy also must have passed the limit of endurance. For the battalion lay there open to him and his guns knew how and where to fire. The night was fair and the air chilled. Visibility was exceptionally good. Carentan, a ten-minute dog trot down the road, stood in sight. Yet the hours of complete darkness passed and the moon rose, fully illuminating the scene, without changing the situation. Over the marsh lay a great quiet. D plus 4 ended; D plus 5 (June 11) began.

Night on the Causeway

At 0330 Colonel Cole went forward again. He found that Captain Simmons was getting his men across Bridge 4 but that Company G's men were where he had left them five and a half hours before. Only now Lieutenant Cortez was up ahead with a five-man outpost on the right embankment, and three men under a corporal were ten yards beyond the bridge on the left-hand side. When Captain Simmons had come up, Captain Clements had said, "I am not sending any more men up. There's no cover." Captain Simmons had replied, "Hell, there must be some if there're men up there." Captain Simmons had then gone forward and made a reconnaissance past the bridge, finding the ground as barren as Clements said. He crawled on along the left side of the road until he heard Germans talking within a few yards of the spot where he lay in the roadside ditch. Then he crawled on back to his radio and asked for artillery fire along the hedge where he had listened to the Germans; he was told by fire-control center that the guns couldn't fire at night.

At 0200, Colonel Cole had confirmed the arrangement of the companies as they then stood with Company H taking over the lead from Company G and moving along the left embankment. He figured that Company G was the more beat-up of the two, and that he would have to wait another hour or two before he could tell whether Company I was ready to fight again. Captain Simmons, taking over the lead position, could hear wagons creaking along the enemy front and calculated that the Germans were getting either more machine guns or mines into position. Captain Clements dropped his company back to support; a few hours later he was wounded and taken from the battle.

MORNING

By 0400 Company H had taken over the lead position from Company G. Captain Simmons was putting his men through the gap at Bridge 4 at a rate of one man per minute. Though the enemy was not firing Captain Simmons thought it best to space his men that way so that if fire were opened suddenly not more than one or two men would be caught. But Colonel Cole, who had gone to regiment and had received orders to continue the attack, on his way back to the battalion had walked right down the middle of the causeway without one shot being fired at him. This made him optimistic. He told Captain Simmons to send his men on through the gate as rapidly as possible and not to hesitate about bunching two or three of them there. Company H completed the passage without loss. Company G followed. Company I for the time being pulled back of Bridge 2. Colonel Cole had looked over the company and decided it would be folly to order it forward immediately. There were only twenty-one men and two officers left of the eighty who had started the action. But Cole now had two companies on the Carentan side of the bridges.

Company H moved on along both sides of the road toward the hedgerows and the farm house, 84 men in the company. Company G with 60 men and Headquarters Company with 121 men moved on to the solid ground to the left of the road, thus entering a very small meadow bounded by hedgerows. Captain Simmons' men were going forward in column. They had been told to advance along azimuth 195 which would take them on a cross-country route over high ground to Hill 30, near La Billonnerie, where the battalion was to stop the German retreat from Carentan.

The lead scout, Pvt. Albert W. Dieter, went forward in the thin light until he was within about five yards of the hedgerow which ran at right angles to the main road and behind the farm buildings. The platoons were strung out behind him in squad column for about two hundred yards. As he took his last few steps to close on the hedgerow, German rifle, machine-gun and mortar fire opened up on the company all along the line. Dieter, in the lead, got the full effect of it and his left arm was shredded from wrist to shoulder by the opening volley. Without ducking or quickening his pace he walked right back along the line of fire to where Captain Simmons had taken cover in a ditch. There he stopped. He said to his commander, "Captain, I'm hit bad, ain't I?" "You sure are." Dieter said, "Well, I didn't ———— up

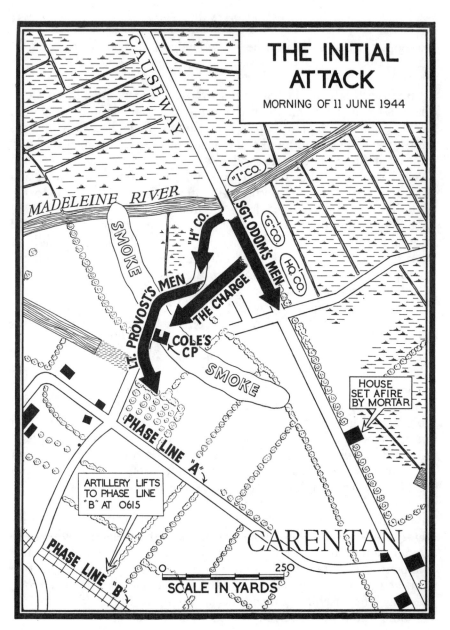

Map 26.

on you, did I, Captain?" Captain Simmons replied, "No, you sure didn't." Dieter then went on back.

Up forward, a couple of men had been knocked down by machine-gun bullets. Five or six others from the leading platoons had been wounded and had crawled over to dress their wounds. Simmons needed some kind of a table on which to work while putting rough splints on one man's arm. There was a dead German in the ditch lying cold and stiff and ready for his purpose. He took the corpse's pack off, rested it on the stomach, and went to work with the first-aid pack.

Colonel Cole, in the Company H area, was crawling along a ditch. Forty or fifty yards behind him was Captain Rosemond, the artillery liaison officer. The colonel asked him to shell the farmhouse and the hedges. Captain Rosemond told him he couldn't get the fire because the artillery commander wasn't present with the guns to approve the request. Cole said: "Goddam it! We need artillery fire and we can't wait for a general." He got the fire in fifteen minutes.

The time was then about 0530 and for the next twenty-five minutes the artillery pounded the hedgerows around the house; it looked as if the stuff was going in where it was needed. Still, there was no slackening of the enemy bullet fire. On Colonel Cole's order, the artillery fire was changed from air-burst to delay, and then changed back again. It made no difference. Bullets still whipped through the thorn above the ditches and tore into the embankments in as great volume as before. Colonel Cole was puzzled. He felt no assurance about what to do next. For a fleeting moment, he considered moving his men back the way they had come. He wondered whether he should try to get them forward by infiltration along the main road, and against this, he weighed the possibility of making a heads-up assault against the house. Then he made his decision.

THE CHARGE

Major Stopka was right across the road. The colonel yelled to him: "We're going to order smoke from the artillery and then make a bayonet charge on the house." Major Stopka replied: "OK." Colonel Cole told Captain Rosemond what he wanted. Within a few minutes, the smoke was being laid in an arc which had the house in its center and extended past the Madeleine River on one end and over the main road to Carentan on the left. Colonel Cole waited while the smoke was being put down. About fifteen or twenty minutes passed. Colonel Cole adjusted the smoke farther leftward to meet the wind. He was especially concerned that the screen should be just right.

Across this field Lt. Col. Robert G. Cole led his 3d Battalion of the 502d taken from Bridge 4. The road to the left leads to Carentan. The

Company G, deployed and pinned in the small meadow to the left of the main road, was being sprayed by fire from a machine gun and a machine pistol in a covert along the hedgerow on the southern border of the field. The men in the meadow tried to crawl over to the hedgerow next to the main road as this fire fell among them. Others of the company who had not got up to the meadow were sent scurrying from the road by fire which swept right down the causeway. They dug in beside the road and remained in their foxholes while the action thickened around the farmhouse.

First Sgt. Hubert Odom of Company G, taking three men and a machine gun, worked along the hedgerow which bounded the road to the hedgerow covering the enemy fire trench. The men moved crouched over, walking in the ditch and sticking close to the embankment. At the same time, Private Emery, the mortar man, went to work on a house about eight hundred yards down the road from where machine-gun fire seemed to be spilling into Company G's position. He bracketed the house and hit it with his third round, setting it afire.

in the first bayonet charge of the Normandy invasion. The picture was house which was the objective of the charge is at the extreme right.

Then he put two more shells on the target for good luck. He picked out a second enemy position, and working the mortar by himself, continued to fire. Sergeant Odom was still toiling forward with the machine gun. At forty yards' range, he saw a German stand up behind the hedge and fire a burst from a machine pistol. Sergeant Odom was fifteen yards ahead of his own gun. The German's first burst hit all three men who were behind him carrying the gun. One of them, Pvt. William P. Evans, got the gun in action and kept on firing. Odom crawled forward through the water of the ditch which ran along the hedge. He was low enough that the enemy fire could not find him. He yelled to Sgt. Anthony L. Zeroski to toss him some grenades. Zeroski did so. Sergeant Odom, one of the best baseball players in the Division, threw three grenades over the hedge and heard a scream. Then a German rose out of a trench and disappeared so quickly that Odom had no chance to fire. Zeroski crawled up and covered Odom while he crawled on through the hedgerow. The gun was knocked out but the four Germans who were with it had gone back through

Lieutenant Colonel Robert G. Cole, who won the Medal of Honor for his part in the Causeway fight. He was killed in Holland.

a trench toward Carentan. Odom knew there had been four. They had been eating breakfast. The sausages on their plates were still warm.

Colonel Cole had passed the word to Major Stopka—and the word was supposed to have passed on down to the company commanders and from them to the men—that they were to fix bayonets and reload rifles with a full clip. Three companies—G, H and Headquarters—were supposed to have received the order. At 0615, Colonel Cole gave the command. The artillery lifted its fire to the railroad track beyond the house. As soon as Colonel Cole heard the shells come over, he blew his whistle and took off across the ditch. Only about twenty men followed him. There were about fifty more men with Major Stopka over on the left and the major was yelling: "Let's go! Over the hedge!" But it was a little company which bounded forward. Company H and Headquarters Company were hardly represented.

Colonel Cole looked back over his line and what he saw almost stunned him; he thought, "My men have let me down."

What had happened? Some small part of this slack was due to men who had gone to ground at the first heavy volley from the enemy and had remained mentally pinned. But there were other contributing factors. In the din of the battle and the natural excitement of the moment it was not easy to get the word around to a command which was widely distributed and, for the most part, hugging the earth. Some men, some officers, never got the order. They heard something passed on to them about "whistle" and "bayonet" but in the confusion they could not tell what was said. Others heard nothing. Still others got the order, but didn't know the advance was on until they saw the trickle of men crossing the field. Then a few raced on trying to catch up.

Colonel Cole trotted halfway across the field. Then he stopped, knelt on one knee and looked back. Fire was clipping the grass all around him and more of it was passing overhead. He saw that his men were trailing behind him in single file. So he waved both arms at them trying to get them to fan out. Instead, they hit the dirt. He started working on them one man at a time, urging them to go on. He kept firing his Colt .45 wildly in the general direction of the farmhouse and as he fired he yelled: "Goddam, I don't know what I'm shooting at, but I gotta keep on." Some of the men who heard him, in spite of the danger all about, couldn't help laughing.

About five or six men were killed by bullet fire as they lay there. Colonel Cole's radio operator, T/5 Robert E. Doran, got up to his commander, his SCR-300 on his back; then they ran on together. The smoke was gradually clearing from the barrage fire and through the rifts in it, they could see the farmhouse. Major Stopka kept yelling: "Let's go! Let's go!" and ran on, hurdling the first ditch. Colonel Cole leaped a low hedge and came down in a ditch almost up to his neck in water. He yelled back to Doran, "Don't follow me!" and Doran took both hedge and ditch in one leap. Others caught up with the leaders and passed them. Major Stopka saw two men go down in front of him. He yelled to Pvt. Edwin S. Pastouris, one of them: "How are you?" Said Pastouris: "I'm OK. You keep going!" Fifteen men from Company H and Headquarters Company, who had come belatedly to the action, ran on up the road to the hedgerow which formed the rear boundary of the house, then turned and ran down the hedge on the outside till they came to the building. They kept on going into the orchard. That was the way the colonel wanted it. He was standing by the house, waving the men on; all of them wanted to stop as they came to the building. He told Company G to assemble on the brush pile behind the house along with Company I which was now coming up from behind Bridge 4. Company H and Headquarters Company were to collect next to the right of the house before continuing. The enemy machine-gun groups which had been well fortified on the high ground to the right of the house had now pulled back for the most part. There were dead Germans lying thick over the ground and in the foxholes, but most of the live ones had retired through the orchard toward the railroad.

For his charge across the field Colonel Cole was awarded the Medal of Honor, the first man in the Division so honored. He did not live to know about it, being killed in Holland by a sniper's bullet. Major Stopka, for his part in the charge, was awarded the DSC, receiving it a few days before he was killed at Bastogne.

THE ODYSSEY OF PRIVATE STERNO

The experiences of Pvt. Bernard Sterno of Company H were typical of those of many of the men who followed Colonel Cole on this bayonet charge, the first made by American troops in the invasion. Although his M1 was jammed, Sterno started with Colonel Cole across the open ground toward the farmhouse two football-field lengths away. Halfway across he saw a dead German sprawled in a slit trench behind a clump of bushes. Set up in the bushes in front of the German was a pistol with a cord leading back to the body. Sterno wanted the pistol, but figuring that the cord might be set to a mine he took his knife out and slashed the cord. He felt something "bump into a finger" on his right hand. But his gloves were on and he didn't realize at once that he had been hit by a bullet and had lost a finger. He got the pistol and crawled on. A few feet farther along Sterno saw another man from Company H. He went to the man but saw that he had been shot through the chest and was near death. An aid man came along and told Sterno that his hand was all bloody. He bandaged the stump of the finger and Sterno kept going. Then he heard someone call, "Help me!" It was a sergeant from his own company. Sterno crawled up to him. The sergeant was hit in the stomach and leg. Next to him was the medical man who had just bandaged Sterno. But he was dead now with a bullet through his head. Sterno got the medical man's kit and canteen and gave the sergeant rude first aid. By that time enemy fire was breaking around the CP in heavy volume and Colonel Cole was telling the men to move away from the vicinity. Sterno went on about twenty-five yards beyond the house, found a place in the fire

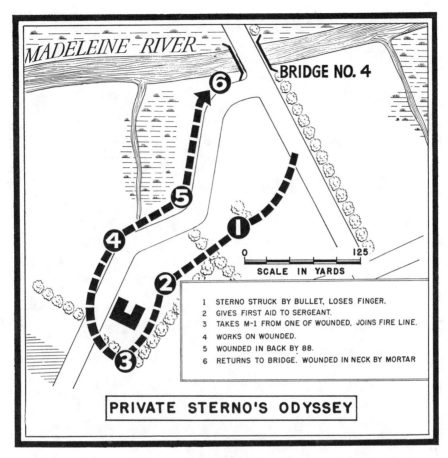

MADELEINE RIVER

BRIDGE NO. 4

6

5

4

2

1

3

0   125

SCALE IN YARDS

1   STERNO STRUCK BY BULLET, LOSES FINGER.
2   GIVES FIRST AID TO SERGEANT.
3   TAKES M-1 FROM ONE OF WOUNDED, JOINS FIRE LINE.
4   WORKS ON WOUNDED.
5   WOUNDED IN BACK BY 88.
6   RETURNS TO BRIDGE. WOUNDED IN NECK BY MORTAR

PRIVATE STERNO'S ODYSSEY

Map 27.

line, flopped down in a water-filled ditch and began to fire, using an M1 he had taken from one of the wounded. His bandage worked loose. Another first aid man came along, looked at the wound and told Sterno to get to the rear. There were a number of wounded lying in the ditch along the road and Sterno figured he'd better help them. They begged him to stay there and flag the ambulance that came along. The ditch and the road were now being raked by 88mm fire from the direction of Carentan. One man lying next to Sterno had had an eye torn out by shrapnel. He didn't know whether the eye was gone and he asked Sterno about it. Sterno didn't want to tell him the truth so he replied: "Well, even if it is, you should be glad you have the other one." He prepared a sulfa pad and put it on the man's eye. Then he started to work on some of the other wounded. There was the sudden swish of another 88 shell. Sterno jumped for the slit trench but didn't

ST. COME du MONT

NO.1 NO.2 NO.3

FARMHOUSE

BRIDGE NO.4

DOUVE RIVER

MADELEINE RIVER

ORCHARD

The Carentan causeway and scene of the bayonet charge, looking toward St. Come-du-Mont. The fields on each side of the causeway had been drained.

quite make it. He felt "something terribly heavy" land against his back
—jarring him as if he had been kicked hard. He wasn't sure whether
he was wounded again or had only felt concussion. In fact, a shell
fragment had ripped into his back and stopped in the groin although
this was not known until he was thoroughly examined on the LST
the next day. The man who had lost an eye was now yelling, "My
arm, Oh, my arm, Oh, my arm." Sterno was groggy for a few seconds.
When he looked at the man he saw that his arm had been smashed by
the latest explosion. Another man next to him, who had been alive
a few minutes before, had lost half of his head. It felt to Sterno as
if there was blood running from his own back but he wasn't certain;
he thought still it might be shock and imagination. He looked at the
others in the group of wounded. One man who was just five feet from
him had blood streaming from his ears, nose and mouth; he was
conscious but was so shocked that he couldn't utter words and was expressing himself in a little babble. Sterno figured that most of these men
were beyond his power to help. He crawled on rearward to Bridge 4.
There was a foxhole and he dropped into it. About one-half minute
later a mortar shell hit just outside the hole and a piece of it got
Sterno in the neck and another piece hit an officer lying beside him.

Aftermath of the Charge

First Sgt. Kenneth M. Sprecker and Private Roach of Company H
reached the farmhouse twenty yards in front of Colonel Cole. They
shot the lock off the door and dashed inside. The place was empty.
Sergeant Sprecker moved on to the brush pile and saw two Germans
in the orchard, rifles in hand, getting ready to fire. Sprecker fired
first with his tommy gun. Both Germans fell.

Lt. Edward A. Provost of Company H had nine men with him as
the charge started. Five got hit or lost crossing the field and he carried
on with the four who remained. They worked up the road skirting
the right of the house. A hedgerow paralleled the road; just opposite
the house was a solidly constructed machine-gun position which had
been dug deep into the embankment overlooking the Madeleine. The
men crept in behind the cover of the farmhouse wall. Lieutenant
Provost was not giving them any orders; they moved in silence. The
mail orderly, T/5 James O. Brune, threw a grenade over the hedge.
There were five Germans at the gun and in the V-shaped fire trench
which adjoined it. The grenade hit and exploded fair among them.
Some were stunned; others stood there screaming. Lieutenant Provost
and Brune saw them, so they bounded up the eight crude steps from

the road to the gun position without giving the gun crew a moment to recover. Brune started to fire as he ran. Lieutenant Provost yelled: "Don't waste bullets! Use the bayonet!" This they did. Then they retraced their steps and went on up the road, picking up men from Companies I, H and Headquarters Company as they went along—ten men altogether. As they drew abreast of the orchard, they looked left and saw about two squads of Germans milling around beyond the first few rows of trees, as if getting ready to pull out. The men with Lieutenant Provost propped themselves up behind a hedge and fired. A few of the enemy fell at the first volley. The others went to ground immediately and formed a line, then began shooting. Lieutenant Provost was wounded and returned to the farmhouse for first aid; Sergeant Sprecker came up and took charge. Soon after he got there the orchard was cleared of Germans.

When the German fire had broken over the head of the column during the advance of Company H along the Carentan road Company I had been in movement from behind Bridge 2 to a point behind Bridge 4. The survivors of Company I heard the sounds of battle up ahead, in and around the farmhouse. The German fire, however, had again engulfed Bridge 4 and bullets were rattling off the iron gate as they had the afternoon before. The men of Company I had to run for the narrow opening through this bullet fire; they did it one man at a time, each man with head down. Those who made it then jumped down to the protection of the embankment. The last two officers, Lieutenants Burns and Gleason, were hit trying to get through the gate. About one-third of the other survivors were lost at this point. The rest went on leaderless. They attached themselves as individuals to any group they could find and joined the skirmishing around the orchard and through the hedgerows. For the time being, Company I ceased to exist as a unit. The entire 3d Battalion was by now completely scrambled and the junior leaders fought on with little scratch groups.

The fire had not lifted from fields which were immediately south of Bridge 4. Most of the men who had been under cover there when Colonel Cole and his group charged the house were still pinned. Many of the enemy were positioned behind the hedgerows which ran at right angles to the Carentan road. It was from this direction that much of the automatic fire had poured into the fields and had kept the men from Company H and Headquarters Company confined to the ditches. The charge had moved off obliquely to the right from the direction of this fire, though the original movement, extended into the orchard, would have outflanked it. The enemy's point of greatest strength, insofar as command of the causeway was concerned, had been on a ridge of high ground between the house and the Madeleine, a tributary of the Douve which Bridge 4 crossed. The charge had routed the force there and Lieutenant Provost's dash with the bayonet had stifled the last flicker of resistance at this position. However, the Germans in the hedgerows along the opposite flank had not been dislodged by the charge. When the smoke began to clear away they could again volley into the fields south of Bridge 4. This was their natural line of fire.

Captain Simmons, pinned between the farmhouse and the Madeleine, hadn't heard Colonel Cole's order. Trying to attend to his wounded, the captain had heard someone yell something about a "whistle" and "bayonet" but the words didn't register as an order. He shouted to S/Sgt. John T. White who was working a light machine gun nearby, "Well, what about a ———— whistle?" but he got no reply and so continued with his work. The charge across the field got away without his seeing it.

A few minutes later a shell exploded near Captain Simmons and knocked him cold. He came to with Sergeant White shaking him by the shoulders. "What happened?" he asked. Sergeant White told him that the battalion had been ordered to charge across the field and that some of the men were already at the farmhouse. Simmons said, "Then let's get the hell out of here." His head still was not clear. He motioned to the men around him to follow. A group got up; they advanced straight up the ditch and toward the corner of the hedgerow which ran back of the house. A German machine gun was still firing from that point into the field where Captain Simmons' men had been. This last anchor of the German forward line gave way as Simmons and his men ran on toward the hedgerow. A few of the men with Simmons fell under bullet fire in crossing the ditch. The Americans ran on firing their rifles toward the gun. A few Germans were killed; a grenade knocked the gun out.

Captain Simmons had started the day with 84 men; when it was over he had 30.

The fighting slackened for a few minutes. The right flank had been cleared. The left flank was clear to the first hedgerow. Colonel Cole, making a random estimate of his own strength, sent Pvt. Doyle Bootle of Headquarters Company back to Colonel Cassidy of 1st Battalion to tell him to bring his men on through. Cole figured that 3d Battalion was washed up at least for the time being. In point of fact his situation was even worse than he knew; the meager parties which had closed up to the hedgerows were not even sufficient to compose a thin fire line.

The mission of 3d Battalion remained unchanged; it was to go on to Hill 30. But Colonel Cole figured that a fresh battalion would come through in sufficient momentum to complete the assignment that day and he so advised the regimental commander. He also asked for ammunition and men and an ambulance.

By this time the engineers had rigged a temporary span at Bridge 2 and had torn away the jammed gate at Bridge 4. It was possible for vehicles to come through to the farmhouse. Colonel Cole was in the court of the farmhouse where he had just finished splinting a man's leg with a pick handle. Next to the door was a young private. He had taken off his shoe and was putting sulfa powder on a minor wound in his heel. Colonel said to him, "Get out of here right now. This is a dangerous spot." The boy said, "I want to be safe, Colonel. I might get blood poisoning if I don't fix this." As he spoke the last word he was hit straight-on by a flat-trajectory missile, which smashed him up against the stone building and dropped him in a bloody heap on the flagstones.

A vehicle duly arrived, carrying ammunition. There were no Red Cross vehicles present and so an ordinary truck had been rushed to the scene. It brought ammunition up and took the wounded back, under fire in both directions. There were so many wounded that they were carried out double deck, some riding in the body of the truck and others in stretchers across the top. Two jeeps were also pressed into service. In the aid station at Pont-du-Douve Capt. Frank Choy, 1st Battalion surgeon, and Capts. Adolph Blatt and Charles Althoff, 3d Battalion surgeons, worked over the wounded. The truck ambulance on its third trip brought a group of aid men from First Army. Later the regimental aid station was set up across the street.

By this time 1st Battalion had joined in the battle. Also, Colonel Cole's staff had caught up with him; they had been scattered about with the various elements. Lieutenant Gehauf, dead tired from his exertions of the two preceding days and nights, had gone to sleep in a ditch in the early morning and Colonel Cole had decided to let him sleep. He came into the CP cursing the colonel for leaving him behind. Lt. Ralph A. Watson, S-1, had been at the fourth bridge and had then gone on up the road which wound past the farmhouse to help organize the men.

The staff collected in one room. Colonel Cole was in the room next to them working on the wounded. A shell (whether it was mortar or artillery no one was certain) landed on the doorstep outside. The steel sprayed in through the open doorway. All three of the staff were hit, along with an enlisted man. They were packed away in an ambulance. 1st Battalion Enters the Fight

Colonel Cassidy suspected that 3d Battalion had probably broken the back of the enemy resistance but had spent its own strength in so doing. The first part of this impression was gradually dissipated as 1st Battalion got in motion. Company B came under heavy fire immediately. It was automatic fire and the worst part of it seemed to be coming from well concealed positions in the marsh off to the right of the road. When the lead elements reached Bridge 4, the bullet fire became so thick that a man could scarcely raise his head. Lt. Robert Rogers of the lead group had two of his machine guns set up on the embankment at Bridge 4 and put a traversing fire over the marsh. Still the fire from the marsh did not diminish. Company B lost eight men that morning—three of them killed—just in finishing the move across the causeway.

Lieutenant Rogers led his men forward; he was still thinking that he would crash them through a thin line of enemy and then march on to Hill 30. They reached the open field across which Colonel Cole had charged and were able to deploy over toward the house without many additional losses. At that point Colonel Cole warned them that the house was becoming a target for artillery and mortar fire and that they had best get on quickly. They did so. Lieutenant Rogers found to his amazement that there were only small fractions of squads from 3d Battalion holding any part of the ground. So he disposed his men generally up along the hedgerows to the right of the house and on the far side of the road which ran alongside the house. He saw that 3d Battalion had no real defensive position, and that he would have to relinquish for the time being any idea of advancing beyond his initial line among the hedgerows. The advance of the company stampeded the small number of enemy who had continued to cling to the immediate foreground. They were pursued beyond the houses at the crossroads and small groups from the company kept on going for several hundred yards farther. Lt. Homer J. Combs led six men all the way to the railroad track. Meanwhile another group of men got a machine gun forward to the crossroads and then searched all of the houses. The men found the houses empty, except for a few French civilians.

The group which had gone on to the railroad track saw six Germans some distance away off to their left. They fired at them; but as they themselves were already being fired upon by riflemen their aim was not good; the enemy vanished. The group held a council of war. The men wanted to go on hunting for the six enemy. Lieutenant Combs figured he was getting too far away from the main body and led them on back. They stopped at the road and built up a fire line along it, distributing themselves just in front of the houses and employing the ditch and hedgerow cover abounding the road. This line, or rather a part of it, held until the battalion was relieved late that night. It had no moments of quiet; it was counterattacked numerous times. On one occasion it was almost completely shattered and during much of the day was subjected to a continuing pressure from twenty yards range. The Germans came back to the road line almost immediately after Lieutenant Combs' sortie, and took up position in the ditches on the other side of the road. There they were protected by a high brick wall. Thus locked with the enemy and virtually isolated from their own main body, the men at the forward line on the right maintained themselves by dueling with grenades, and in two instances turned the Germans back at the point of the bayonet. They had one machine gun which was set up initially to fire diagonally across the crossroads and into the field beyond. For a time this machine gun position was able to hold firm. The group, however, had no line of communication to the rear. One thing helped them; as they had come forward they had found a grim tableau at the crossroads. Set up there was a German machine gun with a dead gunner behind it. Sprawled across the gun and the gunner was a dead American paratrooper. He had been there many hours, but next to his hand were two boxes of American machine gun ammunition. The group took this gift along and before the morning was out they had need of it. At first, there were only a dozen men on the forward line. More came as the morning wore on, until at its strongest the position had about two-thirds of 1st Platoon and twenty-five men from the 3d.

The backstop of the right flank had been set up, however, at the No. 1 hedgerow on the side of the hedgerow which faced toward the orchard. There S/Sgt. Harrison Summers, who on D-day (to quote the ETO Historian, Col. S. L. A. Marshall) had given as distinguished an account of himself as any soldier in the American Army, had set up two machine guns—one at the corner and the other at the rear—where they could sweep up the road.

While these arrangements were going on disaster had already over-taken Company A. The two leading platoons came over the causeway and through Bridge 4 under a heavy shelling by artillery and mortar. They lost a few men along the way. Then they started across the clear field as Company B had done. One of the heaviest concentrations of shell that day—mainly mortar but with some 88mm mixed in it—fell right among the men as they reached the middle of the field. Fifteen men were hit; the shock scattered the others in all directions and they scrambled four ways in search for cover. The deep ditch was directly ahead of them. Some jumped head-first into the water. But others ran back to Bridge 4. It took an hour and a half to get them together again and up to the firing line, the mortar fire continuing meanwhile though in less volume. The 3d Platoon (these platoons had only fifteen to twenty-five men apiece) then came up, started across the field and got caught in the same meat grinder. This platoon lost nine men on the identical spot and the others scattered, looking for any kind of cover. But cover was not easy to find by that time; the more convenient ditches and foxholes were already filled by the wounded and stragglers who had been caught in the backwash of the battle. Company A had lost six men in crossing the causeway, most of them from bullet fire. That made it thirty all told before the company approached the fire line.

It was at about 1100 that this first heavy blow fell on Company A. The same barrage had engulfed the farmhouse where Colonel Cole was sweating out the regulation of his artillery and the finding of his own flanks. The American artillery was firing toward the railroad and Carentan. That the colonel knew. He knew also that some elements of 1st Battalion had gone on and were working at the hedgerows somewhere beyond. But he did not know how the battle was forming or whether the men forward in the orchard and along the hedgerows were closely engaged. By now most of the forward line—to call it that was an exaggeration—was manned by 1st Battalion.

Between Colonel Cole and Colonel Cassidy, both preoccupied with what they saw directly before them, there was little exchange of information. In the long run it probably made very little difference. For 1st Battalion's role in the Carentan fight was simply to build up on the ground where 3d Battalion had exhausted itself. Without actually relieving 3d Battalion, 1st Battalion took over, got its shoulder in the door, and there became wedged. Such of Colonel Cole's men who were still in the fight filled in along Colonel Cassidy's defensive line. After Company A had been ripped apart while trying to move up left of the farmhouse so as to push the enemy from high ground lying west of Carentan, five men who had jumped forward to seek cover in the ditch picked themselves up and tried to keep their assignment. They got as far as the left end of Hedgerow 4 where they reinforced the leftmost element of 3d Battalion—four riflemen and a light machine gun. At this position two successive gunners had been hit by bullets bouncing off the gun and hitting them in the face. They tried to resume fire and did so twice. But the gun finally went out of action because they grew too weak and there was no one to take over. When Colonel Cassidy's men reached the hedge all four of Colonel Cole's men were lying in the ditch, bleeding badly and unable to defend themselves. The newcomers took up fire positions behind the hedge. But the German automatic fire from the right swelled to such proportions that they could not raise their heads to take one shot. They pulled back before noon, taking the wounded. But they had reached the most advanced ground to be held during the day. In that time they had not seen a single enemy. Indeed, this was characteristic of the whole day's fighting. Keeping well covered, the Germans advanced along the perpendicular hedgerows and ditches, then moved to the flank on the inside of the hedgerows which ran at right angles to the road. They understood this manner of advance very well and rarely exposed more than a shoulder or the tip of a helmet. The men of the 502d knew that a new line of fire had been built up opposite them only from the rising rattle of the guns. Many of them fought all day and saw no one. (Later two-thirds of 3d Battalion who were under fire around the farmhouse said they saw Germans only after the Germans had become corpses.) They fought on, pouring their small-arms and machine-gun fire at the hedgerows, hoping that volume of fire alone would keep the enemy back. In this work the rifle was their most useful weapon. (In after-battle questioning only thirteen men could remember having made some use of the grenade; only six were certain that they had killed any of the enemy with it. More by accident than by design about ten of them closed with one or two of the enemy in the scurrying around the hedgerows and used their bayonets.)

Too, the scrambling which had resulted from the manner in which the two battalions were committed was made worse by the geometric pattern of the countryside. Some of the fields in this part of Normandy are square, some oblong and some triangular in shape, and range from tennis-court size to fields large enough for Cub planes to operate from; they average about the size of a baseball field. Their outline, rather than the rise and fall of ground, determined the lines of advance and of resistance. The units had to accommodate themselves tactically to the situation as they found it. Large units could not remain forward as a group. To greatly increase the strength along any stretch of hedge was to multiply the chance that a number of men would be killed. Small groups, moving out on separate missions, sometimes advanced on converging lines or returned from a completed mission to find their companions gone, then joined another group. Each company lost some of its number to the ditches and other cover as the advance continued under fire. When these stragglers were rounded up and put into action by a passing officer or noncom, they included men of every company.

The weakness of the general position, as both battalion commanders realized, was that it had no rear. As the diffusion of the assault forces increased, any chance for organization which would allow for a local reserve was swallowed up. There was nothing to fall back upon. If the front cracked, those who were still on two legs would have to retreat back over the causeway. Captain Rosemond, who was trying to direct the support artillery from the second story of the farmhouse, was being plagued by the hedgerows. They blanked out the fields so that he couldn't see where the shells were falling. So he had to sense and regulate by sound whether he was getting the shells where he wanted them. From noontime on for several hours he did his forward observer's work without a hitch. This forward observer job should have been Lieutenant Spruel's, but he had been killed in the charge across the field with Colonel Cole. Lieutenant Spruel had had a hunch about it. He had said to Captain Rosemond as he arose to jump off, "Well, I didn't want to go back to England, anyway. They'd just give us another training schedule."

But until the sun stood high neither battalion had gotten enough feel of the enemy to be sure whether he intended to stand and fight or to cut and run. During the first heavy blaze of artillery and mortar fire which broke over the American front in mid-morning, the rattle of burp guns had crept closer and the men had said to one another, "They're coming now." Machine guns from far over to the west of Carentan road had put Bridge 4 under heavy fire and enveloped the area immediately south of it. The 1st Squad, 3d Platoon, of Company H, lost six men in less than ten minutes while they were lying in the ditches; the men said later that more of their comrades died in ditches that day than died going forward. A man from Company G had a mortar shell land almost on his head as he lay flat in a ditch with arms outstretched. It wrapped the helmet around his skull and he had to crawl to a medico to have it pried loose.

The Lull

There was a lull. What caused this break in the morning action is not known for certain, though it may have had its source in certain moves which at this hour, unknown to the two battalions, were taking place in the higher headquarters of both camps. But it was the greatest boon that came to the 502d all day, for it enabled 1st Battalion, which up till this moment had not been able to take hold firmly, to complete its defensive arrangements.

Company C came forward and moved to ground just ahead of Hedgerow 2 and along the main highway. The deep ditch which forms the boundary of the field between the Carentan road and the farmhouse turns about even with the Hedgerow 2 and the stream flows under the road and through a culvert. Beyond the ditch at this point and extending almost to Hedgerow 3 was a large cabbage patch. This patch was to become the pivot of the 1st Battalion defense along the left flank. Company C moved up among the forward cabbages. There its rifles and machine guns were positioned so as to put a flanking fire on the Germans as they crept down the inside ditch and the hedgerow paralleling the main road. Company A's line was built up along the rear of this one, taking in the base of the cabbage patch south of the ditch. From this ground the company could fire toward the top of the orchard and against Hedgerow 3. The line extended across the road and past the culvert, so that the machine guns stationed there could fire frontally against the Germans coming down the ditch on the outside of the road. These were to become the lines along which the enemy was to press his further attacks. The attacks varied hardly at all throughout the hours of the afternoon.

The men spread themselves among the cabbages because the plants themselves provided fair concealment. They did not realize at first that this plot of ground was a hub covering the enemy's axial lines of advance. Colonel Cassidy had been over to Colonel Cole and they had discussed where 1st Battalion might find room to dispose its upcoming platoons so that they would have some usefulness in the event of a counterattack. They agreed that the area next to the Carentan road was the least manned and the most vulnerable sector of the front at the moment. So the platoons were told to go that way and the men took up their positions among the cabbages.

While the two companies were fixing themselves on this ground Lt. Wallace A. Swanson of Company A, Sgt. Jay Schenk of Company C, Sgt. Stanley Czarniak of Headquarters Company, and two machine gunners from Company G took advantage of the respite from mortar fire to go up the main road to the house which was on the left side of the road. The house was just a little beyond Hedgerow 4. They saw Germans in the next house. The Germans saw them at the same time and engaged them with rifles and machine pistols; two Germans were hit by machine gun fire. Czarniak then got hit in the face by a bullet from a machine pistol and he started back for a dressing. The machine gun ran out of ammunition. It was 1145; Lieutenant Swanson decided he'd better fall back. The situation, insofar as the enemy infantry were concerned, was quiet. Lieutenant Swanson had seen no enemy activity off toward his right. But while he was retracing his steps he saw Germans moving along Hedgerows 3 and 4 toward the road. Lt. George R. Cody, who was then in the cabbage patch, could look ahead and see these same activities. No one was firing at the enemy during this time and it mystified Swanson.

Sergeant Odom, who had got up to this same forward ground early in the morning, continued to hold it with his two men after knocking out the enemy machine gun. He had been there when Lieutenant Swanson came up and he remained there after Swanson withdrew. But he could not see what was happening to Swanson's group because, though they were spaced only a few yards apart, a hedgerow intervened. However, Pvt. Allen C. McLean of Company G had been keeping a solitary post in this same field between the road and the house. Not far from him, although McLean did not know it, were Cpl. Leroy Drummond of Company H and a small group of men from 1st Battalion. Corporal Drummond had stopped in the field to help a wounded comrade, Pvt. Claude F. Fletcher, who had been hit in the stomach by a shell fragment. After getting Fletcher to the road he met the 1st Battalion men who were coming along. By now Lieutenant Swanson and the machine gunners had already begun to move back. As Private McLean saw it, a few German grenades had fallen among Swanson's men and while no real hurt had been done to them it quickened their belief that a lack of machine-gun ammunition argued for a slight withdrawal. Corporal Drummond and the others saw the Germans coming down the hedgerow on the right of the road. It looked like there were thirty or forty of them. The group figured it was time to move back. They withdrew carefully, not running or exposing themselves. At the position where Sergeant Odom had grenaded the German gunners early in the morning, they found an American machine gun set up; the sight of the gun encouraged them. Drummond and three riflemen from 1st Battalion and one machine gunner thereupon decided to make a stand. They put down a line of fire on the Germans moving along the hedgerow, killed a few of them and forced the others to deploy and then withdrew.

During these actions Sergeant Odom (who was to receive the Distinguished Service Cross and a battlefield commission) and his two men stayed right where they were in the forward ground.

Well over to the right of the regimental front Pvt. Robert I. Boyce and about five other riflemen moved up the road past the right-hand corner of the farmhouse. They saw a German machine-gun squad coming down the road. Two women were marching in front of the squad. At first they thought the Germans intended to surrender. Then one man of the party saw that two of the enemy were lugging the gun and he yelled to the others that it was a trap. They shot into the group and killed two of the Germans. The women ran, but where they disappeared to no one noticed.

Captain Simmons' men who had been in the water-filled ditch finally worked off flankward toward the Madeleine River. They reached its bank just in time to see two squads of Germans pull out of a dugout and flop into position behind a hedgerow. The two squads poured so much fire toward the American party—rifle fire supported by one machine pistol—that the men had to get down into the water again. Having spent one hour in the water of the ditch they spent another hour in the water of the river.

Lieutenant Swanson in the meantime had gone on a sight-seeing tour. He had made one prior trip to reconnoiter the situation on the extreme right where Thompson and the others were fighting at the crossroads. He again moved forward to see how things were going there. But before he ever reached Thompson he bumped bodily into a group of Germans who came from behind a hedgerow. They grabbed him and blindfolded him and held him for an hour. Then they turned him loose and he returned to his own lines.

All of this mystified Lieutenant Swanson very much.

The Germans Counterattack

The enemy infantry had been pressing their only strong counter-attack of the morning. Swanson had seen their right flank come on along Hedgerow 4 as he had walked back along the Carentan road but he had moved on before the two forces opened fire. Corporal Drummond and his men had turned back the attack on the right flank without knowing that this was part of a general engagement. But the fight had flamed along all the hedgerows and through the orchard. Firing machine pistols and rifles, the enemy moved straight along the hedge bordering the orchard toward the two machine guns commanded by Sergeant Summers.

A lieutenant was moving along Hedgerow 2 trying to round up some men. There were two or three 502d riflemen near him. They began to feel the heat of the German fire as the enemy came on through the orchard. A sergeant was hit in the arm and ran toward the farm-house to get first aid. The other men, seeing him go, moved out fast along Hedgerow 2 toward the highway. They had not seen the bullet hit the sergeant but they had seen him run, and they took alarm and followed him. The lieutenant, seeing his men run, took out after them.

Lieutenant Rogers, who was at the hedgerow next to the house, heard the cry as it passed along, "The order is to withdraw." The word passed from man to man—"Withdraw! Withdraw!" Then an officer repeated it. "Don't say that unless you're sure!" Rogers yelled at him. The officer stayed at his post and was shot dead by a German bullet a few seconds later.

The rift at Hedgerow 2 dropped the weight of the attack squarely on Summers' two guns at Hedgerow 1. Fire from the enemy's burp guns ripped the trees and cut the ground all around the gunners. They gave back everything they had, raking the orchard hedgerow and Hedgerow 2 with steady fire. After closing to within thirty yards of the gun the Germans faded back. It is not too much to say that the salvation of the position turned on the effectiveness of Summers' fire at that moment, coupled with the courage of the few riflemen from Company B who supported him.

For what had been most feared had happened on the left. The sudden run by the three men along Hedgerow 2 and the cries of "Withdraw!" brought panic to the stragglers and the wounded who were lying in the fields and ditches to the rear of the cabbage patch. They arose on all sides and ran toward Bridge 4. There they were stopped and turned back by a small group of supply and communications officers and noncoms. This retreat was not even felt in the cabbage patch; the men were too busily engaged in firing at the enemy to know that it had taken place.

Colonel Cole, who was still directing the battle from the farmhouse, did not know there had been a breach on his front. But of a sudden he felt a vague uneasiness. He thought from the way that the enemy fire was building up and from the prolonged rattle of his own machine guns that the Germans were counterattacking. He asked for more artillery.

It was different with Pvt. Allen T. Emery of 3d Battalion Headquarters Company. He was in the hedgerow just beyond the house. He sensed nothing unusual until he heard a cry, "The Germans are counterattacking! Get behind the bridge!" He heard several men yell it. Then he saw men from 1st Battalion come running back. At first they were not running rapidly but at a kind of slow trot, as if doubtful whether they were doing the right thing. Emery and Pvt. Eugene W. Saver of Company H, who was with him, watched them go. Some of the 1st Battalion men were firing as they fell back. Emery and Saver jumped in a foxhole to keep out of the line of fire. In the hole they found a large bag of food—sausage, butter, bread, and fudge—and they proceeded to eat it while they peered out of the foxhole and watched the 1st Battalion men stream back to the bridge. Mortar fire had been falling spasmodically all along the line. Then it came quite suddenly in large and persistent doses. There was a pick-up in machine-gun fire also from the hedgerows. Being in the foxhole, Emery and Saver saw no Germans. They didn't believe that any were coming and they kept on eating and wondering why the others had fallen back to the bridge. They thought the fudge was very good.

THE TRUCE

A few minutes after noon regiment sent word by radio that all hands were to cease firing; the enemy wanted a truce. Colonel Cole dispatched runners to tell the men that they were to hold their positions but that all hostile activities along the front were to cease. Some of the groups never received this order. The men had taken cover in such a scattered way that it was impossible to circulate any message completely. Lieutenant Swanson wandered right through the early part of this truce without hearing about it. That was how he happened to be captured when he blundered into an enemy position and how he happened to be released later without any explanation. The men on the right who had established the forward line near the crossroads heard nothing about the noontime truce. So far as they knew the war was still going on. They had no radio nor were any runners getting up to them. Far off on their left they could see the Germans moving around and concentrating toward them with more freedom than before, but they had no awareness that the American left had suddenly quieted. The Germans who were behind the wall opposite them were still carrying on fighting with percussion grenades, machine pistols and a few rifle grenades. They replied to this fire as best they could but they were having to hoard the last of their ammunition. The free movement of the Germans up ahead of them during this general respite was something they could not curb in any case. The road curved sharply beyond the intersection. That, and the intervention of the hedgerows, made futile any fire toward the left flank. The men there simply sweated out the German regrouping and wondered what was happening.

Rumors ran like wildfire. Along the road someone yelled, "They've

surrendered." Another story went the rounds. "We have captured a
German field marshal." However, those who figured that they were
through fighting for the day and that the battle was over were in a
small minority. The majority had only a limited idea of the truce. They
thought it had been called to permit them to remove the dead and care
for the wounded. These things they proceeded to do. The impression
was strengthened a few minutes after the cease-firing order came
through. An American officer with a Red Cross flag came across
Bridge 4 behind two Germans who were bearing white flags and took
the road into Carentan. He was Maj. Douglas T. Davidson, the regimental surgeon, acting as a direct agent of the division commander, to
ask whether the Germans were ready to yield Carentan.

His mission failed; the military commander in Carentan wouldn't
see him. Nothing came of the truce except that the men got an hour's
rest. There was occasional firing by riflemen and mortar men from
both sides during the lull, coming apparently from outposts which
hadn't received the order. One German machine pistol man in the
forward hedgerows broke the silence with a few rounds. A few riflemen joined him and others answered him. The regiment heard these
sounds and called Colonel Cole to ask who was firing. Upon being
told that the enemy was guilty, the regiment replied, "Don't let our
men fire except in self-defense."

During the truce all wounded men were taken to the rear except six
who were behind Bridge 4. A chaplain came up into the forward
ground, collected about thirty of the casualties and started them out.

Capt. Adolph Blatt, the 3d Battalion medic, also went up. He wrote:

Major Davidson wanted all the ambulance jeeps to come forward to pick
up wounded, so I hopped into one and went up. Just as I crossed the first
bridge I saw the two German prisoners with a huge white flag walking back
to our lines with Major Davidson about a hundred yards behind them. I went
up to the fourth bridge and there were some wounded there to be evacuated,
but I thought there might be some ahead across the bridge, so I had the jeep
go about three hundred yards beyond the bridge to our very own front. . . .
I asked one of our officers in a ditch if we had any wounded there and he
said they had all been taken back; and just then the bullets began to fly again.
The truce was over. We turned the jeep around in about nothing flat and tore
back across the bridge, stopped the jeep and dived behind the embankment
where the wounded were. The fire for the next half hour was terrific, but
then it slackened and we loaded up the jeep and drove back to the aid station.
I don't believe that anyone was actually shooting at us, but there was so much
lead in the air that there was a considerable amount whipping past our ears
until after we had recrossed all bridges. When we got back to where the aid
station had been [at Pont-du-Douve] we found that it had been moved back

about a mile to a little town [St. Come-du-Mont] because the fire around the original place was too heavy. So we drove back to the little town and unloaded.

Major Davidson got back to his own lines about 1300. The men didn't see him return. But they didn't need to be told that he was back. As he crossed Bridge 4 on his way to the Regimental CP, the Germans cut loose with everything—rifle fire, machine guns, mortars, and artillery—in what was by far the most intense concentration of the day.

It fell with power and precision over the entire area held by both battalions, and casualties mounted all up and down the line. Colonel Cole called the regiment and asked for permission to return the fire. He was told to wait. As far as the regiment knew Major Davidson had not returned. Colonel Cole waited; then he called again. The regiment was still hesitating. It had not received official notice that the truce was ended. Just then a shell hit the farmhouse directly above the colonel's head. "Listen to that!" Colonel Cole said. "How about me telling my men to fire?" They again told him to wait. All of this, however, was slightly beside the point. The men of the two battalions were already bearing down with every weapon they had. When the Germans had opened fire, the men had taken the situation into their own hands and the belated order from the regiment to resume fire wasn't even passed on to the men by Colonel Cole.

THE AFTERNOON FIGHT

The afternoon battle wore on much as the morning fight had done, though to the men on the fighting line it seemed to have a more deadly monotone. In the morning the enemy had acted indecisively as if not certain whether to fight or retire. In the hours which followed the truce there could be no doubt that the Germans intended either to drive the 502d Regiment back across the causeway or annihilate the two battalions on the ground around the farm.

All offensive vigor by this time had been spent in the American force. That was almost as true of the individuals, taken one by one, as of the units. In Colonel Cole's battalion the last residue of offensive dash had been exhausted during the charge across the field and the brief advance into the orchard and the first few hedgerows beyond. Colonel Cassidy's men had become so spread over the wide front that the separate groups could no longer feel the strength of the larger unity. For both battalions, therefore, the afternoon was a period of grim holding on. The volume of German fire rose steadily, and the paratroopers felt again the pressure of an invisible enemy who revealed himself only through the swelling of sound as his mechanisms pushed nearer.

Pvt. Peter Dunsky of Company H spoke for the men all along the line when he said, "We had to play it by ear. When we heard rifles and machine pistols fire at us from two hundred yards away for half an hour, then from one hundred yards, then fifty yards, we knew they were coming that much closer to us. The *B-r-r-r* sound of the machine guns would double, then treble in volume—not more shots, but more sound. We could hear them working the bolts of their rifles. We could hear their cartridge shells rattle. And the nearer they came to us the more accurate they became."

Up at the crossroads on the right flank the onfall was swift and furious when the truce ended. The Germans swept in force around and within the curved line of the American position throwing rifle, machine-pistol, grenade and mortar fire ahead of them as they crept along the hedgerows. They got to the crossroads and from the ditches and trees just beyond the intersection they poured automatic fire into the ground beyond the road in great volume. The thirty-five men from 1st Battalion who were situated there had to break back precipitately. There is a place near the farmhouse where a long man-made inlet from the marsh and river gets almost to the roadway. They fell back to that neck of land and set up a new defensive line. So far as they knew the whole detachment on the right had been forced to make this withdrawal. But they were wrong about it; seven men on the extreme right had stuck it. They continued to stick—a little island of resistance which lasted throughout the day.

Hour after hour the Germans pressed on through the orchard and along the abounding hedgerows. About ten men from Company B had taken position along Hedgerow 2 next to a small detachment from Company H. The fire from the flank found them. Seven men from Company B were hit by bullets and the others quit the hedgerow in order to help get their wounded back.

All that saved the Americans was that the enemy did not have enough artillery. There were not more than two guns, probably 88s. After firing six or seven rounds, each gun would break off for a while. The mortars never let up. They had the range and they stayed on it. This was just as true of the automatic weapons. After the men from Company B had fallen back from Hedgerow 2, the ten men from Company H stayed on, holding it by themselves. They were on the north side of the hedge in one spot and the Germans held the rest of the hedge on the other side. Neither group could get at the other because of the thickness of the hedge. But they grenaded each other.

The enemy kept coming. Sergeant Summers' No. 2 gun at the front

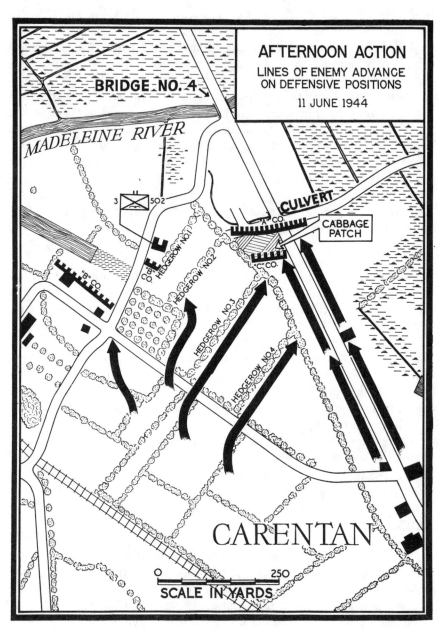

AFTERNOON ACTION
LINES OF ENEMY ADVANCE
ON DEFENSIVE POSITIONS
11 JUNE 1944

BRIDGE NO. 4

MADELEINE RIVER

CULVERT

CABBAGE
PATCH

3 502

"A" CO.

"C" CO.

"B" CO.

"D" CO.

HEDGEROW NO.1

HEDGEROW NO.2

HEDGEROW NO.3

HEDGEROW NO.4

CARENTAN

0   250
SCALE IN YARDS

Map 28.

of the last hedgerow was knocked out and the three crew members were killed. The right-hand gun kept on firing down the road. Probably the interdictory effect of this fire helped save the seven men who were isolated in the forward position on the right. Pvt. William J. Burt, who had effectively used his machine gun on D-day at the WXYZ position, had no idea that there were any Company B men ahead. But to him, firing along the road seemed like a good idea at the time.

The seven men—Sgt. Ted Kaus and Pvts. Luther Davis, James Parham, Burton Petit, John Kokrugga, Anthony Foglia, and Redmond Wells—had watched their original number dwindle steadily. Lieutenant Combs had been hit; fifteen others had been wounded and three killed in the forward line. Late in the afternoon Private Wells, who was the acting squad leader, got a bullet in the shoulder. "I think that's about enough," Wells said to the others. "Leave me here. The rest of you had better drop back to the next hedgerow." His comrades said nothing; they just looked at him and shook their heads. The seven men were still holding out when the American barrage came over and the Germans faded back.

Twenty-eight men had been helping Sergeant Summers and Lieutenant Rogers hold the ground around the machine-gun position at the farmhouse. Twelve remained in the fight. The others were dead or wounded, mostly from bullet fire.

Company C and what remained of Company A had had almost no hedgerow maneuvering to do. In the cabbage patch, where they had been disposed during the late morning, they held their ground for more than six hours against all enemy counterattacks. They were in pretty solid; alone among the units which had distributed over the front they had maintained a semblance of their tactical organization. This was a marked advantage. The men knew one another and knew their leaders. Company A had about thirty men with three machine guns among the cabbages. Company C's strength was a little less. They took losses from German fire throughout the afternoon, but as evening came on there was still enough fire power distributed through the cabbage patch that the flank never faltered.

Nor was the position ever dented. In the first German onfall which followed the truce, the enemy came right on down the hedgerows, moving in parallel lines toward these two companies on the American left. At the same time other enemy riflemen came crawling along the ditch on the outside of the road. These lines of advance were continued throughout the afternoon. Each attack had the same pattern. Though toward the close of the action the Germans had trouble coming forward because they were obstructed by the bodies of their own dead, the machine guns covering the ditches were still cutting down enemy riflemen within twenty-five feet of their own muzzles. From both sides of the culvert the machine guns covered the two parallel ditches. Pfcs. Charles L. Roderick and Franklin E. Cawthon on the right-hand ditch kept their gun going six hours. Roderick got a hit on the operating handle while his gun was firing. It drove a piece of the handle through his shoulder, but he refused to be evacuated. Pvt. Leroi C. Nicolai and Pfc. Alfred A. Fitzsimmons stayed on the left-hand gun. They fired usually in bursts of six or seven. It took a lot of ammunition. They counted ten German dead within twenty-five yards of their gun when the action closed. The banks of the ditch were irregular and these enemy were able to crawl almost to the gun position before Nicolai could get a clear shot at them.

Through most of the afternoon the Carentan road could not be traveled as far as the culvert by either jeeps or men carrying ammunition, so intense was the fire. To the rear of the guns the ditches were so clogged with wounded that ammunition carriers could not come forward over their bodies. Yet one of these hardships compensated for the others. Men—the wounded, the faltering and all those who for one reason or another could no longer face the fire—were strung out along the ditches and along the causeway for more than a mile on both sides of the road. These two chains of battered human beings served as a moving belt. Ammunition boxes were given into one pair of hands back beyond the causeway. They passed through hundreds of hands on the way up but, always, they came along. The wounded would crawl the three or four yards which might be necessary to get the upcoming ammunition and then crawl back to pass it to the next man up the line.

The congestion at the road got worse as the afternoon yielded more wounded who took cover in the ditches. As their numbers increased the need grew for new hands at the front. Some of these men, rounded up by officers and noncoms working the rear, were stalled in the ditches as they tried to come up. Sgt. Charles R. Derose, who had stepped in a hole and broken his leg just as he got up to Company A's position, stood up in the same hole on the broken leg for four hours and served as a traffic director. He shuttled the wounded back and he urged the able men on toward the cabbage patch. To all who witnessed he was one of the splendid figures of the day.

CRISIS

The time was about 1800. In the farmhouse Captain Rosemond stood at the second story window for a few moments looking out over the hedgerows. Colonel Cole joined him there. They noted the pitifully scant numbers of the paratroopers around the house and along the first two hedgerows. They were firing as rapidly as they could. Compared with the volume of sound from the close-up enemy bullet fire, however, the sound of his own pieces seemed to the colonel like a dying rattle. The relative noise of the two fire lines convinced him that he was beaten; he knew then that his line was cracked.

Crawling along the inside of the hedge, Captain Simmons made a last trip up to carry ammunition to the ten men who were holding out along Hedgerow 2. Their machine gun was jammed and they were engaging only with rifles and grenades. Captain Simmons then came back and with a handful of men around him built up a line of resistance in the last hedgerow next to the house. They figured this was the final reserve. If the Germans got through the second hedge and the men there had to fall back from the last field, they could at least be covered during the withdrawal.

There was no longer any attempt to evacuate the wounded. They moved back along the ditches if they could crawl; if they couldn't they stayed where they had been hit. The few remaining aid men tried to care for these cases on the spot after getting up to them through the ditches. So close-joined had the battle become that the litters could not be brought up past Bridge 4.

To Colonel Cole and Captain Rosemond, straining their eyes eastward, it seemed now that the play was ended. They could see nothing of the enemy but they could feel his presence all around them. Rifle fire was buffeting the house from two sides and knocking slates from the roof above their heads. They said nothing; they simply nodded their agreement to each other that the fight had been lost. In Captain Rosemond's mind there was a question whether it would be best to stay and go down fighting or try to retreat over the causeway with all the hazard that such a retreat entailed. He said a prayer. In Colonel Cole's mind there was no question at all. He figured that his men had already "fought to the last" and that he had no right to ask any more of them. He believed it was his duty to pull out. He decided that in pulling out he would leave his wounded. There were five or six of them in the house. He told the first-aid men that if a withdrawal was ordered, they were not to encumber themselves.

At 1630 he talked by radio to Maj. Allen W. Ginder, the regimental S-3, who was Colonel Michaelis' acting executive officer. Colonel Cole

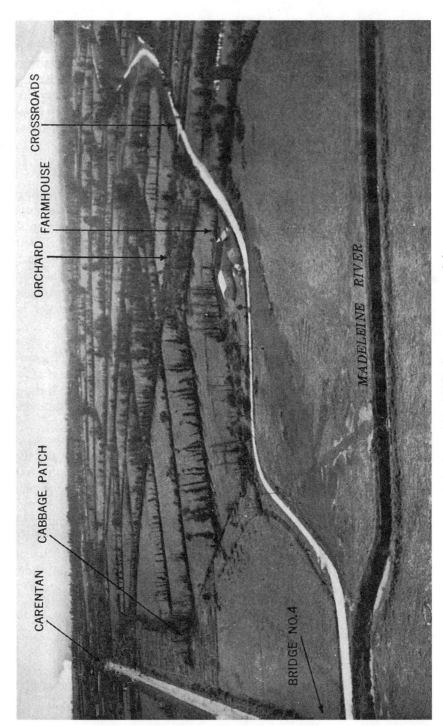

CARENTAN

CABBAGE PATCH

ORCHARD FARMHOUSE CROSSROADS

MADELEINE RIVER

BRIDGE NO. 4

Last phase of the 502d's Carentan causeway fight.

told him he'd had enough for the day. He said that he thought the regiment had better get set to rearward so that the forward battalions could be covered when they withdrew. He asked that the 2d Battalion build up a fire position on the dyke behind the Madeleine and along the right side of the highway so that a fire screen could be put around the farmhouse when the appropriate moment came. He asked also for the artillery to get ready with smoke, so that they could put down a curtain around the farm and the highway area when the battalions began to funnel back into the causeway.

But after he had given Major Ginder these forewarnings, he marked time for a while and waited for a further sign that the battle was turning more radically against him. Major Stopka, moving around the farmhouse to watch the fighting, could hear the Germans working their bolts in the hedgerows. He said to the colonel, "It is getting goddam hot."

There were few local arrangements for the withdrawal. The colonel thought the best thing was to get out as fast as possible. He told Major Stopka to regulate the movement on the right while he, Colonel Cole, took it in the center. Capt. James H. Hatch of 1st Battalion would do the same on the left.

One last chance remained. That was the American artillery. But Captain Rosemond's radio was jammed. The men had been working over it frantically but were getting only German jamming. What was coming over from the guns was insufficient in quantity and too far from the front lines to turn the enemy back. Captain Rosemond knew that the situation required everything the artillery could give it, planted just as close to the farmhouse as possible. He got through at last to Capt. Charles Aldrich at the artillery CP. As he made contact Cole said to him, "If this doesn't work, we'll get the hell out of here right now." Captain Rosemond told Captain Aldrich what he wanted. Captain Aldrich replied, "We're almost out of ammunition." Captain Rosemond said, "For God's sake, get some!" He was pleading with him as a man pleads for his life—"Get it! We must have it!" Captain Aldrich drew back for just a moment to make further inquiries. Then he returned to the instrument and said, "Fresh supplies of ammunition are just now coming into the battery positions."

The Tide Turns

The shells came over at last and they sounded like sweet music. During most of the day only two battalions had been firing in direct support of the farm position. This time every gun within the command was brought to bear. Without asking Colonel Cole what he wanted, Captain Rosemond pulled the fire back so close that it was just arching over the farmhouse roof and falling in the field beyond.

For some few, who had survived the battle thus far, it was too close. Sergeant Derose was still standing in the hole next to the roadway, leg broken, doing his duty. He saw a shell land twenty-five feet in front of him. He said to those around him, "The next one will fall here." But he continued to stand there, waving the men on. The next shell landed within five yards of him and blew him apart. Lt. Frank Magri, already dying from a bullet wound, was also killed by the burst. Captain Cody and Lieutenant Swanson escaped death by a few feet. They heard a whistle and dove head first into the water-filled ditch.

The men of Company A talked about these things afterward, but they did not have the usual reaction of infantrymen who have lost men through their own artillery fire. "We lost good men but we had to have that fire," one of them said and the others agreed. They had seen the last onslaught as the Germans came down Hedgerow 2 and the hedgerow bordering the orchard and started to close on the house from both sides. They knew as surely as the colonel how close a thing it was.

The barrage lasted not more than five minutes. The infantrymen who heard the shells go over and saw them explode along the line later described the fire gratefully as "very intense." The explosions took enough of the advancing German infantry to turn the tide of battle. When the American guns ceased fire, Colonel Cole listened carefully. What he heard told him that the crisis had passed. There was enemy fire—bullet fire—still beating around the farmhouse. But the volume no longer sounded ominous. Captain Rosemond also listened and got the same idea. They waited five, ten minutes; the recession continued. They could still hear the crackle of small-arms fire, only it sounded now as if the pieces had been muted. The enemy machine guns were moving southward.

"Listen to it!" Colonel Cole said to Captain Rosemond. "Just listen to it!"

The colonel went outside and sent about ten men up to the field which lay well beyond the farmhouse between the road and the Madeleine. They moved on as far as the crossroads. Four Germans came out of the woods shouting *"Kamerad!"* But they still held their arms. Two men of Company H had been killed by this same trick within a few hundred feet of the same spot earlier in the day. So the patrol shot into them. Two went down and the other two jumped back into the woods. Otherwise the patrol found nothing but dead Germans. They came back and reported it. Colonel Cole sent a second force of twenty-five men under Lt. George H. Craft and Lt. George E. Bean, both of Company G, to prowl the orchard. They crossed the first field in a skirmish line—a scratch force drawn from all four companies. There was no German fire; however, the advancing line continued to fire into the base of the hedgerow as it went forward. The second hedgerow and orchard were about seventy-five yards away and it was another hundred yards across the orchard. From the area embracing the field and orchard had come most of the enemy fire throughout the day. The artillery had cut a few convenient holes in the hedgerow. Some of the men jumped through them. Others went by the gate. They stayed in the field and orchard for more than an hour. A German machine gun fired loosely at them from far over on the left. Next to the hedgerow they found an American 60mm mortar which the Germans had been using against them. Colonel Cole came up to them where they had formed a fire line along the hedgerow. He told them to hold it until 2d Battalion came to relieve them. The German fire could still be heard faintly in the distance, but the whole front had cooled along the bank of the Madeleine. By morning the Germans had disappeared from this sector of the front.

During the afternoon fighting the medics had plenty to do. Captain Blatt's account is typical:

Major Davidson wanted to set up a forward aid station, so he and I took some litter teams in a jeep down across the first bridge. He was to stay there and I was to go forward with the litter teams on foot. Then I would send the patients back by litter to the barn we had selected and he would send them back to the aid station by jeep. I started up along the road but the fire was so heavy that the litter team couldn't come along, so I sent them back and worked my way up to the fourth bridge and treated several wounded on my way. There was a platoon (Bud Rainey's) just crossing the bridge under machine-gun fire. The men ran across one at a time and then dived in a ditch along the road across the bridge. They called back that a man had been wounded so I grabbed a litter that had been left behind when I was there with the jeep earlier, and ran across the bridge and dived in the ditch. The man had been shot in the arm so I dressed it and had him run back across the bridge. Then they yelled that there was another wounded man up forward so I crawled along the ditch treating the men I found.

There was a house on the left of the road about four hundred yards ahead and earlier in the day I had been told that Colonel Cole was in a house on the left of the road with the CP there so I thought I would try to get up there. I kept sneaking along the ditch and finally when I got within about 150 yards of it someone asked me where I was going, and I told them. They said. "Good God, Doc! That building is a German machine-gun nest. The house you are looking for is back along the other fork of the road." I was startled, to say the least, and I remember thinking to myself, "I thought that was awfully far forward for a CP."

Just then, after I had worked my way back a little, the firing suddenly ceased and the enemy had disappeared. It was about 6:00 p.m. After the shooting stopped I went across the field to the house where Colonel Cole had had his CP. There were quite a few wounded along the hedgerows and they brought up some jeeps and we got them all back to the aid station. It was about 7:00 p.m. by this time and still quite light.

When we had cleaned that area I took a jeep to go along the road along which I had crawled earlier in the afternoon because I knew that there were wounded there and I did not know if they had been evacuated. Sgt. [John P.] Durka, the 2d Battalion staff sergeant, who had come up, asked if he could go along. We went to the road just in front of the fourth bridge and I started walking along the ditch on the right, he along the ditch on the left, and the driver slowly drove the jeep down the center of the road. About 150 yards from the bridge I found a wounded man, so the jeep came over there and Sergeant Durka came over and we put the man on a stretcher and then onto the jeep litter brackets. Then I started along the road again on the right and Sergeant Durka on the left, and suddenly there was the whistle of an artillery shell and it burst just behind Sergeant Durka, killing him by concussion. I dropped to the ground when I heard the scream of the shell and neither I nor the jeep driver nor the wounded man felt a thing, but Sergeant Durka gasped a couple of times and then died. We ran over to him immediately but he was dead before we could put him on the stretcher. We took him and the wounded man back to the aid station (another jeep came up just after Sergeant Durka was injured and told us that there were no more wounded along the ditches). His death hit me pretty hard because he was such a fine person. I had liked him better than any other soldier in the detachment and because he had volunteered to go on a job that he actually didn't have to do.

About 2000 2d Battalion arrived and took over the position. Cole ordered a roll call of his men; there were 132 left to make answer. While they were forming in the orchard about 2100 there was one last burst of shelling from the German artillery. Three more men were killed and eight were wounded.

The little battalion started back over the causeway which during the last two days they had renamed "Purple Heart Lane." They passed through the now open gate at Bridge 4. That morning four companies, man by man, had wedged through the gate; the largest company had put 121 men through. Now the entire battalion numbered just that. Thirty hours before, one of the companies, I, had come onto the north end of the causeway with eighty men and officers. Now less than a dozen were going back. A week before they had been a battalion of green troops few of whom had ever seen violent death. They had jumped and had helped clear the causeways from Utah Beach so that the seaborne troops had had almost a dream landing. Now they themselves had come to a nightmare causeway; in the dusk as they returned across it they saw on either side the price of their passage.

At 2330 the battalion reached St. Come-du-Mont, walking. One of the men said to the colonel, "Did you know today is Sunday?" Said Colonel Cole, "Jesus Christ! Why didn't somebody tell me?"[2]

Linkup of the Beachheads

During the night of June 9-10, the 327th Glider Infantry had crossed the Douve and on the 10th, as the 3d Battalion of the 502d began its bloody probing of the Carentan defenses along the northwestern highway, the 327th was fighting down the Carentan side of the Douve, approaching the town from the east.

At the time—June 10—the 327th had the only American troops across the Douve in the Carentan area, though the 3d Battalion of the 502d was beginning that night to pass a few men across the Douve along the St. Come-du-Mont–Carentan causeway. The 327th force was also the nearest Utah Beach unit to Omaha Beach and that afternoon the first link-up of the beaches was made.

General Taylor had received a report that unidentified troops were in Auville-sur-le-Vey, a village on the banks of the Vire River three miles southeast of Brevands. Shortly after noon he ordered Colonel Allen of the 3d Battalion, 327th, which was in Brevands, to send one company to the village to investigate and report to him within an hour. Allen assigned the mission to Company A (the battalion, still officially the 1st Battalion of the 401st Glider Infantry Regiment, retained its A, B, C, D company designations), reinforcing it with a section of heavy mortars; and he went along with the company.

About halfway to the village they ran into small-arms fire. Instead of stopping, the company, which had been hurrying anyhow, broke into a run. Two men at the head of the column (one S/Sgt. John R. Gacek, a professional boxer and wrestler, ETO champion in the latter sport, later killed near Opheusden, Holland), each took a light machine gun in his arms and, as he ran, sprayed the countryside. At about 1400, in the village of Auville-sur-le-Vey, the first known contact between troops of the two beaches occurred. Sitting in front of a store was a group of 29th (Blue and Gray) Division soldiers with some German prisoners. One of the glidermen, who had seen his sergeant and his lieutenant wounded and left behind on the road from Brevands, became enraged at the sight of these Germans and attempted to kill one of them with the machine-gun tripod he was carrying; Colonel Allen had to come between him and the German.

Carentan. At the upper center is the Bassin-à-Flot and the narrow woods along each bank. Troops of the 327th moved through these woods into Carentan.

Colonel Allen radioed the news back to General Taylor that V Corps had established the bridgehead that morning. Then he borrowed a jeep and accompanied by Maj. Paul H. Danahy, Assistant Division G-3, who had made the trip with the company, crossed the Vire over the blown but repaired highway bridge and drove to 29th Division Headquarters and then on to V Corps Headquarters. The two officers gave the Corps Commander, Maj. Gen. Leonard T. Gerow, a picture of the 101st situation. Late in the afternoon the two officers returned to Auville, picked up the company and six light tanks looking for a mission, and returned to the battalion at Brevands. Along the way they counted twelve machine-gun positions they had knocked out on the round trip.

The 327th Begins Its Attack Toward Carentan

The joining up of the two beachheads as thus accomplished did not lessen the importance of the capture of Carentan. The linkage was still very thin and the only good roadnet passed through the town.

About the time Company A rejoined the 3d Battalion, Col. Joseph H. Harper crossed the Douve and took command of the 327th, relieving Col. George S. Wear. Colonel Harper was regimental commander of the 401st Glider Infantry Regiment, but due to the split-up in March which sent the 2d Battalion to the 82d Division he was without a regiment and was acting as beachmaster on Utah Beach. He found the 327th attacking toward Carentan.

The 327th fight was on the western side of a wedge of land between the Douve and Vire Rivers, an area the clearing of which had been assigned the Division by General Bradley. The highway which runs from Cherbourg to Carentan in a southeasterly direction swings due east at Carentan and proceeds across the wide part of this wedge five miles to the Vire. It crosses the Vire at Auville-sur-le-Vey, five miles from Carentan, and continues east through the nearby town of Isigny and on back of the Omaha Beach country. The causeway bridges just northwest of Carentan cross the Douve and some of its tributaries; east of the town the counterpart highway and railway bridges cross the Canal de Vire-et-Taute.

The Canal de Vire-et-Taute leads off the Douve a mile north of Carentan and runs inland almost due south, skirting the eastern edge of the town, where it is bridged by the east-bound highway and railway. These last are continuations of the Cherbourg highway and railway which enter Carentan from the northwest. On that side of Carentan, the northwest side, there was hardly a yard of the last seven or eight miles into the town along which the 101st had not fought; from Blos-

Troops of the 101st passing through Ste. Marie-du-Mont on their way to Carentan.

ville to La Croix Pan to St. Come-du-Mont to Dead Man's Corner to Pont-du-Douve to the four causeway bridges across the Douve—where at this very time Cole's 3d Battalion of the 502d was fighting along the final couple of miles before Carentan. Soon an approach to the town was to be made along the same highway but from the opposite direction.

Colonel Harper found the 327th advancing with the immediate objective of cutting the escape route of the Germans in Carentan to the east and of securing the bridges on that side of the town. The regiment had reached almost to the highway bridge across the canal. The left flank extended back along the highway toward the Vire and the right flank was on the general line of the canal between the highway and the Douve to the north. After learning the situation and plans from Colonel Wear, Colonel Harper went forward to look over the battalions and their fight. The 1st Battalion Headquarters he found in a house in St. Hilaire-Petit-Ville along the main road east of the bridge. The battalion CO, Maj. Hartford T. Salee, was in the CP, wounded. Major Salee reported that he had a few men in a house near the bridge and that the remainder of his men were along the road. Company A was in the houses on both sides of the road. Company B was south of the road, toward the railroad which paralleled the highway at a distance of a few hundred yards. Company C was in reserve farther back down the highway. After inspecting his 1st Battalion, Colonel Harper moved across the road and located the 2d Battalion to the north of the highway. The 3d Battalion was in reserve in the village of Le Rocher, about a mile and a half to the east.

The situation, as Colonel Harper saw it, was not too favorable. The attack was bogged down. Enemy fire and the casualties suffered had so disorganized the units that the men were in little groups scattered from place to place; there was no real line and no movement was being made. He determined to have the two battalions push forward.

The attack was to begin at 2200; the late hour was selected because it was just twilight and the faint light would allow the companies to organize for the attack while the forward movement would be cloaked in darkness. The two battalions were to attack, two companies abreast, using the highway as their boundary, and were to push forward to the last line of hedgerows, about three hundred to four hundred yards from the canal. The 321st Field Artillery Battalion, which had crossed the Douve during the day and had its guns set up near Catz, was to keep the enemy occupied with fire laid on the far bank of the canal. The 2d Battalion's heavy machine guns were brought up and put into position north of the highway to support the movement.

The attack got off on time and by midnight the men were organized and in position on their objective, the hedgerow just short of the canal. During the night the positions were improved and strengthened. Also, a patrol from the 2d Battalion was sent to a small, partially wrecked footbridge which crossed the canal where it joined the Douve. The patrol moved right up to the bridge and set up a position.

So ended June 10 along the highway east of Carentan. Along the same highway to the northwest of the town Cole's 3d Battalion of the 502d lay recovering from its first day of fighting on the open causeway after trying to pass through the narrow opening of Bridge 4.

The 327th Attacks Carentan

When the 327th objectives had been taken word was sent back to Division, and General Taylor ordered the regiment to continue the advance on Carentan. General Taylor offered Colonel Harper his choice of trying either the north or south flank; neither officer considered the possibility of a direct assault on the main highway bridge because of the strong defensive positions held by the Germans at that point. Colonel Harper had seen the swamps to the south of the railroad and had no desire to try an attack there, and the railway bridge was blown. So he told the general that he would try a crossing on his right flank over the footbridge at the juncture of the canal and river. The 3d Battalion would be brought up to make the crossing.

Colonel Harper knew that, even though a crossing was made at this point, the way into Carentan might not be easy. For at the same point where the Canal de Vire-et-Taute joins the Douve another canal also connects and parallels the Canal de Vire-et-Taute to Carentan. This mile-long canal is known as the Bassin-à-Flot and allows barges and medium-small vessels to come from the Douve into the town of Carentan proper. Since the Bassin-à-Flot is to the west of the Canal de Vire-et-Taute there is formed between the two waterways which runs from the river to Carentan a several-hundred-foot-wide peninsula. Thus, when the footbridge was crossed troops would have to move up this restricted peninsula which offered very little terrain protection except that afforded by a line of woods. It offered to the Germans some of the defensive potentialities which were making the causeway approach from the northwest so expensive for the 3d Battalion of the 502d.

Just at dawn of the 11th Colonel Harper made a personal reconnaissance of the footbridge to determine its capabilities. He found that the bridge had been blown and was partly in the water, but with the aid of members of the patrol present at the position he managed to get planking and building materials into place and established a firm footing across the canal.

The colonel's plan was that once the troops were across the Canal de Vire-et-Taute he would put part of them on over the Bassin-à-Flot, crossing the Bassin's locks, and then move up both sides of the Bassin-à-Flot through the woods that grew along it. He and his orderly crossed over the bridge, looked around and drew no fire. Meanwhile, Colonel Allen and the 3d Battalion had come up. Colonel Harper explained to him the plan of attack. Company A of the 3d Battalion was to attack down the left, or east, side of the Bassin and Company G of the 327th was to attack down the right of the Bassin. Company C of the 3d Battalion was to remain farther back in reserve. The 1st Battalion of the 327th, which was in position along the Canal de Vire-et-Taute between the railroad and highway bridges, and the 2d Battalion, which was behind the last hedgerow along the canal from the highway bridge up to where the 3d Battalion was to cross, were to fire heavily into the town of Carentan and on enemy positions on the peninsula between the canal and the Bassin until the 3d Battalion began its attack, then were to lift their fire. The 65th was to support the attack with artillery fire on the enemy positions. Several tank destroyers with the 327th along the canal banks fired at point targets and 4.2 chemical mortars covered enemy positions close to the canal.

The crossing began at 1000 with General Taylor observing. Even before the crossing began the Germans had become aware of the activity around the bridge and had begun mortaring the area, but the passage was made without casualties. The two assault companies advanced through the woods on either side of the Bassin for several hundred yards before the German rifle and machine-gun fire began finding them. The fire was heavy and was not necessarily aimed at individuals because the narrow wooded areas assured a high percentage of hits. The companies were pinned down. Colonel Harper and an artillery observer went forward with a radio to try to get more effective fire on the German defenses and got caught by machine-pistol fire fifty yards ahead of the American front. The observer was wounded but they managed to crawl back to safety.

The fire was coming mostly from the northeast edge of Carentan and from positions on the west bank of the canal, across from the 2d Battalion. The artillery wasn't proving effective, the glidermen couldn't advance into the heavy fire, and the attack bogged. No progress was made during the rest of the day.

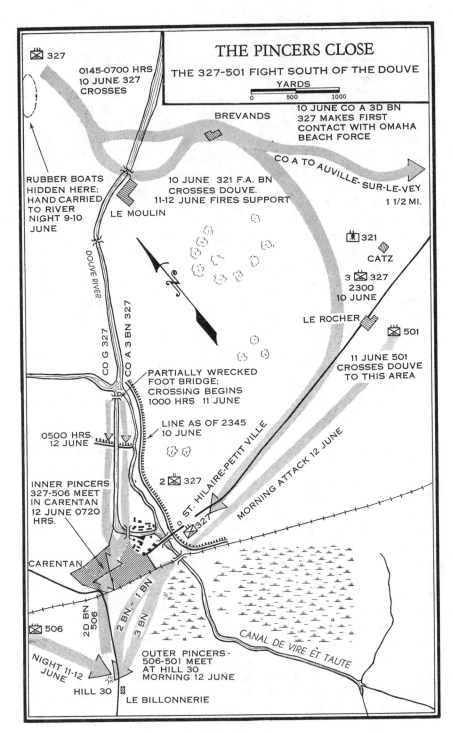

THE PINCERS CLOSE

THE 327-501 FIGHT SOUTH OF THE DOUVE

YARDS

0   500   1000

327

0145-0700 HRS
10 JUNE 327
CROSSES

BREVANDS

10 JUNE CO A 3D BN
327 MAKES FIRST
CONTACT WITH OMAHA
BEACH FORCE

CO A TO AUVILLE-SUR-LE-VEY

1 1/2 MI.

RUBBER BOATS
HIDDEN HERE;
HAND CARRIED
TO RIVER
NIGHT 9-10
JUNE

LE MOULIN

10 JUNE 321 F.A. BN
CROSSES DOUVE.
11-12 JUNE FIRES SUPPORT

321

CATZ

DOUVE RIVER

3 327
2300
10 JUNE

LE ROCHER

501

11 JUNE 501
CROSSES DOUVE
TO THIS AREA

CO G 327

CO A 3 BN 327

PARTIALLY WRECKED
FOOT BRIDGE;
CROSSING BEGINS
1000 HRS. 11 JUNE

LINE AS OF 2345
10 JUNE

0500 HRS.
12 JUNE

INNER PINCERS
327-506 MEET
IN CARENTAN
12 JUNE 0720
HRS.

2 327

ST. HILAIRE-PETIT VILLE

MORNING ATTACK 12 JUNE

327

CARENTAN

2D BN
506

2 BN - I BN

3 BN

CANAL DE VIRE ET TAUTE

506

NIGHT 11-12
JUNE

OUTER PINCERS -
506-501 MEET
AT HILL 30
MORNING 12 JUNE

HILL 30

LE BILLONNERIE

Map 29.

At 2000 Colonel Harper got word to report to Le Rocher, which was now the regimental CP. At the CP he found the First Army's Deputy Commander, Lt. Gen. Courtney H. Hodges, Generals Taylor and McAuliffe, and Colonel Johnson of the 501st. General McAuliffe had been placed in charge of a task force whose mission was the capture of Carentan. This force consisted of the 327th and the 501st. The formation of this force was prompted by the difficulty of coordinating, with the poor communications available, the direction of this combat team with that of the 502d-506th force on the other side of the town.

THE PINCERS CLOSE

At the time of the conference on the night of the 11th the 101st had extended the arc of a pincers 180 degrees about Carentan. At one end, along the Carentan–St. Come-du-Mont road, and within a mile of Carentan, the 2d Battalion of the 502d anchored the ground taken that day by the other two battalions of the regiment. These two battalions, dog-tired and depleted, were now slowly moving back across the causeway, their work done. From there the arc circled along the bend of the Douve and up the Bassin-à-Flot to where the 3d Battalion of the 327th was pinned half a mile from the town; and sharply on around the Canal de Vire-et-Taute, within pistol-range of the town, where the 327th lay along the hedgerows nearest the canal.

General McAuliffe began closing this pincers from the east. Leading out of Carentan were four surfaced highways and three rail lines. The northbound highway and railway were held by the 502d along the causeway and, farther north, by the 506th; the eastbound highway and railway were held at the canal bridge by the 327th. The other two highways ran southwest out of the town in the general direction of Hill 30 and there was a west-bound single-track railroad just to the north of the hill. If the 502d could complete its pincers on around to Hill 30 it would cross and cut both the remaining highways and the single-track railroad. But Colonel Michaelis, looking over his exhausted and depleted battalions, had asked that some other outfit be sent on around to Hill 30. The 506th was selected for the job and after it passed through the 502d the 502d went into Division reserve.

To complete the encirclement the 501st, which had been in Division reserve and had that day been alerted for an attack on Carentan in case Major Davidson, 502d's surgeon, brought back an unfavorable reply to the demand for the town's surrender, was ordered to cross the Douve and approach Hill 30 from the east. If the 501st from the east could contact the 506th from the west at Hill 30 the ring about the town would be complete. The German 6th Parachute Regiment defending the town would then have an opportunity to carry out their implicit orders to "defend Carentan to the last man."

The 506th Advances

Both the new attacking regiments, the 506th and 501st, had had a day or two in which to rest and recuperate. That morning in their bivouac areas across the Douve they had held religious services, well attended (it was Sunday), and had received and distributed PX rations. Motor pools and horse corrals had been established and the captured and liberated vehicles and horses were collected at these places; up to that time some units of the 506th especially had begun to look like airborne cavalry. Kitchens had been set up and hot meals were being served, some of captured German rations. News bulletins were issued, men had a chance to heat canteen cups of water and shave. The dead were collected, far-dropped paratroopers, just getting through the enemy lines, were welcomed back, French underground members turned up with information and offers of help, very occasional enemy planes came over, war correspondents dropped in at the CPs to get stories, rumors of gas attacks and booby traps went the rounds. Now the companies issued extra ammunition and started out.

The 501st moved out first. That afternoon, Sunday, June 11, while the 502d and the 327th were still engaged on the approaches to Carentan, the 501st crossed the Douve on the engineers' now completed treadway bridge near Brevands and bivouacked in the vicinity of the village of Segueville, southeast and to the rear of the 327th. To get to Hill 30 it was necessary to cross the Canal de Vire-et-Taute. Colonel Johnson decided to make the actual crossing the next morning at first daylight.

That night, June 11, at 2100 General Taylor arrived at the 506th Regimental CP at Angoville-au-Plain and personally delivered the order for the regiment to attack through the 502d. The artillery which had been supporting the 502d during the past day and a half on the causeway was attached to the 506th. The 1st Battalion got under way while it was still light and began crossing the causeway before midnight. Having crossed the causeway it turned right at the farmhouse where Colonel Cole's battalion had made its charge that day. The 1st Battalion was followed by the 2d Battalion and Antitank Battery A of the 81st Airborne Antiaircraft Battalion, commanded by Capt. Thomas P. Moran. Advancing in single file, the battalions moved on an azimuth a mile almost due south to Hill 30. Only at the high ground itself did the troopers meet any real opposition; there they drove in a German outpost line. The 2d Battalion set up to the west but in contact with the 1st Battalion. The movement closed the right arm of the pincers around Carentan another 60 degrees, putting 506th troops astride the last two highways and the last rail line out of the town. Now the only wide-open escape corridor for the defenders was through the marshy section just south of Carentan and between Hill 30 and the Canal de Vire-et-Taute.

Back across the Douve Colonel Sink had moved his CP from Angoville-au-Plain where it had been for the past four days to Dead Man's Corner, just below St. Come-du-Mont. Having witnessed the 502d's struggle on the causeway he figured that his own column would probably run into a good deal of opposition and that his CP wouldn't be too far behind his assault force when morning came. But as the messages from the advancing units came back, "No trouble yet," "We're going right along," "We're getting no fire," he realized that he had better follow up his battalions. Just before 0100 that morning, June 12, he struck his CP and started across the causeway toward Hill 30, following the troops. After leaving the road past Bridge 4 the group failed to follow a true course and veered to the east. The head of the column came to what Colonel Sink recognized as the Carentan racetrack. Just across the fence was a German sentry. After debating whether it would be best to shoot or grenade him. Sink decided, since it might betray their position, to do neither. Moving back about four hundred yards the CP group dug in, set up an all-around defense, and established radio contact with the battalions.

Just before daylight the CP radio chanced onto a circuit and heard General McAuliffe tell Colonel Higgins to soak a hill—which happened to be the one the CP was on—with white phosphorus. Some rapid cutting in on the circuit cancelled the mission.

Daylight revealed the CP to be just outside Carentan and between the town and the two battalions. Daylight also brought down enemy rifle fire from many directions onto the CP group. Major Hannah, the regimental S-3, managed to contact by radio Capt. Lloyd Patch of 1st Battalion. "Can you hear all the commotion?" asked Major Hannah. When Captain Patch said he could Hannah ordered him to start a company in the direction of the firing and to take care of the enemy machine guns. After about 30 minutes the Headquarters party heard the deep slow cadence of the American light machine guns and a few minutes later they were relieved.

It is a 506th claim that the first American into Carentan was a member of that regiment, driving a cartload of mortar ammunition.

The lone cart had crossed the causeway from St. Come-du-Mont, missed the right turn at the end of the causeway, and, in the small hours of the night, had continued on the highway into Carentan. In the deserted center of the town the only sounds outside those of the perimeter fighting, were the horse's hooves and the steel tires on the cobblestones. Fires, unfought, burned in various sections from phosphorus shells being lobbed in by 4.2 chemical mortars and naval guns. In the center of Carentan the horse stopped. The soldier-driver, suspecting that he might not be in the right place, began to feel conspicuous in the still, deserted town square. Suddenly, the unnatural silence was broken— in the duffel on the cart a forgotten alarm clock began ringing, the sound echoing among the stone buildings.

The Fall of Carentan

As the dawn of June 12 lightened, the poised forces began moving in on the almost encircled town. Earlier General McAuliffe had sent out a reconnaissance patrol which had reached the edge of the town but had been unable to force an entry. He suspected that a large part of the town's defenders had withdrawn but that a force had been left to put up something of a fight. This view was justified by events. The 3d Battalion of the 327th, at 0500 renewing its attack along the Bassin-à-Flot from the northeast, ran into sniper fire at the edge of town and some opposition along the west side of the Bassin, but it was the fire of a covering force; Colonel Harper and General Taylor, following them, saw only two German dead. Before 0700 3d Battalion was well into the town.

On the southwest side of town, at Hill 30, Colonel Sink had ordered Colonel Strayer to attack with his 2d Battalion at the same hour, 0500, while the 1st Battalion was moving to relieve the attacked regimental headquarters group. The 2d Battalion started out toward Carentan, moving astride the main road. Under harassing machine-gun fire most of the way it found that the enemy had ranged in artillery on the junction where the two highways out of Carentan on that side of town joined; but the lead company, F, got past before the shells began to fall and moved right into town. Company E, following F, had nine casualties from artillery and the fire of a few German pockets of resistance. Capt. R. D. Winters of E flanked his company to the right and in an hour wiped out this remnant of resistance.

At 0720, in Carentan, Company F contacted the 3d Battalion glider-men coming from the opposite direction. There was a good deal of shooting, mostly by troopers firing into doubtful buildings, but few

*Glidermen of the 327th watch a captured gun
and a jeepload of medics arrive in Carentan.*

Germans were found and Carentan was well cleared by 1000. Most of the final German opposition had been centered in the area around the railroad station in the southwest section of the town. There, shortly after the junction of the 327th's 3d Battalion and the 506th, Colonel Harper, Colonel Strayer of the 506th and Colonel Allen of the 3d Battalion, 327th, met. The three officers went into a nearby wineshop and got a bottle to drink to the victory.

Meanwhile, to the south of Carentan the 501st was running into some stiff opposition in its efforts to get to Hill 30. The regiment launched its attack across the Canal de Vire-et-Taute at dawn under cover of smoke and following a preparatory artillery barrage. The attack was made by 3d and 2d Battalions advancing abreast, 3d Battalion being on the right and with the Carentan-Isigny highway as a right boundary. The canal was out of banks but the extent of the flooding was not realized until the attack; the whole valley was under water. The original plan called for an attack aimed directly toward Hill 30, avoiding the edge of Carentan. The flooding ruined any chance of an orderly advance and most of the men crossed the canal itself in single file over the partly wrecked railroad bridge several hundred yards south of the highway.

The lead company across the bridge, H, commanded by Capt. Felix Stanley, was about half way between the canal and the hill and wading waist-deep across the flooded bottomland where the Germans opened up on them with mortars, machine guns, and 20mm fire from anti-aircraft positions on the hill. Fortunately, the first members of Com-

231

pany H had gotten to the base of Hill 30 when the barrage began and were able to successfully attack and destroy most of the AA guns. On Company H's right Company I, after crossing the bridge, had continued up the railroad tracks to the Carentan station and had then swung up the hill on H's right. At the top of the hill both companies were stopped by small-arms fire supported by a tracked vehicle.

The supporting artillery was working well (although the chemical mortars had dropped some short rounds of white phosphorus among the paratroopers as they waded across the flooded bottoms). About 20 battalion volleys were laid on the enemy, very close in, and the German resistance was broken.

From the hilltop 3d Battalion moved down to the tiny settlement on the southern edge, La Billonnerie, and there set up a defense against a counterattack from the south. Late in the morning the attack came, up the highway which ran north into Carentan. The 501st called for artillery. The volleys broke up the German attack and also a 506th outpost which was, unknown to the 501st, a short distance to their front.

About this time 2d Battalion of the 501st came down the highway from Carentan, deployed astride the road, and reinforced the line held by 3d Battalion. When the 1st Battalion came up it replaced the 3d Battalion and that battalion withdrew. The 3d Battalion had suffered about 50 casualties during the morning, bringing its total casualties for Normandy to about 65 percent of the battalion's original strength. "I had about a boy scout troop from then on," said the CO, Ewell. Although the fight did not rank, in casualties, length, nor tactical importance as the battalion's outstanding engagement the circumstances under which it was fought made it one of the bitterest. Looking back on the experience after the war Colonel Ewell wrote: "The strain of wading across a shallow pond with 20mm spraying the water was terrific. We were really shot—I was so damned exhausted emotionally that I just didn't care about anything. The people who did the real fighting were worse. This attack as far as I personally was concerned was the most trying one that I went through in all our fighting in Europe."

THE ENEMY REACTION

Obviously the enemy had decided not to defend Carentan from within. After the bloody, almost suicidal, defense against which the 502d and the 327th's 3d Battalion had butted the day before, the opposition the troopers met coming into Carentan amounted to little more than interdictory fire. French civilians, who were beginning to come out of their cellars, reported that there were never more than two hundred troops in the town itself; the defense had been set up and broken on the approaches. The German LXXXIV Corps had reported to the German Seventh Army that Carentan had fallen at 1800 on June 11 after a bitter hand-to-hand struggle. While this report may have seemed half a day premature to riflemen shooting and getting shot at trying to get into the city proper, it was undoubtedly the bloody, determined fighting of the 502d on the previous day, and the final life-saving artillery barrage, that convinced the enemy that Carentan was lost. Most of the defenders managed to get out of the town during the night before the encirclement to the south was completed.

The loss of Carentan was the cause of a certain amount of chagrin to the German High Command. The German 6th Parachute Regiment which on June 9 had been ordered to defend the town to the last man had, on the 11th, fought in a way which indicated that such a stand might be made. However, on that day the regiment reported that the situation was becoming critical because of failing supplies of ammunition, and the High Command attributed the loss of the town to the 6th Parachute Regiment's lack of ammunition. The German Seventh Army war diary reveals some buck-passing as to just who was to blame for the shortage. The Americans who attacked Carentan, dodging or absorbing the unprecedented amount of automatic-weapon and mortar fire, had no doubts about what became of the ammunition. The loss of the town must have nettled even Hitler himself; at any rate on the 12th he issued an order that "explicit orders by Der Führer demand that everyone in strongpoints, points of resistance, and other defensive positions surrounded by enemy units must defend his position to the last man and to the last bullet, in order to allow time for preparation for the counterattack and the reconquest of the coast. No orders to retreat will be issued."

A German counterattack was planned for the morning of the 13th; it would probably have been attempted on the 12th if all the units which were to be employed had arrived in time. The main attack, which was to retake Carentan, was to be made along the peninsula of high ground that extended southwest from the town. The 37th SS Panzergrenadier Regiment of the 17th SS Panzergrenadier *Goetz von Berlichingen* Division, reinforced by a company of the 17th SS Tank Battalion and a platoon of self-propelled guns from the 17th Antitank Battalion, was to assemble about three miles west of Carentan on the night of the 12th-13th and attack east the next morning. Attacking with them were the remnants of the battered 6th Parachute Regiment. As soon as the Americans were driven out the parachutists were to

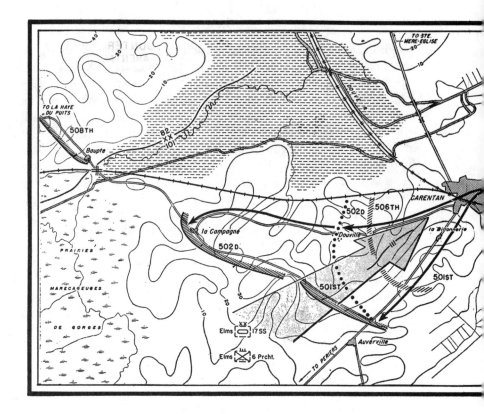

set up a defense in the town which they once lost, while the panzers moved north on St. Come-du-Mont, reestablished a bridgehead across the Douve, and pursued the fleeing 101st. The action was to be protected from counterattack from the 82d area across the Douve to the north or from the V Corps area across the Vire to the east by Combat Team Heintz, a battle group made up of elements from both the 17th SS Panzergrenadier Division and the 352d Division. This combat team was to carry out continuous counterattacks, by night as well as day, to keep the Americans off balance. (It was this group which the 327th later was to run into near Montmartin-en-Graignes.) Farther to the southeast, near the Vire, the 38th SS Panzergrenadier Regiment was assembled to repulse a breakthrough anywhere along the Douve–Vire front and to form counterattack groups. To give artillery support to the Carentan attack there was attached to the 17th Artillery Regiment the 2d Battalion of the 191st Artillery Regiment, the 2d Heavy Howitzer Battery of the 352d Infantry Division, and the guns of Artillery Group Ernst. Air support was also promised.

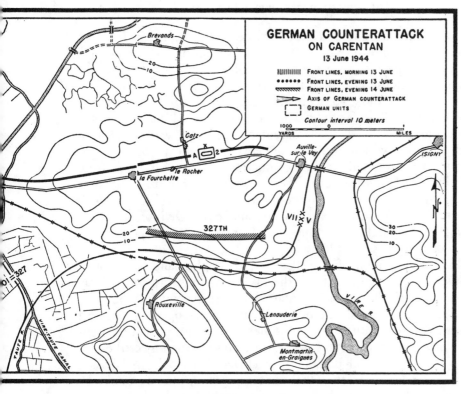

GERMAN COUNTERATTACK
ON CARENTAN
13 June 1944

|||||||| FRONT LINES, MORNING 13 JUNE
•••••• FRONT LINES, EVENING 13 JUNE
〰〰〰 FRONT LINES, EVENING 14 JUNE
➤➤➤ AXIS OF GERMAN COUNTERATTACK
⌐⌐⌐ GERMAN UNITS

Contour interval 10 meters

Map 30.

Many of the German troops met up to this time had not been first-class fighting men. Not so the 17th SS Panzergrenadiers. They were tough and skillful, part of an experienced combat team, with organic tanks and artillery. They allegedly took very few prisoners.

The Division Prepares to Defend Carentan

That the logical direction for a German counterattack to retake Carentan was from the southwest along the peninsula of high ground leading into the town from that direction was recognized in the 101st headquarters where a defense against such a drive was being planned. It was also recognized in Division Headquarters that from a tactical standpoint the chief gain from the Carentan victory was not the town itself but rather this high ground. General Taylor decided to push out several miles to the west where the peninsula ran narrowly between swamplands, and there set up defensive positions. This job fell to the two regiments already available on the southwest approaches—the 506th and the 501st. As a matter of fact as 2d Battalion of the 506th

235

was moving into Carentan 1st Battalion, near Hill 30, had had to turn one company around to repel a German attack on its rear. When the town was occupied that morning the 501st and 506th formed the southwestern defense line, with the 501st to the left of the 506th.

That afternoon the two regiments got orders to push out their defensive fronts. The 506th was to advance toward Baupte on the railroad and highway west of Carentan; the 501st was to advance toward Sainteny which was on the Périers highway southwest of Carentan. Already small German counterattacks had been made from the southwest and a good deal of German artillery fire from that area was landing in town, some quite close to the house in southwest Carentan where the 506th had its command post. Division had foreseen this danger and had set up its advance command post in the woods along the Bassin-à-Flot.

By 1530 2d Battalion of the 506th, on the right flank, had got as far as Douville, a village between the eastbound highway and railway and more than a mile out of Carentan. Up to that point they had met little opposition. Just outside of the village the troopers ran against the German forces gathering for the next morning's attack. A fight began which continued in this general position for the rest of the day. At 2200 that evening 3d Battalion, which had been held in Division reserve, was released to the 506th and was committed through the 1st Battalion about midnight, coming in on 2d Battalion's left.

The 501st, on the left of the 506th, was unable to come up alongside the 506th though it pushed forward a thousand yards from Hill 30 before being stopped by dug-in German resistance. That evening Company D of the 70th Tank Battalion, a light tank company, was attached to the regiment and with this armored support some further progress was made.

Across the Douve preparations were being made to motorize the 2d Battalion of the 502d, then bivouacked near St. Come-du-Mont, and the battalion was alerted to move out on an hour's notice. Just before midnight Colonel Sink, Colonel Johnson, and the commanding officers of the supporting artillery met in Colonel Sink's command post in Carentan. They decided on an attack, to begin at 0500, with an artillery barrage at 0430. Possibly behind the German lines a similar meeting may have been taking place among the unit commanders who were to launch their attack against Carentan at about the same time.

THE ENEMY COUNTERATTACKS CARENTAN

The 101st attack of June 13 began on schedule with both the 501st and

506th committing their reserve battalions. Almost at once it became obvious that the two regiments were heading into trouble. The 501st was immediately pinned down by heavy fire but managed to hold its defensive position on the left flank during the day. The 506th started out as scheduled. But the area in which the regiment was launching its attack happened to coincide with the German line of attack. The advancing 506th columns found themselves passing German columns and armor going in the opposite direction. A good deal of confusion resulted. The Germans were determined and were using a considerable part of their available armor; a high proportion of the infantry was armed with light machine guns or machine pistols. The 506th found itself in the toughest spot it had ever been in. The regiment had attached to it nine light tanks; two were knocked out almost at once. Within a few minutes it became a question not of conducting an attack but of improvising a defense. By 0700 the right flank was in danger, heavy casualties were being reported from the companies, and Colonel Sink was asking for support. By 1000 he had been given 2d Battalion of the 502d on his right flank, some aerial support by strafing P-47s, and a couple of additional antitank guns. Identified in the attacking force were elements of the 37th and 38th SS Panzergrenadier Regiments, the 17th SS Tank Battalion, and the 6th Parachute Regiment. The German paratroopers, panzermen, and artillery proved too much for the outnumbered defenders and the 506th was backed almost into the town itself. Then came welcome news from General Taylor— American armor was on the way. At 1030 elements of Combat Command A of the 2d Armored Division under command of Col. John H. Collier and accompanied by Brig. Gen. Maurice Rose reached Carentan; how they happened to get there will be explained later.

General Taylor met General Rose and in about fifteen minutes worked out a plan for the use of the armor. At noon Colonel Collier and Lt. Col. Charles H. Chase, 506th executive officer, went forward to reconnoiter. At the same time the rest of the 502d, except for 3d Battalion, crossed the Douve and entered Carentan. At 1400 a task force composed of the 1st Battalion of the 66th Armored Regiment and the 502d less its 3d Battalion, with the 3d Battalion, 327th, attached, moved out on the highway to the southwest, passing through the 506th. Another task force composed of the 3d Battalion of the 41st Armored Infantry Regiment and the 2d Battalion of the 66th Armored Regiment attacked along the road to Baupte. The task forces received close support from the 14th Armored Field Artillery Battalion, both of which had been attached to the Division that day.

German tanks knocked out on the Baupte road during the fighting of 13 June, southwest of Carentan.

The armor and the paratroopers worked out a scheme of action which proved effective. The tanks started down the road in column with the paratroopers deployed on each side, a squad assigned to a tank. The tanks, when they hit the enemy lines, deployed and ran down the hedgerows where the Germans were hiding. As the Germans got up to run or change position, the infantrymen shot them down. Behind this combination came two battalions, mopping up those who had been overlooked. The drive pushed the enemy back several miles and the joint action inflicted approximately five hundred casualties.

One of the companies involved that afternoon was F of the 506th. The company historian, George Goodridge, describes the action:

An enemy tank broke through the Third Phase Line and came clanging toward the Second. It stopped about 150 yards away and was spraying Fox's hedgerow line with cannon and machine guns. One of the tank crew had opened the turret to man the topside machine gun. Everybody was yelling, "Get that damned tank!" In the face of such direct fire a hedgerow cannot stop everything. Kenneth Steinke, Robert Janes and Lester Hegland (lost his Adam's apple) were hit and evacuated. Colonel Chase and Captain Mulvey crawled over to Ostrander, a rifle grenadier. "Why don't you fire at it?" the Fox CO asked.

"The tank's too far away, sir, and I've only got a few rounds left."

"Fire anyway; I'll get you more," said Colonel Chase.

The first grenade bounced off the tank. Ostrander loaded again and fired. Hollywood was out-Hollywooded. The grenade dropped smack inside the tank, dragging the machine gunner back into it and killing the rest of the crew.

"That's one of my boys," Captain Mulvey said proudly to Colonel Chase, patting Ostrander on the back.

A few minutes later Major Horton, S-2 chief, came along with an armful of rifle grenades for Ostrander. Colonel Chase kept his word. Noody and Flick

knocked out a tank also, with their bazookas. But other tanks took their places.
. . . Clyde Jeffers' shoulder strap was cut in two by a piece of flying shrapnel.
"Boy, that was close!" he ejaculated. Yochum let out a wild Indian yell when
a bullet struck his heel. A medic looked it over. "Hell, you don't need a medic,
you need a shoemaker . . ."

Two enemy tanks broke through to the rear and were knocking the battalion
aid building down. When they saw the Red Cross flag in front they stopped
firing, went into the station for some medical supplies and took off again. . . .
Mather worked his way through two hundred yards of murderous fire to
retrieve a machine gun someone had left behind. It had no bipod but he
brought it back anyway. Vogel held it, while Mather fired. Fox men were
fighting well but they were fighting a losing battle. They knew it in their bones.
Kraut machine guns were raking the hedgerow from all angles. Stone, Aebischer
and Ours were evacuated.

At 2:47 clanking sounds were heard above the din of battle. The men kept
glancing in the direction of the road toward Carentan, hopeful. Six light tanks
came flying down the road. The men's spirits reached the sky. German 88 fire
greeted these tanks when they approached the bend and they scooted back
from where they came. Fox men were more depressed than they were before
these tanks arrived. But not for long. At 3:00 sharp a fierce rumbling shook
the road—big, beautiful Shermans of the 2d Armored [Division] came roaring
with armored infantrymen trailing them, men fresh from the beaches and
spoiling for a fight. Fox men didn't yell a single "Hurrah!" or utter a spoken
word. They were simply overwhelmingly thankful.

The tank leaders spotted Fox Company's line and fanned out in front. Those
equipped with bulldozer ploughs crashed through hedgerows as if they were
stiff paper, permitting others to race through. It was wonderful to watch them
at work and many retired to the high ground, the better to watch them. A
tank would stop in a hole made by a brother tankdozer, then turn a sharp right
or left, wherever the Krauts were, and sweep every foot of the hedgerow. When
and what they missed were mopped up and destroyed by the armored infantrymen. The men were treated to an awe-inspiring show of violence and destruction of the highest order. The enemy dissolved before the calm, deliberate fury
of this 2d Armored unit.

The 101st's defense plus this tank-infantry counterattack ruined the
enemy's big chance to retake Carentan and cut the link between the
beaches. That evening the 501st, assisted by tanks, launched an attack
in its sector and by dark was dug in in new defensive positions two
and a half miles from Carentan astride the southwest highway. At
the same time and about the same distance from Carentan on the
501st's right the 502d and the 3d Battalion of the 327th were digging
in to hold the new Division front astride the Baupte highway and
railway. At 2300 the 506th was withdrawn to Division reserve in
Carentan. By the next afternoon, June 14, 506th troops were pulling
town patrol and queuing up for haircuts in the reopened Carentan
barber shops.

While the fighting along the southwest approaches to Carentan was going on another fight was under way to the southeast. Running along the peninsula of high ground to the east of Carentan was the line of the Carentan–Paris railroad. VII Corps had assigned this line to the 101st as an east-west line to be held against the Germans to the south. General Taylor assigned the mission of securing this line to the 327th. In order to insure a successful defense he had extended the assignment to include some connecting high ground to the south of the rail line. This high ground was just south of Montmartin-en-Graignes, a hamlet five miles southeast of Carentan.

Early on the afternoon of the 12th, the 327th, less 3d Battalion and Company G which was left with the 3d, about-faced in its position facing Carentan and started east toward its new objective. Attached to the 327th was the Division Reconnaissance Platoon and five tank destroyers. The march was to be a fast one in column order down the main highway east to the vicinity of Le Mesnil, there to swing south on the road to Val Laquais. At Val Laquais the battalions were to divide, 2d continuing south down the road while 1st moved east, then south, along secondary roads. The battalions were to cross the railroad at 1500, converge on Montmartin-en-Graignes, and pass on through the town to the high ground beyond. Little resistance was expected.

That was the plan of the advance. However, long before they reached the railroad the battalions found themselves under heavy fire from small arms, mortars, and 88s. The 2d Battalion, moving down the main road, found that even the tank destroyers were of little help in maintaining the advance and the battalion moved off the road. In trying to work his battalion forward Lt. Col. Thomas J. Rouzie had noticed that the German resistance seemed to come from small groups scattered through the wooded and heavily underbrushed country. He decided that the best bet would be for the companies to split up, advance in platoons, and reorganize up ahead at a given phase line. A number of casualties had already been suffered including Capt. Ira E. Hamblin of Company E, killed.

Company E, followed by Company F, advanced in the area west of the road and met very strong resistance in the vicinity of Rouxeville and Deville, villages about two miles due west of Montmartin-en-Graignes. Here 2d Battalion took additional casualties including the fatal wounding of the battalion executive, Maj. Warren D. Stubblefield, Jr., and Lt. Willard C. Harrison, Company F executive officer. It was now about 2100 or 2200 hours. Lieutenant Harrison is reported to have died when, after his men had been pinned down for quite a while by

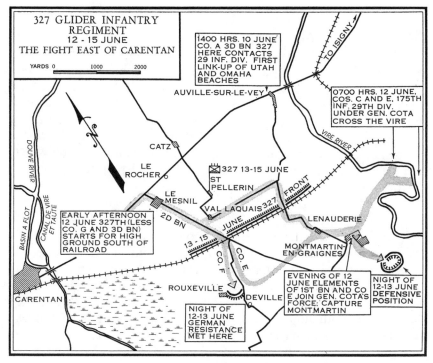

Map 31.

machine-gun fire, he stood up, shouted "Make like a tank!" and charged for the machine-gun nest. The fire cut him almost in two.

Colonel Rouzie moved with a platoon of Company E. This platoon was attacked and lost several killed and wounded in beating off the Germans. During this fight Rouzie's radio operator and 300 radio disappeared, leaving him without contact during the rest of the move through the woods.

Meanwhile, 1st Battalion, under Capt. George P. Nichols, had pushed down to the village of Lenauderie, less than a mile north of Montmartin-en-Graignes. Here it was joined by most of Company E and in a few minutes by the E platoon with which Colonel Rouzie had travelled. Colonel Rouzie borrowed Captain Nichols' radio and raised Colonel Harper, who told him to take command of what there was there of the two battalions. He also ordered Rouzie to push on to Montmartin and take the high ground south of the village; and he gave him news of the rest of his 2d Battalion which was held up but which was to keep going and join him in Montmartin. Company F at that time was still fighting to the west in the vicinity of Rouxeville.

Shortly after his meeting with Nichols and battalion, Colonel Rouzie

241

saw some men wearing the blue-and-gray patches of the 29th Infantry
Division. They told him that they had been fighting off Germans
from all sides, that they were very glad to see him and that their
assistant division commander, Brig. Gen. Norman D. Cota, was with
them. Colonel Rouzie went with them to General Cota. The general
was also very glad to see him and to hear that the 327th was driving
through to Montmartin. They decided to join forces and take the
village and the high ground to the south of it. It was a decision which,
by a devious course, was to effect the fate of the 101st regiments fighting
on the other side of Carentan.

"150 German Tanks in Montmartin"

The 29th Division, one of the divisions landing on Omaha Beach,
had been ordered on the 12th to send a rifle company west across the
Vire River toward Montmartin-en-Graignes to reconnoiter, and to
capture two highway bridges across the Canal de Vire-et-Taute. It
was believed that the Germans might try an armored attack from the
direction of St. Lô against this thinly held section between the two
beachheads; if such an attack developed possession of these bridges
would be of major importance to the American forces. The mission was
assigned to the 175th Infantry Regiment of the 29th, and that regiment
sent two companies, C and E. Accompanying them was General Cota.
The two companies were separated during the crossing of the Vire,
were ambushed and badly shot up. That afternoon, fighting in a tight
spot near Montmartin-en-Graignes, they heard a fire fight going on to
the north; it was the 327th.

The attack on Montmartin-en-Graignes was carried out by the
combined force, Company A of the 327th attacking from the west,
Company C and a platoon of E enveloping the town from the south,
and General Cota's 150 troops attacking straight into the center of the
village. Though Company A was cut off and did not reach the objective
the attack succeeded, Montmartin was taken and some enemy equipment, including a number of bicycles, was destroyed. However, the
enemy continued to fire into the town, so General Cota and Colonel
Rouzie decided to move out to the high ground eight hundred yards
to the south, the 327th's objective, and set up a defense there. This
they did just as dark came.

Meanwhile, back at the 327th command post on the main highway
south of Le Mesnil, Colonel Harper knew very little of what was
developing in these confused actions. He had lost contact with everybody. So he moved his command post down the highway between

1st Battalion and Company E fighting to the east and Company F to the west. With a 300 radio he finally contacted 1st Battalion; they reported that they were pinned down. Another report came that Colonel Rouzie was believed killed. At dark the situation was so disorganized that Colonel Harper ordered 1st Battalion to withdraw to the edge of a woods south of Lenauderie and reorganize. Company F was ordered to withdraw from its position to the west, if possible, and join the regimental command post group. Colonel Harper did not know that Montmartin-en-Graignes had been taken. That night he called Division to ask for armor to push the attack toward the high ground. Col. Gerald J. Higgins, Chief of Staff, told him that there was none available; that, in fact, some was needed at Carentan to use against the Germans southwest of the town. Colonel Harper remained in this command post that night, drawing occasional fire from 327th men who were wandering twisted around in the dark.

Shortly after daylight of the 13th a major walked in and asked if he were in the 327th command post. When told he was, he said that he was from Gen. Omar N. Bradley's First Army Headquarters and had been directed to turn over to Colonel Harper a company of medium tanks, a company of light tanks, and a battalion of armored infantry. To Harper it was an obvious mistake; the gift was undoubtedly for Division at Carentan. When the major insisted, Colonel Harper called Colonel Higgins, telling him that he had enough armor to go on through to St. Lô. Higgins got General Taylor on the phone. General Taylor said for God's sake to hold on to it until he called Corps. In a few minutes he called back and said to send the armor on to Carentan with all speed. The German attack against the 506th was then at the very edge of the town.

Shortly thereafter a message came through from Division for the 327th to draw back to the original corps objective, the line of the railroad. The regimental command post was established in an orchard near St. Pellerin, about half a mile north of the rail line. Colonel Harper went forward to meet the battalion S-3s and to show them their units' new positions. On his return to his command post he found an important message from Division—150 German tanks were in Montmartin-en-Graignes. Just then a naval support fire-control party arrived at the command post with the same story as the armored force major—they had been sent personally by General Bradley and had some cruisers and a battleship offshore to support the 327th. The message from Division made clear to Colonel Harper why he was getting all this armor and fire power and he now realized that he needed it. Almost immediately another stranger arrived—this time a major from the 29th Division with word that General Cota was in Montmartin. If General Cota was in that town, Colonel Harper said, he was either dead or captured. He thereupon told the naval lieutenant to prepare to fire on the town immediately. He also ordered the 65th Armored Field Artillery, the 321st Glider Field Artillery, five attached tank destroyers, and all his 37mm antitank guns to take positions on the high ground back of the railroad. He ordered Company B of the 326th Airborne Engineers, who were attached to the 327th, to destroy the railroad bridges in the sector.

Preparations completed, the 327th and the artillery awaited the German armored attack. The salvos from the warships came over. Harper and his force knew that the town of Montmartin-en-Graignes and, they hoped, the German armor in the town, were taking a pasting. Along the rail line the Americans continued to wait. No attack came.

What had happened was this: During the night, General Cota had reported by radio to the 29th Division that he had observed from the high ground where he was dug in 150 German troops reentering Montmartin-en-Graignes. The message had been garbled in transmission so that it read "150 German tanks." There already existed considerable anxiety in Corps and Army at the time about the possibility of a German attack in this section and the report tended to confirm the belief that this was to be the big attack to cut the connecting link between Omaha and Utah Beaches. Therefore, the formidable support, including the tanks and armored infantry from Combat Command A of the 2d Armored Division, had been sent to Colonel Harper and from him, providentially, to General Taylor in Carentan.

General Cota and his force, fortunately on the high ground back of but not in the shelled town itself, that night managed, after an unsuccessful air resupply by a Cub plane, to fight their way back to the Vire, recrossed, and rejoined the 175th Regiment at midnight of the 13th. Colonel Rouzie, who had been with them, helping hold what had been his own assigned objective, rejoined his 1st Battalion of the 327th that same night. For his part in the fighting of the 12th (at one time, during the close quarters action, he had personally accounted for two Germans) Colonel Rouzie received an Oak Leaf Cluster to the Silver Star he won over a quarter of a century earlier in World War I.

The 327th continued to hold along the railroad during the 14th, maintaining contact with units of the 29th Division on the left. Enemy pressure against this line dwindled. That night the 327th was attached to XIX Corps, which had become operational at noon that day and

A number of 101st men can be identified among these wounded being returned to England on the Queen Empress. The club design on the helmets indicates the 327th.

was on the 101st's left flank, and directly to the 30th Division which had just come ashore. On the morning of the 15th the 30th Division passed through the 327th in an attack to the south. During the afternoon 2d Battalion of the 327th was attached for a few hours to the 120th Infantry Regiment of the 30th Division as a reserve, but reverted back to the 327th, and that night the 327th reverted back to the 101st. By dark of the 15th the 327th was on its way to Carentan, bivouacking that night just out of town.

AFTERMATH AT CARENTAN

On the morning of the 14th the 502d and 3d Battalion, 327th, southwest of Carentan, continued to push out from the Carentan area, mopping up as they went. By 1600 the 502d contacted the 508th Parachute Regiment of the 82d Division at Baupte; the 508th had crossed the Douve and marched down to Baupte that day. This new contact with the 82d Division relieved a possible threat to the western flank in the northern sector of the Division, and the 3d Battalion of the 502d which had been held across the Douve near St. Come-du-Mont, was therefore moved down to join the regiment. The 502d, along with the 501st on its left, also secured the road which runs southeast from

Regimental commanders of the 101st, just decorated with the Silver Star, receive a bouquet from a little girl in Carentan, 20 June. Left to right: Colonels Johnson, Michaelis, Harper, and Sink. Just after this picture was made, German artillery rounds began falling in the square, dispersing troops and civilians.

Baupte to join the Carentan–Périers road. The cleaning out at the triangle Carentan–Baupte–road junction went on rapidly; by night only a few snipers remained in the sector.

The 3d Battalion of the 327th advanced in the general direction of Baupte but ran into little opposition and later in the day went into an assembly area at Auvers, a village east of Baupte. In Carentan, the 506th, now Division reserve, set up a reserve defense just west and southwest of the town.

On the 15th there was a further strengthening of the lines west of the city, but little action. During the afternoon air reconnaissance reported an armored force approaching Carentan from Périers. Plans were made to meet this attack by sending armored elements of Combat Command A forward and by putting the two reserve battalions of the 506th in their prepared defensive positions just west and southwest of Carentan. The attack did not materialize, however. On the 15th the Division was relieved of assignment to VII Corps and assigned to VIII Corps.

Through June 15 the number of prisoners evacuated through the

101st amounted to 876. However, this was no true number; for in the early days many prisoners were taken directly to the Utah Beach Prisoner-of-War Inclosure or were turned over to other units by members of the 101st who failed either to get a receipt or to keep a record of the number.

The next morning, June 16, the 327th was put into the line and given a defensive sector between the 502d and the 501st, reducing the front to be held by each unit. Defensive work continued and the 326th Airborne Engineers put in barbed wire entanglements and laid an antitank-mine belt across the front of the entire Division sector.

On the 17th limited objective attacks were made by the 501st and the 327th to push the outpost line forward on the left in order to improve observation to the south and southwest. The objectives were attained and the new outpost line was established by evening.

Actually, these final small actions of the 16th and 17th represented the last real fighting of the Normandy campaign for the Division. For the next two weeks, until the 83d Division relieved the 101st on June 29, the parachutists and glidermen continued to hold their defensive position south and southwest of Carentan. The position was a strong one, linked on the right near Baupte to the 82d Airborne, and flanked on both sides by swamps. Any attack would have to come along the peninsula of high ground which the Division now had well covered and well mined. The main fault of this line was that nowhere was it more than four miles from the east-west highway and railway through Carentan, so that for many days the bridges near the town were subject to shelling by guns of caliber as small as 88mm. This vulnerability was made evident during a presentation of the Silver Star to officers and men of the Division in the Carentan town square on the evening of June 20. As representative platoons of the various Division units stood in formation for the ceremony artillery shells began to fall in the square. The square quickly cleared.

One purpose of the engineer-built bridge downstream near Brevands was to provide some insurance against the capture or blocking of the Carentan bridges. Cutting of the link between the two beaches in the vicinity of Carentan would have presented a real danger during these days when units were being shifted up and down the peninsula. The small number of troops assigned to hold this corridor, as represented by the 101st and its attached units, was a calculated risk which the First Army assumed in order to keep the bulk of its troops available for the cutting of the peninsula and the capture of Cherbourg, after which the forces could be brought back to drive the enemy farther

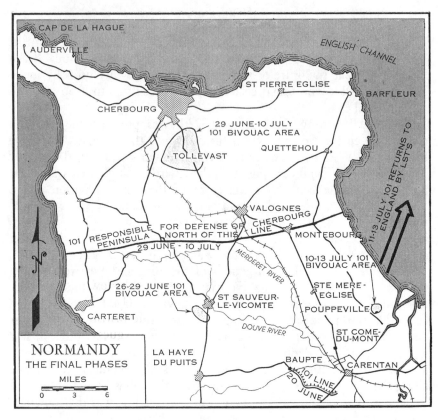

Map 32.

to the south. It was a gamble which, due in large measure to the 101st's alertness and courage, worked.

St. Sauveur-le-Vicomte

On June 26 the 101st received orders from VIII Corps to send one combat team to the vicinity of St. Sauveur-le-Vicomte, fifteen miles northwest of Carentan, to take up a defensive position astride the main road south of the town. The remainder of the Division would follow the next day and the entire Division would take up a tactical bivouac position generally west of St. Sauveur-le-Vicomte. Accordingly the 501st, the 907th Glider Field Artillery and Battery C of the 81st Antiaircraft Battalion took up the assigned position by dark. The rest of the Division, except for the 2d Battalion of the 502d, followed on the 27th, the Division command post closing at Carentan at 2100 and opening at St. Sauveur-le-Vicomte at the same hour. The 83d Division took over the old sector. The 2d Battalion, 502d, joined the Division the next morning. At noon the 101st was ordered to move to a bivouac area at Tollevast, four miles south of Cherbourg, and was given the responsibility of defending the Cherbourg Peninsula north of an east-west line through Montebourg, about half way between Carentan and Cherbourg. VII Corps troops had taken complete control of the city of Cherbourg on the 27th and on July 1 had wiped out the last resistance on the North Cherbourg Peninsula near Cap de la Hague.

The movement to Tollevast began on the 29th and all elements of the Division closed in the new area by 2100. For the first time since England the Division was assembled in one area. The next day sectors of responsibility were assigned to the various units and patrolling of the area began.

On July 7, standing on a German pillbox near Cherbourg, General Taylor looked down on his now battle-tested veterans. "You hit the ground running toward the enemy. You have proved the German soldier is no superman. You have beaten him on his own ground, and you can beat him on any ground." Then Gen. (later Field Marshal) Sir Bernard Law Montgomery pinned on him the British Distinguished Service Order. Probably nobody there that day guessed that in less than three months the Division would go into its second action under the overall command of this Englishman.

After not quite two weeks in this quiet sector the Division was relieved and on July 10 moved by trucks to a bivouac area just back of the beach proper at Utah. There, in the vicinity of where they had jumped, glided, or come ashore the officers and men of the Screaming Eagle Division loaded onto LSTs. On July 13 the Division's LSTs put into Southampton, England. During the month of June the 101st had suffered a total of 4,670 casualties; of the six divisions in VII Corps only the 4th Division had a greater casualty total. The 101st had completed all its missions. Two years before Gen. William C. Lee had told his men, "You have a rendezvous with destiny." Those men now knew they had kept faith with Bill Lee.

NOTES

[1] A somewhat different account of the capture of La Barquette locks is given in Capt. Laurence Critchell's history of the 501st Parachute Infantry Regiment, *Four Stars of Hell.*

[2] "I followed this same battalion through the airborne invasion of Holland in September, 1944, and through the winter fighting in the Ardennes, and I doubt that there has ever been a finer fighting unit in the Army of the United States. It never tasted defeat nor was it ever given an easy assignment. At least three of its engagements are historically noteworthy examples of heroically successful achievement against great odds." Col. S. L. A. Marshall in *Men Against Fire.*

Col. George Van Horn Moseley, Jr., who broke his leg on the Normandy jump, welcomes his old regiment back to England. Facing Moseley is his successor, Lt. Col. John H. Michaelis. Behind Michaelis is Lt. Col. Paul A. Danahy, G-2. Behind Moseley, G-2. Behind Moseley are three members of the 502d's Medical Detachment, Captains Allen Ramay and Rice J. Turner, Jr., and Major Douglas T. Davidson (Hands on pack).

English Summer

To the airborne troopers returning from their first combat experience England in the summer of 1944 was a pleasant place. Almost the only ground troops to come back had been the wounded; the Channel crossing was still one-way for soldiers. The successes of the two American airborne divisions had been well publicized and the English greeted them with enthusiasm. The troopers responded in kind, glad to find civilians who spoke a language they could understand. They spread out on passes, furloughs and leaves to London, to Scotland, and to the familiar neighboring towns.

When they got back to their camps the re-equipping, reorganizing and training began. After that came rumors, true and false, trips to the marshalling areas, dry runs and finally the wet run to Holland. It was, for the 101st, a summer of alarms and excursions.

THE WESTERN FRONT: SUMMER 1944

When the 101st left the Continent in July the Allied forces there consisted of the U. S. First and the British Second Armies which together formed the 21st Army Group commanded by Field Marshal Montgomery. By the middle of July these armies had expanded the original beachheads to include the entire Cherbourg Peninsula and the key road junctions of St. Lô and Caen. From the vicinity of these towns General Eisenhower ordered a breakthrough and a drive across France.

The breakthrough began on July 18 when, after the heaviest and most concentrated air assault ever employed to support a ground operation, the British Second Army attacked south and southeast of Caen. The U. S. First Army, which had been scheduled to attack southward out of the Cherbourg Peninsula the following day, was held up by bad weather until the 25th; then it attacked and broke through west of St. Lô. This drive unhinged the German left, anchored at the port town of Avranches, and opened the way for the armor of the newly formed and highly mobile U. S. Third Army. General Patton poured his tanks through the gap and by the end of August the Allied armies had freed Paris and were across the Seine both east and west of that city. By the middle of September the Canadian First Army, which became operational on July 23, had isolated the Channel ports of Le Havre, Boulogne, Calais and Dunkirk and had reached almost to the Scheldt (Escaut) Estuary in Holland; the British Second Army had reached Antwerp and had established a bridgehead across the Escaut Canal in Belgium; the American First Army had reached the Siegfried Line from Aachen to Luxembourg; and the American Third

Army in southeast France had established bridgeheads across the Moselle River both above and below Nancy.

The First Allied Airborne Army

During the summer something new was added to the Allied lineup— an airborne army. The effectiveness of the airborne operations in aiding the Normandy landings had convinced General Eisenhower that large airborne forces could and should be used as part of major offensives. After going over the matter with Generals Marshall and Arnold, General Eisenhower formed the First Allied Airborne Army. Included in this Army were the U. S. 17th, 82d and 101st Airborne Divisions, forming the U. S. XVIII Airborne Corps; the Polish 1st Parachute Brigade; and three British divisions, the 1st and 6th Airborne and the 52d Lowlanders (air-transported). Also incorporated were the U. S. IX Troop-Carrier Command and its British equivalent, the RAF 38th Group. As commander of XVIII Corps, General Eisenhower selected Maj. Gen. Matthew B. Ridgway of the 82d Airborne Division. To lead the airborne army he named Lt. Gen. Lewis H. Brereton, commander of the Ninth Air Force and the officer to whom, in 1918, Brig. Gen. William (Billy) Mitchell had given the job of working out the details of the first planned use of airborne troops.

The "First Triple A," as the Army was called, began operations on August 8. Quickly assembling a staff, General Brereton put it to work on plans for using his divisions in the battle going on across the Channel. Even before that date, though, plans for the employment of airborne units were being turned out and becoming obsolete as the fast-moving ground troops in France overran what were to have been the airborne objectives.

Operation Cancelled

That Supreme Headquarters, even before the invasion, had in mind other possible summer missions for the 101st is indicated in a statement in the Neptune plans: "There is a strong possibility that it will be necessary to re-emplane personnel from the 82d and 101st Airborne Divisions a second time at approximately Y [Ready day] plus 35." This date was based, of course, on the assumption that the airborne divisions would be very quickly relieved and returned to their home bases—an assumption which was often made but, in the case of the 101st, never realized during the war. After the Division returned sixteen Allied airborne operations got into the paper stage and several came close enough to execution that airborne units went into the marshalling areas and were only hours away from emplaning.

Of the operations planned by the First AAA to be carried out during the summer of 1944 the 101st figured in three: Transfigure, Linnet I and Linnet II. Operation Transfigure, planned for the latter part of August, was to be a drop in the area southwest of Paris to close the Paris–Orléans gap. Orléans, on the Loire River, is seventy miles south of Paris, which is on the Seine. The destruction by the Allied Air Forces of the bridges over these two rivers had forced the Germans to route part of their supplies from the east to Normandy through this gap between the rivers; in the face of the German defeat in Normandy and Brittany it was apparent that the gap was one of the most convenient avenues of retreat from Western France. An airborne drop into this gap might cut off reinforcements and supplies from Germany to the forces in the west and block it as an escape route.

The airborne force for Operation Transfigure, under the overall command of Lt. Gen. F. A. M. Browning, commander of British airborne troops, was to be made up of the 101st Airborne Division, the British 1st Airborne Division, the Polish 1st Parachute Brigade and the U. S. 878th Airborne Aviation Engineer Battalion. A follow-up force, the British 52d Lowlanders Division, was to be airlanded on seized landing strips.

The British 1st Airborne was to drop in the vicinity of Rambouillet, twenty-five miles southwest of Paris. The Polish Brigade was to land southeast of Rambouillet. The 101st was to make a daylight landing on D-day morning in the Sonchamp–Ablis area, south of Rambouillet and on the Paris–Chartres highway.

Within the Division zone the 502d, with a detachment of the 326th Engineers, was to land near the village of Sonchamps, seize a glider landing area and link up with the British at La Hunière. The 506th, with an engineer attachment, was to block the Chartres–Paris highway and to seize the road center of St. Arnoult on that highway. It was also to block the highway east out of Chartres. The 501st was to assemble north of the village of Ablis on the Chartres–Paris highway and to seize and protect a glider landing zone there. Later it was to move to the area east of St. Arnoult-en-Yvelines and assume the defense of the sector. The 327th Glider Infantry Regiment was to come in by glider and assemble at the village of Chatonville.

The planning allowed an earliest possible D-day of August 19; on the 17th General Patton's armor reached Chartres and Dreux and by the 19th the gap was blocked. Transfigure became a might-have-been operation. The 101st and the other alerted divisions moved from the marshalling areas back to their camps. One thousand forty officers and men of the 101st's seaborne "tail" who had landed on Omaha Beach on August 14 and left their marshalling area at St. Laurent-sur-Mer on August 22 and returned to England.

The rapid advance of the Allied armies across France during the summer not only tended to overrun the Airborne Army's planned drop zones before the airborne missions were carried out, but it also diverted the planes necessary for these missions. Because of the German decision to hang on to the Brittany and Channel ports the Allies had to depend on the overworked Normandy bases for their supplies. There weren't enough trucks to shuttle the supplies up the ever-lengthening roads to the fronts. Consequently, the transport planes assigned to the First AAA as well as bombers had to be diverted to hauling supplies.

The withdrawing of the planes [reported General Eisenhower] caused considerable embarrassment to the Airborne Army's commander, Lt. Gen. L. H. Brereton, whose program of training was thereby interrupted. He justly pointed out that there was a risk that continued cargo carrying would render the troop carrier commands unfit for a successful airborne operation. Since the procedure and training required for the two functions were in many respects diametrically opposed, combined exercises by airborne troops and the air transport personnel were of the utmost importance. I consider, however, that my decision to use the planes for ground resupply purposes was justified by the fact that thereby the speed of our armies' advances was maintained, and as a consequence of this the projected airborne operations in France were rendered unnecessary.

Transfigure was followed by Linnet I, an operation planned for the area near Tournai, Belgium, a large town just across the border from the city of Lille in the northwest corner of France. The operation was to put the airborne forces down in front of the British Second Army and expedite its drive into Belgium and across the Escaut Canal. It would also present a major threat to the enemy lines of communication and thereby cause him to divert from the main battle going on in France troops he could hardly spare. This, it was believed, would create opportunities for enveloping and destroying a large enemy force by a combined action of the airborne troops and the oncoming British Second Army. Taking part in the operation would be the 82d and 101st Airborne Divisions, the British 1st Airborne Division, the Polish 1st Parachute Brigade, and the U. S. 878th Airborne Aviation Engineer Battalion. The British and the Poles were to land several miles north of Tournai, the 82d immediately to the north and east of the town, and the 101st on DZs and LZs on three sides of the town. The 101st mission was to seize the road center of Tournai and the town's bridges.

The 501st, less its 3d Battalion, was to land two miles west of Tournai,

seize the village of Marquain and nearby high ground and block off
any enemy movement from the direction of Lille. The 3d Battalion
was to land two miles south of Tournai and seize the village of St.
Maur. The 506th was to drop on the same drop zone as the 3d Battalion
of the 501st and was to move north and seize the half of Tournai that
lay west of the Escaut River (the river flowing north through the
town). The 502d, with Company C of the 326th Engineers, was to
land two miles east of the town and, leaving one battalion to protect
a glider landing zone, was to take the section of Tournai east of the
Escaut. The 327th, after a glider landing, was to assemble southeast of
Tournai, put out patrols to the east and south and be prepared to
support the action of the Division.

On September 2 the Guards Armored Division of the British Second.
Army captured Tournai; that night Linnet I was cancelled.

An alternative plan, Linnet II, calling for the general groupings and
drop patterns, was projected at about the same time as Linnet I and
was cancelled on September 3, one day after Linnet I. This plan would
have landed the airborne force in the area between the Belgian fortress
city of Liège on the Meuse River and the Dutch border city of Maas-
tricht. The 101st was to have dropped to the west of Liège and to have
seized the high ground dominating the roads running east and southeast between the village of Viernay and the Meuse bridges at Kessala
and Bressou.

Preparation for Operation Market

Planning for Operation Market went into high gear immediately
following the cancellation of Linnet I and II. By September 11 the
developments had reached the stage where the Division's unit commanders and certain other officers were briefed.

The following is a transcript of the briefing by Colonel Millener,
the Division Chief-of-Staff:

Colonel Millener: There is a possibility of an operation to take place in the
area northeast of Antwerp. The entire airborne effort is designed to assist the
advance of British 2d Army into Holland and into positions from which it
can attack eastward into Germany. Using as axis of advance for this movement
and establishment of bridgehead over the delta streams of the Rhine; De Groote,
Eindhoven, Uden, Grave, Nijmegen, and Arnhem. The over-all mission is the
securing of that route and various crossings and critical points for use of British
Second Army by airborne forces. Airborne Forces will be 82d Airborne Division,
British First Airborne Division with Polish Brigade attached and 101st Airborne
Division and probably 878th Engineer Battalion attached to 101st. British First Air-
borne Division landing in position to secure crossings at Nijmegen and Grave. Our

mission, as described by General Browning, is to form a carpet along the axis of advance to assist and assure the speedy advance of British Second Army, which will be spearheaded by British XXX Corps. Air lift will be the same as for Linnet. No double tow. Signals as for Linnet with certain additional radio links between 101st Airborne Division and British XXX Corps and British Second Army. Air supply to be figured ten days. Seaborne tails will be set up as for Linnet and be scheduled to leave after departure of airborne elements. The earliest possible time is September 14, Thursday. Decision to be made by General Brereton late this afternoon as to actual time. This decision is to be based on seventy-two hours after receipt of photographic coverage and as yet none has been received. One or two points are obviously the same as for Linnet. Our parachute elements and small glider echelon which was scheduled for first day in Linnet will be the same. First priority will be for parachute elements on D-day and small glider echelon, and balance of glider echelons to be scattered over three-day period. All elements will be sealed upon departure of first unit to marshalling area. As far as money is concerned, the Finance Officer is trying to get the coin of realm now. Exact plans for several points cannot be discussed by me at this time. Object of this conference was primarily to give a general idea of the area to go into and as operation and warning order for what to expect. It is hoped that all units will go to the some departure airdromes as much as possible. There will be some shifting in order for certain units to be dispatched in their proper sequence.

Colonel Sherburne: Passes are off now?

Colonel Millener: No, regular 2300 passes for tonight and depending on what we get later today.

Colonel Moore: Some units have lost their battle casualty booklets. Contact AGO to get replacements of these booklets. Partial payrolls will not be feasible at this time. Teams from Finance Department will be detailed to each field to swap money. If each man doesn't have at least a pound note left, it will just be tough!

Major Danahy: Civilians inside of camp areas will have to be expelled. Of course, those civilians that work or have to enter camp will be admitted but not to unit areas.

Captain Robinette: Unit commanders send in this afternoon their actual strength of participating parachute units, so correct lists may be made up.

Colonel Moore: Parachute school has some men in school at the present time that are not due to graduate until Saturday.

Colonel Millener: Let the school run throughout today and we will probably cancel same tomorrow.

Colonel Harper: How about letting them make a couple of jumps?

General Higgins: Let you know later about that. Will talk to you after the meeting.

Colonel Millener: Any more questions? Well, that is all I have.

For Operation Market the takeoff fields and the D-day parachute serials were as follows: from Aldermaston, 90 aircraft with the 501st less the 3d Battalion; from Chilbolton, 45 aircraft with the 3d Battalion of the 501st and 45 aircraft with the 3d Battalion of the 506th, each battalion with a platoon of the 326th Engineers; from Membury, 90 aircraft with the 506th less the 3d Battalion; from Welford, 45 aircraft with the 1st Battalion of the 502d, 9 aircraft with Division Headquarters, 7 with Company C of the 326th Engineers, and 3 with personnel from Division Artillery; and from Greenham Common, 90 planes with the 502d less the 1st Battalion. The D-day glider serials, all departing from Ramsbury, were as follows: Division Headquarters, 8 gliders; Signal Company, 14 gliders; Reconnaissance Platoon, 15 gliders; 326th Medical Company, 6 gliders; Division Artillery, 3 gliders, and 24 gliders carrying jeeps for the three parachute regiments.

The D plus 1 (September 18) glider serials were to be as follows: from Ramsbury, 23 gliders with the 327th, 19 gliders with Division Headquarters, 18 gliders with the Division Signal Company, 8 gliders carrying 502d jeeps and 2 carrying 501st jeeps; from Aldermaston, 58 gliders with the 327th, 20 gliders with 501st jeeps, and 2 gliders with General McAuliffe and his party; from Welford, 54 gliders carrying the 326th Medical Company and an attached medical platoon and 6 gliders carrying 502d jeeps; from Greenham Common, 7 gliders with 506th jeeps, 8 with 502d jeeps, 40 with the 377th Parachute FA Battalion and 25 with the 426th Quartermaster Company; from Chilbolton, 65 gliders with the 326th Engineers and 15 gliders with 506th jeeps; and from Membury, 80 gliders with troops of the 2d Battalion, 327th.

On D plus 2 (September 19) the following glider serials were to take off: from Welford, 18 gliders with troops from the 327th, 21 gliders with Division Artillery personnel, 22 gliders with the 377th FA Battalion, and a glider assigned to the 81st AA Battalion; from Membury, 41 gliders with the 1st Battalion of the 327th, 40 gliders with the 907th FA Battalion, and 1 glider from the 326th Engineers; from Aldermaston, 40 gliders with the 81st AA Battalion and 40 gliders with the 321st FA Battalion; from Chilbolton, 41 gliders with the 1st Battalion of the 327th and 40 gliders with the 907th FA Battalion; and from Greenham Common, 40 gliders with the 81st AA Battalion, 31 gliders with the 321st FA Battalion and 9 gliders with the 907th FA Battalion. Two of the 327th gliders failed to make the flight and 22 Division Artillery gliders instead of 21 took off.

On D plus 3 a parachute serial, Battery B of the 377th Parachute FA Battalion, was to take off from Ramsbury in 12 aircraft.

The last glider serials to make the trip into Holland took off on D plus 6: from Greenham Common, 20 gliders of the 907th FA Battalion, 11 gliders of the 81st AA Battalion, 3 gliders of the Signal Company and 1 glider each of the 326th Engineers, 327th Glider Infantry, 321st FA Battalion, and the Division Ordnance Company;

and from Membury, 39 gliders of the 907th FA Battalion and 8 gliders of the 327th. These were all gliders which had returned to their departure bases on D-day, D plus 1, and D plus 2.

On D plus 8 (September 25) the last of the Holland-bound troops to go in by air left England, approximately five hundred officers and men of the 327th and the 907th FA Battalion taking off in C-47s from Aldermaston and airlanding near Brussels.

Sergeant Koskimaki's Summer

Sgt. George Koskimaki, who jumped into Normandy in General Taylor's stick as his radio operator, chronicled the summer with all its pleasures, worries, preparations, rumors, alarms, and dry and wet runs.

July 13: Landed at 3 P.M. Our Division band played as we marched off the boat. Arrived in Newbury at 5 PM. Got "beered up" at Maggie's tonight. *July 14:* Got paid $160 today. Had a beer party; then Goosen, Chapman, Hickman and I left on furlough. We drank my champagne on the train. *July 15:* We got to Edinburgh, Scotland, this afternoon. *July 17:* We took off for Newcastle. It looked like God's country with no GIs. *July 18:* People here look at us as if we were oddities. I guess they've never seen airborne troops before. *July 22:* Got back to Newbury at 0300. *July 24:* Had reveille this morning but no training schedule to follow. *July 25:* Start training Thursday for the new mission. I'd like to know how this one will work out. *July 26:* Rumors are out that we will take a boat trip to the Mediterranean area soon. *July 27:* The training program started this morning and it is really rough. *July 29:* Had an inspection today in barracks, first one since the first of May. *July 31:* Hart got back from the hospital today. He had been hurt in one of the glider crashes that killed some of our boys.

August 1: We fired all weapons on the range today. I shot the carbine, M-1, Thompson sub-machine gun and the .45 Colt. *August 4:* We got back from a night problem today. *August 6:* We helped a British farmer with his wheat this afternoon. We shocked wheat all afternoon and then went swimming in the mill pond. *August 7:* Listened to the 299 radio today to Axis Sally, the German gal who plays swing music for the American soldiers. *August 8:* Things are beginning to move fast again. Something is gonna pop. *August 9:* Lt. Carter said today that we had been scheduled to jump Sunday morning on the Brittany Peninsula but conditions improved so we are off the alert again. *August 10:* Had a Division review today at Hungerford for Gen. Eisenhower. He inspected all the troops. Troop Carrier Command was also there. We'll be in combat soon again. *August 12:* Got 50 more guys in the company today. We started getting our brand-new equipment today. We're hot again so it's combat again soon. *August 13:* Packed our bed rolls today. Turned them in before midnight. All the boys are running back and forth not knowing what is going on. *August 14:* Really busy today. The seaborne troops left today. We got our chutes again today. Second combat jump is coming soon. *August 15:* Sweating out our second D-day. We know what it is like now so it is a lot harder. We leave for the marshalling area today. *August 16:* Had our briefing tonight. Scheduled to jump near Paris tomorrow morning for our second D-day. *August 17:* Jump was postponed 24 hours so we got in some more briefing. Scheduled to jump at 0850 tomorrow morning. *August 18:* During the night the mission was called off because General Patton had reached our jump area with his tanks. We returned to our company area at Newbury at noon. *August 21:* "Moose" Lawler is back with the company today. He was hurt in a D-day glider crash. *August 22:* Seaborne troops got back from France today. Having real Limey weather (rain). Lawler and I took in a show in town. *August 23:* Were to have jumped today but the weather was bad. *August 24:* Have a Division CPX problem tonight and tomorrow. *August 25:* Furloughs are gonna be given again so maybe I'll get the one I didn't get this spring. *August 26:* Some of the boys left on furlough this evening. *August 29:* Today all furloughs and overnight passes were cancelled. Again we are making rapid preparations for a mission. Got parachutes today. *August 30:* Had a company dance in town. A company formation was called at midnight. Had to pack our bags to leave at 0800 for the marshalling area. *August 31:* Arrived at the marshalling area this morning. First ones there this time. We get foreign money again tomorrow after the briefings. It isn't France.

September 1: We helped the glider boys load up today. I found out that we are scheduled to jump in Belgium, just behind the Maginot line. We get briefed tomorrow. *September 2:* Had our briefing today. This should be our toughest mission. I'm jumping a 50-lb. radio on my leg. We take off at 0702 tomorrow morning. *September 3:* Our mission was called off at midnight because the American 1st Army reached our objective. We shall wait here until we get a new mission. *September 4:* Were scheduled to jump at Liège near the German border but the weather became too bad for any flying. *September 5:* Today is our 1st anniversary overseas. Got paid today and most of the boys lost it all at craps. We're back at Newbury. *September 6:* A lot of rumors are floating about of our leaving soon for the South Pacific or India. It looks like a long way back to the States. *September 8:* Are planning loads for C-47 planes in case we are used as air-landing troops or maybe we shall fly part way to the South Pacific. *September 9:* Rumors of a movement to the South Pacific continue so there must be some truth in it. It may come this month—we don't know. *September 11:* Twenty-four-hour passes were cancelled again today and the war room is under strict guard. If we go to the marshalling area again we'll go on a "wet run." *September 12:* We had our first football practice today— also the heat is off again. *September 13:* We got some new football equipment today but something may start cooking before our uniforms arrive. *September 14:* Things are mighty hot for us again. We leave for the marshalling area. One officer said that this was positively a "wet run." *September 15:* I learned we were gonna pave the way for the British 2d Army. Mission is in Holland to capture and hold vital bridges. *September 16:* Were briefed today and received our foreign currency. Got ammo and made final checkups. We land in Holland at 1330 tomorrow.

Sergeant Koskimaki's next entry, that of September 17, began: "I'm writing from a slit trench . . ."

Holland

Holland is the story of a road—of the men who fought and died to get it and keep it open.

It was not a long road—not in comparison with the tremendous distances of this war—running less than one hundred miles through Holland from the Belgian border north to the Zuyder Zee.

The 101st's part of it was much shorter, twenty miles or less, from Eindhoven through Zon and St. Oedenrode to Vechel and Uden.

The 101st will not forget how it landed near those cities, drove the enemy out, took the bridges and kept the road clear, waiting for the clank of British armor moving up the corridor they created.

Long they waited. But finally they heard the rattle of the treads, and the tanks rolled past them. They knew they were doing their job.

The 101st was lucky. Farther north other men waited for the clank of those same tanks. But they never heard them.

The Eagle Division remembers many things about Holland. A "parade ground jump." Clean people whom they liked. Strangely spelled city names that they learned to pronounce correctly. Easy victories, followed by desperately hard ones. And a succession of maneuvers and movements up and down and around that road that left them trying to figure out just what happened.

It is not hard to understand why this fighting was always unusual and frequently desperate. Twenty miles of road is more than a division is supposed to defend, especially when the road is a corridor inviting attack from both sides, a corridor that threatens to cut off a desperate enemy whose available resources of men and matériel are much greater.

Against such odds, the troopers had the advantage of surprise, individual courage, and of joint resourcefulness. Men were not afraid to carry out their orders. Nor were they afraid to ignore them.

Airborne soldiers had never been trained for joint attacks with British tanks. But the closest kind of cooperation was quickly worked out, successfully. When battle lines became confused, division artillerymen sent shells over the nearest enemy units into the rear of more distant German groups which were blocking a paratrooper advance not away from but toward their guns. Nor was such improvising confined to the battle front. Airborne ordnance over a long period made fifth-echelon repairs with third-echelon equipment. In a way entirely different from Normandy, Holland presented a challenge.

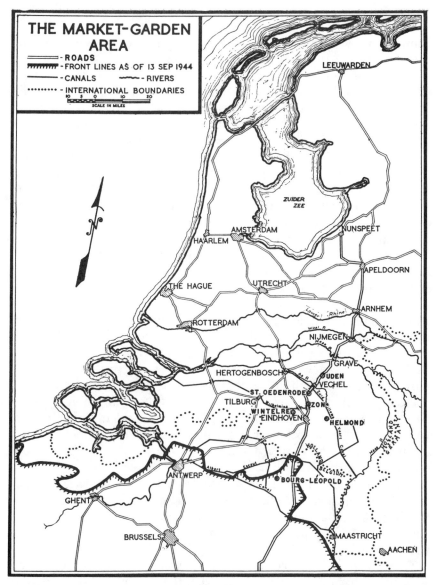

Map 33.

The Why of the Operation

It was one of the unusual combinations of circumstances characteristic of war that placed the 101st Airborne Division on that stretch of road on September 17, 1944.

Throughout August and early September the German armies were on the run, retreating across France and Belgium. The American

261

Third Army was advancing on Nancy, and getting ready to take the city. The First Army had cleared out portions of Belgium and France, and was crossing the German border to approach Aachen, a city whose name was shortly to make daily appearances in American headlines. To its north the British Second Army also had driven across Belgium and was fighting along the line of the Escaut Canal, with one bridgehead across the canal barely touching the Dutch border. Since the Germans had had no opportunity to establish solid defense lines, the British did not expect to be stopped in Holland. But they did fear interminable delay, for the many canals and rivers would make it easy for the defenders to hold them up at one point after another while the Germans built up a real line of defense on their own frontier.

In contrast, Allied grand strategy required breakthrough progress here. Germany must be invaded first from the north. The reasons for this conviction on the part of the High Command have been the subject of much controversy since the war. General Marshall perhaps put the case for the choice of this northern route to Germany most effectively when he advised interested parties to take a look at the map of Europe. In spite of the rivers and canals, the terrain up here is obviously much more suitable as an invasion pathway than that which confronted General Bradley down in the central part of the battle line. There must also have been the hope that quick success in the north would make it possible to get the port of Antwerp functioning quickly, with all that that meant in the relief of the supply problem, which otherwise must get worse before it got better. And there no doubt existed the feeling that the northern route would lead more quickly to the elimination of the Ruhr industrial area from the war.

The major advantage to be gained from the September operation was readily apparent. A thrust north across the Rhine would flank the Siegfried Line and place the Allied armies in a position to pour out across the Westphalia Plain, an area where armored maneuver was possible.

The British Second Army, unaided, was probably incapable of such a thrust at that time. Though captured, the nearby port of Antwerp was not yet operating, for German troops still dominated its approaches. Second Army supply lines stretched 250 miles from Normandy ports. All its transport was being used to the limit to keep one corps fighting.

But in the month before, the High Command had forged an instrument designed for such a situation—the First Allied Airborne Army. In early September, when the High Command began to wonder how to "beef up" the British to help them across the Rhine, General

Brereton was enthusiastic about having his Airborne Army do the job. For his part, General Montgomery insisted that this airborne assistance, in addition to quantities of American supply units and equipment, was essential to the plan. So, on September 10 the operation was decided on in which airborne troops were to play the initial role, unrolling a carpet before advancing ground forces.

The road was the key to the operation—the road and the towns through which it passed and the bridges over which it ran. The road and its bridges were all-important because they were the only way to get armor over the canals and rivers that crisscrossed this part of Holland.

Not the least remarkable thing about this operation is the fact that this road runs north, not east. But it does lead across the Rhine and that was what counted.

First Allied Airborne Army was to drop from the skies behind enemy lines and seize key spots all along this road, converting it into a corridor through enemy land. Simultaneously breaking through the German defenses around its Escaut Canal bridgehead, the British XXX Corps was to strike north up the road, led by the tanks of the Guards Armored Division. With all strategic points already in Airborne hands it was felt that XXX Corps could rapidly push through to the Zuyder Zee, hitting the coast in the vicinity of Nunspeet. However long it took to get to Nunspeet, it was to reach Arnhem within forty-eight hours—for airborne troops, without standard artillery, tanks or effective resupply, were not expected to hold out longer than that. Two flank British corps, VIII and XII, would follow later to widen and strengthen the corridor. Once this corridor across the Rhine had been established, other larger operations would exploit its usefulness in the defeat of Germany.

Far to the north where the road ran across the Lower Rhine, at Arnhem, the British 1st Airborne Division was to drop. South of it where the road crossed the Waal at Nijmegen and the Maas at Grave the American 82d Airborne was to seize it.

The 101st's job was the 16-mile stretch that began behind the German front line, at Eindhoven, and ran north through Zon, St. Oedenrode, Vechel and Uden.

As outlined originally by General Browning, the plan called for a scattered drop by the 101st, and the simultaneous seizure of seven points along the highway from south of Eindhoven to north of Uden. General Taylor, mindful of the Normandy experience, protested this over-dispersion to General Browning but the best he could do was to obtain permission to visit General Dempsey, British Second Army commander in Belgium. After listening to General Taylor, General Dempsey readily agreed to the plan actually employed, whereby the Division landed in two principal areas, sheltered by water barriers. General Dempsey also agreed that Eindhoven had to be a secondary objective on the time schedule, a fact which later became of great importance.

The 101st was to seize the rail and highway bridges over the Aa River and the Zuid Willems Vaart Canal near Vechel, the highway bridges over the Dommel River at St. Oedenrode, over the Wilhelmina Canal near Zon and again over the Dommel River at Eindhoven. The Division was to hold those towns.

This job was crucial and had to be done fast. The Guards Armored was to reach the 101st first; it had to pass through the Division's area to get to the others farther north. In recognition of this fact the 101st was given priority on resupply until XXX Corps had reached it. XXX Corps received operational control over the Division as soon as it landed.

Even after the Guards Armored had passed through, the 101st was responsible for the security of its section of the corridor. As it turned out, the heaviest fighting took place during this second phase, after XXX Corps had advanced beyond the 101st area, but before the British flank corps had come up.

The Division's stretch of road was too long to be held as a tactical unit. The best that could be done was to set up perimeter defenses at the crucial points and attempt to cover the ground in between and keep the Germans off balance by strong aggressive patrol actions.

The whole operation was a novel and risky one. Sixty miles of corridor that, like a chain, was only as strong as its weakest link— airborne troops dropped 16 to 60 miles beyond their front lines—a corps advancing up a single road with two German armies on its left flank doomed to be cut off should the operation succeed. It could be called an operation on a shoestring, and the road would be the shoestring.

Hope for the success of the over-all operation could be based on the element of surprise, and on the condition of German troops in the area. Some of them were known to be still disorganized after their wild retreat across France. Others were rear-area outfits which were not expected to show much stomach for battle.

They didn't. And there were times when the offensive seemed to come within a hair's breadth of success. But such times were fleeting, and perhaps illusory. An indication of this was that the German High Command never pulled troops back from the front-line fighting in the Antwerp region to use against the corridor. Had the enemy really feared the corridor, he would probably have used all possible troops against it.

THE TERRAIN

The proverbial pancake is no flatter than much of Holland through which the 101st Division fought. Only the sand dunes of the Weibosche-Eerde area rise appreciably above the surrounding country. The fields, whether they are large meadows or small cultivated plots, are generally lined with rows of poplars. Such tree rows, however, are merely tree rows; not the complicated hedgerows of Normandy. Small patches of woods dot the area. The only real forest that affected the action was just to the north of the Wilhelmina Canal, between Zon and Best.

Water was ever-present. It came down as rain. It was found in the numerous small drainage ditches and in the rivers and canals. These canals were the major water barriers, sixty feet wide, and deep enough to drown in. The rivers, like so many European rivers, were ridiculously small, the Dommel at Eindhoven less than 15 feet across; the Dommel at St. Oedenrode and the Aa at Vechel not more than 25 feet.

Towns and villages were of solid Dutch construction, with brick and stone predominant.

Tanks were road-bound primarily because they could cross the canals only at the road bridges. When it became necessary for them to lash out through the fields, they were frequently able to do so until they were forced to cross another water barrier.

The road itself was of asphalt in some places, brick in others. Automobiles could pass each other comfortably on it. But for large trucks passing was a tight squeeze. The shoulders were solid. There was nothing wrong with the road. It was the fight to keep it as a corridor that made men call it "Hell's Highway."

DZs, LZs AND REGIMENTAL MISSIONS

The flat terrain made possible a wide selection of drop zones. But, mindful of the Normandy experience, General Taylor insisted on a high degree of concentration. So it was arranged to drop both the 502d and the 506th in the area northwest of Zon, on Drop Zones B and C respectively, and to use the same area for the later glider landings. Only the 501st was to be dropped separately.

To the 506th was given the mission of seizing the Wilhelmina Canal bridge at Zon, then moving on to the south and taking Eindhoven, with its four highway bridges over the winding Dommel River.

The 502d was to guard the LZ, to capture the road bridge at St.

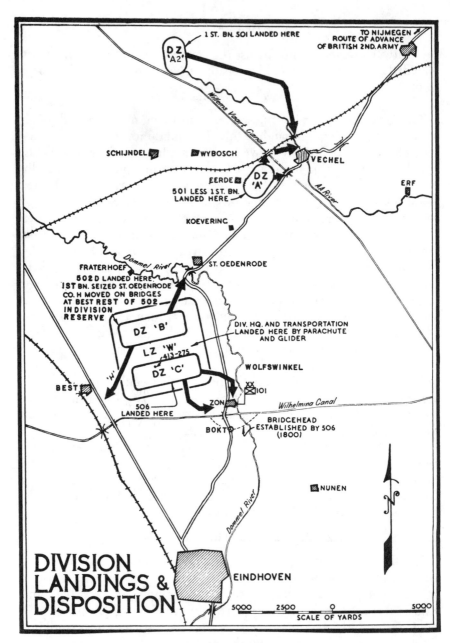

Map 34.

An Army nurse bids paratroopers farewell, 17 September.

Oedenrode, and to be ready to take over the defense of Zon and support the 506th in its move south to Eindhoven. General Taylor gave it the additional mission of sending a company to seize the road and railroad bridges at Best, on the flank of the zone of responsibility.

The 501st had the job of capturing the highway and railroad bridges over the Aa River and the Zuid Willems Vaart Canal at Vechel. To place it closer to these bridges it was given the separate DZs, farther to the north.

THE D-DAY FLIGHTS

Early in that hectic week of planning between September 10 and September 17, General Brereton made one bold decision that changed the whole character of the operation for his airborne troops. It would be a daylight jump. Gone was to be the endless, aimless stumbling around through the hours of darkness that sometimes characterized Normandy. This was to be a grand gamble on Allied superiority in the air.

The atmosphere in the C-47s was tense, for there was plenty that a man could worry about. Many of the veterans, aware of what was coming, were more nervous than they had been before Normandy. Worse than the newcomers, they were sweating it out.

In the ears of those who had heard him, the words of General Brereton stayed on: "On the success of your mission rests the difference between a quick decision in the west and a long-drawn-out battle." Maybe it would all be over pretty soon, and a man could go home.

Waiting to take off for Holland.

Taking off from airports in England, the planes bearing the paratroopers of the 101st circled into formation and set out along a southern route, over Belgium. The men noted the clear skies all the way which meant more chance of making the right DZ. It also meant that the job of German interceptor planes would be easier. But none of these dared come close. That part of the daylight gamble was won.

Swinging left at Bourg–Léopold, the planes went squarely toward the front lines. As they neared them the flak began to fly. Five minutes from the DZ it was thick.

It was thick, but it was not impossible. For just prior to the C-47 flight, Air Force fighter planes had gone to work on the flak points, and knocked out many of them—enough that that part of the daylight gamble was also won.

But this time there was no breaking of formation, no evasive action as there had been in Normandy. Even as motors started to burst into flame and wings to break, pilots held their planes in place for the crucial seconds that gave the troopers a chance to jump where they were supposed to jump.[1] Entire regiments came down in full view of one another. Men landed close to their friends and close to their equipment. Battalions were assembled and operating in less than an hour. Considered from any standpoint, it was the most successful

General McAuliffe talks to Air Corps Colonel William Whittacre
at Aldermaston Airdrome, just before the take-off for Holland.

landing that the Division had ever had, in either training or combat.

Only two planes of the 424 carrying parachutists and one of the four pathfinder planes that preceded the regular formations failed to reach a DZ. Between 1300 and 1330 hours, 6,769 men were jumped with casualties of less than two per cent for personnel, and five per cent for equipment.

The glider landings on LZ W an hour afterward were not so fortunate. Of the 70 gliders that were towed off from England, only 53 came in without accident. Three more crash-landed on the LZ. Nine came down in other places on the Continent, two in friendly territory, seven behind enemy lines. Two were dropped back in England and one in the Channel.

Men in the seven gliders that came down in enemy territory, striving to rejoin their outfits, went through experiences that make the ordinary adventure story seem pale by comparison.[2] Even for many of those who came directly in, it was not a quiet trip. There was for instance the experience of Cpl. James L. Evans of Divarty Headquarters, riding in the lead glider of the first serial. The flak which wounded him simultaneously knocked out both the pilot and the co-pilot of his glider. Somehow Evans managed to crawl forward and, though unfamiliar with the controls, steadied the plunging glider. He then roused the

Wreckage of a CG4A glider which collided with another CG4A on the 506th drop zone near Zon, early on the afternoon of D-day. Fifth from the left is Chaplain Tilden McGee. Looking at his hand at the right is Stanley Spiewak. Survivors look out from the wreckage in the center.

dazed pilot and passed the controls back to him. A severed artery in the thigh of the co-pilot demanded immediate attention, and Evans applied a tourniquet. Fortunately, the landing was not rough.

The gliders successfully brought in 252 officers and men, 32 jeeps and 13 trailers. No artillery came in on D-day. But artillery observer teams did, and fought with the infantry regiments until their guns arrived.

What the Division had as it set out on its mission was a fighting arm —the three parachute regiments, with platoons from the 326th Engineers attached; and a control arm—elements of Division Headquarters Company, Division Artillery Headquarters Battery, Signal Company, Medical Company, and Reconnaissance Platoon.

Seven days were taken to get the entire Division into the fight. During this period the Division Commander was not only handicapped by lacking sorely needed personnel, but he also had to divert part of his forces to do the job of standing guard over an LZ. If Allied air strength had been sufficient to bring in all the Airborne elements connected with the operation in the first two days, all tasks would have been easier, and the over-all operation would have had a better chance of success.

506TH: ZON

An entire parachute regiment, in bright sunlight, landing on a single field, is a pretty sight. And if the field happens to be behind enemy lines, it is also a reassuring sight. More than one man in the 506th had both these thoughts as he came down to DZ C shortly after 1315 on the afternoon of September 17. This looked good!

It looked good to Colonel Sink too as he hastened to a check point on the southern edge of the field where his 1st Battalion was assembling. He and the Battalion CO, Maj. James L. LaPrade, had agreed in advance that as rapidly as the men appeared they should be organized in groups of 15 to 25, placed under an officer and hurried on their way south. Colonel Sink helped speed this process.

Minutes counted. To the 1st Battalion had been given the first part of the 506th mission—securing the main bridge and if possible two smaller bridges over the Wilhelmina Canal at Zon. This done, the rest of the regiment was to rush through and finish the job, going south to Eindhoven to take that city and the four bridges over the Dommel River which it contained.

Minutes counted. According to the over-all plan, the British XXX Corps at the moment when the paratroopers were stepping out of their planes, had started attacking north toward Eindhoven from its bridgehead fifteen miles away. It was the job of the 506th to have the welcome mat out in front of that city by the time the corps reached it.

Major LaPrade had most of 1st Battalion on its way forty-five minutes after the jump. His instructions were to move due south keeping well to the right of the main road and the town of Zon until he reached the Wilhelmina Canal. Then he was to swing left and move on the bridges from the flank. General Taylor accompanied the battalion.

Meanwhile, 2d Battalion and 3d Battalion were completing their regular organization. A few men had been confused by the smoke signals of the 502d on DZ B and were late in reporting. The arrival of the glider echelon meant a further delay.

On Colonel Sink's order 2d Battalion moved out, down the main road to Zon. He followed it; and after him came Regimental Headquarters Company and 3d Battalion.

Marching down the road, Colonel Sink remembered several enemy tanks near Wolfswinkel which he had seen from his plane, and he sent a patrol over to investigate. Before the patrol could get there American fighters came in overhead, saw the tanks, attacked, and knocked them out. Here was another demonstration of the air superiority that had made a daylight jump possible. The feelings of the men, already favorable toward the Air Forces on account of the almost perfect drop, warmed even more.

Without encountering any serious opposition, 2d Battalion reached the outskirts of Zon. But there, while members of the point were questioning a German soldier who had bicycled unsuspectingly into their midst, an 88mm covering the road suddenly opened fire. The point went down. The advance party, one platoon from Company D, swung out to the right and around the first row of buildings. Its members were protected from the fire of the gun by the surrounding houses and walked to within fifty yards of it without any difficulty. Evidently the Germans had put out no flank protection. With his bazooka Pvt. Thomas G. Lindsey of the 2d Battalion Headquarters bazooka section fired one round at the 88. His rocket hit the gun near the elevating mechanism and finished it. One German was killed by the blast and six others fled toward the bridge. With his tommy gun Sgt. John F. Rice, of D, who was near Lindsey, killed them all. Meanwhile, other D men had overwhelmed another 88 to the right of the first. The action was complete in ten or fifteen minutes.

The 2d Battalion moved on toward the center bridge, its leaders wondering what had become of LaPrade's battalion. The companies, deployed, began a search of the houses, with D to the right of the

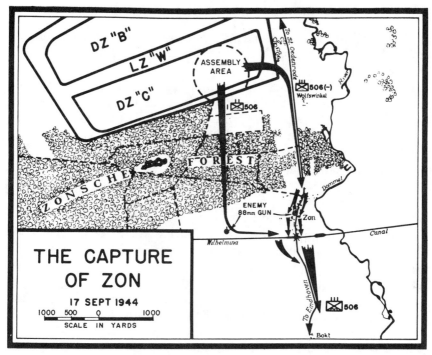

Map 35.

road, and E to the left of it. Company E men saw a few Germans run from the buildings and scatter out before they could fire on them. A platoon was sent after them but succeeded in cornering only two Germans on the road east of Zon.

Meanwhile, the center was receiving rifle and machine-gun fire from a house on the far side of the canal. The battalion began getting casualties, about ten men being wounded at this stage. Rifle, machine-gun, bazooka and finally mortar fire were placed on the house. It became silent. The men continued to advance. Leading groups of all three rifle companies moved to within fifty yards of the bank. Colonel Sink was about seventy yards to their rear. The first men from 1st Battalion had appeared on their right flank.

Suddenly, with a roar, the bridge went up. Debris fell around the infantrymen, already stunned by the blast. Lt. Sterling Horner ran forward to look at the wreckage. He found three Germans crouched down under the concrete of the north pillar—badly dazed, but otherwise unhurt.

Colonel Sink came on up, looked things over, and noted that the central pillar was undamaged.

Only a moment after the bridge exploded, Major LaPrade, along

273

with Lt. Millford F. Weller and Sgt. Donald B. Dunning, came running up to the end of the canal. Pausing for but an instant they dove in and swam to the far side.

From other officers, Colonel Sink quickly learned why 1st Battalion had been delayed. Going directly south to the canal it had run into heavy fire from a group of 88s, fire which included flak that exploded when it hit the trees just above them. The Company A men leading the battalion were forced to the ground, taking casualties as they lay.

Among those hit was Capt. Melvin C. Davis, Commanding Officer of A, who may be the originator of one of the classic remarks of the war. As he was receiving first aid for one wound, another bullet hit him, and he quipped, "You better hurry up, medics. They're gaining on you." Captain Davis is also remembered for a remark he made during the briefing sessions back in England. When told that his mission was to get the Zon bridge and hold it for the British to cross, he promised to charge each of them a toll of one shilling.

The guns that shot up Company A were finally overwhelmed and 1st Battalion resumed its advance with Company B in the lead. It was within 150 yards of the bridge when the explosion occurred.

Even while Colonel Sink was learning these facts some 1st Battalion men obtained a rowboat. Several squads were ferried to the south bank. Together with the group that swam across they dispersed the enemy firing from nearby houses. The position was won.

Meanwhile reconnaissance confirmed a piece of bad news that had been brought to Colonel Sink shortly after the landing—the two smaller bridges had both been blown several days earlier.

To provide against such an emergency, the 3d Platoon of Company C, 326th Airborne Engineer Battalion (the Battalion's Parachute Company) had jumped with the Regiment. It went to work and in an hour and a half had improvised a footbridge. But the footbridge was so weak that it could bear only a few men at a time. Getting the regiment across was a process that dragged through the evening till midnight.

Meanwhile, what of Eindhoven? And what of the British who were to be helped through it? Plans to take the city by 2000 were obviously washed up. Colonel Sink considered a night attack, but rejected it as being far too risky, especially in view of a civilian report that a German regiment had just moved into town. So he had his regiment set up a defense area based on Bokt, about a mile south of the Canal, and went to sleep hoping that the blown bridge at Zon had not put a crimp in the entire operation.

As it turned out, his fears were groundless. Unknown to him the British had run into unexpectedly heavy opposition and had gotten only half way to Eindhoven in the D-day fighting before stopping for the night.

Nor was it necessarily a part of the over-all plan that Eindhoven be taken on D-day. General Taylor in his conference with General Dempsey, had pointed out that it might be impossible to secure all the Division objectives in the Zon area on D-day and to take Eindhoven as well. Now talking with Colonel Sink while the bridge was being repaired he agreed that an overnight wait was advisable. So Eindhoven became the number one job for D plus 1.

501st—Vechel and Eerde

"It's the wrong field again."

That was the thought that flashed through the mind of Lt. Col. Harry W. O. Kinnard as he stepped out of his plane shortly after H-hour. He should have seen Vechel, and he didn't. He should have seen a rail line, and he didn't. But he had gotten the green light, and he put his stick out along with the rest of his battalion, the 1st Battalion of the 501st.

The mission of this regiment was to secure the four rail and highway bridges over the Aa River and the Zuid Willems Vaart Canal at Vechel. According to the original plan, the whole Regiment was to be dropped on DZ A, west of both these waterways.

But Colonel Kinnard had pointed out that if his battalion were put down between the two streams it would be able to get to the river bridges without risking the delay of a fight at the canal bridges. The necessary approvals for this change of plan had been given, and arrangements made to drop his battalion on a field just north of the rail bridge over the canal.

But he obviously was not coming down there. Suspended in air he tried to figure out where he was coming down, but there was little time for that. So tight had been the drop that he had to side-slip several times to avoid collisions with other paratroopers. And it was not until he hit the ground that he learned from one of the many Dutch civilians who crowded around that they were near Kameren, about three miles northwest of where they were supposed to drop. The rewards of initiative were disappointingly slight.

Less than an hour was needed to organize the battalion and get it moving down the main road. Going toward Vechel, the battalion encountered no enemy except isolated German cars which were cap-

Landing of the 1st Battalion, 501st, near Kameren.

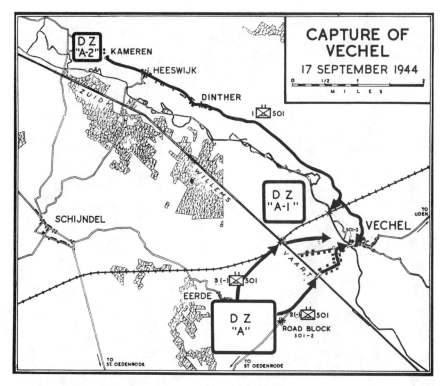

Map 36.

tured before their occupants recovered from their initial surprise. But as fast as the battalion moved down the road it was preceded by several of its own men who had requisitioned trucks and bicycles right after the jump and taken off for the bridges. By the time Colonel Kinnard approached the town, they had seized the Aa River railway bridge, but a fire fight in Vechel was slowing further advance.

Meanwhile 2d and 3d Battalions had landed on DZ A, both with excellent drop patterns. Organizing without opposition 3d had moved out toward Eerde within forty-five minutes, and seized the town. At the same time it sent a detachment to place a block across the Vechel–St. Oedenrode highway.

With its rear thus secured 2d Battalion moved out toward Vechel. Company E headed directly for the railroad bridge over the canal. Company D, under Lt. Richard G. Snodgrass, led Headquarters and F up the road. Against negligible opposition the rail bridge and the two road bridges were taken. Hastening on, 2d Battalion scouts bumped into 1st Battalion scouts in the center of Vechel. All that remained was to knock out the few Germans who were still fighting, and the

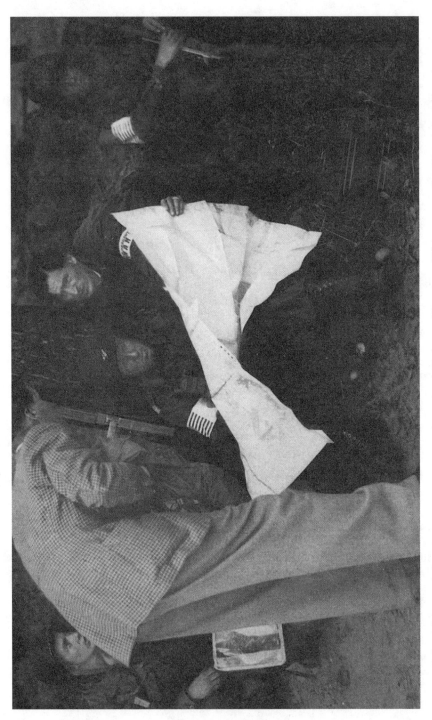

Colonel Johnson of the 501st goes over a map with two Dutch Underground workers. These men met the 501st at the drop zone.

town, along with fifty prisoners, belonged to the 101st Airborne.

Defense dispositions were ordered immediately but were made slowly, for by this time the enthusiastic welcome of the good people of Vechel had made all military moves difficult. Throngs of civilians gathered around any group of soldiers, chattering and offering them goodies. It became hard to believe that there was still a war to be fought. But, starting from the top and working down, discipline reasserted itself, and the town was organized for all-around defense.

The two engineer platoons which had jumped with the 501st went to work on a supplementary truck bridge over the canal so as to permit two-way traffic should it become necessary.

There was a minor flurry of excitement when a lone German tank came up the road almost to the newly established block. Its occupants were as surprised as the troopers, but they recovered first, and managed to get their tank away unscathed.

One misfortune dimmed the general luster of this picture. In moving so rapidly from his DZ, Colonel Kinnard could take only a portion of his equipment with him. He had left the remainder in the hands of a miscellaneous detail of 46 men, including eight jump injuries, under Capt. W. S. Burd. He did not expect Captain Burd's detail to have any difficulty closing in on the rear of the battalion. But shortly after the battalion left, Germans had unexpectedly attacked the group and forced it to retreat to a large stone building. Word of its plight reached Colonel Kinnard in late afternoon. He at once asked for permission to send a company in relief. The regimental CO, Col. Howard W. Johnson, did not feel that a company could be spared from the mission, the defense of Vechel, and would agree to nothing larger than a platoon.

As darkness fell, this platoon was dispatched under Lieutenant Rafferty. Eight hundred yards short of its goal it was stopped by German fire and forced to dig in. At first light on D plus 1 German strength made it obvious that the platoon either had to be supported or pulled back. It was pulled back. The detachment under Captain Burd was captured.

502d—St. Oedenrode and Best

Watching fire envelop a nearby plane so engrossed Lt. Col. Patrick Cassidy, commanding officer of the 502d's 1st Battalion that for once he failed to see the green light. General Taylor, who was jumping right behind him, had to tell him: "Cassidy, the green light is on."

"Yes, sir."

And out he went, closely followed by the general.

General Taylor and Lt. Col. Patrick C. Cassidy, 1st Battalion,
502d, taking off from Welford Airdrome, 17 September.

The men in that plane had seen all the sights on their way over—the war-blackened country behind the front lines—the colored smoke at the turning point at Bourg–Léopold—American dive bombers giving enemy AA positions a workout—C-47s returning from earlier flights. One went down while they watched. Their own plane shook from the concussion of AA explosions. A few moments later one of Company A's planes burst into flames. Colonel Cassidy counted seven of his men leaping out before it was lost to view. And then he saw flames breaking from Lt. Col. Raymond D. Millener's plane, the flames that had distracted him when the green light went on. He found out later that the pilot had held that plane on course until the last man had jumped, and then crashed with it.

Coming down hard on a barbed-wire fence, Colonel Cassidy took a bit longer than usual to get off his harness. Then he headed toward the battalion assembly smoke he thought was his own. Not until he reached it did he find out that it belonged to the 1st Battalion of the 506th and that consequently his own assembly point was somewhere to the north. Later he learned that his entire battalion had been dropped two miles south of the planned DZ.

Colonel Cassidy experienced only two of the possible delays that slow up the organization of a battalion after a jump. There are many others. Only men who have landed via parachute can describe them.

When you hit the ground and stop, all you feel is gratitude for still being alive. All you want to do is relax. Then you remember there is a war on. You have trouble getting out of your harness, maybe a lot, maybe not so much. Especially if you hear firing, you hop to the nearest ditch. You are suddenly aware of five hundred other parachutists dropping through the sky right at you and you start dodging. By this time you have lost all sense of direction. So even if you remember that the assembly point is in the southeast corner of the field, and the planes came in from the west, it does no good. You get out a compass if you have one. You study landmarks and try to remember your briefing sessions.

A smoke signal has gone off somewhere. Everyone seems to be moving in one direction. You join a group. When you get there you find out that it is the right battalion but the wrong company. Someone says you are supposed to be four hundred yards farther south, across a brook. On the way there you see a buddy with a bad ankle and stop to help him. Finally arriving you find your platoon leader, but not your squad leader. But what a relief to be back with your own crowd.

Thus the minutes fly.

Colonel Cassidy this time avoided many of these sources of delay, but did go to the wrong smoke. Picking up what men he could he set off to find his own assembly point.

St. Oedenrode, cleared of Germans by the 502d on 17 September, thanks its liberators.

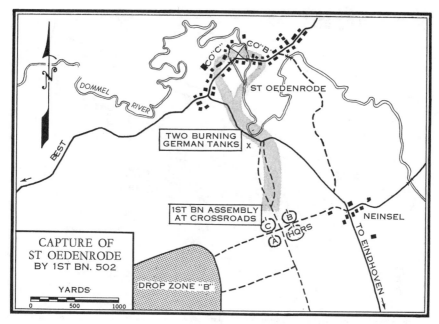

Map 37.

Some men, in speaking of that trip, tell of the six C-47s that they saw shot down. Others mention the gliders coming in. But most talk only of the way the afternoon heat, intensified by the heavy jump clothes, became nearly unbearable.

Colonel Cassidy finally reached his road junction assembly point, found the rest of his men, and reorganized for his mission. In general the 502d was being held just north of Zon in Division reserve, but Company H was dispatched over toward Best.

And to 1st Battalion fell the task of taking St. Oedenrode, a main junction point in the corridor. Colonel Cassidy's plan was to send elements of C, Headquarters and A directly north to the town with C in the lead. Their left flank was to be covered by a squad sent out one thousand yards to set up a roadblock. On the right B was to advance into town using a footbridge, and still farther to the right a platoon was swung out to investigate reports of enemy forces in a nearby village.

Going north, the main attack ran into increasing small-arms fire and Company C was finally pinned down. But two Mark IV tanks—which might have given the 502d a hard time—lay peacefully to the left of the advance, knocked out by the fighter-bombers. Company B, looking for its footbridge, came across a second highway bridge that had not been considered in the planning. Even while they were investigating, a

283

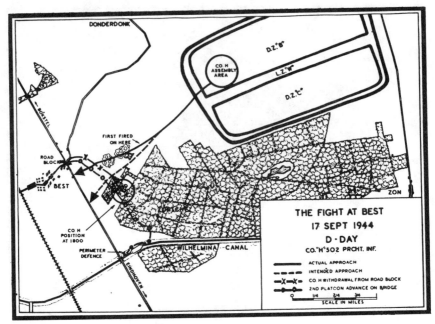

Map 38.

German squad advanced to blow this bridge. One bazooka round finished off that squad's explosives—and the squad. But a larger German group had already taken positions in a nearby cemetery, covering the bridge. There was an extended fire fight, in which Company B finally gained superiority and successfully rushed the bridge. Meanwhile, Company C had freed itself and also advanced into town. The clean-up went fast, and a perimeter defense was soon established. Twenty of the enemy had been killed and 58 captured in this fight.

St. Oedenrode had been easy.

But the story was different for Company H, which had been dispatched toward Best. Its mission was to seize the rail and highway bridges over the Wilhelmina Canal there. Since these bridges were not on the direct route of advance of XXX Corps, they were not included in the Division mission and General Dempsey had shown no interest when specifically asked about them. But to General Taylor's mind they did provide a good alternate route, should the Zon road become unusable (as it now had), and their seizure would help to secure the flank of the entire Division. He decided to take them. But it was originally felt that only a platoon could be spared from the main missions of the Division for this seemingly routine job. At the request of Lt. Col. Robert G. Cole, 3d Battalion commanding officer, Col. John H. Michaelis, 502d CO, ordered this increased to a reinforced company.

So Company H set out, accompanied by a section of light machine guns from battalion headquarters and the 3d Platoon of Company C of the 326th Engineers under Lt. Charles W. Moore, Lt. James B. Watson and Lt. Otto J. Laier. The men did not know it at the time, but this "platoon" mission was later to require a battalion, then two battalions, then half the Division plus a squadron of British tanks.

Misfortune dogged the footsteps of Capt. Robert E. Jones, Company H commander, right from the start. He chose a route that should have brought him out on the Eindhoven–Bokstel highway a thousand yards southeast of Best. But going through the woods he lost sight of his church-steeple marker, and came out on the highway within four hundred yards of the Best crossroads.

Small German groups immediately opened fire on him. While his company tried to push them back and seize the crossroads it became widely dispersed. The Germans were meanwhile reinforced by a twelve-truck troop convoy. As he was adjusting his lines to meet this new threat, Colonel Cole radioed him to get the engineers, the light machine guns and his 2d Platoon down to the bridge at once. Without these groups his position would have been impossible, so he pulled his entire company back into the woods.

As soon as he had a new defensive position, he ordered his 2d Platoon and the engineer platoon to take off south through the forest and get the bridges. Taking charge of this group, Lt. Edward L. Wierzbowski, leader of the 2d Platoon, could not but realize how much the earlier fighting had cut down his punching power. He had only eighteen men in his own platoon. Lt. Andrew Duffy, his assistant platoon leader, was missing. So was one squad of the engineers. So was the entire section of light machine guns. The group was small, and it was destined to fight alone. It made mistakes. But it stuck tenaciously to its mission. And for its failure it exacted a high price from the enemy during the next forty hours. To one of its members the Medal of Honor was to be awarded.

The sun was down even with the horizon but light still filtered into the woods as Lieutenant Wierzbowski and his men set off for the bridges. They found themselves going through a plantation of young pine planted in even rows, with fire breaks cutting the woods every twenty-five yards.

As they crossed the first fire lane, a machine gun opened up on them. Germans had already infiltrated into the forest and set up guns to cover some of the lanes. Wishing to preserve every man he had, Wierzbowski insisted that each lane be checked, and those under fire be taken in individual rushes. As an added precaution, he had the entire column swing seventy-five yards to the left, away from the machine guns. His men chafed at these delays, for they were eager to get to the bridges while there was still daylight. But darkness fell while they were picking their way through the woods, and with the coming of darkness it began to rain.

At last they came to the final fire break and the last small patch of woods. Hoping that they were now unobserved they crawled forward into the open. Beyond the first rolling terrain was a small area of marsh. Pfc. Joe E. Mann, the lead scout, skirted farther left to avoid it and finally came out on the dike bounding the canal.

Crawling over this the group went down to the bank of the canal and turned west, toward the bridge. They felt their way slowly along the bank until they came to a spot where a loading zone and two large derricks blocked the way. Pausing to check, Wierzbowski saw that it was about 2100. He guessed that they were still five hundred yards east of the bridge.

Willing to gamble, he led the group along a wet and slippery catwalk suspended around the derricks out over the canal. No flares went off while they were thus exposed. Regaining the bank, they continued west, feeling their way in the darkness.

After an hour of slow progress Wierzbowski felt that they must be close to the bridge. He crawled up to where Mann was still leading the way. Not yet seeing the bridge, the two crawled on forward. They crawled too far. The Germans covering the bridge had been changing guards and the old sentry had withdrawn to the bridge entrance. Thus they missed him. But the new man came on back past them, and Wierzbowski and the scout discovered that they were within his beat. They did not want to jump him: there was a guard on the far side and their sentry kept shouting to the guard and firing his rifle periodically. And they couldn't leave: they were so close to him that any movement would reveal them. They stayed there, not knowing what to do.

The men who had been left behind on the side of the dike were confused by Wierzbowski's absence and not quite certain whether they should proceed. A half hour passed: they had grown very uneasy.

Then without warning some potato mashers were thrown toward them from the other side of the canal. Really scared, a couple of men began to scramble up the bank. Others followed. As the fourth man gained the top the enemy opened on them with machine guns and rifles from both sides of the canal. The sudden fire stampeded a number of the party; they ran for the woods. The others scrambled down the far side of the bank and began to dig in.

This firing proved a release for Wierzbowski and Mann. They jumped up and ran back to the platoon. With artillery and mortar fire falling around them, Wierzbowski had his men retreat another sixty yards along the canal. While they dug in, he checked. He had 15 men and 3 officers left. In the position there was a machine gun with five hundred rounds, a mortar with six rounds and a bazooka with five rounds. But he was on his mission, and had no thought of retreat.

At 0300 the enemy firing ceased. The rain continued.

Unknown to Lieutenant Wierzbowski, Captain Jones had sent three patrols, and finally the entire 3d Platoon to find him. All had been stopped. The rest of Company H remained in the woods where it had dug in during the late afternoon. It took thirty-nine casualties that night.

As soon as the first reports on Company H's rebuff came back, Colonel Michaelis realized Best was no company mission. More power was needed, and the bridges made it worthwhile to send the power.

So at 1800 the rest of 3d Battalion was dispatched to join H. It had come within a mile of Best when heavy artillery and mortar fire blocked further advance. Darkness fell and maneuver was dangerous, so the men dug in. Patrols sent out to Company H were unable to find it. Radio contact was the only link Company H had with its battalion until after first light the next morning.

Division CP—Zon

General Taylor and General Higgins, along with other members of the command echelon of the Division, jumped with the 502d. The gliders coming in an hour later brought the Division Reconnaissance Platoon, units of the Signal and Medical Companies, and additional command personnel. Radio contact with the three parachute regiments was established within minutes after the gliders landed.

Thirty-one parachuting signal men had already set up communications for the first CP in the woods south of the LZ. By 2100 this CP had been moved to a schoolhouse in Zon. Wire was laid to the 502d, the 506th, and the provisional Division Artillery headquarters, also in the woods south of the LZ. This headquarters in turn was in touch with the skeleton staffs of the artillery battalions. Next morning the wire was run on up to Vechel.

Another wire unit the next day followed the 506th in its advance to

A Dutch girl and her father welcome the 101st into their town.

Eindhoven, splicing civilian lines to use in place of the military wire lost on one of the missing gliders.

Among the other gliders missing was the one containing attached British signal personnel. Without them it was impossible to make immediate contact with XXX Corps headquarters. But forty-five minutes after landing the Signal Company was in touch with Division Rear Base in the United Kingdom, and through them it was possible to communicate with British Second Army and hence with XXX Corps. However, this was not satisfactory, and that night General Taylor did not have any precise idea of where XXX Corps was.

There were two other ways in which that information might have been obtained. But on D-day, neither one worked. The first was direct communication with Second Army. Late in the afternoon the Signal Company succeeded in establishing this, and a question as to the exact location of XXX Corps was flashed to them. But for some reason this query was never answered.

That evening XXX Corps itself was reached over the now famed "Phantom Net." But in the rush of getting the attack organized within a week, signal operating instructions had not had a chance to filter down to the XXX Corps operator, and he did not recognize the signals being used. The next morning, however, when he was addressed in accordance with some known British SOPs he responded.

On D plus 1, direct radio communication was secured with British 1st Airborne Division headquarters, and the 82d Division. The 506th going into Eindhoven made radio contact with the Division's own radiomen attached to XXX Corps. This was done over the "Orange

Net," a method of communication through the use of the same frequency at all levels, first worked out by Division Signal Company for
the Normandy campaign.

On D-day the 326th Airborne Medical Company found its job less
difficult than anticipated. Fifty-two men, including an attached surgical team, who arrived in the glider echelon, set up a temporary hospital
on the southern edge of the field, and by 1500 they were treating casualties. The first major operation was performed at 1700. An hour later
they moved to a small hospital in Zon. Here in excellent surroundings
107 casualties were treated during the remaining hours of D-day.

SUMMARY OF D-DAY ACHIEVEMENTS

After the most perfect drop in its history the Division had succeeded
in seizing all its immediate objectives along the road. The blown
bridge at Zon was disappointing and delayed the capture of Eindhoven
but did not hold up the over-all operation.

The 502d was running into serious difficulties at Best but that fight
was over a secondary objective, not a part of the Division mission. Zon,
St. Oedenrode and Vechel were in Airborne hands and the stretches of
road in between were clear. The civilian population was friendly and
the Dutch underground was already showing how steadily it could
furnish vital information about enemy strength and movements. The
enemy had been taken by surprise. Except at Best only rear area troops
had been encountered. A few more daylight hours, and the 101st section
of road would be clear.

D PLUS 1 (SEPTEMBER 18)—502D—BEST

Many men of the 520d speak with greater pride of the attack of the
2d Battalion at Best than of any other single event in the history of the
regiment. Even though unsuccessful, that attack showed the extreme
of combat discipline to which the paratroopers were trained.

The Battalion was ordered to Best early on the morning of D plus 1,
when Colonel Michaelis realized that 3d Battalion was up against more
than it could handle. "I'll be glad to see you when you get here,"
Colonel Cole told Lt. Col. Steve Chappuis of 2d Battalion over the
radio. The 3d had succeeded at first light in making contact with
Company H, but heavy fire from an enemy who had obviously been
reinforced had driven it even farther back into the woods all along its
perimeter. As for getting the bridge unaided, that seemed to be out
of the question. Wierzbowski's group had already been given up for
lost.

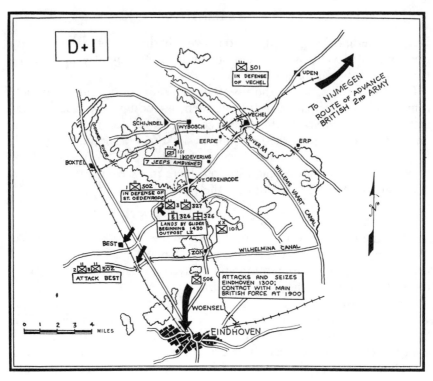

Map 39.

Colonel Chappuis' orders were to advance on the right of 3d Battalion, establish contact with its right flank, pivot on it, and attack on through ·Best down to the bridges. So he brought his battalion across the fields, Company D on the left, E and F to its right. Company D men reached the 3d Battalion area and the line pivoted.

It was just like the book. The Dutch had been haying and the fields ahead were full of small piles of uncollected hay. That was the only concealment. From left to right the line rippled forward in perfect order and with perfect discipline, each group of two or three men dashing to the next hay pile as it came their turn. It was as if the piles were of concrete. But machine-gun fire cut into them, sometimes setting the hay afire, sometimes wounding or killing the men behind them. That did not stop anyone except the dead and wounded.

Someone yelled "Sergeant Brodie, you're next." Another man behind the hay pile shouted: "Brodie's dead, but I'm coming on," and he jumped up and ran ahead.

It was like a problem being worked out on a parade ground. The squad leaders were leading, the platoon leaders urged them on.[3]

But it could not continue like this. For the battalion was taking such

290

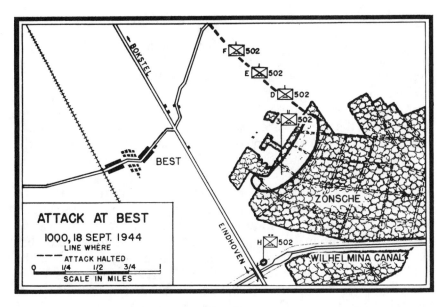

losses that continuing the advance would mean its destruction. The whole area was being plastered with artillery, mortar and automatic fire from beyond the highway. Eight officers already lay dead or wounded in the wheat field and about twenty per cent of the men were casualties. The attack had been put on without artillery and the battalion was getting support only from its own mortars.

A soldier who was in that charge thought little of what it might prove about paratrooper discipline. He described it more directly. "We had no artillery and the Krauts had beaucoup of it. We lost a quarter of our men that day." Colonel Chappuis stopped it and pulled his men back.

Again enemy reinforcements had moved into Best faster than the Americans—instead of five hundred Germans there were probably over one thousand. The job at Best was much bigger than it had appeared.

While 2d Battalion was reorganizing, the enemy maintained his artillery fire on 3d Battalion. As 3d attempted to counter this with further dispersal, small enemy groups infiltrated its lines.

Almost as a last resort Colonel Cole called for air support. The P-47s came in low, and began to strafe his own battalion positions. He hastened out to direct the laying of identification panels. The P-47s began hitting the enemy lines and fire from the Germans along the highway slackened. Colonel Cole walked out in front of his men and

291

beyond the woods, stood there for a few seconds with his hand shield-
ing his eyes, looking up at a circling plane. Suddenly a sniper's bullet
from a house a hundred yards away hit him through the temple. He
died instantly.

Lt. Ralph A. Watson was right behind him. He couldn't bring himself to phrase the words: "Cole is dead." So he sent Maj. John P. Stopka
only this message: "You are in command of the battalion," and for the
next hour the executive officer thought it was only a temporary matter.

Right after Colonel Cole dropped, a German ran from a corner of the
house and one of the battalion machine guns cut him down; the men
figured this was the man who had killed Colonel Cole. They couldn't
be certain of it but they continued to say to one another that it was so.

Enemy fire continued to harass 3d Battalion through the day, but
that afternoon, Major Stopka was able to get patrols forward to the
Eindhoven–Bokstel highway and cut the road. A road block was set up.

In the course of the afternoon 2d Battalion reorganized. At 1700
Colonel Michaelis ordered Colonel Chappuis to move out through 3d
Battalion in a southeasterly direction and make another attempt at
the bridge. He had no way of knowing the Germans had blown it that
morning. The battalion went forward about a thousand yards before
fire from 88s posted along the canal made further advance impossible.
Drawing back to the nearest woods the battalion organized for the
night and prepared to renew the attack in the morning. Although its
advance had been stopped, 2d Battalion had succeeded in driving out
the enemy groups whose fire had harassed 3d Battalion.

Back in St. Oedenrode Colonel Cassidy's 1st Battalion spent the day
under Division control so that the 502d command group would be free
to concentrate on the Best struggle. Although the Germans had sent
strong patrols into the battalion positions during the night they were
thrown out. The day would have been quiet had it not been for the
"Incident of the Seven Jeeps."

Two of these jeeps belonged to the Division Reconnaissance Platoon
and had been assigned by General Taylor to conduct the other five up
to the 501st in Vechel. Also present was a guide from the 501st who
had come down from Vechel to Zon that morning. The cavalcade was
under the charge of Colonel Cartwright of First Triple A Headquarters.

Who was at fault is still in dispute, but tearing through St. Oedenrode
all seven jeeps took the road to German-occupied Schijndel rather than
turning right toward Vechel. Company C outposts tried to flag them
down, but they sped past unheeding. They learned of their mistake
only after the Germans opened fire on them with mortars and small

arms about three miles up the road. One jeep was set on fire immediately, and several men were wounded. The others took to the ditches. The only jeep to make a getaway was the one containing Colonel Cartwright. He returned to St. Oedenrode and requested the rescue of his party.

The request put Colonel Cassidy on a spot, for his mission was to hold the town, and he did not want to become involved in a distant fight of unknown proportions. However, Company C already had a three-man patrol on the road under Lt. Joshua A. Mewborn. Gambling on Mewborn's ability to pull off the rescue quickly and without loss, Colonel Cassidy directed him to increase his patrol with two squads from the 2d Platoon and do the job.

Keeping to the ditches on both sides of the road, Mewborn and his men set out. But they were still a thousand yards from the jeeps when the enemy saw them, and threw an interdictory fire on the road ahead.

This was so hot that it stopped most of the men, and Mewborn went ahead accompanied only by the three original members of his patrol, Pfc. Culverhouse and Privates Leafty and Duval. Running through the German fire, Mewborn and Leafty took a position near the jeeps. With their tommy guns they sprayed the area while Culverhouse and Duval jumped into the first two jeeps, turned them around and dashed off. Both jeeps were hit several times but got safely away. Meanwhile Lt. Troy Wall had brought the other two squads up close enough to lay a base of fire. Under this cover Mewborn and Leafty along with two medics were able to get hold of the wounded. Having suffered two wounded of its own, the entire party withdrew. The rest of the day was quiet.

For Lieutenant Wierzbowski and his little group down by the bridge, D plus 1 was a day of disappointment. In the clear light the bridge turned out to be a single-span concrete structure, over a hundred feet long. The sentry had been withdrawn from the north approach before daybreak and it seemed unguarded. But there was a barracks south of the canal just twenty yards from the bridge with dug-in positions around it. These positions were well filled with soldiers. Another group of Germans was on the far side of the road, only eighty yards away. "Every time we raised up to start toward the bridge, we drew heavy fire from both sides."

As the morning wore on they saw German infantrymen straying toward them through the trees along the northern bank of the canal—stragglers from the 2d Battalion attack. They held their fire and their ground and when the Germans got to within fifty yards mowed them down, killing about thirty-five.

Around 1000, the watching men saw a German soldier and a civilian —they thought he was Dutch—come up to the far side of the bridge and stand around for twenty minutes or so, apparently talking. They thought little of the incident. In any case, they could not get a clear shot at the soldier.

At exactly 1100, there was a terrific explosion. The span shook and lifted and then they had to bend low in their foxholes as the concrete and steel debris from the ruin fell all around them. The German and the civilian had evidently set a time fuze to an already prepared demolition. But of this Lieutenant Wierzbowski could get no word back to the regiment. It continued to think the prize was still within its grasp.

Mann and Hoyle made one sortie. They saw a German 88mm dump, with ammunition and spare parts, lying about a hundred yards from them; they sneaked out and Mann destroyed it with a few rounds from the bazooka. Staying in their new position they shot six Germans coming toward them from the north. Then Mann was hit twice by rifle bullets. Hoyle took the bazooka and with his first round destroyed an 88 about 150 yards up the canal.

The P-47s, which came over that morning in response to the call of Colonel Cole, strafed the group, but no one was hurt. Both before and after this escape the men could hear the fire of the two battalions in the woods. This encouraged them to go on believing that they would shortly be relieved.

In mid-afternoon they got an attack along the canal bank from the north and drove it off. To get a better view of the retreating enemy, Lieutenant Watson of the engineers sneaked out in front of the position. He was hit in the mid-section and went down. Pfc. James Orvac, first-aid man, crawled out and treated him. Then Lieutenant Wierzbowski went out to look him over.

Watson thought his testicles had been shot off and he begged Wierzbowski to take his .45 and kill him. Wierzbowski dragged him 150 yards back to the lines. His testicles were all right.

Now the German fire increased. Private Onroe H. Luther was hit and killed by a shell fragment in the head. Private Northrup was hit in the base of the spine. Little could be done for him. Two more bullets bored into Mann. They bandaged him and put both his arms in slings. He begged Wierzbowski to let him stay with the defenders instead of sending him off to a safer foxhole with the other wounded; the request was granted.

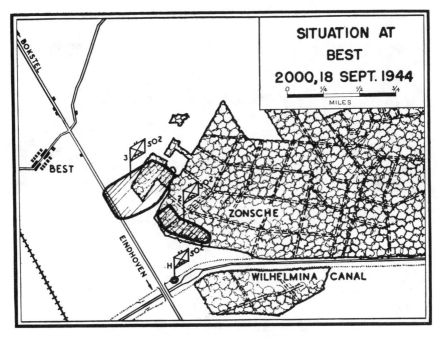

Map 41.

By this time medical supplies were exhausted. Lieutenant Otto J. Laier and Sergeant Betras of the engineers volunteered to try to break through for aid. They crawled away. A few minutes later Betras came back wounded. They had been ambushed and Lieutenant Laier had been knocked down by a bullet and captured.

But they thought their troubles were over when a British armored car, accompanied by a British reconnaissance car, appeared on the other side of the canal. When the Germans immediately opened fire on them, they pulled part way around the corner of a building, blazing away at the Germans with all of their machine guns. The German fire quieted and soon the German garrison on the other side of the canal got out.

Cpl. Daniel L. Corman found a small boat at the bank, rowed across to the armored car and came back with a medical kit. Lieutenant Wierzbowski yelled across asking them to call Division on the radio and explain the need for relief. The car couldn't get Division. So Wierzbowski started to move his men to the bank, planning to row them across to its shelter. But the British commander shouted to him: "Stay where you are! I am sure that help will be here soon."

Privates Koller, Waldt and Laino prowled down toward the derricks and came back with three German medics and one wounded German

295

Bridge at Best, looking west from the derricks. In the right foreground Lt. Edward L. Wierzbowski's squad was dug in, and here Pfc. Joe E. Mann won the Medal of Honor. (Water color by H. Standley)

officer. Lieutenant Wierzbowski told them to get to work on his wounded, which they did. What he really needed was plasma. Lieutenant Watson was in bad shape; Northrup was slowly dying from loss of blood.

Again things seemed to take a turn for the better when a patrol from Company E stumbled into their position in the early evening. Departing, it promised to take back word of the destruction of the bridge and the plight of the group. But the report was distorted so that when it reached Colonel Chappuis it told only of the destruction of the bridge.

Later an entire platoon from Company D which had become separated from its battalion during the afternoon attack appeared. Lt. Nicholas D. Mottola, its leader, decided to have it spend the remainder of the night with Wierzbowski.

Lieutenant Wierzbowski accordingly reorganized his lines with the Mottola group holding one flank. His men, utterly fatigued, dozed off. In the middle of the night the Mottola flank was beset by a larger German group attacking from the direction of Best and fell back across the canal, some men swimming and others rowing. They ultimately recrossed the canal well to the east and the survivors rejoined the battalion two days later.

Strangely enough, Wierzbowski's men were scarcely aware of this attack being pressed against the Mottola group. To complete their misfortune, the British cars, hearing Americans come into the position, had concluded that the relief was accomplished and had pulled away from the far bank. The survivors stayed in their foxholes awaiting the morning.

With first light on D plus 2, Lieutenant Wierzbowski and his men found themselves enveloped in heavy mist. They had not moved to

Pfc. Joe E. Mann, Company H, 502d, who won the Medal of Honor at Best on 19 September. The picture was taken in the U. S. before Mann left for England. A Victory ship has been named for him.

redistribute themselves so as to cover the open flank left by Mottola's abrupt departure which they still did not comprehend. As the light grew, Wierzbowski looked around. Twenty feet away he saw a group of Germans coming toward him. He yelled. Sergeant Betras threw a grenade, and then several of the others threw. But the Germans had beaten them to the throw and grenades were already on their way to the foxholes. Two hit the top of one embankment and rolled down among the wounded. Betras threw the first one out. Someone else got rid of the other. The third went wild. The fourth hit the machine gun and exploded directly into Laino's face. It blew his left eye out, blinded the other eye and made a bloody pulp of his face.

A bullet hit Koller in the temple. Another grenade came over Wierzbowski's head, hit Laino on the knee and bounced off into his foxhole. Laino, still blinded, reached down groping for it, found it and tossed it from his foxhole just a split second before it exploded.

The next grenade came toward Mann. He was sitting against the back of the trench—a large trench containing six other men—and he saw it come over and felt it land behind him. But his arms were bound

297

and useless because of his four wounds from the day before. Yelling "Grenade!" to the other men and fully conscious of what he was doing he lay back and took the explosion with his own body.

It blew his back apart. He had saved the other men, though Pvt. Anthony Atayde, at his side, was wounded in the body and Privates Paxton and Wienz were both hit in the hip by fragments. He said quietly to Wierzbowski: "My back's gone," and a minute or two later died, without a groan or a whimper—the bravest man, his comrades said, that they had ever known.

Mann, from the state of Washington, had been a popular soldier in his company; and his citation for the Medal of Honor reads, "His outstanding gallantry and his magnificent conduct were an everlasting inspiration to his comrades for whom he gave his life." He and his battalion commander were to be the only members of the Division to receive this highest award granted an American soldier; both awards were to be posthumous, and both men died within a day of each other.

The Germans kept coming in. By this time his men had exhausted their supply of grenades and all other ammunition. Only three were unwounded. Further struggle seemed pointless, so Wierzbowski and his group surrendered.

Later, after 2d Battalion's successful attack that afternoon, the survivors of Wierzbowski's group managed to free themselves and in turn make prisoners out of the Germans who had been guarding them.

D Plus 1: 501st—Vechel and Eerde

The defense of Vechel had been reorganized shortly before dark on D-day and in the resulting confusion the men of Company E, which now had the northwest sector of town, did not get an exact idea of their new area. Nor did they have a chance to register their mortars. So they were not well prepared when in the midst of the fog of that night a company of Germans came down the east bank of the canal and launched a surprise assault upon them. Fighting centered around a huge warehouse (later to be the Division CP). At 0200 burp-gun fire was heard to the front and a few minutes later the outposts were overrun or pushed back to the main line of resistance. There were three attacks with the heaviest about 0400. At one critical stage Lt. Joseph C. McGregor, though badly wounded, managed to hold off the Germans with a tommy gun until his men were able to draw back to a defensible line. He was later dragged back to safety. Seven men were killed by German grenades or machine pistols, and 26 more wounded. Among the latter was the company commander, Lt. Frank A. Gregg, who was to be wounded twice more in the Holland fighting. His wound this time was light but two of his officers, including Lieutenant McGregor, sustained serious injuries. With the coming of daylight, Lieutenant Gregg was able to commit his reserve platoon effectively, and the Germans were forced back.

Two other company-sized attacks were launched against the Vechel perimeter that night. They also were beaten off. But the Germans pressed more strongly a D plus 1 assault on the 3d Battalion position at Eerde. Company I took the brunt of the morning attack on its road-block near the railroad station. The attack was finally broken and 43 Luftwaffe NCOs were captured. When the Germans once more took the offensive shortly after noon they were again beaten off.

But these continuing attacks on an exposed battalion worried Colonel Johnson. So he decided to have 3d Battalion become regimental reserve and move to Vechel. The battalion's withdrawal was made with Company I fighting the delaying action.

REINFORCEMENT AND SUPPLY

The fighting power of the Division was considerably strengthened by the D plus 1 flights, which were eighty per cent glider. Arriving from 1430 on through the afternoon 428 of an original 450 gliders came in safely on LZ W. More infantry was the first thing they brought in, the 2d and 3d Battalions of the 327th. They carried parts of the 426th Quartermaster Company, the 801st Ordnance Maintenance Company, one-third of Division Artillery Headquarters, and an advance group from 377th Parachute Field Artillery Battalion. They delivered the remainder of the Division Signal Company, the Medical Company, and the Engineer Battalion.

In all it was 2,579 men, with 146 jeeps, 109 trailers, two bulldozers and other supplies. No effort was made to bring in the guns of the artillery.

Later on the same afternoon 121 Eighth Air Force bombers parachuted more supplies in, but less than half of these was recovered. Unless recovery could be improved on succeeding days, it was apparent that the Division was soon going to suffer from lack of gasoline and lack of food.

As the gliders landed on LZ W the men made their way in small groups to the Zon–St. Oedenrode highway where units were soon assembled. A control section had been established by Division Headquarters and this speeded the operation. Mortar fire on the northwest section of the LZ had the same effect.

Nor was this fire the only evidence that Germans were not far away

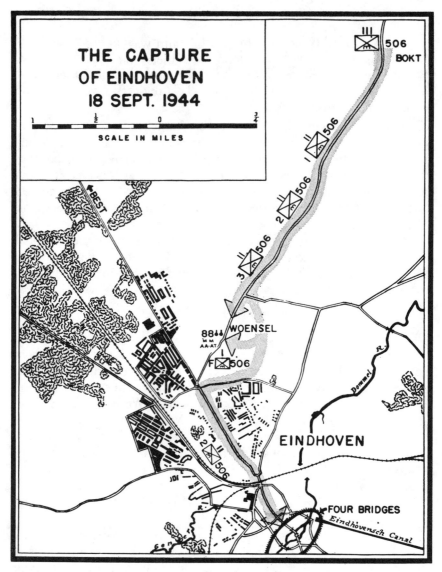

Map 42.

from the LZ. One group from the 377th was pinned down by German rifle fire, and an impromptu rescue party had to go to its relief.

Among the first to arrive was General McAuliffe. The tug plane for his glider had been hit on the way over and one engine caught fire, but Col. William Whittacre, senior pilot from Aldermaston Field, by skillful flying, had managed to keep the fire under control.

Going over the front lines, the glider-riders had seen German soldiers lined up in columns firing at them. Their aim was generally poor, but in Colonel Harper's glider the ping of bullets going through fabric could be heard and telltale holes of light began to appear. Colonel Harper and his jeep driver returned the fire with their own weapons.

Landing, Colonel Harper reported to Division Headquarters at Zon. He then established his CP in the forest south of LZ W with 3d Battalion in position nearby. One of the two pigeons carried by the message center chief, S/Sgt. Dallas E. Walker, was released to fly back to England with the message that the glider landing had been made and giving the coordinates of the assembly. The 3d Battalion's immediate job was to provide local protection for the LZ and the Division Service Area. The 2d Battalion was a thousand yards to the east at Wolfswinkel. The regiment was alerted immediately to go to the aid of the 502d at Best but no move was ordered that night. All through the night the men of the 377th and the 3d Battalion of the 327th worked with the Quartermaster Company recovering supplies from the gliders and chutes scattered over the LZ.

That night the litter-bearer and ambulance sections, who had come in with the Medical Company, were sent to their respective regiments.

THE 506TH TAKES EINDHOVEN

"If you see any Germans just let them filter on through you and I guess the Ducks [502d] will take care of them. We have got to get to Eindhoven this morning, and we can't waste any time killing Germans." With these words to his battalion commanders, Colonel Sink put his regiment on the road to Eindhoven, a city of over one hundred thousand, where enemy concentrations had been reported.

The 506th had spent D-day night just south of the Wilhelmina Canal, across from Zon. A heavy rain made the few hours of sleep uncomfortable, but D plus 1 dawned clear.

The 3d Battalion led the morning march with H and I astride the road. To guard the bridge site a platoon from Company A along with the engineer platoon was left at Zon.

Only six hundred yards beyond the Line of Departure the battalion encountered rifle and machine-gun fire, and from that point all the way into Eindhoven, the column was opposed by little groups of infantry and occasional artillery fire. For about two miles, the 3d Battalion butted its way through, either driving the small groups back by fire or eliminating them where they stood. Then as it moved into the outskirts of Eindhoven it began getting direct fire down the main street from two 88s and mortars. The battalion came to a stop.

Capt. John W. Kiley, battalion S-2, exposing himself, was killed by a sniper in the Woensel church tower. Someone got off a bazooka round, hit the tower and silenced the sniper.

Colonel Sink came forward. He decided that to attempt to force the issue with the 3d Battalion would cause unnecessary losses. So he ordered the 2d swung around it to the left.

Colonel Strayer moved the 2d Battalion quickly down an adjoining road toward the center of Eindhoven, peeling off Company F to make a flank attack on the Germans holding up 1st. The 2d Platoon, the lead element of Company F, was moving west on Pastorie Straat, when at the corner of Klooster Dreef they met the battalion executive, Capt. Charles G. Shettle, who told Lt. Russell Hall that his platoon was to clear out the German 88 battery. The platoon continued to advance during the conversation and fell in behind the Dutchman who had given Captain Shettle information about the gun location and promised to lead the men to it.

Strung out, the column went on up Klooster Dreef without any of the men being sure of the situation or aware of the nearness of the gun. Lieutenant Hall called his rifle grenadiers (Pvts. Homer Smith and Robert W. Sherwood) and tommy gunners (Cpls. Marion J. Grodowski, Willard A. Sharp, Robert E. James and Pvt. Clarence L. Shrout) to get forward to the head of the column. At a corner the Dutchman stopped them and explained in English that the gun was just around the bend in the street.

Once he understood, Lieutenant Hall sent his men to the attack. The block which lay between him and the gun was triangular in shape, with Dutch homes on all three sides. The 2d Squad under Lt. Robert Pardue took the left side of the block—Woenselsche Straat. The 3d Squad was kept in a reserve position in the center of the block and the mortar was set up just a little forward of it. Lieutenant Hall and S/Sgt. John H. Taylor went with 1st Squad which was to move to the left and deploy between the houses of Klooster Dreef. Both assault squads took off through the backyards and then moved up cautiously to the front of the houses. Not a shot was fired. The enemy seemed to have no idea of their presence.

As the 1st Squad got in position, Sgt. George Martin saw a German soldier walking south on Klooster Dreef, shot at him, and missed. Lieutenant Hall, S/Sgt. Hugh Borden, Taylor, and Sherwood, moving through a space between two of the buildings on Klooster, saw a Dutchwoman in a second story window across the street. She waved furtively at them, pointed down the street and held up three fingers. The men stopped. Three German soldiers passed, walking northwest toward the gun. Lieutenant Hall, Taylor and Borden jumped out into the street ten feet behind them, Taylor yelling "Hold on!" and the other two yelling: "Stop!" The Germans seemed completely unnerved though they must have known American troops were in the neighborhood. Offering no resistance, they were moved back into one of the houses.

From the other side of the street, two Dutchmen motioned the squad on toward the Woenselsche intersection, indicating the direction of the gun. Sherwood and Taylor had started out onto the street, when they saw the 88 at the crossroads—150 yards away. Taylor stood on the curb and fired a full clip from his M1 at six Germans who ran toward the gun. Two of them dropped. Later it was learned that they had only been wounded. The M1 jammed. Taylor ran behind a building to clear the clip and reload.

While he was doing so, the Germans got the 88 into operation. The first round knocked a corner off the building about twenty feet above Taylor's head. Sherwood and Taylor pulled back behind the house to get better protection. The gun fired two more quick rounds. Using a tree just behind the gun as an aiming point, Sherwood fired two grenades at a high angle. The second landed five yards behind the gun. At the same time, the grenadier with the 2d Squad, Smith, fired from a position on Woenselsche Straat only seventy-five yards from the gun. To keep under cover he had to fire from his left shoulder. But his second round was a direct hit. Sherwood saw it land, realized that the gun was out, and yelled to Smith, "We got that bastard!"

Sherwood and Taylor ran across the street and there met Sgt. Frank D. Griffin, the mortar leader. Together they went ahead to within sixty-five yards of the gun, where Griffin saw the target clearly for the first time and returned to put his mortar in action. They all felt that though the crew had been driven back by the grenade's fire, the 88 was still operative and needed another touch or two.

Taylor saw a German officer come up behind it. He drew a bead on him as the first mortar round landed—fifteen yards to the right of the gun. The mortar burst hurled the German officer toward one of the houses. Taylor squeezed the trigger, shot him in the leg, saw him get up and run on again. The second mortar round hit directly on the gun. This was quick adjusting, especially since the men had only a mortar tube which they were holding between their legs to fire.

Sherwood put a grenade pointblank into the house after the officer. Unwittingly he achieved a small shamble. The grenade exploded inside the house and wounded ten Germans.

Top: German prisoners guarded by the 101st and British soldiers at the Vechel bridge. Americans in the foreground are from the 326th Engineers and the 501st. Bottom: Prisoners haul a cart of jerricans, K rations, and water bags for 101st paratroopers. The prisoner pushing gave his age as fourteen.

Up to this time the 1st Squad did not know there was a second gun north on Woenselsche Straat. But the 2d Squad had already stumbled upon it and was trying to get into position. As the first gun was knocked out, the second gun opened up with three quick rounds aimed loosely at the houses where the 2d Squad was operating. Smith replied with rifle grenades at a range of 150 yards. None hit the gun.

But the crew couldn't take it. They blew the breach of their gun with a grenade and tried to make a getaway. Six 2d Squad men moved fast across Klooster Dreef and took up a position near the end of the houses. Fourteen Germans from the second gun came running, ducked through a house and started to clear through the beet field beyond it. The Americans fired. They dropped down among the beets. The Americans yelled for them to come out and surrender. They came.

During this action the platoon suffered only two casualties. The Germans lost 13 killed and 41 prisoners.

While these two 88s were being destroyed the body of the 2d Battalion kept on moving downtown toward the bridges.

Late in the morning the 506th made contact with the British XXX Corps, over the Orange Net. They learned that it was still five miles south of Eindhoven, still having difficulty with enfilading German 88 positions along the highway.

General Taylor, who had just driven up, directed that word be sent of the blown bridge at Zon, and that the British be asked to put suitable Bailey bridge equipment at the head of their column. This was done.

The general asked about the 506th situation in Eindhoven. Colonel Sink told Colonel Chase, his executive officer perched up in the top of the Woensel church steeple, to get the latest report from Colonel Strayer. "We hold the center of town and we are sitting on the four bridges over the Dommel River."

General Taylor, disbelief on his face, climbed to the top of the church steeple to talk with Colonel Strayer himself. Convinced, it did not take him long to realize the importance of the news—the 101st's section of the road was clear.

With light hearts the 3d Battalion men now started to move forward through the 88 positions that Company F had taken care of that morning. Where the opposition of a large enemy group had been feared, the 506th had found but one over-strength and badly placed battalion. (The large group civilians had described probably left for Best that morning to add to the difficulties of the 502d.)

Eindhoven was free, the first Dutch city to be liberated. Joyfully its inhabitants crowded around the advancing paratroopers. They made the men welcome with schnapps, beer and other delicacies. Orange streamers appeared everywhere.

In the midst of such difficulties, defense positions were organized, and patrols sent out.

At 1230 two British armored reconnaissance cars entered the city from the north, having bypassed it during their morning patrol. This was the Division's first actual contact with the British column. These cars, it is probable, were the two that shared the vigil of the Wierz-bowski group later on that afternoon.

Not until 1830 did the men of the 506th hear the sound that they had long been waiting for, the clank of tanks of the Guards Armored Division. Looking battered by their day and a half of fighting, they pushed through Eindhoven and on to the north. Advance units reached Zon at 1700.

Here members of the 326th Airborne Engineers had been working all day to clear debris from the bridge site. As Colonel Sink had surmised, they found the center trestle sound. British engineers took over, and during the night installed the Bailey bridge that they had brought along for this purpose.

At 0645 the following morning (D plus 2, thirty-six hours behind schedule) the Guards Armored thudded across this bridge, and the operation began to move according to the original plan—a British armored column attacking up a road cleared by airborne units. Through Zon and on to St. Oedenrode. The individual soldier holding a perimeter defense had been told even less about the progress of the British than his superior officers. All he had known was that he was in the middle of an enemy country, and that something had gone wrong. To him the sound of the tanks, the sight of their guns, was both an assurance and a promise; an assurance that there was a plan and a promise that the plan might work.

Past St. Oedenrode, and on to Vechel. Through Vechel. On to Grave and the territory of the 82d. The first part of the mission of the 101st was accomplished. The road had been opened.

VICTORY AT BEST

Now that the British column had complete use of the highway through the Division area, the 101st began the second phase of its mission—guarding the corridor. The fight at Best had always been for this purpose. This day it was to end in a smashing victory.

Because the Germans had chosen from the first to concentrate on Best, and had been able to bring in men and artillery faster, the fighting there had been a series of disappointments to Colonel Michaelis and his men of the 502d. In sucking enemy reinforcements to Best from all over the Division area, the 502d had made a real contribution to the success of other Division fighting; but that was scarcely apparent to the 502d at the time.

On D plus 2, the balance turned in favor of the Division. As the result of a combined effort by the 502d, the 327th and a British tank squadron, a German force of two to three thousand men was destroyed.

Because of the inconclusive nature of the action at Best and to avoid further piece-meal action General Taylor decided to gather everything together into a task force under General Higgins and to clear up once and for all the Best situation.

The day's first move was inconclusive. Colonel Michaelis ordered 2d Battalion forward at 0600 to resume the attack of the preceding evening toward the bridge. Immediately drawing fire from the woods to the right and from the line of the canal it went about two hundred yards, taking small losses on the way. Not till then did the patrol from Company E report in with word that the bridge was blown. The patrol had lost its way and remained immobile in the darkness. Colonel Chappuis reported to Colonel Michaelis who told him to pull back and take up a defensive position along the line from which he had jumped off. The battalion remained there. Twice German groups attacked it. Both times they were beaten off.

Other enemy groups, coming from the direction of the DZ, had also hit at the flanks of Company G during this exchange, Company G having been uncovered by 2d Battalion's advance toward the bridge. Company G held its lines.

At daylight, General McAuliffe had gone to the 327th CP to order the 2d and 3d Battalions attached to the 502d. Lt. Col. Ray C. Allen moved the 3d out as soon as he learned of the assignment, then he turned it over to his executive officer and hurried ahead to the 502d CP.

Looking for it he stumbled upon a group of two hundred Germans marching south to reinforce those in the Best area. They opened fire on him. Escaping with nothing worse than a hit on a K-ration box in his pocket, he hastened back to his battalion column to deploy it quickly enough to destroy this enemy group. But the Germans sensed danger and gave up their formation to hurry on as fast as they could. Three times 3d Battalion groups hit them, and each time were just a little late. Seventy-five of the rear stragglers were captured and some were killed.

By 1100 the chase was over; the battalion was reorganized and Colonel Allen reported to the 502d CP, now in the woods west of Best.

By this time 2d Battalion of the 327th had reported in, together with the squadron of British tanks and the small amount of British artillery assigned to the forthcoming attack. General Higgins, who had taken charge of the combined forces, shortly outlined the role of each. His purpose was to clear all Germans out of the area northeast of the canal and the road. To accomplish this the 502d, assisted by the tanks, was to place its right flank on the highway and drive south to the canal. This would take care of the main body of the Germans. To get the numerous groups which were known to be scattered through the Zonsche Forest the 2d Battalion of the 327th was to push two smaller forces west and south from Oude Meer, the lake in the middle of the forest. Together they were to crush the enemy against the canal. Simultaneously the 3d Battalion of the 327th was to go north in a move designed to isolate the enemy by the canal and protect LZ W during the landings that afternoon. The time of the attack was to be 1400.

Maj. Roy L. Inman, CO of 3d Battalion, 327th, gave the active assignment to Company G, under Capt. Hugh Evans. He ordered the 1st Platoon to become the right part of the enveloping force and the rest of the company to become the left. Company F he held in reserve.

The left moved off at 1400, with 2d Platoon leading 3d and Weapons. As it followed the road down into the forest, the 2d Platoon split again, placing its 1st and 2d Squads, under Lt. Frank H. Hibbard, on the right of the road, and the 3d Squad, under T/Sgt. Manuel Hidalgo, on the left. The squads advanced quietly down in the ditches until suddenly rifle and machine-gun positions opened fire on them. They hit the dirt and a slight hump in the road ahead gave them the protection they were seeking.

Lieutenant Hibbard notified Captain Evans and he immediately sent two machine guns forward to serve as a base of fire, one on each side of the trail. Due to the same hump one was ineffective and a BAR had to be substituted.

Then, trying a new double envelopment, Lieutenant Hibbard led the 1st and 2d Squads off the trail and through the woods to the left. Hidalgo's 3d Squad moved to the right. Hibbard's men advanced by crawling through the thick growth until they could see and hear a German group of seven men and a machine gun to their left. One of the glidermen who could understand German listened and said he thought they wanted to surrender. A German stood up in his hole, perhaps with this in mind. Someone shot him in the leg. Hibbard yelled, "Cease firing!" but the Germans became uncertain—afraid now to surrender.

Lieutenant Hibbard, wishing to take advantage of the low morale of the enemy, sent back to the machine-gun position for Sgt. Lloyd J. Gross, who spoke German, but without waiting for Gross the squad moved on around these positions.

Sergeant Hidalgo, on the other flank, saw a German with one leg over his bicycle, talking to a man just off the road. Apparently the noise of the 1st and 2d Squads moving through the brush caused the German to believe that the Americans were not going to come down the road. Hidalgo noticed the German had his rifle slung so he fired his first shot over the German's head. The German quickly recovered from his surprise and jumping on his bike started to wheel toward the canal. Hidalgo took a second shot with his M1 and hit the man in the head. The comrade from the foxhole sprang to the bicycle to try to escape. Hidalgo shot him in the leg.

By this time both elements of the platoon had gotten in behind the Germans. It was a double envelopment right out of the textbooks and, with German morale so low, it did the trick. Completely disheartened, the Germans began to surrender individually and in small groups.

Two men went beyond the textbook precepts—Sergeants Hidalgo and Carl J. Hanlon, who now moved up and down the center of the road shouting for the enemy to give up. Backed by the numbers and position of the Americans, this also worked. One group which Hidalgo coaxed out had just taken as its prisoner the commanding officer of the 377th Parachute Field Artillery Battalion, Maj. Harry W. Elkins. Freed, he helped Hanlon guard the Germans by holding a hand grenade threateningly with pin out.

Having knocked out these positions and sent their prisoners to the rear, the men moved on to the canal. They encountered no more enemy until, moving west along the canal, they came to a group of buildings in a clearing. The company was broken into groups of half squads to comb through these.

This brought about a second series of captures. The majority of the prisoners were Germans fleeing the combined infantry-tank attack of the 502d farther west or fugitives from the forces hit in the morning by Colonel Allen's men. Some of the German noncoms were so cowed that it was thought safe to send them back into the forest to bring others out.

The other wing of the Company G dragnet, the 1st Platoon under Lieutenant Morrison, had also started at 1400. It was halted almost immediately by enemy small-arms fire. The platoon deployed. Rifle, machine-gun, rifle grenade, and mortar fire was placed on the enemy positions and after a considerable delay the Germans were forced back. The platoon then moved along its designated route.

It received sporadic rifle fire, mostly overhead, but during the remainder of the march did not encounter any Germans. Now, joining the rest of the company, the men helped round up enemy troops coming in from the west. In all, 159 prisoners were taken. Many more Germans had been killed, without a single casualty to Companies G or F. Temporarily, at least, the woods were clear.

Meanwhile, the 502d had put on a smashingly successful attack that broke the back of the enemy at Best and avenged all the frustrations and defeats which it had experienced at his hands during the preceding forty-eight hours.

The plan had been for the first tanks to go to Companies G and I which with three apiece would move through the area just to the left of the road, down toward the canal. The 2d Battalion, also with six tanks, would stay in place until the 3d Battalion companies came abreast of its position, then join the advance.

But at 1420 while Company I still waited for its tanks, Company G got its three and started forward without an order. With their 17-pounders (76mm) the tanks fired toward the German positions. These rounds, backed by the roar of their motors, seemed to terrify the enemy. For even as Major Stopka ran forward to hold Company G until Company I was set, seventy-five Germans came out of the patch of woods with their hands in the air. The infantrymen rounded them up and the tanks continued firing. To the right Company I was now coming along with its tanks, flushing prisoners out of the roadside ditches.

Major Stopka realized that the whole situation was turning; this attack was going to work. To him, it was clear that "the rumbling of the tanks and the noise of their fire had taken all heart out of the enemy." So he radioed regiment: "Send us all the MPs available." The battalion had a hundred prisoners in the bag before it had started to attack as a whole.

Company I came abreast of G. As the line straightened, Major Stopka yelled, "OK, now, take off!"

The 2d Battalion was already ahead of 3d, going along with its six tanks, through the fields and the patches of woods. Here, too, "the tanks were the decisive factor," according to Colonel Chappuis. One strange development Colonel Chappuis reports—he saw Germans "get up from their fire positions and move toward our lines only to have their own comrades mow them down with machine-gun fire as they were trying to surrender." The operation was hardly more than a mop-up. In two hours 2d Battalion captured seven hundred prisoners.

The 3d Battalion likewise moved right along with prisoners coming into its lines by the hundreds. Major Stopka told his assault force not to bother with the prisoners. "Let them come on back and we'll find some way to take care of them." So the British tanks and American infantry continued to bore forward and the beaten Germans, singly and in little mobs, sifted back through them, neither force paying much attention to the other.

The 3d Battalion's acting executive officer, Capt. Frank Lillyman, mustered a crew of cooks, messengers and oddments and took over the guard detail until the MPs arrived.

The advance went on as far as the canal, sweeping through fields which were littered with enemy dead. That evening, Major Stopka had a detail check the field, and it counted six hundred German bodies. The final prisoner count for both battalions was 1,100.

At the canal, Lt. Champ L. Baker of Company I took one platoon over to the right of the road and cleared out patches of wood along the highway for four hundred yards. The rest of the two battalions held steady along the canal. Jeeps came into the American lines to carry out the wounded. Through it all the Germans in Best itself kept up a desultory artillery fire.

At 1830 Division sent word that the CP was under attack, and the squadron of tanks was dispatched to Zon.

The 502d later returned to a defensive position extending north and east from the blown bridge back into the forest. To its north the 327th dug in for a night that was quiet except for the artillery fire from Best.

Thus were three days of fighting at Best finally crowned by complete victory. The bridge over the canal whose capture had been the mission given to Company H when it was dispatched on D-day had been blown, it is true. But the victory nonetheless was of great importance. For the Germans wiped out at Best had to be defeated somewhere. Otherwise they would have been in a position to overrun the LZ or to keep it under such a steady rifle and artillery fire as to render it unusable. And without the LZ all subsequent glider landings would have been imperiled, if not impossible. Even though Best had started as a diversion, victory there became a major mission of the Division. With that victory, the entire Division position became stronger.

An artilleryman of the 377th Parachute F.A. Battalion comes down on his head.

For the sudden and complete collapse of the hitherto victorious Germans, there was no adequate explanation. But it is known that most of these men, battle-weary and confused, had just retreated across France and Belgium. At some collecting point, possibly Boxtel to the north, they had been shoved into a strange unit and rushed to this new struggle. Initial success cheered them. But they were queasy about fighting paratroopers. And when they heard the tanks as well, it was just too much.

As must be apparent, unit identifications among the prisoners were completely confused. Of the outfits opposing the 101st, the one most completely resembling a division during these first days was probably the 59th Infantry Division.

REINFORCEMENTS

Last-minute exchanges with the 82d Division resulted in the 101st being allotted 385 gliders for the flight on D plus 2, more than twice as many as had originally been planned. But fog and bad weather en route took a heavy toll, and only 209 of these gliders landed safely on LZ W.

Men on that flight spoke of being able to see nothing except three feet of tow rope, stretching out toward nowhere. Some glider pilots failing to bank when their planes did, turned over and had to cut loose. Eighty-two tow planes missed the LZ completely, and after flying circles over Holland, France, or Germany returned to England. Twenty-six gliders on that trip were never accounted for. Sixteen were known to have crash-landed in enemy territory, for some of the men in them got back. Thirty-one landed in friendly territory on the Continent. Most of the occupants managed to rejoin their outfits within a few days.

In all, 1,341 men arrived safely on the LZ, 554 of whom belonged to the 1st Battalion of the 327th and 159 to the 81st Airborne Antiaircraft Battalion. The rest were artillerymen, 337 from the 321st Glider Field Artillery, 190 from the 377th Parachute Field Artillery, 24 from the 907th Glider Field Artillery and the remaining 77 from Division Artillery Headquarters.

An idea of the way this flight was cut to pieces by the fog can be gained from the equipment figures. Of 136 jeeps that left England, only 79 safely reached the LZ. Of 68 guns only 40 came in. The 321st lost 3, and the 377th lost 1. Hardest hit was the flight of the 907th. All the planes towing its twelve 105mm howitzers turned back.

Most of what didn't get in on D plus 2 stayed out for several days. Battery B of the 377th did come in on D plus 3 by parachute. But the next glider flight was D plus 6, and it was small. More than five hundred men and essential equipment were later flown to the Brussels airport. Men and equipment, in most cases, were with their outfits by D plus 10.

One battalion of the 327th spent the night unloading the gliders and protecting the piled equipment from bands of marauding Germans.

The twenty howitzers of the 321st and the 377th that did come in were the first guns to reach the Division during the Holland operation. A combination of reasons had led to the exclusive emphasis upon infantry in the flights of the first two days. With Division objectives so scattered, and the Division itself broken up into small perimeter defenses, General Taylor had felt that no matter where it was placed, artillery could not cover the entire area. And as between allotting space not only for guns, but for transport and ammunition, or giving it to infantry, General Taylor chose the infantry. Then, too, there had been the thought that 101st artillery observers who came in on D-day could direct the fire of British guns. This plan had not worked because the distances involved were too great for the radios. Especially in the early fighting at Best the Division had sorely felt the absence of its artillery.

It was plain hard luck that when the artillery was brought in, the weather cut it to pieces. But the artillerymen simply took this in their stride. For days afterwards small groups came trickling in to their units. Some of them, with the assistance of the Dutch underground, had stubbornly held on to parts of their equipment, and brought it in with them through the enemy lines. One group came in in its own jeep. The 321st took pride in a *Stars and Stripes* story about three of its men:

No one but three airborne boys would ever find themselves in German-held territory 62 miles from their own headquarters with a gliderful of ammunition the way Mike Lewis, Artie Ketterman and Jack Kessel did.

Their tow plane got off course and lost and when their glider finally came down they were deep in a section of Belgium still held by the Germans. The boys abandoned their glider and lugged their trailer load of ammunition into a woods near a main road. They went out on the road, just hoped there were no German troops in the immediate vicinity and flagged down a car. Luckily the first one was driven by a Belgian. When he stopped they dragged their trailer out of the woods and hitched it to his car. He stopped near the Holland-Belgium border, so they climbed out, unhitched the trailer and waited for another hitch-hike. Finally they got back to their outfit, ammunition and all.

The persistence of these few was matched by the work of all the artillerymen during the days of heaviest combat. For the artillery battalions did not have the transport to move themselves and their equipment as frequently as the tactical situation required. Wagons, and even wheelbarrows, were frequently pressed into service to haul ammunition and spare parts.

Even aside from the question of transportation, the job of the artillery battalions was not an easy one. They were expected to do a man's job with a boy's equipment. For the 321st and the 377th had only pack 75s, and the 907th had the infantry cannon, the 105. With these they had to do a bigger job than the more heavily equipped regular division artillery, supporting four infantry regiments instead of three.

Although it does not appear in many of the records, the Division obtained one extra gun on D plus 2. Through accident a glider in the 82d Division tow of that day landed on LZ W. The men of the 377th knew what to do.

The Enemy Attacks Zon

For Division Headquarters in Zon D plus 2 was a day of uneasiness, full of conflicting rumors. They knew how completely the Division was committed to the fight at Best, and they could only hope that the day's action would be decisive. For the Division could hardly afford the concentration of men required there.

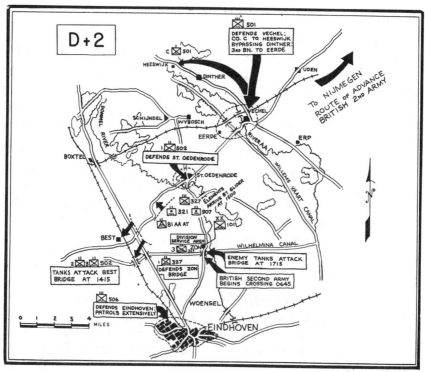

Map 43.

There were reports of German armor massing to the southeast. There were also reports of the British flank corps coming into the 101st area. So about 1700 when tanks rolling toward Zon were reported south of the canal and east of the road, no one was sure whose they were.

Lt. Frederick Starrett, General McAuliffe's aide, along with a liaison lieutenant from the Dutch army, had just come up from the south in General McAuliffe's jeep; General Taylor turned them right around to find out. Leaving the jeep just south of the canal they went forward on foot.

General Taylor also directed Lt. Col. Ned D. Moore, G-1, to investigate the report of German armor. Colonel Moore crossed the bridge. Here Lieutenants Starrett, Adams, Dubois (the Dutch lieutenant), about ten men from Division Headquarters, Private J. J. McCarthy and another man from the 506th joined him. The group had proceeded along the canal for about two hundred yards when they saw movement in the trees along the canal about three hundred yards to the front. A well camouflaged tank burst from the trees and headed along the canal bank toward the bridge. It opened fire on the bridge and soon set a truck on fire on the bridge. Lieutenant Dubois was sent back to

315

the bridge to telephone the CP that the woods contained at least six German armored vehicles accompanied by infantry. The German tank with four riflemen trotting along under its cover kept on toward the bridge, firing with machine guns and tank cannon. People on the bridge returned the fire with small arms and Colonel Moore's group was trapped between the two fires. Lieutenant Adams and a few men jumped into the canal, where Adams drowned.

Colonel Moore, Private McCarthy and the man from the 506th found shelter in a small hole. McCarthy had a bazooka and three rounds of ammunition. The rest of the party dispersed to the rear. As the tank advanced, McCarthy and Colonel Moore opened fire with the bazooka. The first two shots missed and although the third was a hit, it failed to stop the tank. One man jumped out of the hole to find better cover and was killed by the riflemen following the tank. McCarthy and Colonel Moore remained in the hole until the tank and riflemen went by at ten yards distance headed for the bridge. • Another German tank and about a company of infantry moved up and began to dig in about thirty yards from Colonel Moore and Private McCarthy. Every time the two moved the Germans would shoot at them. Why grenades were not rolled into the shallow ditch, only the Germans knew. As darkness came on, the Germans set fire to a barn and a haystack fifty yards south of the canal. The fire highlighted every movement, and the two Americans were pinned in the ditch until about 2200 when the fire died out and they crawled through the German positions. In a roundabout way, they made their way to the bridge and back to Zon where Colonel Moore reported the German strength and positions to General Taylor. Private McCarthy rejoined his platoon on the bridge after being treated for minor wounds. He was killed the following morning in an attack to drive the Germans out of the woods.

After he left the Moore group, Starrett moved northeast into a patch of woods to practically bump into a second tank. The grenade he had been carrying in his hand, pin out, he threw and took off with the tank after him. The grenade had evidently damaged the dispositions of the tankers rather than the tank, which was buttoned up. Gathering some British soldiers on his way, Starrett ran behind a nearby house. The tank continued to follow and fired at the house, wrecking it. But then the main action boiled up and the tank had more important things to worry about. This gave Starrett a chance to organize the scattered groups south of the canal into a line of defense along the road. Here they stayed until the main fight slackened off. Then under cover of darkness they tried to move north to Zon, only to find a truck burning on the canal bridge. The Americans in Zon, seeing them in its light, and mistaking them for more Germans, opened fire. It was 2200 before they could send a messenger across the canal and then get back to town themselves.

In the course of the fighting, General McAuliffe's jeep had been moved along the canal, and then deserted. The members of a German patrol must have had fun that night as they pushed it into the canal.

As the first shells screamed into town that afternoon the Headquarters and Signal Company men hurriedly organized a defense line on the eastern and southern edges of the school yard, north of the canal. Engineers grabbed rifles and became infantrymen again. A machinegun crew from Battery C of the 377th joined in. But their lack of AT weapons prevented them from dealing with the six tanks effectively.

Enemy guns got five direct hits on the schoolhouse, putting the switchboard out of commission and bursting the water pipes. Repairs were started even as the firing continued and wire communications were reestablished that evening.

Radio communication was never interrupted, due to T/5 Gordon B. Gissenass, who stayed at his post throughout the attack.

Meanwhile General Taylor had gone back to the LZ and had led up what was available of 1st Battalion, 327th, and a 57mm gun from Battery B of the 81st. The arrival of the gun was providentially timed. It wheeled into position north of the canal and neatly knocked out the Panther tank that was concentrating on the CP. Shortly thereafter, bazooka fire disabled another tank. This seemed to make the Germans lose heart and they called off the attack. Some remained in the area but were content with exchanging a few rounds every hour. Why they failed to push this attack harder and at least destroy the bridge was a mystery to those who were there.

That afternoon on account of the fight at Best the Division was so short of men that the sole protection on the eastern flank of the command post had been a thin and poorly organized line of glider pilots. Fortunately the attack came from the south, with some advance warning. And fortunately the attacking group both then and the next morning was part of the 107th Panzergrenadier Division, just arrived from Poland and a little bit skittish about its return to combat on the Western Front. Had the raiding party been a little stronger or a little bolder that action might have had an entirely different result.

Division G-2 did a superior job during the next few days putting together a complete picture of this new German division, both for its own regiments and for higher headquarters.

The glider pilots, the most uninhibited individualists in the Army, cannot be dismissed with the statement that they were holding the eastern edge of the CP. There seemed to be something about flying a glider, or being selected for that job, that freed a man from the ordinary restraints of Army life. Those who wanted to fight, fought like lions. Those who wanted to go back to Brussels managed to get there before anyone else. Once their gliders had landed or crashed, there was no flying for them to do. After each airborne operation it had been recommended that glider pilots be organized into units trained in infantry tactics and given a job on the ground. They were usually right up front during those crucial hours when the need for men is greatest. But they successfully defied all such attempts at organization.

It was only because there was no one else that General McAuliffe commandeered a group of them and put them on duty guarding the eastern edge of the command post area. The necessity for having nothing between the command post and Germany except this row of glider pilots suggests the extent to which the Best fighting had drained the Division of men.

As soon as the attack had been beaten back 1st Battalion, 327th, set up a perimeter defense around Zon. During the night two more guns of the 81st were pulled in and a narrow minefield was laid in front of the position by an engineer platoon. Realizing that the 1st Battalion with only one-half of its men would not be able to hold Zon against a determined attack, Division ordered the 506th's 1st Battalion to come north to Zon from Eindhoven. When the battalion arrived it was put in position north of the canal and east of Zon.

Counterattack at St. Oedenrode

On D plus 2, just as on D plus 1, it was on the road to Schijndel that 1st Battalion, 502d, ran into its major scrap. The Dutch underground had warned Company C's Captain Hancock early in the morning that he could shortly expect an attack from the Schijndel direction. He accordingly hustled a patrol forward under Lt. Harry Larson. Advancing under continuous fire the patrol had managed to push back the enemy outpost line. However, it shortly found itself opposed by a reinforced company which blocked further advance and started to encircle both its flanks. By 1100 Lieutenant Larson felt obliged to have his men fall back down the ditches bordering the road and join Lieutenant Mewborn's platoon which had come up in support. But the Germans continued their advance and tried to flank the larger group In preventing this, all of Company C was drawn into the fight.

Watching from his battalion CP, Colonel Cassidy saw that the company was hard pressed but he had no reserve to send to its aid. Suddenly he remembered a tank that had come limping into town that morning with the Irish Guards column. Unable to go more than five miles an hour it had dropped out of the line and stopped in front of the battalion CP. A messenger was dispatched to the tank commander, Sgt. James M. McCrory, to ask if he would help. "Hell, yes!" was Paddy McCrory's reply.

And with that reply the 502d Parachute Infantry got a new member. He was not a jumper—but he had the spirit and he had a tank.

Paddy was short on crew so Battalion Operations Sgt. Roy W. Nickrent and Pvt. John J. O'Brien, Jr., climbed aboard to assist with the firing, and the tank started its slow course up the Schijndel road.

By the time it reached the rear of the company area there were enough bullets zipping around to drive Sergeant Nickrent inside. But McCrory, with his head still out, spotted a battery of three 20mm guns which had been laying a flanking fire on Company C. He opened up at 150 yards. The Germans had not seen his approach, and before they could get off one answering round he had knocked out all three guns.

The timing couldn't have been more opportune. It came just as C's whole line was getting its heaviest deluge of 88, 20mm and mortar fire in the middle of the enemy assault. The destruction of the battery stifled the enemy offensive and for a few minutes the action remained in balance.

McCrory went on up the road toward Schijndel. Sergeant Nickrent, again on the outside, saw what looked like another camouflaged gun position and he yelled until he got McCrory's attention. McCrory searched for about ten seconds, then cut loose and destroyed the gun with two rounds. The tank limped on. A German truck, parked in a field, started toward the Schijndel road on a getaway. The tank's first round hit it squarely; it was an ammunition truck and exploded all over the landscape.

By now bullet fire was again finding the turret and Nickrent felt that things were too hot. So he slid down off the hull and dog-trotted behind the tank. But the fire on both flanks seemed to be "closing in all around" him and, after going along this way for about fifty yards, he ran and flopped in the ditch on the right of the road. As he flattened he saw three prone figures up ahead of him. While he did not get a clear look at them, he thought they were Americans, or maybe dead Germans. But as he hit the dirt they arose—three Germans surrendering. Before Nickrent could raise his tommy gun Germans were com-

ing at him from all sides anxious to surrender. By this time Company
C men had caught up with him, and the Germans were quickly dis-
armed and sent to the rear.

Within the tank Private O'Brien saw that Nickrent was no longer
acting as observer so he borrowed a Sten gun and climbed up into the
turret. He continued to stand there and spray the ground ahead until
a bullet mortally wounded him.

With the help of the tank the company had advanced about five hundred yards. Even when three more British tanks reported in from Zon,
Colonel Cassidy felt that in stopping the Germans he had accomplished
his purpose. Rather than leading out with the tanks and risking a
longer and larger fight, he called his platoons back to man their roadblock. Fifty-three prisoners had been taken and over thirty Germans
killed.

Sergeant McCrory, upon being thanked for the crucial assistance
which he and his tank had given that afternoon, said only "When in
doubt, lash out." Some still consider that the motto of the battalion.

While this skirmish was taking place on the north side of the battalion sector, Company A men on the south were not idle. A German
patrol hit the platoon under Lt. Delmer O. Idol, then withdrew, returned to hit Lt. E. W. Gaydon's group farther down, and withdrew
again with no one hurt. A patrol under Lt. Maurice LeGrave, striking
southwest, found a German battalion in position near Donderdonk,
got in a fight with a German patrol behind its own lines and returned
with a prisoner.

506TH AND 501ST

The 506th, with a squadron of tanks from the 15/19 Hussars, started
a concerted effort to widen the Eindhoven section of the corridor on
D plus 2. The 3d Battalion was dispatched toward Winterle, a town
about six miles to the west. Before the battalion reached it the ad
vancing British flank corps sent word that it would take responsibility
for it. So the battalion was recalled.

The 2d Battalion was sent toward Helmond about eight miles east.
Before it got there the regiment learned that a German column was
loose in the area. (It was the one which attacked Zon later that afternoon.) The 2d Battalion was recalled to the defense of Eindhoven.
This recall of the battalion probably averted another Best; for Division
later learned that Helmond was a bastion of German defense.

D plus 2 was not a day to be forgotten by Company A men; for,
mounted on tanks, they spent their time dashing from one trouble
spot to another.

As rumors of the threatened German attack reached Eindhoven, the orange bunting disappeared from the windows and store fronts and the civilians became quiet.

Both 3d and 2d Battalions were bivouacked well out in the suburbs. This was fortunate; for that night German bombers gave the central part of the city a terrific plastering. Civilian casualties ran well over a thousand. The British outfits spending the night in town were badly battered. Headquarters and Service Companies were the only 506th units in the city. The men in these companies dove into the trenches dug around their building, which had formerly been a Gestapo headquarters, and suffered thirteen casualties.

On D plus 2 Col. Howard Johnson, commanding the 501st at Vechel, decided it would be more effective to outpost his area strongly than to keep all his forces concentrated passively in the one city. So he sent 3d Battalion to Eerde and dispatched Company C north to the Heeswijk-Dinter area. Both groups occupied their new positions without much difficulty.

Another move occurred on D plus 2 which later events were to make peculiarly fortunate. The Medical Company sent an attached platoon of the 50th Field Hospital forward to Vechel to establish a station there. Two days later a surgical team was sent to join them. They were shortly to get more work than they could handle.

Hare and Hounds With the Heinies

The freeing of Major Elkins of the 377th Parachute Field Artillery Battalion was mentioned in connection with the advance of the 327th through Zonsche Forest. How Major Elkins was first captured is part of a story.

Along with his reconnaissance officer and three enlisted men, Major Elkins had set out in a jeep early in the morning of D plus 2 to report to the 502d CP and plan the artillery support when guns would be available. While going through the unfamiliar woods the party was fired on and then surrounded by what was obviously a greatly superior enemy force. It quickly became a case of every man for himself. Robert Allen had the most luck or the most skill. He eluded detection and found his way back to the battalion CP the same afternoon. The reconnaissance officer gave the slip to the immediate enemy group but shortly ran into other ones. He managed to elude detection and reached the CP on the next day with data on enemy positions.

The other two enlisted men, Corporal Propst and Private Topper, were captured along with the jeep. They offered to use it to pick up

German casualties and were told to go ahead. After doing this for several hours they managed to slip back over to friendly troops with two wounded Germans. Taking on an additional three wounded Americans, they set out to find an aid station. But they lost their way, were cut off once more and wound up in Best in enemy hands.

Slick talking on their part convinced a German captain that they deserved consideration for bringing in the German wounded. They got it. After removing the two Germans he personally accompanied them back to the American lines where they reported in with their vehicle, their wounded comrades, and information about the enemy situation at Best.

Major Elkins alone had a really hard time. He got too close to a German outpost to move and had to hug his one spot of earth for six hours. During this time he was caught in the middle of a machine-gun duel, but was not hit. Finally the Germans realized his presence, surrounded and captured him. But this so engrossed them that they did not realize that almost at the same moment men of the 327th were surrounding them. Recaptured within a few minutes, Major Elkins gladly assisted the glidermen in taking care of the prisoners.

Overall Operation at End of D Plus 2

When the Guards Armored Division thundered north from Vechel on the morning of D plus 2 it was moving into a situation that was not developing according to plan. The 82d, into whose portion of the corridor it advanced, had secured most of its objectives. But it had not been able to capture the crucial bridge across the Waal River at Nijmegen. This was taken only by a heroic effort on the afternoon of D plus 3.

Crossing the Waal on D plus 4, days behind schedule, the Guards Armored found that the Germans had used the extra time to set up defenses along the rest of the road to the north. Further advance was slow and costly.

Meanwhile, what of the British, beyond the Lower Rhine River at Arnhem? Misfortune had dogged them from the beginning. They landed in an area where there were more German troops than were to be found in the American areas to the south. German reinforcements came in faster. Their own airborne reinforcements were delayed by bad weather. Their supplies were dropped into enemy hands. They had not been able to seize the bridge that would give them contact with the south bank of the river. By D plus 3 their position was becoming desperate.

The airborne landings in Holland did not come as a complete surprise to the German High Command. Its members knew that the Allies had large airborne forces ready to be committed. But in their estimate of the situation they had expected the airborne landings to be in some other place and in conjunction with new seaborne landings. They were fully acquainted with all the factors that made the Holland operation such a risky one and they had concluded that the Allies would attempt no such thing. They were therefore surprised on September 17 but the High Command immediately saw the significance of the attack and day by day took more extended countermeasures.

Since the airborne landings had been made in the sector of the First Parachute Army, its commander became responsible for the immediate countersteps. All available Luftwaffe groups in the area were placed at the disposal of his local commanders. Antiaircraft units were formed into battle groups. New fortress battalions were attached to the First Parachute Army, and one infantry division was ordered to move to the landing area. On D plus 1 an armored brigade, an assault-gun battalion and two Volksgrenadier divisions started for the corridor.

The strategy the High Command agreed upon was to contain the corridor at its base, then cut it just as quickly as possible. This seemed especially desirable after the armor of XXX Corps had moved to the north. No great force could be secured to attack the corridor from the west however, for Hitler refused to allow any movement of troops from the Fifteenth Army positions along the Scheldt Estuary. It was his belief that even if a reduced effort failed to cut the corridor in the vicinity of Eindhoven the line of the Waal River could be held, the northern airborne elements reduced and the corridor cut at a later date from the east.

D Plus 3 (September 20): The Defense of Zon

Early in the morning of the 20th the 107th Panzer Brigade renewed its assault on Zon.

To Capt. T. P. Wilder of the Division Reconnaissance Platoon had been given the job of finding out just how and where the German tanks were crossing the river to get into the area from which they were attacking the town. A patrol sent out the evening before had been unable to learn anything.

While it was still dark Captain Wilder and nine of his men piled into two jeeps, crossed the Wilhelmina Canal bridge at Zon, and set out along a narrow byroad leading south of town. A mile out they met a British colonel and his driver in an armored car. They were

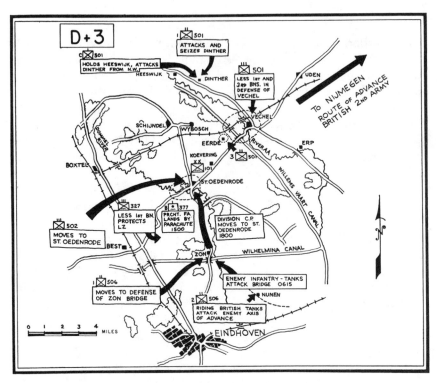

Map 44.

on the same mission but, in addition, wished to find how the British might bring their tanks down into the area to drive off the German armor. The American captain and the British colonel decided their vehicles should form a unit and continue the reconnaissance together.

With the British vehicle in the lead the contingent continued down the road. After perhaps a mile the British armored car suddenly halted in the middle of a narrow road. Dismounting to ask the reason for the delay, Captain Wilder saw a group of about 150 soldiers filing across the road directly ahead of the British vehicle. As he approached the colonel's car one soldier came down a ditch along the road, smiled at the British colonel, and then passed on to join the group.

Captain Wilder, a little startled at the uniform of the man in the ditch, hurriedly asked the colonel why he had stopped. The colonel replied, "These are some of your chaps, aren't they?"

"No, they are Germans," answered the captain.

"Then what do you suggest we do?" asked the colonel. "We'd better try to get out of here in a hurry," replied the captain and, suiting action to words, he piled into his jeep, only to find that due to the narrowness of the road all three vehicles were forced slowly to back their way fifty yards before being able to turn around.

As they were backing the Germans too began to realize that these could not be their own troops. They fired but in the dimness of the early morning caused no casualties. Returning down the road the reconnaissance men deployed and set up two machine-gun nests with cross fire to hold off the German columns. They were relieved two hours later by larger infantry forces.

Even as this bizarre incident was taking place in the morning fog, the Germans moved in force against Company C of the 327th. Company C was holding a 400-yard front south of the canal with its headquarters group, its 1st Platoon, and its light-machine-gun and mortar sections—the rest of the company had been lost en route to Holland. The outpost that first gave the alarm was wiped out in the fighting, and the company commander, Capt. Walter L. Miller, had to shift his men rapidly from one place to another to prevent an immediate breakthrough. Fortunately the terrain offered the attackers little cover. There were a few shallow ditches leading up to the Zon bridge, but Company C men never gave up their grip on these.

The guns of Batteries A and B of the 81st kept the two supporting tanks at a respectful distance and the German infantry was beaten off.

Then the Germans launched an assault against the positions of the 1st Battalion of the 506th north of the canal. These men also held.

An hour after the first attack strengthened German infantry units supported by eight tanks renewed their push against the positions of the 327th. Sharp fighting followed, involving not only the men of the 327th but also a platoon and a half of the 326th Engineers. As the lines began to give and the need for more troops became extreme, thirty company clerks and other headquarters men from 1st Battalion, 506th came marching by. They were rushed into the fight. The howitzers of the 377th which had been set up on the LZ aided with their fire.

The balance turned with the arrival of ten British tanks, which had been requested too late the day before, from Best. The two leading tanks ran into the engineer-laid minefield and were destroyed despite the efforts of the Company C men to warn them. Captain Miller had jumped on the back of the leading tank but before he could get his warning across the tank hit a mine and he was blown off. The German guns chased Miller behind some buildings (he had been hit in the leg but it didn't interfere with his running), then turned their attention to a British gasoline truck coming up the road and sent it up in a spectacular blaze. During this time Pvt. Herschel C. Parker had remained in the open, manning a machine gun against the approaching Germans.

The eight remaining British tanks destroyed four of the German tanks at the cost of one more of their number. By mid-morning a general German withdrawal had started.

This attack temporarily halted traffic on the road. But the Germans had not cut the road. Had they acted more aggressively they might have been able to do so.

Once the German assault was stopped it was necessary to clear their forces from the area. At 1145 a hastily organized attack moved south between the road and the Dommel River. Company A, 327th, reinforced with a platoon from the 506th, was given the open ground along the river, while Company C, also reinforced, moved through the wooded sector with its right shoulder on the highway. Three British tanks advanced directly behind the column to take care of any strongpoints. Four others traveled along the highway to pour fire into the enemy flank. Without maneuvering the attacking companies drove forward. The tanks fired ammunition by the belt. To keep the tankers informed as to the location of the front line a yellow flag on a twenty-foot pole was carried between the advancing companies. Despite difficult terrain and mixed organization the attack cleared the area. While only two men were killed and twenty-eight wounded, the companies had become scattered in the forest, so at Bokt the force halted to reorganize. One hundred eighty-five Germans had been captured in the engagements that morning. Trucks once more started up the road.

This second attack on Zon made it obvious that Division Headquarters should be moved to a town more suitable for control of the Division. So at 0830 it was transferred temporarily to the village of Wolfswinkel, and at 1600 on up to a large castle in St. Oedenrode. Complete wire systems were maintained in both places. During that morning General Brereton and General Taylor had used Colonel Sink's headquarters in Eindhoven as their meeting place.

The Division Service Area remained near Zon with the 326th Engineers as its security.

Another effort to clear the enemy from the Zon area was made later that day by the 2d Battalion, 506th. A report had come in that there were fifty enemy tanks at Nunen east of Zon and Eindhoven and it was thought that this must be an enemy concentration point. So

Company E with a squadron of British tanks was sent out to reconnoiter and perhaps raid it. A German force intercepted them and an evenly drawn tank-infantry battle developed. Company F with another squadron of tanks was sent as reinforcement that afternoon. But the fight never became decisive, and at dusk the British and Americans disengaged and withdrew to Eindhoven.

During the afternoon of D Plus 3 an attempt was made to get the Germans in the vicinity of Best to surrender. The 506th S-2 section had got reports from wounded Germans that their comrades were contemplating giving up. Late in the afternoon a group from the 506th under a flag of truce approached the blown bridge across the Wilhelmina Canal in their sector. The German bridge guards allowed three of the party, Capt. Richard P. Meason, Capt. Samuel C. Feiler (a dental officer acting as interpreter), and a Dutchman, member of the underground, to cross. The three men were blindfolded, led about 500 yards from the bridge, and taken into a CP. They explained their mission to the German commander, a major. The German said there was no possibility of surrender. The three men were again blindfolded and led back to the bridge. Their German guards, who had privately expressed to them their hope that a surrender could be arranged, were downhearted when they heard that the major had refused. Across the canal the Americans and the Dutchman rejoined the group waiting for them and returned to their CP at Eindhoven, reaching there at about 2130.

THE 327TH

When the 502d had won its great victory the day before it had made no effort to clear out the Germans west of the highway in the vicinity of Best itself. The large German group left there was reinforced during the night and remained as a menace to the entire division flank. So on D plus 3 the 327th gradually assumed its responsibility— to protect the Division area from this force and to hold LZ W. During the day its regular support moved in, the 321st Glider Field Artillery and Battery A of the 81st.

The 2d Battalion made another sweep through Zonsche Forest that morning to clear out any Germans who might remain. It later established a defensive position along the east border of the forest and remained there for two days. The forest was patrolled constantly during that time but no more enemy was encountered.

The 3d Battalion was drawn into a skirmish that afternoon protecting the LZ, but the German raiding party got away with small losses.

To this battalion went the responsibility for gathering supplies as they came in and forwarding them to Division.

502D UNITED AT ST. OEDENRODE

When D plus 3 dawned the 2d and 3d Battalions of the 502d were still down near Best. General Taylor wanted to pull them out and send them to St. Oedenrode, but German artillery fire on the area made this impossible, so they stayed in place and took their losses. Again the Germans had reinforced Best during the night. Just before noon two batteries of the 377th went to their support, and by excellent counterbattery work reduced the enemy fire. The same guns also halted several German attempts to move trucks loaded with troops down the road to Best from the north.

By late afternoon movement had become possible, and 2d Battalion pulled out to St. Oedenrode at 1700 with 3d Battalion following.

Throughout the day there had been spasmodic but heavy shelling of St. Oedenrode also. At 1230 the enemy artillery found the range of the 1st Battalion CP. After the shells had killed four men and wounded two, Colonel Cassidy moved his headquarters into the basement of an old factory.

But enemy guns were not yet through with St. Oedenrode. While the advance detail was readying the castle there for Division CP, self-propelled artillery opened up on it with direct fire. Colonel Cassidy took two British tanks and a squad of men from Company A and, as darkness fell, drove off these guns.

Now united for the first time since the drop, the 502d took responsibility for the defense of the St. Oedenrode area. In support it had the 377th Parachute Field Artillery, which had also moved from Best, and Battery C of the 81st.

THE 501ST ACCOMPLISHES A CANNAE

The mission of the 101st in Holland was not to kill Germans but to create and hold a corridor. Aggressive patrolling was taken for granted, but if too many groups spent too much time roaming around the country looking for a fight, the resulting engagements and shifts might seriously weaken the ability of the Division to accomplish its original mission. On the other hand, the road couldn't be defended by sitting on it and letting the enemy organize his strength for an overwhelming attack at one crucial spot.

General Taylor phrased his dilemma thus, referring both to engagements already described and battles still to come:

The only comparable operation in history that I know of was the defense of the western railroad lines against the Indian raids during the period following our Civil War. We were forced to spread along the highway, garrisoning key towns with the hope of being able to move rapidly to meet hostile thrusts before they could become dangerous. When the enemy was close enough to the road to be dangerous to the traffic on it, he had to be fought and destroyed; on the periphery of this vital zone it was a matter of nice judgment to decide how to discourage the enemy from attacking without becoming involved in a serious engagement. The action at Best may appear to have been a piece-meal engagement which got out of control; actually, that is not the case although no one knew in advance that a major engagement would be the outcome of our patrol of the Best bridge. The Germans in that area had to be liquidated in order to protect our vital drop zone area. Had the 502nd not flushed these Germans, they would have had the leisure to mount an organized attack upon the drop zone.

Similarly, the 501st around Schijndel nearly became overly involved and diverted from their mission of defending Vechel. However, the fine leadership of the battalion commanders allowed them to extricate themselves just in time.

The problem was to meet rapidly changing situations, concentrating enough strength in time to prevent a major disaster to the highway. The slowness of the British in coming up and taking over responsibility for the southern towns in our area of responsibility made it most difficult to maintain tactically sound dispositions. For example, the 502d was held at St. Oedenrode for lack of British relief when its presence near Vechel might have allowed us to obtain a more decisive success. Many times the Division Commander was obliged to form improvised tactical grouping under the command of General Higgins or General McAuliffe giving to them all the available means to handle a local situation. Thus, the fight at Best was the work of General Higgins while General McAuliffe conducted the defense of Vechel during its most critical days.

Colonel Cassidy of 1st Battalion, 502d, on D Plus 2 had faced the same problem in his fight on the Schijndel road. He knew that the way to hold St. Oedenrode was not to sit inside it and let the Germans strike when ready. But at the same time he did not want to commit himself too fully on the road from Schijndel, when the real peril might be approaching down the road from Olland or the road from Vechel. He accepted the fight when he had to, but pulled back almost immediately after he had put the German attackers on the run.

This dilemma of the commanders accounts for the speed with which units of the 506th were moved out of Eindhoven in the morning, and back to it in the afternoon. It accounts for Colonel Johnson of the 501st seizing Eerde, then relinquishing it, then taking it again. And it accounts for his next engagement. For on the morning of D Plus 3 Johnson threw doubts to the winds and gave Kinnard permission to use his entire battalion in an offensive sweep up to Heeswijk. His confidence in the offensive was to be abundantly vindicated that day.

The object of Colonel Kinnard's attack was to destroy enemy forces which his patrols had found in this area all along the north bank of the canal.

Company C was already in the Heeswijk–Dinter region, having moved up to outpost those towns the day before. Taking advantage of this fact, Colonel Kinnard converted what might have been an ordinary infantry attack into a maneuver that had as its goal the total encirclement of the enemy, a Cannae.[4]

This was to be accomplished by using Companies A and B to force the enemy back into a killing zone that would be set up by Company C. C, to become the dustpan of the operation, would take positions extending from a point to the south of Heeswijk up to the drawbridge over the canal. Companies A and B, which were to be the broom, would sweep up to C through the five-mile area between the canal and the highway.

Both attacks jumped off at 0930. For the broom, B was on the left with its left shoulder on the canal; A was on the right with a several-hundred-yard gap between the two companies. Capt. Stanfield A. Stach of A had his company move out, 2d Platoon on the left bank of the river and 3d Platoon on the right. The 1st Platoon in support was echeloned to the right and following 3d within seeing distance—about three hundred yards. Behind the 2d Platoon Stach placed a LMG section from Headquarters Company. He, himself, started out with the guns, but soon was up ahead of the 2d Platoon.

He knew in advance that the Aa River, which he was using as a platoon boundary, was going to give him difficulty. He also worried about the gap between Companies A and B. In an effort to reduce the risk from this he told off his left-hand squad to act as a continuing patrol between the two. But this squad soon became lost and was a cipher during the crisis of the action.

The advance proceeded quietly for about half an hour; then a German machine gun in a windmill on the right bank opened fire across the river on the 2d Platoon area. The men dropped fast and no one was hit. Captain Stach went on forward along with Lt. Billy Turner of 2d Platoon and Lt. George Murn. While they were working their way across a field they noticed four Germans in the weeds about a hundred yards ahead. No one fired and Stach called on the Germans to surrender. Instead they flopped into a drainage ditch and disappeared.

Thinking he must be close to the German MLR, Stach called back for two of his LMGs and put them in position on the ground where he had been standing. Then he and his group crawled forward through

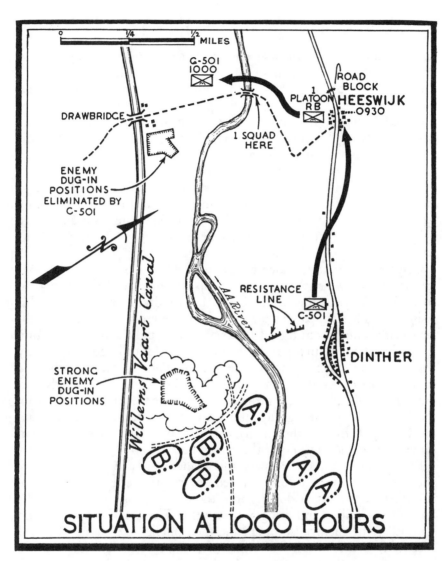

Map 45.

a high-weeded pasture. Ahead of them they saw a line of trees with flanking ditches providing fairly good cover. This they thought was the enemy position. They continued crawling forward. When they were about 125 yards away heavy rifle, machine-gun and machine-pistol fire broke out, enveloping them. But Turner and his platoon sergeant crawled ahead another forty yards, dropped into a drainage ditch, and stayed out of sight. Captain Stach sent one man back with word to get up the whole LMG section. They were on the move in less than

ten minutes, but it seemed so long to Stach that he became anxious
and crawled back to get them himself. One gun and one of his rifle
squads he was able to get forward by fire and movement to the ground
he had just left. The other guns he put on his left flank to fire over
the ground separating him from B Company and keep the enemy
from enveloping his line. More than that he could not do. For his
contact squad had already disappeared and his 3d Squad had lost a
man and had been scattered through the woods.

Even with only this fraction of a platoon Stach was still able to
maneuver. Under pressure from the machine guns on the left enemy
fire fell off, and the rifle squad and the machine guns took advantage
of the lull to get up to the ditch where Lieutenant Turner and his
sergeant had taken refuge.

Despairing of getting much farther without help Stach sent a runner
to 1st Platoon, which had been in support, with word that it was to
cross the river via the bridge near the windmill and come to his
assistance. Then, impatient for more men, he crossed the Aa himself,
detached a squad from the 3d Platoon, and brought it back with him.
This squad he sent up the right flank of the field leading to the enemy
position, meanwhile signalling Lieutenant Turner and his group to
open up with everything they had. A heavy growth of weeds and
occasional wild plum trees provided some concealment, and aided by
the fire from Turner's group, the squad was able to move up from
ditch to ditch toward the enemy. Shortly after it started 1st Platoon
came up and took off along the same route.

Emboldened by the success of this maneuver, Lt. Cecil O. Fuquay
and six men from the left decided to try to speed up the action.
Together they charged directly into the open, going at a run for the
line of trees, yelling and firing as they went. This act of simple bravado
stampeded the enemy. Leaping from their ditches, the Germans pulled
back toward a road on their right (the main position) and to a red
barn farther to the rear. Sgt. Rudolph Brumley of 1st Battalion Headquarters Company, a popular member of the original company, was
the only one killed during this bold rush. The rest of the group
jumped into the ditches that the Germans had just vacated and continued to fire toward their left front.

Far over on the right Captain Stach and the squad he was leading
reached the deserted defense line and commenced firing on the fleeing
Germans.

From there they saw Lieutenant Turner run out into the open field
on the left, stand completely exposed and yell for the Germans to

come in and surrender. Some of them were persuaded, turned back and came toward the American lines. Lt. Sumter Blackman, who had followed Turner out, collected the prisoners and headed them back. Made confident by his success, Lieutenant Turner ran on to the next field, stopped near the center and again called loudly for surrender. But now he was in front of the main body of Germans; he got a bullet through his head and died. Pfc. John C. Webb, one of the machine gunners who had accompanied him, fell dead by his side.

By this time the Germans had completed the occupation of their true MLR, the ditch to the left and the red barn to its rear. They were starting to bring down heavy fire on the Americans. The 1st Battalion soldiers were forced to the cover of the ditches to wait for a new attack to be organized.

While this flight was in progress the 3d Platoon, over on the other side of the river, had not been idle. Under Lt. Henry J. Pulhaski it had managed to wipe out the machine gun in the windmill, whose firing had opened the whole engagement. Learning of this, Stach sent Pulhaski word to press on to the outskirts of Dinter. As the platoon moved forward into the open it began to receive fire from the Germans opposite Stach. But seeing two Germans directly to his front get up and wave white handkerchiefs Pulhaski walked on forward. A shot rang out at close range. Then fire broke out all along the line in front of Pulhaski and he fell, riddled with bullets. His men found cover.

Company B, after some early difficulties, had an experience with the enemy that made it the victim of a similar treachery. Advancing about twelve hundred yards through deserted terrain the men saw white handkerchiefs tied to the bushes ahead. Thinking they had a surrender they pressed forward rapidly and were within three hundred yards of the German positions when heavy fire broke out. Fortunately most of it was high and ineffective; only one man was hit before all went down.

Lt. Ian B. Hamilton was not one to stay on the ground. He sent word up and down his line, "In ten minutes we will get up and go on." When the time elapsed he moved, and his men got up and followed him.

But during this short interval much of the enemy fire had been drawn over to Company A on the right. One other development kept this quick advance from being costly. While they were down a small group of riflemen on the right had noticed that the three 20mm guns which were harassing them had not been dug in. Crawling forward these men with well directed fire drove the Germans away from them.

Mortar fire completed the destruction of these weapons. This crippling of the enemy's principal arm had an almost decisive effect on the action. Ignoring the rapidly diminishing fire from the enemy's six mortars, Company B men moved forward. Reaching a ditch off to the left of the same red barn toward which A was fighting, they concentrated the fire of their LMGs and mortars on that target. By pure coincidence, for the companies were not in close communication at this point, this was well timed to lift the pressure from A.

Discouraged by the double attack, the enemy decided to quit. Hands in air, fifty Germans came out of the red barn. Seeing this, Germans on the firing line laid down their arms. The two companies advanced, made contact and rounded up the prisoners. When they moved forward again it was shoulder to shoulder, for the sector had narrowed. Advance was quick for the back of the resistance had been broken. By 1500 the two companies abreast were only five hundred yards short of Dinter. Patrols were out along the highway to round up any enemy who tried to escape to the northeast.

About two reinforced companies of Germans had been distributed over the position around the windmill and the red barn. All were now dead, prisoner, or fleeing in panic toward the rear where C awaited their coming.

For the "dustpan" was already in place. Under Capt. Robert H. Phillips the two platoons of C which were at Dinter had moved out through Heeswijk and on to the canal early that morning. The platoon at Heeswijk was left there except for one squad, which was moved southwest to cover the bridge across the Aa.

As Captain Phillips and his two platoons approached the canal, machine-gun fire broke out from the houses on its bank. The men dropped into the ditches along the road and volleyed into the houses. The German force disintegrated. Some surrendered; some slipped out to the rear, crossed the canal, and pulled up the drawbridge. Among the prisoners captured in this advance was the German battalion commander.

Company C pressed on to the bank. From behind the covering dike the company drove the Germans back from the opposite shore with rifle fire. One group tried to bring the drawbridge down by cutting the chain with a bazooka round. It was a good idea but it didn't work. So under cover of fire from the rest of the company Lt. Eugene D. Brierre and a squad rowed across in a small boat, fanned out, and then lowered the bridge. Captain Phillips moved a platoon across the canal to hold the bridgehead.

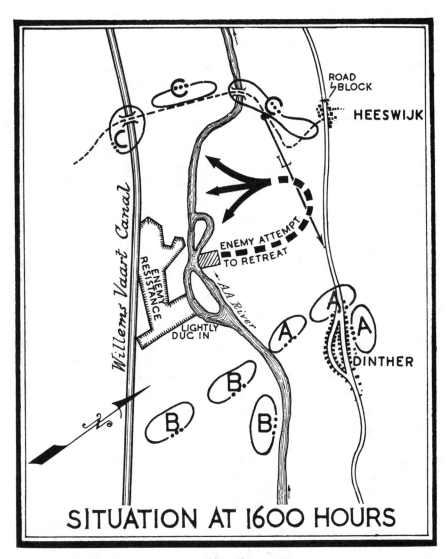

Map 46.

Around noon C received its first fire from within the "trap" area. Small groups moving northwest got within range, took up ground in a disorganized fashion and fired uncertainly in C's direction. Phillips used his mortars to keep these enemy groups from coming too close.

It was not till about 1500 that the Germans made their all-out attempt to break out of the trap. With a rush they moved toward a wooded area along the canal. But Captain Phillips had carefully placed a machine gun to cover their route. It caught them in the flank, mowed some of them down, and drove the others back.

335

They then tried a trick, shouting, "Kamerad!" but coming forward with their weapons. Captain Phillips sent word by messenger that they'd have to put down their weapons or he'd fire. The messenger returned. "They said they have plenty of time," he told Captain Phillips. "It is too early in the day to surrender." Phillips yelled in reply, "I'm going to kill every damned one of you." His mortars had not fired on this large group at all and the machine guns had gone quiet during the negotiations. He signalled them to let everything loose at once.

Within five minutes he saw the Germans clinging to earth, throwing their rifles and pistols high in the air in token of surrender. So he told his men to hold their fire. In the first group 120 Germans came in, dragging forty wounded. Others came after them; some who had managed to cross the canal now came back to surrender. Phillips had only eighty men at the position, so he pulled his 3d Platoon down from Heeswijk to help handle the prisoners.

Colonel Kinnard in the meantime had circled around the north end of his advancing line and had reached C's position in time to see the trap close. B and A came steadily on, and at 1730 B's scouts moved into C's position. Company A had swung more toward the highway to cut any final attempt at a breakthrough. The total bag netted 418 prisoners, 40 dead, 40 wounded—all from the same unit, the *Ewald* or *Jungwirth* Battalion of a parachute training regiment. The battalion losses for the day were four killed, six wounded.

This annihilation of a German force was accomplished by inferior numbers which initially had no advantage whatever in potential fire power. Prisoners taken that afternoon say that at the time the line confronting A and B crumbled, the defenders, without wire communication, did not know that C had moved into the backstop position. Hence the first surrenders were induced by the close-up fire fight and not by maneuver. The larger group which surrendered to C, however, was already beating back from the direction of the A-B assault when first brought under fire from C. It appears probable that this was their first intimation that there was an American force on their rear. However, they did not know whether it was a picket squad or an organized position, and their early bickering with Phillips was probably a probing gesture. It took only two well placed machine guns and four 60mm mortars to convince them that they were powerless.

As the companies came together C pushed its bridgehead about two hundred yards farther south of the canal; B set up a perimeter defense around Heeswijk for the night, and A around Dinter. They stayed there all through D plus 4 and were not engaged.

For the rest of the regiment D plus 3 was a quiet day. The 2d Battalion in Vechel assisted 1st in late afternoon by caring for the prisoners as they came in. Some of its men remember watching three C-47s, returning from a trip to the British at Arnhem, shot down near their position.

The 3d Battalion remained at Eerde. Its patrols reported Germans digging in in the Schijndel area.

SUPPLY

The sole reinforcement received on D plus 3 was Battery B of the 377th Parachute Field Artillery Battalion. The planes in which this battery was flown encountered such heavy flak on their first try at the DZ that they had to turn around and approach from a new direction. Both men and guns were jumped in the late afternoon. There were few jump casualties and almost all equipment was quickly recovered.

The seaborne echelon docked at Omaha Beach in Normandy that morning and started the long trek northward to the fighting.

By D plus 3 supplies were short and getting shorter. There was only a thirty per cent recovery of the paradrop that day, no gasoline and only one meal for the troops. The story on D plus 4 was to be substantially the same. Each soldier had come in with one K ration and two D rations, but these were already used up. Civilians wanted to help but their supplies were meager. Captured German rations were used by those lucky enough to get them. But many soldiers, especially those far from LZ W, were not getting enough to eat. Some of the sluggishness and contrasting desperateness which may be detected in the fighting after D plus 5, was due to lack of rest, and some of it was due to lack of food.

Throughout the first three days of the campaign there had been no evacuation of casualties from the Division area. The road had been too crowded with north-bound traffic to permit it. But on the morning of D plus 3, thirty ambulances and four 2½-ton trucks took the Division wounded through to the 24th Evacuation Hospital in Bourg–Léopold, Belgium. Except during the hours when the road was cut these trips would continue through the rest of the fight.

D PLUS 4 (SEPTEMBER 21): 506TH

In contrast to the checks it received on D plus 3, the 506th succeeded

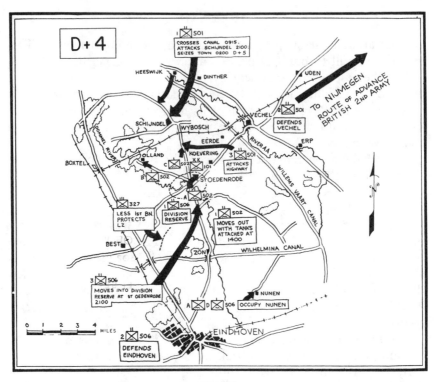

Map 47.

in widening its part of the corridor on D plus 4. Companies A and D pushed out into Nunen, the town which the Germans had so strongly defended the day before. This time the two companies occupied and held it without a fight. The remainder of 2d Battalion stayed in the Eindhoven area, the rest of 1st Battalion in the Zon area under Division control.

By this time both of the British flank corps, VIII and XII, were in touch with the 506th and well on the way to taking over its original area of responsibility.

So Division prepared to shift the rest of the regiment north where the need for it was greater. The 1st Battalion at Zon was alerted to march north of Vechel and occupy the corridor town of Uden. Though it was in the 101st area, it had not yet been either defended by the Division nor attacked by the enemy. Colonel Sink made a reconnaissance and drew up plans to move an advance detachment of 175 men with some supporting weapons to Uden early the next morning. The rest of the regiment would be shuttled in later that day.

At nine that evening, 3d Battalion moved to St. Oedenrode to become Division reserve.

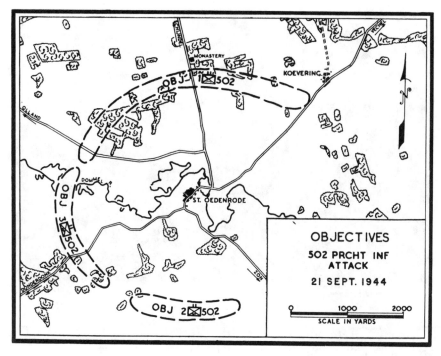

Map 48.

502d; The Triple Attack from St. Oedenrode

Colonel Michaelis felt that his newly assembled regiment's first move should be to clean out the stray groups of Germans which had been reported in its area. So he ordered 3d Battalion to search out the ground for two thousand yards to the west; 2d was to move a thousand yards south, driving off or destroying any Germans that might be between St. Oedenrode and the LZ area. The 1st Battalion had the big assignment—it was to advance groups along the road to Olland, the road to Schijndel and the road to Vechel. The 2d and 3d Battalions were to move out at 1100, 1st at 1400. The tanks of an attached British squadron Colonel Michaelis divided among his battalions.

The 2d Battalion reached its objective in less than an hour without discovering any Germans. The 3d quickly encountered dug-in enemy positions, backed up with mortars and light artillery. After four hours of fast-moving fighting in which it knocked out an 88 and took 105 prisoners but lost one of the British tanks accompanying it, it reached its objective.

For the 1st Battalion attack, Colonel Cassidy told B to move up the Olland road, C again to move north toward Schijndel, and one

Sgt. Stanley F. Czarniak, Pvt. Charles J. Murz, and Sgt. Roy W. Nickrent, during a lull in the Holland fighting. Czarniak and Nickrent helped man Paddy McCrory's crippled tank.

platoon of A to advance along the Vechel road to Koevering. The rest of A along with the mortars he kept in a reserve position.

The platoon from A moved rapidly down the corridor road to Koevering. Company B at first advanced without difficulty, but C had rough going from the start. Its difficulties were increased when the two British tanks, which were supposed to move along just behind the first riflemen, through some misunderstanding went a hundred yards out in front and were both knocked out by rockets. But the paratroopers slowly continued the advance. In each platoon the squad nearest the road went up the roadside ditch and the other squads spread out to the flanks, following whatever line of cover looked best to them. The enemy had dug in along these ditches and their positions were well concealed. They knew that there were hardly any avenues of escape available and so they usually went on fighting until overwhelmed. By the time the paratroopers came up even with the two tanks, their attack was stalling. The reserve platoon was committed on the left.

When word of loss of the tanks got back to Colonel Cassidy, he asked Sergeant McCrory, whose crippled tank had had a crucial effect in the fighting the day before, if he would go in again. "Sure!" was Paddy's reply.

Sergeant Steve Czarniak climbed aboard to fill out the crew and the crippled tank started forward. When they came to the two smashed

340

Shermans McCrory got down to see if he could do anything for one of the commanders, lying half out of the hatch. Though still breathing he was beyond help. Then McCrory suddenly ran forward about twenty yards toward the right-hand ditch, pulling his revolver as he ran. Four or five times he fired at the ground. Czarniak, alarmed, was just getting ready to follow him when he returned with a suckling pig in his hand. He threw it up to Czarniak saying, "Tonight we'll eat." The tank went forward into battle.

By this time the reserve platoon had begun to turn the tide. German fire was slackening all along the line except from one house, where an 88 and several machine guns were still going strong. McCrory crept up the main road, with the 88 doing its best to knock him off. In line with the house he stopped, fired three rounds into it and then skipfired three into the garden. He got the 88 and the house quieted.

With this strongpoint destroyed the going became easier, and the entire company moved forward. McCrory continued on up the road with twelve infantrymen on each side of him. He saw an armored car and got it with the first shot.

Soon after, an AT gun farther along, behind a large monastery building, saw him and sent three rounds in his direction. Since he was far ahead of most of Company C and just about out of ammunition, he decided to withdraw. So he fell back to the company which in the meantime had received orders from Colonel Cassidy to stabilize its position. This it did, about five hundred yards short of the monastery. For his exploits in these two days of fighting, Paddy McCrory was recommended for the Silver Star.

Company B, meanwhile, after its rapid early advance on the road to Olland, had been stopped by a close-up engagement in which it lost one tank but took several prisoners. It had still gone less than a thousand yards when it received Colonel Cassidy's order to hold and to send a patrol of platoon strength to search out the woods between and make contact with C. The patrol ran into difficulties at once. Colonel Michaelis decided to send in two 2d Battalion companies to fill the gap. As they moved up Colonel Cassidy had the platoon from A come back from Koevering, and he placed the entire company just to the right of C. Darkness had fallen by this time and the men dug in for the night.

Even while this assault was in progress PW and civilian reports indicated that the Germans were shortly going to launch a strong attack from Schijndel, probably with the intention of cutting the corridor. As a matter of fact this afternoon advance of 1st Battalion,

502d, probably forestalled a preliminary German attack. These reports received further confirmation when at 1700 trucks carrying two thousand Germans were reported moving through Schijndel toward St. Oedenrode. It was realized then that the attack would be heavy. In early evening, air observers of the 377th managed to direct fire on the now empty German trucks, and several of them were destroyed.

Meanwhile Colonel Johnson of the 501st, again wholly confident of the usefulness of offensive fighting, was making plans which if carried through unhindered would have converted the next day's fighting into an even larger Cannae. No such Cannae occurred. But his battalions and those of the 502d cooperated in such a way as to keep this reinforced German group on the defensive throughout the day.

Johnson's plan was to use two of his battalions (1st at Heeswijk and 3d at Eerde) for an attack on Schijndel which would put them in the rear of this whole German force.

501st: The Night Attack on Schijndel

After a quiet day in the Heeswijk area Colonel Kinnard had gone to 501st headquarters at 1600 that afternoon and received his orders for the attack on Schijndel. His battalion was to cross the canal and move right down the main road to the town. But just as he was about to take his company commanders on a route reconnaissance, the regimental S-3 radioed him an order from Colonel Johnson to start the advance at once. Colonel Kinnard questioned the wisdom of this projected night assault on a strange city filled with an unknown number of the enemy. But Colonel Johnson could not be reached and there was nothing to do but obey. No one was able to determine why the time of attack was moved up so suddenly.

Leaving a platoon from C to hold the canal bridge, Colonel Kinnard put his battalion on the road at 1900—C, B, Headquarters, A—in column of companies. Such concentration was risky, but the danger of getting completely scattered in the dark, should he order an open formation, weighed more heavily on his mind. Perhaps he regretted this feeling a few minutes after the start when from a group of houses up ahead a 20mm and a machine gun simultaneously opened up on his column. The men took to the ditches on both sides of the road, putting small-arms fire on the houses until at last they heard a motor vehicle pull away in the opposite direction. The fire ceased.

The men again moved forward without further incident except that twice the truck, which evidently mounted the two guns, halted at a bend in the highway ahead and gave them a few rounds.

Around midnight the point entered the outskirts of Schijndel. Colonel Kinnard called his company commanders and outlined his plan for the seizure and occupation of the town. Company A was to take over the southeast end; C would dominate the business district and the northwest; B would get the thinly populated area between the other two. They were to clear out all enemy that night, then set up a strong close-in defense just outside the built-up areas. Company A was also to send a patrol as far as Weibosch Church to meet the 3d Battalion as it fought its way up.

These orders were carried out. A few surprised Germans were encountered, but the town was taken without a real battle. The large German groups had evidently moved on to the south.

By 0150 the town was completely in hand. A priest, head of the Dutch underground, came to the 1st Battalion CP and introduced himself, asking what he could do to help. He said that the majority of his members, now hidden in a factory, would do whatever the Americans wanted. Colonel Kinnard told him to get the man who could speak the best English and present him at the CP. A little bald-headed Dutchman arrived in about ten minutes.

Colonel Kinnard's first words were "Keep your people off the streets. Tell them not to get out their bunting. Tell them to act as if we are unwelcome. Get that word to them tonight." For Colonel Kinnard felt that his stay in Schijndel would be short. He did not want all the people of Allied sympathies to reveal themselves and their orange flags, only to be betrayed when the Germans returned a few days later. Back at Heeswijk he had failed to foresee this succession of events, and he felt like a Judas as his withdrawal from that town became imminent.

Then he asked the Dutchman if there were any Germans in the vicinity. The man replied that there were large forces down by the Schijndel station and on the moor. "Can you send small patrols of your men on bicycles to both of these points," Colonel Kinnard asked, "and have them report to us what they find?" He agreed, and the mission was carried out, the patrols reporting back in about two hours with information as to the enemy dispositions.

Once again the Dutch underground had risked its neck to get information about German movements and plans to Allied troops. This time the information had been specifically requested. Usually it came in without being asked for. Men on bicycles brought it; it was phoned in on underground cables that the Germans never had been able to locate. Practically all of the dispersed glidermen, who later rejoined their units with the assistance of the underground, came in only after a thorough briefing on enemy installations in the locality in which they had landed.

Such information, of course, had to be carefully evaluated. But especially before the British flank corps came up, it was information that could have been obtained in no other way, and was absolutely vital to Colonel Danahy and his G-2 Section.

What Colonel Kinnard did not get until after daylight was any positive word about 3d Battalion and the progress it was making in its night march to Schijndel. That march was rough going, but not nearly so bad as Colonel Ewell anticipated when it was first ordered. He described his feelings then with the remark, "I thought I might as well turn in my soldier suit."

Fearful of having his battalion scattered across open country, Colonel Ewell got its left shoulder on the railroad embankment just as soon as he could, and it moved forward with I on the right, H on the left, and G and Headquarters in the rear. The going was slow; many times enemy patrols opened upon them. Twice the column was fired on by the same gun-carrying truck that had bothered the 1st.

So it was not till first light the next morning that between Weibosch and Eerde he ran into the 1st Battalion patrol. Shortly thereafter, steadily increasing fire opened up on 3d Battalion from the south. Rather than risk a major engagement, Colonel Ewell had 3d Battalion veer off to the north of the tracks and head straight for Schijndel. When he met Colonel Kinnard he admitted, "Those buildings looked damn good to me, and I thought I'd get my men where they could put their backs up against something."

So D plus 5 opened with the men of the 101st getting into position where an annihilating attack upon the large enemy group south of Schijndel would be possible. Two battalions of the 501st were in Schijndel ready to move south, and two battalions of the 502d were on the St. Oedenrode–Schijndel road ready to move north.

But the four battalions never met; before they had a chance to unite another German force had thrown all such plans into the scrap heap by cutting the road northeast of Vechel.

Thus D plus 5, rather than being the story of a successful attack, became the story of a desperate defense in which brilliant planning and luck combined to ward off disaster.

The day opened with Vechel being held only by the 2d Battalion, 501st; 3d Battalion, 502d was in St. Oedenrode; 506th, except for its 1st Battalion at Zon, was getting ready to move to Uden that morning.

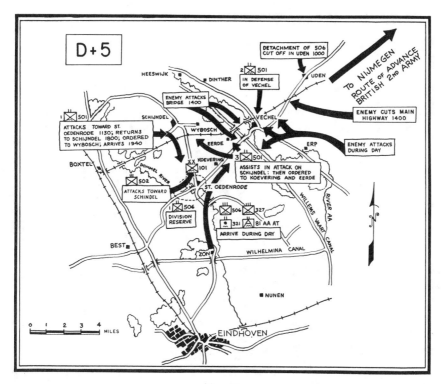

Map 49.

The 327th was still in the Zon LZ area. Patrols of XII Corps had already been in touch with it just below Best, so it was getting ready to move out to Vechel. But before the story of the defense that almost failed comes the story of the attack that almost succeeded.

D Plus 5: The Double Attack

During the early morning hours at Schijndel Company C of the 501st, out on the flank, was having a field day against enemy vehicles coming in from the west, with Lieutenant Howard cautioning his men to "shoot high so you can knock off those men without ruining a good motor car."

At 0715 Lt. Hamilton of B suddenly reported that two tanks and an infantry force were pushing hard from the southwest, coming astride the road. All other companies were alerted to send bazooka and grenade teams to this sector. Colonel Kinnard tried to get observation from the church steeple but found that a heavy ground mist effectively screened the enemy. Hamilton phoned next that the tanks were still coming and that the platoon which had been outposting the

345

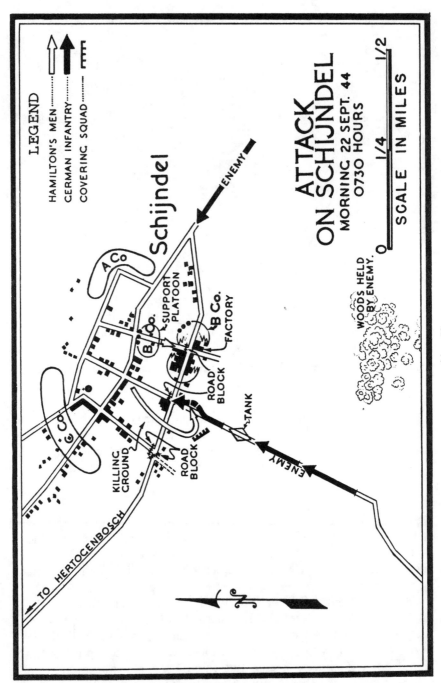

LEGEND

HAMILTON'S MEN ....
GERMAN INFANTRY ....
COVERING SQUAD ....

Schijndel

A Co

ENEMY

B Co.

SUPPORT PLATOON

B Co.
FACTORY

ROAD BLOCK

C Co

KILLING GROUND

ROAD BLOCK

TANK

ENEMY

TO HERTOGENBOSCH

N

WOODS HELD BY ENEMY.

ATTACK
ON SCHIJNDEL
MORNING 22 SEPT. 44
0730 HOURS

SCALE IN MILES

0   1/4   1/2

Map 50.

road was pulling back past the factory and through the hedgerows. "I'm leading the support platoon up to restore the position," he said to Colonel Kinnard.

"What size is the enemy force?" Kinnard asked.

"Two tanks and two hundred men."

"Go ahead," was Kinnard's command. Hamilton jumped for the door and ran to the next house. The 2d Platoon men were still sleeping in the doorways along the Klooster road.

He ran from door to door collecting men, yelling at them as he went "Come on! We're taking off." He found a platoon scout, Pvt. Ruel O. Hoskinson, pointed toward the nunnery building on the next road over and yelled, "We're heading that way. I think we can get them from the flank."

The advance body of the Germans was already drawing into the edge of the town, a matter of 150-200 yards away. Hamilton could not see them but he calculated that, if 3d Platoon had withdrawn, the Germans would come straight in on the same line. This checked with his estimate of where he thought he heard them firing.

Hamilton's idea was immediately to make an end run around the buildings to his right, emerge on the line of the enemy advance between the main body and the advance party, take the latter in rear and so bring the whole movement in check. They took off through the back yard of the nunnery—Hoskinson in the lead, Hamilton following, and thirty men behind them—all moving at a dead run. They crossed a street, circled around the barns and houses to the right of the road and swung back to the road. Hamilton had guessed correctly; the enemy advance party was now between them and the rest of the battalion. Hamilton spread one squad out behind the sheds and manure piles to the right of the road to do the out-fighting and contain the elements of the German main body, which were coming up on his right flank. Hoskinson still leading, the remaining men then turned left and back into the road. A gate blocked them right at the last moment. Hardly pausing in his stride, Hoskinson shot the bolt off with his M1 and kept on going. The whole thing had taken place so quickly that the enemy, advancing cautiously along the line of houses on both sides of the road, was taken totally by surprise. Hoskinson shot five Germans as he came at them from the rear; the supporting fire from the other men behind him killed five others, and that broke up the threat. The remaining twenty Germans between this flying wedge and the battalion threw up their hands in surrender.

But the enemy flank confronting the detached squad held its ground, and was not cleared out until Hamilton went after it with tanks later in the morning.

Meanwhile, elements of the larger enemy group had gotten into other parts of town; by a united effort of both battalions they were ejected by 0930.

Colonel Johnson arrived about 1000 with the tanks that had been promised. He gave six to each battalion, but three of 1st Battalion's were immediately dispatched with a platoon from A to clean out Weibosch, where what was thought to be an enemy platoon had been bypassed by 3d Battalion. Company B and one tank were sent to clean out the area immediately south of Schijndel in the vicinity of the railroad station. Two 1st Battalion tanks were kept in general support in the center of town.

Prior to B's departure the railroad station area was given a good shelling by the howitzers of the 377th, dug in back at St. Oedenrode, and fired with the guidance of an observer at Schijndel. This created a situation rare in the history of field artillery. The observer was on the gun-target line, but out beyond the target. All through D plus 5 the 377th, when supporting the 501st, was firing over the nearest battle line into the back of the enemy, and only a little short of the friendly troops it was helping. It was a case where a long round might have proved fatal to Americans.

Of course, the original responsibility of the 377th was to support the 502d in its attack; support of the 501st was an additional job.

While burdened with this double responsibility, the members of the 377th did not exactly welcome a report that enemy infantry were near the howitzer positions. A detachment of fifteen Battery B men with a machine-gun section from Battery C attacked and dispersed this enemy group, killing five of its members, wounding five and capturing two.

That day three of the Battalion's five forward observers were wounded and had to be evacuated.

All Division artillery work was hampered when one of the liaison planes was shot down. Both the pilot, Lieutenant McRae, and the observer, Captain Brown, became prisoners. Later on in the fighting they were recaptured.

The 502d attack at the day's beginning had been marred by an accident. Several short rounds in the pre-attack barrage landed among the men of Company C, causing eight casualties. But with morale unhurt Company C men advanced north with the rest of the two battalions at the set time, 0630. More than that they advanced standing up, firing as they walked.

Resistance was encountered from the first, but the audacity of this advance as skirmishers cowed the enemy to such an extent that his fire was erratic. To the marching infantry it appeared that the Germans were doing little more than putting their rifles and machine guns out over the edge of the holes, keeping their heads down and firing without aiming. The fire was heavy in volume but there were no American casualties during this stand-up advance. The machine guns leapfrogged forward and provided a covering fire for the riflemen. Five tanks assigned to each Battalion added their fire. In twenty minutes Company C had covered the five hundred yards to the monastery.

At that point two squads of the 3d Platoon under Lt. William Everding peeled off to reduce the monastery position in detail. A double apron of barbed wire surrounded the grounds; it had to be cut strand by strand before the group could get in. Fortunately there was little fire from the monastery. Once in, the men ran through the yard firing into the windows. A thirty-minute prowl of the grounds yielded nothing, and the men finally concluded that the enemy had used some escape route while they were cutting the wire. So they cut the wire on the other side, and went on through to catch up with their company line.

Meanwhile a German shell had struck the heaviest single blow of Division history. Colonel Michaelis early in the day moved his CP forward to be near the action and located it in a ditch traversing a field to the right of the road. He was there with members of his staff, demanding changes in his supporting artillery fire, when a tree-burst exploded above the entire group, dousing the whole area with steel fragments. Colonel Michaelis was wounded in arm, leg and stomach, and Pfc. Garland E. Mills, his orderly, was killed. His S-2, Capt. George Beuker, and his S-3, Capt. R. B. Clements, along with Capt. Henry Plitt, the assistant S-3, were hurt. Also downed were Lt. Col. Paul H. Danahy, G-2, and Lt. Col. Harold Hannah, G-3, Division officers who had been visiting the CP. Major Elkins of the 377th and Lt. Thomas B. Swirezinski, one of his forward observers, were both hit although Major Elkins' wound was light and he continued to run his battalion through the day. Altogether fourteen men were casualties. Although he had a fragment in his arm and was dizzy from concussion, Colonel Cassidy took command of the regiment until Colonel Chappuis, the senior regimental officer, could be brought to the rear.

When Colonel Chappuis took over the regiment his 2d Battalion companies, against light opposition, had already reached their objectives and halted. Thinking that contact with the 501st was imminent, he ordered the 1st Battalion companies also to halt. When nothing happened he told 1st Battalion to move on forward. He knew the 501st was in the vicinity but expected them to advance from the direction of Eerde. Again the men started at a walk, firing as they moved. But this time the Germans made them pay a price for their courage. Losses were heavy and the advance slowed down. Just as it was stalling, British tanks knocked out the 88s and SP guns causing the heaviest damage. The men moved forward again. The Germans, who by this time may have gotten reports of Americans to their rear, became discouraged and began to surrender. They continued even after the battalion reached its objectives at 1230 and halted. From the 1st Parachute Regiment and the 49th and 59th Grenadier Divisions 125 prisoners were taken.

While C waited, a four-man patrol under Cpl. Raymond Charron went forward several hundred yards and blew up several unguarded German field pieces which stood there loaded and aimed at the company. Later a Tiger tank crossed the company front about six hundred yards out. A gun crew from the 81st gave it a shot which hit the front part of the tank and caused it to turn around. A British Sherman then sent three rounds into its rear. It exploded and burned itself out.

As Colonel Chappuis by this time suspected, the German attack on Schijndel that morning and then the necessity for clearing out Weibosch and the railroad station area had badly delayed the 501st advance. These jobs done, Colonel Johnson gave to Colonel Kinnard's already depleted battalion the additional job of holding Schijndel during the attack. Two platoons of A were left there with Captain Stach in charge.

Moving out, Colonel Kinnard put B, the only full company he had left, in the front with two tanks following immediately after. Behind B what remained of C was echeloned to the right. A's one remaining platoon was to the left, moving directly down the main road.

Going down to the railroad which was the agreed-upon line of departure for the two-battalion attack, B shot a few enemy stragglers and destroyed some enemy vehicles. C reported that it was getting 20mm fire, and saw a German infantry force approaching from the west about a thousand yards off its right flank. Men from the Dutch underground patrols came in with the same information, and a squad from A was sent out to confirm it.

The 1st Battalion drew abreast of 3d along the railroad line at 1330, and the attack jumped off. The 3d Battalion was well to the left of the highway, but as the ground was perfectly flat, the gap between the two battalions did not become a source of trouble. Advance was swift. From behind the infantry the tanks engaged the German strong points. As fast as these were softened the infantry groups moved up the ditches to places where they could be brought under small-arms fire, or wracked with grenades, and then overwhelmed them. In the first hour 25 enemy were killed by 1st Battalion alone and 45 captured, with a loss to that battalion of only eight casualties. Though the men had been on the go for twenty hours straight, this was heady stuff; they pressed on forward.

But then at 1430 came the news that turned the whole day topsy-turvy. Division radioed that a German armored force had attacked Vechel and cut the corridor. The British tanks must be returned at once. Colonel Johnson ordered them back.

Then he began to worry. Vechel after all had been his responsibility, so he ordered 3d Battalion to abandon the attack and leave immediately for Eerde, ready for any new assignment that might become necessary.

In an unusual military movement Colonel Ewell halted his battalion's attack, had all his men execute left face, and walked them off the battlefield with their right flank entirely exposed. The Germans by that time were so disorganized that the battalion got away with it, as Colonel Ewell thought it would.

Colonel Ewell reorganized his battalion at Koevering and proceeded back to Eerde. By this time the Germans had taken possession of the town and the Battalion had to fight its way in. It did.

This sudden withdrawal of Ewell's force left 1st Battalion in a bad spot. An attack on the right flank was expected momentarily. The left flank was now exposed; the rear might be insecure. So on Colonel Johnson's order 1st matched 3d Battalion's sudden withdrawal to the left by executing an about-face, and returning to Schijndel. At 1800 Colonel Johnson ordered it to withdraw to Weibosch. Before he could move Colonel Kinnard had the problem of disposing of his four surpluses—too many prisoners, too many wounded prisoners, too many trucks, and too many Dutch who had helped him too much for their own good.

With 170 wounded Germans, conditions in his aid station had become so bad that Colonel Kinnard had already put captured German medics to work on their own men. Now he decided there was nothing to do but leave all of them behind, even though this meant that they were restored to their own army. The eight Dutchmen who had actively and publicly aided him felt that they could not stay in Schijndel after he left, and he was glad to take them along. He set them to work guarding the 250 unscathed prisoners that he also took with him. The autos, trucks and motorcycles which 1st Battalion had captured he turned over to the Dutch underground, except for one rolling kitchen complete with peeled potatoes and two sides of beef; this he kept for his own men.

The column closed on Weisboch at 1930 and the prisoners were escorted on to Vechel. The battalion set up an all-around defense and thus became the northwestern flank of the larger Vechel defense.

At 1615 the 502d realized that a junction with the 501st was not going to occur and it fell back on St. Oedenrode. What had begun as a converging movement by four battalions was now concluded. The 3d Battalion, 501st, pushing on the left of the northern force and 2d Battalion, 502d, moving on the left of the southern force had encountered the least resistance and advanced the fastest. These two battalions might have successfully encircled the opposition, had the situation elsewhere permitted such a maneuver. Save for the destruction of enemy personnel and guns, the action had been fought to no tactical conclusion. The corridor was now no wider than before. Two days later the British took heavy losses in fighting their way through to the same monastery.

The Corridor Is Cut But Vechel Is Held

Division leaders knew from the beginning how easy it might be for the Germans to cut the corridor, and what a disastrous effect such a stroke would have on the entire operation. It was obviously good German strategy to stop the flow of traffic somewhere near the base of the corridor and then deal at leisure with the Americans and British up north near Nijmegen or Arnhem. Nor was there an apparent defense against any strong German group that was determined to grab a section of the road. The Division could not be strong everywhere; parts of the road were totally unguarded.

From D plus 3 on it was evident that strong German groups were in the Division area. The only question was when they would strike and where. With each passing hour the tension mounted.

On D plus 5 the blow fell. It should have been disastrous—a combination of fighting men and smart leaders with a lot of luck prevented that. Men somehow reached the right place at the right time and the enemy was finally hurled back.

Vechel was the German point of attack, probably because destroying the bridges there would keep traffic stopped long after the attackers had gone. To the east of Vechel they had Combat Team Walter composed of the newly equipped 107th Panzer and 280th Assault Gun Brigades. It was part of the 107th Panzer which had made the unsuccessful attack on the Zon area two days before, and had so easily let itself be driven off. Now it was in a fighting mood. West of the road were the many groups being fed down from Boxtel. From D plus 3 on, G-2 had found an increasing number of regular units from the First Parachute Army. The 347th Infantry was also known to be in the area. But numerically, the strongest division was still the 59th Infantry.

On D plus 5 these eastern and western groups launched a coordinated assault on Vechel from the southeast, the northwest and the north, that resulted in the biggest battle thus far in Holland.

Again the Dutch underground warned the Division. In the early morning of D plus 5 they sent in reports of enemy movements east of the corridor near Helmond and west of it near Boxtel. The eastern force, consisting of more than four hundred vehicles, was soon rolling up toward Uden and Vechel. In the west the Germans were moving down along both banks of the Zuid Willems Vaart Canal, and at 0925 an infantry force with five mobile guns was ready to strike. It is not known whether they realized the maneuvers of the preceding day had left but one battalion of the 501st in the town, but certainly they could not have anticipated the speed with which the rest of the Division massed to turn them back.

The Division opened the day with an effort to rush the 506th to Uden, as had previously been planned. That hitherto undefended town might be the main point of German attack. Riding trucks and every other kind of vehicle that could be got, the advance party, under Colonel Chase, the regimental executive, managed to get there by 1100. Right after it passed, the Germans cut the road north of Vechel, and it was isolated until 1700 the next day. Had they realized that it consisted only of Regimental Headquarters Company and a platoon from the 2d Battalion, the Germans might have overwhelmed it. It was touch-and-go all the time, but Colonel Chase made masterful use of his meager forces, rushing them back and forth across town, firing, creating an impression of strength. And the Germans never went all-out against them.

Shortly after 1100 Colonel Ballard's men of the 2d Battalion, 501st, saw the tanks and trucks of CT Walter come swinging up the road from Erp. The battle was on. They wished the rest of the regiment were still with them.

From houses and foxholes just outside the Erp road section of town they fought desperately. They managed to ward off the first attack, but they could see part of the German column swing around to their left toward the Uden road, and cut it. Who was to stop it there?

That same problem was facing General McAuliffe. He had come up to Vechel that morning to select a new location for the Division CP. When the direction of German attack became apparent General Taylor had told him to stay and take charge of the defense.

Just as his situation became critical the 2d Battalion of the 506th came riding into town. He rushed it out the Uden road in time to meet the advancing Germans in the outskirts.

Spotting Lt. Col. X. B. Cox, CO of the 81st, he yelled "Get one of your guns up that road and smash a tank; that may stop them."

Colonel Cox hopped into the nearest of his gun-towing jeeps, and the men who were in it were automatically his crew—Battery B commander, Capt. Adolph Gueymard, Cpl. William Bowyer, and Pfc. Rogie Roberts. Together they tore out the Uden road toward the sounds of firing. It was a dismal sight that greeted them. A Mark V already across the road was still shooting up a British 40mm AA outfit, which had been caught there when the attack started. Banging away bravely at the German tank was an American 37 gun crew.

There was no time for Colonel Cox and his crew to get into a covered position. Swinging their 57 around in the middle of the road a hundred yards from the tank, they jumped to the ground. As they started to ram home a shell they saw the gun on the Panther swing over toward them. The tank fired first; they felt the flash and thought they were goners, but the shell hit the house behind them and merely showered them with masonry. Squinting through the dust Colonel Cox aimed and fired. His shot hit the tank, disabling it. His second shot, quickly gotten off, set it on fire.

Each recoil carried the 57 some yards back. Roberts was hit by the carriage and got a broken kneecap. But the tank was done for, and its loss had taken the sting out of the German attack.

Once again the 81st had justified its place in the hearts of the infantrymen. They were not afraid of tanks, but when two infantry forces are pitted against each other and one is equipped with tanks, it frequently goes hard with the other. That was the situation in which airborne men found themselves all too frequently. Their most effective counter to the German tanks was the 6-pounder guns of the 81st.

Such was the function of the 81st. But in this particular instance its story does not go unchallenged. The 327th claims that tank, and assigns just as minor a role to the 81st in its destruction as the 81st has given it in the foregoing account, which was based on interviews with all the available participants from the 81st. Here is the 327th's version of the story as told by Sgt. James C. Weatherford. Even though the German tank is differently identified, it is the same event.

On September 22, 1944, 327th's 3d Battalion was moving toward Vechel, Holland, from the landing field. The Antitank Platoon was following the column. Col. Joseph Harper met the platoon just after it had left the field and ordered it to follow him to Vechel by truck. As we got into Vechel, Colonel Harper met Colonel Sink of the 506th Parachute Infantry. They studied the situation on the map, as Colonel Sink's regiment was in the town. About this time the 1st Battalion Antitank Platoon of the 327th arrived, Colonel Harper having ordered them to Vechel. Colonel Harper came back and gave orders for both antitank platoons to go to the Uden highway just outside of Vechel and set up their guns for a tank attack. The 3d Battalion was leading, and, under fire by enemy machine guns, it pulled into a side road. One of the antitank guns set up right in the middle of the highway. The other two lined up twenty yards apart to the left of it on the side road.

This gave a field of fire down the highway for all three guns. The 1st Battalion platoon pulled into the side road to the left of the 3d Battalion platoon. They also had a field of fire down the highway. As we came through the edge of the town, there were no American troops, only the troops that were driving the British convoy of trucks which were jammed up together, the Germans having stopped them down the road about four hundred yards to the front. The antitank platoons had just gotten their guns into action when two German Mark IV tanks with infantry behind attacked. Someone said they might be British tanks, but I recognized them as German tanks and gave the order to open fire as they were only about 150 yards to our front. My position was right between the three guns of the 3d Battalion Antitank Platoon, and, being platoon sergeant, I was commanding all three guns. Just before we opened fire, they started firing on us. Fire from one of the tanks hit one of the British ammunition trucks and exploded the ammunition. The tanks were firing point-blank at us with 88mm guns and machine guns. Our guns fired several rounds and set one tank on fire. The ammunition in the tank started exploding, and the Germans evacuated it. With a light machine gun I opened fire on the Germans and killed one. Meanwhile, the gun in the road engaged the second tank as it was coming across the field toward our position. This gun, commanded by Cpl. Melvin Fossmeyer, hit the tank causing it to turn and start back toward its own lines. The guns from both platoons engaged this one tank that was knocked out, but Corporal Fossmeyer's gun was the only one that engaged the other tank.

Two of my men went out later that afternoon to the tank that was knocked out and counted at least twenty holes through it, through the barrel of the gun and the body of the tank. These were small holes and were made by 37mm shells as we had squeeze-bore attachments on our guns and were firing the British squeeze-bore ammunition.

Afterward, one of our men went back to the village to attempt to make contact with Colonel Harper. Upon his return, he told me that one of the 81st antitank guns was set up about one hundred yards back of us. I will not say that the 81st gun did not fire anything because I do not know as there was so much popping around, but I do know we engaged the tanks and stopped them as we were the only troops up there at that time.

The Germans kept up their assault on both battalions, at the same time sliding on around to the left flank of 506's 2d Battalion. More troops were needed. Where were they to be got?

Anticipating the Vechel attack, General Taylor the night before had ordered the 327th to march from its bivouac in the Zon woods to that town this morning. But he had to tell them to keep to secondary roads so as not to interfere with British Second Army traffic which had priority in the corridor.

As his column reached St. Oedenrode, Colonel Harper returned from Vechel with news that the German attack had already materialized. He rushed his motorized antitank platoons forward as described, telling Colonel Allen as he left to get 3d Battalion ready for a similar rush. He returned shortly with fourteen trucks. Into these Colonel Allen piled his mortars, heavy machine guns and the two rifle companies, B and C. He took off for Vechel. The rest of the Battalion came up by foot with the remainder of the regiment.

Colonel Allen tells what happened:

When we arrived at Vechel I found Colonel Harper at the 501st CP. He immediately took me to the CP of Colonel Ballard out on the outskirts of Vechel toward Erp. Then I got the situation from Colonel Ballard and made my plans to attack the enemy right flank which had enveloped around to the north of Vechel. My A.T. guns had already been thrown into action on the Uden Road to the north, and had been pretty badly shot up but were still engaging the enemy.

After issuing my attack orders I accompanied the leading platoon on the advance to the L.D. We turned northwest, advanced toward the railroad station, keeping buildings and fences between us and the enemy. We then circled toward the west and attacked in a column of companies, C Company leading. We took the enemy by complete surprise when we found them just west of the Uden Road. Company C under the command of Capt. Preston R. Towns hit them with so much automatic fire power that he had no trouble in rolling the Germans across the highway, but not without losses. So successfully was the attack progressing that I did not have to use my mortars. Nor did I commit my reserve company. I was saving it for a knockout blow to clear the enemy away from Colonel Ballard's troops. But hardly had we driven the enemy across the highway when Capt. T. P. Wilder arrived with an order from C. G. to disengage the enemy and assemble my battalion in the vicinity of the railway station northeast of Vechel. I was thoroughly disappointed at having to disengage from such a successful attack—but I obeyed the orders—not, however, without some delay. We just couldn't walk off and leave our wounded. That was when our medical detachment under the command of Maj. Martin Wiseley did its stuff, but not without lots of trouble and daring exploits. They had to advance all the way under fire, crawling most of the time in ditches. Not having enough litters to carry out all the wounded at one time, they had to dart from house to house, dodging fire from artillery and mortars and small arms, procuring ladders and tearing doors from houses to use as litters. During the fight

Lieutenant Armstrong, leader of the platoon making the initial assault on the enemy, was severely wounded. He was placed on a ladder and started to the rear. The ladder broke; he was dragged to safety while Major Wiseley went back through fire and tore off a door to use as a litter. Several men were evacuated from houses through the windows, because fire on the doorways was too intense. The medics then had to drag each improvised litter down ditches for two or three hundred yards to safety.

The battalion was assembled in the vicinity of the railway station about 1700 and immediately went into an all-around defense of its own. Darkness caught us well organized, but as yet we didn't have A Company. However, A was finally contacted by radio and told when to report. Sometime after dark I received an order to shift my positions slightly and go into an all-around defense with the rest of the Division. Upon making contact with units on my right and left I felt much better about the whole thing. This left my battalion in a position to the west across the Dinter highway and northwest around the railway station toward Uden. We received a heavy shelling but the men were well dug in and not hurt from it.

Throughout the day British artillery and armored units which had been caught in town when the road was cut gave badly needed support to all the defending battalions. Air support was frequently requested, but was unavailable because of the poor weather.

At intervals through the afternoon Colonel Sink buttonholed General McAuliffe saying, "We have got to do something about Charlie Chase up there in Uden." But the road was cut, all available forces were deeply committed, and nothing could be done.

The second major assault developed about 1400, when the German infantry and guns in Eerde started to move east against the highway bridge over the canal. Learning of this new attack, General McAuliffe rushed down taking Colonel Sink with him to organize whatever defense was possible here. Luck was with them for on the way they saw Company D of the 506th headed toward Uden, hardly aware that the road was cut. They turned the company around and took it back to the bridge with them.

The German force already had cleared the bridge with fire from its mobile guns. It had driven into the ditches the crews of some British 3.7-inch AA guns that had crossed just before they appeared. General McAuliffe got these men back to their weapons, using their fire as the only possible answer to the heavier German guns.

While the British were still getting into position a group of Sherman tanks appeared, coming toward the canal from the south. For them to venture on the bridge would have been suicide, for the Germans had it completely covered. But they seemed to be unaware of their peril, and kept coming forward. There was only one thing to do—dash across the bridge through small-arms fire to stop the tanks in time, and Colonel Sink did it.

Discouraged by the British fire and the appearance of the infantry the German force pulled back slightly to the west. The 3d Battalion of the 506th arrived in town a few minutes later and was held in reserve, the first reserve that General McAuliffe had had in the day's fighting.

Reorganizing from their unsuccessful attack on the bridge, the German force from Eerde moved on south and cut the Vechel–St. Oedenrode highway, encircling the town.

While this group was still moving across the highway, the rest of the 327th with the 321st Artillery came marching up from St. Oedenrode and made contact with its flank. Quickly deploying Company A under Capt. Joseph B. Johnson to the right of the highway and Company C under Captain Miller to the left, the regiment went on forward, the attacking companies using walking fire. The assault was successful and by 1600, when the companies reached the canal bridge, seventy prisoners had been taken. Communications to the south were again established.

The 327th marched to an assembly area in the northwest part of town, from which 1st Battalion was immediately dispatched back to take a position astride the St. Oedenrode highway west of the canal. There was quiet in this area for the rest of the afternoon, but after dark the enemy attacked in strength, and sharp fighting took place before the Germans were beaten back.

The rest of the regiment, consisting of one battalion and one company plus the headquarters group, stayed in the assembly area until a 35-minute shelling forced it to change to a new position south of town. Although this shelling was especially heavy, the entire town was being plastered by German artillery throughout the day.

The 321st was subsequently moved to the south of Vechel to support 501st's 2d Battalion. It was unable to register its guns before the next morning.

Later in the afternoon the enemy launched another attack against the town from the north. It was finally halted just short of the railroad bridge by a group from 501st's 2d Battalion and a platoon from Company H, 506th, which had gone in position there a few minutes earlier.

The Germans probed the perimeter all through the afternoon, but as evening came on their assaults diminished and finally ceased.

Thus ended D plus 5, in some respects a preview of Bastogne. The Division had held on to Vechel against the fury of a triple assault. The bridges were intact; the road to the south was open. For D plus 6 remained the job of opening the road to the north.

Men who were there don't need to be told that the enemy's cutting the road did not mean simply his walking across a piece of asphalt. That road was loaded with British transport vehicles of every type. Cutting the road meant fire and destruction for the vehicles that were caught. It meant clogging the road for its entire length with vehicles that suddenly had nowhere to go. For the men at Nijmegen and Arnhem, cutting the road was like severing an artery. The stuff of life—food, ammunition, medical supplies, no longer came north.

The 101st knew this. It had to open the road again.

This day had seen a complete change in the disposition of the 101st. It was beginning to lose its string bean appearance and was starting to fight along a solid front. Everything was now concentrated in the St. Oedenrode–Vechel area except for the small detachment in Uden, 506th's 1st Battalion in Zon, and the service units on LZ W.

Communications fortunately were intact and XXX Corps promised that the Grenadier Guards, part of the Guards Armored, would move down from Nijmegen to assist in clearing the road between Vechel and Uden. Of almost equal importance to the Division, though unknown to it at the time, were the two bridgeheads which the British VIII Corps had thrown across the Zuid Willems Vaart Canal near Helmond that day. They were a direct threat to the communication lines of CT Walter.

Weather prevented any reinforcements or supplies from being flown in on D plus 5. On this day the Division passed from the XXX Corps to the British Airborne Corps.

D Plus 6 (September 23)

Soon after dawn the enemy again attacked the southern part of Vechel in the area of 501st's 2d Battalion. Though the assault was on a small scale, it produced some of the heaviest fighting that the battalion had been through, especially for Company E. Losses were increased by the heavy mortar fire which the Germans maintained on battalion positions.

By 1000 these attacks had been stopped and the Germans did not renew the assault until 1300, when they concentrated on the Company D area. This new attack lasted for only an hour and was beaten back without any loss of position.

During this fighting a German tank blasted its way forward to a Company D flank where there were no antitank weapons. Picking up a bazooka, T/4 Jack B. Rider, a cook, and Pvt. Ben Stoner ran the entire length of the company line, exposed to enemy fire, and disabled the tank.

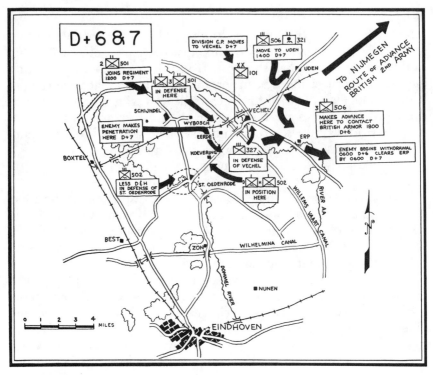

Map 51.

Late in the afternoon the battalion launched a counterattack and found that the enemy had withdrawn from their front.

During the morning the enemy west of the canal sent several small attacks into the position of the 1st Battalion of the 327th in a renewed effort to seize the bridge, but these were all repulsed with heavy casualties for the enemy.

General McAuliffe that morning pulled back 327th's 2d Battalion to take up a new position along the canal southeast of town. The 3d Battalion of the 506th was moved to the northeast to cover the flank of its 2d Battalion.

This put the 506th in position for the most important operation during the 23d—the clearing of the road from Vechel to Uden. At 1500 the two battalions moved out astride the highway and advanced two thousand yards against negligible resistance. There they met the Grenadier Guards who were attacking from the north toward Vechel. The road was open; the traffic that had been blocked could roll again.

A second phase of the Vechel–Uden attack was aimed at pivoting the armored and infantry force in such a manner as to come in behind the enemy southeast of Vechel.

As General Taylor describes it:

Failure of the British to cooperate briskly at Vechel made us miss a great opportunity to destroy the German column from Erp. I sent Captain Wilder with the Division reconnaissance detachment west of the highway on D plus 5 to contact the Guards Armored column which was to help us from the north. Wilder made a most hazardous trip through German-held territory to his destination carrying my plan for the use of the British troops. In brief, it was to make a deep envelopment of the German right (north) flank in conjunction with a frontal attack by our troops in Vechel. I was in contact with Wilder by radio and for hours urged him to get the British moving. When they did move they were painfully slow and declined to budge away from the highway. The result was that they pushed the Germans off the road but we did not bag the lot as we should have. Wilder's radio code name was "Sugar." I'll always remember the silly feeling I had standing in the middle of Vechel shouting, "Hello, Sugar!" over the radio while the Germans shelled the town.

The 2d and 3d Battalions, 506th, did however, make a quick turn and strike the right flank of the enemy southeast of Vechel. The enemy withdrew at once to the south and contact was lost at 1830. Vechel was never again threatened from this direction or by this force.

West of the canal 501st's 1st Battalion moved from Weibosch to Eerde as its 3d Battalion moved closer to Vechel and faced north along the railroad; this further consolidated the Division. The 502d continued its defense of St. Oedenrode with the 377th in direct support.

While fighting was still going on around Vechel, the last 101st glider serial brought 77 of 84 gliders safely to LZ W, gliders which had been turned back by weather on September 19. These contained the 907th Glider Field Artillery Battalion and remnants of the 327th. The 105mm guns of the 907th, now having made three trips across the Channel, were a welcome addition to Division strength. As quickly as possible the units moved to Vechel, and the 907th was placed in direct support of the 501st. This freed the 321st to go to Uden with the 506th. The seaborne tail of the 101st, chiefly motor vehicles, arrived at Zon on the nights of D plus 5 and D plus 6.

Included in it were Batteries D, E, and F of the 81st AA, which were assigned to protect the Division Service Area, then near Zon.

Late that afternoon command of the Division passed from the British Airborne Corps to the British VIII Corps.

D PLUS 7 (SEPTEMBER 24)

The day dawned heavy with fog and rain after a night of relative quiet. Traffic rolled north again along the road.

A patrol sent out by the Reconnaissance Platoon in the early morning

Sand dunes at Eerde.

found that the Germans to the south had continued their withdrawal. As a precautionary measure, 2d Battalion of the 327th was sent south to Erp to hold the bridge there until it could be blown by the British.

Redistributing itself, Division sent the 506th along with the 321st and Battery B of the 81st on up to Uden to join its advanced elements there. The Division CP was moved from St. Oedenrode to the warehouse in Vechel to be close to the new center of activity.

The 501st CP and 2d Battalion, along with the 907th and Battery A of the 81st, moved to Eerde to consolidate that regiment. While crossing the railroad bridge this group took heavy casualties from enemy artillery fire.

It was in this Eerde area that the day's pot of trouble was brewing. Down from the north came a stronger German force, made up of the 1st and 3d Battalions of the 6th Parachute Regiment, the 1st Battalion of the 1st Parachute Regiment, and the 1st Battalion of the Hermann Goering Regiment. There could be no question that on D plus 7 the Division was dealing with the best that the German Army had to offer. However, the appearance of the 6th Parachute Regiment on the Division front caused elation rather than dismay. The 101st had already taken its measure in the Normandy fighting, battering it in the swamps before Carentan and in the town itself.

Throughout the day this enemy force probed all along the Division line west of Vechel. Some of the heaviest fighting took place in the section of 1st Battalion, 501st, the sand dunes of Eerde.

THE SAND DUNES OF EERDE

On D plus 6 501st's 1st Battalion had moved from Weibosch to take

Windmill at Eerde used as a German OP. In the foreground is a British Sherman tank knocked out during the fight on 24 September.

over the defense of the little town of Eerde. It established itself generally west of town with its three companies on line, tied together by patrols. Company C was in the middle, just to the south of the railroad. B was to the north along the railroad embankment; A was at the south end of town. In front of C's section of this line was a row of sand dunes, fifteen to forty feet high, covered by grass and occasional fir trees. Colonel Kinnard sent one platoon to outpost these dunes.

Early on the morning of D plus 7 the outpost platoon came rushing back with word that the town was about to be attacked by five tanks and two hundred infantrymen, coming down from Schijndel. By the time Colonel Kinnard got the report, the enemy was in the dunes, looking down the throats of his men.

Colonel Johnson at once alerted 3d Battalion and sent nine British tanks to 1st's assistance. When the tank observer and the forward observer from the 907th reported in shortly thereafter, Colonel Kinnard told them to put all possible fire on the dunes. This they did. But when both hesitated to brave the 88s which were now converging on the area and go up the Eerde church steeple to adjust the fire, Lt. Harry Howard volunteered for the job. Later in the day another 907th forward observer, Lt. Gerald C. Taylor, did excellent work from this same steeple.

Colonel Johnson arrived at 1000. While still getting a line on the situation he and the British liaison officer were both hit by fragments of a mortar shell exploding nearby. Colonel Kinnard, who was standing between them, escaped with an earache.

Another shell landing a few minutes later had more tragic conse-

363

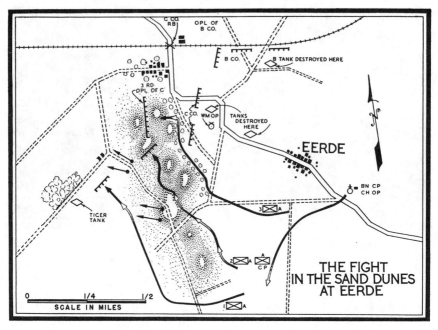

Map 52.

quences. A truckful of ammunition had come up and stopped near Company C's CP. Lt. Robert S. Schorsch, battalion supply officer, and his sergeant along with the company supply sergeants approached to unload it just as a shell came in dead on the truck. The load blew, and every man in the group was killed or wounded.

By this time the fight had been extended to the area north and east of Eerde. Company B was in touch with Company I which had gone into position north of the railroad tracks. The two of them were able to bring a large part of the area under a crossfire that the Germans found impassable. But fighting all along the line was close and heavy.

Feeling that the dunes were the crucial terrain feature of the area, Colonel Kinnard concentrated on cleaning them out.

His first attack plans hinged on the tanks. Three of these, exposing themselves, were quickly knocked out. The British commander withdrew the rest, saying that with so many antitank guns in the dunes the risk was too great. The day's battle was to be an infantry affair.

Colonel Kinnard's new plan was to use C as a base of fire while A advanced into the dunes from the south. Captain Stach of A was given a section of light machine guns, a mortar observer, and a prayer. The rest of the battalion was to throw everything it could into the dunes when the attack started at 1215. The location of the attacking

364

platoon had to be estimated by guess or by God but Colonel Kinnard succeeded pretty well in keeping the artillery moving three to four hundred yards ahead of his men.

Captain Stach, in the attack northward, kept 2d Platoon under Lieutenant Fuquay out front, followed by 1st Platoon under Lt. Harry L. Mosier, the latter echeloned to the left and rear so as to cover the open flank. On line with 1st Platoon was the section of light machine guns from Headquarters Company under Lieutenant Murn; to the rear of the guns were Headquarters Company and 3d Platoon under Lt. Harry J. Mier, Jr.

As Company A moved out Mosier directed Lt. James C. Murphy, his second in command, to take one squad of 1st Platoon and clear the woods to the west of the line of dunes. The group got through the first wood patch without incident, emerged in a clearing and in an instant came under such a volume of rifle and machine-gun fire that the line went flat, with one exception. Without waiting for orders Pvt. John Bleffer ran with his machine gun to the left of the squad line, flopped down, got the gun in action and put so much lead into the enemy position that the German fire gradually lessened. Lieutenant Mosier was able to get the rest of his platoon up to the engagement and deploy his three machine guns on line. They opened fire.

With Mosier leading them and yelling "Let's go!" the platoon charged across a hundred yards of open field to the flange of dunes along which the enemy on this flank had taken position. Mortar fire buffeted them and machine-gun fire clipped the grasses through which they ran directly into the German fire positions. As they closed, a number of the enemy threw down their arms and fled, though a minority attempted to stand and defend the position. All control vanished at this point, and in twos and threes the attackers dropped on the men in the foxholes and machine-gun positions; sometimes clubbing them or giving them a bullet at close range.

Lieutenant Murphy was galvanized by the spectacle, such was the ferocity of his men. "What we did in those moments we could scarcely remember afterward because we had no time to think. It was courage such as I had never imagined possible, almost foolish courage, and I doubt if any group of men could have held their ground against it."

When the dunes again became quiet 15 of the enemy were dead, 7 were prisoner, and an estimated 50 had fled back through the dunes. The platoon had overwhelmed five machine guns and one mortar to accomplish this destruction of enemy personnel.

The men held steady there for a brief period, reorganizing. Then they moved so as to cover the left flank of the company and at the same time achieve an optimum field of fire against any enemy trying to turn west under the pressure of 2d and 3d Platoons' advance into the dunes. The light machine gun section under Lieutenant Murn became the base of this action and its fire destroyed a great number of the enemy as they tried to clear out of the high ground. The guns and the men around them were given no quiet, however, as the German mortars and artillery to the west continued to rake their ground.

The 2d Platoon had continued to move northward and at 1410 it came under machine-gun, mortar, grenade and small-arms fire from the enemy positions in the heart of the dunes. The men advanced around the bases of the dunes using the thick scrub as cover, going on a few feet, taking cover again, putting more fire forward, watching for any move in the scrub ahead, concentrating fire toward it, moving on again. In this manner they gradually pushed the enemy back from the southern dunes. The 60mm batteries were kept in constant operation and in the men's view were the most useful weapon; their own artillery was falling so far in front of them that they scarcely sensed it.

The platoon came at last to a wide break. The highest dune of all rose ahead of them, but there intervened for more than a hundred yards a stretch of flat and barren ground. They were considering what to do next when a German tank opened fire on them from about a thousand yards off to their left not far from 1st Platoon's ground. The first bursts found their target. Lieutenant Fuquay was killed and Bronislaw Kraska, a squad leader, had his face blown away by the same explosion. Sergeant Kushner, the platoon sergeant, was terribly wounded. Prior casualties during the advance had eliminated all but one squad leader.

Captain Stach sent for Lieutenant Murphy and told him to take command of the 2d Platoon. Murphy got up there, reorganized what was left of the platoon, and after looking his situation over and deciding that 2d was no longer in shape to spearhead the attack, got ready to move it into the company support position.

Before he could do this he was recalled to the 1st Platoon, for a shell had critically wounded Lieutenant Mosier and killed the platoon sergeant, George H. Adams. Private Bleffer acted as platoon leader until Lieutenant Murphy got back.

The 2d Platoon, left leaderless, found itself suddenly the object of a strong German counterattack, supported by an increase of fire from the base of the big dune. There was no choice but to hold the ground and slug it out, and this the men did on their own initiative.

By this time control had become virtually impossible everywhere. It had turned into a "soldiers' battle." The advance progressed because of the initiative of individuals.

"I saw one man throwing rocks into the scrub to one side of him," said Lieutenant Blackman. "The rocks hitting the scrub produced motion. The enemy fired at it; he got a line on the enemy fire position and knocked it out. I saw three men consult among themselves, then get their heads down and charge straight into an enemy machine-gun nest twenty-five yards away, and take it without loss. That was the way the thing went all day." Meanwhile the men of the company headquarters, on their own initiative, had become either ammunition bearers or had joined the assault platoons as riflemen. First Sgt. Frank Seymour and one of the company runners had taken over two of the machine guns.

As 2d Platoon continued to operate as a base of fire against the big dune, 3d Platoon under Lieutenant Mier was committed on the right with the mission of driving the enemy to the west from the remaining dunes, so that they would break out into the open fields where the fire of 2d Platoon could get at them. The attached section of light machine guns had in the meantime been passed up from 1st to 2d Platoon.

Lieutenant Mier moved his men up through a copse to the east of the dunes which were still to be taken, the platoon going north in close squad column until its forward files reached a point even with the northern end of the dunes. Then the platoon faced left and moved ahead rapidly, the men closing in at a run. They completely overran the enemy positions, and the Germans who tried to get away dashed out in front of the machine guns along 2d Platoon's front.

The rest was a foregone conclusion. Within half an hour the dunes were once again free of Germans. Lines were rearranged and the men dug in; German artillery fire continued into the darkness.

The Enemy Cuts the Road Again

Having been thrown back in its probing attacks on the 501st and adjacent areas, the German attack sideslipped to the right. A small force of about two hundred men, an SP gun and a few tanks moved along an auxiliary road toward Koevering. Outposts of the 502d, still stationed in the St. Oedenrode area, reported its movement and Companies C and H were rushed up to Koevering to intercept it. But they arrived only seconds before the Germans. Guiding away from them the Germans reached an undefended section of the highway

British trucks knocked out between Koevering and Vechel on 24 September.

northeast of Koevering. Here they stopped a British convoy, burned its vehicles and knocked out three counterattacking British tanks. The two 502d companies attacked but were repulsed.

Once more the road had been cut. During the night the 377th and the 907th fired into the German salient, but the Germans succeeded in building up their strength with tanks, SP guns, and more infantry. By morning they had a substantial force astride the highway.

The adaptability of airborne men was well illustrated by the experience of the 907th that afternoon and night. It was in position near the highway just south of the canal, firing in support of the 501st.

The artillerymen first felt something was wrong when traffic on the road ceased and firing was heard to the rear. Soon they saw smoke from burning vehicles on the road not more than four hundred yards from Battery B.

Still ignorant of the size of this new menace they called their battalion commander, Lt. Col. Clarence F. Nelson, who was up at 501st headquarters. He ordered Battery B to defend the battalion. Able was to continue on the fire mission in support of the 501st.

The Battery B commander, Capt. Gerald J. McGlone, ordered his guns out of the pits and had them placed in position for direct fire. One .30-caliber machine gun and two .50s were ground-mounted. The twenty-eight bazookas in the battalion were brought out; the attached infantry platoon took positions in a ditch running as far east as the main road. As evening came Captain McGlone sent out an eight man patrol under Cpl. Robert A. Durienshen to get more information about the enemy.

An hour later, at 1930, the battalion executive officer, Maj. William J. Pasley, and Captain McGlone went down the main road to make a personal reconnaissance. Though it was practically dark they could see clearly by the light of a burning truck. Near a small trail they met the British brigadier who commanded the tank unit that had been caught by the German move. The brigadier had formed a platoon of tank-crew men, truck drivers and twelve glider pilots armed with tommy guns who had been on their way to the rear. These he placed along the road to fight off a further German penetration. While they talked the Durienshen patrol returned with word that it had been able to contact only one small enemy group which was moving across the road rather than up it.

At 2100 a new patrol moved out, not for reconnaissance but for the purpose of destroying the SP gun that the battalion had heard firing. Its leader, Lt. Edwin A. Blake, had thought of the mission and secured the five volunteers who made up the patrol. It wandered around for hours, never finding the gun, but it did manage to lay its hands on a lot of British, Dutch and German equipment left on the highway. From one trip it returned with a civilian car, from another with a British trailer and a quantity of arms. The trailer was loaded with five hundred reels of valuable German film previously captured. Eventually the Germans realized what was going on and laid an interdictory fire on the road.

The vital wire which connected the 907th and the 501st ran to Eerde along a secondary road that seemed to constitute one boundary of the German salient. Five times that night it was knocked out by shell fire, and five times artillerymen crawled up the ditch on the right side of the little road to repair it under the noses of the Germans. On one such trip S/Sgt. Raphael E. Meyers and Pvts. Harmon Hunter and Joseph H. McCoy noted an abandoned British truck containing a keg of beer. Cautiously they crawled to it, removed the keg, and rolled it several hundred yards along the enemy flank to a place where it could be opened in safety.

The only casualty suffered by the battalion was its liaison plane and pilot. Not realizing that the enemy was in the area, the pilot flew low over the road; the Germans killed him with small-arms fire.

Another larger communication problem had to be solved that night, for the trunk telephone lines of the Division ran along the main road and had been cut by the Germans. This isolated the 502d and Division

Paratroopers of the 101st move alertly past a burn ing British-operated American six-by-six truck during the fighting of 25 September 1944 to reopen the "Road." The lead man is from the 326th Engineers.

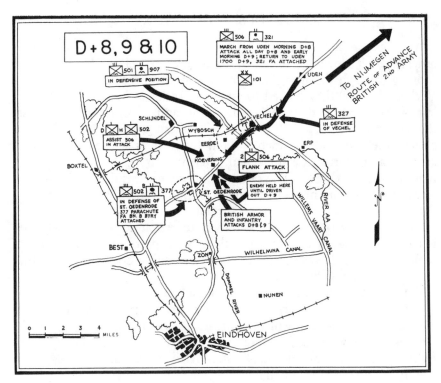

Map 53.

rear, which had joined it in St. Oedenrode that day. Communication was imperative so Signal Company sent out a wire team along with six guarding infantrymen. Together they proceeded over unfamiliar territory well to the east of the main road. Although they frequently came close to enemy groups, they managed to get through to St. Oedenrode with their wire by 0500. Plans for the concerted attack of that day were agreed upon before the new wire was cut at 0600.

Nor was this the only group that went through the darkness of that night from Vechel to St. Oedenrode. The 2d Platoon of Battery C of the 81st had also been ordered south. The sudden cutting of the road had left the 502d without any antitank protection, and they needed it. Division ordered the platoon down. Travelling well to the east, the platoon with both its battery commander, Capt. William Lockman, and its own commander Lt. Martin Stutman, made the trip and played its part in the next day's fighting.

D Plus 8 (September 25)

The job on D plus 8 was to get the road open again. The Division almost succeeded.

At 0030 the 506th with the 321st and Battery B of the 81st was ordered back down from Uden to attack and clear the highway. Moving through the heavy rain of that night, the weary men passed Vechel. At 0830 they moved to attack the salient, 3d Battalion to the left of the road, 1st Battalion to the right, and 2d in reserve. At first the advance went smoothly; strong artillery support from Vechel cleared the way and the men walked forward. But then the enemy artillery and mortar fire thickened. German tanks, dug in along the road, joined the chorus. The two battalions were fighting on a narrow front and this concentration of fire was murderous. The 3d Battalion had to halt and dig in, and then the 1st.

Now was the time for 2d Battalion to repeat its run around the left end that had been so successful in the capture of Eindhoven. It took off on a wide sweep east of the road, with a squadron from the 44th Tank Regiment in support.

But with it also advance was slow. Some tanks were quickly knocked out and the others necessarily became cautious. Germans using captured Shermans added an element of confusion. Too, knowing the Queen's Guards, along with 1st Battalion and Company H of the 502d, were fighting up from the south, Division Artillery battalions had to be extremely conservative in the support they gave this group.

Finally at 1940 contact with the southern force was established, and the job was just about done. But when the attack halted for the night, the German force still held one small section of the highway.

While this fight was on the 502d continued its defense of the St. Oedenrode area, the 327th its defense of the Vechel area, and 501st its defense of the Eerde area. All three regiments suffered several small-scale enemy attacks, but beat them off. The 2d Battalion, 501st, was moved into the line near Eerde. Members of the 377th Artillery in St. Oedenrode received their first mail since the jump.

D PLUS 9 (SEPTEMBER 26)

The job on D plus 9 was still to reopen the road. Men of the 506th moved out in the early morning and advanced down the highway unopposed; the Germans had already started their retreat to the northwest. Coming up from the south the Queen's Guards wheeled to the left against the retiring force, and shortly pinched out both the 506th and the 502d.

But the road was not yet open to traffic. The Germans had done a thorough job of mining their section of it. The 326th Engineers had to sweat hours at the dangerous work of mine-clearing before the British column could move again. In the meantime a very poor alternate route had been opened to the south. It was given little use.

At 1300 the 506th marched back to Uden. The rest of the Division maintained its positions along the highway.

D Plus 10 (September 27)

Traffic continued to roll up the road.

The Division had now stabilized itself with the 501st defending Vechel from the west and northwest, supported by the 907th, Battery A of the 81st and Company A of the Engineers. The 502d was still at St. Oedenrode with the 377th and Battery C of the 81st. The 506th was up at Uden with the 321st and Battery B. The 327th had one battalion in line northeast of Vechel. The rest of the regiment was Division Reserve, with several British tank, antitank and field artillery units attached.

The command post remained at Vechel, with Headquarters Company, Division Artillery, Headquarters Battery, Signal Company and Reconnaissance Platoon in the immediate vicinity.

Quartermaster, Ordnance and the rest of the Engineers were at St. Oedenrode. The Medical Company was still at the hospital at Zon.

German forces made several small but sharp attacks against the 327th and the 501st positions. They were repulsed.

The 501st had two Germans come through their lines that morning to dicker for the return of their battalion commander, who had been captured in the previous fighting. In exchange for him they offered Chaplain R. S. Hall of the 502d. Without attempting to fix the place of religion in life, the 501st rejected the offer; war, they figured, was not a chess game where under some circumstances a bishop may be exchanged for a knight. The whole incident ended anticlimactically when Colonel Johnson learned the Germans had not been blindfolded before they were brought through his positions. He ordered them held.

In the late afternoon the men in Vechel cheered as they received their first mail since leaving England. This strengthened the general feeling that the initial phase of the campaign was over. Some said that for the Americans it was all over.

As it turned out, they were wrong. But this was correctly regarded as a pivotal time for both the Division and the over-all operation. What had been happening up north during these days of the Division's fight at Vechel and its fight at Koevering had determined this.

The Overall Operation at the End of D Plus 10

Ever since the Nijmegen bridge had been seized on D plus 3, the British XXX Corps had been trying to blast a way north from the Waal to the Lower Rhine. But rainy weather made the fields impassable to tanks. The road, raised several feet above the surrounding countryside, was ideally suited to antitank defense. This the Germans had had a chance to organize because of the delay at the Nijmegen bridge. They had the entire road enfiladed with 88s. British progress was expensive and slow.

Finally on D plus 5 a group of light armored cars managed to cut loose to the left and rush up to the Lower Rhine at Driel where they joined forces with a group of Polish parachutists who had been dropped there. With their guns they were able to give a small measure of support to the British across the river. But that night when they tried to send DUKWs to the other side with supplies they bogged in the mud.

Later on about five hundred infantrymen were ferried across the river, but it was too late.

During the intervening days the British 1st Airborne Division had been completely surrounded by greatly superior German forces and steadily pushed back until finally it was confined to a small perimeter west of Arnhem and just north of the Lower Rhine. Its continued resistance there lives on as one of the great actions of modern war.

But feeling the hopelessness of that position the commanders of XXX Corps and the Airborne Corps agreed on D plus 8 to pull the survivors back across the river. The withdrawal was made that night. All told, the British had taken 10,095 men north of the Lower Rhine; 2,490 came back.

That same day all expectation of an advance to the Zuyder Zee was given up. The situation began to stabilize with the British accepting the Lower Rhine as the northern limit of their advance and attempting only to widen the corridor up to that river.

There was no getting around the fact that the over-all operation was a failure. It had not gotten Allied troops across the Rhine; it had neither encircled the German armies in Holland nor bared the right flank of the Siegfried Line. It was admittedly a gamble, designed to exploit German weakness and disorganization in a decisive way. Obviously, the Germans were not as disorganized as had been thought. Many people feel too that the British still lacked the equipment for such an operation as this one. The risk was so desperate that if it were taken at all, it had to be all-out; the British could not afford to go all-out and knew it.

Though the operation was a failure, there were gains to the Allied cause that resulted from it—the northern flank was advanced sixty-five miles over a series of obstacles that included two major canals and the difficult Maas and Waal Rivers. Large parts of Holland were liberated. This additional territory provided a buffer of defense for the vital supply port of Antwerp, and played an important role in the attack across the Rhine the following March.

The 101st Airborne Division could be satisfied that it carried out its part of the operation with credit. General Brereton paid tribute to his men:

> The airborne mission in this operation was accomplished. Airborne troops seized the fifty mile corridor desired by the Commander in Chief of the Northern Group of Armies, and held it longer than planned. The fact that the weight of the exploiting troops was insufficient to carry them past . . . Arnhem in time to take advantage of the airborne effort detracts in no way from the success achieved by the Airborne Forces.

Along with the 82d, the men of the 101st could take pride in the evaluation of their work included in a study by the Historian of the European Theater of Operations. "Did the American divisions act aggressively and in keeping with the bold nature of the entire Market-Garden Operation? Of this there is no doubt. The gallantry of the officers and men of the 82d and 101st Airborne Divisions in all of their actions showed an excellence which has not been surpassed in any operation in the European Theater. In every operation from the crossing of the Waal River in canvas boats to the surrounding of a superior force near Vechel, this feature is accentuated."

No group in the Division escaped unscathed, for during this operation, no one was very far from the front. The units that came in by glider had more men missing than those that came by parachute. This was to be expected. While the parachute drops were almost ideal, the glider trips were broken up by weather, in the fashion already described. Some of the men listed as missing were landed in other parts of Holland and Germany and managed to report in days or weeks later. Others were never heard from.

During this same period the Division took 3,511 German prisoners. The total number of Germans who were killed or wounded has not been estimated; it could not have been small.

Division CP at St. Oedenrode. Lt. Col. Roger Parkinson,
Division Ordnance Officer, was killed in the foreground.

Breathing Spell

Fighting was not a full-time job for everyone after D plus 9. Battalions went into reserve and stayed there for twenty-four hours or more. There came a chance to live a more human kind of life.

The people of Vechel were happy to help the men do this. They converted the rear annex of a large dairy plant into a huge shower which the muddy airborne men were only too glad to use whenever they could get into the city. The cup of milk proffered by an old man at the finish of the bath was a luxurious touch.

In another part of town, eight barbers were put to work clipping hair.

Even when their day out of line did not take the men to the Vechel showers it gave them a chance to wash their clothes.

Brussels passes were inaugurated on a limited scale, which meant that a few lucky men had a chance to get away from it all, however briefly. Their reports on returning were so enthusiastic as to start that preference for Brussels over Paris as a leave town which the Division always felt thereafter.

The slowing down in the tempo of the fighting helped not only the combat soldier but gave the servicemen a chance to breathe again. The Signal Company had felt the strain as much as the others, trying to maintain lines over the more than twenty-five miles from Eindhoven to Uden during the various peaks of combat. Its difficulties were increased by the fact that it could not secure any alternate routes, such as would be possible in a less extraordinary Division area. Everything followed the road. During the entire operation the Division used 4,800 miles of wire, of which 3,275 were laid by the Signal Company itself.

In an effort to tidy up the landscape the engineers went to work burying the cows which actually had been hit by artillery fire.

For the ordnance men, still at St. Oedenrode, these days meant little change. Three officers and nine men had come in by glider on D plus 1. Their first job was to get the ammunition supply point set up. Then they secured the light equipment they had brought in with them, scrounged replacement parts and set up shop. All had to be triple-threat men, able to work on a howitzer, a jeep, or a rifle with equal facility. The greatest need for repairs was on the crew-served weapons. Because of the importance of getting these back to the fighting fronts as quickly as possible, many of the repairs were unorthodox in nature, but they worked. This unorthordoxy was especially apparent before the arrival of the seaborne echelon with its heavier equipment, and two more officers and twenty-eight more men.

After the later move up to the "Island," the life of the Ordnance Company became more ordered. Regularly teams visited the battalion that had just moved into reserve, and made on-the-spot repairs.

The last few days in Vechel saw changes in the top positions in the Division. Lieutenant Colonel Hannah, G-3, had been seriously wounded by the unlucky shell burst on the road north from St. Oedenrode. As his successor, General Taylor selected Lt. Col. Harry W. O. Kinnard, for reasons which should be apparent. Quick, bright-eyed Colonel Kinnard, West Point 1939, thus became one of the youngest G-3s in the American Army. His former place with the 1st Battalion of the 501st was given to Maj. Raymond V. Bottomly.

Lt. Col. Roger W. Parkinson, Division Ordnance Officer, was killed by a surprise burst of German artillery near his shops in St. Oedenrode on September 26. Capt. John S. Patterson, commander of the Ordnance Company, held the additional position until October 16 when Lt. Col. Carl E. Anderson took the job.

Lt. Col. Thomas F. Sutliffe took charge of the 2d Battalion of the 502d when Colonel Chappuis became regimental commander.

On September 28 the Division went under British XII Corps.

THE CAMPAIGN GOES ON AND ON AND ON

The rest of the Holland fighting was a long anticlimax for the 101st. This was especially true because officers and men alike had expected to be pulled out when the emergency period of the action was completed. Some men jumped from their planes believing that they would

Lt. Gen. Sir Miles C. Dempsey, commander of British Second Army,
talks with Brig. Gen. Gerald J. Higgins, Assistant Division Commander.

be relieved within seventy-two hours. It actually took seventy-two days.

Of course the seventy-two hours was just a rumor. But everyone thought the Division was simply on loan to the British Second Army to help them with a particular attack. When the attack was over it would be treated as shock troops were supposed to be treated and sent back to prepare for the next emergency.

Surprise and disappointment therefore greeted the announcements made during the days following D plus 10. Instead of going back it was going forward, forward, to the "Island." This was the name given to the long narrow area north of Nijmegen between the Lower Rhine and the Waal where the British had established a front line. There would have been not only surprise and disappointment, but also utter disbelief if anyone had known in advance that while there the Division was going to set a new record for continuous service in the front lines. No one would have credited a report that unit journal entries which identify days as "D plus 4" or "D plus 23" would this time run up to "D plus 71."

It is now evident that the British badly needed help. They had become involved in clearing the Antwerp area, and were using so many troops there that they had none to spare for the "Island." But the Division did not know this then. All that was known was that an army not its own was giving it a rough deal.

The trek north started on October 2 (D plus 15) when the 506th moved up to Nijmegen, taking with it the 321st, Company B of the Engineers, and all the batteries (except C) of the 81st. Firing in support of the 82d, the 321st got off the 101st's first round to fall on German soil.

The next day the 506th moved out to take over a front-line position from the British near Opheusden. Other Division units followed it north in the course of that week, and joined it on the Island.

Fighting on the Island

By the time the Division was ordered up the British had extended their front line along the south bank of the Lower Rhine as far west as Opheusden. Three or four small German bridgeheads still existed and these were destined to give trouble later. But the ground behind had been cleared out. This ten-mile-long area between the two rivers from Opheusden on the west to Elst on the east was to become the Division responsibility.

Most of Holland is flat and low, but the Island is an exaggeration of both these characteristics. There is no rise in the ground, other than the dikes holding back the two rivers. The land in between is farmland and orchards, cut up by drainage ditches and tree rows. The dikes themselves are twenty-foot earth structures, with a road along the top, and sides sometimes steep, sometimes sloping so gradually as to make the dikes two or three hundred feet wide at their base.

The Germans in contrast had hills on their north side of the Rhine. With perfect observation, German artillery dominated the entire Division area and made all daytime movement dangerous.

Men lived in foxholes—foxholes that usually had to be covered as a protection against German tree bursts. But they couldn't dig the foxholes very deep, for at three feet water seepage started. This got worse as the rains of October raised the level of the two rivers.

Waters in the rivers finally rose past the danger point and plans had to be made for a quick evacuation of the Island if the Germans blew the protecting dikes. The Americans were spared that experience, but the British who took over in late November went through it.

Although the Division never had the observation granted to the Germans, it did have the guns. Whole regiments of British artillery were placed in its support. Added to its own units this gave it more firepower than ever before. Island battles were artillery battles, in a sense that the 101st had never experienced before.

In this fighting everyone learned to have a great respect for what a rocket-firing Typhoon plane could do to help the ground fighter. Whenever enemy strongpoints gave trouble, the British Typhoons were sent for. Usually their rockets did the job.

It was while on the Island that the men first had the "Screaming Meemie" used against them. Here they first saw the German jet planes, and here they heard the ill-famed V-2 pass over their heads on its mission of terror. During their last few hours here Lt. William D. Hardie, Jr. and a FO party from the 377th saw what they believed was a daytime launching.

In a sense the use of the word "anticlimax" to describe this later fighting is incorrect. The men who fought at Opheusden feel that it was as terrible a battle as any they were ever in. There were other moments of sharp fighting and excitement.

But for most of the men most of the time, the Island was a long, dull experience which well-directed German artillery fire made constantly dangerous. A man's inability to do anything about that artillery fire contributed to a general sense of frustration. For the combat men there was the additional strain of the constant patrolling which characterized the last weeks. Patrolling brought casualties and the realization cut more deeply as a man's turn to go out came closer.

To top off all this the length of the Division's stay there necessarily restricted the freedom which usually compensates a man engaged in front-line fighting. The veterans of Carentan and Vechel could not but wonder what it was all about when their front-line positions were inspected for cleanliness. "That Island was the worst period of my life" was the way one officer summed it up.

The Division was on British rations all this time—and that served to make matters worse. Parts of the 14-in-1s were not so bad. But the ox-tail soup, "the grease that had bones floating in it," and the heavy pudding, extra heavy, were points of irritation. Bully beef became as monotonous as it had been in World War I. There was no coffee, and Americans tire of tea. For some men the crowning blow was British cigarettes. They finally took to smoking *Stars and Stripes*—when they could get a copy.

Local wine stocks helped out and the traditional British rum ration was a welcome innovation, though the distribution of a ration of alcohol created the usual problems for company commanders. It had its source in the ten or fifteen men in any company who did not drink. If each one had his own thirsty buddy to whom he promised his ration, all was well. But if six or eight of the extra drinks all went to the same man there was trouble ahead.

Diet was further aided by "Operation Jam Factory." There was a deserted cannery beyond the American MLR near Dodewaard where jam was to be had for the taking. It made the British hardtack more palatable, and many a good man risked his life taking some.

As further compensation, the bounties of Dutch agriculture were showered upon the entire Division. Sometimes the process was helped by shaking a tree or two. Apples were to be had everywhere, and pears and nuts. There were cows, many of them obviously suffering from not having been milked. There were pigs and sheep. There were even houses to cook them in, and plates and silver to use. Some men had the most elegant meals of their lives during that stay in Holland.

Things were so wide open because civilians had been hastily evacuated when the British realized that the Island was going to be a fighting area for a long period. The stuff was there to use. And soldiers, feeling that both they and the stuff might be blown to bits the next morning anyway, used it.

Some of the things that happened were contrary to the law, strictly interpreted. But those in authority at first adapted the rather tolerant attitude typified by the experience of one company commander. This lieutenant had already decided to stay in the Army, and was especially anxious not to get any black marks on his service record. One day he was walking down the road with his regimental commander. To his chagrin they came suddenly upon a group of his own men emptying their carbines into the pig they had chosen for their dinner. "Look at that pig, lieutenant," drawled the colonel, "attacking your men."

But such natural toleration could lead to real abuses, and it did. Along with the British, Dutch civilians, the Germans, and the 82d, all of whom were or had been present, the 101st had to accept a degree of responsibility for the disappearance of property in some of the Dutch towns. When the situation began to get serious from a divisional standpoint there was a crackdown. Officers were relieved. New orders against looting were read to all troops, and stiffer penalties were invoked.

Worried about the British rations, and believing that much of the trouble was due to the wrong kind of cooking, General Taylor procured a British warrant officer in late October to run a school for Division cooks. Eating was further improved when the Division was transferred from the British Second to the Canadian First Army on November 9. The Canadians had baking units to serve their front-line troops. Relatively fresh bread took the place of the now-hated hardtack.

The food situation was only part of the long headache that the stay on the Island constituted for G-4 and the Quartermaster Company. The British did not know American supply procedures and the Americans did not know theirs. Nor was it only a matter of procedure, for even vocabulary was different. Supplies were scarce, everything having to be trucked from Cherbourg or Utah Beach. Even with the help of the American truck companies that had been given them the British were still short of transport.

Occasionally the Division obtained permission to send its own trucks south to the American zone to fetch crucial items. The only other shortcut was to have special materials flown in to Brussels and truck them on up from there. But most items had to descend to the Division slowly through channels—British channels.

It was during the Holland campaign that the 397th Quartermaster Truck Company began to work for the Division—an association practically unbroken from then to the end of the war. So complete was their identification with the Division that some soldiers began to call its members "The Airborne Negroes."

One of the triumphs for the Quartermaster Company was getting the civilian laundry at Beek into operation for the Division on a 300-bundle-a-day basis. The company of course had to furnish the coal. PX supplies were first brought in October 4, and came irregularly thereafter. The company's major failure was not getting Thanksgiving dinner to the men. A real one was served out of British rations the first Sunday after the Division came out of the line and returned to the American zone.

During the Island stay all the rear-area activities, Quartermaster, Ordnance and the rest, were concentrated in one end of a large monastery, a few miles southeast of Nijmegen. The building was relatively safe, but occasional shell fire meant casualties for each group.

Nijmegen was also the home of the new hospital of the Medical Company, with the advanced field hospital unit working up on the Island. In all 2,765 casualties were handled during the campaign. The changed nature of the fighting after October 22 reflected itself in the eighteen Schü-mine cases that were received that week, all of them in advanced stages of shock.

Though it was plainly marked, German planes bombed the hospital on October 29, and three Medical Company men were killed and six wounded. Fearing similar attacks in the future the company moved across town to the monastery where other Division Rear activities were congregated.

German artillery fire, by playing hell with the roads and wire lines kept both the Engineers and the Signal Company busy with repair work. The almost continuous rain of the preceding six weeks helped make road repair an unending job. In between times the Engineers deloused Dutch villages which for a month had been occupied by nothing but British or American soldiers.

The Engineers also operated a set of showers at Nijmegen, but most of their duties were up toward the front. Once again they had the job of clearing German mines from Division areas. In front of defense lines they prepared minefields of their own and set up trip-flare systems. But they were probably proudest of another activity of theirs. "The Engineers fought as infantry in every major action of the Division." Company B was in the thick of the Opheusden fighting.

Signal Company's work was made easier when it found a submarine cable under the Waal. Up to that time all its wires to the regimental areas had fed across the Nijmegen bridge along the road and had accordingly taken a pounding from German artillery. But the cable led into a quieter section, and fewer wire repairs were required.

Before this change had been made M/Sgt. Conrad E. Russell, a Signal Company wireman who had been with it since activation, was lost to shell fire around the bridge.

The Division command post was moved to the Island October 4, and reestablished in tents in an orchard near the little village of Slijk Ewijk. Late that month, German artillery found the range of the orchard. The command post was moved to the houses of Slijk Ewijk itself.

In connection with all these Island activities was a crucial fact—the

Division had moved up without having received replacements for the losses it had taken in the earlier engagements. Colonel Ballard's battalion of the 501st, for instance, which had left its planes on D-day with 34 officers and 574 enlisted men went up to the Island with 26 officers and 426 enlisted men. The 506th Regiment on D-day had an effective strength of 159 officers and 2,093 enlisted men. It moved into the line at Opheusden with 119 officers and 1,800 men.

The Battle of Opheusden

After one night in Nijmegen the 506th Combat Team on October 3 was ordered forward to Opheusden to take over a section of the front line from the British 43d Division. The relief, like practically all troop movements on the Island, was accomplished at night.

Terrain here was as flat as everywhere else on the Island. The Lower Rhine and the Waal moved closer together so that there was only 4,500 yards between them. Breaking up the flat expanse was a two-track railroad running east and west whose embankment rose more than five feet above the surrounding land. North of the railroad was the main drainage canal of the Island, ten feet wide with about three feet of water in it during early October. Opheusden, a small town of about one hundred brick buildings, lay between the Lower Rhine and the railroad. It could be approached from the east by two roads, one along the dike and the other running between the railroad and the drainage ditch. Just east of town the latter ran into a north-south road which bridged the ditch and crossed the tracks near a small station. As was to be expected the hills north of the river gave the Germans excellent observation on both roads.

A curious point about the Allied front line here was that it faced west; the Americans were fighting toward the U. S.

Going into position, Colonel Sink placed his 2d Battalion on the south bank of the Lower Rhine extending from Heteren west of Opheusden. The 3d Battalion section ran south through Opheusden across the tracks to the Waal in the vicinity of Dodewaard. G was north of the railroad with Battery B of the 81st. I was south, and H was in reserve. The 1st Battalion became regimental reserve. The British said the section was quiet, and no trouble was anticipated.

British intelligence, in turning over to the Division all information of possible use, reported that the German 363d Volksgrenadier Division was somewhere east of Arnhem. It had been reorganized as a Volksgrenadier outfit after getting knocked to pieces at Avranches, and was believed to be ready for combat again.

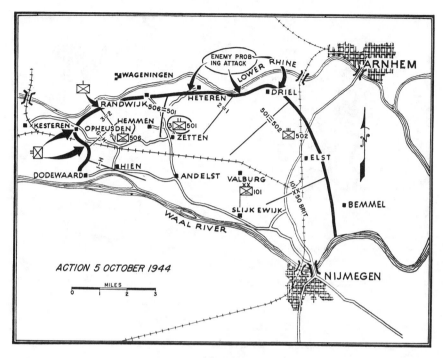

Map 54.

Unknown to the British and unknown to the 101st this division had been given the mission of clearing the Island. It was already moving west behind the German lines to Rhenen. Here, fortunately, the bridge over the Lower Rhine had been knocked out and its units had to make the river crossing by ferry, necessarily a prolonged operation. This perhaps was the reason for the piecemeal fashion in which they were committed. The odds against the 101st in the fighting that followed were bad enough; had the Germans been able to use the division as a unit, they would have been much worse. It was sent forward a regiment at a time, to be chewed to pieces.

The men of the 506th had no idea what was in store for them when, early in the morning of October 5, the Germans started to probe the lines of the 3d Battalion. At 0600 men saw the trip flares that Division Engineers had set close-in to the battalion positions go off. This signalled the launching of a full-scale attack. Simultaneously the 2d Battalion reported increased artillery fire.

The 3d Battalion held the first assault. But a second one with more artillery support forced Major Horton to commit Company H and send back a call for help. Colonel Sink and his S-3 rushed to the area. Seeing the need for more troops, Colonel Sink directed that the 47th

385

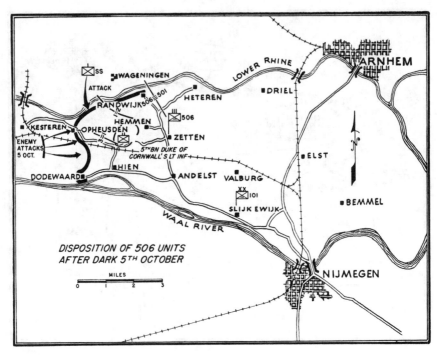

Map 55.

Tank Squadron and his own 1st Battalion, less one company, be brought into the action.

The one company had to be kept in reserve because 2d Battalion was sending increasingly serious reports. A company of SS troops in what must have been a diversionary attack came across the river to assault their positions at 0830. Another half-company followed later on. Both were driven back with heavy casualties.

The rest of 1st Battalion worked its way forward, taking losses from German artillery on the road. Company A reached Opheusden first and its platoons were attached, one to Company G on the right and two to Company H on the left.

German artillery continued its fire on Opheusden. Shortly after 1000 Major Horton was hit, and a few hours later died. Maj. Robert F. Harwick took his place as battalion commander.

Early in the afternoon the Germans launched another infantry attack supported by tanks. It was thrown back with the help of accurate supporting fire from the 321st, who had nine forward observer teams with the 506th. In the course of the day's fighting the 321st fired 1,700 rounds. The British 79th Field Artillery Regiment did a comparable job.

Late in the afternoon the Germans attacked again, this time in the

386

Company I area south of the tracks. At first Company I held. But it was overextended and could not keep the Germans from turning its flank along the banks of the Waal. A desperate counterattack later restored the lines. Casualties for the 506th Regiment that day were 6 officers and 86 men.

In the course of the fighting Company B of the Engineers was again thrown in to fight as infantry. A British antitank unit and a squadron of armored hussars were used, as well as two batteries of the 81st.

That evening Colonel Sink decided to move the entire 3d Battalion south of the railroad and to put all of the 1st Battalion into the line in Opheusden itself. The 5th Battalion, Duke of Cornwall's Light Infantry, had been brought forward to give him a new reserve. These movements were made under cover of darkness. But as Company H pulled back to readjust its line the Germans were lucky enough to use the opportunity to move down the railroad tracks and into the area around the tiny railroad station placed where the road crosses the tracks.

In early dawn Company G was ordered to attack west along the railroad and clear them out. It advanced easily for about six hundred yards when it ran head-on into the 957th Infantry Regiment attacking east along the same tracks, one battalion on each side. After a bitter struggle in the open Company G retreated to its original lines where the 3d Battalion managed to hold for the rest of the day.

Matters went more unfavorably for 1st Battalion, fighting in Opheusden itself. Company A, just north of the tracks, was pushed back to the eastern edge of town. Lt. William C. Kennedy, its commander, was wounded and was replaced by Lt. Anthony N. Borrelli. The 506th men suffered from what they considered the heaviest artillery of the Holland campaign. The 321st fired 2,600 replying rounds that day.

The antiaircraft batteries of the 81st were used as ground troops, with their .50-caliber guns right on the MLR. The antitank batteries were so close to the front line that when a German attack forced a partial withdrawal, one gun had to be left. It was recaptured the next day.

In the early afternoon the 5th Battalion, Duke of Cornwall's Light Infantry, was committed on the left of the 1st Battalion. Attacking, it managed to regain about three hundred yards of the lost ground before it was stopped. The enemy counterattacked, but the Allied line held firm.

Late that day the 3d Battalion of the 327th was attached to the 506th.

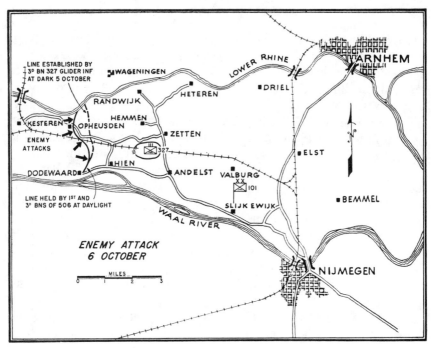

Map 56.

Rather than trying to squeeze this battalion into the current front line, it was decided to have it create a new defensive position 1,200 yards to the rear. Under cover of darkness the 1st Battalion, 506th, and the Duke of Cornwall's Light Infantry battalion, both badly shot up, would be withdrawn from the battle. The 3d Battalion, 506th, would fall back and take a new position as the southern portion of the newly established line. This maneuver would clear Allied troops out of Opheusden and leave it open for Typhoons and artillery to blast what Germans they could the next day.

The withdrawal order forced the 1st Battalion to face the problem of what to do with its 120 seriously wounded men. During the day they had been given treatment in the aid station that Capt. Joseph Warren, the battalion surgeon, had set up in the windmill on the east edge of town. They were now lying in the basements of the houses along that last street, hoping their battalion could keep its grip at least on that.

It was not so hard to get out those who could walk. About fifty of these in two groups were evacuated through the ditches in late afternoon.

But the others were going to be difficult. After darkness made the

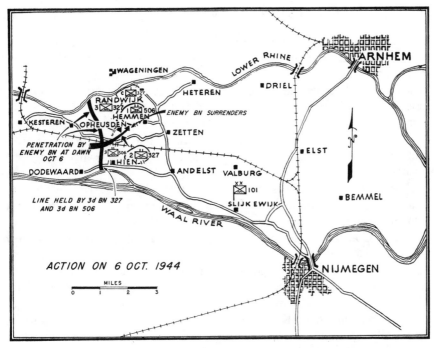

Map 57.

dike road partially usable Maj. Louis R. Kent, regimental surgeon, sent up all the transportation he could get his hands on—six jeeps and an ambulance. These removed twenty of the litter patients; about fifty were left. Six captured German artillerymen were pressed into service as litter bearers, and they took care of three more. The rest had to be taken out by the unwounded, two men to a patient, using the seat carry with the M-1 rifle.

Only one vehicle came forward to help the line companies and some of the crew-served weapons were placed on it. Everything else was hand-carried as the weary battalion started to the rear with one platoon temporarily left behind to screen the withdrawal.

Taking a roundabout route the battalion arrived about 0400 in an orchard behind Tienhoff, just 1,200 yards west of Hemmen, and settled down for a hard-earned rest. The four companies bivouacked in an area approximating a square, with Headquarters Company closest to the front and Company C farthest away.

Battle casualties for the 506th that day were 11 officers and 91 men. And the fighting was far from finished.

For that night the Germans brought up a fresh battalion, and just at dawn they sent it attacking east along the railroad. Breaking through

389

a thinly held section of the new line, the battalion plunged directly
to the regimental rear and then for some reason headed slightly to
the north. This meant it was headed toward the area where the 1st
Battalion had settled down for its rest only two hours before. Sentries
spotted the advancing groups of men, but in the dim light were not
sure whether they were British or German. The group came closer;
a machine gun chattered and the whole battalion stirred. Fortunately, even in their exhausted condition the men had dug slit
trenches.

There was great confusion as each group tried to learn the identity
and intentions of the other. The word "surrender" ran through both.
During this interval the mortars were sent to the rear. With Headquarters Company, they had been so close to the Germans that they
would have been of no use.

Finally the situation began to clear—first to the men of the 506th
where the murmuring converged into "They want *us* to surrender."
Men started firing. Someone in headquarters sent out the message:
"There is a bunch of Krauts in here and they aren't supposed to be
here. We are taking a rest." Company C was immediately dispatched
around the left flank. At that time it consisted of Lt. Albert N.
Hassenzahl and twenty-six men.

The Germans, too, sent a company to their left. But mortars of the
506th caught them in the middle of an open field, and broke up the
maneuver. By this time Company C had been stopped by the German
mortars. Lieutenant Hassenzahl called for mortar fire on the German
positions and got it. Free once more it went on and completed a
180-degree turn, striking the Germans in the rear.

The Germans were already in confusion. Their plight was made
worse by the advance of the 2d Battalion, 327th, into their right flank,
and the reserve Company C of the 3d Battalion, 327th, upon their left.
The 2d Battalion had been bivouacked nearby, and had heard the
noise of the firing.

Seeing the Germans in such straits, Captain Warren, the surgeon,
boldly strode into their lines and by his presence helped to give the
impression that the fight was over. The Germans surrendered; over
two hundred prisoners were taken and more than fifty dead bodies
were lying on the field. The 1st Battalion of the 506th had suffered
two dead and five wounded from this early morning battle.

Among the prisoners was the German major in charge. On him
was a map indicating that he had been expected to take his battalion
right on through the American positions to the Nijmegen bridge.

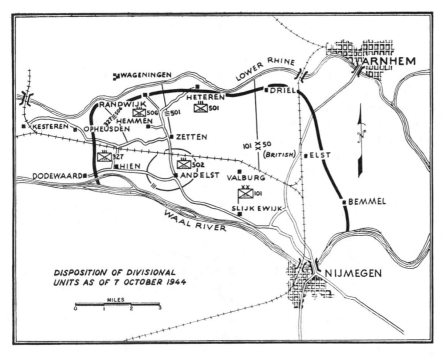

Map 58.

The emphasis was now to shift from the 506th to the 327th, which was shortly to have entire responsibility for this area. It had been kept in Vechel until the morning of October 6, then brought forward with the 907th to replace a British unit in the Elst region. But at noon, in view of the losses the 506th was taking at Opheusden, the mission was changed and the 2d and 3d Battalions were temporarily attached to the 506th. Late that afternoon Colonel Allen of the 3d Battalion was told that he would be responsible for the northern half of a new defense line 1,200 yards east of Opheusden to be set up that night. His area ran two thousand yards from the Lower Rhine River south to and including the railroad tracks.

At 2100 he issued his orders to the battalion, now assembled at Groote Hel. Companies A and B were to go on the line with Company A on the north. There would be five hundred yards of open space between the two that would be covered by fire only. Company C was in reserve. All positions were to be occupied by 2330.

It was a wild night, for Germans had already infiltrated the area that the front line companies were to occupy. Capt. Robert J. Mac-Donald, Company B's commanding officer, and his runner, T/5 Lawrence A. Harris, returning from a reconnaissance walked into an

391

enemy patrol. Captain MacDonald immediately fired on it, killing four Germans, capturing one and forcing the rest to flee. A few minutes later Harris, delivering a message by himself, bumped into another German group. He blazed away and broke up that one, too. Lt. Clarence J. Ryan, company executive officer, had a similar experience; he used hand grenades.

In spite of such occurrences and in spite of German artillery that kept up a continuous fire on the area the positions were occupied. Supply and communications services were established. Defensive fires were worked out with the mortar officer and the liaison officer from the 321st. By midnight the battalion was ready for action. It did not have long to wait.

At 0430 the next morning an enemy force of about three hundred men was seen moving east along the tracks on the left flank of Company B. Burning buildings silhouetted the enemy group, so it was safe to hold fire even as they approached. At seventy-five yards Lt. John T. O'Halleran gave the word. The entire left platoon blazed away along with a section of heavy machine guns. BAR men had a field day. Taking heavy losses the enemy group retreated in confusion.

Toward dawn enemy artillery and mortar fire increased and another German battalion supported by four tanks advanced down the tracks. Again men of the 327th opened on them with everything they had but the tanks with their heavy close-in fire made a difference. A large portion of this new group managed to break through and continue east. How it ran into the 1st Battalion of the 506th, was surrounded and forced to surrender by that battalion and 327th units, has already been told.

Heavy German artillery fire continued but there was no new attack until 1330, when a small force again advanced against the left flank of Company B and a larger group moved across the open space between B and A. They found the open space a death trap. Combined artillery, mortar and small-arms fire, working according to plans made the night before, wiped them out.

The smaller force, with the support of a tank, managed to get into a defiladed position south of the railroad track. Realizing that a bayonet assault was likely, T/Sgt. James C. Single, who had taken charge of the flank platoon when its leader was wounded, readied his men for it. The Germans advancing across the embankment were met with a shower of grenades that killed or wounded thirty-five of them and forced the remainder to withdraw. A bazooka knocked out the tank.

In late afternoon it was apparent that the enemy was gathering opposite the battalion for a new attack. The fire of 148 guns was massed to break up his formations. When the assault came an hour later it was directed primarily at Company A. Seeing the danger of its flank being turned, Colonel Allen rushed Company C to its assistance. The line was held.

Throughout the day similar attacks were being hurled at the 3d Battalion of the 506th in its new position south of the tracks, but they were all repulsed. With the coming of darkness the 1st Battalion of the 327th was moved up to relieve it and the switch was accomplished that night. Company E stayed on line in the position astride the tracks to which it had moved that afternoon. The rest of the 2d Battalion moved into reserve position near Hien. The whole area became a 327th responsibility.

The 506th that day lost 3 more officers and 95 men. Since the landing its officer strength had been reduced one-third, and its enlisted strength one-quarter. Only when this is thought of in terms of the fighting units—rifle squads with one rifleman, mortars with no one left to operate them—can the size of the job that the survivors had to do be appreciated.

Despite the losses which they had already taken around Opheusden the Germans were determined to break through, and from October 7 to 14 there were scarcely six hours when the 363d Division did not launch some kind of attack against the 327th. But the positions originally chosen were ideally suited for defense action. Supporting artillery was prompt and powerful. The men of the 327th fought well. The 363d Division simply smashed itself to pieces.

Fog and poor visibility on October 8 deterred the enemy from repeating the dawn attacks of the 7th. It was not until 0800 that a reinforced company moved out against A's positions. As the right flank again began to waver the support platoon was sent over to assist it. Even as that platoon moved out an enemy patrol of twenty men, which had probably taken position the night before, attacked Company A in the rear. A detail from company headquarters wiped it out. Meanwhile, heavy artillery and mortar fire had helped to repulse the main attack. The enemy withdrew, leaving fifty dead on the field.

At 1000 a formation of Typhoons went to work on Opheusden. Enemy pressure slackened noticeably as a result.

Nothing further happened until mid-afternoon when a patrol of fifty men with four tanks moved against the right flank of Company B. The men were sucked into the open space where machine-gun fire from both B and A caught them and wiped them out. The tanks caused heavy casualties in the Company B ranks before artillery fire drove them off. Early that evening Company C was sent forward and exchanged positions with B.

Heavy artillery fire bore down on the 1st Battalion positions throughout the day.

By this time the 327th numbered among its supporting units not only the 377th, Battery C of the 81st and Company C of the Engineers, but also the 116th Royal Artillery (British), the 61st Reconnaissance (British), and a squadron of the Scots Greys Tank Regiment (British).

Strong enemy patrols roamed the area that night, but all attempts to penetrate the American lines were thrown back.

German artillery fire took on a faster tempo on October 9, and there was a feeling of expectancy in the air. At 1700 the fire increased still further to a stage which British observers described as the worst since El Alamein—two thousand rounds were estimated to have fallen in one fifteen-minute period. The barrage landed so heavily on Company C, 1st Battalion, 327th, that the company was thought wiped out and a platoon from Company A was sent to plug the gap; but when the barrage lifted all but two Company C men were alive and waiting for the time to begin shooting.

It was not far off. At 1745 eight tanks and two regiments of infantry moved forward. The weight of the attack was directed against the 1st Battalion area to the south where the 1409th Fortress Battalion and two battalions of the 959th Infantry made up the assaulting group. British and American artillery opened up on their advancing lines. In the emergency air bursts were requested to explode only seventy-five yards beyond the front line. The infantrymen opened up with small-arms firing so fast for so long that their gun stocks began to burn their hands. The first enemy wave was caught in enfilade fire between Companies A and C and wiped out. But others kept coming. All non-fighting personnel were put to the job of ammunition resupply, so that the machine guns, rifles and mortars could continue firing.

In the 3d Battalion area two speeding tanks, part of the initial attack, managed to run over the foxholes of an OPLR before bazooka fire could be brought to bear on them. But the riflemen held their positions and kept the German infantry back. A 37 finally destroyed one of the tanks and the other withdrew.

By darkness the main attack had been broken with heavy losses for the enemy but the glidermen were to get no sleep that night. Whistles screamed in front of their lines as German officers organized small groups and drove them forward. Shouting German soldiers advanced through the darkness. Fighting desperately, the 327th stopped each group, but morning light revealed German bodies less than an arm's length from some of the foxholes.

A small group of Germans attacked the northern flank early the next morning but they were quickly driven back. The next group to come forward did so under a Red Cross flag, to ask permission to remove their wounded and dying. There were many of these stretched out in the fields between their lines and their cries filled the air. Colonel Harper gave his permission.

German artillery started again as soon as the fields had been cleared. There was no major attack but several small patrols were sent over to probe the American lines.

Fearful of an armored attack along the dike road 3d Battalion moved one of the 57mm guns of the 81st to cover it. Later, under cover of darkness, a string of mines was laid across the road. That night Company G came forward to relieve Company E. Company F relieved Company C and was attached to the 1st Battalion.

Further patrol activities and the inevitable artillery characterized the morning and afternoon of the following day, the 11th. But at 1800 smoke was thrown across the front of the Company A positions on the north. A half hour later out of the smoke two rifle companies advanced, supported by machine guns, mortars and four tanks. Artillery and small-arms fire stopped this attack except on the right flank of Company A where German artillery with a direct hit had knocked out two light machine guns. A caliber .50 was rushed forward to replace it. One of the tanks, advancing up the dike road, hit a mine that had been laid only the night before. It stood motionless but continued to fire until the 57 knocked it out. As the German infantry came close the company put all its fire over in this direction, including canister from one of the 37s and the enemy was stopped.

The 12th was comparatively quiet. That night the 2d Battalion relieved the 1st. In the 3d Battalion Company B relieved A.

On the 13th the northern flank was again attacked but no more successfully than before. In a heavy rain that night the 2d Battalion of the 502d relieved the 2d Battalion of the 327th and the latter in turn relieved the 3d Battalion of the 327th, moving from the southern to the northern part of the line.

The German attack on the 14th again was directed against the northern flank now held by Company G. A heavy barrage concen-

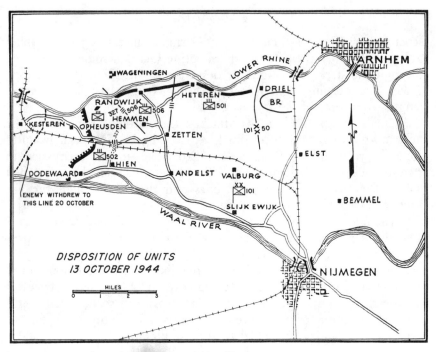

Map 59.

trated on its position at 1630. After thirty minutes it lifted to two
hundred yards behind the company line, and the German infantry
advanced, elements of three companies worn down to about seventy
men each by the earlier attacks. Company E assisted in the protection
of G's left flank, and the G men held their own right flank. The
enemy was once again forced to withdraw with heavy casualties.

Again on the 15th the Germans launched a company-size attack on
the northern flank, supported this time by six tanks. The attack was
repulsed and Battery A of the 81st, which had recently been moved
to this section of the line, knocked out three of the tanks.

By this time the 363d had been virtually wiped out. Giving up all
hope of a breakthrough on the Island the Germans fell back 2,400
yards. Both sides settled down to patrolling the no-man's land thus
created.

Other Units, Other Fights

Opheusden was by all odds the largest single battle of the Island
campaign. But other units were not idle during the days it was fought.

The 501st with Company A of the Engineers left the Vechel area
on the morning of October 4 under orders to replace the British that
night on the south bank of the Lower Rhine between Driel and

Colonel Howard R. Johnson (right), CO of the 501st, and Lt. Col. Robert A. Ballard, shortly before Johnson was killed. Ballard became regimental CO at Bastogne after Colonel Ewell, Johnson's successor, was wounded.

Heteren. This was going to be more difficult than anticipated for the British had held the section so lightly that the Germans had been able to build up three small bridgeheads on the south bank. Half a battalion was working to expand one of these even as Company C moved up into the area. German artillery and small-arms fire caused great difficulties as the British were relieved, and Company C settled down to a battle that was to last all through the next day. At one time it was completely surrounded by stronger German groups. Not until late afternoon was the reserve, Company A, able to break through

Lt. Col. Julian J. Ewell, who succeeded Colonel Johnson as CO of the 501st.

to it. Seventy-five prisoners were taken in the final victory, and a German tank was destroyed. Against lighter opposition Company B and the 2d Battalion had succeeded in taking over their new positions the night before.

The beachheads, protected from direct assault by overwhelming German artillery on the north bank, continued to be a headache. One group of Germans who had taken possession of a brick factory and a storage yard opposite Company E were impervious even to a rocket-carrying Typhoon attack that would have destroyed an ordinary position.

But the 501st managed to contain them, and finally to wear them down and eliminate them. This process, lasting for several days, was interspersed with numerous patrol actions and small-scale attacks. The Germans launched one of the most serious of these in the late afternoon of October 6 in the Company F area. It was finally repulsed with heavy losses to the enemy.

Shortly after this attack Colonel Johnson went out inspecting front-line positions in the 2d Battalion area, accompanied by Lt. Richard O. Snodgrass, commander of Company D. As a heavy-caliber German shell gave its characteristic whistle, everyone ducked but the colonel. With his usual disdain for danger he walked on. The shell exploded practically at his feet. Fragments penetrated his arm, his neck, and the base of his spine. Capt. Louis Axelrod, 2d Battalion surgeon, was hurried to the scene and the colonel was shortly started on his way to the Nijmegen Hospital. But he died before he got there, breathing out his last words, "Take care of my boys."

With his hands and brain Colonel Johnson created a regiment in his own image and led it into battle. When he died part of the 501st died with him. Neither officers nor men would soon forget that terrible energy, that lust for color, that amazing combination of self-will and complete identification with the regiment which characterized him.

Moseley . . . Wear . . . Johnson . . . only Sink was left of the original regimental commanders.

Colonel Ewell became regimental commander, his slow Texas ways seemingly designed to contrast with the previous abruptness. In his drawl he described the change, "The days of the flash-and-dash are over." Colonel Ewell, West Point '39, was generally considered one of the best tacticians of the Division.

Colonel Ewell placed Lt. Col. George M. Griswold in his old post as commander of the 3d Battalion. Two weeks later he chose Lt. Colonel Ballard as regimental executive officer, and Maj. Sammie N. Homan became commander of the 2d Battalion.

General Taylor too was a victim of German fire. A round from a self-propelled gun wounded him on November 9 while he was inspecting front line positions along the Lower Rhine and he was out of action for two weeks.

The 502d Regiment and its attached units, moving up from St. Oedenrode on October 3, were held in the Nijmegen area for two

days as a reserve for the 82d Division. Then it went forward to the
Island and took a position in the Elst area. Its stay here was relatively
quiet. On October 10 the regiment went into Division reserve near
Andelst. Three days later it took over the southern half of the 327th
line near Opheusden. This might have led to large-scale action, but
shortly thereafter the Germans made their retreat, and both sides
settled down to continuous patrolling. In late October Lt. Colonel
Ginder, the executive officer, was wounded, to be replaced by Lt.
Colonel Cassidy. .

The 506th continued to maintain its one-battalion front on the
Lower Rhine. It was here on the night of October 22-23 that the escape
of the last survivors of the British Airborne's effort at Arnhem was
engineered. These were men who had been cut off from the main
body in one way or another, and had missed out on the major evacuation of late September. They were living in semi-concealed fashion
with the assistance of civilians. Their leader was a British Lt. Col.
O. Dobey, escaped from a German hospital, who had gotten in touch
with the Dutch Underground. The Underground had a wire underneath the Lower Rhine which made coordinated planning possible.

The scene was described by the 506th Historian:

Saturday evening British pontoon boats were placed under cover of the
orchards, along the edge of the river in the 2d Battalion area. Night routes were
laid out with engineer tapes and everything seemed ready. For the last few
evenings a Bofors gun had fired tracers into the sky so that the enemy might
not be too curious when those tracers became a signal. Artillery was boxed to lay
on outside a square of four hundred yards along the Rhine, in case of emergency.
Mortars and MGs were set up on each flank to be used if necessary.

Night fell, the ever present murk and drizzle adding to the obscurity. Assault
boats were edged over the dyke and into the water. By midnight all was ready.
A company had posted the river on either flank of the focal point of the operation
to fight off any enemy attempts to counterattack or infiltrate. Men who would
make the crossing lay shivering as they waited. The artillery was silent, ready to
lend instant support should we need it. The Bofors erupted an arc of tracers
across the night sky in a prearranged signal visible to every Kraut—and to the
men who were to assemble underneath their line of flight. At 0100 a red flashlight blinked the old V-sign from a point several hundred yards upstream across
the river.

It was the signal we had waited for. Boats were slid into the water and were
lost in the darkness, visible only in the flashes from German artillery and
nebelwerfers. One barrage landed on Colonel Sink's CP several hundred yards to
the rear. The boats got across OK and Lieutenant Heyliger (who was known as
"Moose" because of his face) was welcomed shortly by a British brigadier as the
finest looking American officer he had ever seen. Meanwhile, one officer and six
men moved to either flank and waited for the deal to be completed. A German

flare lit up the area, but apparently could show nothing and so the shuttle was begun. In thirty minutes everyone was safely back.

The British troopers, the fliers, and the civilians were guided back along the tape to a small town where they were fed coffee and—you guessed it—jam! The boats were hidden in a nearby patch of woods. The British took over with their welcoming committee, moved all back another several hundred yards and gave them tea and cakes, so on into Nijmegen where at last they were put to bed.

Not one man had been hit; the operation could not have been more successful, the British said.

In all, 138 British soldiers and four American pilots were thus redeemed from life in a *Stalag*.

When the Division's area of responsibility was enlarged on October 28, the 506th was shifted to the east on the river bank just opposite Arnhem.

After the German withdrawal of mid-October, the whole front was relatively quiet. Battalions and even regiments were again able to go into reserve. Of course both the comfort and safety of the rear areas were questionable. But it was a chance to clean up.

Life was more leisurely, even in the front lines. Men listened to "Arnhem Annie" as she invited them across the river. Through some miracle of supply *Yank* and *Stars and Stripes* came through. The Division's own daily news sheet, *The Kangaroo Khronicle,* reappeared at this time. There was even a German propaganda leaflet shot over the lines in early October, *Why Fight for the Jews?* And the Division went in for some international persuasion of its own when the 506th Prisoner of War Interrogation Team made a broadcast to the Germans on November 2.

But there was still the German artillery to keep a man awake nights —and there were still patrols. Some of the most hazardous were in the Opheusden area where there were those 2,200 yards between lines, most of them well sown with Nazi mines and booby traps. Constant patrolling of this area and the German lines beyond it was a necessity, and it took its toll. The Division Reconnaissance Platoon leader, Captain Wilder, lost a foot. In the 327th the reconnaissance officer, Lt. Fred J. Rau, and his sergeant were both killed. One of the 502d patrols lost seven men and an officer.

Patrols were of all types sent out for all purposes. A 35-man patrol from the 502d under Lt. Paul Dovulok was sent out with the mission of getting prisoners. This patrol picked up eight. What gave it particular significance was the fact that one of the eight was a staff sergeant who obligingly drew a map of all the German mine locations in the area. The work of future patrols was made considerably easier.

The Incredible Patrol

Some of the patrols became masterpieces of advance planning, with artillery fire, river crossings, smoke signals and the other paraphernalia of war all incorporated into one enterprise. Perhaps the most famous of this group was the Sims patrol of the 501st.

General Higgins, in visiting the front line, on the tip end of the American boundary along the Lower Rhine, talked with Lt. Hugo Sims, Jr., regimental intelligence officer of the 501st Parachute Infantry Regiment. In emphasizing the importance of capturing prisoners, the General pointed out to Sims that "we must find out what units are opposing us in order to determine whether the Germans have withdrawn their main forces to another front."

"Sims, can you get me a prisoner?"

"Yes, sir," Sims answered.

For about ten days Sims sent out one or two patrols each night with the single mission: "Bring back a prisoner." But it was to no avail. These patrols were ineffective because there was a strong feeling that this patrolling was unnecessary. The feeling penetrated the patrols. The men in the patrols were unwilling to risk their lives for what they felt was no good purpose. This feeling of injustice was so strong that members of a patrol were known to puncture the rubber boats to be used for their crossing, so that the patrol would have to be called off. Other patrols crossed the river, and when they reached the German shore, would rest in some place hidden from view, returning several hours later with a negative report.

Sims decided to go and get the prisoners himself. He put his request to lead a patrol in writing to Colonel Ewell, concluding: "I feel that this patrol is necessary as a stimulus for the battalions." The regimental commander wrote across the request: "OK, J.J.E."

While the 23-year-old lieutenant was busy making preparations for what he hoped to be a model patrol, a number of officers dropped in to talk with him. Ray Hoffman, Sims' No. 1 assistant, requested that he be given permission to lead the patrol. Capt. Les Cady said, "Hugh, you are doing a very foolish thing." Major Roberts, the regimental operations officer, chided, "Poor Huey, age 1," referring to Sims' son.

Sims wanted Cpl. William R. Canfield, of Selman, Oklahoma, as his assistant. Canfield was big, he was quiet, and, most important, he was dependable. On being informed that his chances of returning were less than fifty-fifty, Canfield volunteered.

Canfield then picked out three of the best scouts in the intelligence section: Roland J. Wilbur, Robert O. Nicolai, and Frederick J. Becker. They were each informed of the spectacular patrol that was being planned and of the dangers involved. They all volunteered to go.

Sims called M/Sgt. Peter Frank. Frank knew nothing about patrolling. He interrogated prisoners. He spoke German fluently. Frank had requested some weeks earlier that he be allowed to go on a patrol. Sims' decision to carry him along made him jubilant.

Twice before the patrol left on this spectacular enterprise, Sims called the members together. He had aerial photographs of the area through which they would move. Over and over he explained the route. Finally, he required each of them to give the route from memory. He explained to them that four times each hour, two rounds of artillery would fall in a small clump of woods about three miles behind enemy lines. The artillery would be a check for each member of the patrol on his direction. Each man would know that the artillery was falling in that same clump of woods he now saw on the aerial photo. Sims also told the group that before leaving he would synchronize his watch with the observer's watch. This was essential in that the mortar observer was to fire a flare every thirty minutes. Sims pointed out that in this way the patrol would be able to observe German positions to their front while the flares were burning just as if it were daylight. Knowing that the flares were to be fired, the members of the patrol would all be concealed at the designated time each half hour.

The plan of the patrol was simple. The group was to move north, about six miles during the first night. They were to conceal themselves in a house on the main road between Utrecht and Arnhem before daylight. The following day they were to observe the traffic on this main highway, and that night capture a German vehicle and drive back to the American line. The idea of riding back in an enemy vehicle exhilarated the whole group.

Sims told the group of his plan to get through the enemy front line. At night, he said, the German troops would occupy a line along the northern bank of the river. But since the area north of the river was open ground and there was no concealment behind which troops could hide, the Germans would be forced to withdraw before daylight to a 75-foot embankment covered with trees about two-thirds of a mile north of the river.

On the American side of the river, at the patrol's departure point, Sims reminded them, "There is a high dike at the very edge of the river. This means that the patrol can hide behind the dike at the

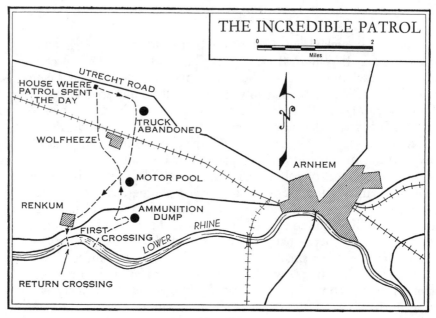

Map 60.

river's edge, until it gets dark, and then travel across the river while the Germans are moving from their embankment two-thirds of a mile down to the river. The plan is for the patrol to cross the river and move two or three hundred yards toward the embankment and then lie down and let the enemy front line pass over them."

The patrol was interviewed by Cpl. Russ Engel after its return, and his story of its exploits appeared in *Life* for January 15, 1945.[5]

. . . Pfc. Frederick J. Becker of Atlantic, Iowa, took over the story. "All of us were a little nervous in the last few hours before the patrol. We all had blacked our faces and we began to look as if we were really going on this deal instead of planning it. I was stuck with one of the musette bags with half the radio in it. One of the other boys was to carry the other half and I was a little griped because I was stuck with the heaviest part. But the other boys had their jobs, too. They had demolition blocks for blowing the railroad we planned to cross on the return trip.

"Instead of the steel helmets we had been wearing for the last month or two we wore our soft overseas hats. Each of us had our pockets full of extra ammunition plus grenades and honed knives. We were really going prepared. In addition to our regular weapons we all carried .45 pistols. Wilbur was the only one of us taking an M-1 rifle, the rest of us chose the Tommy gun for more firepower. We tried to talk him out of the M-1 but we knew it would be nice to have him along with it. Wilbur has the reputation of being pretty accurate with that gun and is famous for never shooting a man unless he can aim dead center for the head. He doesn't miss.

404

"After a dress rehearsal in front of headquarters, where Lieutenant Sims checked over our equipment, we decided we were set. Now it was only a matter of waiting for darkness. We sat around for a while and then went in for some hot chow. The cooks seemed to know what was up and the boys in the mess line gave us a few pats on the back. Lots of our buddies came up and wished us well and said they were sorry they couldn't go along. They really were, too. We all tried to act as if it meant nothing at all. After we washed our mess kits one of the cooks came up and gave each of us three K-ration chocolate bars and said when we came back he'd have a swell hot meal waiting. It was getting dark now and we all sat around the S-2 office getting fidgety."

Here Pvt. Roland J. Wilbur, the M-1 rifle expert, took over. He comes from Lansing, Mich., where he used to work for Nash-Kelvinator. Now he almost looked like a soldier in one of their magazine ads, sitting there with a grim look on his face, cleaning the M-1 as he spoke.

"The S-2 office wasn't too far from the dike on the Lower Rhine. We took off about 7:39. We rechecked all our stuff and piled into two jeeps. In a few minutes we were up near the area where we planned to cross. We stopped and got out of the jeeps and began to wonder if the clothes we had on were enough to keep us warm. It was overcast and cold and it had begun to rain. We were wet before we had really gotten started. A couple of hundred yards away we ran into the group who had the boats ready to take us across.

"We were awfully careful about reaching the dike because a lot depended on these first few minutes. We knew that a couple of other patrols had been knocked off before they had gotten to the water. Our main hope was that the Jerries weren't on the alert because we were going over a little earlier than the other patrols. We started to go down toward the bank when a whisper from Lieutenant Sims halted us in our tracks. He thought he heard a sound from the other side. After a couple of minutes of shaky waiting we decided to take a chance. Edging down the bank, we came to the two rubber assault boats. Lieutenant Sims and two of the boys carefully slid into one and the rest of us crouched low at the bank and waited with our guns ready in case Jerry should open fire as they crossed. It seemed to take them hours to get across and we could hear every dip of their paddles in the water. We were certain they would be heard and the whole deal would be off, but they weren't. They made the opposite side and crouched low to wait for us.

"Finally we landed. Arrangements were made with the men with the boats so we could signal them by flashlight when we came back. They wondered if we had any idea when it would be and we told them that we hoped it wouldn't be until the next night. We hunched down and told the boatmen to be quiet going back. We could just barely see them as they hit the opposite shore."

Pfc. Robert O. Nicolai, a former member of the Merchant Marine who comes from Midlothian, Ill., now broke into the story. He was given the Bronze Star for his part in the Normandy campaign and is the cocky member of the group.

"All of us started up the bank to the top of the dike, Lieutenant Sims in the lead. Nothing ahead looked like a Kraut, but there was something that we hadn't expected. A little way ahead there was a big pond directly across the route we had planned to take. We decided that it would be better to go around and change our route a little.

"We skirted the edge of the water but found we still had to do some wading in the dark. By the time we passed the pond our feet were slogging wet. Lieutenant Sims seemed to have on a pair of boots about ten sizes too large and they squished with every step he took. Someone said, 'Dammit, pick up your feet.'

"Suddenly the first of our mortar flares lit up the sky and we were all flat on the ground. We cautiously looked around the countryside but there wasn't a Jerry in sight. It was now 8 p.m. and the flares were working just as we had planned. As soon as the flare died out we got up again. About 200 yards ahead we saw a light and a few shadows moving. We held a confab and decided that because we didn't want to take prisoners too early we would alter our course again. We by-passed the light and circled around to the right. Then we heard the unmistakable sound of Germans digging in for the night. It was the sound of folding shovels digging into the earth and the clunking noise they made as they were tapped on the ground to loosen the mud. We now turned left again and as we did someone stumbled into the brush in the darkness. Immediately we stood still as statues and waited. Then we heard the zip of a German flare going up. We hit the ground and froze as more of the flares lit up the country-side. To either side of us we could hear Germans moving around. Now and then one of them shouted to ask what the flares were for. They had heard something and had whole batches of flares ready to shoot off. Each time a flare burned out we crept forward between the two enemy groups. In a half hour, when our own flare next went up, we had covered less than 300 yards.

"Then we crossed a road and found ourselves within 20 yards of a lighted tent. I was all for going in and taking whoever was there a prisoner. I thought it might be a Jerry officer and a good bag but once again we decided that it was best to skirt the area. We went one way and then the other through the fields. Every time we heard activity we edged in other directions."

Cpl. William R. Canfield of Selman, Okla. now interrupted the story. "I was a little to one side of the group and suddenly I heard someone blowing his nose. I moved over to the left and saw a group of Jerries stopped for a minute on the road. I asked Lieutenant Sims if I might capture them and take them along but he said not now. I was sure feeling cocky.

"A little later I heard Becker make a noise and as I glanced at him he began to pull himself out of a slit trench he had slipped into. I walked over to him and saw a big, fat Jerry snoring away in the hole. For a moment we thought he might waken and looked down ready to pounce on him if he made a noise. When he remained asleep we went on and joined the rest up ahead. Now we were in a wooded area and we had to be careful of every step. At a clearing in the woods we came to a small road and not ten yards away we saw a couple of Jerries walking down the road, with something on their shoulders. Nicolai sneaked along the road and looked more closely. He came back and reported that they were carrying a mattress. A little farther down the road we saw them walk into a house with their mattress. We waited but they didn't come out so we figured they must have turned in for the night.

"Farther on we crossed the road and stumbled right into an ammunition dump. Sergeant Frank, the interpreter, went over to check the writing on the boxes. He found they were shells for a heavy 150-mm. infantry gun which Lieutenant Sims marked down in a little book he was carrying. He also marked the position of the ammo dump and the location of the mattress house. Just as we were starting to make a more thorough inspection around the ammo dump we heard the unmistakable sound of a German Schmeisser gun belt being snapped back. In a second there came another. We stood rooted to the spot, afraid to breathe. The things seemed to come from just across the road. There wasn't much else for us to do but to go sneaking back through the area of the sleeping men."

Sergeant Frank now pointed out that he hadn't been too scared when the belts snapped back. He had a story all ready for the situation. Every time they came to a new emergency he would review in his mind a story that might work the patrol out of it. This time he was ready to raise hell with the Jerries for making so much noise with their machine-gun belts. Frank continued: "Now we cut straight across the fields for about two miles. Nicolai was getting hungry and he simply reached down and grabbed a handful of carrots from a vegetable patch and began to eat them. Soon we had enough of the fields and decided that we were deep enough in the enemy territory to brazen it out on the road. when we came to a good paved road we walked right down the middle of it. Just ahead we heard the clank and rumble of a Jerry horse-drawn vehicle. We crawled into the ditch along the road and waited for it to pass. In a couple of minutes we were on the road again.

"Farther on we checked our compass course and started off to the right. We hadn't gone more than 20 yards when I saw Becker throw his hands in the air. Right in front of us was a huge German gun emplacement. The gun and pits for the ammunition were there but there didn't seem to be any Jerries. About a hundred yards farther on we came to a strange collection of silhouettes. We couldn't be sure what they were and kept on going until we made them out. It was a Jerry motor pool with all types of vehicles parked for the night. We were all for taking one of the cars but Lieutenant Sims again turned thumbs down. He pulled out his map and noted the exact location. Soon we were on the edge of the town of Wolfheeze and decided that it would be best to work around it. As it later turned out, this was a good thing. The place was lousy with SS troops.

"We skirted the town pretty closely and could even smell the smoke from stinking German cigarettes. We now crossed the railroad which we knew marked the two-thirds point on our trip. We were some distance behind the enemy lines and had the feeling we would be able to bluff our way out of almost any situation that might arise. The last three miles of rushing through the fields was pretty hard. The tall grass slowed us down but it also sheltered us from observation. Nicolai was in the lead, eating carrots again. When he heard the rush of a car going by he whispered to Sims that this must be the road we had crossed so much country to reach. Within a few hundred yards we came out on the road."

Nicolai broke in again: "We all waited a few minutes at the side of the road while Lieutenant Sims brought out a map and checked our location. We were right behind a house that marked the exact spot where we had planned to hit the road. This was only luck but it made us feel as if everything was going according to plan. Lieutenant Sims, looking over the house and the area, decided we might as well occupy the house for cover. We sneaked up carefully, listening for the slightest sound. Becker and Canfield now went through a window and a minute or so later came back to whisper that all was clear inside. But after a conference we decided that this was not so good after all. If Jerry were to see any activity around a house which he knew to be empty he would become suspicious. Becker and Canfield climbed back out and we headed down on the road again. In front Sergeant Frank was carrying on a monolog with Becker in German. This was funny because Becker didn't understand a word of it. We all fell into the spirit of it, feeling we could fool any Germans who came along. Soon one of the boys was singing *Lili Marlene* and we all joined in.

"After about a mile of walking along the road without meeting a single German we came to a couple of houses. One of them had a Red Cross marking on the front. It was a small cross and the place hardly looked as if it were a hospital. At any rate it looked like the better of the two houses. As Sergeant Frank and myself edged close we could hear what sounded like snoring inside. We walked to the back door and found it open. In the front room of the house we found two Germans sleeping on piles of straw. They wore big, shiny boots and I was sure they were officers. Sergeant Frank said they were cavalrymen. Leaving Frank on guard I went back outside and reported to Lieutenant Sims. He said we would take the men prisoners and stay at this house. I told Frank the plan and he began to shake the Germans. One of them finally began to rub his eyes. He stared at us and Frank kept telling him over and over that he was a prisoner. They just couldn't believe it."

After the dazed Germans had been thoroughly awakened they were questioned by Sergeant Frank. He got all the information he could from them and relayed it to Lieutenant Sims. Sims was now up in the attic setting up the radio with another man. In about ten minutes the men heard him saying into the radio, "This is Sims, Sims, Sims. We have two prisoners. We have two prisoners." They knew the radio was working and everyone felt swell. Soon Sims was sending information about the things he had noted along the way.

After questioning the prisoners Sergeant Frank told them to go back to sleep but they just sat and stared. Frank asked them if they expected any more soldiers in the area. They said that another man was supposed to pick them up at about 5:30 in the morning.

After the radio had been set up everything was quiet until daybreak. The men took turns watching the road while the others tried to get a little sleep. At about 7 a.m., Nicolai, reported the arrival of a young civilian at the front door. The civilian proved to be a boy of about 16 in knee pants. He was both surprised and pleased to be taken captive by the "Tommies." The men took some time to explain to him that they were not Tommies but airborne GIs. When this had been taken care of Sergeant Frank was allowed to go ahead with his questioning. The boy explained that the house belonged to some friends of his and he had just come over for some preserves. He knew the people had been evacuated and said they might not be back for some time.

The boy went on to say that his older brother, who was a member of the local underground, would also be along shortly. Almost immediately the brother was brought in by Nicolai. He was a slick-haired, effeminate young man and the patrol had doubts about him. He spoke a little English and produced papers to prove that he was a member of the Dutch underground. He began to tell the men about the various enemy installations in the area. He gave them artillery positions and unit numbers and all this was immediately relayed back over the radio.

In the following hour six more civilians were guests of the patrol. They all seemed to know that there was no one home and all wanted something from the house. They were told they would have to stay until after the patrol had left. The civilians were happy to see the men, but they didn't like the idea of having to stay. One of the captives, a very pretty Dutch girl accompanied by what appeared to be her boy-friend, wouldn't take no for an answer. The men said she was not averse to using all of her charms to get out, either, but they were firm.

At noon the traffic on the road began to increase. Convoys of big trucks appeared to be heading from the Utrecht area toward Arnhem. The men observed all kinds of vehicles and guns. Presently an unsuspecting Jerry entered the courtyard for a drink of water. Opening the front door a little, one of the men pointed his Tommy gun at the German and commanded him to come in. The German came in laughing, apparently not quite convinced that the whole thing wasn't a joke. He turned out to be a mail orderly who had lost his way after taking mail to a near-by town. He seemed to be an intellectual type and was very philosophical about being captured.

Shortly afterward the idea of food occurred to everyone in the house. The men in the patrol got out their K-ration chocolate and the civilians began to dig into the little bags they all carried. It began to look as if the civilians had been going to a picnic. They brought out bread and cheese and shared it with the Americans. An hour or so later the German who was supposed to meet the first two prisoners at 5:30 finally showed up with two horses and a cart. The men let him enter the courtyard and water the horses. Then they called out to him, "Put up your hands, you are a prisoner." He didn't seem to understand and it was necessary to repeat the order. Then he answered calmly, "I must feed my horses." Finally he raised one hand and came toward the house, muttering that it just couldn't be true. Now the civilians helped in the questioning because the Germans were not too sure about the names of towns where their units were stationed.

Once the men watching from the windows were tempted to whistle at a passing car. It was driven by a pretty German WAC. The men said that the only thing that restrained them was the fact that their lives depended on it. Because everything had gone so smoothly the men were feeling pretty cocky. They began to figure out their plan for the coming evening. They wanted to capture a truck, a couple of staff cars with German WACs and drive back to Renkum. Along the way they would stop briefly to blow up the railroad.

At 4 p.m. two more Germans entered the courtyard and were immediately taken prisoner. They were very sore, mainly because they had come along the road just to goldbrick away a little time. By this time a big fire had been built in the front room where the prisoners were kept. The prisoners kept the fire going and the men argued to see who would stand guard in the warm room.

As darkness approached the men began to assemble their equipment. Becker was left on guard in the house with the prisoners and civilians while Lieutenant Sims and the others went out to look for a truck. The German mail orderly, who seemed the happiest to be captured, was chosen to help them. He agreed that as soon as Sergeant Frank told him he would help stop the truck by shouting, "Halt Kamerad." As they waited the German said to Frank, "I am happy because the war is over for us." Frank replied that it would all depend on the next few hours and that he would be able to say with more certainty the next day.

Becker reported that when the lieutenant and the others left the house the remaining prisoners looked a little scared. Finally one man came and asked Becker in pantomime if they would be shot. Becker told them that such things aren't done in the American Army. All of the Germans in the house wore the Iron Cross and had seen service against the Russians.

While the men were waiting along the road a whole German company passed on bicycles. As each German rode by he would shout *"Guten Abend"* to the men along the road and they shouted back the same. One man stopped and asked Sergeant Frank if this were the right road to the next town. Rather than become engaged in conversation, Frank told him he didn't know.

Getting impatient after an hour and a half, the men decided they would stop the next truck that came along, no matter what kind it was. In the meantime a motorcyclist stopped by the road and went into the courtyard of the house. Nicolai rushed across the road and grabbed him. It developed that he was checking up on the absence of the other men. When Nicolai brought him across the road he saw the mail orderly and rushed up to shake his hand. They were old friends and had served together for years. A few minutes later the men heard a truck coming down the road and told the two Germans to step out and shout *"Halt Kamerad!"* When the truck came all the men shouted at once and the truck stopped. It turned out to be a big five-tonner carrying 15 SS men. Nicolai jumped on the back and herded the Germans off, taking their weapons as they got down. They were all very surprised. At first the driver refused to leave his seat, but after a number of strong threats, namely shooting, he finally got off. He was a tall man and very cocky. When asked to put his hands up he said, "Who says so?" When he was told that he was a prisoner of war he looked astonished and said that it was impossible. As he spoke, he put one hand up and with the other drew a pistol, but only to hide it in his pocket. Sergeant Frank took it away.

The driver was told to get back in the truck and pull it off the road. He seemed reluctant and Frank had to hold a gun against his ear while he started the motor. He seemed unable to keep the motor from stalling every few seconds and when he moved into the courtyard he had trouble turning. It was obvious that he was stalling for time. He kept looking at Frank and saying in German, "Jesus, I'm mad. This can't happen to me." He told Frank he was on his way to meet the captain of his battalion. When he was told he was to drive the truck and the men to the Lower Rhine, he said there wasn't enough gas. He was told that if that were true then he would be shot, so he said that there was enough gas for 20 miles.

Now Becker and the prisoners in the house came out and piled into the truck with SS men. The Americans spaced themselves around inside the truck so they could keep guard. Lieutenant Sims and Sergeant Frank sat in the front with the driver. When they were on the road the truck stalled again. As the driver tried to start the motor an amphibious jeep pulled up and a tall SS officer began to bawl him out for blocking the road. Canfield was off the truck in an instant and had brought the officer inside. As it turned out, this was the captain the truck driver had been going to meet.

Again the sergeant concentrated on getting the driver to start the truck. He worked hard at stalling the motor and had to be threatened before he would drive at all. Finally he got the truck under way and they set out on the return

route they had mapped out before the patrol. Every now and then the driver
would get temperamental, folding his arms and saying, *"Hab' ich eine Wut!"*
("Am I mad!") After a prod or two with the gun muzzle he would go back
to safer driving. Farther along the road toward Arnhem he was told to turn off
to the right. Shortly the truck came to a muddy place in a woods and bogged
down hub-deep. No amount of trying by the SS driver was able to move it.
It was now 10 p.m. and the patrol decided they might as well try to make it
back on foot.

Now the men regretted having so many prisoners. As they piled down from
the truck the SS captain bolted to the side of the road in the darkness. In a flash
he was in the woods. Nicolai shouted for him to stop and ran after him. In a
moment the others heard two shots and Nicolai's only two words of German,
"Hände hoch, you son of a bitch!" followed by a great crashing in the under-
brush. Becker also ran into the woods to see if he might help. Following the
noise he found Nicolai and the captain. Nicolai was still shouting *"Hände hoch"*
and with every shout he would kick the captain in the seat of the pants. When
they came back to the truck the captain was cowed and willing to go quietly.

Lining the Germans up in two columns, Sergeant Frank now gave them a
little lecture. He said they could just as easily be shot as taken back and that all
six Americans were risking their lives to get them back safely. He told them that
if anyone tried to escape or made an unnecessary noise he would be shot immediately. Starting out again with the SS captain and Sergeant Frank in front,
the column made its way along the road toward the river. As they walked the
SS captain told Frank that it was useless to try to cross the Rhine with the prisoners.
He said the Americans might as well turn over their guns because they would
surely be caught by the Germans along the river.

The captain also asked if he might have a cigaret. He was told he couldn't
have one now, but that later he would have more and better cigarets than there
were in all of Germany. The captain said the Germans had nothing against the
Americans and he couldn't see personally why the Germans and Americans
didn't get together to fight the Russians and Japanese. We are both white races,
he said. Sergeant Frank answered that the Russians were also white. Yes, replied
the captain, but they are inferior. Finally the captain asked if it were not possible
for them to rest a while, or at least to slow down. He was told that he had the
misfortune to be a captive of American paratroopers, who just didn't walk any
slower. Now as they walked along they constantly heard German voices.

Arriving at the railroad crossing, the patrol decided finally that they didn't
dare blow up the tracks with the two-and-a-half minute fuse they carried.
Reluctantly they crossed the tracks and ditched their demolition charges in bushes
by the road. Along this last stretch of the road they passed countless houses
with Germans inside.

When they came to the town of Renkum the patrol marched boldly down the
center of the main street with a great clicking of German hobnailed shoes. It
was obvious from the sound alone that they could be nothing but a group of
marching Germans. They went through the town without incident and headed
straight for the near-by dike. Everyone was feeling wonderfully lightheaded.
Arriving at the dike, they had marched right down to the water when they saw
a squad of Germans at a river outpost. As they came close Sergeant Frank
called out to them in German that there was nothing to worry about. When

Paratroopers of the 506th dug in on the reverse slope of a ridge overlooking the German positions near Heteren.

they stopped, two of the men rushed over and told the Jerries to put up their hands. The columns moved on, cleaning out two more posts along the river. The six-man patrol now had a total of 32 prisoners.

On the dike Lieutenant Sims gave the prearranged flashlight signal to the other side. Soon the answer came—three blinks. The SS captain, his truck driver and one of the patrol were the first to get to the other side. Part of the patrol stayed behind to cover the crossing while the rest of the prisoners were ferried over. Finally the last three men touched the Allied side of the Rhine. The incredible patrol was over.

The Island and Corporal Derber

For at least one other paratrooper the Island was an exciting place; and when there wasn't excitement enough he stirred up his own. Twenty-one-year-old Cpl. Glen A. Derber of 2d Battalion Headquarters Company, 501st Parachute Infantry Regiment, had arrived in Holland on September 17 via parachute with a healed shoulder wound received near Carentan in June, a light machine gun in a leg bundle, and an old 1903 Springfield rifle for which he had a real affection. After the war he reconstructed from his combat diary the period on the Island.

After crossing the Nijmegen bridge which had become a constant target for German artillery, we dismounted and dispersed in an orchard to await our march to the front where we were to relieve the Limeys, who were glad to see us because the Germans had given them a pretty hard time of it. We started our march to the front late in the afternoon and it was dark by the time we got there to move into our positions. The Limeys had already moved out before we got there so the Germans could have walked right thru if they had known.

I didn't get on the MLR that night but stayed back near the CP to furnish the brass some protection. Next day I moved up to the MLR which was on the reverse slope of a dike which was anywhere from fifteen to twenty feet high with a road on the top of it. I had to work my way through lulls in a mortar barrage to get to the MLR for this was indeed a hot spot. Our platoon suffered several casualties the very first morning.

There was a continual exchange of artillery barrages on this front. We had lots of Limey artillery to back us up and this was strictly a defensive position so we felt pretty secure. The following morning on the nineteenth day of this mission I got orders to move to a new position. The gun crew which had been there had been hit by a direct hit from a mortar shell. The Krauts were about six hundred yards off and moving about freely. It seems the Limeys didn't give them much trouble. I opened fire on them and sent them for cover. A few minutes later mortars dropped in around me.

I decided my foxhole wasn't deep enough and started digging. When I had it to what I thought was a good safe depth, I chased the Krauts back to their holes again and got some more mortar fire, close ones too, so I decided I wouldn't use the MG again.

After a dinner of C rations which we hadn't had yet and which tasted pretty darn good after eating those Limey rations, I borrowed a pair of field glasses and started some sniping activities with my '03. I could fire the rifle without drawing any mortar fire because it didn't attract as much attention as an automatic weapon like a machine gun with its tracers. I saw a Kraut about six hundred yards or so away lying outside of his hole in the warm sun, so I tried a shot. He didn't move. I guessed the bullet couldn't have gotten to him so I set my sights up to seven hundred yards and tried again. He scrambled to his feet and ducked into his foxhole, then looked around wondering who was shooting at him. The next time I fired he ducked into his hole. When he came up to look around again he had his rifle. I tried another shot, and down he went again. I checked with the field glasses after each shot and when I looked after my last shot he was aiming at me!

I got ready to fire again and a bullet cracked above my head. It seemed pretty wide to me and I was all for this game. This was something I could enjoy, for I had great confidence in my rifle and my ability to use it. The next shot I fired must have hit him in the head for he bounded out of his hole as if by reflex action and went tumbling head over heels down the side of the dike. Some other Kraut came running over to take a look at him and I scared him off with a shot.

I had a lot of fun that afternoon, wounding two more and two probables. That not being enough excitement for one day, I spied some wild ducks in a pond to the rear of our lines and started chasing them around with my '03. I finally hit one. That done I went off to one of the nearby houses, or what was left of it and went into the fruit cellar and found a couple of jars of canned cherries. . . . Those canned goods were too much to pass by, for the chow we were getting was terrible.

The following day I got in some more sniping with no definite results. There was the usual exchange of artillery and mortar barrages. The nights were getting cool now and dense ground fog would move in on us. We'd send men out in front of the lines on what was called listening posts to detect any enemy movements. This one foggy night while I was on guard two men who were out in front of us got scared in by a Heinie patrol and it so happened that they decided to come over the dike right where my gun was located. One of them stuck his head up and looked around suspiciously. It was too foggy to make out whether the helmet was American or Kraut so I just eased the safety off my rifle and sat quiet, waiting. Then he starts crawling across the road toward our side of the lines on his belly. That looked too suspicious to me, why would one of our men be sneaking back into his own lines? I leveled the gun at his head and then startled him by asking what company he was from. We didn't have pass-words at the time. I could have simply asked him if he was American, but some Germans could speak pretty good English and he simply would have answered "yes." But a German wouldn't be liable to know what company was on the line. When I told the guy later how close he came to getting shot he heaved a sigh of relief and was very glad I didn't have an itchy trigger finger.

The next day, D plus 21, proved to be an exciting day too.

About four hundred yards down the dike to my right the Germans had managed to move up in the night and had dug in directly across the dike from our positions. Here were our lines on one side of the dike and directly across the road not thirty feet away the Germans were dug in. The only thing they could do was toss grenades up and back trying to get each other out but they simply rolled down the dike and exploded harmlessly at the bottom so our men devised the clever idea of taking a length of parachute suspension line about forty feet long and tying the grenade to the end. Then when they threw it across it could only roll down so far.

Someone came along looking for a grenade launcher, saying they had a machine gun position down that way to knock out. I was coaxed by my crew members to take the job so I took my rifle and grenades and went to look into the situation. The machine gun was located about seventy-five yards out from the other side of the dike and could be reached with grenades if one was willing to stand up and expose himself above the top of the dike. I agreed to do it if someone would cover me. I put three of my four grenades right on the position and then fired some armor piercing bullets at the machine gun to make it useless. I went after more grenades and when I returned I found out the Krauts had pulled out leaving the gun laying in a ditch. My first sergeant bawled me out afterwards because I left my gun position to go out hunting Krauts . . .

The next day I was sent back to the CP again to get a couple days rest. Our platoon had dwindled from eight gun crews down to five gun crews and only four were used at once on the MLR, which left one extra which stayed at the CP to pull guard. They changed about so each crew got a chance for some rest. I didn't like the boredom back there though so I would go up to the dike when I got a chance and do a little sniping. I just loved to fire my rifle.

Well, it seems the Germans had caught on to this sniping too and they had a well concealed sniper at work on a certain section of our lines. Two men had been hit in the head when they stuck their heads up over the dike to look around. I was itching for a rifle fight this day so I thought I'd try and find him and have a little duel. I tried all the tricks I knew, I'd push my helmet up one place and then sneak up near a place where I had a background against which I couldn't be easily seen. Then I'd poke the glasses through some grass and look around the landscape trying to locate that sniper. He must have had a powerful telescope or something because he never would shoot at just a helmet stuck up in view. And I can thank my lucky stars that he wasn't too good a shot because here I was looking around through the glasses when all of a sudden a bullet hit the sod directly across the road from me. Six inches higher would have put it right through my head.

I figured maybe I'd forget about sniping for a while and especially so on my own time, when I didn't even have to be on the lines. Next day, my twenty-third day of this mission, turned out to be my birthday. It was a terribly dull day; it rained and there wasn't any excitement to speak of so I just sat in my foxhole and wrote letters home. The following couple of days were very quiet and so one evening I headed for the dike again to find some excitement. Visited some buddies and fired tracers at the tail of a Limey plane which got shot down and landed in the river in front of our lines. Then we found some grenades which the Limeys had left. And one said white phosphorus so we says "let's toss it over the dike and watch the pretty sparks fly." So we tossed it over and the sparks flew all right but they left a great big white cloud of smoke. And right on the front lines. Well, we got out of there in a hurry—just in case the Krauts got suspicious and fired a few rounds at it.

Finally our turn came to go into Division reserve, so we were relieved and marched about seven miles back to an orphans' home where we billeted. We stayed back there for five days during which time we had to work like mad

cleaning our guns and equipment for inspection. But we did get a truck ride
to Nijmegen to take a shower. Then some more inspections and a little visit
from the division commander and we are ready to go back up to the lines again.
I never liked being in reserve because it was too much like garrison life. Reveille
every morning, chow lines, details, formations and all that. At the front you
could do, within limits, more or less as you pleased. There were usually four
men in one gun crew whose duty it was to man the gun and keep it in working
order. We'd each stand watch for two hours at a time, so between times we'd
have six hours to ourselves. During the day we wouldn't follow that schedule
very strictly. A glance over the dike now and then to see if any Krauts were
around was all that was necessary.

So I felt better when on the thirty-first day in Holland our period of acting
as division reserve was over and we moved up to the front again. It was a
quiet night with a steady, light rain falling. We moved to different positions
from those previously held. The outfit we were relieving had all the positions
and foxholes dug in for us so we simply took their positions, crawled into their
holes and settled down to guard our gun. As soon as it was light the following
morning we came out and took stock of our surroundings. It was usually quite
a surprise to find that the real situation was entirely different from what you
had conceived it to be in the darkness. This day we had our first American
10 in 1 rations which were a wonderful treat after a month of nothing but
Limey chow. The stew, harricot oxtail, and kidney pudding got pretty sickening,
but what really hurt was when we'd see some of our Limey friends eating American lend-lease food. Even the chocolate candy in their rations finally became so
sickening that I couldn't eat it. But I really couldn't complain, perhaps I was
just getting too choosey, because after all I was taking on considerable weight.
Of course we just loafed around all day so who wouldn't take on weight?

For lack of excitement I would think up all sorts of things to do. Someone
picked up a tommy gun and having never fired one I had to try it out. Then
everyone else along the line would raise a fuss because they were afraid it would
draw enemy fire so I'd have to quit. Then I'd go and visit the 60mm mortar
crew of the rifle company we were attached to. They were continually firing at
houses across the river or any other place where Germans might be. I'd get them
to let me fire a few rounds and that would be another weapon on my list.

I found lots of time to write letters during these days. I had found some
stationery in the wrecked houses along the dike. In addition to the V-mail forms
which were rationed out I could do a lot of writing. That is about the weather
and abstract subjects. We could never tell any of the exciting things we saw
and did. I tried it once in a letter which I was really proud of. The Company
Commander called me down to the CP for a severe reprimand.

Then one day having nothing better to do I decided to zero in my '03. So
I set up a target against the dike and went off a ways to shoot at it. The results
were pretty disappointing and I began to wonder how I ever managed to
knock off a Kraut at seven hundred yards with such a rifle. I was continually
thinking up crazy things to do and stunts to pull. Like one time when my pal
the "Greek" [Pvt. Manuel M. Dandis] came over to visit me. As he was walking
away I got a wonderful idea for a good practical joke and I picked up my '03
and fired a shot into the ground about three feet behind his heels. But the
"Greek" was as crazy as I and it didn't scare him at all. He just turned around

and grinned. Later he admitted that it startled him a bit. Another stunt was to get some increments from mortar shells and when everyone was sitting around the fire eating, or better yet while they were reading mail just after a mail call, one of us (the one who didn't get any mail) would slip an increment into the fire unnoticed. When they burned there was a big flash and a swishing sound like a shell coming in and everyone being on edge anyhow they'd scatter like mad. Big joke!

We liked to play with demolitions too. We'd get hold of some prima-cord, which is an explosive which looks like a piece of fuse. We'd tie it around a fence post, unscrew the cap from a grenade to set it off and then see what results it would have on the post. Another good stunt with a hand grenade which some of the men in our platoon pulled on each other was to unscrew the fuse and dump out all the powder. Then they'd have the pin come out "accidentally" and the grenade would start sputtering and smoking while everyone ran for their lives. There'd be a harmless little pop after which everyone would look around sheepishly at one another.

At night whenever we suspected any German patrols were out in front of our lines the 60mm mortars would fire some parachute flares to light up the area. After the flares burnt out the chutes would land out in front of our lines in no-man's land. They made good souvenirs but rather than chase out from behind the cover of the dike to get them I thought I'd take one of the shells and get it out of there. I couldn't get the shell apart so I thought of the idea of setting the shell off and when it popped open I'd have my chute. There is a twenty-nine second fuse on them which is set off when the shell hits the bottom of the mortar tube. To set this off I'd hang the shell on top of a post and then set it in a hole in the ground and run like mad. I got one chute that way but the flare usually burned it up. Needless to say I heard about that from one of the officers, too.

Our ten-day stay at the front went by in a hurry. The weather was pretty favorable, we were getting enough to eat, the mail came regularly, and the enemy wasn't causing trouble any more. We seldom saw any infantry any more, just mortar and artillery fire on our positions occasionally to keep us on our toes. There were orchards all around and there was a good crop of apples so we never had to worry about getting enough fresh fruit to eat. On the forty-first day we were relieved and had to march back to the orphans' home again for some more garrison life. The enemy tossed some shells over while we were making the march back and there were some tense moments but no one hurt.

Again there were the inspections and details and the usual garrison routine which became worse the longer we stayed on the lines. Halloween night found me pulling CQ duty . . .

Next day they showed us a movie and I don't believe I will ever quite appreciate another movie as well as I did that one. As I sat there fresh off the lines with my rifle between my knees watching the scenes which were so much like home, it suddenly dawned on me what a huge gap there was between my two lives. Looking at that show was like looking back into another world.

That night we again moved to positions on the front. This time we went up in trucks instead of marching which was a great relief because after lying around without exercise on the lines all the time we were getting pretty soft. We had calisthenics every day while in reserve but they didn't help too much.

We were amazed one night to see over on the German side what appeared to be a meteorite going the wrong way. We thought they might be buzz bombs. Next day we were amazed again when we saw a missile of some sort rise high in the sky leaving a trail of white smoke in its wake. They turned out to be the new German V-2 bombs which were being aimed at Amsterdam.

The Germans were also fond of sending over "screaming meemies" which when they took off sounded like a dozen huge trucks screeching to a halt on cement pavement. They always gave the impression that they were coming straight at you. It would be amusing to see everyone duck for cover and then have the shells land a half mile away. This time instead of being on the dike we were kept a few hundred yards to the rear in a position with the reserve platoons. I didn't like that very well because the safest place was up on the dike. Artillery couldn't reach you there because it would either strike the opposite side of the dike which merely shook the ground and rattled loose dirt down your neck, or else go on over and hit about fifty yards to the rear of the dike. Mortars were the only thing which could reach us there. So when the shell fire got too heavy the first night of our stay there it was decided to move to a different position. That necessitated digging a new foxhole to live in which idea I didn't relish at all. A few stray shells in the area put new vigor in me and by nightfall my partner and I had dug quite a cozy little home. It had a roof and straw on the bottom. The following day I thanked myself for having built such a neat shelter for it was cold and miserable weather. In the afternoon it hailed and then turned to snow.

I went up to the dike to visit the "Greek" and his gang again. I didn't have a thing to do all night but sleep so I told him I'd come and stand guard with him that night. Everyone thought I was crazy to volunteer to stand guard for anyone on such a miserable cold night, but I enjoyed being with the "Greek" and we had fun talking things over out there in the darkness.

Next day the sun shone warm and bright again and everyone felt better. To amuse myself I went up to the dike and fired some rifle grenades at targets in front of our lines, just for practice. The next day was November 11, Armistice Day and to celebrate we had a big surprise for the Germans. At 11:00 a.m. everything we had was going to open up on the Germans. Artillery, 81mm mortars, bazookas, machine guns, grenades, everything on the line opened up. I was at the CP on some errand when it started so I rushed up to the dike and began target practice with my '03 and to see what was going on. It certainly was an impressive array of firepower and must have made the Krauts wonder.

But they were right there and about five minutes later answered our "Call" with a mortar and artillery barrage of their own. It wasn't much in comparison with ours only I just happened to get caught out in the open with only a shallow ditch for cover. As I lay there listening to the shells whistling down at me I had visions of myself flying in all directions as one landed in with me. And what scared me more than that yet was the fear of having one land just close enough to badly mangle me. There is a sudden feeling of smallness at times like that and you wish you could crawl right up into your helmet and hide.

The fifty-seventh day found us in turn to be relieved again so we made ready for the march back to the "rest" area again . . .

The sixty-fourth day we had to move up into positions on the lines again. No one seemed happy about going this time for by now we had all become pretty much sick of the whole thing. We knew winter would be setting in and we wanted action. The positions at the dike were a mess now. The rain had leaked into the poorly constructed positions and had even caused some to cave in. Most of the foxholes on the dike were soaked and it was impossible to keep dry. All holes on level ground were filled with water to within eight inches of the surface. The only dry places left to stay were the basements of demolished houses along the front. There was no such shelter near enough to my gun position to be made use of because we had to stay on the gun, especially at night. During the day all but one of us would go to an old barn for shelter. We cooked meals in there and built a fire to dry out. I used an old raincoat over my machine gun to try and keep it dry but to no avail. It was just mud and water everywhere. The side of the dike got so greasy with mud that we could hardly crawl up and down it to our gun position and steps had to be cut in. One poor chap got caught in a mortar barrage while traveling on level ground to the barn. He jumped into a foxhole and was soaked to the waist.

The nights were getting longer now and the cloudy weather lengthened them still more. It took four turns at watch now and to get out of your hole once you were settled down was especially hard to get used to. Sleeping with my shoes on didn't work so good anymore either because they were always wet and muddy and they'd get cold at night.

Thanksgiving came and as a special treat we were to get a day's supply of American 10 in 1 rations. Everyone was so eager to get some good food that they even took our platoon's rations so we had the prospects of no food at all for Thanksgiving. But some one came to the rescue with some fresh liver from a cow which had "accidentally" been killed by "enemy" fire. So we had fried potatoes and liver for Thanksgiving. That tasted even better than the 10 in 1's would have. We weren't worrying about food anyhow for the rumor was flying around that we were finally to be relieved. It seemed too good to be true. Sure enough the next day we were kept busy policing the whole line up in preparation for our leaving. A Canadian unit was going to take our place. We worked hard carrying all our extra ammo together to be hauled away. All the loose hand grenades we found we'd toss into the water filled foxholes and watch the geyser of water which would fly into the air. At 2200 that evening of the sixty-eighth day the Canadians finally came to take over our positions after what seemed an eternity of waiting, and we marched off to the rear and safety . . .

Of the men in the platoon who flew into Holland with me two months before only a little better than half marched away that night. I recalled how the men who were assigned to my crew after Normandy jokingly called me a jinx and didn't want to be in my crew for it had sustained the highest rate of casualties in the Normandy campaign. Now I would surely be called a jinx for I had gone through three gun crews during this campaign. Of the eight gunner corporals only three remained to make the march back that night. And of the new replacements used to fill our ranks, depleted from the Normandy fight, one lone survivor marched with us that night.

We stayed with some civilians that night and after everyone was settled down they came around with a double ration of rum which is issued regularly in the Limey army. I never would touch the stuff while on the front for I had found that the best way to stay alive was to always have a clear and alert mind. But now we were in safety and I could relax. There wasn't much for each one of us so someone suggested that we draw cards and then some one of us could have enough to do some good. I collected two gun crews rations which made two thirds of a canteen cap full. I was in a pretty jovial mood for the remainder of the evening, but was finally convinced I had better go to bed so I could march in the morning.

DEPARTURE

Fall deepened into early winter, cold was added to dampness, and still the Division stayed on the Island. The hope for change got its first real encouragement in mid-November when units began to send advance parties to a new place no one had ever heard of before, Mourmelon-le-Grand, France. Finally, in late November, unit by unit, the Division pulled out.

The Dutch had not forgotten that the Airborne were the first to free them. As the trucks rolled back down the road "September 17" was what people shouted. The Island and all the miseries associated with it were soon left behind. Down the road to Uden, on to Vechel where the Dutch were already at work repairing their damaged buildings—"September 17" they yelled as they recognized the Screaming Eagles. Down through St. Oedenrode and Eindhoven, and September 17 became a memory—the Division was going to rest.

NOTES

[1]From the diary of Lt. Col. H. W. Hannah, Division G-3: "September 17, 1944 . . . When we passed over the British Second Army and into hostile territory the flak commenced raining on us from Eindhoven. My plane was hit in the left engine and left tail section and some of it came through the floor at the front of the plane where no one was seated. The fire became so intense that the motor cut out and we had to jump prematurely. However, the pilot held on so tenaciously that we were able to jump within the edge of the DZ. The crew chief jumped out after we had gone (I saw him in Zon later) but the plane went down in flames. I have not learned about the pilot, co-pilot and navigator, but I'm afraid they didn't make it—perhaps because they stuck it out for us." Later, Troop Carrier Command officers visited Col. Hannah in the hospital in England relative to posthumous awards for the plane's crew.

[2]One of these gliders, with fourteen members of Headquarters Company, 3d Battalion, 327th Glider Infantry Regiment, and their pilot were taken in charge along with 32 British soldiers by a Dutch underground group and cared for until they were returned through the American lines on October 20. A day-by-day account of the activities of this group, written in English and illustrated with maps and 75 photographs, was sent by the author, A. A. M. Veltman, (referred to throughout the manuscript by his underground name, "The Gangster") of Elshout, Holland, to one of the Americans, Sgt. Tinsley G. Connell of Minden, Louisiana. The account, too long to be included in this history, well illustrates the resourcefulness of these friendly Dutchmen and the great danger they underwent to aid their American and British friends.

[3] "There are many episodes from the late war which equal this one in gallantry. Its unique quality lies in the fact that with an entire nation under arms and with thousands of our well-trained infantry units engaging the enemy, we would search in vain for other examples illuminating the possibility of achieving almost perfect order in infantry maneuver under modern conditions of fire. This is the only clear example in my experience or which has been called to my attention. There were other movements in this same campaign which achieved tactically a great deal more. But there was no other advance with the same clarity and precision." Col. S. L. A. Marshall in Men Against Fire.

[4] "Here is an example of a soldier thoroughly in command of his own situation rather than permitting his situation to command him . . . I know of no better illustration in the book of war of the quality of mind needed in the combat officer." Col. S. L. A. Marshall in Men Against Fire.

[5] "The Incredible Patrol," by Cpl. Russ Engel, Life, January 15, 1945. Copyright 1947 by Time, Inc. Reproduced through courtesy of the editors of Life.

Mourmelon: December

Camp Mourmelon the 101st found to be a former French artillery garrison just outside the village of Mourmelon-le-Grand (there was also a nearby Mourmelon-le-Petit) twenty miles from the cathedral town and champagne center of Reims. The village and surrounding plain had for centuries been an encampment and battlefield; Caesar had camped there and the ground was still marked with artillery craters and ruined trenches of World War I. During the German occupation the camp had been used as a tank depot.

The barracks were low stucco buildings and were in poor shape. One of the first jobs was the repair of these buildings. Meanwhile the Division began granting the leaves and passes which had been held up by the two months in the lines. The first generous allotment of passes to Reims was too much for that old city, especially now that it was SHAEF headquarters and filled with generals and colonels; the number of troopers sent in thereafter was drastically reduced. But the goal of everyone was Paris. And many got there.

Looking forward to a possibly long stay in the winter quarters of Mourmelon each battalion was initially given a period of ten days to improve its area, to check its clothing and equipment needs and to give all personnel a rest period, with training confined to close-order drill and calisthenics. Overhauling of weapons, vehicles and equipment got under way, Red Cross clubs were opened, athletic equipment was requisitioned and football and boxing teams were organized. A number of reinforcements were received and in most cases the battalions set up a training company to give these new men a week or ten days of indoctrination training.

During the stay in Mourmelon an additional parachute field artillery battalion joined the 101st—the 463d. The 463d Battalion had been organized in February 1944 in Italy, had fought on the Anzio beach and on up to Rome. It had then parachuted into Southern France as part of the August 15 invasion. The battalion arrived in Camp Mourmelon on December 12.

Sgt. George Koskimaki's diary tells how the Mourmelon period looked to one man:

November 27: Arrived at our new garrison in France today at 0400. Is almost like Fort Bragg. Must go back to model soldiering again. *November 29:* Had a drill on garrison marching today . . . Had a regular retreat formation with cannon firing and inspection. *November 30:* My morale climbed 100% when a lot of mail arrived . . . Had one of my best army meals as we celebrated a late Thanksgiving today.

December 1: First passes were issued to the boys today and a lot of them got drunk on champagne . . . It is now more like home with American fighters flying overhead instead of Spitfires. *December 2:* The company has taken it easy thus far with only a half hour of drill per day. *December 4:* Lt. Kovrasik made 1st Looey this morning. We had a party in our room with about a case of champagne. Lt. Kovrasik was the life of the party. All our passes were canceled because the boys won't behave in town. *December 6:* Nothing to do today so Chapman and I volunteered for a wood-cutting detail . . . We worked up a good appetite. This area still has scars from the first war. *December 8:* Chapman, Schmidt and I went to town on pass today. Got a haircut in a French barbershop. Schmidt had his hair waved before he knew what was happening. *December 10:* Some boys left for 30-day furloughs to the States yesterday. Butler from the MPs was the lucky man in Special Troops. *December 11:* Saw a swell movie tonight, "The Impatient Years." *December 14:* The mail is beginning to come in now and the boys are getting cheerful. Our training program is filled with a lot of calisthenics. We'll be back in shape in no time. *December 15:* We cut wood at the famous old Marne battlefield of the last war. The shell holes and trenches have been healed over somewhat in the past 26 years by nature. *December 17:* It has been another quiet Sunday . . . The radio announced a big German attack on the First Army front. This should break the back of the German armies. *December 18:* We were alerted at 0100 today to get ready to assist in repulsing the German attack. The enemy breakthrough is serious enough to send us back into the lines. Leave this afternoon. *December 19:* Today we are in Belgium . . .

Bastogne: The First Eight Days[1]

The siege of Bastogne is one chapter in the history of the battle of the Ardennes. On December 16, 1944, the Germans launched their greatest offensive of the war in the west. Achieving a considerable success in their first attacks, they broke through, penetrated 65 miles into Allied territory, halted the Allied offensive then going on, and threatened the entire front in the west. The failure of this German drive was due in part to the American resistance at St. Vith and Bastogne.

The background of Bastogne dates from the fall of 1944. At that time three American armies, forming the 12th Army Group, were in position on the central part of the western front. The U. S. First and Third Armies were along the Siegfried Line and the U. S. Ninth Army was facing the Roer River in Germany some thirty miles from the Rhine. All three armies were pushing for the Rhine over difficult terrain, across swollen rivers, and against determined enemy resistance. Except in the Aachen sector, where an advance was made to the Roer, the line did not move during October and November. The Third Army fought near Metz; the First and Ninth Armies made their advance farther north, near Aachen. In between these two major efforts the First Army held an extensive line of defense. Of this line the southern and major part was maintained by the U. S. VIII Corps.

On December 16, VIII Corps, under the command of Maj. General Troy H. Middleton had its headquarters in Bastogne, Belgium. Its area extended from Losheim, Germany, north to a point where the Our River crosses the Franco-German border. Generally parallel to the German frontier along eastern Belgium and Luxembourg, its front was 88 miles wide. The country, the Ardennes, has rugged hills; there are high plateaus, deep-cut valleys and a restricted road net.

The mission that First Army gave VIII Corps was to defend this line in place. New divisions were brought into this part of the front for battle indoctrination, and battle-worn divisions were sent to VIII Corps for reequipment and rest. As divisions were rotated into the sector, they took over existing wire nets and other facilities.

At the beginning of the German attack in December, the VIII Corps front was held by two battle-weary divisions, a green infantry division, part of a green armored division, and a cavalry group. The battle-tested divisions (they had both seen months of fighting) were the 4th Infantry Division, which in November had fought a costly action through the Hürtgen Forest below Düren, Germany, and the 28th Infantry Division, which had sustained heavy casualties in the First Army drive to the Roer. The 106th Infantry Division, newly arrived on the Continent, entered the Corps line four days before the German offensive began. The 14th Cavalry Group, consisting of the 18th and 32d Cavalry Squadrons, held the north flank of VIII Corps, and the 9th Armored Division, minus Combat Command B which was with V Corps, had the most of its units attached to the divisions.

The enemy facing the VIII Corps was estimated at four divisions. From north to south these were the 18th, 26th, 352d and 212th. Early in December the 28th Division took prisoners and reaffirmed the presence of the 26th and 352d Divisions, but rumors that one or more panzer units were in rear of these infantry divisions were not confirmed. From December 12 on, the American outposts along the VIII Corps front heard sounds of a great volume of vehicular movement behind the enemy lines.

On the morning of December 16, the VIII Corps front, which had been quiet since the latter part of September, suddenly flared up. For more than a month the enemy had been concentrating some 25 divisions. It had been skillfully done and the extent of the concentration was not fully known to our forces. At 0500 heavy artillery concentrations struck along the entire VIII Corps front and these were soon followed by tank and infantry attacks. The strongest attacks were in the north near the V and VIII Corps boundary.

The infantry-tank attack on the north flank of the VIII Corps began at 0800 on the 16th, and in three hours the enemy had penetrated the position of the 14th Cavalry group three miles. Group reserves were committed and the 106th Division put out flank protection to the north. Through the right of the 106th Division the enemy advanced rapidly for a mile and a half, but then as reserves were brought up his progress was slowed. The German gains threatened to isolate two regiments of the 106th Division. Captured documents showed that on this day the enemy hoped to take St. Vith. This he did not do.

Against the 28th Division the enemy used two panzer divisions, three infantry divisions and one parachute division in an infantry-tank attack on the "Ridge Road" just west of the Our River. In this operation, two enemy divisions assaulted each regiment of the 28th. In the center and right of the 28th the enemy made advances up to four and a half miles and crossed the north-south highway at several points. In the southern part of the VIII Corps the 9th Armored and the 4th Infantry Divisions were also attacked by the enemy. These attacks were diversionary to prevent our shifting troops to the north.

At the start of the German offensive the VIII Corps reserve consisted of an armored combat command and four battalions of combat engineers. The engineers were- assembled during the first morning, and as the seriousness of the enemy thrust became apparent, additional troops were made available. In the north on December 17, Combat Command R of the 9th Armored Division was released from V Corps and the 7th Armored Division was ordered to close into an assembly area near St. Vith. In the south the 10th Armored Division was moved toward an assembly area near the city of Luxembourg. Orders were also issued to move the 101st and 82d Airborne Divisions to the general area threatened.

From captured documents and from the direction of early thrusts it seemed evident to VIII Corps that the objective of the attacks was Liège and possibly Namur. This, however, was a clear case of VIII Corps misunderstanding the enemy's intent, though the same misunderstanding prevailed in the entire Army for months afterward. It was finally found, however, that Hitler had given his commanders in the Bulge attack specific and inflexible orders to stay on the south of Liège.

On the 17th, the second day of the offensive, the enemy increased his pressure along the whole front especially in the north. The right flank of V Corps was forced back and in the VIII Corps, German infantry and armor had by 0900 cut off two regiments of the 106th Division. To stem the advance on St. Vith the 168th Engineer Combat Battalion fought a delaying action north and east of that town, Combat Command B of the 9th Armored Division was put into the line, and the 7th Armored Division was committed piecemeal to defensive action as it arrived during the evening.

In the 28th Division sector the Germans began their attacks early and made large gains. The left flank of the 28th was forced to withdraw to the west bank of the Our River and the right was pushed back an additional one to four miles. But it was in the center of the division that the enemy made his deepest penetrations, thrusting one salient of eight miles and another of six. Everywhere the American withdrawal had been four to six miles. At some points the enemy was within 11 miles of Bastogne.

On the southern flank of the VIII Corps the 4th Infantry Division defended against strong attacks, but the enemy did not make the heavy effort here that he had made farther to the north. The 10th Armored Division reached the Luxembourg area in time to assure its defense.

On December 18, the third day of the offensive, the enemy increased the momentum of his drive in the center of VIII Corps. The Corps north flank was bolstered by the arrival of the 7th Armored Division but remained extremely critical because of the deep German penetra-

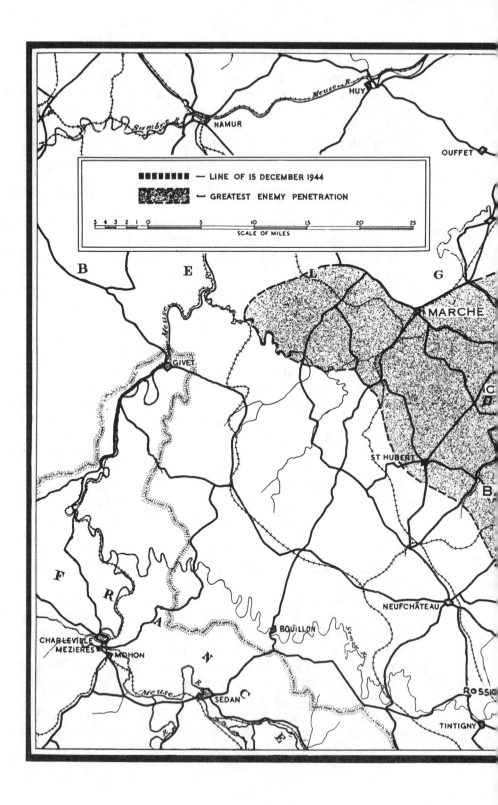

LINE OF 15 DECEMBER 1944

GREATEST ENEMY PENETRATION

SCALE OF MILES

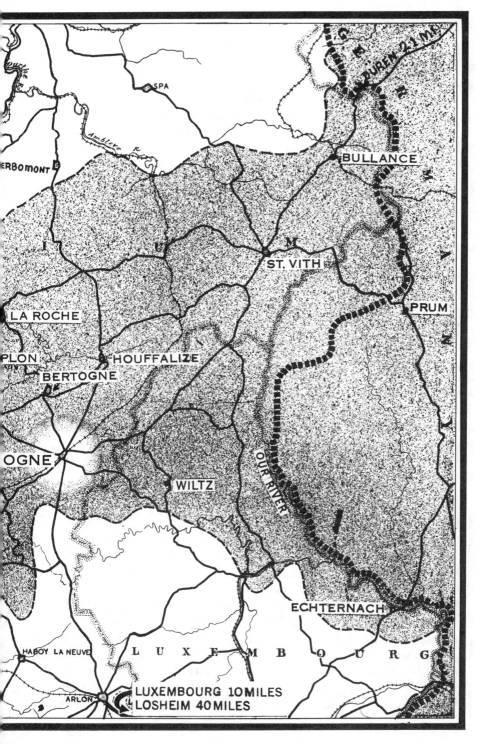

Map 61: Total Extent of the Bulge.

tions into the V Corps sector. But the weight against the 28th Division was so overwhelming that its thin defenses disintegrated and the enemy achieved a breakthrough. The right flank of the 28th, which pulled back across the Our River on the upper eastern border of Luxembourg the previous night, was unable to stabilize its lines. In the withdrawal a wide gap was created through which the enemy pushed a great deal of armor. In the center, enemy thrusts between strongpoints encircled companies and destroyed or captured them one by one. To the 28th Division headquarters the picture was obscure throughout the day because of lost communications, but the appearance of many enemy columns behind the regimental sectors and the tragic tales of stragglers indicated a complete disintegration of regimental defenses. The 28th Division Command post itself was attacked when the enemy approached Wiltz. The 44th Engineer Combat Battalion, the 447th Antiaircraft Battalion, and miscellaneous headquarters personnel from the division were used to defend the town. The command post had communications left with only one regiment.

Directly behind the 28th Division, on the St. Vith–Bastogne road, were roadblocks established by the Combat Command Reserve of the 9th Armored Division. One block, known as Task Force Rose, was attacked by the enemy in the morning and was overrun by 1400, December 18. A roadblock on the Wiltz-Bastogne road, known as Task Force Hayze, came under heavy attack by 1815. The Germans overran this roadblock during the night of December 18-19 to come within three kilometers of Bastogne. The defense of Bastogne now became the task of airborne and armored units which had been ordered into the sector.

The Concentration on Bastogne

On the morning of December 17 at SHAEF two members of the Supreme General Staff looked at the map and pondered the question of where best to employ SHAEF Reserve, which at that moment consisted of the two American divisions, the 82d Airborne and the 101st Airborne, recently withdrawn from the lines in Holland.

"I think I should put them there," said Maj. Gen. J. F. M. Whiteley, the SHAEF, G-3, "the place has the best road net in the area."

Lt. Gen. W. B. Smith, General Eisenhower's Chief of Staff nodded and said to go ahead and do it. He based his decision purely on the thought of how advantageous Bastogne's radial highway net appeared on the map. It was his idea at the time that both 101st and 82d Airborne Divisions should be employed in the Bastogne area. It was in this way that the Airborne Corps happened to make its start toward Bastogne.

SHAEF's general concept was subsequently modified by decisions made at lower headquarters although the initial impetus had been given in the required direction. The change in direction for the 82d Division, which was to have some of its greatest days in the fighting around Werbomont on the northern flank of the Bulge, came after the XVIII Airborne Corps (82d and 101st Divisions) had passed from SHAEF Reserve into the command of 12th Army Group, which was already forming other plans both for the defense of Bastogne and the employment of the airborne strength. But out of the difference in the SHAEF concept of how to employ the airborne force and the ideas which were already forming at 12th Army Group there came some early confusion to the two Corps commanders directly concerned and to their forces. However (as later reported in this chapter) the situation was clarified before any real harm was done.

On December 17 and 18, three battle-tested organizations, by different routes and under separate authority, began their moves toward the town in the Belgian Ardennes with whose name their own fame was to be thereafter inseparably linked. Orders from 12th Army Group were received on the 16th directing the 10th Armored Division to be temporarily attached to VIII Corps, First Army, to counter the serious German attempt at a breakthrough. At 1320 on December 17, in compliance with the order, Combat Command B, 10th Armored Division, took its first step toward Bastogne when it moved from a rest area at Remeling, France, to the vicinity of Merl in Luxembourg. That evening at 2030 the 101st Airborne Division, which was then re-outfitting in a training area at Camp Mourmelon (France), received telephone orders from Headquarters XVIII Airborne Corps that it was to move north though at that time Bastogne was not the destination given. On the following night, December 18 at 1800, the 705th Tank Destroyer Battalion, then in position at Kohlscheid, Germany (about 60 miles north of Bastogne) was ordered by the Ninth Army to march to Bastogne and report to VIII Corps.

Bastogne, then the Headquarters of VIII Corps, was the natural place for rendezvous and for stabilizing the defense. The town is the hub of the highway net covering the eastern Ardennes—a countryside that is forbidding to the movement of mechanized forces except when the roads are available. By holding at Bastogne the VIII Corps could unhinge the communications of the Germans who were striking west toward the line of the River Meuse.

Combat Command B closed into the vicinity of Merl at 2155 on the 17th. On the following morning it was ordered to move independently of the 10th Armored Division to join VIII Corps. It took the road through Arlon to Bastogne. On the way Col. William L. Roberts, the commander, received a request from Maj. Gen. Norman D. Cota, commanding the 28th Infantry Division, to support his force at Wiltz by putting Combat Command B into position south and southeast of the town. But this Colonel Roberts could not do and comply with his Corps orders, so he took his column on into Bastogne and reported there to Major General Middleton at 1600 on the 18th.

At Camp Mourmelon, the 101st Division was short many of its soldiers who were on leave in Paris. The commander of the XVIII Airborne Corps, Maj. Gen. Matthew B. Ridgway, was at the rear headquarters of the Corps in England. The 101st Division commander, Maj. Gen. Maxwell D. Taylor, was in the United States. Upon hearing of the attack and of the fact that the 101st had been committed to battle, he immediately took a plane for Europe. The assistant division commander, Brig. Gen. Gerald J. Higgins, was giving a lecture in England on the earlier airborne operation in Holland. With him were five of the senior commanders of divisional units and sixteen junior officers. The night would pass before these men were to hear that the division had been alerted for movement to the front and it would be noon of the next day before they were all rounded up and ready to emplane for Mourmelon. So the senior division officer present in France, the artillery commander, Brig. Gen. Anthony C. McAuliffe, got the division staff together at 2100 on December 17 and outlined the prospect in these words:

"All I know of the situation is that there has been a breakthrough and we have got to get up there."

General McAuliffe directed the Division to move out in combat teams without waiting for the men on pass in Paris or elsewhere to get back. However, the destination of the 101st as given at this time was not Bastogne but Werbomont to the northwest of Bastogne.

At 2030 on the 17th, Lt. Col. Ned D. Moore, Chief of Staff of the 101st, had been called on the telephone by Col. Ralph D. Eaton, Chief of Staff of the XVIII Corps, and the mission had been outlined in that manner. In moving to Werbomont, the 101st would pass within a short distance of Bastogne and to the westward of it. There was no later modification of this order while 101st remained at Mourmelon.

On the following morning, December 18, the Acting Commander of the XVIII Corps, Maj. Gen. James M. Gavin, attended a meeting at First Army at which it was decided to attach the 82d Division to the V Corps (since the XVIII Airborne Corps could not move in and become operational until the morning of December 19), and the 101st Division to the VIII Corps. However, no word of this change got down to the 101st Division; throughout that day its staff was unaware either that Bastogne was the destination or that VIII Corps was now their next higher headquarters.

An advance party was then set up to precede the 101st Division to Bastogne. In the party were a representative from each major unit and a company of Engineers who were to be used as guides to lead the combat teams into their Bastogne assembly areas. During the morning of December 18, there had been no time to brief the advance party. Just as the party was pulling away from Camp Mourmelon during the noon hour Colonel Moore ran out of the division command post and advised them that XVIII Corps was to handle the operation and that they should go to a rendezvous with a part of the XVIII Corps staff. They were to meet them at the crossroads in Werbomont. This they did.

General Ridgway arrived at Mourmelon about an hour later, having flown from England. He went to the command post of the 101st and Colonel Moore gave him the situation as he had given it to the advance party. Then occurred an odd sequence of events in which Fate might have played a stronger hand against 101st Division had it not been for several providential circumstances. Ridgway went into General Taylor's empty office and called a higher headquarters—presumably his own Corps. In this conversation he learned that 101st's destination was Bastogne, not Werbomont. On the heels of this conversation, General Higgins entered the room, having just reported from England. Ridgway told him that 101st Division was to go to Bastogne. Ridgway then left Mourmelon for the front. Higgins soon followed. McAuliffe had left an instruction that Higgins was to get forward as rapidly as possible, so he picked a route via Sedan, figuring that it would be less encumbered with traffic. But the word that Bastogne was the Division's destination was not passed to Colonel Moore and the units remained alerted for movement to Werbomont.

On reaching Werbomont on the night of December 18 the advance party was told that the operation was being handled by VIII Corps and that they were even then due in Bastogne. In this way the advance party failed in its mission and did not reach the objective until 0300 on the morning of December 19. But others were doing their work for them.

Some few minutes before the advance party had left Mourmelon, General McAuliffe had started for Werbomont taking with him his G-3, Lt. Col. H. W. O. Kinnard and his aide, 1st Lt. Frederic D. Starrett. They drove as fast as they could, passing many elements of the 82d Airborne Division along the route. The 82d had been out of the lines in Holland longer than the 101st and was more fully equipped. The 82d was therefore ordered to move out ahead of the 101st. Come to the road juncture south of the Bois de Herbaimont (nine miles northwest of Bastogne) General McAuliffe turned southeast to Bastogne instead of continuing north along the road leading to Werbomont, which is some 25 miles north of Bastogne. He had decided to go to the VIII Corps headquarters and get briefed on the general situation. It was some time following his arrival at General Middleton's VIII Corps command post that he heard definitely for the first time that the 101st was to fight at Bastogne. General Gavin, who had left Werbomont late in the afternoon of the 18th to hand-carry the message to VIII Corps did not arrive until after dark. The delay caused General Middleton a considerable doubt; he had learned from higher authority that the 101st Division would fight at Bastogne but he did not know that the Division was his to use as he saw fit. General McAuliffe's party arrived at the VIII Corps command post, which was located in a former German barracks at the northwestern edge of Bastogne, at 1600 and from that time forward its members concerned themselves with getting ready to receive the Division. At that same moment Colonel Roberts, who had arrived ahead of his column, presented himself to General Middleton and reported that Combat Command B was on the road and would soon be in Bastogne.

Middleton asked Roberts, "How many teams can you make up?"
Roberts replied, "Three."

The General then said, "You will move without delay in three teams to these positions and counter enemy threats. One team will go to the southeast of Wardin, one team to the vicinity of Longvilly and one team to the vicinity of Noville. Move with the utmost speed. Hold these positions at all costs."

Roberts accepted the order without demur though at that moment he believed that the distribution of his force over so great an area would make it ineffective. But he made the mental reservation that the Corps commander must know the situation much better than he did himself. Middleton's decision was the initial tactical step which led finally to the saying of Bastogne. Combat Command B continued on its way moving north and east to carry out its orders.

The first two teams got through the town during daylight. The lead team, Team Cherry, under Lt. Col. Henry T. Cherry, proceeded toward Longvilly, which was considered to be in the direction of the most immediate danger. The second team under Lt. Col. James O'Hara headed toward the village of Wardin in the southeast. It was dark when the last team began moving through Bastogne. Its youthful commander, Maj. William R. Desobry, went to see Colonel Roberts with whom he had an especially close relationship. For. a number of years Desobry had known the older man well; he was talking now to a man who was not only his commander but whom he regarded as a second father. Roberts pointed northward on the map to the village of Noville and told Desobry that he was to proceed there and hold the village. "It will be a close race to get there before the enemy," Roberts said. "You are young, and by tomorrow morning you will probably be nervous. By mid-morning the idea will probably come to you that it would be better to withdraw from Noville. When you begin thinking that, remember that I told you that it would be best not to withdraw until I order you to do so."

There were no maps at hand; one of Colonel Roberts' staff officers grabbed a Corps MP and sent him along with Desobry to put the team on the Noville road. A cavalry platoon leader from Desobry's column was sent on ahead to reconnoiter Noville, clear it if there were any enemy present, and then outpost it until the arrival of the main battle group. Desobry then dismounted one platoon of armored infantry, placed them on the backs of the three lead tanks and gave the word for the column to move north. Small groups of stragglers were already passing them, drifting southward. The column paid them no heed. The dark had already slowed the armor to a five-mile-per-hour pace and Desobry figured that he had no time to waste.

While McAuliffe and his party were on the road, at Mourmelon the Division was working on the problems of the move. The few hours before the Division began its march were utilized in preparations for departure and in partly providing those combat supplies which had been lost in Holland. Such things as mortars, rifle ammunition, entrenching tools, Arctic overshoes, blankets and gas masks had fallen far below the normal and needed amounts in the tables of basic allowances. In the great emergency, Transportation Corps and Oise Base Section acted with utmost dispatch and rallied truck groups from Rouen and Paris. Many of the truckers had already been long on the road when they were ordered to Camp Mourmelon. They were intercepted, the trucks unloaded on the spot, and the drivers directed to their new destination.

The 3d Platoon, Company E, 506th, bound for Bastogne, loads into ten-ton trailers in front of Division Headquarters in Mourmelon on the afternoon of 18 December. Cpl. Francis J. Mellet and Pvt. Patrick H. Neill (both carrying ammo boxes) were killed at Bastogne.

The first trucks arrived at 0900, December 18. The last of the 380 trucks needed for the movement of 11,000 men arrived at the camp at 1720 the same day. At 2000, eleven hours after the arrival of the first vehicles, the last man was out-loaded. As far as Bouillon, Belgium, the column ran with lights blazing. It was a calculated risk, taken by 101st for the sake of speed. The night was clear and the stars shone brightly. Had the Luftwaffe come on then, the story of Bastogne might have taken a different turn.

In Bastogne, General Middleton sketched the situation to General McAuliffe and Colonel Kinnard very roughly, telling them, "There has been a major penetration . . ." and ". . . certain of my units, especially the 106th and 28th Divisions, are broken." In the absence of the advance staff party Kinnard tried to function as a whole division staff during the conference. But after discussing matters with both the G-2 and G-3 sections at VIII Corps, he had only the vaguest picture of what was happening and felt altogether uncertain about both the friendly and enemy situation. He gathered that some of our armored elements—the 9th Armored Division and 10th Armored Division were mentioned—were out in front of Bastogne, but he could not pinpoint the spots where their roadblocks were. Because of their own uncertainty, both he and General McAuliffe became acutely concerned over plans

434

for the night bivouac. Further than that, they worried that the column might be hit while it was still on the road or that it might even be caught by the German air while still a long way back.

While there was still light, they took a quick swing out over the area west of town and McAuliffe pointed out to Kinnard where he wanted the Division placed. It was a snap decision, yet it influenced the campaign importantly because it placed the Division in a sheltered forward assembly area until it was ready to strike. In the emergency Kinnard grabbed an MP private from the Corps and sent him to the crossroads at Sprimont to meet the division as it came on. He and General McAuliffe then went to the junction of the Arlon and Neufchâteau roads in Bastogne to make another attempt to find the advance party. Colonel Kinnard had with him nine 1:100,000 and six 1:50,000 maps of the area. This was all that the Corps staff could give him with which to fight the operation ahead. When he returned from the reconnaissance, Kinnard searched at Corps headquarters for more maps but found that the map section was already moving out. From Corps he obtained an administrative order giving him the location of ammunition dumps, water points, evacuation hospitals and other installations.

However, despite Colonel Kinnard's best efforts, in the speed of the preparations to receive the Division, a good many points had not been securely pinned down. Trailing the last of the 82d Division's column through Sprimont, Col. T. L. Sherburne, acting commander of the 101st Division's artillery, and an assistant, Capt. Cecil T. Wilson, arrived at the vital crossroads where one road leads off toward Bastogne and the other toward Bertogne at about 2000, December 18. Along the way leading north the rear elements of the 82d Division were blocking and stopping. Colonel Sherburne then wondered whether he couldn't get north and on to Werbomont more rapidly by veering from the Bertogne road and taking the long way through Bastogne. He asked an MP at the intersection whether any units of the 101st had gone that way; the MP wasn't certain about anything but referred him to an MP sergeant in a near-by house. The sergeant told him that General McAuliffe and his party had come along some hours before and had gone into Bastogne. So Colonel Sherburne returned to the man who was directing traffic and told him to turn all 101st Division parties toward Bastogne when they came to the intersection. He then continued on.

It appears likely that this small incident smoothed the whole path for the 101st Division. Two officers from the 502d Regiment, who were supposed to have gone with the advance party to Werbomont but had missed it, were re-routed by the MP a few minutes behind Sherburne to VIII Corps Headquarters.

They joined Kinnard and Starrett and drove west to Mande-St. Étienne. Here they met a jeepload of 327th Infantry officers who had also missed the advance party. Kinnard now had enough personnel to set up the assembly area. An officer guide was posted on the Mande-St. Étienne road to direct the incoming column and Starrett went to work setting up a Division command post in a near-by farm house. The other officers reconnoitered their regimental areas and made their plans for the night dispositions. The hour was a little after 1800 on the 18th and there was not yet any sound of combat in the vicinity. A heavy maintenance company from 28th Division was already in Mande-St. Étienne. The company commander told Kinnard this was his area and he could not leave. Kinnard had to return to Bastogne to get an order from the corps commander to clear the area. Around General Middleton in the Corps command post there were now only six or eight officers.

From First Army, Gen. Courtney Hodges, its commander, had called General Middleton and advised moving VIII Corps Headquarters to the rear. This had been done but General Middleton had stayed on in Bastogne with Colonel Stanton, his Deputy Chief of Staff, and several other members of his staff for the purpose, as he thought, of acquainting Maj. Gen. Matthew B. Ridgway, the commander of XVIII Airborne Corps, with the situation, and of helping General McAuliffe get his situation in hand.

General Ridgway arrived at General Middleton's command post in Bastogne about 2030. He was still acting on the not wholly complete information which he had received from his several sources while at Camp Mourmelon. He understood that the 101st Division was to fight at Bastogne, but he thought that it was to operate under his Corps (the XVIII Airborne) though some 25 miles of distance intervened between the two airborne divisions. His acting corps commander, General Gavin, who had come and gone by this time, had brought the word to the 101st that it was to fight in the VIII Corps under General Middleton. But the situation still had not been clarified by higher authority. From Bastogne, General Ridgway called Headquarters First Army. It was at this time that the two Corps commanders got the new instructions which changed the problem of each and which at last set the lines along which the 82d and 101st Airborne Divisions, late of the SHAEF reserve, would operate in the Ardennes. Bastogne was to remain an VIII Corps problem and the 101st Division would operate under that Corps in that town. General Ridgway's XVIII Airborne Corps, less the 101st Division—so General Ridgway now learned for the first time—was to operate on the other side of the Bulge. On the strength of this new assignment, General Middleton subsequently called Gen. Omar Bradley, Commanding General, 12th Army Group, and gave it as his estimate that the 101st Division and other troops assigned to defend Bastogne would probably be surrounded, since he had no reserve. General Bradley said that would be all right with him —to stand and defend even though it appeared probable that Bastogne would become encircled.

General McAuliffe decided to stay at Corps headquarters to get his mission for the next day. During the conference of the two corps commanders, Brig. Gen. Gerald J. Higgins, assistant division commander of the 101st, who had been called from England by General McAuliffe, arrived.

General Higgins and Colonel Kinnard went out to the Division assembly area. Lieutenant Starrett had found that the local schoolhouse was a better command post than the dwelling which Kinnard had designated and on his own initiative had made the change. He already had telephone lines strung to VIII Corps Headquarters and to the 501st Parachute Infantry area. An officer from the 506th Parachute Infantry who had missed the advance party reported at the command post and was given his sector.

In general, things were now looking a little more snug although one point of irritation had not been entirely eliminated. That was the captain commanding the heavy maintenance company who had refused to move his people out at Colonel Kinnard's request until Kinnard brought an order direct from General Middleton. General Higgins found him now completely blocking the highway over which 101st Division was coming in. His vehicles were parked three abreast and six or seven rows deep. It was an absolute impasse. General Higgins sought out the captain and made his protest. "I can't do anything about that," said the captain. "I have received an order from the General to move my vehicles out. I've made this block to make sure that none of my vehicles get by and get lost; it's the best way to collect them." Even after the situation was explained to him, he said he'd stay where he was. General Higgins then gave him a direct order to get his vehicles in single file along the road at once and himself set about urging the drivers over to the side of the highway.

This was but one incident in a night-long fight with the outgoing

Trucks and stragglers head west through Bastogne. Note men without equipment. Many of these were later collected, re-equipped, and formed into Task Force Snafu.

traffic. Every time the column of retreating vehicles came to a halt for a few minutes, some of the drivers fell asleep from exhaustion. When the road was again free for a few minutes and the forward vehicles got in motion, these sleeping drivers formed new traffic blocks back along the column. To keep things moving at all, it was necessary for officers and MPs to continue patrolling up and down the column, ready to rouse any slumberer who had tied things up.

That night in Bastogne was quiet, largely because the 28th Division was holding in place on commanding ground around Wiltz and fighting the enemy off for a few vital hours. Many stragglers were falling back through the town and the roads were jammed to the south and west but no attempt was made to hold any of these men at the time. VIII Corps was busy with its evacuation and Combat Command B of the 10th Armored Division and the 101st Division were engrossed in their own problems. Colonel Roberts, who had set up his command post in Hôtel Lebrun at 1800, December 18, found that it was difficult to persuade other units that were about to withdraw out of the Bastogne area even to give up their motor parks so that he could get his own vehicles off the streets.

The third major part of the Bastogne garrison, the 705th Tank Destroyer Battalion, under Lt. Col. Clifford D. Templeton, got its marching orders at 1800 on December 18. It left Kohlscheid, Germany, at 2240, but could not proceed by the shortest route—Liège, Houffalize,

Bastogne—because the enemy was already around Houffalize. The column of the 705th therefore moved by way of Laroche where it went into a defensive position along the heights six miles south of the town at 0915 on December 19. Colonel Templeton looked Laroche over and was thoroughly alarmed at what he found. American units were in confusion along the road. They were making little or no effort to adjust themselves to the situation or to set up a local defense. So in mid-morning Templeton sent two platoons with four tank destroyers to set up a roadblock to the north of the town. Leaving the battalion at Laroche, he then went on to Neufchâteau, where VIII Corps Headquarters was newly established. There General Middleton told him to get on into Bastogne and attach his outfit to the 101st Division. An officer was sent back to Laroche to bring the battalion on but to leave the roadblock force in place.

Colonel Templeton and his command section, after reporting to General McAuliffe, started northwest to meet the oncoming column. At Bertogne the section was ambushed by a German party armed with two machine guns, one self-propelled gun and several small antiaircraft guns. The opening fire wounded three men, destroyed a jeep and forced the abandonment of the armored command vehicle. Templeton's men withdrew along the road for about half a mile with all their weapons engaging the enemy. This action took place about 1500 on the 19th and was over in twenty minutes.

Templeton radioed to his battalion to expect the German roadblock at Bertogne. He then told them, however, that the roadblock could be overwhelmed and the battalion was to "come any way possible to Bastogne, but *get* there." He did not know that the Bastogne road was impassable because the bridge above the town was out. In the late afternoon the command section returned to Bastogne to establish its command post. Templeton then radioed the commander of the supply train to "find a haven in the west and hook up with some big friends." He felt quite certain that his train would get through safely because the one M18 accompanying it was capable of dealing with any roving enemy tank or infantry group along the way. Colonel Templeton's 705th Tank Destroyer Battalion reached Bastogne at 2030, December 19, by the route Laroche–Champlon–Bastogne.

With the arrival of the 705th Tank Destroyer Battalion, all the major elements which would be present in Bastogne during the siege (the first phase of the defense of the town) were gathered. The 101st Division and Combat Command B had begun the fight that morning and the tank destroyers were now ready to link their power with that of the armor and the infantry. Men of every unit had morale of the highest quality and with their weapons each was capable of stiffening the other. It was a matter of finding the way through courage, resource, and good will.

TEAM CHERRY

*On the evening of December 18, Roberts ordered Team Cherry of his Combat Command B to move out along the road leading east and go into position near Longvilly. It thereby became the first of the Bastogne reinforcements to move out and engage the enemy. The force under command of Lt. Col. Henry T. Cherry included the 3d Tank Battalion, Company C of the 20th Armored Infantry Battalion, the 3d Platoon of Company C of the 55th Engineer Battalion and the 2d Platoon of Troop B of the 90th Cavalry Squadron.

By 1920 they had reached a point just west of Longvilly. The streets of that village seemed filled with the vehicles of Combat Command Reserve of the 9th Armored Division. About midnight Combat Command Reserve began withdrawing along the Bastogne road and Team Cherry took over the defense of Longvilly. Before the last of the vehicles of CCR were clear of the town the road was blocked at Magéret by a German force, cutting off Team Cherry and part of CCR from Bastogne. Cherry, who was on the Bastogne side of Magéret when the road was blocked, was cut off from his command except by radio.

By the morning of the 19th it was obvious that Team Cherry's position in Longvilly was untenable. A fight went on all morning by a patrol from Team Cherry, troops and armor of the trapped Combat Command Reserve, and collected American stragglers to break the block in Magéret. In the afternoon the remainder of Team Cherry was ordered to withdraw from Longvilly, and it joined the force trying to break through the block toward Bastogne.

The line of tanks, tank destroyers, guns, half-tracks, and vehicles stalled along the road made a perfect target for the Germans who got twenty tank destroyers and some 88s onto the targets. Each wrecked or stalled vehicle increased the jam and in a few hours the road was littered with burning or destroyed American armor and vehicles. The survivors meanwhile fought their way into Magéret.

Team Cherry had by the night of the 19th come to such a pass that it could no longer confront the oncoming enemy and most of its energies had to be directed to saving its remaining elements and covering its own flanks and rear. Whether the German advance into Bastogne from the eastward could be checked and thrown into recoil now depended on the forces of the 101st Division itself.*

First Meeting With the Enemy

At Bastogne, the 101st Division played in luck from the beginning and the luck began weeks before the siege started. In the early part of November Lt. Col. Julian Ewell, commanding the 501st Parachute Infantry on the Lower Rhine front in Holland, took a busman's holiday and spent two days of his leave at Bastogne.

It was the luck of war that in giving the march order before leaving Camp Mourmelon, General McAuliffe had put the 501st Parachute Infantry at the head of the column. It was the luck of war again that Ewell got away well in advance of the column on December 18 and was the first commander to arrive in the vicinity of the bivouac. He ran into a wire-stringing detail there, asked what they were doing, found that they were men from the 101st Division and then followed the wires into the Division command post. Then he got ready to guide his own men in.

All down the route over which he had come Colonel Ewell had found the traffic blocking and stopping, and he didn't expect his 501st to come up to him before 2300 because of this congestion. But it beat that schedule by half an hour and Ewell's unit was closed into its area by 2400. McAuliffe knew at 2400 that by then he had one regiment ready.

Earlier in the night (December 18) Ewell had talked to Generals McAuliffe and Higgins. The one thing on which all three commanders agreed was that no one could be sure of anything. Ewell said of himself that he was as much in the dark as any man present. But he told his commander, General McAuliffe, that he thought he should be given a definite assignment. It was a big request, the situation considered. McAuliffe and Middleton conferred on it.

The commander's index finger pointed out along the road running eastward—toward the ridges where Ewell had walked in November —although neither General Middleton nor General McAuliffe ever knew that he had seen the ground. The enemy was coming that way. At Corps headquarters the 9th Armored Division was thought to have a roadblock somewhere around Longvilly and the 10th Armored Division a block farther west toward Neffe. The 9th's block was thought to be surrounded; the 10th's block was supposed to be engaged but not yet surrounded.

General Middleton had described the situation at these blocks when General McAuliffe had reported to him, and he had said: "There is a battle now going on for Bastogne." He spoke of the block out along the Longvilly road as "surrounded" and indicated the positions of the three blocks which Combat Command B of the 10th Armored was maintaining to the east, northeast and southeast of the city. The Corps commander had no specific plan for the employment of the 101st Division. The news that he was to have that division had come so recently that he had had no time to prepare a plan. At first General McAuliffe could think of nothing. At 2200 he suggested to General Middleton that a combat team be sent east to develop the situation. That idea appealed to General McAuliffe simply as a "good old Leavenworth solution of the problem." It was wholly consistent with General Middleton's concern for the preservation of the other elements of his command. As General Middleton reasoned the problem, so long as the 10th Armored team was already employed in the east, it was not urgent that the 101st Airborne Division develop the situation there, although it was sound practice to reinforce the armored team's roadblock, since it was becoming evident that the weight of the enemy attack was coming down the Longvilly road.

Middleton and McAuliffe sent for Ewell. He had been spending a part of his time unprofitably at the road intersections trying to get information from men who were straggling in from the north and northeast. All talked vaguely and dispiritedly. Man after man said to him: "We have been wiped out," and then stumbled away through the dark. They did not know where they had been. They had no idea where they were going. Colonel Ewell and his officers tried several times to draw these men out, then gave them up as a bad job and paid no further attention. Ewell reached his separate conclusion that any quest for information concerning the enemy, other than going out bodily after it, was useless.

The exact mission given Ewell was to "seize the road junction at 676614 and hold it." That would put him out the eastern road well beyond Longvilly. Middleton told him that combat Command Reserve of the 9th Armored Division had a roadblock at that point which was supposed to be "isolated" and that the 110th Infantry was supposedly still maintaining a command post at Allerborn. From the assembly area of the 501st Parachute Infantry, it was nine and a half miles to the road junction. However, that distant point did not enter into General McAuliffe's instructions to Ewell or into Ewell's estimate of what the 501st would be able to accomplish. McAuliffe was not sure where the enemy would crowd him first, but he thought it most likely that they would roll on him from the east. That had as much to do with his assignment of Ewell as did the fact that the armored roadblocks were involved with the enemy.

Map 62.

Then General McAuliffe simply pointed to the map and moved his finger along in the direction of Longvilly. He said "Ewell, move out along this road at six o'clock, make contact, attack and clear up the situation."

Ewell didn't ask a question. He said: "Yes, sir," saluted and went on his way.

Recalling that scene some days afterward, General McAuliffe was to remark: "There were many men and commanders in my operation who did outstanding things. But Ewell's was the greatest gamble of all. It was dark. He had no knowledge of the enemy. I could not tell him what he was likely to meet. But he has a fine eye for ground and no man has more courage. He was the right man for the spot I put him in."

Of the few maps which the 101st Division had obtained from VIII Corps Headquarters, twenty went with Ewell's combat team as it started to march. It wasn't enough to go around. Lt. Col. Clarence F.

443

Nelson, commanding the 907th Glider Field Artillery Battalion, had only one map scaled 1:100,000 from which to provide his firing data. So as the movement got under way, he had sketches drawn up for the forward observers. On the sketches all control points and critical features—such as crossroads, bridges, woods and towns—were marked and numbered. The observers knew the locations of the batteries. In this way the artillery operation was coördinated.

The offensive mission was limited to the one combat team, Ewell's. McAuliffe had decided right at the beginning that a successful defense of Bastogne depended on the utmost harboring of his reserves at every stage of operation, and having sent Ewell forth, he decided to sit on Bastogne with the rest of his Division until something new developed.

That same idea—conservation of force—guided Colonel Ewell in his opening moves. In giving his battalion commanders the march order, he told Maj. Raymond V. Bottomly, Jr., who was leading out with the 1st Battalion of the 501st, that he was not to put out flank security until he reached Magéret; otherwise, the progress of the column would be much too slow. But in line with the governing principle he added the instruction to all commanders that if they met opposition, they were to "take it slow and easy." Being familiar with his men and their methods in past campaigns, he knew that they tended to throw themselves directly on the target. These methods had worked in Normandy and Holland. But from what he had seen of the Bastogne terrain in November, he had concluded that his main chance lay in "fire and maneuver" rather than in shock action. He felt that his whole operation should be guided by this principle. He said to them: "I don't want you to try to beat the enemy to death."

The regiment took off at 0600, December 19, passing its command post on the minute. Battery B of the 81st Airborne Antiaircraft Battalion—seven 57mm guns—moved out behind 1st Battalion. The 101st Airborne Division's Reconnaissance Troop, which had been attached to Ewell's 501st Parachute Infantry, started through the town ahead of Major Bottomly's men. The observers and the liaison party from the artillery moved out with the lead infantry company. The artillery battalion stayed in the bivouac area two miles west of Bastogne waiting for the infantry to find the enemy.

Ewell went forward at 0700. The light was just beginning to break. Already, he felt vaguely familiar with the terrain and the first thing that happened strengthened his confidence in his memory. At the first intersection past the town, he found the 1st Battalion moving down the wrong road—toward Marvie. He saw from memory of the

The 501st goes out of Bastogne toward Magéret to meet the oncoming Germans, 19 December. Note the number of bazookas. The weather was rainy and misty but had not yet turned cold; few of the men are wearing overcoats.

ground, without looking at the map, that they were going the wrong way. He recalled them and got them pointed toward Longvilly. The Reconnaissance Platoon, having proceeded farthest along the wrong road, thus got behind the battalion column, and raced to catch up.

Ewell's column passed on down the road that follows the line of the creek toward Neffe. To their left the hills rose evenly from the edge of the right-of-way—fairly easy slopes up which an infantryman might run without undue exertion. Ahead, they could see very little. The road dipped and turned around the hill facings of the little valley and the morning fog lay so thick that the visibility toward the south, where the land opens up beyond the line of the creek, was limited to 500 yards.

The 1st Battalion had been on the march for a little more than two hours, and the advance party was being passed through by the Reconnaissance Platoon, when the column was fired on by a machine gun from along the road and just westward of Neffe. The first burst of fire did no damage but the battalion hit the dirt. They had need to, for they were looking straight down the groove toward the enemy position; for the last 700 yards the road runs straight and almost level into Neffe.

To right of the road, the ground fell off sharply to the creek. To the left were the gently sloping hills, and Bottomly deployed his men that way. Ewell told him to go ahead and develop his situation. Shells began whipping along the road and Bottomly sent word back to Ewell that he thought he was being opposed by two tanks and two platoons of infantry.

Colonel Ewell took himself off, leaving Bottomly to direct his own fight. He had already tasted the shellfire and he didn't want to tempt it, unnecessarily. Back beyond the road's first turning, about 100 yards from Bottomly's skirmish line, there was a pocket in the hillside to left of the road where a stone house fitted snugly. There Colonel Ewell set up his command post.

It soon became clear to him that his 1st Battalion would not be able to overcome the roadblock because of the German tanks. The tanks were firing from a defilade close into the hillside where the road runs down to Neffe from Bizory. Bottomly couldn't bring the 57mms to bear because the Neffe–Bastogne road ran so straight for the last half mile. About 1000, convinced that his 1st Battalion was stopped, Ewell decided to bring the rest of his regiment out of Bastogne. But this was easier said than done.

The VIII Corps was rushing the evacuation of its last units and their troops were streaming through town across the line of march the rest of the 501st Parachute Infantry would have to take. The 2d Battalion fought its way through this traffic during the next hour and Colonel Ewell ordered them on to an assembly area on the reverse of the gently sloping ridge north of Major Bottomly's position. He figured that he would put them out to the left, closed up so that they could be deployed at the most advantageous moment.

Lieutenant Colonel Nelson, commanding officer of the 907th Glider Field Artillery Battalion, and Capt. Gerald J. McGlone, commanding officer of Battery B, 907th, had gone forward to Colonel Ewell the minute the radio flashed word that the 1st Battalion of the 501st had met fire at Neffe. McGlone got his battery into position 500 yards northeast of Bastogne on the left of the Longvilly road, and opened fire as soon as he was in position, which was only a few minutes after 1000, December 19. The fog was still thick and the battery was working under several other handicaps—its radios had never been tested and five of its guns had never been fired. But they spoke now from a distance of only 1,000 yards behind Bottomly's skirmish line. Having weighed the risk that the enemy might flow on around Ewell's narrow front—and accepted it—Nelson decided that one battery was enough in that particular posi-

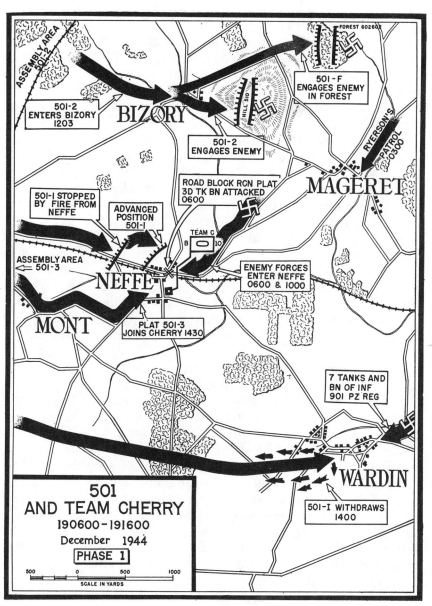

ASSEMBLY AREA
501-2

501-2
ENTERS BIZORY
1203

FOREST 602602

501-F
ENGAGES ENEMY
IN FOREST

BIZORY

HILL 510

501-2
ENGAGES ENEMY

RYERSON'S
PATROL
0300

MAGERET

ROAD BLOCK RCN PLAT
3D TK BN ATTACKED
0600

501-1 STOPPED
BY FIRE FROM
NEFFE

ADVANCED
POSITION
501-1

TEAM C

B   10

ASSEMBLY AREA
◄— 501-3

ENEMY FORCES
ENTER NEFFE
0600 & 1000

NEFFE

MONT

PLAT 501-3
JOINS CHERRY 1430

7 TANKS AND
BN OF INF
901 PZ REG

WARDIN

501-1 WITHDRAWS
1400

**501
AND TEAM CHERRY**
190600-191600
December 1944

PHASE 1

500   0   500   1000
SCALE IN YARDS

Map 63.

tion. He put Battery A, under Capt. Lowell B. Bigelow, into the action from a position near the battalion command post, 1,000 yards west of Bastogne. Luck rode with him. The defilade where he had placed Battery B on the spur of the moment was so well chosen that the guns were to work there for almost a month without receiving a single round of German counter-battery fire.

This day, however, the batteries had no need to worry about anything coming in on them. The only heavy support for the German attack was from their tanks and it was all close-up fire directed against Ewell's infantry units. The American artillery fire was turned mainly against the tanks and the small groups of German infantry. There were many such targets.

Colonel Ewell sized up his situation. In 1st Battalion, Companies B and C were in skirmish line, while Company A was collected in reserve. Major Bottomly had deployed most of his strength to the north of the highway but he had managed to find room for one platoon in the ground south of the creek and rail line. The battalion had put two mortars into operation almost immediately and their fire was shaking down the houses around the enemy roadblock in Neffe.

But an attempt to get the 1st Battalion's left flank forward had failed. From Neffe, the north road climbs gradually through a shallow draw to the small farming community of Bizory. The country hereabouts is all uninterrupted grazing land except for the small but thick tree plantations and clusters of farmhouses which appear as villages on the map. The dominant terrain features are the long and quite regular ridges which run generally in a north-south line. These hills are gently undulating and the hillsides are quite smooth. From the tops of the commanding ridges one can see great distances on a clear day. The reverse slopes of the hills are smooth and usually accessible from either end of the hills, making them highly useful to artillery and armor. The roads are close enough together so that vehicles can move to the ridges from either direction. When the country is covered with snow, nothing obtrudes on the landscape except the small black patches of forest. The ridges fall away in gently sloping draws which provide clear fields of fire to the flank and make it easily possible to cover the main lines of communication. The road from Neffe to Bizory rises gradually for a distance, providing a perfect slot for fire from the low ground around Neffe. Bottomly had made one pass in this direction and shells from the enemy armor had fairly blistered the little valley.

Ewell decided that as long as the enemy tanks were in Neffe, his 1st Battalion couldn't move in any direction. He ordered the 2d Battalion to seize Bizory. That hamlet is in the same draw up which the tanks had shot at Bottomly's men, but the ground flattens out at Bizory so that the place can't be seen from Neffe. This detail, however, Ewell couldn't see from the rear, but he was curious to find out about it. The map told him that the ridge adjacent to Bizory was the high ground and would be of use to him. He wanted to see if the enemy force east of there was holding a continuous position and he sent his 2d Battalion forward to find out.

His decision, so casually made, probably contributed as much to the salvation of Bastogne as anything that happened during the first few critical days. Colonel Ewell was still strongly of the opinion that he was being opposed by only a minor roadblock. But when he determined to extend the 501st and sweep forward, he made it a certainty that the oncoming Germans would suddenly collide with Americans who were attacking along a broad front. This was the thing the Germans least expected. Until it happened they had been meeting small or disorganized units, which they quickly encircled and overcame.

The shock of the discovery threw them off stride. They recoiled, hesitated and lost priceless, unreclaimable hours and opportunity because of their own confusion. In that action, a few American platoons hardened the fate of armies. But Ewell thought of none of these things as he ordered his 2d Battalion, 501st Parachute Infantry, to seize Bizory. He reflected on them later in his command post in the Bastogne monastery which the German artillery had made one of the best-ventilated buildings in all of Belgium.

EAST OF BASTOGNE

The 3d Battalion of the 501st Parachute Infantry had been caught in the traffic snarl west of Bastogne and was at a standstill. Colonel Ewell checked on them at 1200, December 19, and found that they had scarcely moved at all. After trying to get out of town, the battalion had backtracked, only to find that other routes were likewise clogged with outgoing troops. Yet even this delay had its benefits. Some of the infantrymen lacked helmets, rifles and ammunition. They begged them from the armored troops of Combat Command B, 10th Armored Division, who were in the town, and thus in the interval the battalion became somewhat better equipped. Colonel Ewell ordered Lt. Col. George M. Griswold, commanding the 3d Battalion, to march his battal-

The Bastogne road entering the outskirts of Mont. (This and the other drawings illustrating Bastogne are by Tech. Sgt. Olin Dows, who entered Bastogne while the fighting was still going on.)

ion to Mont, a little hamlet lying south of the Neffe road. It seemed like the best opportunity to get the battalion out of Bastogne. Ewell also directed that one of Griswold's companies be sent down the Wiltz road to cover the 3d Battalion's right flank as it moved. Colonel Griswold was told to send the company to the bend in the road directly east of the village of Marvie. Colonel Ewell planned to send the 3d Battalion against Neffe from the southwest after it had reached Mont, but he issued no orders to the effect at the time. He followed his usual plan of giving his subordinate commanders only a limited objective.

At 1203 the 2d Battalion took Bizory without opposition except for unobserved fire from the German tanks in Neffe. Still convinced that the Neffe roadblock was the only immediate threat to his front, Ewell ordered his 2d Battalion to advance and seize Magéret. By this move he figured he would box the tanks in so that he could then move against them either from front or rear according to the advantages of the ground. But he specified that Maj. Sammie N. Homan, commander of the 2d Battalion, send one of his companies to seize the patch of woods directly north of Magéret. This wood is a small plantation of very tall spruces. Ewell saw that the long ridge running across to the spruces dominated Magéret in the valley. It seemed to him that putting one company there might cover the approach to Magéret.

Major Homan started out by road from Bizory to Magéret, but his rout march ended quickly. At the crest of Hill 510 he ran into

German infantry in dug-in positions: they were the Reconnaissance Platoon of the 26th Volksgrenadier Division. Homan took this first jolt almost without loss; not so, the enemy. Their line was moving forward from the foxholes and coming over the hill when the 2d Battalion mortars and Nelson's artillery caught them with full blast. The paratroopers saw a number of the enemy fall before the survivors ran back. Deploying the rest of his battalion, Homan sent Company F to the left to seize the coveted wood. When this extension was completed he reported to Colonel Ewell by radio that his hands were full and he was now engaged along his entire front. "For the time being," he said, "I cannot think of taking Magéret."

Colonel Griswold's 3d Battalion reached Mont and found one of the engineer roadblocks outposting that point, but the further operation of the main body of the battalion was compromised by the nature of the ground between Mont and Neffe. The two villages are little more than a mile apart and from Neffe one can look right down the little valley and see Mont clearly. The tanks of Panzer Lehr, which were at Neffe, were shipping a few shells toward Griswold's infantry. It seemed possible that a small party might work its way toward Neffe but the ground was much too naked for the exposure of any large force. Colonel Griswold stopped his 3d Battalion where it was.

Company I, which had drawn the assignment on the extreme right flank, was instructed to prowl the three large woods west and northwest of the village of Wardin. At 1330 Company I reported that they had checked the three woods and found no enemy. Colonel Ewell then told Company I to advance to Wardin and make contact with a friendly armored roadblock that was supposed to be there. Ewell had not been told officially of the existence of this force but had heard of it quite casually from someone walking down the road. The company went on to make the contact Ewell had ordered. But for all practical effect, the stranger who had mentioned that there was a friendly roadblock nearby might just as well have left his words unsaid.

This was Team O'Hara of Combat Command B, 10th Armored Division, which on the night of December 18 had taken up position on the high ground south of Wardin just short of the woods. The night had been quiet except for the stragglers coming through—mostly rear echelon people from the 28th Division whose idea of the enemy situation was confused. The morning of December 19 opened with fog. About 1000 the trickle of stragglers stopped altogether. This worried Team O'Hara for they figured it must mean that the enemy was coming next. They put out a platoon as a reconnaissance screen to

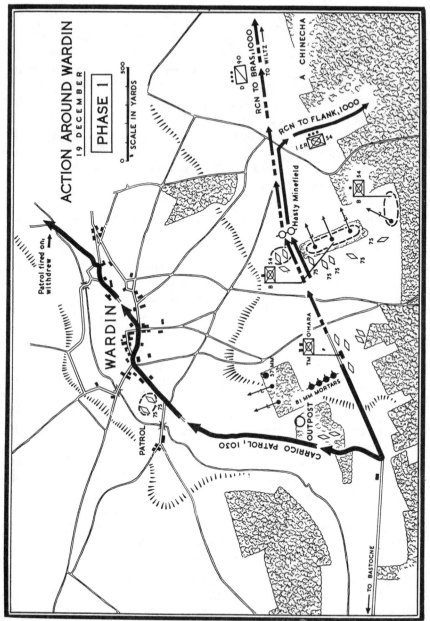

ACTION AROUND WARDIN

19 DECEMBER

PHASE 1

SCALE IN YARDS

0   500

RCN TO BRAS, 1000

TO WILTZ

D 90

A CHINEHA

RCN TO FLANK, 1000

I ER 54

B 54

Hasty Minefield

75

75

75

75

B 54

75

75

75

Patrol fired on,
withdrew

WARDIN

PATROL

75
75

TM O'HARA

57 MM

81 MM MORTARS

OUTPOST

CARRICO PATROL, 1030

TO BASTOGNE

Map 64.

the east which moved slowly along the road to Bras. At 1140 they engaged and destroyed a Volkswagen on the Wiltz–Bastogne highway. Just as they opened fire they saw the head of the enemy column break through the fog a few hundred yards away—two Mark IV tanks and a personnel carrier. The platoon had nothing with which to fight armor so it cleared out rapidly, reporting its findings by radio. As a result of the message, unobserved fire was put on Bras by the 420th Armored Field Artillery Battalion.

At about the same time Capt. Edward A. Carrigo, Team S-2, and First Lieutenant John D. Devereaux, commanding Company B of the 54th Armored Infantry Battalion, were entering Wardin from the southwest and finding it unhealthy. The town was wrapped in fog; they could scarcely see anything at fifty yards' range. But they prowled on through the town and just as they got beyond it a projectile of antitank size hit the front bumper of their jeep. Nothing was hurt, but the two officers increased their speed and reported that there were people moving into Wardin who were quite unfriendly.

By noon of the 19th the visibility lengthened to 800 yards. 2d Lt. Theodore R. Hamer, observer for the 420th Armored Field Artillery Battalion, moved forward to the top of a small hill. There were five tanks of Team O'Hara on the crest when he got there. But before he had a chance to observe for fire, his own tank was hit twice from the left by a high-velocity gun, wounding Hamer and three other crew members. One man was incinerated inside the tank. Another medium tank was hit in the turret by a shell that killed the gunner. The driver backed the tank down the hill wildly, not stopping until his vehicle became bogged; the tank could not be salvaged and later had to be destroyed. The other tanks cleared away from the hill as rapidly as they could. Direct-fire artillery began to hit the force's main position from north across the valley. On the road ahead, the team had hastily set up a minefield. At 1300 a few Germans jumped from a Volkswagen and tried to remove the mines. From only 200 yards away to the west, five of the infantry half-tracks and five medium tanks opened fire on the German party. But they were able to jump in their car and make a clean getaway. Shortly after, an outpost at the south of the position saw another enemy group moving through woods northeast toward Wardin. One of the medium tanks moved up and put them under fire.

These were the things that had happened before the time when Team O'Hara saw men coming toward them from the woods at their rear. These men were in patrol formation and wore an unfamiliar

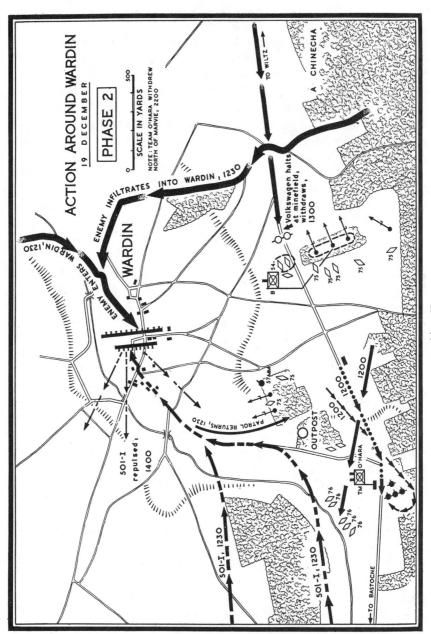

ACTION AROUND WARDIN

19 DECEMBER

PHASE 2

SCALE IN YARDS

0 — 500

NOTE: TEAM O'HARA WITHDREW
NORTH OF MARVIE, 2200

ENEMY INFILTRATES INTO WARDIN, 1230

ENEMY ENTERS WARDIN, 1230

WARDIN

Volkswagen halts
at minefield,
withdraws,
1300

75

75

75
75

75

B 54.

PATROL RETURNS, 1230

57 MM

75
75

501-I
repulsed,
1400

OUTPOST

1200

1200

1200

1200

76
76

76
76
76

TM O'HARA

501-I, 1230

501-I, 1230

TO WILTZ

A   CHINECHA

TO BASTOCNE

Map 65.

green uniform, which looked tight around the legs. The tankers were just about to fire and then someone in the approaching party yelled. The approaching men were the point of Company I, 501st Parachute Infantry. Their green jump suits had almost been their undoing. The main body of the Company was right behind them in the woods and the company was on its way to Wardin—good news to the tankers. The first infantry support had arrived and they could now withdraw their own patrols which had been reaching out toward the town.

Some fateful minutes passed and nothing was done to unify the action. With the enemy crowding in on them, the forces acted like two ships passing in the night. The paratroopers went on. Two medium tanks were placed so as to cover the exits from Wardin. That was all.

Lt. Col. James O'Hara, commander of the 54th Armored Infantry Battalion, 10th Armored Division, and Team O'Hara of Combat Command B, had thought that the enemy would push west on the Wiltz–Bastogne highway. But he was wrong about it. The Germans bypassed his group—except for a few who squeezed a little too far over to the west and got themselves killed for their pains and went on to Wardin, moving along a deep gully where O'Hara's tanks couldn't bring their fire to bear. The tankers could see the German infantry infiltrating by twos and threes, moving northwest toward the town, until a hundred or more had passed. They asked that artillery be put on the gully but the Bastogne artillery was occupied with the defense of Noville. Then the enemy began to fret O'Hara's immediate front again: one group came close enough to fire at a tank with a rocket that fell five yards short. Half-tracks sprayed the area with machine-gun fire and the tanks pounded away with their 75mms. Thus preoccupied, Team O'Hara paid no mind to Wardin. They knew there was fighting going on but the situation was "obscure."

At 1415, December 19, Colonel Ewell heard that Company I was being fired on in Wardin. The reports trickling in during the next few minutes indicated that the company was doing pretty well. Armor was now opposing them, but they had already knocked out two tanks and were pushing the enemy infantry from the town. By 1600, Ewell was pretty much content with his general situation. He had three battalions approximately abreast, he was in contact with the enemy all along his front and there was a friendly roadblock—Team O'Hara —on his extreme right flank. But he felt that he had gone as far as he could with his offensive action and that such strength was now being committed against him that he could no longer think about his specific mission (to "seize the road junction at 676614 and hold it"). He therefore ordered his battalions to make plans to break contact at dark and draw back to defend a general line along the high ground to the west of Bizory–Neffe, and in an approximate extension of this line to the southward of the creek. At Division headquarters, General McAuliffe and Colonel Kinnard looked over his plan and approved it.

As he was walking back through Bastogne he met a sergeant from Company I who said to him, "Have you heard about Company I? We've been wiped out." Ewell got to his radio; he didn't believe the sergeant, but the story was nearer right than he thought. Company I had lost 45 men and 4 officers at Wardin and the survivors had scattered so badly that it was no longer possible to form even a platoon. The news was a shock. When he first heard that Company I was becoming involved in Wardin, Colonel Ewell had ordered it to disengage and withdraw. But before the company could comply, it had come under the full shock of an attack by seven tanks and one infantry battalion from Panzer Lehr. The survivors got out as best they could.

This news simply strengthened Ewell's conviction that he must abandon all further offensive intention and tighten up his position. Colonel O'Hara had reached the same conclusion and for much the same reason. Four of the walking wounded who had gotten out of Wardin had come into his lines and told him the news. He saw his force now in an exposed position with no one on his right, an aggressive enemy on his left and pressure along his whole front, and he asked Combat Command B headquarters for permission to withdraw.

By radio he received his reply, "Contact friends on your left, hold what you have." This told him that headquarters still didn't understand the situation. So he sent his S-3, Capt. George A. Renoux, to Bastogne to explain in person what he couldn't with safety discuss over the air, and then went to his rear to reconnoiter a better position. At 1715 he was ordered to withdraw to the high ground north of Marvie—the place he had by then already picked as the best defensive line in the area. The Headquarters Company, Heavy-Weapons Company and engineers were first to start digging into the new slope. When they were in place, the rest of the force came along, except for four medium tanks and one platoon of infantry which covered the withdrawal. Throughout the whole move, the 420th Armored Field Artillery Battalion put a heavy covering fire into the ground where the enemy had been seen during the day. Not a shot was fired in return.

Because of the loss of Company I and his feeling that the enemy was building up on his right, Colonel Ewell asked Division headquarters to attach one battalion to his regiment for a right flank and reserve. He was given the 1st Battalion of the 327th Glider Infantry under Lt. Col. Hartford F. Salee. They were put in behind Ewell's 3d Battalion which put them next to Team O'Hara.

Between 1700 and 1800, December 19, the 501st Parachute Infantry fell back to the new defensive line. Estimating his gains and losses, Ewell didn't give his regiment too much credit. He thought that Company I had probably killed some Germans at Wardin, but since the enemy still held the town he couldn't be sure. His impression was that the execution done by his own right and center had not been very great. The honors of the day belonged to the artillery. Colonel Ewell said, "Any actual killing of the enemy that day was due to the artillery."

Captain Ryerson's force (Company C, 20th Armored Infantry Battalion, 10th Armored Division) of Team Cherry, having spent the day hoping that the infantry would get up to them, clung to three houses in the northwest edge of Magéret after dark. The enemy shot up flares and blazed away at Ryerson's vehicles with antitank guns, destroying three of them. Their infantry then came on but was driven back by the fire of the 420th Armored Field Artillery Battalion.

At 0030, December 20, Combat Command B Headquarters sent orders for Ryerson to withdraw before dawn, and to make contact with Colonel Ewell at Bizory. One line in the special instructions said, "The lead vehicle will inform outpost line of number of vehicles in his column to insure that no Germans follow column into our lines."

Captain Ryerson got ready to move his wounded to a point beyond the crest of the first hill—the first step on the way out.

Holding the Château

Colonel Cherry had been sitting on the hot seat. Having failed to get to his forward elements the night of December 18, he went to his command post, which was set up in the château 300 yards south of Neffe. A signal company from VIII Corps which had hastily pulled out of this building had scribbled signs on the walls saying, "We'll be back—The Yanks." One of Cherry's men read it and snorted, "We'll be back—Hell! We're here to stay."

At 0600 on December 19—just as Ewell's men were passing the initial point—Cherry's Reconnaissance Platoon, 3d Tank Battalion, which was outposting the road junction at Neffe, was hit by enemy tanks and infantry from the east. The platoon knocked out one tank with a bazooka but the enemy kept coming, and after taking some losses, the line broke back under a storm of German rifle, machine-gun

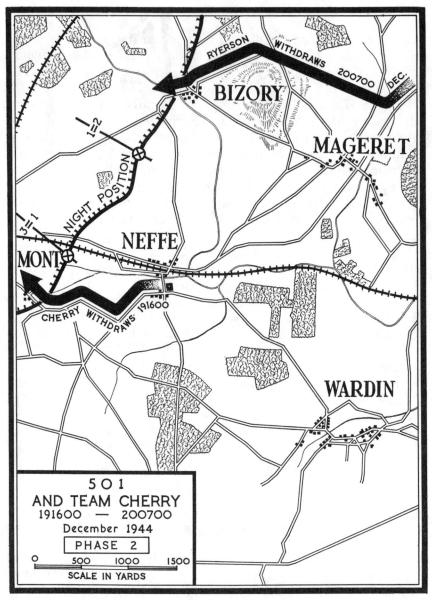

Map 66.

and direct artillery fire. Most of the outpost fell back along the Bastogne road up which Major Bottomly's men (1st Battalion, 501st Parachute Infantry) were coming. But three of them were able to get through to Cherry in the château and they carried the word that the enemy had come to Neffe with two tanks and two infantry platoons.

458

Neffe, captured by the Germans on the morning of 19 December. The Neffe Château is in the clump of trees on the right; the road to the left leads to Bastogne.

At 1000, while Colonel Ewell was committing his 2d Battalion of the 501st, Colonel Cherry saw four more German tanks (one was a Tiger Royal), an armored car and 97 more infantrymen enter Neffe from the direction of Magéret. Right after that they hit his force, and they spent the rest of that day trying to crush him with their left while poking at Ewell's troops with their right . . .

Some time around mid-afternoon on the 19th a platoon from Ewell's 3d Battalion of the 501st in Mont worked its way carefully forward, taking advantage of the cover afforded by the forest patches and the rise and fall of the ground, and entered the château. It had turned out this way, that whereas the fire of the German tanks had kept Colonel Griswold's 3d Battalion from closing on Neffe, his infantry fire had compelled the Germans to release their tight hold on the château. Too, the enemy must have felt mounting concern for what was occurring on their right. The platoon had come as reinforcements—to help Cherry hold the fort. But by that time the roof was blazing over his head and his men were being smoked out by another fire lighted by German HE shells. He waited until the approach of darkness and then led all hands out of Neffe and back to the infantry lines at Mont.

Before leaving, Colonel Cherry sent Combat Command B this message, "We're not driven out . . . we were burned' out. We're not withdrawing . . . we are moving."

Team Desobry at Noville

*It was the belief of the commanders at Bastogne that the 28th Infantry Division had absorbed much of the shock of the attack before the enemy reached their front on that first day, and that the harassing of the German flank and rear by the armored forces which had gone out the Longvilly road further lightened the burden upon their own men of the 101st. In those critical hours the armor out along the roads

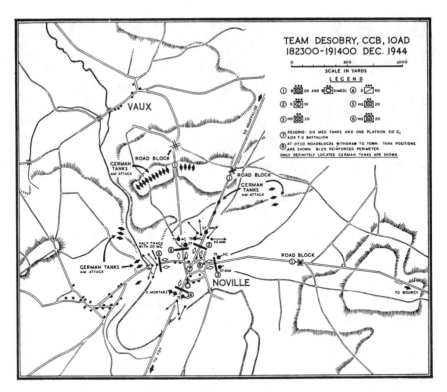

Map 67.

leading north and east was to the infantry in Bastogne like a football end throwing himself in the path of interference so that the secondary defense can have a clean chance to get at the man with the ball.

One of the most desperately placed of these small armored forces was Team Desobry which assembled in the Noville area at 2300 on December 18. Major Desobry, commander of the team, set up a perimeter defense with small tank-infantry outposts on the Bourcy, Houffalize, and Vaux roads. Attempts to install minefields in support of these roadblocks, which were about half a mile from Noville, were thwarted by the steady stream of stragglers coming down these roads. Every vehicle was searched for infantrymen and those found were incorporated into the defense, though with a few exceptions most of these strays were so beaten in spirit that they took to the cellars when action started. Before daylight of the 19th both the Bourcy and Houffalize outposts beat off German attacks. At daylight in accordance with their instructions the three outpost groups fell back on Noville.

At 0830 two Tiger tanks nosed out of the fog on the northern edge of the town and were knocked out. At 1030 the fog lifted and revealed

460

the whole countryside filled with German armor. For the next hour events were shaped by the flash of the heavy guns and the vagaries of the ever-shifting fog, but aided by a platoon from the 609th Tank Destroyer Battalion which arrived providentially while the shooting was going on, the American gunners knocked off the enemy tanks like ducks in a shooting gallery. One line of fourteen tanks appeared on a ridge near Vaux; ten of them were knocked out. All around the perimeter the story was the same; by noon the firing had died down and smouldering German tanks and dead tankers and infantrymen littered the areas in front of the American positions.

In spite of its success the position of the Noville force, with the enemy on three sides, was not too good, and there was a strong possibility that they might be surrounded. So Major Desobry called Colonel Roberts and asked permission to withdraw to the high ground around the village of Foy.*

Colonel Roberts sparred with the request from Noville. He still possessed authority to sanction the withdrawal of his own elements but he reckoned that the situation required steadfastness for the time being and until the 101st Division was solidly established in Bastogne. So at first he gave no answer. He left his own CP and started for General McAuliffe's headquarters to see what could be done. Before he had gone halfway he ran into Brigadier General Higgins, assistant division commander of the 101st. Even as he rapidly sketched the situation to Higgins (the time was 1050) the 1st Battalion of 506th Parachute Infantry, under Lt. Col. James L. LaPrade, passed by in the street. At the head of the regimental column, accompanying LaPrade, was the 506th's commander, Col. Robert F. Sink. Convinced by Roberts' words that the Noville situation was fully desperate, Higgins on the spot ordered Sink to send a battalion to Noville and LaPrade automatically drew the assignment. Colonel Sink was further directed that his 2d and 3d Battalions should be put in Division reserve just north of Bastogne on the Noville road. At the same time the 1st Battalion, which had been given the Noville mission, was detached from Regiment and put under Division control. Colonel Roberts returned to his CP and called Major Desobry. "You can use your own judgment about withdrawing," he said, "but I'm sending a battalion of paratroopers to reinforce you."

Desobry replied, "I'll get ready to counterattack as soon as possible."

Colonel LaPrade and his staff got up to Major Desobry at 1130 and told him the battalion was on the way. It was not quite clear to either of the local commanders whether there had been an attachment of one force to the other but they decided that for the time being they would keep it a "mutual affair." Colonel LaPrade and his command had just one 1:100,000 map to serve them for the forthcoming operation.

The commanders agreed that the next order of business was to attack due north and seize the high ground the enemy had tried to use as a springboard during the morning. Infantry and armor would jump off together at 1400. However, Colonel LaPrade's battalion didn't arrive until 1330 and couldn't get ready that soon. So the jumpoff was postponed until 1430, December 19, since meanwhile there was a small matter of supply to be finally adjusted.

The 506th Parachute Infantry had left Mourmelon in such a hurry that many of the men did not have helmets and others were short of weapons and ammunition. Colonel LaPrade told Major Desobry about this embarrassment and the armored force's S-4, 2d Lt. George C. Rice, was sent packing to Foy to bring up ammunition. On the way he met the upcoming 1st Battalion and asked for their supply officer; but this officer was in Bastogne beating the woods for weapons and ammunition. So Lieutenant Rice asked the company officers what they needed most, and found that rocket launchers, mortars and all types of ammunition were the critical shortages. He then dashed on to Foy and loaded the jeep with cases of hand grenades and M1 ammunition. The jeep was turned around and the stuff was passed out to the paratroopers as they marched. On his next shuttle, Rice got back to the moving battalion with a jeep and a truck overloaded with weapons and ammunition. The matériel was put alongside the road in five separate piles so that the men could pick up the things they needed as they went by. He made one more trip and caught the head of the column just before it reached the limits of Noville. A load of 81mm mortar ammunition came into town after the battalion got there.

These details caused a slight delay in getting the battle under way again.

Attack and Withdrawal

Colonel LaPrade and Major Desobry wanted the high ground and this was their plan—that three tanks would strike northward along the Houffalize road and four tanks would hit east toward the high ground west of Bourcy. With this group of tanks would go one and one-half platoons of infantry for their close-in support. In between these two armored groups moving along the road, LaPrade's paratroopers would spread themselves over the middle ground. One company would advance south over the Bourcy road, another off to the left of it would extend to the Houffalize road and the third company would go toward

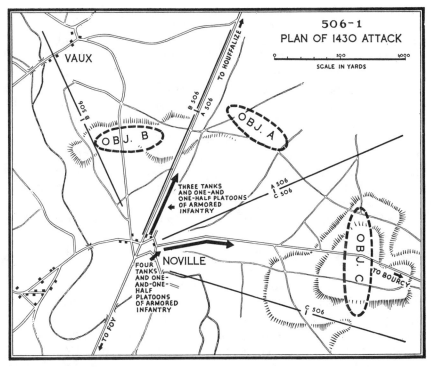

Map 68.

the high ground at Vaux. In this way, armor and infantry would spread out fanwise as they left Noville and started for the commanding ridges.

However, the preliminaries were not propitious. Noville was already taking a pounding from the enemy artillery. The Germans were firing by the clock and dropping twenty to thirty shells into the defensive position every ten minutes. The houses and several of the vehicles were afire. A proper reconnaissance became impossible; the assembly went off badly. Still, the attack got away at 1430, December 19, though somewhat unsteadily.

The line had scarcely moved out from the houses when an artillery concentration landed in the middle of Company C of the 506th Parachute Infantry, which was on the right flank. A number of men were hit but the company kept moving. Bullet fire from enemy positions on the high ground bit into the infantry ranks and slowed their advance. The little groups worked their way along, dashing on to favorable ground, stopping there to fire, then making a rush on to the next point of cover.

But elsewhere along the line, except on the far left where Company B

463

kept moving, the attack was already flagging. The tanks and armored infantry decided the attack was impossible so moved back to their holes, not even realizing that the paratroopers were continuing to attack in any strength. Company A was blocked by heavy tank fire immediately and after a small advance was forced to return to the village. But on the flanks, B and C went on until they reached the lower slopes of the objective ridges and started to climb. At that moment the enemy tanks came against them, supported by some infantry. A few of the paratroopers kept going; their snow-covered bodies were found on the ridges weeks later. But the greater part of the two companies went to earth and sought whatever cover was at hand. Then they continued to slug it out with their small arms as best they could. They could hardly see the enemy at any time. The fog was closing down again and it was mixed with the smoke drifting over from the fires of Noville.

They held the ground until dark. Then Colonel LaPrade's men fell back on Noville. The fighting on the slopes had cost the battalion heavily but the men thought they had caused equal losses to the enemy. From the town itself three tank destroyers had exchanged fire at about 1500 yards with the enemy tanks and had kept them from coming on. But whether they had done any real hurt to them could not be seen.

For about an hour after the return to Noville the front was deathly quiet. LaPrade's men had had no chance to dig in prior to the attack so they sought refuge in the houses. Colonel LaPrade improved his command post by moving a heavy clothes closet in front of the window. The ·Germans resumed their bombardment of the town and in the middle of the shelling a platoon of tank destroyers from the 706th Tank Destroyer Battalion reported for duty. Further tightening the defense, General Higgins, having arrived at Noville just as the American counterattack was fading, took the essential steps toward unifying the local command. Major Desobry and Colonel LaPrade were in agreement that one man should be in control, and LaPrade, being the senior, drew the assignment. LaPrade told General Higgins that he thought he could hold on until dark but that he was convinced that the enemy would attack in strength shortly thereafter. Soon after that, Colonel Sink got up to Noville for a personal reconnaissance. He talked to LaPrade and the latter shortly issued his orders for the combined defense. The plan was for Company B to defend to the northwest and Company A to the northeast and Company C was to cover the southern half of the perimeter while the armored group was held in the center of the town ready to strike out in any direction. A few minutes after

LaPrade was placed in command, an 88 shell landed in the street outside the command post. The explosion shattered the clothes closet and both commanders were struck down by fragments. Colonel LaPrade was killed and Major Desobry wounded. Major Robert F. Harwick, LaPrade's executive, who had rushed back from a leave in Paris to join his battalion and had arrived in Noville just at the close of the afternoon fighting, took command of the combined force. The armor passed into the hands of Maj. Charles L. Hustead.

For the men of Combat Command B who were within the town the rest of the night (December 19-20) was comparatively quiet. Their peace was punctured at times by the dropping of a few artillery shells and out beyond the wall of fog they could hear the noise of an enemy build-up. There was little quiet, however, along the infantry perimeter. Enemy tanks in twos and threes, supported by infantry, probed toward them. When warned by small-arms or bazooka fire, they checked and blazed away at the positions from which they had seen the flashes. The accompanying German infantry tried to infiltrate through the lines. These small penetrations and the resulting fire were such that it was almost impossible to maintain wire communication with the outposts. For the paratroopers those hours were a nightmare of surprise fire, ominous noise and confusion. But when morning came the light revealed that two of the enemy tanks had been knocked out by bazooka fire.

These opening blows in the first round at Noville had been enough to convince General McAuliffe that the enemy was full of fight. After that first day they would never seem as strong to him again and the impression would deepen that their attacks were coming on in diminishing volume. But on the first day he looked toward his northern sector with increasing concern. In the afternoon of December 19, the 3d Battalion of 506th had been ordered to move up to Foy between Bastogne and Noville and establish a line there, with the 2d Battalion moving to Luzery as a regimental reserve. When this move was made, Company H on the right made contact with the 501st Parachute Infantry by patrol and Company G on the left joined with the 502d Parachute Infantry, maintaining a strong point in Recogne. That night all platoons of Company C of the 705th Tank Destroyer Battalion were attached to the 506th Parachute Infantry and General McAuliffe got ready to employ as much of the strength of 502d along his northern flank as the morrow would prove necessary.

This small, confused action had reverberated all the way back to Corps. On returning to Bastogne, Higgins had reported to McAuliffe as follows: "I think we're way out on a limb. These is too much distance between LaPrade in Noville and Strayer in Foy. It is my judgment that the Noville force had better get out." Colonel Sink, having carried out his independent reconnaissance, had reached exactly the same conclusion. At around 1820 he called Division and said that it was getting very hot at Noville; he urged that his forward battalion be withdrawn to a point north of Foy. But in view of the fact that General Middleton had ordered that Noville be defended and that the armor which had gone forward in response to that direction was still acting under Roberts's orders, it looked like a matter for decision by the higher headquarters. General McAuliffe called General Middleton and relayed Higgins's and Sink's reports of the situation, adding his personal recommendation that the force be withdrawn. Middleton said, "No; if we are to hold on to Bastogne, you cannot keep falling back." Sink was called and told that the Noville force would have to stick. By then, Major Desobry had ceased to worry about the local problem. He was unconscious when they removed him from the CP to the nearest field hospital. He was still out, when a few hours later, the Germans overran the hospital and took him prisoner.

Doubts and Decisions

Yet on the whole, that first night in Bastogne, the situation was good, and it was largely the intuition and hunch and driving energy of the leaders that had made it so. The day of the 19th had proved that in the few minutes allowed him the night before, General McAuliffe had sized up the position properly. He had been tossed into a battle in which nearly all the major facts about the movement of forces were either unknown or obscure. He had rejected Corps' idea that the 101st Airborne Division be assembled to the southwest of Bastogne. It was a point that didn't give particular concern to General Middleton so long as General McAuliffe got his troops in where they were best placed to defend the town. However, VIII Corps Headquarters' reasoning was based on the long-range thought that after the enemy found he could not get through Bastogne, his next important move would be to the southwest. In his hasty reconnaissance out to the westward with Colonel Kinnard, his G-3, late in the day on the 18th, General McAuliffe had selected the ground for his camp from the short-range point of view. He wanted an assembly area which would place him at maximum advantage with respect to his own immediate deployments and the movements of the enemy in the immediate future. Though he had no way of knowing it at the time, his center of equilibrium was on the ground farthest removed from the early dangers of the encirclement although his two eastward-facing regiments were pointed directly toward the avenues along which the Germans would make their first approaches. The first day's results proved that the angels had been with him as he made his first decisions.

In the opening arrangements one decision was taken which worked out adversely. Lt. Col. David Gold, the surgeon of the 101st Division, and Lt. Col. Carl W. Kohls, the Division supply officer, had picked out a conveniently located crossroads to the westward of the Division assembly area and decided that this must be the rear, if there were such a thing. The Division hospital was set up on the crossroads. Near midnight of December 19 the 327th Glider Infantry was told to send a motorized patrol to crossroads X—the site of this evacuation center. The patrol was to investigate and clear up reports of machine-gun fire in that vicinity. They encountered no fire but the hospital was gone— Colonel Gold and all his officers and the men of the clearing company had been captured by the enemy. The 327th patrol decided that there must have been a fight, for dead Germans dressed in civilian clothes were found strewn over the ground, though there were no bodies of American soldiers. The bulk of the Division medical supplies had been captured or destroyed.

*What had happened to the medical company was cleared up the next day. Two dental officers, Capts. Jacob Pearl and John Breiner, and a medical officer, Capt. Roy H. Moore, Jr., had ducked into the woods and had worked their way back into Bastogne where they told their story. A few other men also managed to get away and piece in the details.

At about 2230 an estimated six armored vehicles—tanks and half-tracks—and a hundred infantrymen had come down the Houffalize road and had attacked the clearing station. During the attack a convoy of trucks came out of Bastogne. Pfc. Don M. Dobbins who had been captured a few minutes earlier by Germans in civilian clothes while taking a truckload of wounded to the clearing station saw the trucks coming down the highway.

All of a sudden all hell broke loose. Here is the way the scene was set. About seven of us were standing behind a truck and along the highway were twelve trucks on their way back to the Division at Camp Mourmelon to get more supplies. All of this was taking place at a crossroads. On one side of the road was a tank destroyer—American, of course. There wasn't anything we could do about it. The Germans had killed the men in it and were manning it themselves.

Well, the tracers started flying and hitting everything around there. Why the few of us behind the truck weren't hit is beyond me. I suppose the good Lord was with us that night. The bullets were so close that I thought I would have to brush them off. We all made one big dive for the ditch.

We were having trouble with a trooper who had a head wound, and the medic who was taking care of him told me that he was gone or something to that effect. I suppose the boy died. There was nothing we could do for the boys in the truck. To stand up on the road was suicide. The Germans fired on every truck standing there and set them on fire. I remember a Negro truck driver in one of the trucks who got up in his cab and blasted away at the Germans with a fifty-caliber gun mounted on his cab. He didn't last long, for the Germans turned everything they had on him. If they had fired a second longer they could have cut the cab away from the rest of the truck.

I looked at the trucks and saw every one of them on fire. Our truck was burning fast because they had fired right into the gas tank. During all of that we didn't hear any outcry from it. I suppose all of them were dead. The guns were trained on them long enough.

In the confusion Dobbins managed to escape, but was not able to get back into Bastogne until the siege was lifted. (Among those in Dobbins' group who escaped was Capt. Samuel C. Feiler, 506th dental officer. Feiler took charge of the wounded escapees and turned them over to a major of the 10th Armored who had come up with a vehicle. Then he started on foot to Bastogne to give the news of the hospital's capture. About half-way to town he met a 327th patrol and told them what had happened. A little farther on he was joined by a 506th aid man, T/5 Alvin Kidder, and a wounded soldier. The three men hailed a jeep and rode into Bastogne at 0400 to give a first-hand report of the capture.)

The machine-gun fire sprayed not only the trucks but the tents in which medical treatment was being carried on; the big crosses on the tents were quite visible in the light of the burning trucks.

After fifteen minutes of the firing a German officer came up to the station and questioned the senior officer, Lt. Col. David Gold, the Division Surgeon. With no alternative Colonel Gold surrendered his unarmed medical company and used the thirty minutes the Germans gave him to load up his wounded and the medical personnel and equipment. Then into the German lines went 11 medical officers and 119 enlisted men of the 326th Medical Company, 3 officers and 2 enlisted men of the Division Surgeon's office, and 4 officers and 3 enlisted men of the 3d Auxiliary Surgical Group.*

Division then called on VIII Corps for medical help, and all 101st Division units were notified that casualties would be evacuated to the aid station of the 501st Parachute Infantry in Bastogne itself. One platoon of the 429th Medical Collecting Company, then located at

Jodenville (about one mile west of Sibret), was made available to the 101st. Until the night of December 21 the platoon used its five ambulances and two weapons carriers to carry some of the wounded back to the 635th Medical Clearing Company. Then the Germans cut across the road and contact was lost with the clearing unit. An abandoned medical supply dump and the chance discovery of another depot in Bastogne containing blankets, litters, splint baskets and other hospital items helped the situation. Yet there continued to be a critical shortage of bed clothing, litters, penicillin, surgical instruments and surgeons.

The losses of the first day of battle had not, however, put any unusual stress on the medical facilities. But later in the fight when Bastogne became encircled, many of the wounded would have to lie on concrete floors with little or no cover. The blankets of the dead were collected so that there would be a chance for the living, and the shattered homes of Bastogne were searched for any kind of quilting.

*Lt. Charles S. Phalen, a litter officer of the 326th Medical Company who served in the makeshift Bastogne hospital, recorded the effect of the siege on the medical service.

The 501st Regiment aid station, which was occupying a stone church in Bastogne, was made the central collecting point . . . The casualties continued to come in while none could be taken out. The wounded were laid in rows along the floor of the church with barely enough room left between them for aid men to walk. To one side, in front of an altar in an alcove, two battalion surgeons worked steadily, hour after hour, under the silent gaze of the Blessed Virgin.

A new collecting point was imperative, both because of the overcrowding and the fact that the church was located near one of the main intersections and was under intermittent artillery fire. Already two ambulances and two jeeps had been disabled in the courtyard.

To fill this new need a building formerly used as a maintenance garage by the Belgian Army was taken over. The larger room, originally intended for vehicular storage, was set aside for casualties, while the former tool storage room was designated as surgery. In charge of the new installation was Major Wisely, the regimental surgeon of the 327th Glider Infantry, and under him were the battalion surgeons from the antiaircraft and artillery units. These few were divided into shifts for twenty-four-hour duty . . .

In the main room the wounded were laid in rows on sawdust covered with blankets. Each row had a shift of aid men and an attempt was made to segregate incoming cases into specified rows depending upon the seriousness of their wounds. Over against the back wall were laid the ones who would not recover. As they died they were carried out to another building where an impromptu Graves Registration Office was functioning . . .

With the coming of the snowstorms and cold weather, the trench-foot cases presented a new problem. Another building was set aside for this type of disability. The men were laid in rows similar to the other stations and covered from neck to ankles. Their feet were left bare and exposed.

Once again the collecting point was filled, so all casualties who could walk were moved to a former rifle range about fifty yards away. This sported a sand floor and the roof was open at intervals. It was not a warm place but it was the most solidly constructed building in the town. The walls and roof were composed of several feet of reinforced concrete. These compensated for the discomfort.

Despite the fact that we had found some medical supplies in an abandoned First Army depot, the shortage was becoming fairly serious by the end of the third day. Items needed most were blankets, litters, morphine, large and small Carlisles, plasma, and surgical dressing.

Nor was the eating situation too good. The staple food became pancakes for each meal, although the more seriously wounded got small portions from 45 cases of 10-in-1 ration which had been given to the collecting point by the tank destroyers.

The flour for the inevitable pancakes came from a civilian warehouse. Quite a supply of sugar was made available when an enterprising aid man spent afternoons pounding on cellar walls, searching for hidden loot. A hollow sound was investigated and produced a sealed room containing bags of sugar, some coffee, and an American carbine.

With the change in the weather came the C-47s with the aerial resupply . . . The bundles were picked up by every unit who could spare a truck or jeep and then broken down according to their content. About sixty of them contained medical supplies, each bundle holding an identical quantity of Carlisles, morphine, and plasma. There were no litters or blankets.

However, the bundles themselves made up for the lack of the latter. They were made of a long strip of canvas, about ten feet long and four feet wide, and lined with heavy felt-like material. These, along with the chutes, were very warm.

Most of the fighting occurred in the small perimeter towns surrounding Bastogne. The only units in the town were the various headquarters, supply, and medical units.

The battalion aid stations were set up in the usual manner with the main section in a farmhouse or convenient building and a forward section in a timber and dirt covered foxhole near the battalion headquarters. Usually each battalion had two medical jeeps—one forward and one back. As the battle proceeded many of them were reduced to one jeep to evacuate the entire unit.

The denseness of the forests where much of the combat occurred prevented jeeps from getting near the casualties. As airborne units are not equipped with litter-bearer sections in the regiments, the strain on the aid station personnel was great. Some units solved the problem by tearing corrugated metal sheets off of the roofs of sheds and forming them into very acceptable toboggans . . . Rations varied according to the fortunes of scavenging and sometimes the diet became ludicrous. Flour was fairly plentiful so pancakes were always available. Every once in a while someone would stumble across stores of oatmeal, cartons of bonbons, and once quite a large supply of fresh grapes was located in a partially demolished store.

Each aid station had one doctor per battalion, with the exception of one or two in the glider units who were lucky enough to have two, the normal strength. Instead of the authorized ten [Medical] Administrative Corps men, there were three. What few jeeps were available often had but one driver who had no assistants to relieve him.

Christmas Eve arrived. The snow was deeper and the weather had returned to its former state of cold and cloudy skies . . . In the collecting points the wounded were staring at the same ceiling and the doctors and aid men were carrying on as usual. To break the monotony the G-4 sent over a supply of Cognac which the Division had impounded. Each man was given a shot or two.

One of the aid men had been tinkering with a civilian radio and about 2100 he got it adjusted to an AFN wave length. He turned up the volume and Bing Crosby's voice filled the room. He was singing "White Christmas."

All sound ceased and one of the MCs looked out of the operating room at the long silent rows of men and said "By God, if you saw that in a movie you'd think it was the corniest scene since Sonny Boy died."

What other entertainment was to be offered no one found out, for Charlie came over with his presents and one of the collecting points was hit by an incendiary. Everyone available spent the next hours trying to get the wounded out. Despite all efforts more than half of the litter patients were burned to death, and most of those rescued had to be treated for burns. They were transported to the upper floor of another building, as no more space was available below. Included in the death toll was a young Belgian nurse who had voluntarily stayed in the town to help care for the wounded.

Shortly before dawn of Christmas day, Charlie tried again. One of the bombs hit next to the building where the rescued men had been moved. But whoever is in charge of such things decided they had had enough. It was a dud.

The weather broke again in our favor and once more the 47s came in. This time in the medical supplies were collapsible litters. The other items were the same as before with the exception of several containers of whole blood. The whole blood was never used, however, for a shell burst in the room where it was stored. The place looked like a slaughter house.

On the sixth day Major Wisely got permission from the Division to try and evacuate the wounded through the German lines. Casualties were dying that could be saved if given adequate care and treatment. In an action of the day before, a German doctor had been captured. He had been put to work taking care of the forty or fifty enemy wounded. When told of the proposal, he agreed to accompany the regimental surgeon into the German lines in an effort to obtain permission to take the most serious casualties out. A jeep was draped with a huge bed sheet with a red cross made out of a supply chute tied over it. At noon the two went into the enemy lines.

In the afternoon a glider was dropped into Bastogne containing a volunteer surgical team. They set to work immediately. Most of the surgery consisted of amputations. Shortly after this the parley jeep returned with the word that the German commander would give his answer on the next day. The surgical team worked all of that night and on into the morning.

The answer to the evacuation request will never be known. Before the party could set out for the German lines, word came that the airborne engineers were in contact with Patton's spearhead, the famous 4th Armored. Behind the armor had come forty ambulances so there was no time to celebrate. The task of selecting the first to go out had to be accomplished.*

Col. W. L. Roberts, commanding Combat Command B, 10th Armored Division, had been at Château-Thierry in 1918 and he well remembered the things that happen during the rout of an army. In his first conversation with General Middleton in which the VIII Corps commander had outlined the missions that sent the three combat teams of Combat Command B to Wardin, Longvilly and Noville on the night of December 18, Colonel Roberts had foreseen one of the main problems.

General Middleton said to him, "The 28th Infantry Division and the 9th Armored are ahead of us. They are badly cut up. The situation is fluid."

Colonel Roberts replied, "Sir, there will be stragglers. I want authority to use these men."

Middleton agreed orally and later confirmed it with a written message: "Major General Middleton directs that you have authority to take over all or any part of Reserve Command, 9th Armored Division, in case they show the slightest inclination to retire. Anything you do to prevent falling back in that area will be given fullest backing."

Colonel Roberts set his net to catch those drifting back. His Headquarters Company was instructed to keep hot food ready all day at a central point in Bastogne. A detail stood by to get these men from other units into billets around the town square. MPs were stationed at the road crossings in the south of Bastogne with instructions to stop every soldier who was trying to get away from the battle and turn him back to the Combat Command B area. About 250 stragglers were thus reorganized in Bastogne on December 19. Some were men from the 9th Armored; most were from the 28th Division. In this way Team Snafu was born, and within the next week it came to include 600 men, led by casual officers; but this outfit was severely handicapped by the fact that they were short of equipment and transportation as long as the siege lasted. Team Snafu was mainly a reservoir for the defending force. The stragglers went into it; the regular units drew from it as they had need.

Any organized units heading south were also commandeered. At 1400 on December 19 the 73d Armored Field Artillery Battalion of Combat Command Reserve, 9th Armored, moved through Bastogne. Colonel Roberts watched it go by before suddenly realizing that it was his for the taking. He sent a staff officer to bring the battalion back and within a few minutes the battalion commander reported at his command post. Roberts told him to put the battalion in position with the 420th Armored Field Artillery Battalion. The commander returned to his battalion but found that there was insufficient fuel for his vehicles and could not make the return trip. The 58th Armored Field Artillery Battalion was stopped and put into position with the 420th, where its twelve guns fired during the next day. Just before the Germans closed the roads to the southward, this unit heard that it had been cut off from Bastogne so it moved to the west. The 969th Field Artillery Battalion—a Negro unit—was commandeered on December 21 and their 155mm howitzers gave body to the artillery throughout the siege. Colonel Roberts also found in Bastogne eight new undelivered tanks, complete with their Ordnance crews, and he inducted them forthwith into his organization.

Colonel Roberts had worried a lot about the security of the town itself for he had only part of his Engineer battalion and the Antiaircraft Artillery battalion as reserve. General McAuliffe wanted to keep his own reserve as mobile as possible and couldn't see assigning one of his battalions to garrison the town. A task force from Combat Command B, 9th Armored Division, entered Bastogne to learn the situation but was ordered by higher authority to withdraw to Leglise, six miles southeast of Neufchâteau. A request to 10th Armored for the use of the Reserve Command was turned down. So finally Colonel Roberts committed Team Snafu, under command of Capt. Charles Brown of 110th Infantry, to the close-in defense of Bastogne. Team Snafu's complexion was somewhat changed on the following morning, December 20, when Brig. Gen. George A. Davis of the 28th Division arrived in Bastogne with a request that Combat Command B attack toward Wiltz. It couldn't be done, for by that hour all of Colonel Roberts' forces were fully committed. Not long after General Davis departed, Combat Command B was ordered by Corps to release all 28th Division stragglers to their own command.

Throughout the first day of battle there had been losses and a few minor gains in the 101st Division's already strained supply situation. In the 907th Glider Field Artillery Battalion, Lieutenant Colonel Nelson, worried because his ammunition supply was rapidly reaching the vanishing point, dispatched searching convoys toward what he thought was the Division rear. They moved westward and had been gone about six hours before Colonel Nelson grew aware that he had actually sent his trucks into enemy ground and that they were cut off. A second convoy of five trucks and trailers was sent toward Neufchâteau under S/Sgt. Vincent Morgan, a supply sergeant. Sergeant Morgan was told that if he could not get M3 ammunition (standard for the 105mm M3, a gun especially adapted for glider use) he was to bring back some M2 ammunition which the manual said could be used in an emergency. The fortitude with which this young noncom carried out his assignment was one of the finest things of the siege. He returned late that night through heavy shelling and small-arms fire about one hour before the Germans cut the road of his inbound journey. He had first gone to Neufchâteau and on being disappointed there he had driven far to the northwestward, covering in all about 75 miles. On his trucks were 1,500 rounds of M2. It was the only resupply of ammunition received by the 101st Airborne Division before the air resupply came in.

That partly compensated for a stroke of bad luck. The two convoys of the Division Quartermaster and Ordnance companies reached the Division rear area late at night and were told to remain at a crossroads in the woods (P448630). Lacking time in which to reconnoiter the area, the two companies left all trucks parked on highway N4 facing west. Shortly after midnight on December 20, Division headquarters was notified that the service area was receiving machine-gun fire, and a few minutes later came the message "Evidence indicates service troops have disappeared."

That alarm was enough; within five minutes a message was on its way to Corps headquarters asking for Quartermaster and Ordnance help.

After being flushed by the fire the two companies had headed west and then south. Most of the trucks got through to the Corps rear and on the next day Capt. John L. Patterson of one of the units, the 801st Ordnance Maintenance Company, taking a different route, got into Bastogne with two trucks bringing 500 gallons of gasoline. He then turned south again to bring the rest of the convoy forward. But by that time the Germans had already closed the road. Such was the shortage of gasoline in Bastogne through most of the siege that vehicles were fueled only just before they went out on a run so that there would be no loss of gasoline if any standing vehicle was hit.

The Repulse

It was a night for drifters, the night of December 19-20. As the darkness grew, more men from the elements which had been shattered to the east of Bastogne came moving back through the regimental lines of the 101st. Few of them stayed. Colonel Ewell and his officers talked to these men. They could tell very little of what had happened to them. Many of them were inarticulate. Infantrymen from units of

Map 69.

the 28th Division still trickled into the area in groups of three or four. They made no attempt to organize themselves and they did not for the most part wish to be organized by anyone else. Some of these straggling infantrymen would ask Ewell's men, "What are you doing?" Upon being told, "We are fighting Germans," they would look at the paratroopers as if they were stark mad.

But not all were like that. Some who seemed utterly wretched and spent when they came to within the lines, upon being handed a K ration, would eat it and look around and ask where they could get a rifle. They were ready to fight again. But to others food and companionship made no difference. They had been shocked so badly that they wanted only to keep on drifting. They were allowed to do so. This disorder had no ill effect on the combat force. The demoralization did not seem to bother the nerves of the men who were still fighting and they accepted it as the natural product of battle it often is.

A battalion of Field Artillery, the 109th of the 28th Division, came through as a unit and attached itself to the 907th Glider Field Artillery Battalion. Those groups from the 9th Armored Division which had been compelled to withdraw from the advanced ground along the Longvilly road were in good order and high spirits when they reached the lines around Bastogne. One platoon of armored infantry attached itself to Major Homan's battalion (2d Battalion, 501st Parachute Infantry) and helped them carry the fight during the next several days. Seven tanks arrived from the 9th Armored Division and constituted themselves a small task force operating in support of the battalion. At 0200 the 2d Platoon of Company B, 705th Tank Destroyer Battalion arrived with four tank destroyers and took position on the south edge of Bizory.

These reinforcements got there in the nick of time. At 0530, December 20, while the 501st Parachute Infantry was patrolling toward its front, the 2d Battalion got an attack over the same big hill to the east of Bizory where they had been stopped by the German reconnaissance force the day before. At a range of 3,000 yards, the tank destroyer men saw six enemy tanks rolling toward them from the southeast. Sgt. Floyd A. Johnson led his section to the hill north of Bizory and put the two tank destroyers on either side of the road. 1st Lt. Frederic Mallon led the second section to the higher ground southeast of town and waited for the German tanks in an open field.

The firing opened at 0730, the tank destroyers withholding their fire from the enemy infantry so as not to compromise an engagement with the enemy armor, which by this time comprised one Mark IV, one Mark V and two 75mm self-propelled guns. These were following the infantry line by 400 yards—it was a full battalion of infantry, the 2d of the 76th Regiment, 26th Volksgrenadier Division. In the first long-range exchange of fire, one tank destroyer was disabled and its loader killed by a direct hit on the turret; it limped away to the rear. The second tank destroyer in this section, after knocking out the Mark IV tanks, pulled back into Bizory where, in taking up another position, it damaged the tube of its gun by running against a building and became incapacitated. The other tank destroyer section opened fire at 600 yards on the Mark IV tank and one self-propelled gun, destroying both.

This was the crux of the engagement: most of the in-fighting of that morning of December 20 was done by the heavy guns. Major Homan's machine guns had opened up on the German infantry while the tanks were coming on and by so doing had kept them at a distance. Within a few minutes of this first body check to the German battalion, all the artillery that General McAuliffe could turn eastward from Bastogne blasted them. Homan's infantry along the ridge was too far distant to do much bullet damage to the advancing German formations but his men had a clear view of the German ranks coming on slowly, of the automatic fire making them hesitate, of the shells falling among them, of the attack gradually spending itself and of the enemy that was left then breaking away to the northward to escape the fire.

Colonel Ewell's own infantry losses were almost nothing, but two tank destroyers were out of action for the time being and the defense had also lost two tanks. So ended the first, though not the most ruinous, of the piecemeal efforts which on this day presaged the failure of the German battle. This particular fighting had lasted about two hours, the artillery barrage perhaps twenty minutes. Prisoners-of-war letters captured from the 76th Regiment said that their losses had been terrible.

There followed a day-long wait along Colonel Ewell's 501st Parachute Infantry front. About 1900 the Germans put a heavy shelling from tanks and self-propelling guns on sensitive points over the ground held by the 501st—Bizory, Mont and the road junctions. The bombardment severed all the telephone wires connecting the battalion with the rear.

As the German artillery slacked off, the 1st Battalion of the 501st radioed to Ewell that the enemy was charging straight down the road from Neffe. Maj. Raymond V. Bottomly's 1st Battalion could hear the tanks coming on but it was so dark that they could tell little else. All the guns from the eleven artillery battalions in Bastogne dropped a dam of fire across the road one or two hundred yards west of Neffe— the heaviest and most effective American defensive fire during the siege. Three German tanks, two of them Panthers and one a Tiger Royal, were hit and destroyed just as they drew past the last houses in the village. Some German infantry, which had moved down the Bastogne road before the barrage dropped, met their fate from machine guns Company B had posted in a house by the side of the road. That company took the shock without having to yield one yard of ground. Their strongpoint controlled the terrain so well that not one German drew near enough to close on the infantry line. They were killed to the last man, and for weeks later, their grotesque forms along the roadside, heaped over by the Ardennes snows, showed where the German death march ended. The most forward of these bodies was 300 yards ahead of the shattered tanks.

The German thrust from Neffe coincided with an assault on the 3d Battalion's position at Mont, though here the battle took a quite different form because of Major Templeton's tank destroyers. The

Enemy preparing to attack the left flank of the 3d Battalion, 501st, on the night of 20 December. The American position is on the crest of the hill to the left. Mont is in the center draw. The barbed-wire fences, so costly to the enemy, are to the right of the grove of evergreens. The action was reconstructed by Artist Olin Dows.

1st Platoon of Company B, 705th Tank Destroyer Battalion, under command of 1st Lt. Robert Andrews, had arrived to reinforce Colonel Griswold's 3d Battalion position on the evening of December 19. One tank destroyer was posted at the bend in the road. From here it could cover both the dirt road winding across the valley from Neffe and a draw leading off to the southward. A second tank destroyer took position by the last house, which put it somewhat behind, but in line with, the tank destroyer blocking the Neffe road. The other section was placed on the north side of Mont to check any tank advance from directly across the valley. The tank destroyers held these positions until the hour came when they were most needed, on the night of December 20.

Between 1900 and 1930 on that night the enemy struck through the fields lying between Neffe and Mont, advancing against Colonel Griswold's left. But the presence of the tank destroyers had intimidated the German armor. It took refuge in the little wood lying just west of the Neffe château and from the grove it shelled Mont. The German infantry advanced under this fire. Enemy self-propelled guns moved along the railway line from Neffe a short distance (the rails here ran through a cut) and went to work on the same target. These two lines of fire converged on Griswold's positions at almost a right angle; the men in the forward line had to give ground, falling back on the village. The most forward of the tank destroyers, commanded by Sgt. George N. Schmidt, became their rallying point. Schmidt unloaded most of his crew and told them to join the fight with small arms. He then joined the infantry machine gunners who were already searching the down slopes with every automatic gun the Battalion could bring to bear; in the next few minutes he threw 2,000 rounds of caliber .50 at the enemy. Lieutenant Andrews used a radio-equipped jeep as his command post and central control station, and used his security section as ammunition carriers to feed the stuff up to whichever tank destroyer was calling for it most urgently. The other three tank destroyers, under Sgt. Darrell J. Lindley, were shooting at the railway line. They tried at first to spot the self-propelled guns by firing at muzzle blasts; when that failed, they put flares up over the valley.

The fighting died about 2300. By that time, the three self-propelled guns were out, and lines of German dead littered the hillside. Because of the dark the defenders of Mont had no clear idea of why their automatic fire had made such a clean reaping of the German attack or of where the attack had broken. But in the light of the next morning, December 21, they could see what had happened. The hillside between Neffe and Mont was crossed in both directions by barbed-wire fences spaced between thirty and fifty yards apart, with five or six strands in each fence. In ordinary times they were used apparently, as feeder pens for cattle. With the tank fire behind them the Germans tried to come right through this fenced area without first destroying the fences in any way or equipping infantry to cut them. On coming to the fences they tried to climb through but the spaces were small and their individual equipment was bulky. Griswold's men had perfectly clear fields of fire and so did the tank destroyer supporting them. The fences were as effective as any entanglement. The evenly spaced lines of dead told the story. They had charged right into a giant mantrap.

Colonel Ewell had the impression that night that the 901st Panzer Regiment had about expended itself and that it could no longer muster enough men to be an effective offensive force. They had been somewhat roughly handled before they got to Neffe and his own men furthered the good work.

So on December 19 the Germans, having gained contact with the 501st Parachute Infantry on a wide front, at first drew back to defensive positions. On December 20 the enemy made three attacks and the infantry, armor and tank destroyers in Colonel Ewell's sector beat them all down. One of these fights was tactically less spectacular but strategically more useful than the others.

During the period of the fighting at Noville and Neffe there had been an action between the flanks of the 501st and 506th Parachute Infantry regiments which, although just a minor affair in itself, was to have an important effect on the general situation. When the two regiments moved out to their positions on December 19, one going east and the other going north, they could not initially form a common front. In theory they were joined somewhere along the railroad track below

Lahez (1½ miles south of Foy) but in fact there was a considerable gap between their closest elements. Each became so closely engaged in its local situation that the matter of contact was neglected. Colonel Sink was alarmed about the peril to his right flank from the beginning, but it was not until late on the night of December 19 that Colonel Ewell fully shared his apprehension.

Company A of the 501st was in reserve in a small wood just north of the quarry on the Neffe road, which made it the most rearward element in the 501st's general position. Several hundred yards to its rear were the guns of the 907th Glider Field Artillery Battalion's forward battery.

At 2300, December 19, a German patrol of thirty men came in between the company and the battery, moving from out of the northeast. A man on outpost duty for Company A saw the patrol and alerted the company. The patrol was permitted to come on. As it drew near the wood where the company had bivouacked, both the artillery and the infantry opened fire. The enemy dispersed into a nearby wood, though one member of the patrol was taken prisoner. Upon being interrogated he said that the patrol had come forward through the gap between the two infantry regiments and that its mission had been to get in behind and cut the Bastogne road. The incident gave the artillery grave fears about the security of their base and it also called Colonel Ewell's attention to the most vulnerable sector of his front.

Sometime on the morning of December 20, after the Germans had attacked at Bizory and then sideslipped northward, Company A of the 501st was attached to the 2d Battalion with the mission of occupying the woods south of the railroad and making contact with the 506th Parachute Infantry. However, it did not proceed immediately on this assignment and during most of that day the effort to join with the 506th was limited to patrol actions out of Company D, 501st, which was in reserve in the 2d Battalion. Four times during the day patrols from Company D tried to move north along the general line of the road running to Foy. But they were always turned back from the vicinity of Halt, where the enemy had taken up fire positions.

At the same time Company D, 506th Parachute Infantry, was pushing rightward toward the railroad station at Halt against stubborn resistance. When evening of the 20th came the company had reached the Foy-Bizory road. It stayed there with its right flank some hundreds of yards distant from the railroad station at Halt, which was held by an enemy force. There had been no contact with the 501st. Colonel Sink, commander of the 506th, called both Headquarters, 501st Parachute

Infantry, and Headquarters, 101st Division, and urged that the 501st swing leftward to meet him. He said that his force was standing on the railroad line which was supposed to be the regimental boundary— but this overstated the case.

The first three patrols which had gone out from Company D of the 501st to search for the 506th's flank had been turned back by fire from the Bois Jacques. They got no idea of the enemy strength in the forest area for they were beaten back by a scattering small-arms fire at long range whenever they moved to right of the Foy-Bizory road in an attempt to gain the railroad.

Corp. Frank Lasik of Company D, 501st, led out his fourth patrol of the day just as the evening twilight of the 20th came on. There were eight men with him, and instead of beating over the same ground as the earlier patrols they swung around to the westward of the Bizory-Foy road. When within a short distance of the railroad Lasik dropped six of his men and continued on with two others. They reached the rail line and moved east along it to within a hundred yards of the Halt station. At that point they saw a force of seven German tanks supported by a body of infantry moving straight toward them down the railroad track, and only 75 yards away. Private Manzi fired one shot toward the enemy force and then the three men withdrew as rapidly as they could. Lasik knew that Company A had been given an assignment and was supposed to be moving toward the same ground which the Germans were approaching. He rushed to the Battalion command post and told them to get word to Company A, 501st, that tanks were coming down the railway track.

Company A had moved out about 1600 on December 20 and was already engaged in clearing the woods that lay south of the railroad and west of the Foy-Bizory road. They found no enemy in the first wood and so they continued on to the next plantation lying south of the tracks and between them and the station at Halt. In the middle of this journey they met a patrol from the 506th Parachute Infantry. Until that meeting they had believed that the 506th was already on the railroad track. But from the patrol they learned that the actual flank of the 506th was about 600 yards north of the railroad track and that Company D, 506th, had been having a running fight with small groups of the enemy for control of the station at Halt.

From the second woods, Sgt. Lyle B. Chamberlain of Company A, 501st, was sent with a four-man patrol eastward along the tracks to search for the enemy. This was at just about the time that Lasik was getting back to warn the battalion. Sergeant Chamberlain's patrol moved through the swampy ground that lay to the left of the tracks and had gone but a short distance when they sighted a German patrol coming toward them. It looked to Chamberlain like the point of a company. Darkness was already closing around them and the German group did not see Sergeant Chamberlain's patrol. The patrol fell back on the company and reported what they had seen. Hastily, the 3d Platoon of Company A was deployed along the edge of the woods north of the railroad track to lay an ambush, for the enemy group which Sergeant Chamberlain had sighted was all northward of the track. While the platoon was deploying thick fog closed in around the woods and this coupled with the darkness reduced visibility to almost nothing. The Germans were allowed to approach within 10 to 15 yards before Company A opened fire. The surprise volley wholly disorganized the leading German platoon and the men who were not cut down ran to the rear to the swampy ground.

The whole Company A front had by this time become engaged. The enemy had been advancing with two companies abreast astride the railway track. On Company A's right, the 1st and 2d Platoons did not get the same chance to close with the enemy at short range, and after the dispersion of the German right, mortar, grenade and automatic fire from the German force south of the tracks beat heavily against the two platoons. Because of the darkness and the fog the men of the company could get no idea what losses they were taking themselves and could only judge the progress of the action by the build-up of the enemy fire. They saw little or nothing of the Germans they were engaging. The skirmish went on with both forces firing toward the flashes and sounds in the position of the opposite force. Company A lost fifteen men in the night engagements, three of whom were killed in action. But in the black darkness the men of the Company thought at the time that they were taking much heavier losses. The fog made more vivid their impressions of the opposing fire while keeping them from feeling their own strength. The murk was so thick by this time that it was only by the sounds of fire that a man could tell where his nearest comrade was fighting.

While the fire fight on the south of the tracks continued, the Germans who had fallen back toward the swampy ground on the north of the track gradually collected themselves again. For half an hour or more there was a lull in the action on this side except that both forces tried to carry on at long range with hand grenades. Then the 3d Platoon of Company A heard the enemy moving out through the woods around their left flank.

Apprehensive that they would be outflanked if they maintained themselves in the forward ground, the 3d Platoon pulled back its own left flank to the westward so as to cover the rear of the company position. This change in the form of the enemy attack was also indicated on the right flank. Pfc. William C. Michel, a German-speaking soldier who was with the company executive officer, Lt. Joseph B. Schweiker, could hear the enemy shouting commands and telling his men to move out around the left and right of the American force. The order may have been a ruse intended to cover a withdrawal, but as the fire fight began to build up again it seemed to Lieutenant Schweiker that the enemy was actively pushing out around the flanks of Company A and threatening his rear.

At about 2230, December 20, Lieutenant Schweiker ordered the company to fall back to the line of the second woods. Lt. James C. Murphy called all of the squad leaders together and told them that the signal for withdrawal would be a long burst of machine-gun fire and that all of the other machine guns were to be kept quiet until this signal came. The withdrawal was made in reasonably good order, the circumstances considered.

When Company A took up its position in the second wood it was deployed to right of the railway line. The company was not pressed there at any time during the night. Apparently the Germans had ordered a withdrawal at about the same time. After staying in the woods for somewhat more than an hour the company withdrew a little to the southward and bivouacked in a third plantation.

The advance of the enemy down the railroad track had put them on the rear of Company D, 506th Parachute Infantry, but it was not until 0400 that Company D, which was somewhat engaged by small groups hitting directly at its front, discovered that its flank had been turned. Lieutenant Colonel Strayer reported to Colonel Sink that he believed an enemy force of about two platoons had penetrated between his battalion of the 506th and the 501st. But he did not know that Company D, 501st, was meeting this force frontally. Colonel Sink ordered Company D, 506th, to face some of its men toward the rear and hold their present ground. This they did. The 1st Battalion, 506th, then in reserve at Luzery, was ordered to send Companies A and C forward to help contain the penetrating force. Both of these companies were badly depleted from the fight in Noville.

When morning of December 21 came the situation was about as follows: Company A, 501st, which had not been further disturbed during its bivouac, moved back up without opposition to exactly the same positions it had occupied during the night engagement. Company D, 501st, which had bivouacked just to the south of Company A's bivouac area under the mistaken impression that it had moved into the woods lying south of the railroad tracks, discovered its error when the light came. It immediately moved farther north, with one platoon going directly toward the objective woods and the others detouring east to clean out another small wood which they thought might contain enemy forces.

Through the accident of these shifts, the 501st Parachute Infantry thus had forces advancing from west, southwest and south as if to bring about a general envelopment of the German force at the Halt station. Coinciding with these movements from the south and west the two reserve companies (A and C) of the 506th reached the area to the north- ward at about 0815 and were committed in companies abreast to beat through the forests lying south and west of Company D's position. The morning of the 21st was heavy with fog; none of these approaching forces moving in on them from northeast, north, west, southwest and south was visible to the Germans dug in around the Halt station and in some of the plantations to westward of it. They were so completely misled as to their own position that when the platoons that had marched east for Company D, 501st, started their sweep north toward the Halt station, several of the enemy glimpsed them through the fog and came walking up to meet them, thinking they were friendly troops.

The line of the 506th came slowly but methodically on toward the railway tracks. Some of the Germans stayed to fight. Others gave up. Still others, in trying to get away were forced back into the killing ground established by the semicircular advance of the different forces of the 501st. By about 1100, December 21, the envelopment was com- plete and Companies A and C of the 506th had made full contact with units of the 501st along the railway line. The two companies were then ordered to return to Luzery, leaving Company D to solidify the front.

But in moving south and westward through the forest Companies A and C, 506th, discovered that the job was by no means completed. The morning advance had forced many of the enemy into the woods to the westward beyond the lines of Company A, 501st Parachute Infantry. The rat hunting continued throughout the day and it was almost dark before the 506th was convinced that the mop-up operation was complete. By that time it was realized that the original estimate of two platoons of enemy—these were troops of the 77th Volksgrenadier Regiment of the 26th Volksgrenadier Division—had far undershot the mark. The Ger- man force was more nearly the size of a battalion. About 100 of the enemy were captured and 55 killed by the units of the 506th Parachute

Infantry in an operation that cost them only five or six casualties. About 80 Germans were driven into 501st's sector, where they were either killed or captured. Later, when the whole battle could be reviewed clearly, the senior commanders of 101st reckoned that the enemy missed his finest opportunity on this ground and during these hours. A strongly weighted attack straight down the railroad track could have carried through to Bastogne and turned the flanks of 501st and 506th Regiments.

With the end of this engagement on December 21, the sectors of both the 501st and 506th became relatively quiet until after January 1. But there were other important consequences. Firm contact had been established between the two regiments, and it was never broken or weakened after that time. The Germans were served notice that the road to Bastogne from the east and north was not open.

Out of these things also developed a new feeling of confidence among the artillery in the Bastogne area. They were now fully covered on the north and east by a reasonably strong shield and they could more easily direct their attention to the other parts of the defensive circle, wherever the danger mounted.

From December 21 on, the Germans gave over their attack against the 501st Parachute Infantry's part of the Bastogne front. The road to Bastogne did not lie through Colonel Ewell and his 501st.

Running Battle

In Noville they were running short of armor-piercing shell as the morning of December 20 dawned. In Bastogne, General McAuliffe was wondering whether Noville was worth what he might have to pay to hold it, and was about to reach a decision. Deprived of any support from the commanding ridges, Noville is not a military position but just another village on low ground, and a perfect sinkhole for fog. The issue was already hanging in the balance because of the ammunition situation and the miscarriage of the American attack on December 19; only a little more pressure would tip it.

On left flank of the 506th Parachute Infantry, the 502d had passed a quiet night. In midafternoon of December 19 the 502d had moved to Longchamps and established a perimeter defense there. Its 3d Battalion deployed on a high hill to south of the village. Its 1st Battalion was in the Bois de Niblamont which was southward of the hill. Initially, the 1st Battalion had held half of the front, but at 2400 of the 19th General McAuliffe told Lt. Colonel Steve Chappuis, commander of the 502d Parachute Infantry, that inasmuch as his regiment was the Division reserve he could leave one battalion on the northward-facing line. The 2d Battalion drew the assignment. It made no difference in any case, for though the battalion was stretched seven thousand yards, there was no action anywhere along its front that night.

But to the eastward where 506th stood guard, the boys who had prayed for morning soon wondered why. At 0730 two enemy tanks came hell-roaring through the field along the Houffalize road, swung in beside the first building of Noville, wheeled so as to protect each other and then stopped. On their way in they had knocked out a jeep with one shell, and had sprayed forward with their machine guns as they rushed. Unseeing, they came to a halt within ten yards of a bazooka team and the first rocket fired set one of the tanks on fire. S/Sgt. Michael Lesniak, a tank commander, had heard the German armor roaring along. He dismounted from his tank, walked up the main street for a look, then went back and swung his gun in the right direction and moved to the center of the street. He fired before the enemy realized that he had gone into action and his first round finished the German tank. A third German tank that stayed just north along the road but out of sight in the fog threw a few loose shells into the town and one of them hit Sergeant Lesniak's tank, damaging the turret.

That was the beginning. Almost nothing that followed could be seen as clearly. During the next two hours the defensive perimeter was under constant attack from the German armor and infantry. But the enemy pressure developed quite unevenly as if their forces, too, were groping or were keeping active simply to conceal some larger design. It was battle with the bewildering shifts of a montage; there were momentary exposures and quick shiftings of scene. The enemy came on in groups of a few tanks supported by small parties of infantry and were held off by the armored infantry and paratroopers with their own weapons just long enough to let a friendly tank or tank destroyer get into firing position. Fog mixed with smoke from the burning buildings again mantled the country between the village and the ridges, diffusing the efforts of both forces. It was all but impossible for anyone to get any impression of how the tide was moving; the combatants could tell only what went on right before their eyes.

Curiously enough the tank destroyer men of 2d Platoon, Company C, 705th TD Battalion, who had taken position in the south of Noville, had the impression that in these early morning hours the infantry was standing off a full-fledged attack. They could see only a hundred yards beyond their own guns and they could hear large numbers of enemy tracked vehicles moving toward them through the fog. Their imaginings were further stimulated by a direct hit on one tank destroyer at the outset which killed the gunner, Corp. Stephen Cook, and wounded several of the crew. For two hours they fired in the general direction of where they thought the German armor was massing; they could see no targets but they thought their unobserved fire might have some deterring effect. At 1000, December 20, the fog quite suddenly lifted and the sky became almost clear. In the field within view of the tank destroyer force were 15 German tanks; they were proceeding toward their own lines at about 1,000 yards range. Four of the tanks were hit and disabled and the tank destroyer men were confident that their own shells did it. They had seen their shots hit home and watched Pvt. Steve E. Reed empty seven boxes of caliber .50 ammunition into the German crews as they tried to flee across the fields.

Just before the fog had cleared a Tiger tank had charged right into the heart of Noville. Visibility among the buildings was just about zero. The tank stopped in front of the command post of Company B, 20th Armored Infantry Battalion. The tanker swung his gun uncertainly toward the door. Capt. Omar Billett said a quick prayer. A joker beside him remarked, "Don't look now, but there is an 88 pointing at you."

Sergeant Lesniak's tank was within twenty yards but the German had failed to see him in the fog; by rotating his damaged turret just a short space to the right Lesniak had his gun dead on the Tiger. At twenty yards he fired three rounds of 75mm. at the German tank without doing any apparent damage. The German quickly put his tank into reverse. But the left track ran up and over a jeep. The jeep was completely crushed but at the same time it fouled the track and beached the tank. The German kept on pushing back—the jeep under him. He next collided with a half track and the tank tipped dangerously over on its right side. That was enough for the German crew. They jumped from the tank and ran out of the town, going through the American lines without getting a shot fired at them, such was the thickness of the fog.

The radio inside the Tiger was on a busy channel, and talk flowed on inside the dead tank. It looked like a wide-open opportunity, but before the command post could round up anyone who could understand German, the channel went out. The tankers destroyed this Tiger with thermite and later on they caught hell from Colonel Roberts for not bringing the tank back to Bastogne. But they had a good excuse. The losses among the tank drivers were already such that they did not have enough men to maneuver their own armor. Two tanks were without drivers and partly without crews. So the tankers asked the paratroopers

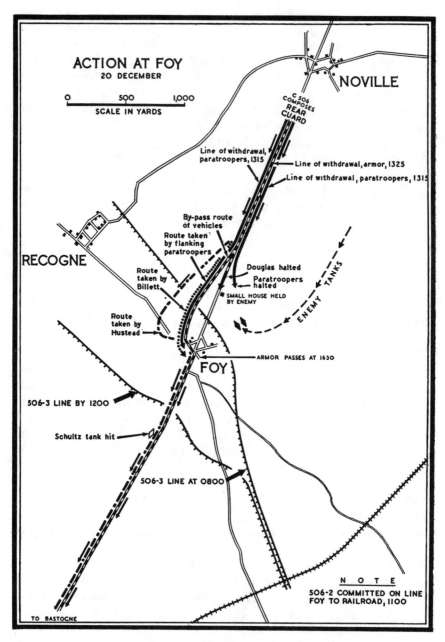

ACTION AT FOY
20 DECEMBER

SCALE IN YARDS
0   500   1,000

NOVILLE

C 506
COMPOSES
REAR
GUARD

Line of withdrawal,
paratroopers, 1315

Line of withdrawal, armor, 1325

Line of withdrawal, paratroopers, 1315

By-pass route
of vehicles

Route taken
by flanking
paratroopers

RECOGNE

Route
taken by
Billett

Douglas halted

Paratroopers
halted

SMALL HOUSE HELD
BY ENEMY

ENEMY TANKS

Route
taken by
Hustead

ARMOR PASSES AT 1630

FOY

506-3 LINE BY 1200

Schultz tank hit

506-3 LINE AT 0800

NOTE
506-2 COMMITTED ON LINE
FOY TO RAILROAD, 1100

TO BASTOGNE

Map 70.

if there were any men among them who could handle tanks and two of Major Harwick's men of the 1st Battalion, 506th Parachute Infantry, climbed aboard and started out with the Shermans. Later on both men were killed in their tanks during the withdrawal.

They knew now that they would not be able to hold Noville much longer. The clearing of the fog revealed to Major Hustead (now commanding the 20th Armored Infantry Battalion) and his staff a situation they had already suspected. During the night of the 19th the men on the outposts had heard enemy armor moving across their rear, particularly to the southwestward. In the morning, patrols had gone out, and although they couldn't tell much because of the enveloping fog, they found enough to confirm the fact that enemy forces were between them and Bastogne. Hustead had lost radio contact with Combat Command B Headquarters during the night. So in the morning he sent 1st Lt. Herman C. Jacobs to Foy; he was to get to Headquarters, 3d Battalion, 506th Parachute Infantry, in Foy and use their radio to inform Combat Command B of the situation and request that the Noville garrison either be withdrawn or reinforced. He carried out the mission in a half-track and several times on the way to Foy he blundered into enemy parties and had to shoot his way through. But at Foy he found no one; by this time 3d Battalion was engaging the enemy to the south of the village. Lieutenant Jacobs continued on to Bastogne and found Colonel Roberts who sent his only available reserve—an antiaircraft platoon—forward. But the platoon was blocked by enemy forces before it could get to Foy. The Germans were coming across the road from both sides. When the fog rolled away the men in Noville could look southward and see the circling armor. To make their isolation more complete, they had lost all contact with the main body of 506th Parachute Infantry and they did not know whether the situation at Foy was developing for or against them.

The Germans had already made their onfall against Colonel Sink's support position. In early morning, December 20, the 3d Battalion of the 506th received light shelling and flat-trajectory fire along its lines at Foy. During the night and through the first hours of daylight the enemy had taken advantage of the heavy fog and moved in very close to the American outposts, though it seems probable that they knew very little about the location of the U. S. lines and were groping.

At 0800, December 20, a force of about two companies of infantry supported by three tanks attacked toward the ground defended by Companies I and H. By 0900, they had driven in far enough to put direct fire on the American positions with their supporting weapons. The tank destroyers of 3d Platoon, Reconnaissance Company of the 705th Tank Destroyer Battalion were not in position to give the infantry any direct fire support during the engagement. They were in the woods south of Foy when the attack came on, and in the later stages of the action they were established as roadblocks, but during that morning they did not fire on any enemy armor. Company G in Recogne was engaged by another company of German infantry supported by three tanks. The command post of the 3d Battalion in Foy came under direct fire from an enemy tank. Until 1030 the Battalion held its ground in Foy and then withdrew to the high ground south of the village. Here it reformed for the counterattack.

It was about mid-morning when 101st Airborne Division Headquarters called the 502d Parachute Infantry and directed that its 3d Battalion (under Lt. Col. John P. Stopka) attack through Recogne and gain contact with the American force at Noville, thus reestablishing the left flank. The battalion crossed the line of departure at 1130 and then pushed right on, meeting little opposition.

But when the 3d Battalion, 502d, reached Recogne a change in the order came. At somewhere around noon General McAuliffe had decided that Noville wasn't important enough to warrant a last-ditch stand on the inferior ground around the village. Colonel Stopka was accordingly instructed to make a limited attack forward to cover the extrication of Major Harwick's men of the 3d Battalion, 506th. That battalion was to fight the same kind of action on the other flank. It was figured that the Noville force could sideslip into the area of the 502d once Stopka's battalion got up to it. However, his Battalion had fought its way only a short distance past Recogne when the plan was again changed.

Colonel Sink, commanding the 506th, had looked the situation over and decided that the best way out was for Major Harwick's force to retire down the Bastogne road. Colonel Stopka's battalion remained in position on a line running through Recogne with its left flank extended westward to join the 2d Battalion of the 502d. Its advance had been made wholly without artillery support because of the dense fog.

Radio communication between Bastogne and Noville was not reestablished until 1300. The order then came through on the artillery radio net to Harwick and Hustead that their command would withdraw to the Bastogne perimeter of defense. They were told that an attack on Foy was being made immediately to relieve the pressure on Noville. When they saw that the attention of the enemy was diverted to the Foy attack, they were to make a break for the south.

A few local problems had to be solved in Noville preceding the with-drawal. A considerable amount of ammunition had to be destroyed. There were more than fifty wounded men waiting evacuation. But the shrinkage of manpower in the Noville force through battlefield deaths and casualties already evacuated had totalled so many men that, despite a steady loss in vehicles, there were enough tanks, half-tracks and trucks left to move back all the casualties and permit all the armored units and most of the paratroopers to ride out of Noville.

Company C of the 506th was already south of Noville in a reserve po-sition, and accordingly, it was nominated as the advance guard to move out on foot. Three tanks would support Company C. The half-tracks and jeeps loaded with the wounded would come next in the column. Then would follow the main body, the personnel carriers and armor. Those of the infantry who couldn't find a ride would move out in file on both sides of the road. Company B of the 506th was to be the rear guard, supported by four tank destroyers. One platoon from that com-pany was detailed to destroy everything useful that could not be evacuated.

At 1315, December 20, Company C took off. At 1325 the first vehicles quit Noville. Major Hustead and his engineer officer had prepared the ammunition dump for demolition; the dump was alongside a building and they were hopeful that the blast would lay the building low and block the highway. Hustead waited until the last vehicle had passed the ammunition point. He then gave the engineer the signal to set off the delayed charge. They heard the explosion as they moved on down the road.

The start was good. Until 1300 the air had been crystal clear for most of the noon hour. Then, as if Providence again chose to intervene in their favor, the fog closed around them and screened their departure from the enemy. They knew that they could be heard and they won-dered whether the Germans would try to take them in flank while they were on the move. But the fire which might have been turned against the road was spared them and they moved along quite easily, except for an occasional flurry of bullets.

A little protecting belt of armor—one armored M8, followed by four half-tracks and five medium tanks—moved in front of the vehicles con-taining the wounded. Just beyond the village, one of the tanks broke down and had to be destroyed with thermite. The armored car took off at full speed without waiting for the others, and got to Bastogne without receiving any fire. The column continued on toward Foy and the half-tracks had come abreast of a farmhouse within 500 yards of the village when occurred one of those chance things which may change the whole course of a battle despite their own intrinsic unimportance.

In the leading half-track the shutter dropped and the driver could not see. The driver raised up and moved his arm to adjust the shutter and Maj. James B. Duncan mistook the gesture and thought that the man had been wounded and was holding his eyes. So Duncan quickly pulled the hand brake. That stopped the entire column. The first half-track was rammed from behind by the second half-track which had lost its brakes. The third half-track pulled up close. At that moment bullets and grenades bit into the column from both sides of the road. The men could not see clearly what they were fighting but they knew that some Germans were deployed in the ditches and that they were also drawing fire from the house. Major Duncan figured that he had to fight it out on that ground. The machine gunners in the half-tracks put heavy fire on the ditches; and the dismounted riflemen, after flattening themselves, blazed away with their tommy guns. In ten minutes the skirmish was over. Some of the enemy had been cut down. Others had dispersed into the fog.

The fourth half-track had withdrawn a short distance to keep from jamming the column. Major Duncan had gone back that way. The amount of firing that he could hear from forward among the half-tracks, mingled with the noise of the firing of the 3d Battalion, 506th, which was attacking north toward Foy, gave Duncan an exaggerated idea of the importance of the action. He asked for the tanks to get forward and fire on the house.

Meanwhile the three half-tracks had shoved on. Back through the column all men had dismounted and taken to the ditches. Major Hustead came forward to see what was blocking the road and he met Major Duncan near the head of the column. Both officers then tried to get the tanks moving again. The crew of the first tank told Major Hustead they had no ammunition. The second tank couldn't fire either; there was no ammunition for the big gun and the machine gun was jammed. Duncan prodded two of the tanks into carrying out the order and they shelled the house until it caught fire. Thereupon, they backed away. Duncan was still worrying because he could hear small-arms fire, so he ordered them to go in. As they moved away they were caught broadside by fire from three German tanks which had slipped through the fog from the eastward. The first American tank caught fire. In the second American tank the driver was hit and the tank came to a halt.

Because of the murk, men who were only a few yards back in the column could get no true idea of what was happening. Capt. William

G. Schultz, the tank commander, was in the fifth tank. He walked up to the third tank, which was short of personnel, and drove it on down the road past the two disabled tanks. They were beyond his help and he thought that if he kept moving, the rest of the column would follow.

But in this he was mistaken. He drove through Foy alone and about a quarter-mile beyond the village his tank was hit by a shell from an enemy tank and disabled, but Captain Schultz and his men got out alive and walked on into Bastogne. Meanwhile, Major Hustead and Captain Billett were striving to get the column moving. A tank destroyer of the 705th TD Battalion whipped up from the rear of the column to try to get a line on the yet unseen German tanks. A Sherman tank from the forward group backed straight toward the tank destroyer and the tank destroyer, reversing direction to save itself, backed over and crushed a jeep. Then the Sherman moved on up to have another go at the house and it was hit by a shell from a German tank and exploded in flames. The turret blew off into the road and blocked the passage. The driver of the fifth tank, who had been with Schultz, had moved up and taken over the second tank just before it was demolished. This left the fifth tank driverless. As the road was now blocked by the turret, Hustead and Billett moved back and forth among the tankers looking for a driver so they could start the column moving across the field to Foy. There was not a single response. Every tanker replied that he was qualified for some other kind of work but couldn't move a tank. The paratroopers and the armored infantry jumped to the conclusion that the men were dogging it. They walked among the tankers cursing them and calling them "yellow bastards"; they threatened to beat up one man whom they suspected of being a driver. But they were all wrong about it. Most of these men were new replacements. Some were cooks, some were mechanics and some were riflemen. They were tankers only in that they belonged to a tank organization. The impasse at Foy could only be charged to the replacement system.

The paratroopers farther back along the road had picked themselves up and moved out through the fields on both sides. The group on the right swept all the way to Foy, met no organized resistance but bagged a few Germans whom they found wandering around in the fog. The tank destroyer force at the rear also became restive and at 1430 1st Lt. Tom E. Toms led his vehicles down a little stream line on the right of the road and by way of this defilade entered Foy from the west. He had gotten there in ten minutes. The paratroopers who had swung out to the right reached the village at the same time. The tank destroyers were not quite through for the day.

The foot troops who had swung out to the east of the road were stopped by the line of fire which the unseen German tanks were throwing at the Shermans at the front of the column. They sent word back to the main body. However, the danger was removed by help from an unexpected quarter. Pfc. Thomas E. Gallagher was driving one of the tank destroyers which had gone into Foy and was on his way to an assembly area in a woods south of the village when he was stopped by an officer of the 3d Battalion, 506th Parachute Infantry. He knew the location of the German tanks and told Gallagher to go after them. Gallagher said he had no crew and no one to work the gun. Two paratroopers climbed into the tank destroyer and took over the gun. Gallagher then moved forward and with the infantrymen doing the firing the tank destroyer engaged one tank at 200 yards range and destroyed it. The other German tank escaped over the hill.

Because of the fog Major Hustead and Captain Billett hadn't seen the infantry parties move out to right and left. Billett felt that he ought to clear a route for the tanks and vehicles to advance and he sent back for his outfit, Company B of the 20th Armored Infantry Battalion. One platoon stayed back in the column with the vehicles and he started out with the other two platoons moving through the fields to the right. Major Hustead had the same idea but didn't know that it had already been put into execution twice on this same flank. He gathered about 20 paratroopers together and made an additional hook to the right. The odd part of it was that although this party groped its way forward over the same ground as the others, they did so in time to reap part of the harvest. The enemy groups around Foy were now feeling the heat from both directions. Hustead's sweep toward Foy resulted in the capture of 43 Germans.

In the village Hustead met troops of the 3d Battalion, 506th, who had advanced from the south and he asked them, "Has our armor come through?"

The men had seen the three half-tracks and Captain Schultz's tank go by and they thought this was the armor Major Hustead was talking about. So they reassured him. Hustead borrowed a jeep and drove to Bastogne to report to Colonel Roberts that he had completed his mission. But when he got to town he learned that he was mistaken and could only tell Colonel Roberts that the column was on its way and should soon arrive.

Major Hustead in Bastogne and Captain Billett in Foy were both on the radio urging the column to come around to the right. But Major Duncan and Second Lieutenant Burleigh P. Oxford were already jockeying the column through the fields. The fifth tank was on its way. A crew of paratroopers had climbed aboard after telling the tankers, "We'll learn how to run the son of a bitch." When the column drew into Foy some of the vehicles got stuck in the soft ground. Lieutenant Oxford dismounted all of the men and got the winches and the manpower working first of all on extricating the vehicles that contained the wounded. At dusk of December 20 the column was finding its way through Foy and past the lines of the 3d Battalion, 506th. The command in Bastogne had intended that the force would go into a defensive position on the high ground south of Foy. But Hustead told Colonel Roberts that the column was dead beat and had better be brought into Bastogne. The tank destroyers under Lieutenant Toms stayed in Foy supporting the 3d Battalion.

Team Desobry had gone to Noville with fifteen tanks; it limped back with only four. The 1st Battalion of the 506th Parachute Infantry was in full strength when it went to Team Desobry's support. It lost 13 officers and 199 enlisted men at Noville. By their combined efforts they had destroyed or badly crippled somewhere between twenty and thirty known enemy tanks of all types including not less than three Mark VIs. They probably damaged or destroyed many more. Headquarters of the 506th estimated that the assaults of the German infantry had cost the enemy the equivalent of half a regiment.

Yet all of these material measurements of what had been achieved were mean and meager weighed against the fact that the men of Noville had held their ground for a decisive 48 hours during which time the defense of Bastogne had opportunity to organize and grow confident of its own strength.

First Action at Marvie

At 0645 on December 20, the enemy shelled Team O'Hara's roadblock on the Wiltz–Bastogne road about 1,300 yards east of Marvie. The fog was thick and little could be seen of the enemy's movements out along the road. But as the light grew, the tankers could hear enemy armor moving somewhere in the fog up beyond the block. At around 0900 the fog lifted a little and they saw a dozen German soldiers trying to break up the block. A concentration from the 420th Field Artillery Battalion caught this group while they were tugging away at the felled logs. Two were killed (they were later identified as part of an engineer working party) and the others fled the fire. The enemy then put smoke on the roadblock—enough to conceal the block and the terrain right around it. Figuring that an infantry attack might be coming, Team O'Hara covered the block with fire from mortars and assault guns. It is believed that this fire fended off the thrust toward Colonel O'Hara's front and deflected it toward Marvie, where five of O'Hara's light tanks had taken up position the night before.

In the meantime Col. Joseph H. Harper, commanding the 327th Glider Infantry, had been getting acquainted with Colonel O'Hara. The 327th had taken over the command post at Mande-St. Étienne at 1500 on December 19, and at 1630 its 1st Battalion had been attached to Colonel Ewell's 501st Parachute Infantry to support his right flank. At 0400 on the 20th the 327th command post and the 2d Battalion of that regiment were ordered into Bastogne and at 0600 they marched on into the town. Without a pause, the 2d Battalion, 327th, moved straight 'on to Marvie and took over that village from the 326th Engineers. The 3d Battalion remained in Flamizoulle (some 2,000 yards east of Flamierge) and established its command post in the woods at (494610).

The 2d Battalion entered Marvie just about as the enemy first opened fire on Team O'Hara's roadblock. Colonel Harper had been told by Division that the reconnaissance group of light tanks would be in support of his 2d Battalion. Going straight away to see Colonel O'Hara, he said to him, "I've been told to hold this sector. I understand from Division that you are in support of me and I would like to go on a reconnaissance."

O'Hara said, "Let's get started." With them when they went out was Lt. Col. Roy L. Inman, commanding the 2d Battalion, 327th Glider Infantry. The officers discussed the relationship of their respective forces as they made the reconnaissance. Under the existing arrangement, Colonel O'Hara's force was not under Colonel Harper's command, for the armored force was still not attached to the 101st Division but was in support only. Colonel Inman had moved his 2d Battalion, 327th, in on the right flank of Colonel O'Hara's force with his line so extended as to secure the village and then bending southwestward to the main road just above Remoifosse. This was a distance of about 2,500 yards. The Engineers had three outposts distributed over this southeastern facing arc and none of them had as yet been engaged. It was agreed that Colonel O'Hara would be responsible for the defense of his immediate front and that Colonel Inman, who would take over from the Engineers immediately, would be responsible for the sector to right of O'Hara's. Harper then left Inman and drove down the main road toward Remoifosse. He established the southwestward extension of his line on the forward slope of the hill over which the main road passes a little more than half way from Bastogne to Remoifosse. The position thus chosen was a few hundred yards north of where the original Engineer outpost had been.

After looking over the situation and making sure that his men were where he wanted them, Colonel Harper drove back to Marvie. The jeep reached the road intersection just west of Marvie. There Harper stopped for a moment and debated with himself whether to go on into the village or take the west-running road and have a quick look at the high ground above the village. He decided in favor of taking a look and the jeep moved on up the hill.

At 1125, December 20, Colonel Inman's command post in Marvie (2d Battalion, 327th Glider Infantry) reported to Colonel O'Hara that they were receiving a great deal of shelling and that they could see enemy tanks coming toward them. This movement had already been observed from within O'Hara's sector. Yet Harper, driving up the hill at the very moment of the attack, was unaware that anything untoward was breaking until he got to the crest of the hill. There he turned about and saw the enemy guns blazing from the edge of the woods directly southeast of Marvie and their point-blank fire hitting among the houses of the village.

Harper could see that the fire came from tanks within the wood but he could not be certain how many. The barrage was followed immediately by an advance out of the woods by four enemy tanks and six half-tracks. They were well spread out and they advanced slowly, firing as they came, apparently drawn on by the prospect of an easy success over the light tanks. These tanks kept dodging in and out among the buildings and the enemy fire appeared to follow their movements closely. The light tanks replied futilely with their 37mm guns and the enemy armor appeared to come on more boldly. Feeling that the presence of his unit, rather than helping Colonel Inman's men, was drawing more high-velocity fire into the town, the light tank commander asked Colonel O'Hara for permission to withdraw. It was granted. By then, one of the light tanks had been set afire by a shell burst; a second had been hit in the suspension system but could make its escape by backing up the hill.

Yet Colonel Harper did not know all of these things. He saw the tanks quit the village and concluded that they had been routed and were deserting his infantry.

Up on the hill behind Marvie, Colonel O'Hara's larger guns kept silent. In front of the oncoming armor a German self-propelled 75mm

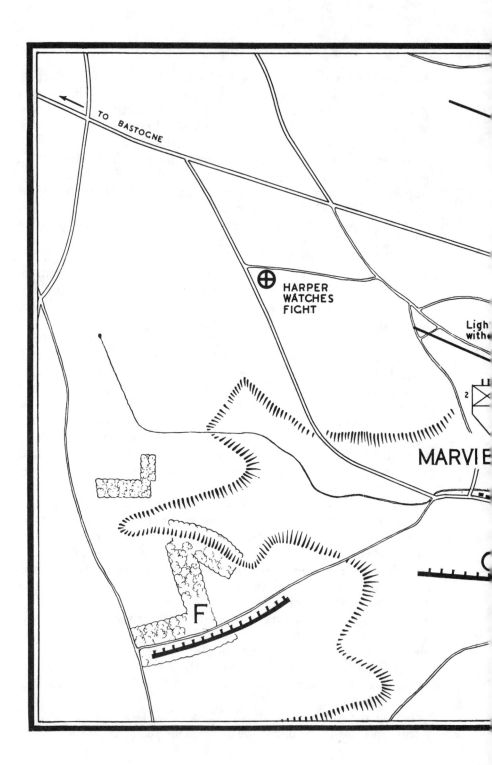

TO BASTOGNE

⊕ HARPER
WATCHES
FIGHT

Ligh
with

MARVI E

F

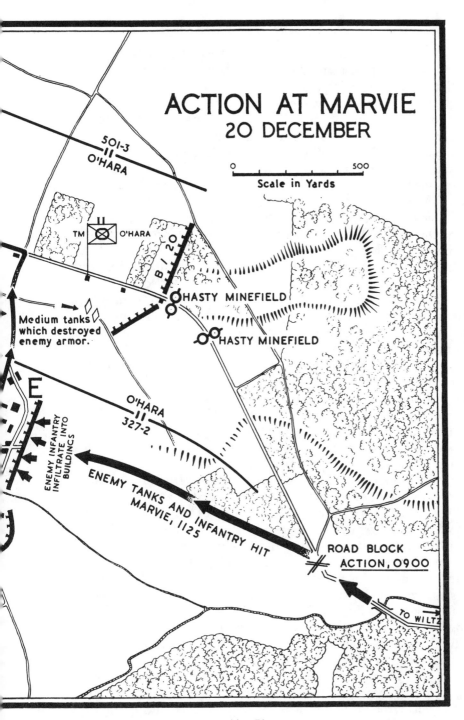

ACTION AT MARVIE
20 DECEMBER

Map 71.

gun was pacing the advance. Its gunner spotted a half-track near O'Hara's command post and fired several quick rounds at it. The shells hit an Engineer jeep, demolished a one-ton trailer and blew through the lower portion of the command post, killing a cow. The command post was in the first floor of the house and this fire was hitting into the basement right under the headquarters.

The tanks were by now almost broadside to Team O'Hara at 700 yards range. Firing at right angles to their own front, two of Team O'Hara's medium tanks opened up on the line of Mark IVs and half-tracks. The Germans never saw what hit them for they were still shooting at the light tanks now pulling out through the end of the village. One Mark IV was blown up by a direct hit from one of the mediums. The other Sherman knocked out a second Mark IV and one of the half-tracks, the fire killing all of the tank crew and most of the men in the personnel carrier. One German tank fled to the rear. The fourth tank dashed for Marvie where the infantry destroyed it with bazooka fire. The self-propelled gun, having gotten almost into the village before the Sherman opened fire, tried to turn about. It was hit from all sides and it went up like a torch.

In the last stage of the German advance, the half-tracks had sped forward and increased their interval so that they were almost closing on the first houses when the tank line was destroyed. They kept going. They got to the streets of the village and the infantry jumped down. With one small exception the glider troops stayed right where they were and met the German on-fall without flinching. The attack had come just as the relief of the Engineer units had been completed, and some of the Engineers were moving out of the north end of Marvie. Men from Inman's heavy mortar section, stationed in an apple orchard, saw the Engineer party leave as the fire began. They could not understand what the movement of troops was about and they thought that part of their own battalion was withdrawing. And so they followed.

Colonel Harper, watching all of these things from the hill, made the same mistake as his mortar section. He thought that his men had been stampeded and that the village was gone. He called General McAuliffe on the radio, told him what he had seen and said that he was on his way to gather the men and that he would make a counterattack. His car sped back over the route it had come and Harper started to rally his men. Then he learned that most of the party were Engineers and that only the mortar squad from among his command had displaced. He told that squad to get back into the battle and they moved at once. This error in judgment is the only instance during the siege of Bastogne when any American infantryman is known to have left his position under fire and without orders.

Colonel Harper, still outside the village, called Colonel Inman on his radio. The executive officer of the 2d Battalion, 327th Glider Infantry, Maj. R. B. Galbreaith, answered the call. He said that both Colonel Inman and Captain Hugh Evans, commanding officer of Company G, which was holding the village, had been hit by a tank shell while making a reconnaissance just as the German onslaught began. He did not know how badly they were wounded. Harper asked him, "Are you still in the village?"

"Yes," Galbreaith answered. "Yes, but the Germans are here also. We expect to drive them out."

The close-in fighting continued into the early afternoon. Inman's men stayed in their foxholes. Some died there, shot at ten yards' range by machine guns as they tried to stop the half-tracks with their rifle and tommy gun fire, their bodies almost cut in half where the machine guns had ripped them through. Their comrades found them later sitting stiffly at their weapons. Colonel Harper himself inspected these positions. He noted that every one of his dead was still facing forward as if trying to engage the enemy. The bazooka men had likewise met the attack head-on. Some of the German infantry, clearing away from the half-tracks, had ducked into the houses. The glider men went in after them and cleaned them out house by house. Within two hours twenty Germans were prisoners and thirty were dead in Marvie. 1st Lt. Stanley A. Morrison of Company G, who had been captured when the Germans first came into the village, was recaptured by his own men. Colonel Inman had lost five men killed, each of them killed in a foxhole while resisting the half-tracks. Fifteen men of Company G were wounded in the action.

During all that time, Team O'Hara sat high and dry on the ridge, taking no part in the engagement except during the brief gun duel. On the right flank that force received some small-arms fire but the enemy made no attempt to close on that side and the armored infantry in Team O'Hara's position was too far away to lend any support to the men in Marvie. That village was again clear by about 1300. At 1400 some of Colonel O'Hara's tankers saw an enemy half-track stuck in the mud about 150 yards southeast of Marvie. It had been with the striking force during the morning and had become bogged. In the previous excitement all hands had overlooked it. The tankers quickly knocked it out.

At 1420, December 20, the enemy put smoke on Marvie. Some of the tanks made another sally from the woods but changed their minds. The situation began to ease and Colonel Inman's men went about improving their positions, digging their foxholes narrow and very deep and right next to the foundations of the houses. The day ended fairly quietly but with a definite change in the weather. The Ardennes was cold and frozen. The ground had hardened enough for the tracked vehicles to get about over the hills in almost any direction. Still no snow had fallen.

Now, as the first skirmish ended around Marvie, the first flurries fell. Soon the ridges were whitening and the snows thickened during the next few days. Increasing cold, light winds, and deep drifts changed many of the characteristics of the battle. One of the problems that now pressed most heavily on the commanders was to get their men indoors and keep them from freezing. Villages became places of refuge not only from enemy fire but from the cold. The Belgian villagers, clinging stubbornly to their homes even in the face of the German attack, had to be evacuated to provide shelter and cover for the infantry. In a world of white, the forest plantations were the only other areas of easy concealment for troops. The local actions swirled more and more around these two objectives—to capture a few houses or to take a line of fir trees.

THE RESPITE

On December 21 and 22 the opposing forces around the northeast sector simply sparred with one another. The enemy had been stopped cold at Neffe and Mont by Colonel Ewell's 501st Parachute Infantry and supporting units. The effort to slip through the ground held by the forces of Colonels O'Hara and Harper had been equally unsuccessful though less costly. After these futile passes, and following the shock action at Noville, the enemy seemed almost to abandon the effort to break through Bastogne and concerned himself with extending the westward flow of his forces on both sides of it so as to complete the encirclement.

The road to Neufchâteau was cut by the Germans on the night of December 20, isolating Bastogne. General McAuliffe had gone that way just a few hours before to talk to the Corps commander.

It was a pregnant conversation. General McAuliffe said that he was certain he could hold on for at least 48 hours and maybe longer. General Middleton replied that in view of the fact that the hour would probably come when communications could not be maintained, General McAuliffe would have to be prepared to act on his own. He pointed out that the 116th Panzer Division coming in on General McAuliffe's flank—in addition to the three German divisions already fighting him. McAuliffe said, "I think we can take care of them." Middleton said that he certainly wanted to hold Bastogne but was not sure that it could be done in view of recent developments. It was important, General Middleton added, that the road to the southwestward be kept open as long as possible.

As General McAuliffe walked out the door, Middleton's last comment was: "Now, don't get yourself surrounded." McAuliffe noticed that he said it very lightly and felt that the Corps commander was simply having a little joke in a tense moment.

General McAuliffe went on out, jumped in his car and told the driver to make for Bastogne as fast as he could get there. He figured he was already surrounded—or just about so. A half hour after he did come over the road, it was cut by the German armor.

That was not, however, an unmixed evil, for it brought an important change in the relationship of the forces in the defense. During its first two days the infantry and the armor had collaborated well but they had not been a team. On the first night, General McAuliffe had asked that the armor (Combat Command B, 10th Armored Division) be attached to him and its commander Colonel Roberts had said, "What do you know about armor?"

General McAuliffe had replied, "Maybe you want the 101st Division attached to your Combat Command."

It was partly because of this division in the command authority, and partly because the armor and the infantry were units strange and new to each other, that during the first stage there was a lack of cohesion. That lack was felt more as a moral than as a tactical thing. To one staff officer of the Division the armor along the front seemed "like a will o' the wisp."

The armor felt the same way about the infantry. Each force had the feeling those first few days that it was propping up the front pretty much unhelped. In general, neither force was feeling the presence of the other strongly nor having a clear idea how much support was being received from it. Liaison was fragmentary. Both tankers and infantrymen had had to come out of their corners fighting and during the first crucial hours they had no choice but to look straight ahead and slug.

But with the cutting of the Neufchâteau road and the isolating of the Bastogne garrison, General Middleton called General McAuliffe and told him that the armor (Combat Command B) and all other troops within the circle were now under his command.

General Middleton also called Colonel Roberts and told him, "Your work has been quite satisfactory but I have so many divisions that I can't take the time to study two sets of reports from the same area." Colonel Roberts reported in person to General McAuliffe to do command liaison and from that time on until the siege was lifted his post was almost exclusively at the 101st Division command post. The result was that the coordination was complete. Roberts, a veteran tank commander, was particularly concerned that the armor be used properly, used to the maximum effect and not wasted. He strongly resisted the attempts of infantry commanders to use tanks as roadblocks. He worked specifically to get his armor quickly released after each engagement so that there would always be a maximum strength in General McAuliffe's mobile reserve for the next emergency. In the middle of the siege he published a mimeographed memorandum to the infantry officers on the right ways to use tanks.

The order to Combat Command B on December 21 from VIII Corps to "hold the Bastogne line at all costs" gives a key to General Middleton's view of the situation during this period. On the evening before, he had talked with McAuliffe and had expressed a doubt whether the strength at Bastogne was sufficient for the task. All along he had been willing to make the gamble of an encircled force at Bastogne, and for a few hours he may have felt that the gamble was dubious. Now he had come to believe the gamble would succeed and that the battle must be fought out on that line. There was no longer any doubt or question anywhere in the camp. From this hour the action of all concerned, the VIII Corps commander, the 101st Division commander, and the armored force commander of Combat Command B—Middleton, McAuliffe, and Roberts—became wholly consistent with the resolve that Bastogne could and would be held.

General McAuliffe now had the answer to all of his questions. No situation could have been more clearly defined. During the first two days he had entertained many doubts and had continued to wonder just what the situation was. He had heard about various groups from the 28th and 106th Divisions which were still out fighting somewhere and might fall back upon him. The 7th Armored Division was supposed to be somewhere up around St. Vith. He had also had to worry about the organization of stragglers. At the first, part of the 28th Division had been screening him on the south flank. Its commander, Major General Norman D. Cota, had called him on the morning of December 20 and said, "I'd like to see you," and McAuliffe had replied, "I'm too damned busy." Cota then said, "I'll come up to see you."

Now, on the 21st, McAuliffe knew that General Cota would not be coming to see him, and that the only situation involving American troops about which he would have to worry for a while was the situation right within the two-and-one-half mile circle of German forces closed around Bastogne. The only support he could expect for the time being was just what he had—all within ranging distance of his own 105mm batteries. It was a nice, clear-cut position and it had materialized in just about the way that he had expected upon first reaching Bastogne.

But what he had not foreseen, something that came like a gift from the gods, was that after the first hard collision, the enemy would give him a comparative respite in which to reflect on his situation and knit his armor and infantry close together, now that both were his to work with as he saw fit. The Germans had spent two days trying to break on through Bastogne. They spent the next two riding hard around it. They had failed to crush it; they would try to choke it. But while they were building up around the west and south, the pressure against the city relaxed.

The flow of bubbles on the G-2 overlays, showing the extension of the enemy to the south and westward, was moving along. Panzer Lehr Division had been the first to break upon the Bastogne rock. But the 26th Volksgrenadier Division had also come in from the east. A captured map showed that it had failed in one of its appointments, for the 26th Volksgrenadier was to have had the honor of capturing Bastogne.

The Germans were traveling light. Their commanders had told them that Bastogne was bursting with American food and that they could eat when they got there. Some had gone hungry for three days while trying to reach the American rations. Too, the enemy fire power manifested a certain weakness. While his heavy mortars and nebel-werfers were shaking down the store fronts in Bastogne and wounding a few soldiers and civilians, his artillery effort was largely limited to the covering fires given by the tanks and the fire of a relatively few self-propelled guns when his infantry charged forward. This, G-2 attributed to a critical shortage of ammunition.

The cutting of the Neufchâteau road, closing the German circle, appears in the 101st Division records as hardly more than an interesting incident. Up till then, the Division's intelligence of the enemy strength and movements was more notable for its blanks than for its specific detailed entries. The G-2 section had, of course, moved cold into an unknown situation and was having to build up its picture of the enemy and friendly forces piece by piece. There had been no pretty "estimates of the situation" to take over and build upon. All that Division could

Map 72.

know for certain was what it learned from examining the enemy dead or questioning prisoners. That was enough for Lt. Col. Paul A. Danahy's (Division G-2) main purpose and enough also to satisfy his taste for melodramatic utterance.

Eleven dead men had been found on the ground where the hospital was captured. The corpses had civilian clothes—and German military dogtags. Colonel Danahy went out to make the identifications. A few hours after this find, a message from 10th Armored Division came through CCB to 101st Division Headquarters saying, "You can expect attacks from Sherman tanks, civilians and almost anything now."

Reports came into the G-2 office through the first day of Germans killed while wearing American uniforms and of Sherman tanks pouring fire on our lines. Danahy checked up. He found that invariably, where the enemy used American dress, it was mixed with some of their own clothing, so that they could maintain they were in uniform. What he had seen gave him fresh inspiration for prophecy.

Map 73.

"Their equipment is augmented by captured U. S. equipment which they do not hesitate to use," he wrote to the commander. "Their morale is excellent but will disintegrate as they come in contact with American airborne troops. It is well known that the Germans dislike fighting. The false courage acquired during their recent successes has so far proved insufficient to prevent their becoming road-bound."

While this message was going out to the regiments of the 101st, the enemy was crossing the Neufchâteau road and cutting the last line to the south, closing the circle around Bastogne. Reconnaissance and combat patrols reported strong enemy infiltrations in the areas west and southwest of the town.

In the morning of December 21, a patrol from Troop D of the 90th Reconnaissance Squadron went down the road to see what the Germans had there. The patrol, under 1st Lt. Arthur B. Arnsdorf, consisted of one tank destroyer and two squads of infantry. They met a group of 101st Division men near Isle-le-Pré (a mile and a half

507

southwest of Bastogne), then moved on some distance farther until they encountered a well emplaced enemy force which made them turn about.

Another armored patrol under Capt. Keith J. Anderson went to Clochimont where it observed a large enemy force—riding in American vehicles and dressed in American uniforms.

Later in the morning of December 21 Team Pyle—14 medium tanks and 200 infantry, mostly from the 9th Armored—moved to the vicinity of Senonchamps to assist the 420th Armored Field Artillery. Lt. Col. Barry D. Browne, in command of the 420th, had received reports that Sibret and Morhet had fallen into enemy hands. He figured that he was out on a limb and that the enemy might come upon him from either flank. So he turned one of his batteries to fire on Sibret and rushed a forward observer out to adjust on the village. At that moment, he saw the motorized column of the 333d Field Artillery Group as it came speeding up the road out of Sibret. Another column came driving hard behind the 333d—men in American clothes and riding American vehicles. They got fairly close to Senonchamps, then stopped, deployed and opened fire with an M8 assault gun.

Even as Colonel Browne realized they were Germans, they started side-slipping off into the Bois de Fragotte which lies just south of Senonchamps. Team Pyle got there in time to help Browne fill those woods with fire; one battery from the 420th Field Artillery Battalion and one from the 755th Field Artillery Battalion (155mms) also engaged in this action. The infantry and tanks moved west into the woods. Almost immediately, one of the tanks knocked out an enemy 75mm self-propelled gun. The force then advanced into a large clearing in the center of the forest. While crossing the clearing, one of the tanks was disabled by a shell from a high-velocity gun somewhere in the woods. The tank lost a track. A smoke screen was laid in an attempt to cover its withdrawal, but the tank wouldn't budge and had to be destroyed.

The force then withdrew to a line farther to the east, but within the forest. Additional support kept coming to it until by night Colonel Browne was commanding 300 infantry and 19 tanks, in addition to running two battalions of artillery. His troops were covering a sector more than 4,000 yards long and running from south of Senonchamps to the Bastogne–Neufchâteau road. All of this had been built up during the day of December 21 as forces were shifted to meet the attack from the new direction.

But the heavy increase of fire on the left found Danahy ready to meet the emergency. "The cutting of the roads," he wrote in his periodic report to the commanders that evening, "had had no effect upon our present situation except to make travel hazardous."[*2]

On the night of the 20th, after the cutting of the Neufchâteau road and the isolation of Bastogne, Harry Kinnard, the 101st G-3, was on the radiotelephone. Miles away an assistant G-3 of the XVI Corps staff was pumping Kinnard in an effort to learn the Division's exact situation. Not wanting to compromise the Bastogne position by giving information to any listening-in Germans Colonel Kinnard brushed off his interrogator by saying, "You know what a doughnut looks like? Well, we're the hole in the doughnut."

"Nuts!"

At 1130 on December 22 four Germans, a major, a captain and two enlisted men, came up the road to Bastogne from Remoifosse carrying a large white flag. They were met on the road by T/Sgt. Oswald Y. Butler and S/Sgt. Carl E. Dickinson of Company F, 327th Glider Infantry, and Pfc. Ernest D. Premetz of the 327th Medical Detachment.

Premetz could speak German. The captain could speak English. He said to Butler, "We are parlementaires."

The men took the Germans to the house where Lt. Leslie E. Smith of Weapons Platoon, Company F, 327th Infantry, had his command post. Leaving the two German enlisted men at the command post, Smith blindfolded the two officers and led them over the hill to the command post of Capt. James F. Adams, commanding officer of Company F. Adams called 2d Battalion headquarters in Marvie, Battalion called Regiment in Bastogne, and the 327th Headquarters called the 101st Division, relaying the word that some Germans had come in with surrender terms. The rumor quickly spread around the front that *the enemy* had had enough and that a party had arrived to arrange a surrender. Quiet held the front. Many of the American defenders crawled out of their cover and spent the noon hour shaving, washing and going to the straddle trenches.

Maj. Alvin Jones took the terms to General McAuliffe and Lt. Col. Ned D. Moore who was acting Chief of Staff. The paper called for the surrender of the Bastogne garrison and threatened its complete destruction otherwise. It appealed to the "well known American humanity" to save the people of Bastogne from further suffering. The Americans were to have two hours in which to consider. The two enemy officers would have to be released by 1400 but another hour would pass before the Germans would resume their attack.

Colonel Harper, commanding the 327th, went with Jones to Division

22.Dezember 1944

An den amerikanischen Kommandeur der eingeschlossenen Stadt Bastogne.

Das Kriegsglück ist veränderlich, diesmal sind die amerikanischen Truppen in und um Bastogne durch starke deutsche Panzerkräfte eingeschlossen. Wietere deutsche Panzerkräfte haben die Ourthe bei Ortheuville überschritten, Marche genommen und über Hompré-Sibret-Tillet vorgehend St. Hubert erreicht. Libramont ist in deutscher Hand.

Es gibt nur eine Möglichkeit die eingeschlossenen amerikanischen Truppen vor völliger Vernichtung zu bewahren: die ehronvolle Uebergabe der eingeschlossenen Stadt. Hierfür wird eine Bedenkfrist von zwei Stunden gegeben, die mit der Uebergabe dieser Note beginnt.

Wenn dieser Vorschlag abgelehnt werden sollte, stehen ein deutsches Artillerie-Korps und sechs schwere Flak-Abteilungen bereit, die amerikanischen Truppen in und um Bastogne zu vernichten. Der Befehl für die Eröffnung des Feuers wird sofort nach Verstreichen der zweistündigen Frist gegeben werden.

Die durch dieses Bombardement entstehenden hohen Verluste der Zivilbevölkerung sind mit der bekannten Humanität der Amerikaner nicht zu vereinbaren.

Der deutsche Befehlshaber.

This is the original of the German surrender demand at Bastogne. It was probably written on a captured American typewriter, since the diacritical marks have been inserted by hand. This is the first reproduction of these documents.

December 22nd 1944

To the U.S.A. Commander of the encircled town of Bastogne.

The fortune of war is changing. This time the U.S.A. forces in and near Bastogne have been encircled by strong German armored units. More German armored units have crossed the river Ourthe near Ortheuville, have taken Marche and reached St. Hubert by passing through Hompré-Sibret-Tillet. Libramont is in German hands.

There is only one possibility to save the encircled U.S.A. troops from total annihilation: that is the honorable surrender of the encircled town. In order to think it over a term of two hours will be granted beginning with the presentation of this note.

If this proposal should be rejected one German Artillery Corps and six heavy A. A. Battalions are ready to annihilate the U.S.A. troops in and near Bastogne. The order for firing will be given immediately after this two hours' term.

All the serious civilian losses caused by this artillery fire would not correspond with the wellknown American humanity.

The German Commander.

The Germans also sent along this English translation of their surrender demand. "The German Commander" was Lt. Gen Heinrich von Lüttwitz, CG of XXXXVII Panzer Corps.

Headquarters. The two German officers were left with Captain Adams. Members of the staff were grouped around General McAuliffe when Harper and Jones arrived. McAuliffe asked someone what the paper contained and was told that it requested a surrender.

He laughed and said, "Aw, nuts!" It really seemed funny to him at the time. He figured he was giving the Germans "one hell of a beating" and that all of his men knew it. The demand was all out of line with the existing situation.

But McAuliffe realized that some kind of reply had to be made and he sat down to think it over. Pencil in hand, he sat there pondering for a few minutes and then he remarked, "Well, I don't know what to tell them." He asked the staff what they thought and Colonel Kinnard, his G-3 replied, "That first remark of yours would be hard to beat."

General McAuliffe didn't understand immediately what Kinnard was referring to. Kinnard reminded him, "You said 'Nuts!'" That drew applause all around. All members of the staff agreed with much enthusiasm and because of their approval McAuliffe decided to send that message back to the Germans.

Then he called Colonel Harper in and asked him how he would reply to the message. Harper thought for a minute but before he could compose anything General McAuliffe gave him the paper on which he had written his one-word reply and asked, "Will you see that it's delivered?" "I will deliver it myself," answered Harper. "It will be a lot of fun." McAuliffe told him not to go into the German lines.

Colonel Harper returned to the command post of Company F. The two Germans were standing in the wood blindfolded and under guard. Harper said, "I have the American commander's reply."

The German captain asked, "Is it written or verbal?"

"It is written," said Harper.

And then he said to the German major, "I will stick it in your hand." The German captain translated the message. The major then asked,

"Is the reply negative or affirmative? If it is the latter I will negotiate further."

All of this time the Germans were acting in an upstage and patronizing manner. Colonel Harper was beginning to lose his temper. He said, "The reply is decidedly not affirmative." Then he added, "If you continue this foolish attack your losses will be tremendous." The major nodded his head.

Harper put the two officers in the jeep and took them back to the main road where the German privates were waiting with the white flag.

He then removed the blindfold and said to them, speaking through the German captain, "If you don't understand what 'Nuts' means, in plain English it is the same as 'Go to hell.' And I will tell you something else—if you continue to attack we will kill every goddam German that tries to break into this city."

The German major and captain saluted very stiffly. The captain said, "We will kill many Americans. This is war." It was then 1350.

"On your way, Bud," said Colonel Harper, "and good luck to you."

The four Germans walked on down the road. Harper returned to the house, regretting that his tongue had slipped and that he had wished them good luck.

The rest of the day was comparatively quiet. The wholesale destruction by artillery that the Germans had promised did not materialize. But, at 1555 there was an attack by some 50 of the enemy against Company F, 327th Glider Infantry, over precisely the same ground where the German mediators had come into our lines. The attack was broken up by small-arms and artillery fire. At 1700 another small attack was again pressed to within 200 yards of Company F's lines but was beaten back by fire.

The terrain at this spot formed a kind of bowl. The Germans came with their tanks into the bottom of the bowl and fired up against the foxholes along the slope. The men under Sergeant Butler, who had the rifle platoon, and Lieutenant Smith, who had the weapons platoon, held their ground and drove the attackers off with infantry fire alone.

The main event for that day was summed up, though not too neatly, in the G-2 Periodic Report No. 4.

"The Commanding General's answer was, with a sarcastic air of humorous tolerance, emphatically negative. The catastrophic carnage of human lives resulting from the artillery barrage of astronomic proportions which was to be the fate of the defending troops failed to materialize.

"The well known American humanity was considerate of the threatened possible civilian losses by firing artillery concentrations directed at the enemy's impudence."

It was a victory for eloquence at some expense to grammar but in keeping with the other grim humors of the day.

That night, December 22, the Luftwaffe began its bombing attack which was repeated on the next four nights.

The Second Marvie Attack

There were two relatively quiet days on the Marvie part of the circular Bastogne front after the snows came—December 21 and 22. Bastogne was searched for enough bedsheets to camouflage the patrols. Early in the afternoon of December 21 the Germans came across the main highway directly south of Bastogne and then began working north toward the battalion lines on the hill.

Colonel Harper shifted the 2d Platoon of Company G, 327th Glider Infantry, from the ground immediately west of Marvie to a place west of the highway. Three of Team O'Hara's tanks were already on the hill where Harper had placed them the day before.

The armor and infantry together were able to turn this thrust back before it became any real threat. The 1st Battalion, 327th Glider Infantry, was relieved from attachment to the 501st Airborne Infantry, reverting to direct Division control. It was moved to the southwest of Bastogne in the vicinity of the woods there and ordered to establish a roadblock along the main highway, and from this point to patrol westward to make contact with the 326th Engineer Battalion. They were also instructed to patrol to Villeroux and Chenogne and make contact with "friendly troops" but before they could do it the enemy had moved through these positions and driven back the 333d Field Artillery Group. The Engineers then set up as small combat groups and covered the ground between Colonel Hartford F. Salee's 1st Battalion, 327th Glider Infantry, which was over the Neufchâteau road and the platoon from Company G, 327th, which was west of the highway leading south from Bastogne.

In Team O'Hara's part of the sector, too, there was a lull. Some time during the night of December 20 the Germans removed the trees from Team O'Hara's roadblock. At 1100 on the next day a combat patrol went forward to investigate. But on approaching the point where the block had been they found that the enemy now had it covered with crossing bands of machine-gun fire. They were able to withdraw without casualty and mortar fire was then put all around the road junction.

In the early hours of December 22 one of Team O'Hara's patrols going forward saw an eleven-man patrol enter their own lines. The night was clear and crisp. The small group from the 54th Armored Infantry first heard the crunching of the snow as the other patrol came toward them. They lay quiet, not firing because they were outnumbered. Too, the strangers were moving as if they were wholly familiar with the ground. They had no visible weapons and they did not carry themselves stealthily. They went boldly over the fences and entered the American lines along the ground that lay between the 327th and the 54th. They walked right by the sentries, moved to within 100 yards of the command post of the 327th Glider Infantry and within 200 yards of the command post of the 54th Armored Infantry.

Four different groups reported the patrol later and all four said they had seen eleven men. Yet the patrol was not challenged anywhere simply because it had moved so confidently. They got in and out without provoking any fire or interest. When Headquarters heard casually how this group had been drifting about, they checked to see whether any nearby unit had put out such a patrol and found that none had done so. Whether the eleven were friend or enemy was never learned. The visitation and its mystery became one of the legends of Bastogne.

At 1725 on December 23, the 2d Battalion, 327th, in Marvie was heavily shelled by enemy tanks concealed in a small plantation of firs within the hollow just above the village of Martaimont. From their position the tanks could shoot directly into Marvie. It was a characteristic enemy action for throughout the siege it was the German practice to use tanks as artillery, perhaps from fear of hitting their own troops if they used field guns from far back.

At about 1735 the 2d Battalion, 327th, was attacked by tanks and infantry coming from the same general direction, though they had debouched from a larger wood lying a little farther away from Marvie. The attack developed very slowly. The German infantry was clad in snow suits and a light snow was falling. They seemed to be waiting until the gloom deepened so they could make the most of their camouflage. The enemy barrage had ignored Team O'Hara's part of the sector but the outposts of the 54th Armored Infantry spotted two enemy machine guns that were firing into Marvie. Flanking fire was placed on them and they were silenced. Heavy automatic fire then searched the position of the 54th. No enemy could be seen and the men of the 54th held their fire except for one heavy machine gun on the left. The enemy spotted that gun. A few minutes later a hand

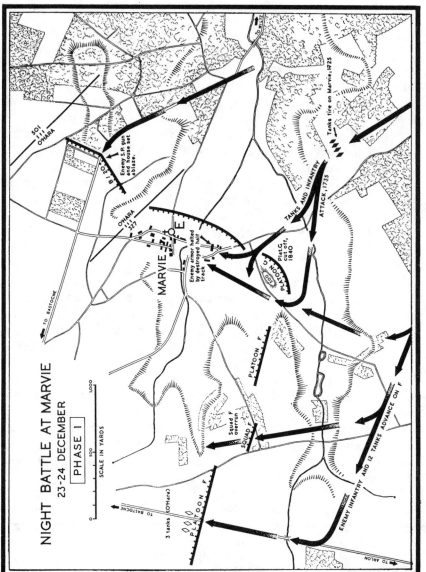

NIGHT BATTLE AT MARVIE
23-24 DECEMBER

PHASE I

SCALE IN YARDS
0 500 1,000

501
III
OHARA

3 tanks (O'Hara)

B l 20 OHARA

Enemy S.P. gun
and house set
ablaze.

OHARA
327

MARVIE

Enemy armor halted
by destroyed half-
track

TO BASTOGNE

TO BASTOGNE (O'Hara)

PLATOON F

PLATOON F

Squad F
overrun

SQUAD F

PLATOON F

PLATOON
G
Plat.G
cut off,
1840

TANKS AND INFANTRY
ATTACK, 1735

Tanks fire on Marvie, 1725

TO WILTZ

ENEMY INFANTRY AND 12 TANKS ADVANCE ON F

TO ARLON

Map 74.

grenade dropped next to the gun killing the gunner and wounding one other man. The rest of the crew quit the position. Next morning a patrol returned to the gun and found the second man still alive but so nearly frozen that he could only nod his head to them. Both he and the dead man had been searched and stripped of their possessions by Germans who had come in fast upon the position after the grenade fire.

Within half an hour the attack was fully developed and soon after 1840, December 23, one platoon of Company G, 327th became surrounded on Hill 500 to the south of Marvie. The enemy had begun a gradual envelopment of the platoon's position by moving into and through houses and yards that were around the base of the hill on all sides. A few members of the platoon were able to withdraw along the flanks of the hill as the encirclement began. The others stayed in their positions and the time quickly came when they could not get out.

Four tanks, which had accompanied the German infantry advance to Hill 500, turned their fire against Marvie, adding to the bombardment that was still coming in from the armored guns in the big wood.

Colonel Harper had worried about this part of the perimeter. Earlier in the day he had asked Colonel O'Hara to put a tank on the hill. O'Hara agreed to station a 57mm gun on the lower slope of the hill where a 37mm gun had previously defended it. The half-track carrying the 57mm gun was just going into position when the German tanks and infantry closed in on Hill 500. The first few German rounds that came his way were enough for the driver; he turned the half-track around and sped north toward Marvie. The troops in the village saw the half-track coming toward them from out of the body of the German attack. They thought it was a German vehicle and they fired at it with everything they had, demolishing the vehicle and killing the crew. Two German tanks that had followed along the same road crossed the stream south of Marvie and got into the village as far as the church. They saw then that the destroyed half-track blocked the road and that they could not advance any farther. So they turned around and withdrew.

Having begun the attack in stealth, the German infantry now came on toward the houses in a frenzy, yelling and firing as they advanced and shooting many flares. To the men in Colonel O'Hara's position it looked as if the tracers were flying in all directions. Bullet fire began to envelop them from the southern edge of the village. A self-propelled gun came charging toward them up the Wiltz road. As it rounded the bend and came abreast the farmhouse there, one of our medium tanks fired and the gun went up in flames. The fire lighted the entire area. The enemy turned their artillery loose on the farmhouse. A loft filled with hay soon blazed like a torch. Because of the intense illumination from these fires, the tanks and infantry of Team O'Hara's line withdrew 100 yards to the west.

Counting an Engineer platoon on the right of Colonel Harper's 327th Glider Infantry, there were 98 men defending Hill 500. Already, a few had been killed or wounded. At the same time that a part of the German force pressed against Marvie from the south, twelve German tanks supported by infantry advanced north along the main road toward the position occupied by Company F, 327th. This body had debouched from the same woods from which the German tanks were firing. Instead of continuing along the Bastogne road, part of the German armor moved rightward toward Hill 500. The infantry were clad in white and were almost imperceptible.

On the slopes of Hill 500 Lt. Stanley Morrison and his men of Company G, 327th Glider Infantry, had dug in around the base of the houses. Colonel Harper in his command post got word that the enemy was attacking. He called Lieutenant Morrison and asked, "What is your situation?"

"Now they are all around me," Morrison replied. "I see tanks just outside my window. We are continuing to fight them back but it looks like they have us." To Colonel Harper's listening ear he seemed perfectly calm and he spoke in a level tone.

Harper called him back in about three minutes. Morrison replied but he said only these words, "We're still holding on." Then the line went dead.

Lt. Col. Thomas J. Rouzie, the executive officer of the 327th Glider Infantry, said to Harper, "I guess that's the end of Morrison."

The men of Hill 500 were never heard from again in the battle. They had been overwhelmed by troops of the 901st Panzergrenadier Regiment of the Panzer Lehr Division. The end came for Lieutenant Morrison's detachment some time after 1900, December 23.

*Commanding the Engineer platoon at Hill 500 was Lt. Harold E. Young. His platoon from Company C, the parachute company of the 326th Engineers, had gone into Marvie on the night of the 19th and had remained there. On the night of the 23d his engineers amounted to about half the defense force defending the hill and he and Lieutenant Morrison had worked out their arrangements together. "For the 101st A/B Division," he wrote later, "Bastogne was a tremendous victory and as a member of the outfit I like to share in that victory. However, I remember Bastogne as the place where my platoon was beaten, pushed back, and many captured, killed or wounded. Even now a peculiar sensation runs through my body as I write about it. I don't recall being unduly scared at the time but my recollections of it are such that I can scare myself now quite easily."

By the 23d Lieutenants Morrison and Young had worked out a system whereby part of the men were in the houses warming up and part stayed out in the foxholes on the alert.

Sergeant Cloutier who had been a mess sergeant at one time put our supper on the farmer's stove and we hungrily looked forward to it. It started to be dusk at about 1630 and just about that time rifle fire started from us and from the Germans. Later I found out that the men under Lieutenant Scott saw the Germans putting up a mortar on the hill opposite. Pfc. Buckley fired on the mortar crew with his BAR. Then rifle fire and machine guns opened up on the ridge to the east and our men returned the fire. By this time it was dark so neither side could see any people moving, just the fire from the guns. Apparently the Germans had planned an attack to start just at dusk so that our BAR only anticipated it by a few minutes.

As soon as I heard the initial firing I ran out, along with Morrison and Saunders. Between 1700 and 1800 I went down to the vicinity of a house on the road where I had two machine-gun crews. They were firing and seemed all right. By this time the Germans were firing at us with two tanks at about 400 to 500 yards—direct tank fire aimed at our machine guns, CP doors and even foxholes. We were receiving .50-caliber machine-gun fire, .30-caliber machine-gun fire, rifle fire, and they were firing mortars for good measure. They may have added some artillery but I'm not sure of that.

A tank shell fragment hit one of my men—Fritz Balboni—and I ran to get the aid man in my CP. I couldn't get to the CP because of machine-gun fire. Then I checked to see what was happening along the road north of my CP. From a house across from the CP I had started down to where I had the two machine guns when I saw three Germans in white suits walking up the hill firing machine pistols. It immediately dawned on me that under the overhead cover of this terrific tank fire and machine-gun fire men were coming up the snow-covered hill in white suits to liquidate my men who were crouched in their foxholes for protection against this all-too-accurate enemy fire. Apparently the enemy had watched us Wednesday, Thursday and Friday and had prepared a well coordinated attack. We had tried not to make our entrances and exits visible to the Germans but I'm sure they knew all but our serial numbers when they attacked.

I realized that I could not get to my machine-gun crews so I decided to warn the men across the road from my CP who had not been fired on to the extent that the men down the road to the east had been, and to re-form our broken lines. While I was doing this Sergeant Digaetano and Corporal Crawley came up to me. His position at the machine guns had become untenable and he had moved his entire squad back toward the CP, and he and Corporal Crawley were the last two to leave the area. How they got back uncaptured I don't know

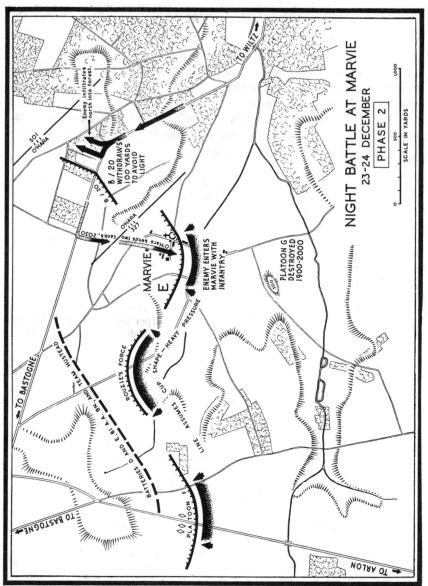

NIGHT BATTLE AT MARVIE
23-24 DECEMBER
PHASE 2

SCALE IN YARDS

Map 75.

because the rest of the squad was captured. Dig's assistant saw Lieutenant Saunders at a house across the road from the machine-gun position and he told him that the Germans were among us; that was the last that he saw of him. We saw a flare go up on the road by Lieutenant Morrison's CP and I figured that that meant the jokers in white were among us and for the tank fire and machine-gun fire to cease. I figured that, for it did cease right after that. Then we heard a tank coming up the hill from the east with a halftrack right behind it. Meanwhile it was as dark as hell and we knew they were walking around among us so that more than once one of us nearly shot another American. I managed to get about fifteen of my men and Lieutenant Shlapak together and we were planning to charge the Germans in the vicinity of our platoon CP when the halftrack reached that house. We had rifles and carbines and I figured that their strength was greater than ours in numbers of men plus the half-tracks and machine guns, so I decided that the hill was theirs. As I moved my men south toward the woods we got out first friendly artillery fire which was short and damned near got us. The tank and halftrack proceeded to fire incendiary bullets into the farmhouses and it seemed as though all of Marvie were on fire. The boys in the white suits moved along mopping up as they went. This was the first action in which the Germans had used snow suits and its surprise effect was terrific.

I moved my men through the various patches of woods to Bastogne. It was between 2300 and 2400 when I located Colonel Harper and reported to him in detail of the action. I told him about the tanks and halftracks in Marvie. Had we had one or more strategically located antitank guns or tanks plus artillery support things might have been different. [With this opinion Colonel Harper agreed. "I'll never again put infantry on a forward slope," said the Colonel, "unless I have tank destroyers or tanks where I can protect them. I lost two platoons separately in defense of the perimeter by making this mistake. In each case they were overrun when there were no tank destroyers to defend them."]*

There had been no tanks or tank destroyers in support of Morrison. Force O'Hara had not fired either in defense of the hill positions or against the German front moving into Marvie from the south. Colonel Harper couldn't understand it. He called Colonel O'Hara who said, "They are attacking me also and are trying to come around my north flank."

This flank had a patch of woods lying just north of the bend of the road but not within the American position and the enemy was striking from out of those woods. Now the snow suits no longer helped them for they reflected the light of the blazing house. From 100 yards away O'Hara's men fired. Some of the figures pitched forward in the snow and others sought its concealment.

One of Colonel O'Hara's men had failed to withdraw in time. He played dead when the Germans came to his foxhole. They said, "Hello, Hello," then kicked him, sat on him, took his BAR and rifled his pockets. But he kept absolutely still. Some time later he heard them bring up two guns on the left, a large one and a small one. They fired the small gun indiscriminately, apparently with the expectation of getting return fire which would provide a target for the large gun. Yet during the night the large gun never did fire. The man in the foxhole also heard the German ambulances make numerous trips into the area for the purpose of taking out their dead and wounded.

Major Galbreaith (executive officer of the 2d Battalion, 327th), reported to Colonel Harper at 2000, December 23, that the German infantry were in the south end of Marvie and were working through the houses. The tanks which had been on Hill 500 and had shelled Marvie from there were now moving toward the houses. Galbreaith asked Harper, "Can't I get tanks?" Harper replied, "I'll try." But the line to Team O'Hara had gone out. Colonel Harper tried the radio but could only hear Team O'Hara headquarters faintly.

Major Galbreaith called Colonel Harper again, and said, "They are all around us now and I must have tanks." "You call O'Hara on your radio," replied Harper, "and say 'It is the commanding general's order that two Sherman tanks move into Marvie at once and take up a defensive position.'"

Colonel Harper had no authority for his action but he figured this wasn't the time to stand on ceremony. A few minutes later the two Sherman tanks moved into Marvie on Colonel O'Hara's orders. The infantry of both sides were already locked in a fight for possession of the houses but the destroyed half-track kept the enemy armor from entering the south of the village.

Colonel Harper's force was now totally stripped of reserve. His line was buckled in and from Hill 500 the Germans were in good position to exploit the break in his center, roll back the flanks of his position, and through this breach enter the heart of Bastogne. But once again in renewing their direct assault on the city the Germans had made the same error of engaging heavily only along one part of the front. The front at Foy had cooled off and Colonel Ewell's forces along the Longvilly road could even doze a little.

At 2145 a platoon of paratroopers from Company A of the 501st Parachute Infantry under Capt. Stanfield A. Stach was sent to reinforce Company F of the 327th Glider Infantry. That company was already in a pretty bad way. One of its squads had been in the small patch of woods just to the southwest of Hill 500 and part of a platoon had been on higher ground to the squad's right rear. These positions had been overrun by the German armored advance from out of the woods around Martaimont.

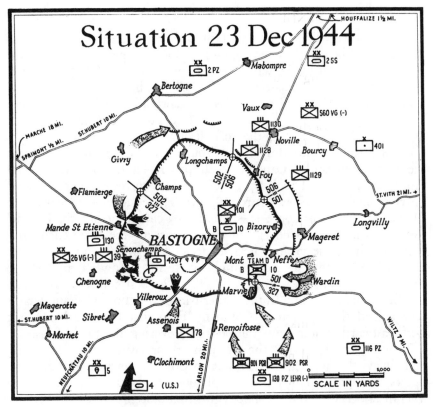

Map 76.

A few of the men got away. Others had been killed or taken prisoner defending their ground. The bulk of the company, in position along the crest of the hill commanding the main highway into Bastogne from the south, had held like a rock. The German assault had come on with its right closing around Marvie, its center enveloping Hill 500 and its left lunging forward along the main highway. The armor that supported the advance of the German left could be stopped only by bazooka fire from Lieutenant Smith's platoon, for this was no place for tank destroyers. Anything that came over the skyline of the hill moving southward from Bastogne was immediately put under fire by German tanks or self-propelled guns firing from defilade. No tank destroyers could be risked at the position. Three of Colonel O'Hara's tanks, known as Force Charley 16, were in support of our infantry line, but the night attack closed in in such manner that the fate of the line depended on the infantry weapons. There was a respite after Smith's fire beat back the first attack but the enemy tanks withdrew only a short distance.

523

The ruptured line north of Hill 500 was quickly patched and strengthened before the enemy could exploit his opening success. One platoon of Company F, which had been astride the Bastogne road, was put in position to east of it. The 327th Glider Infantry was also given Batteries D and E of the 81st Antiaircraft Battalion and Major Hustead's part of Team Cherry. Twelve guns were put in an arc along the high ground in the road triangle just above Marvie.

Colonel Rouzie picked up twenty-four men of Company F and with the forty men under Captain Stach proceeded through Lieutenant Smith's position and took up a defense line corresponding with the distribution of the 81st's antiaircraft guns. These moves—made between 2400 and 0100 (December 24)—temporarily closed the breach. Colonel Rouzie took personal charge of the defense of the threatened area. Upon reaching the ground he had decided he was in no position to attack. He felt that he wold simply waste his strength if he tried to drive the Germans away from Hill 500. The best course open was to establish a defensive line on the "inner part of the cup." Captain Adams reorganized the position of Company F so that the line bent back northeastward to join with the position covering the 81st's guns.

Twice again that night the German armor lashed at the left flank and always the fire fell heaviest, not on Colonel Rouzie's scratch force, but on the position held by the platoons of Lieutenant Smith and Technical Sergeant Butler. The regimental officers of the 327th Glider Infantry said later that Sergeant Butler's courage and energy were the mainstay of the defense. In one of the assaults a pair of German tanks got to within fifty yards of the foxholes held by Lieutenant Smith's men before they were turned back by bazooka fire. By then Smith's command post was blazing, for the tanks had fired fifteen rounds into the house as they came on. Smith and his assistants had set up in the basement and they stayed there while the upper structure burned.

Rouzie's force patrolled southward to the small woods from where part of Company F had been driven and found that it was now held by an enemy outpost. A few Company F stragglers were trying to work their way out of the woods. The patrol mistook them for Germans and fired on them. They hit the ground. One member of the patrol, suspecting that they were Americans, crawled forward, identified them and brought them out. The enemy had captured a number of American mortars around Marvie and through the rest of the night American mortar shells dropped on the ground which Smith and Butler were defending. In the early morning the Germans asked and received permission to remove their dead and wounded from in front of Smith's platoon. It was only when the Germans came forward to collect their dead that the pressure slackened and the mortar fire ceased.

Elsewhere along the sector the issue of the fight was still in balance. Two tanks which had ripped through Harper's forward line had gone right into Bastogne and shot up the houses around his command post, without doing any vital damage. In Marvie the arrival of the two Sherman tanks had stabilized the fighting.

Near midnight, December 23, as the Shermans rolled south into the village, they could hear German armor coming north. They could not see the force nor tell its numbers but the muzzle flashes told them they were engaged at very short range. Again the dead half-track helped save the situation. The leading German tank got up to this accidental roadblock and then tried to turn around, but was knocked out by the two Shermans before it could do so. This loss checked the rest of the enemy armor.

Colonel Harper's infantry in Marvie had dug themselves in very deep right next to the foundations of the houses and they stayed in their holes without flinching. They now had all the best of it because the village was blazing from many fires set by the artillery. Their foxholes were in heavy shadow while the snow-suited German infantry were highlighted as they came across the open spaces. The general assault was quickly checked by bullet fire but enemy parties got a lodgment in the houses at the lower end of the village and pushed slowly northward.

Along Team O'Hara's front things had quieted well before midnight. The enemy advance into the fire-lighted area was checked and then driven back by machine-gun and rifle fire. Later, after the scene had again darkened, an enemy tank was heard advancing along the road. The artillery forward observer fired the 75mm gun from his tank and a 105mm assault gun fired in the direction of the rumble. 2d Lt. Sherwood D. Wishart, tank platoon leader, reported that night that he was certain his shells had bounced off and the tank had backed away. But he had scored a bull's-eye in the darkness and in the morning the tank—a Mark IV—was found sitting to the left of the road with a 75mm hole clear through it. Not a single body was found on the ground which had been held by the enemy infantry, though the snow bore many other marks of death and confusion. The German medical units had done their tasks well.

Soon after dawn of December 24 Colonel Harper went down to look at his lines. He sent a patrol to the hill where Lieutenant Morrison had been and found it was still in enemy hands. His own men still held most of Marvie though the Germans were in some houses in the south of the village. Five men had been killed and seven wounded in the fighting there and one and one-half platoons had been wiped out on the hill. There were no further developments in the situation during the morning.

At 0900 a patrol from Colonel O'Hara's force went to the old roadblock position and found that the enemy had withdrawn except for two Germans who were sitting fully exposed on a nearby pile of beets. They shot the two beet sitters and this drew machine-gun fire on themselves. So they pulled back.

At 1340 six P-47s bombed Marvie, dropping six 500-pound bombs among the American positions. Then they came in over the housetops and strafed the streets with caliber .50 fire. Colonel Harper was walking through the streets when the first bomb fell. Even as he jumped for a foxhole he saw that there were two cerise-colored panels clearly showing where the front of the position was. He thought he saw one of the bombs hit among a patrol that was working through the south of the village toward Hill 500 and he sent two runners after the patrol to see if any damage had been done. Then he walked in the same direction. A German wearing a dirty snow suit dodged out of one house and into another so that he could get into a position from which he could fire on the patrol. Harper fired his M1 at the house in order to warn the patrol. The patrol, which seemed OK from the bombing, went to work on the house too, but on receiving rifle fire from the south of the village, they came on back.

During their brief reconnaissance they had seen a German tank completely camouflaged as a haystack except that the Germans had made the error of leaving the gun muzzle sticking out of the hay. Colonel Harper went to the one Sherman tank remaining in the village and gave the gunner the target—just beyond the last houses. He continued on to the tanks of Team O'Hara along the Wiltz road and told them to start pounding the tank and the houses in the lower part of Marvie which concealed the German infantry. With their first fire the Shermans got direct hits on the tank and blew the hay away. They kept on blasting it and the crews thought they knocked it out. Major Galbreaith (2d Battalion Exec, 327th) said, however, that he saw the tank get away under its own power.

At 1645 the P-47 planes returned again and attacked Marvie with bombs and bullets. At 1945 Bastogne was bombed and strafed by several enemy planes.

At 1800, December 24, Harper was told that he was in command of the perimeter all the way from Marvie to northwest of Hemroulle.

Colonel Harper said to General Higgins, "Look at it! This is half of the Division perimeter."

General Higgins replied, "It's all yours. Do what you can with it. There isn't any other solution."

Higgins reasoned that it was a fairly safe gamble. He had studied the map carefully and had gleaned all that he could from firsthand study of the country just outside the Bastogne perimeter. The landscape to the south was heavily wooded and therefore not suitable for armor. He considered that the only place where the enemy was likely to strike Harper's sector in force was at the Wiltz road. But the opening there was a pretty narrow corridor and he felt that Harper had enough strength across the Wiltz road to deal with any fresh threat at that point. What concerned General Higgins most was the position in the northwest sector, a gently rolling hill country, with no natural obstacles and very little tree growth. Thus far it had been the quietest portion of the perimeter but that fact did not lessen Higgins' apprehension; he felt sure that if a real tank stroke was coming, this would be the point of danger. He remarked to General McAuliffe that they could expect to be entertained out there on Christmas Day.

"The Germans are a sentimental people," he said, "and they are probably thinking about giving a present to Hitler."

Low Ebb of Supply

Despite the deceptively inactive appearance of the front, the defenders of Bastogne had actually reached the lowest ebb of their fortune by the night of December 22. The crisis was a matter of supply.

General McAuliffe's confidence thus far had been well founded. In manpower, he had been able to maintain a very favorable balance between his reserves and his deployments. His infantry losses had been light. The circle of defenses had been scarcely dented. The German forces, which as a whole had been rapidly moving in the Bulge offensive elsewhere, had so signally failed to put on a coordinated attack against his all-around front that he had been able to beat down each of their separate thrusts by massing the fire of his artillery.

The gun pits of all the defending 105mm batteries were complete circles. At different times during the siege nearly all guns fired around the whole 6,400 mils of the compass. Most of the artillery fired in support of each infantry battalion against every major attack the Germans made.

More than that, however, the artillery could not do. All day long the infantry commanders witnessed the enemy build-up opposite their sectors. Tanks and half-tracks loaded with German infantry moved freely and contemptuously along the lateral roads, making no effort at concealment although they were within easy range of the howitzers. It made the defenders frantic.

For by noon of December 22 the 463d Field Artillery Battalion, which was supporting the 327th Glider Infantry, had only 200 rounds of ammunition left and the other battalions were in a similar plight. During the first three days there had been shells enough. Now, in the face of the enemy build-up, the pinch was really hurting and General McAuliffe was about at the point where he would have to ration his guns to ten rounds per day.

There was a delightfully ironic touch even to that restriction, for the supply had dropped very low indeed. Checking the battalions on that day, Colonel Sherburne, the artillery commander, found that with the exception of one battalion which had several hundred rounds of short-range 105mm ammunition which it alone was equipped to fire, the batteries were down to less than ten rounds total per gun. Still, he kept his own counsel, and when men and officers asked him how the general supply of artillery ammunition was faring, he lied cheerfully and skillfully. At times members of the staff became confused between the true figures and the figures which Sherburne was quoting publicly for the sake of morale. The shell shortage continued to be General McAuliffe's worst, in fact, his only real worry. He told his batteries not to fire "until you see the whites of their eyes."

The infantry commanders and the few remaining artillery observers screamed their heads off about it. One commander phoned General McAuliffe, "We are about to be attacked by two regiments. We can see them out there. Please let us fire at least two rounds per gun."

Kinnard listened to this and later recalled McAuliffe's reply, "If you see 400 Germans in a 100-yard area, and they have their heads up, you can fire artillery at them—but not more than two rounds."

At the same time, the Bastogne defenders were running low on small-arms ammunition.

So with somewhat mixed feelings the word was received among the regiments at 1530 on that evening that a column from the 4th Armored Division was coming up from the southwest to support the 101st Airborne Division and would be able to give the 101st relief in time.

It was still a neat question whether that relief would come before the ammunition ran out.

In the smaller units which were attachments to the 101st perhaps the strain was even greater. Confidence can come of numbers around the headquarters of a large organization. Talking with his staff, General McAuliffe gained the impression that none doubted the outcome. But out on the fire line, friends shook hands as the darkness came, figuring that all might be overwhelmed before morning. They could take no measure of the reserve strength of the position. What they saw was how few rounds per gun they had left and how large were the numbers of the enemy. The paratroopers were somewhat accustomed to being surrounded by enemy, but it was a new experience for the units who stood with them, unwavering.

The first message from the 4th Armored said, "Hugh is coming." When General McAuliffe had visited General Middleton (commander of VIII Corps) in Neufchâteau on the night of December 20, he had been told that General Patton was attacking east of Bastogne. The two commanders then set up a simple code, each town along the route getting a letter. Bastogne was "K." Others were designated A, B, C. Now the word was that "Hugh [Maj. Gen. Hugh J. Gaffey, commanding the 4th Armored Division] is on his way."

On the heels of that assurance came another message equally bright. VIII Corps radioed that pathfinders would arrive in Bastogne at 1600 and that resupply by air would start coming in at 2000. Colonel Kohls, G-4, 101st Division, had waited all day long for that appointment, for on the day before VIII Corps had told him to prepare for "resupply tomorrow if weather permits."

Directly west of the houses of Bastogne are large, clear fields on a gentle hillside, close to where the 101st Division had made its command post. This was the designated spot.

Under average operating conditions resupply bundles are recovered by Quartermaster and Ordnance companies and their items of matériel are then segregated in Class I, III and V dumps under Division control. At Bastogne, Colonel Kohls had no Division supply forces available either to pick up the resupply or manage the distribution. The regiments were therefore told to send at least five quarter-ton trucks to the field to handle the supplies directly and haul them to unit dumps. The units were told to report what supplies they had each recovered and then to distribute them according to orders which would be given by the G-4 Section.

At 0730 on December 22, the task of recovering the aerial resupply was given to Maj. William H. Butler, S-4 of the 501st Parachute Infantry, and Captain Matheson, S-4 of the 506th. They went to the drop zone, got the crews and vehicles alerted, put out the panels to guide the plane and then waited.

Nothing happened during the day. In the late afternoon came the message from VIII Corps. At 1605 Corps said that the pathfinders would be dropped at 1723 and that the flight would be two planes with ten men each. Capt. John M. Huffman, Assistant to G-4, went at once to the drop zone to notfiy Major Butler. However, at 1641 the operation was cancelled because of ice conditions.

Then the Division rear base radioed at 1700 that sixty C-47s would drop supplies on the first flyable day. However, VIII Corps had not yet given up. At 2115, it radioed that an attempt "will be made to drop a portion of the supplies."

Colonel Kohls again alerted Butler who went to the drop zone and put out the fluorescent panels. Nothing happened. Out of great expectation came only great disappointment.

Supplies Arrive

From daylight on December 23 all guards stood alerted for the first appearance of the C-47s. At 0935 a military policeman on duty at the entrance to the 101st Division command post carried the word to Colonel Kohls that several large planes were circling the area.

A few minutes later the pathfinders jumped in the area where the 2d Battalion of Colonel Harper's 327th Glider Infantry was deployed. They were quickly rounded up by his men. One minute later, 1st Lt. Gordon O. Rothwell, commanding the pathfinder team, was on the telephone explaining to Colonel Kohls that the supply planes would arrive in about 90 minutes. Kohls told him how to get to the drop zone and where to put the radar set. Again the regimental supply men were alerted. Again Major Butler displayed the panels. At 1150 on the 23d, men all along the front saw the planes coming in; it was the most heartening spectacle of the entire siege.

Men and vehicles were all set for it. The pathfinder radar had given Captain Huffman and Lt. Col. John T. Cooper, Jr. (Commanding Officer, 463d Parachute Field Artillery Battalion) a half-hour advance warning that the planes were coming in and the supply parties reached the field ten minutes before the flight, in time for Huffman to assign zones of retrieving to each unit so that there would be a uniformly quick pick-up. There was very little enemy fire on any part of the field.

Sixteen planes arrived in the first flight, but these were just the beginning. By 1606 of that day, 241 planes had dropped 1,446 bundles weighing 144 tons by parachute into the mile-square drop zone. The drop pattern was excellent and there was about a 95 per cent recovery of the dropped material.

Working against the approaching darkness, the supply crews threw whole bundles, parachute and all, into the jeeps and shuttled between the drop zone and their dumps as fast as they could tear over the ground. All supplies were in the unit dumps by 1700, and even before that time ammunition had been rushed directly to the front lines and the battery positions. The artillery was firing part of the resupply ammunition at the enemy before the drop zone had been cleared.

By the time darkness came on, Colonel Kohls had at hand reports from all the unit supply officers telling what quantities of matériel had reached their unit dumps. It took only a brief checking on his part to see that his supply problem was far from being solved. The contents of the bundles were not in balance with the real needs of the troops. They still desperately lacked certain items and they had received others which they did not need or want. A great amount of caliber .50 ammunition had been sent up but this was not much in demand. The new supply of caliber .30 for the M1, and of 76mm APC and 75mm ammunition was insufficient. The Division needed litters and penicillin badly and though it had collected all of the available bed clothing from the Belgian community, many of its men were still miserably cold at night and were asking for blankets.

Colonel Kohls talked to VIII Corps again at 0830 the next morning (December 24) and said he wanted these things. He asked for additional quantities of ammunition for the 75mm pack howitzer and also of 105mm M3 shell. He asked VIII Corps to investigate the possibility of using gliders in the further resupply. All the early resupply missions had been done by parachute. As they came in the Germans put up a terrific amount of flak. The troops saw a number of C-47s shot down, but these losses had not made other planes take evasive action. Colonel Harper said of the pilots who flew these missions:

"Their courage was tremendous, and I believe that their example did a great deal to encourage my infantry."

While Kohls was talking, the first resupply planes of the day appeared over the drop zone and more bundles continued to rain down on the field until 1530. About 100 tons of matériel were parachuted out of 160 planes during that second day of resupply. Even so, the Division's stocking was not by any means full as Christmas Eve drew on. The shortages weighed more on Colonel Kohls than what had been accomplished. Only 445 gallons of gasoline were on hand. The 26,406 K rations that had been received were only enough to supply the defenders of Bastogne for a little more than a single day. The troops were instructed, for a second time, to forage for any food supplies in their areas and to report them to G-4 so that they could be distributed where they were needed most.

This had been done from the beginning and a large part of the subsistence of the defense had come from the ruined stores of Bastogne or from the stocks of the farming community. From an abandoned Corps bakery had come flour, lard, salt and a small quantity of coffee. Colonel Kohls got these things out to the troops and during the first days of the siege the favorite menu item along the firing line was flapjacks. The coffee, however, was saved for the hospital. The farmers had fairly good supplies of potatoes, poultry and cattle. These were taken over on requisition, to be paid for later by the United States. In an abandoned Corps warehouse were found another 450 pounds of coffee, 600 pounds of sugar and a large amount of Ovaltine. These things were all hoarded for the wounded. Prowling about Bastogne, the Civil Affairs Officer, Capt. Robert S. Smith, found a large store of margarine, jam and flour in a civilian warehouse. This assured flapjacks for several more days. What was equally important, he found 2,000 burlap bags among the groceries and the bags were rushed out to the infantrymen in the foxholes to wrap around their feet where they lacked arctic overshoes.

By Christmas Eve these supplementary stores were pretty well exhausted. Christmas was a K-ration day—for the men who had K rations.

The Situation Improves

Without fully realizing it, the defenders of Bastogne passed their crisis on December 23. They could not measure the change, nor did they know how many elements were acting in their favor. But quite suddenly everything began to come their way. This was not a matter alone of successful local tactics against the enemy. Nor was it only that the measures taken by the VIII Corps and the larger forces concerned with the relief of the defenders were at last beginning to bear fruit, as evidenced by the arrival of the resupply missions. For one thing, such a vital matter as the weather continued to favor the defense.

In the beginning there had been fog and acute dampness which appeared at first blush to doubly jeopardize the situation of a force that was having to feel its way to the enemy and was suffering from shortages of clothing and blankets. Yet all that happened in the opening encounters during the first two days Bastogne's fate was in the balance proved that the atmosphere served almost as a protecting screen for the defenders and wrought confusion among the oncoming forces. Had there not been fog of course there could have been air support. But it is a question whether that support could have been greatly effective during a period when it would have been difficult to distinguish between the retreating remnants of the broken American divisions and the advancing German columns. Again, an early intervention by the air power might have forestalled those concentrations of German armor and other vehicles which were to provide such inviting targets when the opening at last came.

On December 19 Capt. James E. Parker, of the Ninth Air Force, reported into Bastogne as air controller for the defense. His equipment consisted of a pocket full of radio crystals; what he needed was a high frequency radio that would give him contact with American planes. He searched the whole 101st Division without success, then found that the attached 10th Armored Division units had two radios of the type needed—one in a tank and the other in a jeep. The tank could not be spared but the jeep and a technician from Ninth Air Force, Sgt. Frank B. Hotard, were given to Captain Parker. By December 21 his radio equipment was complete and he was ready to work with supporting planes. But the fog still enveloped Bastogne to keep the planes away. Parker had to wait two more days.

While the fog held, the first snow flurries came and the weather grew increasingly cold. On the night of December 21 came the first heavy snowfall, adding to the hardships of the front-line troops and the hazards of patrolling. The overcast was still thick and the ground fog irregular. On the morning of December 23, for the first time since the Bastogne defenders were committed to action, a day dawned fair and clear though with freezing temperatures. It looked like the hour of opportunity.

By then the defenses of Bastogne had become so closely knit, and there was such complete harmony and mutual confidence among the oddly assorted groups of the defense, that it seemed certain that all of the changes in the natural conditions of the battlefield would work only to the disadvantage of the enemy. The defensive lines were set. The crisp clear air insured that if the Germans came on, their snow-suit camouflage would not be overly helpful; at least their features and their weapons could be seen. The roads from Bastogne to all parts of the perimeter were like the spokes of a wheel. They were generally good roads. But particularly around the northern half of the defense they entered the perimeter over ground where a stout roadblock might well hold up an armored regiment for hours. The German armor and its support had largely held to the roads during the period of build-up; and they were still out there, daring the lightning. Wire communications from Bastogne command post to all parts of the perimeter were working as strongly on behalf of the defense as was the axial highway system. Only a few times had the wire gone out. The 101st's practice of emphasizing a net of lateral wires, which set up several ways of reaching the outfits on the perimeter, had saved a number of situations that might otherwise have been blacked out. And foresightedly, the Signal Company had brought in plenty of extra wire.

Now that there was the sure prospect of air resupply, the artillery situation was looking up. It had suffered thus far only from its fears that the ammunition wouldn't last. By the 22d, General McAuliffe's supply had dropped down to twenty-odd rounds per gun and Colonel Roberts' about as low, and some guns were down to ten rounds. But both commanders were certain that as long as the artillery ammunition lasted, Bastogne would hold.

A typical comment was that of Colonel Chappuis of the 502d who, after the siege, said that the most trying thing on his troops in those days was that they had to look out every day and see enemy trucks and men swarming up and down the roads all around them. "We could have murdered those Germans," he said. "The road intersections in front of us looked like 42d and Broadway after a football game. Most of the traffic seemed to be moving to the west. They were in easy reach and were quite contemptuous about it. But we could do nothing about it because we did not have the artillery ammunition."

The opening engagements had reaffirmed the power of an ample artillery properly directed, and by committing their forces piecemeal the Germans had played right into the hands of the defense which had staked its life on the massed fire of its guns. The guns of Combat Command B, 10th Armored Division, were capable of getting 11,000 yards out of their 105mm ammunition while the same ammunition in the short 105 tubes of the Airborne Artillery units could only reach about 4,500 yards. The Armored Artillery was therefore the real power of the defense together with the twenty 155mm howitzers of the Artillery battalions that had been caught in the town (the 755th and part of the 333d Field Artillery Group).

During the first stage, the great natural strength of the position and the vast superiority of the American artillery had worked together for the salvation of Bastogne. The German artillery had been little more than a cipher, save for the fire from the tanks and self-propelled guns. At times it seemed to consist of single guns and their shoots were never very long. The town itself had not yet been given any steady shelling by the enemy guns and the command posts were able to maintain their liaison with little difficulty.

This lack of power in the German artillery and the inability of the German foot and armor to coordinate their assaults against different parts of the perimeter—probably because their communication system had broken under the pressures of the advance—minimized the moral strain which would normally afflict a body of troops that found itself surrounded. The command and staff of the defense were not feeling what they had expected to feel from the lessons they had learned at Leavenworth and Benning. They knew they were cut off. The G-2 reports and the incessant patrol activities against all portions of the defensive circle told them so. But they did not *feel* cut off. They remained mobile and mentally able to promote all of the tactical advantages of their interior position. The thought that there were Germans all around them brought no particular extra worry. They were confident that help from the outside was just around the corner.

However, the most decisive gains of the period had been in the work of the fighting men themselves and in their feeling about one another. In the beginning the different elements of the defense were almost out of communication one with the other. Things had happened so fast that they had been compelled to engage the enemy before giving a thought to their own liaison. But in the course of battle the infantry, the armored force and the tank destroyer crews had taken full measure of each other and found the measure sufficient. The birth of mutual confidence and respect had produced not only tactical cohesion but comradeship in such a degree that before the siege was over these units were to ask their higher commanders whether it wouldn't be possible for them to be joined permanently in one large force. They had come to believe that together they had become irresistible.

After their first tilt in which each had spoken bluntly and made his point, General McAuliffe and Colonel Roberts tabled their feelings and worked together to perfect the team play of their respective forces. As McAuliffe's advisor on armor, Roberts found himself among "the best and keenest staff" he had ever seen. Not only did they radiate extreme confidence but they proved to be "great bird dogs" in detecting early enemy buildups. As soon as the first signs of an enemy attack became apparent, Colonel Roberts would alert his Division reserve and get it moving toward the likely area of irruption. He would then concern himself with building another Division reserve. He never bothered General McAuliffe with these details. If it chanced that

Colonel Cherry, the Division reserve commander, got cut up, or if the 101st Division troops moved over during an action and drew parts of Team Cherry into the front line, there was always Team O'Hara with 14 tanks which he could get out of line quickly in case of necessity.

Colonel Roberts' force had more than paid for itself during the first two days. He had taken his greatest losses in tanks and men in the opening engagement, but that sacrifice had staved off the Germans and gained the exact amount of time needed for the 101st to establish itself solidly. After the first two days Colonel Roberts' two chopped-up teams were consolidated as one and this part of the force became his Division reserve. The number of tanks available for it varied from day to day between six and ten.

Lieutenant Colonel Templeton, the Tank Destroyer commander (705th Battalion), took hold in the same strong way, even having his men fight as infantrymen when they could not be employed otherwise. On the other hand he was never loath to make his point strongly any time he thought the higher commanders were planning to make an unwise employment of his forces. Colonel Templeton's command post was only a hundred yards from the command post of the 101st Division, so coordination was simple. In turn he received from the battalion commanders of the 101st the kind of support that rewarded all of his effort. During relief periods the infantry platoons covering his tank destroyers made the security of Templeton's guns their first concern.

Colonel Roberts, too, was learning from Templeton as they went along. He had reached the conclusion that, properly employed in a defense like Bastogne, some tanks must be up with the infantry and some in reserve in the "socker" role. But what bothered him was the discovery that while his tankers were actually having to work as tank destroyers about 98 per cent of the time, the tank destroyer men seemed so much better trained to get away with it. This was strongly reflected in the ratio of losses in the two forces when compared with the damage done to the enemy armor.

At 1000 on December 23 Captain Parker at his radio heard that supporting planes were on their way. Within a few minutes he was telling them where to strike. The strongest enemy buildups at this time were west and northwest of the town, threatening the sectors held by the 502d Parachute Infantry and the 327th Glider Infantry regiments. The infantry front lines had been hearing and seeing the arrival of these concentrations during the past two days. But because of the shortage of artillery ammunition, there had been no real check against them. The planes dropped low and came in fast against the enemy columns, gaining complete surprise. The German vehicles were on the road facing toward Bastogne when the first bombs fell among them. Such was the execution that one of the pilots later said to General McAuliffe, "This was better hunting than the Falaise pocket and that was the best I ever expected to see."

On that first day the Germans did not use their antiaircraft guns against any of the dive bombers. If this reticence was due to a desire to cover up the positions of the guns, it was a view quickly changed because of the damage the Ninth Air Force planes had done during the first day. For thereafter the German flak was intense over the front at all times and the air units had no further hours of unopposed operation.

They made the most of their opening opportunity. The snow was a great aid. Clearly visible tracks pointed to forest positions which were promptly bombed. The fir forests burst into flames from the fire bombs and before the day was out the smoke from these blazing plantations and from the brewed-up enemy columns made a complete circle around the besieged forces until it seemed almost as if the fog was closing in again. The air people hit every nearby town at least once with explosive and fire bombs. Noville was hit ten times.

The entire air operation was carefully systematized and then supervised in detail. As planes were assigned to the 101st Division by VIII Corps, they checked in with Captain Parker by radio. He put them on a clear landmark such as a railroad or highway as they came in toward Bastogne. Several check points were then given to them from the map. When the approaching planes were definitely located, an approach direction was given that would bring them straight in over the target. This procedure eliminated all need for circling and searching and helped them surprise the enemy. When the bombs and gun ammunition were expended, the planes were ordered up to a safe altitude to patrol the perimeter of the defenses or were given specific reconnaissance missions. Their reconnaissance reports were used as the basis for giving targets for succeeding flights and for giving the ground forces advance information on the build-up of enemy strength. After the first flight there were always targets listed ahead. Captain Parker, carefully monitoring the air, also came across flights assigned to other ground forces battling in the Bulge which had no missions for their bombs. He would then call to them and he often succeeded in persuading them to drop their bombs in the Bastogne area. In a few minutes these planes would be back on their assigned missions.

During the first four days of their support, December 23 to 26, the planes averaged more than 250 sorties daily. After that there were two days of bad weather and then the weather came fair again. But it was on December 23 that the air support clanged the bell most loudly and thereby assured decision for the American forces. Colonel Roberts, watching the planes at work, said with enthusiasm that the effect was worth two or three infantry divisions. General McAuliffe bracketed their work with the overwhelming superiority of his artillery and the supreme courage of the men on the ground in his analysis of why Bastogne was saved.

It was not unusual during the siege to have an infantryman call in that five tanks were coming at him and then see six P-47s diving at the tanks within 20 minutes.

West of Bastogne

For six days the enemy had made only a few swift passes at General McAuliffe's line facing toward the west. That was the way the command and staff had figured the battle was most likely to develop. Kinnard, who had worked out the tactical plan for the defense of Bastogne, felt that the forces could be spread thinnest to the southwest.

Between Colonel Harper, commanding the 327th, and Lt. Col. Ray C. Allen, commanding the 3d Battalion which held the attenuated lines covering toward Neufchâteau, there passed a jest typifying the situation. "How are you doing on your left?" "Good! We have two jeeps out there."

In the northwest sector, the Germans accommodated General McAuliffe's plan of saving the 502d Parachute Infantry for his Sunday punch and that regiment had relatively little fighting though it went through a great many motions.

In the beginning Colonel Allen's 3d Battalion, 327th, became engaged because of the enemy penetration which on the night of December 19-20 reached the Bois de Herbaimont from the direction of Houffalize and overran and captured the 326th Medical Company near crossroads "X." Nine men from the 28th Division—remnant of a group of more than 100 men—got back to Colonel Allen's command post at 2030 and told him how this same German force had ambushed and destroyed their company. It was the first information that the Bastogne–St. Hubert road had been cut and it meant the probable end of any possibility that supplies could be brought in from the northwest. The 101st Division Headquarters became alarmed. At 2200 Colonel Allen was told to move a company out against the roadblock which the enemy had established and destroy it.

Company B under Capt. Robert J. McDonald was two hours in preparing for the attack, but it moved out at midnight, December 20-21, and was approaching the roadblock after about a 90-minute march. The men moved down the ditches on either side of the St. Hubert road with two guides walking on the road to keep contact in the darkness. Ahead, they could see a number of vehicles burning and they could hear the enemy laughing and talking. The horns on several of the vehicles had become stuck, adding volume to the sounds which guided them toward their target. The company moved to a ridge within 75 yards of the roadblock, and there deployed. The din from the German position was such that they accomplished this movement without being detected. They formed up with the 2d Platoon on the left, the 3d Platoon on the right, and the 1st Platoon in the center, supported by the heavier weapons. One squad of the 2d Platoon moved to the Sprimont road and formed a block across it about 100 yards from crossroads "X." On the other flank a squad from the 3d Platoon established a block for the same purpose about 100 yards outside the enemy outposts.

Captain McDonald had figured that the roadblock on the right would take longest to establish, so he directed the squad leader to fire two quick rifle shots when his men were in position. The plan worked perfectly. When the two shots were fired, the center moved forward, the men shooting from the hip as they advanced. The Germans were taken wholly by surprise and most of them fled toward the Bois de Herbaimont just to the north whence they had come originally. So doing, they crossed the killing ground which was covered by the squad on the right under T/Sgt. Mike Campano. Campano's men could hardly shoot fast enough. More than 50 Germans were killed. None were taken prisoner. Company B didn't lose a man.

When the last German had been cleared from the area roadblocks were organized in all directions, with an especially strong block being set up on the highway to Salle (3½ miles southwest of Bertogne). In this general position, Company B became the farthest outpost of the division. In their search of the area the company found three Americans who had been prisoners of the Germans. One was a Negro truck driver and the other two were from the Finance Department of the 28th Division. They also found two dead paratroopers whose throats had been slashed; they guessed that these men had been patients when the hospital was overrun. A number of American trucks were recovered, some containing medical supplies, one carrying a load of mail and another loaded with explosives.

On finding an American light tank among the enemy booty, Company B incorporated it into their defenses along with several caliber .50 machine guns from the recaptured trucks. The noise of the skirmish had drawn an artillery observer from the 333d Field Artillery Group and he attached himself to Company B and stood ready to deliver supporting fire from the 155mm howitzers when it would be needed.

At 0700 on December 21 an enemy column was seen approaching from the direction of Salle. The men at the roadblock guessed it was an artillery battery for it contained nine half-tracks, seven 75mm guns and seven light vehicles. Captain McDonald's men were in a cut above the highway and their position was so well screened that the German column came to within 25 yards before the defenders opened fire. Then they let them have it with all weapons—their rifles, machine guns, a 57mm gun and the guns of the light tank. Only one light vehicle from the column managed to turn and get away. All of the enemy guns were captured intact but they could not be moved to town and they were therefore destroyed with the aid of the recaptured explosives.

Shortly thereafter, two tanks supported by a group of German infantry tried to flank the position from the northwest. Company B crippled one tank with a rocket and the other tank withdrew. The infantry group was driven back by small-arms fire from Company B's position, supported by artillery fire.

At noon the roadblock positions were put under fire by enemy tanks operating to the southward of Salle. The tank fire was silenced by two tank destroyers from the 705th Tank Destroyer Battalion which had just come forward to help Captain McDonald's company. However, by this time it had become clear that the roadblock had little importance. Patrols had been sent out to the northwest and southwest and they returned with information that the highway bridges in both directions had been blown. Since the highway was of no further service as a supply route for the Division, Company B was ordered to return to the battalion sector. It did so in the early evening.

At 0900 on December 22, one German group cut the road to Mont southeast of Flamizoulle (near Mande-St.-Étienne). The outpost which sighted it said that it had set up a roadblock with "two half-tracks, one jeep and a trailer." Just before noon, Colonel Allen put on an attack directly south to clear the road. He took twenty-five prisoners and drove the rest off. The motor vehicles turned out to be ordinary farm carts which the Germans had hooked together for use as a block. A platoon of Colonel Templeton's tank destroyers then reconnoitered the road, the sections covering one another alternately from one terrain feature to the next. They reported to Colonel Allen that the road was open.

In the northwest sector, the 502d Parachute Infantry engaged directly without any long-range sparring with the enemy. That came of the order which initially took Colonel Stopka's 3d Battalion, 502d, to Recogne to help extricate the Noville force. Four tank destroyers accompanied the battalion to Recogne and stayed there, backing up the line. They got no action the first day though two men and a jeep from the 705th's Reconnaissance Company set up as an evacuation team and shuttled the wounded out of the 502d area after a heavy shelling by the German tank artillery.

At 0730 on December 21, the 1st Battalion, 502d, moved to the area just east of Grosse-Hez (two miles east of Champs) on Division order, and with this shifting of the line, Company A was ordered back to its own battalion. (It had been attached to the 2d Battalion to fill out the 2d's long front.) One hour later, the 1st Battalion started up the road toward Recogne. Company G of the 506th Parachute Infantry had been hit at Foy and had pulled back its left flank to high ground. This maneuver exposed Colonel Stopka's (2d Battalion) right flank which was anchored in the first few buildings at the north end of Recogne. Stopka had already swung his reserve, Company G, around to his right and faced it south so as to cover the open flank. He had been helped a little by one of the tank destroyers. The morning was intensely foggy and enemy armor could be heard roaming around just beyond the murk. Sgt. Lazar Hovland got a clear sight of one enemy tank and set it afire in four rounds. A second German tank fired on Hovland and missed; Hovland crippled it with a quick shot but it pulled back into the fog.

By the new order from 101st Division, the 1st Battalion was to clean out Recogne finally and then fill the gap between the 502d and 506th regiments. The order was changed a few minutes later when Colonel Sink (506th commander) reported to General McAuliffe that despite Company G's difficulty the 506th's position was pretty sound. General McAuliffe decided that it made little difference whether he held Recogne. The 1st Battalion, 502d, which had been sweeping forward with two companies abreast, was told to keep on moving but in column of companies. General McAuliffe asked Colonel Stopka if he could disengage, pull back of Recogne and stand on a line running south-eastward to where he could join Colonel Sink's flank. Inasmuch as Company G was already standing on this line which curved crescent-fashion around a reverse slope, Stopka said he would be glad to make the move. At noontime the 1st Battalion was moved back to Grosse-Hez and Company A was moved to the south of Longchamps to stop anything that might come that way. The 377th Field Artillery Battalion had given support to the 502d during the latter stage of this operation and had fired 60 rounds on the highway from Salle to Bertogne. The fire knocked out six vehicles of a German column which was turned back by these losses.

On December 22 the enemy build-up along the Salle-Bertogne road continued at such a pace that at noontime Colonel Chappuis, the 502d's commander, moved Company A to Champs and the rest of the 1st Battalion to Hemroulle (two miles west of Bastogne), which faced them to the westward. A platoon from Company B was set up as a roadblock, where Company A had been, along the Longchamps-Bastogne road.

The 3d Battalion received German probing attacks all day long, but on a limited scale. Two of the tank destroyers which had been with Colonel Stopka's 3d Battalion were switched over to support Company A in Champs. A patrol was sent to Rouette, a mile north of Champs, to check on enemy activities. It encountered a small detachment of Germans in the village, engaged 14 of them in a 20-minute fight, drove them off with machine-gun and rifle fire and withdrew under cover of fire from the 377th Parachute FA Battalion.

On December 23, the positions were unchanged. Another patrol went into Rouette under the leadership of 1st Lt. David E. White. They got close enough to see that the enemy was occupying a line of outposts on high ground which overlooked the roads to Champs and Givry (two miles northwest of Champs). The enemy was feverishly at work setting up roadblocks of farm carts bound together. There was a great deal of digging going on next to the positions.

Farther to the southward the signs were becoming equally ominous. Colonel Allen's 3d Battalion of the 327th Glider Infantry was situated in defense of the area of Flamierge, Flamizoulle and the St. Hubert highway west of Mande-St.-Étienne. This put it well to the west of any other unit, without friendly contact on either its right or left. Feeling that his battalion was overextended, Colonel Allen issued a withdrawal plan to his units on December 21 which was known as Plan A. By this plan Company C would move through Company B in Flamizoulle and Company B would then follow and go through Company A. It was the responsibility of Company A to hold off the enemy until the two other companies were situated on the high ground west of Champs and Grandes-Fanges (a mile to the south). Company A would then withdraw through Company B and Company C would go into reserve position.

At noon on December 23, patrols reported enemy tanks approaching from the woods to the south of the St. Hubert road. On drawing nearer, this force revealed itself as twelve tanks accompanied by infantry in snow suits. About 1330 Colonel Allen's outposts began their withdrawal without trying to engage the German armor. Allen was fearful that the Germans would move to his right and cut him off from Bastogne. Instead, they moved to the left and halted on the ridge just south of the main road near Cochleval. From this ground they fired upon Company C's position, but upon trying to advance, were turned back by the American artillery. In one sortie they lost two tanks to artillery fire and the rest of the German armor then withdrew to turret defilade and continued to fire into Company C for the rest of the afternoon. Six of Colonel Templeton's tank destroyers (of the 705th), along with the reconnaissance platoon, had been in position where with good fortune they might have supported Company C in the first stage of this action. But as they pulled out of the cut just beyond Mande-St.-Étienne, enemy tanks shelled them from the woods off their flank and two tank destroyers were lost immediately. This caused a more cautious attitude on the part of the other tank destroyers and they withdrew slightly while the reconnaissance platoon went forward to screen them on the left flank. The other tank destroyers distributed themselves so as to block the roads leading into Mont and the reconnaissance platoon dug in along the same line.

As darkness came on, Colonel Allen got word that his roadblock at Flamierge had been overrun by an enemy infantry force wearing snow suits. This German column had come down the St. Hubert highway from out of the northwest. Allen's men had been under the mistaken impression that a friendly force—the 4th Armored Division—would arrive by this same route. They mistook the identity of the group and let it come on until the time had passed for successful resistance.

Four tanks moving along with the road column suddenly opened fire on Company C, hitting a number of men and destroying the company aid station, an antitank gun and a pile of mortar ammunition with the first few rounds. The four tanks pressed on against the company position. At the same time the ten tanks to the southward began coming over the ridge. Company C withdrew as best it could.

Colonel Allen figured that by now his whole battalion position was in jeopardy and he ordered Plan A put into effect. But Company C was in such confusion that it couldn't carry out the withdrawal exactly

German propaganda leaflets (two sides) fired by artillery shell into the 101st lines on Christmas Eve.

as planned. One platoon got out to the southeastward by way of the main road to escape being cut off. The other platoons pulled back along the predetermined route. Company B came through Company A as planned and took position on the left flank of the high ground where Colonel Allen had determined to make his stand. Company A moved to the rear in reserve. However, Company C's losses were such that Company A had to come back forward again and take Company's C place in the line. Fortunately, the enemy did not press the attack.

Allen told his men, "This is our last withdrawal. Live or die—this is it."

He had spoken correctly; the battalion was never pushed from that ground though it was still to face its worst ordeal.

The next day was quiet. The men cleaned their weapons and waited for Christmas Eve.

CHRISTMAS EVE

Christmas Eve was quiet. The commanders and staffs took official notice of the occasion. To all of the command posts within Bastogne went a G-2 reminder from the 101st's chief joker, Danahy. It was a situation report over!ay in red, white and green, the red outlining the enemy positions completely encircling the town and the green showing only in the words "Merry Christmas" across the position held by the defenders.

General McAuliffe also rose to the occasion with an inspired communiqué.

24 December 1944

*Merry Christmas!
HEADQUARTERS 101ST AIRBORNE DIVISION
Office of the Division Commander

What's merry about all this, you ask? We're fighting—it's cold—we aren't home. All true but what has the proud Eagle Division accomplished with its worthy comrades of the 10th Armored Division, the 705th Tank Destroyer Battalion and all the rest? Just this: We have stopped cold everything that has been thrown at us from the North, East, South and West. We have identifications from four German Panzer Divisions, two German Infantry Divisions and one German Parachute Division. These units, spearheading the last desperate German lunge, were headed straight west for key points when the Eagle Division was hurriedly ordered to stem the advance. How effectively this was done will be written in history; not alone in our Division's glorious history but in world history. The Germans actually did surround us, their radios blared our doom. Their Commander demanded our surrender in the following impudent arrogance:

December 22nd 1944

"To the U.S.A. Commander of the encircled town of Bastogne.

"The fortune of war is changing. This time the U.S.A. forces in and near Bastogne have been encircled by strong German armored units. More German armored units have crossed the river Ourthe near Ortheuville, have taken Marche and reached St. Hubert by passing through Hompré-Sibret-Tillet. Libramont is in German hands.

"There is only one possibility to save the encircled U.S.A. troops from total annihilation: that is the honorable surrender of the encircled town. In order to think it over a term of two hours will be granted beginning with the presentation of this note.

"If this proposal should be rejected one German Artillery Corps and six heavy A. A. Battalions are ready to annihilate the U.S.A. troops in and near Bastogne. The order for firing will be given immediately after this two hours' term.

"All the serious civilian losses caused by this artillery fire would not correspond with the wellknown American humanity.

The German Commander"

The German Commander received the following reply:

22 December 1944

"To the German Commander:
N U T S !
The American Commander"

Allied Troops are counterattacking in force. We continue to hold Bastogne. By holding Bastogne we assure the success of the Allied Armies. We know that our Division Commander, General Taylor, will say: "Well Done!"

We are giving our country and our loved ones at home a worthy Christmas present and being privileged to take part in this gallant feat of arms are truly making for ourselves a Merry Christmas.

A. C. McAULIFFE
Commanding*

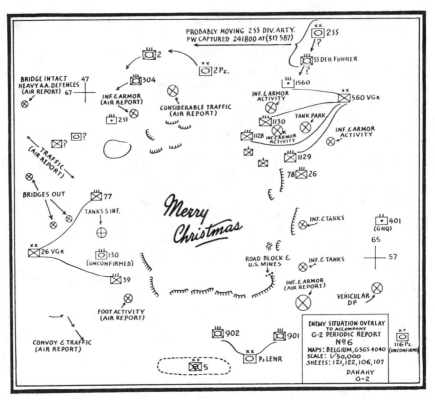

PROBABLY MOVING 2SS DIV. ARTY.
PW CAPTURED 241800 AT (517 587)

BRIDGE INTACT 47
HEAVY A.A. DEFENCES
(AIR REPORT) 67

INF. & ARMOR
(AIR REPORT)

CONSIDERABLE TRAFFIC
(AIR REPORT)

TRAFFIC
(AIR REPORT)

BRIDGES OUT

TANKS 5 INF.

Merry Christmas

26 VGR

130
(UNCONFIRMED)

FOOT ACTIVITY
(AIR REPORT)

CONVOY & TRAFFIC
(AIR REPORT)

2 SS
?

SS DER FUHRER
?

1560

560 VGR

INF. & ARMOR
ACTIVITY

TANK PARK

1130

1128 INF. & ARMOR
ACTIVITY

INF. & ARMOR
ACTIVITY

1129

78 26

INF. & TANKS

401
(GHQ)

65

57

ROAD BLOCK &
U.S. MINES

INF. & TANKS

INF. & ARMOR
(AIR REPORT)

VEHICULAR
DP

902

901

Pz LENR

116 Pz.
(UNCONFIRMED)

5

ENEMY SITUATION OVERLAY
TO ACCOMPANY
G-2 PERIODIC REPORT
No 6
MAPS: BELGIUM, GSGS 4040
SCALE: 1/50,000
SHEETS: 121,122,106,107
DANAHY
G-2

Map 77: G-2 periodic report, 24 December 1944

Privately, on the phone that night to General Middleton, McAuliffe expressed his true feeling about Christmas in these words:

"The finest Christmas present the 101st could get would be a relief tomorrow."

But General McAuliffe's greeting to his troops proved to be in every part a prophetic utterance though the quiet of Christmas Eve did not last for long.

That night the town was bombed twice. During the first raid, in the late evening, a bomb landed on the hospital of the 20th Armored Infantry Battalion near the intersection of the main roads from Arlon and Neufchâteau. It caved in the roof, burying 20 patients and killing a Belgian woman who was serving as a nurse. Another bomb landed on the headquarters of Combat Command B, doing heavy damage and knocking down the Christmas tree in the message center. The men set up the tree again, and in an elaborate ceremony, one of the sergeants pinned the Purple Heart on a mangled doll.

Except for those bombings Christmas Eve passed without unusual

Map 78.

pressure from the enemy. The journal entries of the different regiments all use the word "quiet" in describing the period. But that is a word that simply does not record the tumult in the thoughts and emotions of the men of Bastogne. Such was their reaction to the Christmas and to the memories surrounding it, that for the first time all around the perimeter men felt fearful. It seemed to them that the end was at hand. That night many of them shook hands with their comrades. They said to one another that it would probably be their last night together. Many of the commanders saw this happening, though they knew it had little relation to the still strong tactical situation.

In the 502d Parachute Infantry the officers heard Christmas Eve Mass in the tenth-century chapel of the beautiful Rolle Château which they were using for a command post. It was a happy occasion, well attended by the neighboring Belgians who had rounded out the regimental messes with contributions of flour and sides of beef from their own stores.

547

Singing carols on Christmas Eve in Bastogne. The midnight service was broken up by enemy bombers.

The regimental officers turned in about 0130 on Christmas morning. At 0245 there was an intense shelling of the forward area by the German artillery. Lt. Col. Patrick J. Cassidy, the 502d's executive officer, called Capt. Wallace A. Swanson of Company A who reported that his front had suddenly become active. But he added that the situation was obscure; he could not figure out yet what the Germans intended.

At 0330 Colonel Cassidy called Captain Swanson again. Swanson said that the enemy was on top of him. While they were talking, the line went out. Colonel Cassidy awakened Colonel Chappuis, the regimental commander. Then all lines went out. Chappuis called his 1st Battalion by radio and told them to get ready to move, adding that the commander, Maj. John D. Hanlon, was to come to Rolle as quickly as possible. By radio Chappuis heard from Swanson that Germans in large numbers were in Champs and that his men were locked in a hand-to-hand and house-to-house fight with them. Major Hanlon reported at the command post and was told by Colonel Chappuis to move Company

Bastogne commanders at Christmas dinner. Left to right: Col. William L. Roberts, CO, CCB, 10th Armored Division; Lt. Col. Ned Moore, Acting Chief of Staff; Brig. Gen. Gerald J. Higgins, Assistant Division Commander; General McAuliffe; Col. Thomas L. Sherburne, Division Artillery commander; Lt. Col. Harry W. O. Kinnard, G-3; partly visible is Lt. Col. Carl W. Kohls, G-4; Lt. Col. Paul A. Danahy, G-2; and Col. Curtis D. Renfro.

B to the Champs road just west of Rolle and then get forward into Champs and help Captain Swanson's Company A.

While Swanson was becoming engaged, other German forces had filtered through the woods to the east of Champs on the 2d Battalion's left flank. After reporting this to regiment, Lt. Col. Thomas H. Sutliffe, the 2d Battalion commander, shifted part of his force leftward against this threat. Colonel Chappuis supported his move by instructing Major Hanlon to send one platoon of Company B to the right to join hands with Company E. Hanlon called in at 0545 and said the Germans were still fighting in Champs. He did not want to put the rest of his battalion into the village until it became light because the darkness and confusion were so bad that it was almost impossible to distinguish friend from enemy. Colonel Chappuis told him to hold steady.

As Chappuis and Cassidy estimated the situation at 502d Headquarters, Company B was already backing up Company A and would still be effective if Champs were lost, whereas it might lose its reserve value if it pushed on into the village and the Germans came around it. So

The château at Rolle, CP of the 502d Parachute Infantry.

they waited. They knew that somewhere a real blow was coming but they could not figure where. So far the German pressure had jarred them only at the right and center of the 502d and was coming at them from the north. They looked anxiously to the westward where their sector joined that of the 327th Glider Infantry. Their command post was under heavy artillery fire and was no longer in either telephone or radio communication with Headquarters, 101st Division.

Just as the first light of Christmas morning broke, the S-2 of the 1st Battalion, 1st Lt. Samuel B. Nickels, Jr., came at a dead run into the château where the Headquarters, 502d, was. "There are seven enemy tanks and lots of infantry coming over the hill on your left," he said. He had first sighted them moving along parallel to the ridge southwest of Hemroulle. They were striking toward the ground where the 502d and 327th joined hands.

The Rolle Château was emptied almost before Lieutenant Nickels had finished speaking. Cooks, clerks, radio men and the chaplains collected under Capt. James C. Stone, the 502d headquarters commandant, and rushed west to the next hill. From the château gate at Rolle, the

550

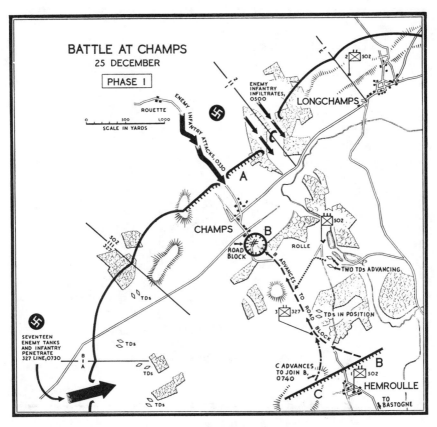

Map 79.

road dips down through a deep swale then rises onto the ridge where it joins the main road into Hemroulle, about two miles northwest of Bastogne. The road line is on high ground all the way until just before it reaches Hemroulle where it drops down again to the village. Captain Stone's scratch headquarters force ran across the swale and took up firing positions close to the road and facing westward. Within a few minutes they were joined by the men of the regiment's wounded who were able to walk. Maj. Douglas T. Davidson, 502d surgeon, had run to the château stable that was serving as a temporary hospital, rallied his patients, handed them rifles and then led them out against the tanks.

They could see the tanks coming on toward them now. From the archway of Rolle Château it was about 600 yards to the first line of German armor. Colonels Chappuis and Cassidy and the radio operator looked westward from the archway and could see just the outline of the enemy movement in the dim light. They were now the only men at the headquarters.

551

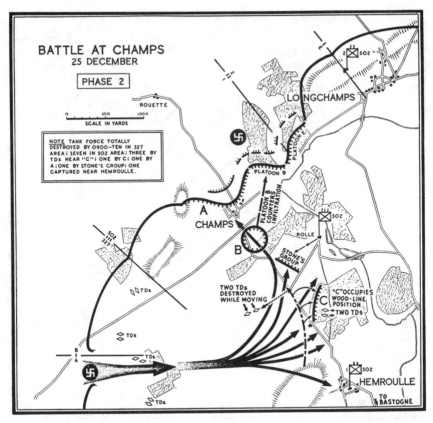

Map 80.

Colonel Cassidy called Major Hanlon and told him to leave Company B where it was but to get the company ready to protect its own rear and then try to get Company C faced to the west to meet the German tanks as they came on.

The 327th Glider Infantry was already engaged. At 0500 Colonel Harper had heard by phone from Company A of his 3d Battalion that 18 enemy tanks were formed for attack just east of Mande-St.-Étienne. At 0710 the German armor supported by infantry of the 77th Grenadier Regiment smashed through the positions held by Companies A and B. In coming through the companies, the tanks fired all their guns and the German infantrymen riding the tanks blazed away with their rifles. The spearpoint of the German armor had already broken clear through to the battalion command post. At the 327th regimental headquarters Colonel Harper heard by telephone of the breakthrough, and on the heels of that message came word from Lt. Colonel Cooper that his 463d Parachute Field Artillery Battalion already had the German tanks

552

under fire. At 0715 Colonel Allen, the 3d Battalion (327th) commander, called and said that the tanks were right on him.

Harper asked, "How close?"

"Right here!" answered Allen. "They are firing point-blank at me
from 150 yards range. My units are still in position but I've got to run."
But Colonel Allen's battalion had not been wholly taken by surprise.
"Tanks are coming toward you!" Capt. Preston E. Towns, commanding Company C, had telephoned to Allen.

"Where?" Allen had asked.

"If you look out your window now," said Captain Towns, "you'll be
looking right down the muzzle of an 88."

Christmas Day was just then breaking. Colonel Allen stayed at his
3d Battalion, 327th, command post only long enough to look out of his
window, and prove what Towns had told him, and to call Colonel
Harper and tell him he was getting out. Then he ran as fast as he could
go and the German tanker fired at him as he sprinted toward the woods.
He could see the muzzle blasts over his shoulder in the semidarkness.
But all of the shots were leading him. The Germans were giving him
credit for more speed than his legs possessed.

Two members of Allen's staff followed him. As they all came out of
the other end of the woods, men of Colonel Chappuis' 502d Parachute
Infantry along the ridge road saw them and promptly pinned them
down with heavy rifle fire. The three then crawled back to the woods,
circled south through a little valley and returned to Hemroulle.

As they came out of the woods the second time, they were fired on
by artillerymen of Colonel Cooper's 463d Parachute Field Artillery Battalion who had formed a skirmish line in case the enemy broke through
the infantry. But Colonel Allen was getting tired of all this and he
waved his handkerchief vigorously until finally the gunners lowered
their rifles and let the party come in.

Colonel Harper, on getting the phone call made by Allen just before Allen had to dash from his headquarters, realized that there was
now no control over the 3d Battalion, 327th. So he sent his own S-3,
Major Jones, with his radio to Cooper's CP and Jones got there just as
Allen did, and he got through at once to the companies with the radio.

In the meantime the forward line had held partly because of the
quick thinking of Captain McDonald of Company B. He had heard
Colonel Allen's urgent report to Colonel Harper over his own telephone
and he at once called Companies A and C by radio. "The battalion
commander has had to get out," he said to them. "I can see you from
where I am. Your best bet is to stay where you are. Hold tight to your
positions and fight back at them."

One of the two American tank destroyers knocked out in the German breakthrough on Christmas morning at Champs. The haystack behind which this TD was concealed still smoulders. This TD was stopped by the German tank on the opposite page.

That was what they did. The main body of German armor rolled straight through Company A's lines—18 white camouflaged tanks moving in column. The men of Company A, 327th (1st Lt. Howard G. Bowles was the acting commanding officer), stayed in their foxholes and took it, replying with their rifles and whatever other weapons were at hand. After the tide of German steel had passed over and through them, 4 men of the company were dead and 5 lay wounded. But the 68 survivors were up and fighting, and in the next round of the battle they captured 92 German prisoners.

Having crashed through Colonel Harper's 327th front, the German armor split as it came on toward the ridge and half of it swung north toward Rolle where Lieutenant Nickels saw it and warned Colonel Chappuis, commander of the 502d Parachute Infantry, in time for him to make his last-minute preparation. Companies B and C, 502d, were even then in column of twos moving up the road toward the village of Champs.

Thus far Colonel Templeton's 705th Tank Destroyer Battalion had played only a minor part in the defense of the sector, but their best moments were approaching. Two of the tank destroyers had been of some assistance to Captain Swanson (Company A, 502d) in his fight for Champs. They were already in position there when the German attack got under way, one destroyer in the center of Champs and another

This German Mark IV tank, captured intact in Hemroulle on Christmas morning, was the only survivor of eighteen which drove through the 327th's lines that morning.

slightly to the west of it so placed that it could cover the road to the southwest and the ridge to the north and northwest. Upon setting up, the tank destroyer crews manned four machine guns on the ground around their centrally located guns. This position held when the German infantry closed on Champs and the tank destroyer force even spared a few of its men to go forward and help the paratroopers root the enemy out of the houses.

Too, the heavy guns were used for close-up interdiction fire to keep the enemy from moving any deeper into the village. In this work, the 37mm. guns, firing canister, were especially effective. Captain Swanson got one of the tank destroyers, under Sgt. Lawrence Valletta, to go forward and blast a house where about thirty Germans had taken cover. Sergeant Valletta moved right in next to the building, trained his big gun on the doors and windows and blew the place apart. He then shelled two more houses and returned to his original position. Just about dawn, he made a second sortie of the same kind.

To the southward of Champs where the crisis of the Christmas action was swiftly maturing, the tank destroyers got away to a bad start but then staged a swift recovery. Two of them from Company B, 705th Battalion, had been in the 327th Glider Infantry area and were out along the road which runs from Rolle toward Grandes-Fanges, a mile to the southwest (this put them to the southward of Company C, 502d Parachute Infantry), when the German attack came over the hill. The

555

On Christmas morning, after breaking through the 3d Battalion, 327th, enemy tanks came across the hills to the left to attack Champs and Rolle. The road to the right goes to Champs. Paralleling the second row of trees a road leads to Rolle. Company C, 502d, was attacked while marching along the center road. It then fell back to join two TDs at the trees in the foreground. From this position seven German tanks were destroyed.

crews had at first put their tank destroyers into concealment behind a haystack and from there had engaged the enemy armor at a distance, knocking out two or three tanks. Yet as the power of the German armor became more obvious, they decided to withdraw. That was how it happened that they were moving back toward Rolle and were directly in line with the German tank fire when Company C of the 502d Parachute Infantry faced toward the enemy.

Both tank destroyers were knocked out almost instantly. The men of Company C saw them reel and stop from the enemy fire and realized that the loss of the tank destroyers had helped spare them the worst part of the blow.

The encounter had had one other powerful effect—two tank destroyers from Company C, 705th, were waiting in the woods behind Colonel Chappuis' 502d infantrymen. The German armor, confident that it was now in full command of the field, came on boldly against the infantry line. Colonel Cassidy (executive of the 502d) had sent a runner sprinting toward the woods to alert the two concealed tank destroyers. The runner had been told to run from the guns on to Capt. George R. Cody's Company C, 502d Parachute Infantry position and tell him that the tank destroyers would be backing him up. But he didn't get there in time.

The guns of the seven Mark IVs were already firing into Company C. About 15 to 20 German infantrymen were riding on the outside of each tank, some firing their rifles. But the ground fog was bad and their fire was erratic. Captain Cody turned his men about and told them to fall back to the edge of the forest. Without any part of its line breaking into a general dash for the rear, Company C fell back to the shelter

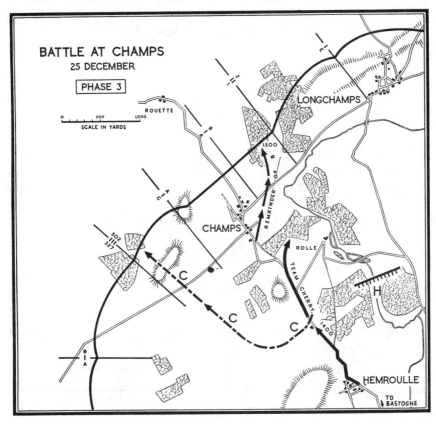

Map 81.

of the trees and there took up positions and opened fire on the tanks with machine guns, bazookas, and rifles. Despite the surprise of the German assault, this movement was carried out with little loss and no disorder.

Then swiftly, there was a complete turning of the situation as Company C's first volleys from its new position took toll of the German infantry clinging to the tanks. Dead and wounded pitched from the vehicles into the snow. As if with the purpose of saving their infantry, the tanks veered left toward Champs and the position held by Company B, 502d.

Until this moment the two tank destroyers in the woods behind Company C had not fired a round. But as the tank line privoted and began to move northward along the top of the ridge, the flank of the German armor became completely exposed and the two tank destroyers went into action. So did Company B, which was now firing at the enemy front. Three of the Mark IVs were hit and knocked out by the

557

Map 82.

tank destroyer fire before they completed their turning movement. One was stopped by a bazooka round from Company C. A fifth tank was hit and stopped by a rocket from Captain Stone's scratch group from Headquarters, 502d. The infantry riding on the tanks were cut to pieces by bullet fire. As Company C's part of the battle ended there were 67 German dead and 35 prisoners, many of them wounded, in the area around the ruined tanks.

One tank did break through Company B and charge on into Champs. Company A, 502d, fired bazookas at it and it was also shelled by a 57mm gun which had taken position in the village. The tank was hit by both types of fire but which weapon made the kill is uncertain.

Capt. James J. Hatch, S-3, of the 502d, had gone forward to reconnoiter Company A's situation and was in the Company A command post at the time. He heard the fight going on outside, grabbed his pistol and opened the door. He was looking straight into the mouth of the tank's 75mm gun at a range of 15 yards.

558

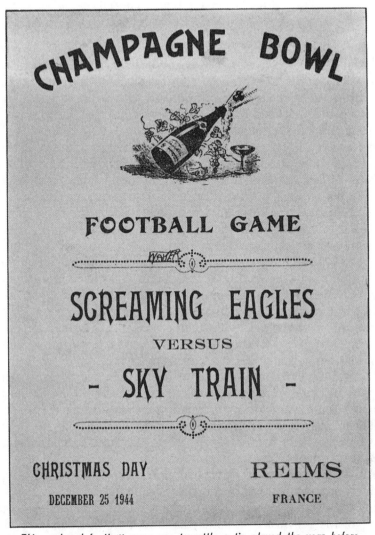

CHAMPAGNE BOWL

FOOTBALL GAME

SCREAMING EAGLES

VERSUS

- SKY TRAIN -

CHRISTMAS DAY
DECEMBER 25 1944

REIMS
FRANCE

This unplayed football game was to settle a tie played the year before in England by the 502d "Screaming Eagles" and the 506th "Sky Train."

Hatch closed the door and said to the others, "This is no place for my pistol."

The seventh tank in the German group—it was later determined that this was the same tank that had knocked out the two tank destroyers—was captured intact at Hemroulle. By 0900, December 25, the action was cleared up around Rolle. Headquarters of the 502d Parachute Infantry had called 101st Division Headquarters and asked about the situation of 327th Glider Infantry over on its left. Colonel Kinnard

(101st Airborne Division G-3) reported that the 327th's lines were generally intact and the situation there well in hand.

In the 327th's sector there had been four tank destroyers behind Captain McDonald's Company B and four behind Lieutenant Bowles' Company A. Captain Towns' Company C was unsupported by tank destroyers but Colonel Harper had sent him two Sherman tanks on hearing that the German attack was coming.

These guns, the bazooka fire of the 327th Glider Infantry outfits and the barrage fire of Colonel Cooper's 463d Parachute Field Artillery Battalion had dealt in detail with that part of the German armor that tried to ride on through toward Hemroulle after breaking Harper's front. The German tanks were fired at from so many directions and with such a mixture of fire that it was not possible to see or say how each tank met its doom. One battery from the 463d stopped two tanks at a range of 600 yards and then some men ran out from the battery position and captured the crews. Eighteen German tanks had been seen on that part of the 327th Glider Infantry's front that morning. Eighteen tanks had driven on through the infantry. But not one got away. When the fighting died at last there were eighteen disabled German tanks, many of them with fire-blackened hulls, scattered out through the American positions along the ridges running from Hemroulle to Champs.

In the 502d Parachute Infantry area, the wire maintenance men had kept on working right through the fire fight and by 0900 the lines were again in solid. None of the German infantry had managed an escape.

The few survivors, upon recoiling, were rounded up by the members of Colonel Allen's overrun 3d Battalion, 327th. The German tankers died inside their tanks.

Although Company C, 502d, had been compelled to engage without artillery support because of the closeness of the action, its losses were negligible. It was put in position along the high ground west of the scene of the skirmish. At about the same time the Company C fight ended, Company A, 502d, was getting Champs under control and was doing the last of its rat hunting through the village houses. Company B was put over to the eastward of Company A to fill out the line as far as the 3d Battalion. In getting to this position, Company B, 502d, took heavy losses from enemy artillery while moving across the high ground north of Champs, but by 1500 the position was complete. Company A counted 98 Germans killed and 79 enlisted men and 2 officers captured in the Champs action.

About 0800 on Christmas, 101st Division moved Force Cherry out through Hemroulle to a position on the high ground along the edge of

Soldiers of the 101st and German prisoner gravediggers look up from their job of burying dead in the Bastogne cemetery to watch the resupply drop of 26 December.

the woods to the southward of the 502d Parachute Infantry. Colonel Cherry stayed there until after dark to cover the restoration of the 1st Battalion, 327th, position. He then pulled back to Hemroulle. A German field order captured during the morning fight showed that the German tank and infantry mission that came to grief along the ridge south and west of Rolle had been attempted by the 115th Panzergrenadier Regiment of the 15th Panzergrenadier Division. Two battalions of the 77th Panzergrenadier Regiment, supported by the division artillery of the 26th Volksgrenadier Division, had implemented the assault against Champs and to the southward which preceded the Panzer advance.

Christmas day closed with Colonel Chappuis and Colonel Cassidy of the 502d sitting down to a table spread with a can of sardines and a box of crackers.

General McAuliffe, disappointed that no relief force had come, called General Middleton and said, "We have been let down."

THE RELIEF

On the morning of December 26, the German forces renewed their pressure against the western side of the Bastogne perimeter. But they did not press their attack in real strength and the American lines held solid. Around the other parts of the defending circle, the day was relatively quiet though both sides intensified their air activity.

The intervention of the air directly hastened the hour when the enemy encirclement of Bastogne was broken through by the arrival of

Map 83.

the armored column from the south. Since 0600 on December 22, the three Combat Commands of the 4th Armored Division had been fighting their way steadily toward Bastogne by three separate routes from their assembly areas north of Arlon. They had met intense resistance all the way along the line and had taken heavy losses in men and tanks. By 1500 on December 26, Combat Command Reserve of the 4th had arrived at the high ground overlooking Clochimont and was preparing to attack toward the village of Sibret. This put the command about four miles to the southwestward of Bastogne with their local objective one mile to their own northwestward. As the attack was about to get under way, the men saw and heard what seemed to be "hundreds" of C-47 planes coming directly over them and bound for Bastogne. The spectacle encouraged Lt. Col. Creighton W. Abrams, Jr., commanding the 37th Tank Battalion, and Lt. Col. George L. Jaques, commanding the 53d Armored Infantry Battalion, to make a break for Bastogne, disregarding their original mission. They believed

562

that Sibret was strongly held. Colonel Abrams' force had been cut down to twenty medium tanks and Colonel Jaques' force was short 230 men. They figured that it might cost less to ignore Sibret and attack straight toward Bastogne.

At 1520, December 26, Colonel Abrams ordered his S-3, Capt. William A. Dwight, to take a light team composed of tanks and infantry, break northeast to the village of Assenois and keep moving until he reached the Bastogne lines. The artillery with Combat Command Reserve, 4th Armored Division—three battalions of 105mm and one battery of 155mm howitzers—was directed to stand ready to place a concentration on Assenois as the team moved up to it. Such was the plan.

In the execution of it, the commander of the leading tank called for artillery support as soon as he came within sight of the village. The guns poured ten rounds apiece against the target, concentrating their fire against the woods north of town and into an area in the southern edge of town where the enemy was supposed to be strongly fixed with antitank guns. Combat Command Reserve's shells were still dropping on Assenois when the first tanks moved in among the houses. There were some infantry losses from our own fire. In the smoke and confusion, the infantry company of Captain Dwight's team dismounted and engaged the enemy in a fight for the village.

But five tanks and one infantry half-track stuck to the letter of their assignment and kept moving toward Bastogne. Three of the tanks had forged several hundred yards to the fore and the enemy strewed Teller mines between them and the rest of the tank force as they were pulling out of Assenois. The half-track hit a mine and was destroyed. Captain Dwight jumped down from his tank to clear the other mines away, so that he could get forward with his two tanks. Meanwhile, the three lead tanks kept going and at 1650 1st Lt. Charles P. Boggess, commanding officer of Company C, 37th Tank Battalion, drove the first vehicle from the 4th Armored Division to within the lines of the 326th Airborne Engineer Battalion, 101st Division, of the Bastogne forces.

This was the beginning. The German encirclement was now finally broken, though some days would pass before the American lines to the south were again firm and several weeks of fighting would ensue before the siege of Bastogne was finally lifted. Captain Dwight, having followed Lieutenant Boggess on into Bastogne, radioed Colonel Abrams to come up with the rest of the breakthrough team.

With them came Maj. Gen. Maxwell D. Taylor, commander of the

101st Division, who had flown back from the United States to join his Division. General Taylor had arrived in time to lead his men through their bitterest days of fighting on the Bastogne ground, the days yet to come.

Captain Dwight then continued on to report to General McAuliffe and arrange for the convoys to enter the town that night. Assenois was cleared by 2000, December 26, with the capture of 428 prisoners. Before morning, the woods on both sides of the road running north from Assenois were cleared sufficiently to assure relatively free use of this line of communication.

Much hard fighting still remained for the other two combat commands of 4th Armored Division before they, too, closed to within the Bastogne perimeter. By their drive north, they had opened an avenue to the south which would insure that the victory won by the Bastogne defenders could be fully exploited by the United States Army and the forces of its Allies.

The relief of Bastogne signaled the defeat of the German Army in the Ardennes offensive. But it had cost the 4th Armored Division a price comparable to that exacted from the defenders of Bastogne themselves. In the seven days during which its forces were moving to the relief of Bastogne the Division lost about 1,000 men. Its total medium tank strength at the end of the period was equal to the full tank strength of a single battalion. As for what this victory—won by the defenders of Bastogne and confirmed by the force that relieved them—availed the Allied cause, and as to how it influenced the emergency of December 1944, there is an official estimate from the command of 12th Army Group. The After Action Report for December 1944 says:

Preoccupation with the key position of Bastogne dominated enemy strategy to such an extent that it cost him the advantage of the initiative. The German High Command evidently considered further extension to the west or north as both logistically and strategically unsound without possession of Bastogne, as that town overlooks the main roads and concentration areas of the spearheads. By the end of the month, the all-out effort in the north had become temporarily defensive; in the west there was a limited withdrawal, and the array of German forces around Bastogne clearly exposed the enemy's anxiety over that position. Until the Bastogne situation is resolved one way or the other no change in strategy can be expected.

THE ENEMY STORY

In one respect, the Bastogne story is complete as told in the preceding pages. There is the battle as it was seen by the defending forces from within the Bastogne perimeter and as it could be clarified for them by all of the normal and accessible sources of information such as our own official documents, captured enemy documents, interviews with our key personnel at all levels, and interrogation of such of the enemy as fell into our hands in the course of operations. To preserve the integrity of the narrative from the viewpoint of the defenders, it seemed essential that the material be presented in that form. Moreover, since it will be noted in reading this added material that the errors caused by so doing were minor indeed, the Bastogne story becomes tangible proof of the competence of our own methods of acquiring intelligence of the enemy and of estimating his capabilities.

There remains, however, the question of exactly what was occurring among the enemy forces while our own forces were defending Bastogne so stoutly. What was their design? How did they view the American action? How did their estimate and judgment of the tactical events modify their own plan and movement?

It has been said in high places that the enemy was not really trying to capture Bastogne. This judgment was taken after a cursory examination of his plan which fell into our hands in the course of the war. But that is not a final truth and if the full importance of all that happened in the first days of the Bastogne defense is to be accurately measured by history, the witnesses must speak from the opposing camp.

In November and December 1945 there took place a series of conferences between the three chief actors in the attack on Bastogne and the author of the Bastogne story (Col. S. L. A. Marshall). Present were Lt. Gen. Heinrich von Lüttwitz, Commanding General of the XXXXVII Panzer Corps, Lt. Gen. Fritz Hermann Bayerlein, Commanding General of the Panzer Lehr Division, and Maj. Gen. Heinz Kokott, Commanding General of the 26th Volksgrenadier Division. Col. Meinhard von Lauchert, the commander of the 2d Panzer Division, was not present nor was his presence deemed necessary. Of the three divisions, the 2d Panzer had had least to do with the direct attack on Bastogne; and further, the Corps commander, having formerly commanded that division and having a sentimental feeling for it and not too much faith in Von Lauchert, had directly supervised its operation during the German advance. With what at least appeared to be utmost candor, the three enemy commanders proceeded to discuss all that had happened to them.

There were in all ten conferences on these matters, during which the commanders worked with all of the necessary maps and such staff notes as were available to them. Inasmuch as the data on the American operation were already complete, it was easy to provide the check points

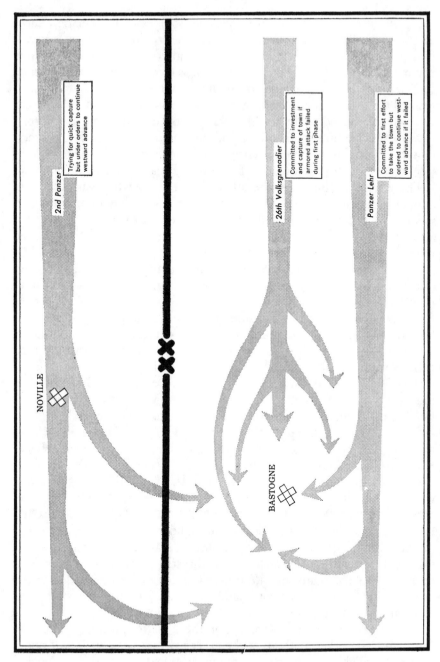

NOVILLE

2nd Panzer

Trying for quick capture but under orders to continue westward advance

26th Volksgrenadier

Committed to investment and capture of town if armored attack failed during first phase

BASTOGNE

Panzer Lehr

Committed to first effort to take the town but ordered to continue westward advance if it failed

Map 84: Bastogne envelopment according to the German plan.

which would establish the accuracy of their story in all particulars. Col. H. W. O. Kinnard, who had been G-3 of the 101st Airborne Division during the Bastogne operation, also attended these interrogations. The meeting with Kinnard was a visible shock to the German commanders. It seemed incredible to them that this boyish-faced soldier had been one of their principal antagonists. They asked several times for reassurance on this score. Lüttwitz said, "Are you certain he was chief of operations? Isn't it possible that he was only the chief for one regiment?"

Lüttwitz is an old-time cavalryman. Now past fifty-eight, he is large, gross and paunchy. His monocle and his semi-belligerent manner of speech would suggest that he is the typically arrogant Prussian, but among other German commanders he had the reputation of being especially kind to troops. He would talk only when he had a map before him; then he liked to lay pencils on the map to represent the movements of his regiments. What was most remarkable about him was that in battle he seemed to have concerned himself more with the movements of squads and companies than with the employment of divisions. He was frequently hazy about how his regiments had been disposed but he could invariably say what had been done by a particular patrol or outpost. Once he starts talking, he is extremely windy. He appeared to be chagrined over the fact that he authored the request to Bastogne to surrender; the other commanders concerned all regard that request as a military *faux pas*. But they believe that Lüttwitz has the "Nuts!" message and that he has hidden it away somewhere as a valuable historical document.

Bayerlein is a short, solidly built man past fifty, sharp-featured and keen of eye. All of his actions are vigorous and his aggressiveness in and out of conversation reminds one of a terrier. This outward seeming hides the fact that he is suffering from a fatal kidney ailment. He prides himself on the fact that in the past ten years he has taught himself to speak English. While working with the American Historical Section, he sat down one evening and wrote as a diversion a fifty-page history of the United States which was quite accurate. His contempt for Lüttwitz is obvious. When Lüttwitz rambles in his conversation, Bayerlein waves a hand in his face and snarls, "Not important! Not important!" He believes that Lüttwitz made the worst fumbles at Bastogne though the record indicates that Bayerlein's individual actions and estimates cost the Corps some of its finest opportunities. About those mistakes and the mistakes of all others, he is brutally frank. They become almost a mania with him. When confronted with his own gross blunders, he puts his head back and laughs with abandon; it seems to be about the one thing that thoroughly amuses him.

Kokott is a shy, scholarly and dignified commander who never raises his voice and appears to be temperate in his actions and judgments. Now past fifty-two, he is doubtless the steadiest man of the three. In his account of battle, he is strictly objective. He shares Bayerlein's opinion of Lüttwitz but is more amused than resentful. Better than any other commander, he saw the true situation at Bastogne though he also made his share of mistakes, as the record shows. He felt, even more strongly than the others, that adherence to the original plan at Bastogne became unwise on December 19 but he is a natural optimist and he expected to win the battle.

The onfall of XXXXVII Panzer Corps against the front held by the American 28th Infantry Division and the general consequences of that onfall have been told in the beginning of this chapter. Having made its penetration, the further movements of XXXXVII Corps were intended to be consistent with the overall policy of the Fifth Panzer Army throughout the German Ardennes offensive: The mobile divisions would by-pass points of resistance and remain free to continue the movement; the clearing out of islands of resistance would be done by the slower-moving infantry bodies. The policy of the Army was duly transmitted from Corps down to the divisions. It was believed that the two armored divisions could quickly overrun Bastogne before resistance there could solidify. In their sweep directly westward, the boundary between the 2d Panzer Division on the right and the Panzer Lehr Division on the left, for the attack on Bastogne, was an east-west line about halfway between Bastogne and Noville. The objective of the 2d Panzer Division was the same crossroads X south of the Bois de Herbaimont which figured so prominently in the American story. The purpose of the Panzer Lehr Division was to take Bastogne by attack from the south. This was the original order as established by the initial plan. It was not changed before the battle opened although it was in a degree modified.

On December 12, Lüttwitz called his division commanders together, and addressing his remarks especially to Bayerlein, the commander of Panzer Lehr, he said to all of them: "Bastogne must be taken. Otherwise it will remain an abscess on our lines of communication. We must clear out the whole of Bastogne and then march on." He added the instruction that if Bastogne was found to be relatively open, it should be attacked directly by the most feasible route, but that if it were defended in strength frontally, the two armored divisions should attempt to envelop and attack the rear or west. These two expedients failing and quick capture of the town appearing impossible, the two armored divisions were to continue their general advance and the 26th Volksgrenadier Division was to undertake the investment and capture of Bastogne. The effect which this conference produced on the minds of the subordinate commanders is to be measured in the story of their separate actions and decisions.

In the attack of December 16 against the general American front, the Corps attacked with 2d Panzer Division on the right flank and 26th Volksgrenadier Division on the left, and Panzer Lehr Division in reserve. Penetrations into our lines having been made, during December 17 the Panzer Lehr Division moved ahead of the 26th Volksgrenadier. On the right, the northern bridgeheads across the Clerf and Our rivers had been built by the 2d Panzer Division; these were the bridgeheads enabling the movement of enemy forces along the road to Longvilly. On the left the engineering units of the 26th Volksgrenadier Division had done the necessary bridging to enable Panzer Lehr to cross the Clerf and Our and push on for Bastogne. The two southern bridgeheads opened onto secondary roads by way of which Panzer Lehr could cut the lines of communication south of Bastogne and attack the town initially from that direction.

The 2d Panzer Division advanced rapidly throughout that day and the next day. Heavy resistance from our 28th Division units in Clervaux slowed its pace on December 17; but after that there was no check to the progress of the 2d Panzer Division until it came almost to the road intersection to the east of Longvilly, where it intended to veer north and proceed toward Noville.

In mid-afternoon of December 17, Lüttwitz, the XXXXVII Corps commander, visited his front lines where his armor was pushing westward from the bridgeheads. He returned late in the day to his CP near Karlshausen on the east bank of the Our River to find a message from his communications officer lying on his desk. It read that he had intercepted an American radio message saying that the American airborne divisions, then near Reims, had been alerted for a fast movement to the battle area. Lüttwitz looked once more at the map and reasoned that they would be sent to Bastogne.

To Lüttwitz, this spoke volumes. In his own words: "Ever since the Arnhem operation our command had feared another attack by airborne forces. When the message came in, we knew not only that there would be no such attack but that the American Army must be extremely short of reserves in the immediate vicinity. Otherwise, it

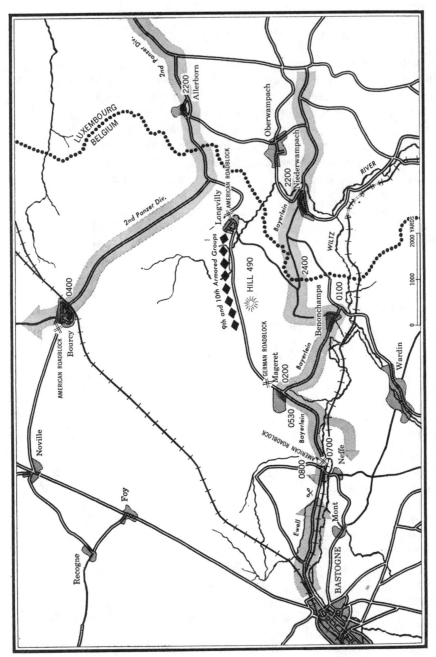

Map 85: *Opening German movements, 18-19 December 1944.*

would not commit airborne divisions of such high standing to the battle." But the knowledge that those forces were bound by ground movement for the same objective as his own forces did not change his plan or his instructions. He was already proceeding toward Bastogne with all possible speed and he calculated that he could get there before our airborne units arrived, and he would be opposed by negligible forces in so doing.

During December 18, the advance continued, with both German armored divisions adhering to the boundaries established in the original plan. Through the day there had been no interruption of progress in either lane that dimmed Lüttwitz's hope of beating the opposing forces into Bastogne. As the night drew on, his divisions were promisingly poised: The forward elements of the 2d Panzer were at the point east of Longvilly where the division was to turn north from the main road. The forward elements of Panzer Lehr were at Niederwampach, to the south.

It is to be noted that the turning movement of the 2d Panzer Division was taking place at such a distance from the roadblock of our 9th Armored Division in Longvilly (which was in process of being supported and then replaced by the forces under Captain Ryerson of Team Cherry, Combat Command B, 10th Armored Division) that both of these armored bodies could have carried out their assignments without head-on collision. The German force was, of course, turning a shoulder and then exposing a flank toward the American armor in Longvilly; moreover, it was assumed by the German commander that the American armor was in march toward him. He therefore took steps to cover the avenues of approach leading toward his exposed flank. At the same time the Americans in Longvilly, knowing nothing of the turning movement, took it for granted that this German column was coming on down the main road. It was therefore almost inevitable that the two forces would engage but the extent of engagement was limited by the mutually exclusive character of their separate missions.

Panzer Lehr, however, was under no such restriction, since Bastogne lay within its boundary. It was only a question of which was the most opportune road and hour, whether time was left to go directly at the town or whether it was the better part of wisdom to strike first at the lines of communication leading south. To do the former, Bayerlein, then at Niederwampach, would have to get his striking force moved northwest to the Longvilly–Bastogne road—the smoothest route into town.

It seems altogether probable that the soaring ambition of this com-

mander was responsible for his decision. He wanted to take Bastogne
in person and the quick thrust was the only way to do it. He talked
to some Luxembourg civilians in Niederwampach; they told him that
the side road through Benonchamps to Magéret was in good condition
and perfectly feasible for the passage of armor. They said, "It looks
bad but will get better and better." In this they misled him but the
intelligence was enough to get him started. The road was narrow and
deep in mud and became steadily worse. But no resistance was encountered and having started from Niederwampach at 2200, the force crossed
the Luxembourg–Belgium border at midnight and reached Benonchamps one hour later. In the force was one battalion of infantry
from the 902d Panzergrenadier Regiment, fifteen Mark V tanks and
one battery of artillery, all under the command of the 902d Regiment's
colonel, although Bayerlein went along in one of the lead tanks and
appears to have personally directed the task force.

At 0200 the force reached Magéret on the main road. There a Belgian
civilian told Bayerlein that two hours earlier an American force of
fifty tanks and forty other armored vehicles under an American major
general had passed through Magéret going east at about midnight. He
was of course referring to Ryerson's scant force of tanks but the degree
of exaggeration in the Belgian's statement was enough to offset all the
damage that might have been caused by his disclosure. It shook Bayerlein badly and from that point on, the farther he moved forward the
more he was constrained to worry about the security of his rear.
Because he now knew that there was American armor operating along
the Longvilly road between him and the German main body, Bayerlein
set up a road block in Magéret composed of three tanks, some supporting infantry and a minefield covering the road from the east—the
same roadblock that split Team Cherry and contributed so much to
Ryerson's subsequent difficulties. The Germans at Magéret were certain
that they could hear American armor moving around in their immediate vicinity but so dark was the night and such the confusion made
by the slow movement of the last of their own vehicles into Magéret
that they could not be sure where the sounds were coming from and
hesitated to open fire for fear of hitting their own. The passage of this
armored striking force onto the Longvilly road with the object of
capturing Bastogne was regarded by the Americans who partially
observed it at the time as only a "strong patrol action." It was so
reported to Colonel Cherry and by him to Colonel Roberts. The
Americans were still expecting the main enemy thrust to come straight
down the main road.

At about 0400 the German force in Magéret began to draw fire from the near-by terrain. Though not greatly harassed, it fought back for about an hour and a half. At 0530 Bayerlein started his tanks on down the road to Neffe. As they worked their way cautiously along toward that hamlet they drew considerable fire from the high ground to right of the road. It is probable that this resistance came from retreating elements of the 9th Armored Division which had taken to the hills at the approach of the German column. The German force kept moving. The lead tank hit a mine at Team Cherry's roadblock just east of Neffe and blew up; the Germans did not receive any fire from the Americans who had been manning the block and saw no signs of these men. So far not a shot had been fired and they got the impression that Neffe was undefended.

While the remaining mines were being cleared away from the road, one infantry company moved south of the tracks and advanced toward the Neffe Château. The company had no close tank support for the ground was still much too wet for armor. So in this double-pronged fashion, the advance got under way again at 0550, with the armor (eleven tanks) riding the main highway. At 0700 the head of the armor reached the Neffe station and there it paused for almost an hour —an interlude that cost Bayerlein his one chance to strike Bastogne before Colonel Ewell could get started. All of the dash had gone out of the man by this time. There was no good tactical reason for the pause. But his own doubt about the situation stayed him. When the order to proceed was at last given, the tanks advanced down the Bastogne road about 200 yards. Then they were struck by American fire. A machine gun in one of the leading German tanks had opened fire at about the same time. It was hard to say who had fired first. [Here note that what Colonel Ewell had considered to be an enemy roadblock was in fact a striking force in motion.] The German recoil was immediate. The loss to the German infantry from Colonel Ewell's opening fire was insignificant but the reaction among the foot forces was enough to deny the tanks the prospect of immediate support. The infantry wouldn't move and the tanks couldn't go forward alone. This deadlocked the advance for the necessary interlude. Then when Captain McGlone's battery went into action against the Neffe position an hour or so later, the impact was great. About eighty Germans were killed or wounded at Neffe within the first hour or so. Bayerlein, convinced by the sound (there was no observation because of fog and he was misled by the sound of the glider 105mm gun M3) that he was being opposed by armor, retired to a cave near the Neffe station.

By noon, Bayerlein's mood was one of extreme pessimism. He had felt out the situation on his right and had found Colonel Ewell's left already advancing. Also, he had been impressed by fire that was coming at him from his left—the probable source of which was the small force of men under Colonel Cherry in the Neffe Château. He imagined that infantry battalions were advancing against both his flanks and that the battalion on the north was about ready to close in on Neffe. So he returned to Magéret, where the American tanks rolling back from Longvilly were continuing to hit against his armored roadblock. He passed through the village during the noon hour, some time before Ryerson's force really went to work against the block. His men had captured an American hospital in Magéret and he asked one of the nurses to look after his wounded. His nerve was working better now. He noted that the nurse was "young, blonde and beautiful." He no longer had any thought of pushing forward with his initial task force and he had about concluded that the capture of Bastogne would require the utmost effort on the part of his entire division.

It is now necessary to follow the course of the 2d Panzer Division through these same hours. That division was under orders to capture Noville as soon as possible. Having made the northward turn to the east of Longvilly, the point of the division advanced rapidly toward Bourcy, meeting no resistance en route. The small action at the Bourcy roadblock, although seemingly inconsequential, was sufficient to convince the division commander that he was blocked in that direction and that Noville was probably strongly held. He so advised the Corps commander and the course of the division was turned north so that Noville could be attacked from several sides. The men at the Bourcy block had mistaken this point for a "reconnaissance element" and concluded that they had made off after completing their mission. Instead the block had changed the course of an entire division. There followed the heavy attacks against Noville on December 19 with the tactical results described earlier. Its road temporarily blocked by this engagement, 2d Panzer on the morning of December 19 was strung out along the road from Noville back to the northwest of Allerborn.

By afternoon of December 19, Bayerlein, commander of the Panzer Lehr Division, had begun to feel himself harassed from every side and was thinking of extricating what he considered to be his "pocketed" forces. In his own words: "As to my own position, I felt that the resistance on my flanks would have to be annihilated before I could again attack. The movement of the infantry regiment which had come out of Bastogne to attack me had reacted decisively on my thinking. Their fire superiority at Neffe was something I had witnessed with my own eyes. I thought and said that we should attack Bastogne with the whole XXXXVII Corps."

In these calculations, an overstrained imagination undoubtedly played a strong part. During the day, elements of Panzer Lehr (Bayerlein's reconnaissance battalion) covered on their south flank by the third regiment of Kokott's Division—the 39th Fusiliers of 26th Volksgrenadier—had pushed on toward Wardin. As we saw earlier, they had a limited success there and one of Colonel Ewell's companies of the 501st Parachute Infantry—Company I, on his extreme right—had been fragmented. But Bayerlein had eyes and ears only for the signs and sounds of enemy fire on his left, a state of mind aggravated no doubt by the activity of Team O'Hara's guns which had not supported Colonel Ewell's attack on Wardin but which were continuing to punish all enemy forces within sight or hearing.

Bayerlein, by his own account, gained the distinct impression that strong American forces had arrived in Wardin and were about to envelop his left; he could not conceive that the American infantry had been defeated there and that the American armor was preparing to withdraw to ground closer to Bastogne. The time had come, Bayerlein concluded, to direct every energy to the extrication of his force. But this was not easy to do. He felt that retirement by the narrow, winding road on which he had come—the road to Benonchamps—was now out of the question. If he were to make it at all, he would have to completely destroy and clear the American roadblock at Longvilly and move by the main highway. These were his thoughts after he had moved farther rearward from Magéret and he so reported them to his Corps commander, adding his personal urging that the plan be changed and that the entire Corps be thrown against Bastogne.

During these same hours, the XXXXVII Corps commander, Lieutenant General Lüttwitz, had received nothing but bad news from any part of his front. In sum, he had heard that Bayerlein had been stopped at Neffe, that parts of the 77th Regiment of the 26th Volksgrenadier Division had been stopped east of Bizory (by the 501st Parachute Infantry), and that the 78th Regiment of the 26th Division had been stopped at Hill 540, southeast of Foy (by Colonel Sink's forces). General Kokott, too, had expressed the same gloomy views as Bayerlein. He realized that the 101st Airborne Division had beaten him to Bastogne. And feeling that his own division might not be equal to the task of dislodging them, he urged that the entire Corps be committed to the task.

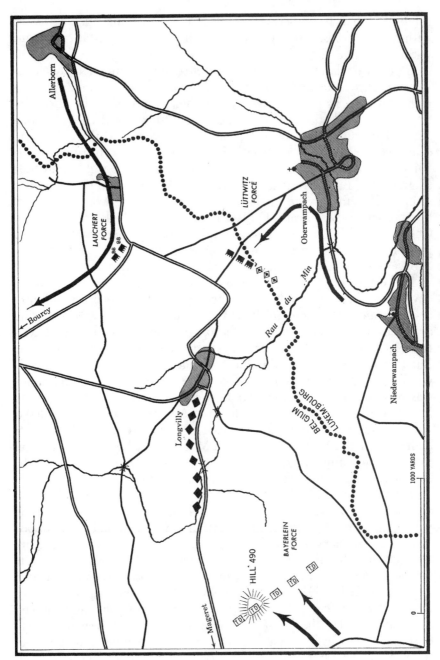

Map 86: Destruction of the Longvilly block, 19 December 1944.

Lüttwitz reported to Fifth Panzer Army that each of his division commanders had gathered the impression that the enemy was in extraordinary strength at Bastogne. He added his recommendation that the original plan be changed and that the XXXXVII Corps be solidly committed to the reduction of Bastogne. Army refused the request, but it added a strange amendment to the previous orders. The Corps as a whole was given permission to renew the attack on a limited scale, since the position of the Panzer Lehr Division had become seriously compromised and so had that of the two northern regiments of the 26th Volksgrenadier Division. This was how matters stood on the highest level at 1600 on December 19.

But on the tactical plane, Corps and all three divisions had been harassed mainly by thoughts of what might happen unless they destroyed the Longvilly roadblock. They had gone to work on that problem in early afternoon with such results that they should have become convinced they had reduced it to a cipher. The consequences to the American armor of the German attack against the Longvilly position on the afternoon of December 19 have been described earlier in their bare detail. But neither Captain Ryerson nor Lieutenant Hyduke had any idea then what major forces had been arrayed against them. In the course of the forenoon, out of Panzer Lehr, the 901st Panzergrenadier Regiment, one tank destroyer battalion with about twenty TDs, and an artillery battalion, had collected in the area of Benonchamps. Bayerlein, worrying about the Neffe–Magéret forces and the probable involvement of his reconnaissance battalion—the Panzer Lehr Division's reconnaissance training battalion—which had been shaken out farther to the south, seized on the Benonchamps forces to break the grip of the Longvilly block.

Bayerlein did not realize at the time that a body of American armor was collected at the position which he was about to attack, for he had received principally mortar and small-arms fire from that direction. He had already begun to discount the story told him by the Belgian the night before and was now swinging around to the idea that there was no American armor on his rear. This is the reason why he weighted his attack heavily with infantry. He ordered the force to attack from Benonchamps through the woods toward Longvilly, going east. Fifteen of the TDs were to give strong preliminary and supporting fires; the other five TDs were directed to accompany the two companies of infantry to the high ground. It was a trick, he said, that he had learned from opposing our 4th Armored Division in Normandy.

This assault force reached the top of Hill 490 a little time after 1400.

From there, they saw the welter of American armor and motionless combat vehicles strung out along the Longvilly road, the tanks trying vainly to break away from their own trap. It was a target they had not expected at all, and it lay fully vulnerable at range of 1,500 to 2,000 yards. The other tank destroyers came forward. The twenty heavy guns of the TDs opened fire and so did all other weapons.

Nor was that all. To support Bayerlein's Neffe position on the right Lüttwitz had ordered one regiment from the 26th Volksgrenadier Division to move to Bizory via the most direct side road. The advance elements of that regiment, the 77th, had already taken the road from Oberwampach going through Niederwampach. The rear elements were still within convenient reach to the southeast of the Longvilly block. Lüttwitz, not knowing of Bayerlein's action, met the commander of the regiment on the road between Oberwampach and Niederwampach and directed him to collect all artillery and heavy weapons in the general area and attack Longvilly from the southeast. He did so, and the force which went forward was heavy in antitank guns. By accident rather than from design it arrived at the high ground south of Longvilly simultaneously with the opening of Bayerlein's attack and its gunpower was added to the impact of the TDs.

Colonel Meinhard von Lauchert, commanding the 2d Panzer Division, had talked with Lüttwitz about the Longvilly block, but since his own people were turning north some distance short of the American armor, it hadn't concerned him overly in the beginning. But when he drew fire from the Longvilly direction (the action taken by the batteries supporting Hyduke) during the morning of December 19 and the shells threatened to interdict his turning movement, he directed that five or six 88mm guns be set up at the road junction below Chilfontaine to counter the American fire. This battery had been in operation for perhaps two hours when the two attacks were launched against Longvilly from the southeast and southwest. Its guns continued to fire and do great execution upon the stalled American column during the hours when the guns along the southern line were raking the armor point-blank. Here was surely the strangest passage in the whole enemy attack on Bastogne—all three divisions engaged at one time, bringing together the greatest fire concentration produced during the first phase of the siege. And their luckless target was a force which already felt itself defeated and was simply looking for a way out!

The bombardment lasted for about two hours, but even after that the German infantry did not close in. After Hyduke and his group fell back on Ryerson, who was trying to break through Magéret and so open a road of escape for what remained of the American force, some few American riflemen remained hidden amid the wreckage of the American armor and kept the enemy at bay with rifle fire—or at least that is the explanation of the German commanders. Dark was almost at hand when the Germans moved out onto the road. Lüttwitz, fascinated by the spot, strolled among the riven hulls and noted that it was a strange place for a battle. This portion of the road was a kind of sacred way, lined on both sides with large stone crucifixes and a dozen or more heroic figures of saints. The burning armor was jammed in among these objects; the sacred images had served to block the way out. But Lüttwitz looked the tanks over carefully and concluded that Von Lauchert's guns had done most of the damage.

It was a melancholy night for Lüttwitz. He was under the impression that a strong American force had arrived at Wardin. And if that were true, it was a serious impingement on any effort to attack Bastogne from the south. His immediate problem was a kind of tactical monstrosity. He could use his entire corps against Bastogne and yet he had to commit it in such a way that there would be no chance of an involvement that would militate against the accomplishment of his basic mission to keep on advancing. He was dropping infiltration for the moment but he was not undertaking siege: there was no time to coordinate a general plan.

In the morning he felt a little better. Word came that Bayerlein's reconnaissance battalion (Panzer Lehr Division) had taken Wardin. Lüttwitz felt that this eased his situation, though no one bothered to tell him that Wardin had fallen into his hands without struggle because there were no Americans there. On the right the 2d Panzer Division took Noville somewhere near the middle of the afternoon, and again the Corps commander grew confident that the Americans were yielding to his superior force. He thought that an outflanking movement directed at Noville by the 2d Panzer Division from the northwest had brought off the capture of the village. He didn't know that the pressure on the American right rear had anything to do with it—a pressure coming from one of Kokott's regiments. Kokott's men had come through the woods and were pressing on Foy. It was this pressure that persuaded Colonel Sink to ask for permission to withdraw. So during most of that day Lüttwitz entertained an illusion that his hit-and-run effort was succeeding.

His hopes were again dashed by what happened to his center. The 901st Regiment, Panzer Lehr Division, tried for Marvie in the hours of the late morning and was repulsed. However, to Lüttwitz that was no more than an incident in the battle; he hadn't expected much. But when Bayerlein hit again from Neffe just after dark fell, and his attack was stopped cold, the whole command reacted gloomily. Again Bayerlein got a slightly exaggerated idea of the forces opposing him. "I was stopped by a tremendous artillery [true enough] and I also found myself opposing a great number of tanks [not accurate]. The effect was overpowering. We were stopped before we could begin." Again, to General Bayerlein the shock at Neffe was decisive. It also spelled failure for the Corps as a whole.

The Corps, meanwhile, had been extending westward to the south of Bastogne. When Lüttwitz heard that units of the Panzer Lehr Division had taken Wardin, he told General Kokott to take his reconnaissance battalion and the 39th Regiment, and swinging on a wide arc toward Sibret, make ready to attack Bastogne from the south. The advance followed the general line through Lutremange to Villera-la-Bonne-Eau to Hompré to Sibret but the roads on this line were so difficult for the armored cars that they had to advance well to the southward of the forest. Sibret was captured about 2000. The 39th Regiment reached high ground one kilometer north of Remoifosse and the wood one kilometer north of Assenois and there was brought in check, chiefly through the efforts of Colonel Harper's 327th Glider Infantry and the engineers. Having taken Sibret, Kokott's reconnaissance battalion went on to Chenogne, where it was brought in check temporarily.

Thus the Corps stood on the night of December 20, with Bastogne almost soldily in its embrace. On the south was Kokott's 39th Regiment (26th Volksgrenadier Division). To the southeast, near Marvie, was Bayerlein's 901st Regiment (Panzer Lehr Division). And next to it, confronting Neffe, was his 902d. The 77th and 78th Regiments of Kokott were on each side of the railway running northeast out of Bastogne. Across the north, blocking all roads, were the elements of the 2d Panzer Division. That division was advancing to the west, and the extension of the general line, in so far as it was concerned, consisted only of roadblock elements whose mission was to protect the flank of the marching column.

Yet despite this apparently excellent situation of the Corps, Lüttwitz felt that night that so far as Bastogne was concerned, he was temporarily defeated. His chief subordinates, too, with the exception of Kokott, believed that the enforced continuation of the advance of the mechanized divisions to the westward, leaving the Bastogne assignment to Kokott's division, dimmed the prospect for a final victory. They had been impressed by the strength of the Bastogne forces and they felt that the task required unremitting pressure from the entire Corps.

In the course of December 21, Kokott's reconnaissance battalion got almost to the highway near Mande-St.-Étienne before being stopped by Colonel Harper's forces. The day was given over largely to the shifting of regiments as Kokott's division took over the general assignment which the day previous had been a Corps responsibility. Panzer Lehr was bound for Morhet. Bayerlein's 902d Regiment was replaced on the Bastogne line by Kokott's 77th, and his 78th Regiment took over the sector which had been held by the 2d Panzer Division. One regiment, the 901st, and some of the special elements of the Panzer Lehr Division were left behind, passing into Kokott's command.

On that day, also, the reconnaissance group of the 2d Panzer Division got only as far as Tenneville. Lüttwitz by now was devoting his entire attention to the progress of the 2d Panzer. He had wanted the reconnaissance group to move fast through the Bois de Bande and reach Bande by nightfall, but for some reason he couldn't get his lead forces rolling and the division strung out all the way from Tenneville to Bourcy. He found out later that the head of his column had been stopped by "strong enemy forces" maintaining a roadblock at a crossing southeast of Tenneville. This was, of course, the block maintained by Company B of Allen's battalion of the 327th Glider Infantry. It held up the progress of the 2d Panzer Division for one whole day, and of this delay much resulted subsequently. On December 22 and 23 the division pushed on only a little way; it was for the 2d Panzer Division a day of endless stopping, starting and turning, the sounds of which gave the defending forces within the Bastogne perimeter the impression that a tremendous enemy build-up was taking place to the north of them. [The patrols into Rouette led by Lt. David E. White of 502d Parachute Infantry were in fact hitting against the outposts covering the flank of this withdrawing division.] Again word came to Lüttwitz that the 2d Panzer Division's road was blocked by a stoutly held enemy roadblock. The report came from the same regimental commander who had engaged Company B, 327th, on December 21.

On the night of December 23-24, Lüttwitz went forward in person to examine the block. He received no fire as he came within range of it, so he rode on to the block and began taking the logs down. The block had been undefended throughout the entire time and the division had lost two days because of the hesitancy of this regimental commander who was subsequently court-martialed for cowardice. It cost the division dear, and not alone in time, for its vehicles were still strung out over these roads when the skies lifted and the American air strike came. Haltingly, and with other similar bad experiences, the division continued on its way toward Marche, Lüttwitz accompanying them.

Kokott, on taking over the main burden of reducing Bastogne, was at first flushed with optimism. On the morning of December 20, he had been at Wardin, where an American shell hit his CP truck, killed the other occupants and propelled Kokott against the wall of the village church. He was badly stunned; it was his closest call of the war. But he had been encouraged by the taking over of the position. After briefing the 39th Regiment and the reconnaissance battalion for the move westward toward Sibret, he went with them, to make certain that they moved as he wanted. So doing, he gained a first-hand impression that Bastogne was wide open on the south and west. He saw certain of the American elements which, either in moral or physical dissolution, were attempting to move south away from Bastogne. But what he saw he mistakenly interpreted. He thought these retreating fractions signified that the Bastogne defense was now disintegrating. This suspicion became a conviction when at Sibret he talked to a Belgian who assured him that the Bastogne garrison was falling apart. Arriving at his CP at Bras at 0200 on the morning of December 21, he was further cheered by the news that the 5th Parachute Division on his left flank (to the south) was making good progress. Kokott had found the roads very muddy, greatly choked by disabled vehicles left behind by both armies and frequently disturbed by artillery fire from within Bastogne.

The next two days were largely given over to maneuver, as Kokott's 26th Volksgrenadier Division extended westward in an attempt to complete the envelopment. The 77th Regiment was shifted to confront Bastogne from the northwest quarter; the 78th was to the 77th's left in the northeast sector; the 901st of Panzer Lehr Division still confronted the Marvie sector; the 39th Regiment was astride all roads leading into Bastogne from the southeast; the reconnaissance battalion had almost closed the circle on the west side and was moving toward the town from the southwest. On the west side between the reconnaissance battalion and the 77th Regiment, there was a small armored force from Panzer Lehr Division. But even so, where the road ran from Bastogne to Champlon, the line had not been rounded out. The American fire upon this artery was so intense that Kokott's forces could not gain the road, though they had it under such fair observation that they could interdict it effectively against American traffic.

For the time being, the 26th Volksgrenadier Division was sufficiently supplied with gasoline, having taken over some American stores during the swing through to Sibret. Mortar and artillery shells, however, were running short and this had become a drag upon operations. General Kokott didn't have the slightest suspicion that the opposing camp was plagued by the same problem. He noted that whenever the American artillery spoke, it did so in heavy concentrations. It was seldom that a single gun fired for in the interest of conserving ammunition there was little use of harassing fires. To Kokott's mind this suggested that the American artillery was being used with confidence and he reasoned that it must be amply supplied with ammunition. Heavy concentrations equal heavy supply: that was how he reasoned it.

Matters worsened on December 23. To the southward there was a near crisis when Kokott's rear began to feel pressure from the American thrusts northward to relieve Bastogne. Kokott's forces first became aware of the pressure when elements of the 5th Parachute Division fell back into their area. There were five newly arrived Tiger tanks near Kokott's CP. He didn't know where they had come from and he didn't stop to inquire. He sent them on down the Clochimont road in an effort to restore the situation. Soon after the German tanks departed, Kokott saw the first American troop-carrier planes come over on the Bastogne re-supply mission. He and his officers saw the parachutes dropping; they thought that additional paratroops were arriving to swell the ranks of the defenders. The effect was, as he expressed it, "to increase the disorder in the ranks of the attackers."

That night, on Corps order, he attacked Marvie, intending to smash through to Bastogne. The 901st Regiment was sent against Marvie, while the 39th Regiment, on its left, moved along the main road from Assenois. In an extension of this same line, forming roughly a half circle, the reconnaissance battalion, 26th Volksgrenadier Division, also moved to the attack and for the first time was able to close its grip on the Bastogne–Champlon road. The attack failed, as related earlier. Kokott received early reports that his forces had "captured" Marvie [an exaggeration] but he never knew that the Panzer Lehr Division had broken the line at Hill 500 that night or that some of its tanks had entered Bastogne. [Kokott's comment on this was: "They took only the first few houses and then reported to me that they had captured the village. I acted on the assumption that they were telling the truth. This is a very common type of error in our operations."]

On the same night, while the Marvie attack was flickering, Kokott was visited at his CP by General Hasso-Eccard Manteuffel, Commanding General of the Fifth Panzer Army. An order had come down from XXXXVII Corps that Bastogne would be attacked again on Christmas Day and Manteuffel had come in person to give his instructions. By this time the German high command was thoroughly alarmed. The continued resistance at Bastogne and the southern action in support of it were holding up the advance of their entire Seventh Army. Manteuffel said it was necessary to hurry the conquest of the town because resistance from the south against the 5th Parachute Division was increasing hour by hour. He added, "Bastogne must be taken at all costs."

Manteuffel asked Kokott what he proposed and Kokott said that inasmuch as he had tried from every other direction and had taken heavy losses, he would now attack from out of the northwest. The 77th, which was the freshest of his regiments and had taken the least losses, was holding his sector. He reasoned, too, that the Americans would be looking primarily to the east and south and that their strength would be deployed in these directions, with weakness in the northwest. [He was all wrong about this. The forces were strongest and freshest in the area he proposed to attack.] His final argument was that the terrain in the northwest was the most favorable for the employment of armor, being relatively open and firm, so that the tanks would not have to be bound by the roads.

Manteuffel then agreed to put the 15th Panzergrenadier Division at Kokott's disposal and directly under his command for this attack. The division was only then moving up, a veteran division with considerable experience on the Italian front, and it would arrive in good condition.

The forward elements of the 15th Panzergrenadier Division reached the sector confronting Champs and Hemroulle about 2200 on December 24. There were immediately available two artillery battalions, one tank battalion (with about thirty medium tanks and tank destroyers) and the spearheads (two battalions) of the first two infantry regiments. For the troops of that division, it was simply a question of how many could get forward to the assembly area before jump-off time. Kokott had decided that he had to attack in the dark because of American air superiority and he had set the hour at 0300 on Christmas morning. He reasoned further that his troops would have to be in Bastogne by 0800, for he felt that he would not be able to continue the attack advantageously after daylight.

The greater part of the first two regiments of 15th Panzergrenadier Division got forward in time to be fed into the attack, along with the tank battalion. Some of these men rode the tanks; others followed in an infantry line that wavered from the beginning, because its members had had little chance to catch breath or get their bearings after arrival at the front. Kokott's 77th Regiment attacked on the left against Champs, and he had the impression that this was the only part of the attack that got off strongly. His reconnaissance battalion, to the southward of the sector where the elements of the 15th Panzer Division struck against Colonel Harper's position, was also supposed to have joined in the attack, although this demonstration made almost no impression on the defenders. The troops confronting the eastern and southern parts of the perimeter were ordered to support the attack with continuing fires to prevent reinforcement of the westward-facing positions.

Thus the plans and intentions of the enemy in the Christmas Day fight. The results were as described in an earlier chapter. By 1000 Kokott knew that his plan was irretrievably lost. At 1200 he asked XXXXVII Corps for permission to stop the attack and reorganize. Corps refused, saying that it had become absolutely necessary to capture Bastogne, since the pressure on the south was becoming uncontainable. But the fight [at the hinge of our 327th Glider Infantry—502d Parachute Infantry front] had run its own course and was already dying. Kokott reluctantly renewed the attack, knowing now that the only effect would be to increase his losses.

NOTES

1Through the coöperation of Col. S. L. A. Marshall and the Infantry Journal Press, *Bastogne: The Story of the First Eight Days,* is included substantially in the form in which it was published in 1946. When the battle began at Bastogne, Colonel Marshall, Historian of the European Theater of Operations, immediately recognized the importance of the action. Shortly after the road was opened by the 4th Armored Division he and two of his assistants, Capt. John G. Westover and Lt. A. Joseph Webber, moved into the town.
Some chapters of *Bastogne* which dealt in detail and almost exclusively with action of the armored units in Bastogne have been condensed; where such condensations have been made or where material which was not in Colonel Marshall's original book has been added, it is indicated by an asterisk (*) at the beginning and end.
Occasional small omissions from the original text are indicated by periods, thus, . . .

2Probably a few individuals and fewer vehicles got into and out of Bastogne after the siege began. One such person, Pvt. Donald B. Straith of Company A, 506th, wrote: "I was wounded in Noville on the morning of December 20 and was sent to the collecting station in Bastogne later that day. The next morning, about 9:30 if I recall correctly, fourteen ambulatory wounded, myself included, left Bastogne in a 1½-ton 6 x 6 truck by either the Neufchâteau or the Arlon road. A short way outside the city our truck was machine-gunned from the left side of the road, killing the driver and a man from either the 501st or 502d. About three hundred yards to the rear of the point at which we rolled to a stop a jeep and a half-track pulled onto the highway from our right, having been attracted by the firing. The machine gun could not be seen due to the fog, and since no more firing was forthcoming the two vehicles led our truck off on the side road from which they had come to a town about half a mile or a mile to the west. Here we were placed in two ambulances and sent to the 103d Clearing Station in a nearby town where, on our arrival, we were informed that the town manned by members of the 28th Division which we had just left was already surrounded." Also, General McAuliffe recalled talking with the driver of a badly shot-up jeep who, lost, drove up the Arlon road and into Bastogne during the siege.

Bastogne: The Continuing Fight

The well fought defense of a closed circle has always had a fascination for Americans. The surrounded places where Americans fought tight shrewd fights and survived or were overwhelmed and destroyed are part of the people's memory. It is a memory stemming from word-of-mouth stories of nameless cabins and stockades, through the encircled wagon trains of the Western plains, to the Lost Battalion of World War I. Now, for the first time, a division of the United States Army had been surrounded and its annihilation was vital to the success of a determined enemy's last great offensive. That enemy, realizing his chips were down, that at last it was survival or defeat, had gone all-out to destroy the division. He had flowed around and closed the circle; had thrown his whole weight, at first confidently, at last with a fanaticism stemming from desperation. And always he was turned back and beaten down. And as he ringed the position with his tanks and bodies there was added to the names Boonesboro and the Alamo and the Little Big Horn, that of a ruined Belgian town, Bastogne.

The Bastogne legend was born even as the men who were making it fought on. It was aided by the universality of the press and radio, of ten thousand daily maps showing one spot holding out inside the rolling tide of the worst American military debacle of modern times. It was aided by a worried nation's grasping for encouragement and hope; for days it was the one encouraging sight that met their eyes each morning. And the War Department, earlier than was its practice, identified the division inside the town, so even before their bloody month in the town was up, to the world the 101st became the Battered Bastards of the Bastion of Bastogne. The elements of drama were there—courage in the midst of surrounding panic and defeat; courage and grim humor in the midst of physical suffering, cold, and near-fatal shortages; a surrender demand and a four-letter-word rebuttal; and a real comradeship that developed among the miscellaneous groups who found themselves in a besieged city. Courage and comradeship combined to develop a team that the Germans couldn't whip, a team of infantry, armor, artillery, tank destroyers, air corps, and a catch-all task force called Snafu; a team, whose Negro truck drivers with no roads over which to drive, volunteered to fill in on airborne artillery gun crews; a team whose wounded refused morphine, cracked jokes as they lay on the floor of their cold, makeshift hospital, and when one of them couldn't get his boots on because of trench foot he borrowed a larger pair and begged to be sent back into the lines. It created a spirit which has ever since driven the men of the 101st to try to straighten out the misconception that only their Division was represented inside Bastogne, a misconception due largely to the fact that for many days only the 101st was specifically identified in the public releases. The Division was willing to apply General Taylor's tribute "It has been an honor and privilege for this division to serve alongside the 4th Armored Division. If we are ever in a tight spot again it is our hope that the 4th Armored Division will be sent to get us out," to all their buddies of the month-long fight in Belgium.

Exactly how important the defense of Bastogne during the first eight days was will long be a subject of argument. Only the very ignorant or very biased will claim that the defenders of the town alone broke the German drive and caused the failure of the December offensive; and there are only a few who, on the other hand, will hold that the action and its effect on the course of events was unimportant. Robert E. Merriam, chief of the Ardennes Section of the Historical Division, ETO, in his account of the Bulge, *Dark December,* tells of the results of his questioning of the defeated German generals about the relative merits of the defense of Bastogne and of St. Vith.

Jodl, Hitler's chief advisor in the fighting, said that Bastogne was not so important at first, but only later "as a big pocket behind our rear when you were attacking." Goering says that Bastogne was the keystone of the entire attack. Jodl, in rebuttal, pointed out that Bastogne could be by-passed while St. Vith could not. Lüttwitz, the corps commander, said that if the Germans had seized Bastogne on December 18, *2 Panzer* and *Panzer Lehr* Divisions would have reached the Meuse River on December 22, and Patton would then have been forced to attack not only those divisions, but also *9 Panzer* and *3* and *15 Panzer Grenadier* Divisions, west of the Meuse. He cryptically added, "Your air force would have stopped us there."

Hitler himself personally ordered Model to forget about Bastogne, once we occupied it, and get on with their work. But the important fact about both defenses, Bastogne and St. Vith, was the physical accomplishment of occupation. The Germans wanted both without a fight, and got neither. These two setbacks threw off the German timetable sufficiently to allow us time to rally our forces, regroup, and attack. Without these defenses the Germans might well have met their schedule. This was the important issue, not the relative merits of the two epic stands. Bastogne should be considered in this light.

That they were making history was not entirely lost on the men at Bastogne. This awareness was greater at the top, where the importance of the position was best understood, than at the bottom where to the men on the outposts, in the little groupings of farm houses called Foy, Champs, Noville or Remoifosse, Bastogne was the place where Division Headquarters was. Some men fought the weeks of the Bastogne action and never set foot in the town itself. Likewise, confidence in the

This poem, illustrated in color, hangs in many Bastogne homes. A translation is on page 808.

After the battle the grateful citizens of Bastogne renamed their town square.

integrity of the position was greatest at the top. General McAuliffe, though his calls for aid were positive and constant, always expected that aid to come as a relief and not a rescue and he never doubted, no matter how long it was in coming, that his garrison would be there to receive it. To correct what he considered a widespread misconception in January he gave to the press the statement: "We resent any implication we were rescued or needed rescue. The whole thing was just our dish . . . I didn't feel the Germans had enough people and enough tanks in their whole offensive to take that place." A few days later he exercised the ETO privilege of privates and generals by writing to the *Stars and Stripes* "B-Bag:" "Our situation was never desperate and I know of no man inside Bastogne who ever doubted our ability to hold it." His confidence pervaded his staff; his G-2, Lieutenant Colonel Danahy issued daily reports which were as cocky as any then being mimeographed in the ETO. There was nothing indicating desperation in the subjects taken up during the meetings on the 20th and 22d of battery commanders of one of the Division's artillery battalions, even though the latter day was, from the standpoint of artillery ammunition, the most critical of the siege. There were discussions of trench foot and of sending some blankets to the makeshift hospital; but there was also a warning about that near-number-one crime of the European war—the wearing of wool-knit caps and sweaters as outer garments; arrangements were made for a place for the men to shave, and a room set aside for a noncoms' club.

This confidence was least out where single men and little groups of men, cold and hungry and hoarding their ammunition, could see in front of them only Germans and German tanks. These men were the ones who wryly repeated the old saying, "They got us surrounded—the poor bastards;" who thought it a not unreasonable mistake on their own part when they took the arrival of the German ultimatum as an enemy

589

offer to surrender; and who passed from hand to hand the Christmas Day issue of the 506th *Para-Dice Minor,* a news sheet published by Pfc. David J. Phillips, which contained the following social note: '

Miss Champagne Belch, your Society Editor, offers the following tips on where to go for dinner and dancing on your night out:

"The Bastogne Bar and Grill" is featuring a tasty little luncheon consisting mainly of *"Ratione de Kay avec Café GI."* Gerald Kraut and his 88-piece band furnish lively and varied entertainment during the cocktail hour. After sundown, the club occasionally bills Mr. Looft Waffe and his famous "Flare Dance."

"The Blue Boche" up the street furnishes a clever program of native folk dances. The most entertaining of these is the renowned German War Waltz in which the chorus performs in intricate circles with hands overhead while singing the hit number of the show, as popularized by the Wehrmacht playboys, entitled, "I'm Forever Shouting Kamerad."

Perhaps the most popular of the Bastogne bistros is the invariably crowded "Cellar Club."

They were the men who killed the Germans and destroyed the tanks.

"All we commanders at Bastogne could do," said Colonel Harper of the 327th, "was to put our men on what we considered the critical ground. When that was done the battle was delivered into their hands. The question of whether we were to survive and win was then up to the individual soldier." For a time during the siege his regiment had held almost half the perimeter. Later, in his after-action report, Harper recorded how they met the challenge. "The private soldier stayed where he was put and in many cases died rather than give an inch."

How Bastogne looked to the relief column and something of the feeling of the cold has been described by a staff officer, Lt. Col. Ralph Ingersoll in his book, *Top Secret:*

I had gone up to see the attack on Bastogne—it was launched an hour's creep over the ice from Luxembourg. It was a hard, stark thing. The wind swept through the broken trees along the roads and the armor in the field, even the tanks that had been hastily smeared with white paint, stood out in sharp relief, cold and naked. The troops built little fires of anything that would burn, even within sight of the enemy, to try to warm themselves. The infantry fought down one hill and up the next. The tanks were not much good then except as artillery. The dead lay frozen and stiff and when the men came to load them in trucks, they picked them up and put them in like big logs of wood. The frozen arms and legs got in their way when they were piling them. But everyone who had come through the summer before commented on how nice it was that the battle-field didn't stink . . .

On the edges of the town you could see, like a picture-story in a book, where the German columns had broken through the perimeter defense and come right up to the edge of the houses themselves. You could see this from the burned-out tanks the Germans had left behind. The Germans had come in and one by one their tanks had been shot through until, standing on a high place, the trail of them was almost like a snake cut into little pieces, winding across the hill on which Bastogne stands. Mixed in with the wrecks of tanks were the wrecks of the gliders that had brought the medics in when the garrison was surrounded—and here and there, black in the sun, were the little basketfuls of charred junk that is all that's left of an aircraft when it comes into the ground at three or four hundred miles an hour . . .

Riding through the Ardennes, I wore woolen underwear, a woolen uniform, armored force combat overalls, a sweater, an armored force field jacket with elastic cuffs, a muffler, a heavy lined trenchcoat, two pairs of heavy woolen socks, and combat boots with galoshes over them—and I cannot remember ever being warm. Not that the temperature was so low, but there seemed a mean dampness in the air and the cutting wind never seemed to stop.

On the afternoon of December 27 there arrived in Bastogne an officer who, because of an unusual set of circumstances, was probably in the best position to understand the larger significance of Bastogne.

Shortly after his arrival in Bastogne General Taylor issued the following message to the troops:

At the time of the recent German breakthrough on the front of the First Army, I was on temporary duty in Washington where I saw the effect of the event on our Country. As the breakthrough developed, the importance of the communication center of Bastogne to the success or failure of the German effort became apparent to everyone. On December 21 the situation map of the War Department first showed the 101st assigned to the defense of this key point and since that time the eyes of the Nation have been fixed on the action of this division.

In returning I passed through every senior American headquarters of the chain of command and received the comments of the senior American commanders upon the recent work of the 101st. Everyone, from the Secretary of War, Mr. Stimson, sends his congratulations. The Chief of Staff, General Marshall; General Eisenhower's Chief of Staff, General Smith; General Bradley and General Patton join in commending the 101st for its magnificent defense of Bastogne.

To the soldiers of this Division who have lived through the day to day fighting in this area it is not possible to appreciate fully just what has been accomplished, but every senior commander knows, the American people know, what the retention of Bastogne has meant in checking the German drive. Bastogne joins with Normandy and Holland as a brilliant feat of arms performed by the 101st Airborne Division.

I wish to congratulate Brig. Gen. A. C. McAuliffe and every officer and man for this job so well done. Your defense has beaten off the German. The time will soon be here to resume the attack and finish him off with a decisive blow.

General Taylor had been called to Washington early in December in connection with a proposed reorganization plan for airborne divisions. After his talks with Secretary Stimson, General Marshall, and other War Department officials, he had begun a round of conferences and inspections (seeing, ironically, for the first time the new recoilless 75mm

Paratroopers of Company C, 502d, eating outdoors.
Standing at the right is First Sgt. Robert Grotjan.

gun and the latest developments in winter clothing, including shoepacs
—items which before a week was out his men would urgently need).
On December 21 he had returned from a visit to the 101st wounded at
Walter Reed Hospital to receive the first word that his Division had
been committed to action. Bad weather held up plane travel, and he
experienced the restless, worried mood of the nation as the bad news of
the Bulge came through. Just before midnight on Christmas Eve the
weather opened up enough for a plane to get through to Paris. He
landed there on the afternoon of the 26th. General Smith briefed him
on the Bastogne situation and forbade any attempt to parachute or
glide into the besieged town, assuring him that the 4th Armored Division would break through that day.

On the 27th General Taylor had driven from Paris south of Bastogne.
There Maj. Gen. Hugh J. Gaffey of the 4th Armored Division offered
to send him up the Assenois road in a tank, but Taylor decided to go up
the narrow corridor in his jeep—a trip which S/Sgt. Charles Kartus,
his driver since the pre-airborne days at Camp Claiborne, remembered
as his own scariest hour of the war.

They drove into Bastogne about 1600. At the CP Taylor asked Mc-
Auliffe about the situation and the condition of the Division.

"Sir, we are ready to attack."

After checking the effective Division strength (as of the 26th it had been 711 officers and 9,516 enlisted men) General Taylor radioed III Corps that the 101st was ready for offensive operations.

Along with the personnel and supplies came the tributes and congratulations. Copies of *Stars and Stripes* gave the defenders some picture of the esteem in which the world held them. The messages were mimeographed and distributed to the troops.

All ranks Canadian First Army have watched with admiration the magnificent manner in which their friends of the US 101st Airborne Division have fought it out with the enemy around Bastogne. Our high regards and congratulations.

Congratulations to all ranks of 101 Airborne Division on their magnificent defense of Bastogne. We are full of admiration.—*British 1st Airborne Division.*

The magnificent spirit of selfless heroism which inspired yourself and the officers and men of the garrison of Bastogne to victoriously defend Bastogne from December 19, 1944, to the arrival of the 4th Armored Division on December 26, 1944, constitutes an inspiring example of discipline, valor and endurance. You and the officers and men of your command are hereby highly commended for a superior performance.—*Lt. Gen. George S. Patton, Jr.*

I desire to take this means of expressing to you and all members of your splendid command my personal appreciation for the superior manner in which the division conducted itself in the action at Bastogne. Without the will and determination of the 101st Airborne Division to stop the superior forces of the German Army thrown against it, there would be a chapter written in history different from the one which will appear.—*Maj. Gen. Troy H. Middleton.*

There were other tributes, backhanded but just as heartfelt. Prisoner after prisoner, experienced combat men, admitted they had never met such a defense. A wounded German corporal who had been in the Afrika Korps and who survived the breakthrough attack on Christmas morning when asked what had happened could only say over and over (as nearly as it could be translated), "We didn't know for nothing, we didn't know for nothing." Another German corporal of an earlier war was also impressed. A transcript of the minutes of Hitler's staff meetings for the period reads, "The Führer again and again stressed the exemplary stubborn defense of Bastogne and said among other things, 'I should like to see the German general who would fight on with the same stubborn tough resistance in a situation which seemed just as hopeless.'" The failure to take Bastogne had come as a surprise to the Führer for on the evening of the 20th at a Military Situation Conference *SS Gruppenführer* Fegelein had said to Hitler: "We shall take Bastogne tonight." (A similar instance of such confidence was a statement attributed by the men of the much-mauled 26th Volksgrenadier Division to their commander, Maj. Gen. Heinz Kokott: "I don't need tanks; I'll take Bastogne with the MP44 machine pistol."), Hitler, worried by and angry at the obstinate Americans in the town, had sent his personal aide, Major Johann-Mayer, to Bastogne to get a first-hand picture of the siege. Lieutenant General von Lüttwitz, commanding the XXXXVII Panzer Corps attacking the town, convinced Johann-Mayer of the stubborn resistance and Johann-Mayer in turn was able to convince the stubborn Führer. Hitler had reluctantly ordered the 15th Panzergrenadier Division from his reserve to join in the attack on Christmas Eve. The transcript read later: "The Führer soon recognized that the situation of the Winter Offensive in the Ardennes was based on the taking of Bastogne and it was for this reason that he immediately developed new plans for a new offensive operation at the Lorraine border which was to start New Year's Eve."

By the time the advance column of the 4th Armored reached Bastogne the German counteroffensive had been brought under control and the Germans had failed in their last gamble. Not that this was apparent to either side at the time, though on the highest level both commanders probably sensed it. For several days the situation remained in a state of flux with both sides trying to seize the initiative.

Robert E. Merriam in *Dark December* says that on the day after Christmas General Jodl, chief of the German Armed Forces Operation Staff, addressing Hitler in the Führer's Berlin headquarters, began a summary of the campaign with these words: "*Mein Führer,* we must face the facts squarely and openly; we cannot force the Meuse River." There followed an all-day conference and all thought of crossing the Meuse was abandoned in favor of a battle east of the river. Merriam continues:

Having made his decision to fight east of the Meuse River, Hitler at once concentrated his attention on Bastogne, about which he had expressed little concern prior to the change in plans. Now with a large battle looming east of the River, Bastogne was a huge rock jutting out of the German sea, and an ever present threat to the German lines of communications. It had to be taken. With this in mind, Hitler ordered a concentrated attack on Bastogne. Suddenly, German divisions from all parts of the Bulge descended on Bastogne preparatory to a new siege of the town. During this time ensued the heaviest fighting of the battle for Bastogne; the casualties were frightfully heavy, much worse than during the actual siege.

First to be shunted south, even though in the midst of an attack on Hotton, the Führer Escort Brigade received orders on December 26 to disengage immediately, march to the southwest of Bastogne, where it was to attack across the narrow neck opening into the town, and once again isolate the defenders of

Bastogne. Then the Panzer divisions of "Sepp" Dietrich's Sixth Panzer Army were to descend upon the town from three sides and throttle the defenders. One by one, Dietrich's panzers shifted their weight from the XVIII Airborne Corps front, to the south. By the first of the year 1, 9, and 12 SS Panzer Divisions were ringed around Bastogne, attacking from three sides. The Führer Escort Brigade, having once failed, was again ordered to cut off the neck of the salient into Bastogne in conjunction with an attack by 1 SS Panzer Division from the east, but the Americans were already too strongly entrenched in this narrow corridor, and the German attacks failed to break through. By the first of the year, eight German divisions were closeted around Bastogne, closing in for the kill.

ARRIVALS AND DEPARTURES

Meanwhile, the days following the breakthrough, December 27, 28, and 29, were relatively quiet days for the town of Bastogne. On December 28 Lt. Gen. Walter B. Smith, General Eisenhower's Chief of Staff, received from his superior an order to "release to Bradley at once the 11th Armored and 87th Divisions, and organize a strong Bastogne–Houffalize attack." These two divisions had been among those held in reserve west of the Meuse. Third Army began planning an offensive using these two divisions; but since they had to be brought up from some distance it was to be several days before the attack could begin. On the 27th the 101st had been attached by Third Army to III Corps.

The main action of the 27th was a small one, in the 327th area. Before dawn the Germans had tried two attacks with an estimated two hundred men and three tanks; both attacks were broken up by artillery fire before they reached the lines. That night just after midnight and shortly before dawn the next morning the Germans slipped over some JU-88s which bombed and strafed the town itself; the damage to the buildings was considerable; casualties, however were light. But the day, cold and misty with flurries of snow, was distinguished by comings and goings; the arrival of the Division Commander and, two and a half hours later, the first convoy since the road was cut six days before.

These were the trucks which, on the night of the 19th, had gotten to within five miles of Bastogne, and had been attacked and chased to the west and south before reaching safety at Neufchâteau. The convoy had been sent from there to wait in Orsainfaing, about twenty-five miles southwest of Bastogne. From Orsainfaing Capt. George W. Horn of the 426th Airborne Quartermaster Company led a convoy of fifty-two vehicles into Bastogne. The 4th Armored furnished an escort of six tanks in the lead and other tanks dispersed through the convoy at the rate of one tank after every fifth vehicle. En route the convoy took a wrong turn, ran into a force of Germans and lost six trucks, a tank and a jeep, before getting out of the trap. Thirty trucks carried ammunition,

A glider brings in 155mm ammunition for the 969th FA Battalion.

nine brought rations, three carried 4,500 gallons of gasoline, two trucks and trailers carried medical and signal supplies, and the remaining vehicles were ambulances and jeeps. At 2025 a second serial of fifty trucks reached Bastogne. These supplies, added to those from the aerial resupplies of the 26th (an outstanding IX Troop-Carrier Command mission, carried out by 301 planes and 11 gliders with the loss of one plane) and of the 27th (of 164 planes 13 were downed by German flak), put both the guns and the men back on regular rations. Part of the aerial delivery of the 27th was made by gliders which had come in just after noon with 736 rounds of 155mm howitzer ammunition; 35 out of 50 gliders dispatched from England landed at Bastogne during the day. Several of these gliders landed alongside the gunpits and the ammunition was put to immediate use. The six days of resupply, from December 22 through the 27th, cost the IX Troop-Carrier Command almost a hundred personnel wounded, injured or missing, 19 planes destroyed by German flak, and 211 planes damaged, 50 of them seriously. The three wings which carried out the resupply mission were the 50th, 52d and 53d; the 50th and 53d were the wings which had taken the 101st into Normandy and Holland. Not only were many of the crews and planes veterans of those operations; some of the gliders were craft which had been salvaged and rebuilt after use in those two missions.

Leaving Bastogne on the night of the 26th were the wounded and the prisoners. At 1800 that evening 260 of the more seriously wounded left in twenty-two ambulances and ten 2½-ton trucks for the 635th Clearing Company at Villers d'Avant, Orval, Belgium. By 1900 that night all the casualties were evacuated. The next day the 495th

Ambulance Company established and maintained routine ambulance evacuation. Jimmy Cannon of *Stars and Stripes* saw some of them pass.

The convoy of wounded came out of Bastogne in a slow trickle. The day was beautiful if you like Belgium in the winter time. The snow on the hills glittered in the sun, and the planes towed vapor trails across the big, clean sky. The wounded sat stiffly in the trucks, and they rose tautly when they came to a rut in the frozen road. The dust of the road had made their hair gray, but it did not look strange because their faces were old with suffering and fatigue.

As soon as the first supply trucks were unloaded they were sent to the PW inclosure, set up in the local *gendarmerie* at the western edge of the town and there they began taking on prisoners. That evening 540 Germans were evacuated to the VIII Corps PW cage at Neufchâteau; the guard escort was forty officers and men of the 28th Division who had weathered the siege in Bastogne, and the glider pilots. Thereafter daily evacuations were made by the 101st's MP Platoon. The bag of prisoners for December ran as follows:

20th	170	25th	110
21st	162	26th	160
22d	20	28th	29
23d	26	31st	34
24th	49		

There were no prisoners turned in on the 27th, 29th or 30th. A check of those captured through December 26 showed that the leading contributor to the Bastogne bastille was the 26th Volksgrenadier Division with 292 officers and men; the 15th Panzer Grenadier Division furnished 128 prisoners; 142 prisoners were from the 2d Panzer Division; and Panzer Lehr Division furnished 78 officers and men. There were also prisoners from the 5th Parachute Division, 2d SS Panzer Division and miscellaneous units.

On the night of December 27, G-2 thought there was some evidence that the quiet might last awhile. The following notation appeared under the heading of "Enemy Capabilities":

Although still capable of attacking and probably will continue to do so there are evidences that he is turning to the defensive. Two instances have been reported of new roadblocks and of digging in positions to the north of our area. The enemy is capable of a tenacious defense to prevent his salient from being cut off.

However, at almost the same hour that the first convoy was driving into Bastogne's streets a somewhat different view of the situation was

Retrieving medical supplies dropped by parachute.

being given to the world. The German news agency DNB, in an English-language broadcast, diagnosed the situation as follows:

> The enemy forces in encircled Bastogne are facing their annihilation. Despite the intensified enemy air activity in the past few days the enemy could not prevent the German offensive from progressing satisfactorily.

If the Division was to be annihilated it was going down with good face; for that morning a message went out to all 101st artillery batteries to have their areas policed and their men shaved for an inspection by General McAuliffe. The men had groused good-naturedly about that and, later in the day, when the supplies came, about not getting at least a little mail.

The 28th was a misty day though not so bad as to prevent enemy observation planes from occasionally coming over to inspect the American lines. The day had begun with a somewhat plaintive journal entry by the 506th—a regiment which had faced SS troops, paratroopers, 88s, and Tiger tanks: "A German police dog was reported operating against us last night." The 506th S-2 explained in his own entry that the dog was being used to smell out 506th positions.

Other visitors from the German lines paid sporadic calls during the day. At 1745 that evening the 3d Battalion of the 327th near Lutre-mange, south of Bastogne, caught an hour-long attack which was supported by mortar and artillery fire. This unsuccessful attack, about a company strong, was the main effort of the day against the 101st. The 501st reported the approach of about a platoon of Germans but turned them back before they reached the main line of resistance. The 501st headquarters remembered the day more vividly because of a 500-pound aerial bomb which during the predawn raid that morning landed on the CP and failed to detonate.

Welcome arrivals continued. At 0930 that morning a platoon of Company G of the 327th outposting the road to the south contacted advance elements of Combat Command A of the 4th Armored Division, following up the original breakthrough command of that Division, Combat Command Reserve. The 318th Infantry Regiment of the 80th Infantry Division, attached to the 4th Armored, also reached this outpost. Three hours later on the Neufchâteau highway to the south-west another 327th outpost contacted advance units of Combat Command A of the 9th Armored Division. Two platoons of Company A of the 705th Tank Destroyer Battalion, the Pioneer Platoon of the 705th's Reconnaissance Company and the battalion's headquarters trains which had been prevented by the encirclement from getting into the town, reached Bastogne and joined the rest of the 705th Battalion there.

More supplies came with the arrival at 2000 of sixty-two vehicles. Twenty-five carried ammunition, nine were loaded with rations, one truck brought in motor oil, six vehicles were from the Graves Registration Service, and nineteen vehicles belonged to the various units of the 101st. The remaining two vehicles brought mail and PX supplies. The PX ration, distributed the next day, amounted to eight packs of cigarettes and five candy bars per man. The mail delivery went on uninterruptedly thereafter and deliveries came in each day from the base camp at Mourmelon. The IX Troop-Carrier Command sent in by glider ten tons of medical supplies during the day; this was the final supply by air, closing the Command's "Operation Repulse."

With the 495th Ambulance Company handling evacuations the 60th Field Hospital was attached to the Division. Maj. William E. Barfield was appointed Division Surgeon and Capt. Roy H. Moore, Jr., took over command of the Division's almost non-existent Medical Company. Captain Moore left that day for Mourmelon to organize and train the replacements of the men captured on the 20th. Col. John H. Michaelis,

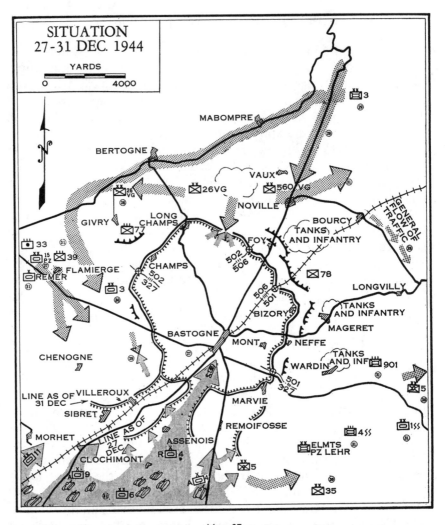

Map 87.

who had commanded the 502d until he was wounded in Holland, rejoined the Division as Chief of Staff, replacing Lt. Col. Ned D. Moore, who had filled the job since the death on December 7 in Mourmelon of Lt. Col. Raymond D. Millener.

With the opening of the road and the arrival of the Graves Registration Service the Bastogne cemetery was closed and those killed after the 28th were taken to a rear area for burial.

On the 28th the 101st Reconnaissance Platoon rejoined the Division. The platoon, after going out with the 501st on the 19th and thereby getting in on the first of the fighting, had again been sent out on the

21st, this time to find a supply route to St. Hubert, sixteen airline miles due west of Bastogne. The platoon had left Bastogne at 1000 and had run into no trouble until it reached the village of Tillet, about halfway to St. Hubert. A dismounted patrol had started into the village and had been chased back by two enemy tanks which entered the village from the west. The patrol met an American column coming toward Tillet from the east and warned it of the danger ahead. The column was made up of elements of two field artillery columns, one being the 58th Armored Field Artillery Battalion, which that morning had left its threatened position near Bastogne, and the baggage train of the 501st.

Since Belgians had already warned that German parachutists were manning a roadblock in the center of Tillet the column decided to try to get through to the west by another route. Reinforced by the Reconnaissance Platoon the column tried an alternate route south of Tillet but at Gerimont, a mile away, it ran into another roadblock. The artillery then went into position, a dismounted patrol of the Reconnaissance Platoon and a forward observer party went forward, and the ensuing infantry-artillery attack destroyed two tanks and thereby knocked out the roadblock. But they found that there was at least one other position still covering the road junction; and darkness and poor visibility closed in to prevent any further action by the artillery. The group decided to wait until morning and then probe for another route. The 101st personnel set up a perimeter defense around their own and the artillery's vehicles. The artillerymen managed to contact Bastogne by radio and asked for help. General McAuliffe could only answer, "You'll have to depend on yourself."

Sometime after midnight the force found out that they were completely isolated. However, the tank commander got word that a friendly column was on the way to relieve them. At 0200 an attack by German tanks was beaten off; but the 101st men on the outposts continued to hear German voices. Before daylight it was decided to draw in the perimeter and to dig close defense positions around the guns. So, like a wagon train facing the encircling Indians and waiting for the U. S. Cavalry, they listened for the Sherman tanks.

The Indians got to them before the Cavalry did. At 0900 about a hundred Germans attacked the position and were driven off. Then the crew of one of the relief column tanks came in on foot and reported that the column had been wiped out.

Knowing now that there would be no relief the artillery officers held a conference with the three 101st officers and decided that, since tanks and self-propelled guns couldn't get through the Germans, their own best hope was to destroy the guns and vehicles and attempt to get the men into the American lines any way they could. The artillery pieces fired their last rounds into the 501st's trucks and jeeps and were then in turn destroyed.

A blinding snowstorm gave the Reconnaissance Platoon, the truck drivers, and the artillerymen—all more accustomed to jeeps and trucks than to walking—the break they needed. With the platoon in the lead and with more than three hundred artillerymen and drivers following, the column started out for Neufchâteau, eleven miles to the south. Passing through the confused lines they made the trip in six and a half hours, reaching Neufchâteau about dark. There the 101st men were attached to the 28th Division, were given a defensive sector, and remained there until relieved and returned, demechanized, to Bastogne.

As the afternoon of the 28th passed and night came on, the fog, which had blanketed the Belgian countryside and made necessary vigorous patrolling, lifted. It would be a good night for the Germans to repeat the air attack made during the early hours of the morning. The Division had no intention of submitting to another such working-over, however, and that day certain steps had been taken. During the afternoon, Lt. Col. X. B. Cox, Commanding Officer of the 101st's antiaircraft battalion, had been appointed as coordinator of all antiaircraft defenses in Bastogne. These defenses consisted of Battery B, 796th Antiaircraft Automatic Weapons Battalion with seven M15s (a multiple mount with a 37mm and two .50-caliber machine guns) and four M16s (four .50-caliber machine guns); and one platoon of Battery C, 467th AA Battalion with four M15s and three M16s. To these he added one of his own antiaircraft batteries, Battery B, 81st Airborne Antiaircraft Battalion with nine .50-caliber machine guns. Earlier that afternoon Battery B had been attached to the 327th for ground use. The other two antiaircraft batteries of the 81st and the three antitank batteries remained on ground-defense missions. Colonel Cox's force continued to build up, and by the end of December he had added another platoon of Company C of the 467th, most of the 778th AAA AW Battalion, and the 217th AAA Battalion with sixteen 90mm guns. That afternoon III Corps had also promised to send Black Widow P-61 night fighters to fly cover over the area during the hours of dark. It was arranged that these planes would stay high for the ack-ack was to fire at anything that came within range. The night passed quietly.

Though the Germans failed to put any planes in the air they did not fail to fill it with words. During the afternoon broadcast to Europe by DNB they admitted that the Americans had "succeeded in reaching with armored vehicles the U. S. forces encircled in the town"; in another DNB broadcast that day they claimed that the "101st Airborne has sustained very heavy losses." The Berlin press service to Europe went even further in its claim: "The 101st Airborne Division has been annihilated or has dwindled to negligible remnants." During the process of the annihilation that day a couple of German artillery rounds fell near the mess truck where Headquarters Battery of the 377th Parachute Field Artillery Battalion was lined up for chow. The main damage, it turned out, was done by an alert individual or individuals who had the presence of mind to steal all the doughnuts before taking cover.

The 29th dawned clear; weather and visibility both were excellent. The day itself turned out to be the quietest since the Division had been at Bastogne. A German patrol of twenty to forty men, was turned back between Monaville and Recogne by the 502d. A before-dawn attack on Company E of the 501st resulted in several casualties including the wounding of the company commander, Capt. Frank "Foxy" Gregg. The only other excitement came shortly after dark when three planes, believed to be JU-88s, braved Colonel Cox's anti-aircraft defenses to bomb and strafe the city; one gun of the 463d Parachute Field Artillery Battalion, a light tank and two halftracks were hit. The ack-ack reported that they knocked down one of the attackers.

However, there were signs of something going on behind the German lines. Particularly was there evidence of a buildup north and northeast of the town. Patrols found the enemy in this section alert and numerous and were unable to penetrate deep enough to get a picture of what was going on. Observation and fighter planes which went over the area met intense flak but were able to report a large infiltration of armored vehicles and trucks and that the wooded areas seemed filled with tanks and infantry. Just who all these people were was not definitely established. It was believed that the 101st's standby opponent, the 26th Volksgrenadier Division, was still in the vicinity and there was a definite report that a new unit had moved in. Corps reported, without confirmation, that this unit might be the 3d Panzergrenadier Division. Whoever it was Colonel Danahy wasn't particularly worried. "It is impossible to tell at this moment," reads his G-2 Periodic Summary for the 29th, "whether the new unit which moved into the north of our position intends to defend or attack, but in either case it will soon be worn down by our action and should not be too much of a problem."

General Taylor strengthened his hand against any attack by withdrawing the 2d Battalion of the 327th Glider Infantry from its position in the line and moving the battalion to the northwest edge of the town in Division reserve.

With the route into Bastogne now fully open supplies and reinforcements continued to pour in. Thirteen truckloads of clothes and other supplies—overshoes and gloves, company mess and maintenance trucks, and Type A rations, including a belated shipment of Christmas turkey, 13,500 pounds followed the next day by 8,500 pounds more—all arrived during the day. The 426th Airborne Quartermaster Company was able to draw and store a reserve of three rations, two being 10-in-1s and one a K. During the morning the first outgoing mail left Bastogne. At 1300 a convoy reached the town with about a hundred 506th men and about forty from the 2d Battalion of the 501st who had been on pass when the Division had left Mourmelon; they were welcomed by their mates and filled in the places of the men who had been lost during the ten days of fighting.

The convoys were also bringing in something new for the artillerymen—the Pozit or proximity fuze. This was a secret development which detonated an artillery round at any set distance from the ground. Its use in the ETO had been set for a later date but the Bulge was considered enough of an emergency to justify its use. Prisoners taken after Pozit-fuzed barrages reported high casualties and demoralizing effects from it.

At 1630 on the 29th the 801st Airborne Ordnance Maintenance Company arrived in Bastogne. The Company had left Mourmelon bound for Bastogne, on the morning of the 19th. It had been part of the convoy which had been turned back by the Germans within five miles of the town. The ordnance vehicles had gone to Neufchâteau and, later, to Orsainfaing. From Orsainfaing the 801st moved to Bastogne where for the remainder of the fight it carried out its functions of ordnance service and supply to the Division. The frozen ground furnished the company with one problem not arising in Normandy or Holland: the artillery howitzers began going out of action due to the trails and spades buckling during recoil. The ordnance jacks-of-all-trades experimented by straightening the bent parts and welding on supports; this worked and the guns were kept in action.

The 29th ended on a minor note of cheer for the commanders of the various units; word had come from Mourmelon that, due to circumstances, rendition of semi-annual efficiency reports for the period July 1-December 31 might be delayed until further notice.

Patton Attacks North

On the 30th of December, U. S. First Army, holding the northern shoulder of the Bulge, found the enemy's pressure in that direction had lessened considerably. "Hostile attention and concentration of strength," reads First Army's Report of Operations for the period, "were directed toward the new threat to the southern flank of his penetration by the relief and reinforcement of Bastogne and by the advance of the VIII and III Corps northward." On the previous day Von Rundstedt had sent his 1st SS Panzer Division south to Bastogne where, on the 30th, it was identified. It was soon followed by other divisions of his Sixth SS Panzer Army, the army Von Rundstedt had counted on using in his revised plan to break into the Meuse Valley. "With them," says the First Army's report, "went the last vestige of hopes for the bold daring drive to Antwerp."

The shifting of divisions from the northern to the southern shoulder of the Bulge was described by General Bradley as follows:

The enemy's schedule for his attack was upset by the heroic resistance of our troops and by the speed made by all three armies [U. S. First, Third and Ninth] in shifting divisions to meet the attack. The result was that wherever the enemy turned along the north flank, groping for a place where he could break out on the Belgian lowlands, he was met by troops of General Hodges' First Army. He found blocking his way the same American divisions which had been soundly thrashing his best ever since the beachhead days of Normandy. An even greater surprise to the enemy was the quick appearance of General Patton's Army on the south flank. Matching the speed with which General Simpson [U. S. Ninth Army commander] and General Hodges deployed their divisions from the north, General Patton's forces first relieved Bastogne, which was, of course, a key to the whole battle, and then attacked with such fury that the enemy was forced to slow his drive to the north. He had, in fact, to move his best SS Panzer divisions across the salient in an attempt to check General Patton's unexpected advance.

On the 29th, General Patton decided that two divisions, the 11th Armored and the 87th Infantry, which had been ordered up as an attacking force, were to attack the next morning, the 30th. The attack was to be launched from the Libramont–Vaux-le-Rosieres area ten or twelve miles southwest of Bastogne. The two divisions were to drive northeast between Bastogne and the Ourthe River toward Houffalize, an enemy-held road junction ten miles north of Bastogne. The 101st's part in the action was restricted by VIII Corps to supporting by artillery fire the advance of the 11th Armored and to be prepared to assist that division in the capture of Noville.

The setup was not too favorable for the two attacking divisions. Neither had had much combat experience; it was to be, in fact, the first action for the 11th. After moving up over icy, snow-covered roads they arrived late in the area. The men were fatigued, the officers unfamiliar with the terrain and they had little time to reconnoiter. But this was an urgent situation; General Patton wanted to hit the Germans before reinforcements from the northern flank arrived. "Had the attack had been delayed long enough for adequate reconnaissance," believes Robert Merriam in *Dark December,* "it is probable the Germans would have launched another attack, and surrounded Bastogne."

The two divisions, 11th Armored on the right, 87th Infantry on the left, jumped off at 0800 on the 30th. Almost at once they ran into the flank of a German counterattack manned by the Panzer Lehr and the 27th Volksgrenadier Divisions heading southeast to cut off Bastogne. At the same time on the other (east) side of Bastogne, the 1st SS Panzer and the 167th Volksgrenadier Divisions attacked the U. S. 26th and 35th Infantry Divisions. "Unquestionably this was the critical day of the operation," General Patton noted in his diary, "as there was a concerted effort on the part of the Germans, using at least five divisions, to again isolate Bastogne."

The fight lasted several days and the four American divisions concerned had a tough fight of it, but the enemy failed to gain his objectives. The 35th caught a particularly vicious attack and lost two companies almost complete, but tank destroyers and artillery of the 4th Armored Division supported the 35th and reported eleven enemy tanks knocked out.

Middleton's VIII Corps attack on December 30, the diversion of troops from XII Corps to Bastogne, continuation of the III Corps attack, and brave and clever defense by the troops in Bastogne, combined to save once again the town from capture, as Germans pounded away with their best divisions: parts of four panzer, two infantry, a paratroop, and Remer's *Fuehrer Escort Brigade.* [Robert Merriam, in *Dark December,* continues]: During these days the conflict was intense, and casualties in the 101st Airborne Division and attached units were the greatest, as German power in force was thrown against Bastogne. But the crisis had already been met on the First Army front. The Germans, bottled in the Bulge, like caged lions furious at their captivity, turned on Bastogne and struck again and again with utter abandon.

Thus did Von Rundstedt continue to expend against the stubborn Bastogne pine knot the divisions he had hoped would, by that time, be rolling past Liège and into Antwerp.

On the day of the Third Army attack—the 30th—General Patton came to take a look at Bastogne. He was jeeped, pearl-handled pistols and all, around the town, and was shown the scene of the 502d fight near Champs. He photographed the German tanks starkly telling their story of the Christmas morning episode. Before he left he pinned the Distinguished Service Cross on General McAuliffe and Colonel Chappuis.

Bastogne, at the center of the fighting, was relatively undisturbed. As a matter of fact, it was for many days to be a hub about which both sides attacked and counterattacked. During two days, January 3 and 4, it was to catch as bitter attacks as it had ever experienced; yet for most of the period, until the 101st began its own attack on January 9, there was to be little change in the positions immediately about the town itself, and most of the days were quiet compared to those in the adjoining sectors.

The nature of the sector dictated that the Division's mission during most of the fighting at Bastogne would be essentially defensive. From the lifting of the siege until mid-January the Division occupied a large salient, about five miles across at its broadest point, about as many miles deep, and with the town of Bastogne at its center. The salient's narrow neck—hardly more than road-and-shoulders wide when the 4th Armored Division created it on December 26—was gradually widened as the divisions on either side of the 101st fought up abreast of Bastogne; but until almost the very end of the period the one, and later several, access roads through the neck were under intermittent enemy artillery fire. It was obvious that the requirements of holding the front all the way around the salient permitted the Division to maintain very small reserves, and certainly none of a size to permit major offensive efforts. This was recognized in higher headquarters, and in the several general offensives for the area ordered by Army and Corps it was always agreed that the 101st would hold in place and join in only after the drives brought neighboring units approximately abreast, and they were able to take over a part of the defensive sector, allowing the airborne division to assemble reserves.

General Taylor's eyes were always on the high ground in the Noville–Bourcy area northeast of Bastogne. But each time a start was made to take this dominating terrain the attacks had to be called off or stopped in midair because of the failure of the neighboring divisions to come up. That his troopers could take Noville at any time the General had no doubt; but he was also convinced that it would be suicidal to attempt to hold the area without support on the flanks. It was not until the 13th that the 101st was to begin a pay drive for this high ground; up until that time its actions were limited to defenses

Following a night skirmish on 30 December 1944 troops set out to rejoin their outfit.
In front are Pfc. M. L. Dickman, Pvt. Sunny Sundquist, and Sgt. Francis H. McCann.

against German assaults and vigorous patrolling to the front to develop enemy concentrations and to anticipate attacks. The preparations for and the beginning of attacks which never materialized or which were called off by higher authorities were to make the action of the 101st during the period appear uncertain and hesitant; but practically it was a tactically sound course and was so accepted by the Corps and Army commanders.

YEAR'S END

Though the fighting was heavy on both sides of Bastogne, there was no enemy action at the town itself during the 30th. But at 0700 that morning Bastogne received the most concentrated bombing and strafing attack yet experienced. The attack convinced many of the remaining civilians that it was time to leave and a number of evacuations took place during the day. Some 101st units also moved; the 327th, which took a direct hit on the S-2 and S-3 offices, moved its regimental CP into Hemroulle. The 506th regimental CP took a hit;

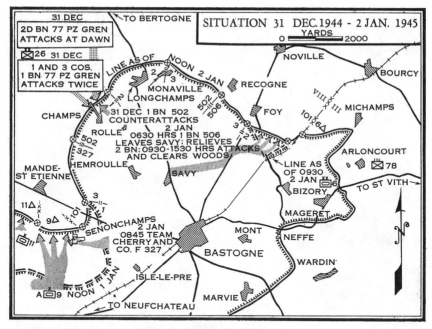

31 DEC
2D BN 77 PZ GREN
ATTACKS AT DAWN

26 31 DEC
1 AND 3 COS.
1 BN 77 PZ GREN
ATTACKS TWICE

TO BERTOGNE

NOVILLE

BOURCY

MONAVILLE
LONGCHAMPS

RECOGNE

MICHAMPS

CHAMPS

FOY

31 DEC 1 BN 502
COUNTERATTACKS
ROLLE   2 JAN
0630 HRS 1 BN 506
LEAVES SAVY: RELIEVES
2 BN: 0930-1530 HRS ATTACKS
AND CLEARS WOODS

ARLONCOURT

78

MANDE-
ST ETIENNE

HEMROULLE

SAVY

LINE AS
OF 0930
2 JAN

TO ST VITH

BIZORY

MAGERET

SENONCHAMPS
2 JAN
0845 TEAM
CHERRY AND
CO. F 327

MONT

NEFFE

BASTOGNE

WARDIN

ISLE-LE-PRE

MARVIE

A   9 NOON

TO NEUFCHATEAU

Map 88.

and Company B of the 326th Engineers lost five men killed and three wounded when one of the bombs hit a squad billet.

The day had begun darkening about noon as an overcast closed down and by 1600 a light snowfall had begun which kept up through the night. During the afternoon the 327th received 480 reinforcements. The gloom of the atmosphere was lifted somewhat when the news got around that some VIII Corps cognac was being distributed to celebrate the New Year the next night.

The morning of the last day of 1944 gave indications that for the 101st the lull of the past few days was about to end. The 77th Grenadier Regiment of the 26th Volksgrenadier Division launched an artillery-supported dawn attack on the sector northwest of Bastogne held by the 1st Battalion of the 502d. During the next few days this sector was to be a focal point for German armored attacks.

The attack, carried out by the 1st and 3d Companies, of the 1st Battalion, 77th Grenadier Regiment, with 2d Company in reserve, was in the nature of a diversion, to draw off American strength from other sections of the front. The two attack companies, with an effective total strength of only sixty men, had the limited objective of taking the three outermost buildings of Champs and holding them until January 1. At the same time, the 2d Battalion of the 77th Grenadier Regiment,

General Patton decorates Colonel Chappuis and General McAuliffe with the Distinguished Service Cross.

with about fifty to sixty men, attacked west of Champs to establish a defensive line on the slope of a hill there and to set up an artillery observation post. These two skinny battalions had support of artillery, mortars, and machine guns. Their attack was at first successful, and the group attacking Champs succeeded in taking the houses which were their objectives; their attack cost Company C an officer and two enlisted men killed, four wounded, and about a squad captured. After about two hours of bitter fighting in the snow, with machine-gun and mortar fire pouring into the German-held houses, the 1st Battalion of the 502d succeeded in capturing the houses and one officer and four enlisted men of the German attacking force. The remaining fifty-five Germans were dead. Company C also got back most of its captured squad. About noon the Germans tried another attack, but gained nothing. The 502d bagged thirty-seven prisoners and the houses and fields were spotted with German dead and wounded.

The 101st was now between two U. S. armored divisions, the 11th on the left flank and the 6th on the right. Between the 327th Glider Infantry Regiment, the extreme left of the 101st units, and the 11th Armored was a sector held by Combat Command A of the 9th

Generals McAuliffe (left) and Patton looking at the scene of Company C, 502d's fight of Christmas morning. Three of the seven knocked-out German tanks are visible.

Armored Division. Both the 6th and the 11th Armored Divisions were attacking north, and during the 31st the artillery of the 101st supported them. The 6th Armored on the right flank had passed through the 501st and had attacked through the 501st's 2d Battalion out the Longvilly road toward Arloncourt. It had then been pushed back to the jumping off line, and reported that it had not enough infantry to hold the ground gained.

The After-Action Report of VIII Corps read:

As the month of December drew to a close the German penetration had been sealed and the enemy had been forced on the defensive. The delay effected by VIII Corps during the initial stages of the Ardennes offensive and the denial of essential road nets through the heroic stand of the 101st Airborne Division at Bastogne gained sufficient time for the Allies to redistribute their forces and contain the thrust. Early resumption of the Allied offensive and pressure brought to bear on the shoulders of the German salient by the First and Third Armies now placed the enemy in a dangerous position from which he had to fight savagely to protect his escape corridor.

On New Year's Eve, Von Rundstedt could hardly avoid the conclusion that his preoccupation with the stubborn salient of Bastogne had helped lose him the initiative which had been essential to make his gamble pay off. To salvage what he could of his blue chips—his panzer divisions—he had to counteract the most dangerous threat to their escape route, Bastogne, a five-mile-deep wedge in his salient. It was clear now that the Third Army to his south, whose spearpoint was Bastogne, rather than the First Army to the north, represented the greater danger. If he had to give ground anywhere it would be better to fall back in the north and west. He must have shared Hitler's concern with this threat to his communications and line of withdrawal.

611

The New Year found him, therefore, building up his forces north of Bastogne and on both sides of the town.

The German build-up around Bastogne was, from their standpoint, a good one; Allied planning for reducing the Bulge was already well along and on both sides of Bastogne American troops were on the move. A coordinated large-scale attack from the north by First Army and from the south by Third Army was scheduled to converge and meet in the vicinity of St. Vith in the northeast. When this meeting of the two U. S. armies occurred, the greater part of the ground the Germans had won in the Bulge would be lost to them. If the two forces could close and meet quickly enough the enemy forces west of the pincers would be trapped and probably lost.

THE NEW YEAR

The new year was welcomed in with a bang, the Division's artillery and mortars joining every gun on the Third Army front in a midnight serenade, all of them throwing high explosives toward the German lines. There was some snow during the night, clearing toward morning. By now the Bastogne area was deep in the snow that had come down at intervals for days. The troops had adapted themselves as well as they could, and some heavy clothing and overshoes had come through to help relieve the shortages which had been felt during the siege. Many of the vehicles were painted white and a few white snow suits had been supplied to front-line troops; others had devised their own. The arrival of many of the Christmas packages which had piled up at Mourmelon during the siege added cheer to the day.

New Year's Day was quiet enough, though occasional paratroopers and glidermen continued to meet death or wounds in sporadic front-line brushes. The artillery stayed busy firing in support of the neighboring 11th and 6th Armored Divisions.

That night things began to stir. In Division Headquarters plans were completed for several limited-objective attacks for the next day; overhead German bombers circled and dropped a few bombs which did little damage. Company F of the 327th was attached to Team Cherry for an attack on Senonchamps, two miles west of Bastogne, and the high ground north of Senonchamps. The 2d Battalion of the 506th was to attack and clear out the woods which lay between Foy and the railroad to the southeast. The 2d Battalion of the 501st was also to attack in the woods along the railroad. These attacks, conceived and executed at Division level, had limited objectives. The capture of Senonchamps, at the base of the Bastogne salient, would widen the narrow neck of the salient and thereby render less dangerous the German threat to the roads over which the Division's supplies had to come. The 501st and 506th attacks were to clear out enemy pockets on the front and to develop the enemy situation. The 501st attack in the woods had the additional purpose of preventing the Germans in these woods from placing flanking fire on the 6th Armored Division when that division pushed up alongside.

The attack of Team Cherry and Company F of the 327th got off at 0810, January 2. By 0845 Senonchamps was occupied. The Germans put up very little fight—in fact the action reminded Company F of maneuvers; a fifteen-minute preparatory barrage, tanks followed by infantry, everything going along smoothly, and just two Germans encountered and captured in the whole affair. Company F rejoined the regiment that afternoon.

The 506th had a more eventful morning. Its 1st Battalion, in reserve, left Savy at 0630 to move up to relieve 2d Battalion, which was sched-uled that morning to serve an eviction notice on the Germans. Just after they left Luzery on the Bastogne–Foy highway, eight or nine German planes bombed and strafed the column; the troops quickly scattered and suffered only three casualties.

The battalion relieved 2d Battalion, holding a line which began at a point a third of a mile south of Foy, extended 1,500 yards southeast to the western side of the Foy–Bizory road, and then followed the road down to the railroad line. The railroad marked the left flank boundary of the 501st area. At 0930 2d Battalion attacked across the Foy–Bizory road into the woods which extended to the north and along the railroad to the northwest. It was the very beginning of a fight for the Bois Jacques—Jack's Woods—which was to become, before it was finally taken, one of the bloodiest chapters of the Bastogne battle.

The objective of the battalion was the minor Foy–Magéret road which ran in the general direction of the line of departure—the Foy–Bizory road—and was about 500-1,000 yards to the east through the woods. The Germans put up a stiff fight initially, but then abruptly fell back, losing seven prisoners and an estimated twenty dead. At 1530 the objective was taken.

At 0930 on the 2d the 501st was notified that its attack would be delayed. The regiment, which had assembled before dawn and had moved to a forward assembly area in the Bois Jacques remained there during the day, catching some enemy shelling—about a third duds—and some sniper fire. The uncertainty and looseness of the lines was brought out during the night when, at 0300 on the 4th, three Germans in American uniforms drove an American jeep three hundred yards inside the 501st lines near Bizory, pulled up alongside a halftrack, killed the driver, and escaped with the halftrack back into the German lines.

That was the extent of the fighting during the first two days of January. There was nothing that night to indicate that the next thirty or forty hours were to be among the busiest, bloodiest and bitterest the 101st was ever to experience.

January 3 and 4: The Bloody Days

"Of all the attacks made by Allied forces in western Europe, the conditions under which this attack [the overall Allied counteroffensive which began on January 3] was made were, by all odds, the worst. The snow in many cases was waist deep, and even short infantry movements were made under the most trying conditions. The few roads were ice coated, and in many places snow blanketed the ice. Tanks were roadbound in nearly all cases, and the Germans, by carefully located antitank guns, aided by minefields to the fore, were able continually to halt Allied tank advances until the infantry could move forward to cope with the German strongpoints. It was unbelievably cold, near zero, and the battle for existence against the elements was at least as difficult as that against the enemy." Thus *Dark December* describes the conditions under which the January fighting in the Ardennes was waged.

There were other factors which handicapped the troops during the fighting. The shortness of the days had a limiting effect on offensive efforts. Full daylight was not until almost 8 o'clock and by 4 in the afternoon dusk was setting in and the men had to begin finding shelter and digging in. And there were the woods. The dense evergreen forests in which much of the Division's January fighting took place were gloomy, eerie mazes, as easy to get lost in as a Mississippi canebrake. The trees, about 35 to 40 feet tall, gave an optimum tree burst to artillery shells. As the level of unmelting snows rose the space between the white floor of the forests and the low-hanging branches became less; to move, a man had to flounder through the snow, bending and clumsily squirming to avoid the tell-tale branches. The woods lent themselves more readily to the defense than to the attack; a machine-gun position or a foxhole was seldom seen until the attacker was within hand-grenade range. When an attack was ordered it meant that the men climbed out of their foxholes and started forward, the fighting beginning as they rose.

In these woods contact between company and company—often even between man and man—was hard to maintain. There were almost no roads, houses or landmarks (the railroad excepted); a commander reporting his position by radio could only give an approximation, and patrols seeking contact between units would take compass bearings and move through the gloom of the woods until they bumped into somebody, friend or enemy. To bring up a case of ammunition or to evacuate a wounded man was generally a hand-carrying job and often the men doing the carrying had no clear idea whether the direction they were heading in was the right one. It is only by taking into account all these factors that the confusion of the later fighting in the Bois Jacques and the other woods around Bastogne becomes understandable.

January 3 started promisingly enough. The previous evening Division had received VIII Corps orders which put into motion the big Third-First Armies' coordinated drives to cut through the base of the Bulge. The 101st, supported by its now tested and trusted attachments—the 705th Tank Destroyer Battalion, Combat Command B of the 10th Armored Division, and the 755th and 969th Field Artillery Battalions with their 155mm howitzers—was to attack northeast on Corps orders and capture Noville. The Corps G-2 estimate which accompanied the field order summed up the enemy situation.

The advance by the III Corps against stiff resistance, together with the gains along the VIII Corps front, bring to the enemy in sharp focus that with the enlargement of the Bastogne salient and with every increase in size of this area, the positions of his forces west of line Bastogne–Houffalize become more untenable . . . Failing to capture Bastogne, and certainly in event of enlargement of territory held by us, his position becomes more precarious. He is fast approaching the point where he must enlarge his holdings, or attempt to salvage what forces he can . . . The build-up in the Houffalize area may presage another attempt to regain the lost momentum of the drive to the west or the beginning of a drive to the southwest.

The German view of the situation at this time was reconstructed after the war by Major Percy Ernst Schramm, who kept the war diary for *Wehrmachtführungsstab der Oberkommando der Wehrmacht* (Operations Staff of the Armed Forces), the highest German headquarters:

Bastogne had been revealed as the point of main difficulty, though our troops had been able to surround it. However, the town itself, with its immediate vicinity and the crossroads, which were unconditionally necessary for the rear-area lines of communications and supply, remained in the hands of the enemy, who defended them with dogged toughness. He was supported by attacks to the south from the vicinity northeast of Neufchâteau, so that he could hope for a

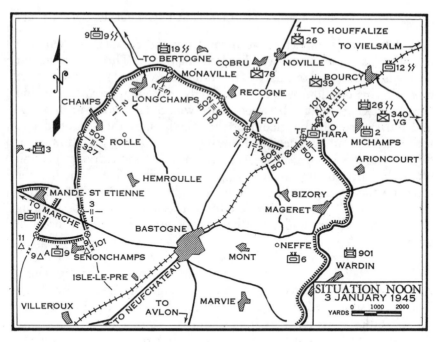

Map 89.

relief. Obviously the enemy command also recognized that Bastogne had a decisive meaning for the success or failure of the offensive. By continually renewed attacks against the southern front he succeeded in opening the pocket and in holding open an at first narrow pipeline to the outside. Reinforcements and everything else necessary could thus be brought in to the encircled troops, so that the hope of clearing up this pocket of resistance further diminished.

... The first goal must be to clear up the situation at Bastogne. On 2 January Commander-in-Chief West ordered Army Group B to so continue the attack that the encirclement would be restored, if possible; Army Group therefore should attack either from the west to the southeast or from the southeast toward the northwest. To this the latter replied that the enemy in the meantime had attained new penetrations and had attempted to cut off the jumping-off ground southeast of Bastogne. The area had grown so narrow that no additional motorized unit could be brought into it. General Field Marshal Model, who was actually there on the spot, answered that the plan requested by the Supreme Command was not feasible, because of the enemy's strength southeast of Bastogne and a terrain unsuitable for tanks. However, more suitable terrain which also provided a prospect of surprising the enemy was available north and northeast of Bastogne. Model wanted therefore to attack with the 9th SS Panzer Division from the north, the 12th SS Panzer Division from the northeast, and the Führer Grenadier Brigade from the east. *Der Führer* agreed to this proposal.

C in C West supplemented his orders on 3 January by a further one which prescribed for the Army Group its future procedure; it should in the future tie up and crush as strong enemy forces as possible, in support of the other operations which were planned for the Western Front. Consequently, it was the Army

616

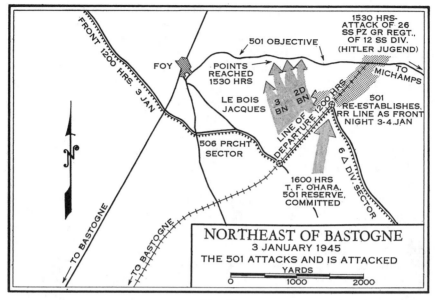

Map 90.

Group's new assignment to retain the newly won territory in all essentials. The assignment to clear up the Bastogne situation under any circumstances remained unchanged. . . .

The action began early on the afternoon of the 3d, on opposite sides of Bastogne and at the points of the perimeter where the lines came closest to the town itself (about two-and-a-half miles in each case). At noon the 2d and 3d Battalions of the 501st launched an attack to clear the Bois Jacques woods. The German position here was a wedge pointing south into the Bastogne lines. Facing them on the left or west side of the wedge was the 506th; facing them on the right or east side was the 501st. This right side of the wedge was along the Bastogne–Houffalize railroad which ran northeast out of Bastogne. It was into this German-held wedge at noon of the 3d that the 501st penetrated.

The objective was the road which ran from Foy east toward Michamps. The road came within a little more than a mile of Noville, which was to become a Division objective upon VIII Corps orders. Responsibility for the railroad line passed to the neighboring 6th Armored Division as soon as the 501st pushed off. During the morning there was a heavy ground fog with occasional snow flurries, and visibility was not much more than hand-grenade range; therefore, the parachute infantrymen had to do their fighting without effective support from the Air Corps or armor. The 501st had 2d Battalion on the right and 3d on the left, two companies abreast per battalion. The 1st Battalion was in reserve. On the 2d Battalion's right flank was the 50th Armored Infantry Battalion of the 6th Armored Division.

The 3d Battalion on the left ran into immediate resistance but managed to move forward until some of its men reached the road, and the whole battalion got to within two hundred yards of it.

The 2d Battalion, two companies abreast, D under Capt. Richard G. Snodgrass on the left, F under Capt. Arthur L. Cady on the right, had easy going at the start and pushed north five hundred yards through the woods, meeting almost no resistance. Within an hour Company F on the right had reached the Foy-Michamps road and had set up a roadblock where that road crossed the railroad.

At about 1430 a runner came down the railroad to where the battalion commander, Maj. Sammie N. Homan, had set up his advance CP six hundred yards below the roadblock and reported that Germans were moving down the railroad out of the territory supposedly held by the neighboring armored infantry battalion. Even before the runner got to him Major Homan had heard the sounds of small-arms fire from the vicinity of the roadblock.

The enemy, finding the railroad blocked by the Company F outpost, moved off the tracks and around to the east and south of the position. After about fifteen minutes of firing the roadblock group was forced to withdraw, and rejoined the rest of F Company in the woods northwest of the railroad.

The 2d Battalion reserve, Company E, under Lt. William P. Heaton, was in a woods just south of the railroad. Major Homan ordered this company to deploy on the east side of the woods up to the railroad, facing east. The battalion now had two companies facing entirely or partly to the east, awaiting the German blow on their exposed flank.

The 50th Armored Infantry Battalion which was to have advanced abreast of the 501st on the right flank of the 2d Battalion had dropped back after reporting eight tanks and a company of infantry moving down along the railroad. It was through this opening that the German attack poured. (This flank—which was the Division's right flank— had been and was to be for days a matter of concern to the Division. Having the adjacent sector held by an armored division using armor as a flexible defense force had not been too reassuring to either the 501st CO or the Division Commander. They were experienced enough infantrymen to know how easily such a front could be infiltrated by small groups of enemy troops. Also, the Bastogne–northbound railroad was the boundary between VIII and III Corps with the 101st the

rightmost unit of VIII Corps and the 6th Armored on the extreme
left of III Corps. Such boundaries have traditionally been weak spots
in a defensive line. The railroad line had other disadvantages. Through
much of the Bois Jacques it was a deep cut between dense forests
[the Foy–Magéret road crossed it on an overpass]. There were no
roads or trails paralleling it. Troops moving forward through the
woods on one side of the railroad could seldom tell whether in the
deep woods on the other side their flanking troops—strangers from
another division and corps—were keeping pace. The responsibility for
the tracks themselves belonged to both sides and, therefore, traditionally to neither. Contact patrols had the dangerous job of having to
cross the open right-of-way, slide down the side of the cut, cross the
tracks, and then up the other side—all the time a fair target for any
enemy weapon trained on the rail line. The problem of this boundary
continued to be a sore point in Division Headquarters, and the question
was eventually taken up with General Patton, who insisted on retaining
it as the only clearly identifiable line in the area.)

The Germans came toward them over the open fields which extend
west from Michamps to the railroad. To the surprise and pleasure of
the waiting paratroopers the advance was made almost in company
formation. With the first fire from the 501st, mostly from Company E,
they seemed to melt away. The open fields and the volume of fire
covering them apparently convinced the German commander that his
best chance was to probe farther south and come around the rear of
the American opposition. By now the strength of the attackers was
being revealed, at least a battalion, and four tanks and six halftracks
could be seen. Beginning to fall about the 501st troops was a mortar
round per second, the most terrific mortar barrage they were to
experience in the war, plus fire from artillery, tanks and infantry
weapons.

At the sight of the tanks and halftracks, Major Homan radioed for
supporting armor. Colonel Ewell told him that Team O'Hara was on
the way. When by the middle of the afternoon Team O'Hara hadn't
shown up, Homan sent his executive, Maj. William E. Pelham, to
the regimental forward CP to guide the armor to the battalion front.

Major Pelham, leading the tanks forward, spotted a German Mark
IV which had penetrated between the battalion and regimental CP.
Unable to tell whether it was friendly or enemy, he drove forward
in his jeep until he was fired on. He returned to his tanks and they
took the German under fire and destroyed him. Team O'Hara then
went into position south of the 2d Battalion and was especially efficient

against the halftracks, driving them back and breaking up the danger of an armored encirclement.

During the fighting on the right flank a notable performance had been given by the 1st Platoon of Company E. Under the leadership of Lt. Joseph C. McGregor (an outstanding officer who was killed a week later) and S/Sgt. Dale R. Smith, the 26-man platoon had worked around to the flank of the enemy attack and with its three bazookas had knocked out a tank and two halftracks. One squad had then set up an antitank gun and had got three more tanks and two halftracks. As the demoralized Germans pulled back the troopers mounted the abandoned vehicles and opened fire with the enemy's machine guns.

There were other instances of effective fighting and courage. An example of deliberate bravery was set during the morning by 1st Sgt. Herschel Parks of Company E. Seeing the company radio operator working out in the open during a heavy artillery barrage Parks got up from his foxhole and ordered the radioman into it. A few minutes later Parks was hit and killed.

Deep in the eerie woods on the 2d Battalion's left the 3d Battalion had fought the Germans with equal courage. Some idea of what their fight was like can be got from following the action of a single platoon.

The 2d Platoon of Company G had been ordered by the company commander, Capt. Felix W. Stanley, to attack a German position which was holding up the company. Under command of Lt. James B. McKearney, who later in the day was severely wounded, the platoon of about 33 men, reinforced by 11 men of the 3d Section of the light machine gun platoon of Headquarters Company, 3d Battalion, moved forward to within 75 yards of the Germans. The automatic weapons fire from the German positions had kept the men down low. A bullet from a German machine gun (an MG42) caught Pvt. Joseph Growney, of the machine gun platoon, in the heel. Pvt. Robert A. Gardner, the only surviving medic with the group, almost got to him when he himself went down with a bullet in the thigh. Sgt. Desmond D. Jones, leader of the eleven machine-gunners, ran forward, tripped on a root and fell; as he went down his helmet was shot off. Sergeant Jones did what he could for the wounded, then centered his attention on the German machine gun. Locating it he crawled forward to within ten yards of its position. The gunners, believing the three men out of action, had begun firing in another direction. Jones raised up with the tommy gun he carried and pulled the trigger; it failed to fire.

He then drew a captured P38 pistol, crawled a little closer, and took aim. It too failed to fire. Now the Germans spotted him and swung their gun onto him.

While all this was going on there had been a lull on another part of the platoon front (in the thick woods even on a platoon front actions could take place unseen and unknown forty or fifty yards away) another machine-gunner, Pfc. John M. Fox, who could speak German, yelled to the Germans to send one of their men out to talk with him. A German started out but one of the paratroopers, not knowing what was going on, shot him. Fire then started up again (it was during this firing that Sergeant Jones was crawling up on the MG42). In a few minutes things quieted down. Fox called out again and this time a German medic, looking like a Crusader with big red crosses on his chest and back, got up and came forward. Not wanting him to spot the light machine gun on which he was serving Fox halted him fifteen yards away and asked if they wanted to surrender. The medic said he would go ask his officer. In a few minutes he came back with the message that the officer would agree only to a short armistice to care for the wounded. Fox then ordered the medic to return and tell the officer that if they did not immediately surrender the Americans would bring up reinforcements and wipe them out. The medic went back and this time returned with a *Feldwebel* (a platoon sergeant with rank equivalent to a technical sergeant). Fox got up and walked out to meet him. He repeated what he had told the medic. To his surprise and relief the *Feldwebel* turned and called his men out of their holes. The officer, the German explained, had been badly wounded and he was acting for him.

Sixty-five Germans lined up for the platoon, which now had fourteen of its own personnel on their feet plus six of the attached machine-gunners—twenty men in all. In the patch of woods were at least an additional 30 enemy dead and wounded.

Meanwhile, back at the machine-gun nest, Sergeant Jones had lain sweating under the muzzle of the covering gun while the negotiations had been going on. When the *Feldwebel* gave up, the men who had held his life in their hands surrendered themselves to Jones.

Just before dark the battalions got orders to pull back. This ticklish maneuver—pulling back fully committed battalions in contact with the enemy—was carried out by pulling back a company at a time, with each company as it came back going into position to cover the company fartherest north. The move, completed by 0300 of the 4th, was carried out successfully. The 501st then reestablished contact with the 6th Armored and the 506th Parachute Regiment on the flanks

During the day Company D had suffered 31 casualties, Company E had 23, 2d Battalion Headquarters 21, and Company F 11. Thirteen of these 86 men were killed and one was missing in action. The 3d Battalion's losses were only a little less, with Company H suffering 38 and Company G 28 casualties each. Most of the casualties were from artillery tree-bursts. One of the worst features of the fighting was the difficulty of evacuating the wounded men.

The near-success of the 501st was long discussed by the commanders and men of the Division. If the 50th Armored Infantry Battalion had held the right flank it is probable that the 501st would have taken the Bois Jacques to the line of the Foy–Bizory road; both 501st battalions had reached the road in places and were nowhere more than two hundred yards away when the Germans came down the railroad on the right flank. The road would have been a natural defense line which the Division could undoubtedly have successfully defended. On the 3d the Germans were still offensive-minded, still hoped to take Bastogne, and as a result had not extensively organized the Bois Jacques as a defensive area. A week later, on the 9th, and again on the 12th, when the 501st attacked in the woods, the Germans had gone on the defensive and the week had given them time to dig in and well fortify the area. It was not until the 15th, after a three-day fight by the 327th and the 502d, that the woods was finally taken. The several hundred casualties suffered in retaking the woods might have been avoided if the 501st's flank had been covered during the critical action of the 3d.

Though the 501st show in the northeast had been scheduled to be the chief feature of the day an even deadlier fight was going on simultaneously on another part of the Division front. An hour after the 501st jumped off the Germans very definitely transferred the Division's attention to another side of Bastogne.

To the northwest of the town a 7,000-yard arc running generally several hundred yards outward of the villages of Champs, Longchamps, Monaville and Sonne-Fontaine, was held by the 502d Parachute Infantry. To hold this long front Lt. Col. Steve Chappuis had all three battalions on line: from left to right, 1st, 2d, and 3d, with Company F held back as a regimental reserve. He also had at his disposal five 57mm antitank guns from Battery C of the 81st AA Battalion and eight of the 705th TD Battalion's tank destroyers.

It was looking like the beginning of a quiet afternoon on this front when at 1310 the phone rang in the CP of the 502d's Company D.

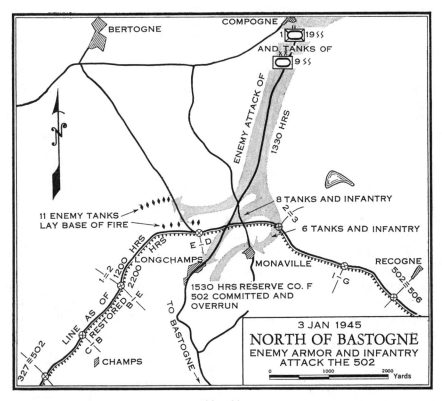

Map 91.

"I hear something." It was Sgt. Lawrence J. Silva calling in from the outpost line. A few minutes later he called back, "I can see fourteen tanks." Then there were eighteen. Then there were twenty. Then more. Finally his voice came: "I can't tell you any more." "Why not?" "There's a tank right over me. I'm lying flat on my stomach." A day or so later he was found that way in his hole, dead.

The attack was not unexpected; for several days patrols had been returning with reports of an obvious buildup, chiefly in the section north and northwest of Longchamps, which was the center of the 502d position and was held by the 2d Battalion. Heavy traffic had been observed on the main east-west highway between Compogne and Bertogne within mortar range of the front lines. But when 2d Battalion got Sergeant Silva's first report they could only estimate, due to the heavy fog—the same fog which was making difficult going for the 501st in their attack on the other side of the perimeter—the strength and intentions of the enemy force by sound and not by sight.

The first report received by Division twenty minutes after the tanks were heard on the 2d Battalion front, said that there were fourteen enemy tanks in front of Lt. Francis F. (Bud) Rainey's Company D, and asked for tank destroyers. Actually, an estimated thirty to forty tanks, mostly Mark IVs, and a battalion of infantry were there in the mist.

The enemy armor had come down the road which runs south from Compogne to Longchamps. On reaching a crossroads north of Monaville and just beyond the 2d Battalion's lines the tanks had fanned out for the attack. In a well planned maneuver six of the tanks moved west across the front of Company D, crossed the Bertogne–Longchamps highway, and from the west side of the road set up and maintained a base of fire throughout the attack. Their fire was very effective against both the antitank guns and automatic weapons defending the sector. Meanwhile five other tanks moved to a point approximately four hundred yards northwest of Longchamps in front of Company E, went into position, and added to the fire of the six tanks. Though these eleven tanks never moved forward the fire from their cannon and machine guns, spraying over the 2d Battalion area, kept the paratroopers down in their foxholes and handicapped their efforts to do anything about the main attacking force.

Some of the officers who had fought since Normandy thought the afternoon set a high in courage. The Germans had enough tanks to use them to shoot or root or gas out individual riflemen. Tanks would stop over foxholes and pivot with the hole as the point of the pivot. Often the hardness of the frozen ground and the depth of the hole would thwart the tank's action; then the man would rise and fire on the following German infantry. Sometimes the tank would return and park over the hole and gun its motor, flooding the paratrooper with carbon monoxide. The man could only lie and take it; but if he was still living when the tank finally went on he would again get up and look for targets against which his rifle might be effective. It was a day productive of fear, frustration and bravery. Pfc. Bruno J. Mecca of Company D, whose hole on the outpost line was early overrun, came back to the CP that night with tears in his eyes: "I'll fight any son of a bitch, but I can't fight those goddam tanks with a carbine."

There was one man on the Company D front that day who did not stay in a foxhole. He was Warren Cobbett, a medic attached to the company. All afternoon Cobbett moved about in the open picking up and bringing in the wounded. To many a man there he was the hero of the day.

This force, made up of fourteen tanks and a follow-up body of infantry, struck in two groups. Eight tanks and infantry, coming from the vicinity of the crossroads northeast of Monaville, hit the 1st Platoon of Company D, commanded by Lt. Thomas Bunn. The other six tanks, attacking from the same place, struck at the point where the 2d and 3d Battalions' sectors joined. In an effort to plug the latter position Colonel Chappuis committed his reserve, Company F.

For the 502d it was the bloodiest fighting since the causeway at Carentan. Company F as it came up was caught in the open by the German tanks and infantry and took a terrible beating, losing 47 men, including the company commander and two other officers, and nine noncoms. Thirty-four of the 47 were missing in action when the tanks overran and captured one platoon almost intact. Company D lost 48 men, 17 of them being killed in action and 13 missing. The losses included two officers, the first sergeant, and ten other noncoms. Neighboring companies, E and I, lost 14 and 10 men, respectively. Company I took over the remnants of Company F.

The attack lasted three hours. General Taylor started everything he could spare toward the threatened sector. The Division's artillery turned a record weight of shells on the Germans and several guns were displaced to antitank positions in anticipation of a possible breakthrough. Team Cherry deployed on the high ground south of Longchamps between the German armor and Bastogne. Tank destroyers attached to the 326th Engineers moved over to help their neighbors. Company A of the 326th Engineers was rushed up with mines and bazookas.

During the three hours the 502d's men held their positions although the tanks were able to penetrate into Monaville and Longchamps. The men in the foxholes risked the fire being laid down by the stationary tanks across the highway and knocked out the German infantry as they came on. At 1620 Colonel Chappuis was able to report to Division, "situation still under control," and asked only for the tank destroyers to come up to handle the German armor. His own men, armed with bazookas and grenades, had already disposed of some of the tanks. A former cowpuncher, Pfc. Franklin R. Blasingame of Company F, had gone into position with a bazooka, had hit and set afire the first tank to approach his position, and then plugged a second tank which also burned. He used his carbine to kill one of the escaping crew and wounded another; he himself was wounded.

Of the five 57mm guns attached to the 2d Battalion four were knocked out during the day but in the meantime they had given a splendid account of themselves. The antitank gunners of Battery C, 81st AAA Battalion were credited with knocking out ten Mark IV tanks.

Seven of these were knocked out by one crew. The section chief was Sgt. Joseph P. O'Toole; the gunner, Sgt. Edward E. Ford; the assistant gunner, Pfc. Arcadio Navarro. Sergeant O'Toole was seriously wounded. Private First Class Navarro, also wounded though less severely, after the ammunition ran out and the gun became useless fought on as an infantryman until the attack was beaten back. Sergeant Ford, when the ammunition was gone, grabbed a bazooka and continued to fight the tanks. The three men received the Silver Star for their afternoon's work.

Besides the tanks credited to the guns of Battery C, the 377th Parachute Field Artillery Battalion was credited with destroying three tanks with seven probables; Company C of the 609th Tank Destroyer Battalion, three with four probables; and Company C of the 705th Tank Destroyer Battalion, two with three probables. One tank was destroyed by a direct hit from a 155mm round fired by the Negro artillerymen of the 969th Field Artillery Battalion.

It was believed that more than two-thirds of the enemy tanks in the attack were either knocked out or damaged, though in some cases the Germans were able to haul off, repair and use these damaged tanks again.

In the early afternoon of the 3d General Taylor formed Task Force Higgins. To General Higgins he assigned the 502d, the 327th, Team Cherry, Companies B and C of the 705th Tank Destroyer Battalion, and Company A of the 326th Engineer Battalion. General Taylor foresaw a possibly difficult situation rising from continued enemy attacks on the 502d-327th side of the perimeter and he wanted General Higgins there to give him a constant estimate of the situation. If communications were disrupted Higgins would be able to take over direction of operations on that front. Task Force Higgins was to operate from the 502d CP. At 1630 General Higgins looked over the situation and found it satisfactory with not too much of the 502d area overrun.

About the time Task Force Higgins was being formed the 1st Battalion of the 327th had begun a movement to relieve the 1st Battalion of the 502d. The German attack against the 502d's neighboring 2d Battalion had held up the completion of this relief until after dark, when the danger of a breakthrough by the Germans was considered checked. The 1st Battalion of the 502d then went into regimental reserve. The 2d Battalion of the 327th had also assembled in reserve in the woods southeast of Rolle just before dark. By 2000 the entire original 502d position was again intact except for a hole near Monaville, and this Colonel Chappuis plugged with Company E of the 327th.

Shortly after dark that evening—January 3—occurred one of the incidents which change the course of battles. A German soldier came up to the machine-gun nest of Corporal Davis of Headquarters Company, 2d Battalion, 502d, tapped the corporal on the shoulder (mistaking him for a fellow German) and asked for directions. The lost German was personally escorted to the 101st interrogators and turned out to be as valuable a captive as the Division ever took. He was a runner from the 19th SS Panzergrenadier Regiment of the 9th SS Panzergrenadier Division; he was delivering messages to company CPs and he had detailed knowledge of another concentrated attack scheduled for early that morning.

Acting on this information, from one to nine battalions of artillery began firing concentrations beginning at 0300 on the area north of Longchamps where the Germans were concentrating. That this fire was effective was verified by another prisoner who said that it had broken up an attack which was to have been launched at 0400. But the Germans were determined; the G-2 periodic report covering January 4 said that the German effort for the day "has probably been the heaviest coordinated attack launched against our positions to date. Fortunately we were forewarned."

The weight of the German attack landed hardest on the 1st Battalion, 327th, which had relieved the 1st Battalion, 502d, near Champs. This relief was not completed until about 2000 hours and, except for the battalion commander and his company commanders, nobody in the battalion had seen the ground by daylight. The village of Champs is on one edge of a large bowl-shaped valley; in the village was the CP of 1st Battalion, 327th. A part of the OP line for the defense of this bowl was on the forward slope away from the main line of resistance. The glidermen, coming up in the dark and cold (during the night and following day it snowed fitfully), found the ground to be frozen shale; the most they could do was to chop out shallow slit trenches.

At about 0530, after a preparatory artillery bombardment which began at 0400, the 104th Panzergrenadier Regiment of the 15th Panzergrenadier Division launched an attack in regimental strength, hitting the battalion on both flanks and in the middle. Approximately eleven tanks and self-propelled guns supported the attack. The tanks, in spite of the dark, drove along the outposts and main firing line, firing with

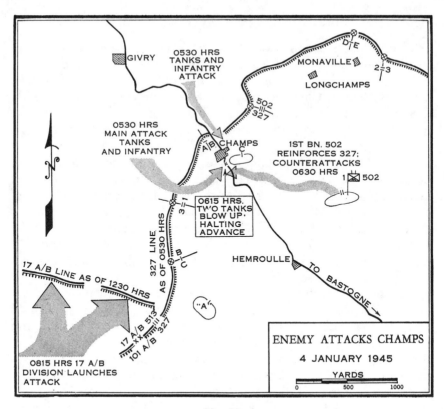

GIVRY

0530 HRS
TANKS AND
INFANTRY
ATTACK

MONAVILLE

LONGCHAMPS

0530 HRS
MAIN ATTACK
TANKS
AND INFANTRY

502
327

A/B CHAMPS

1ST BN. 502
REINFORCES 327;
COUNTERATTACKS
0630 HRS

1   502

0615 HRS.
TWO TANKS
BLOW UP·
HALTING
ADVANCE

HEMROULLE

TO BASTOGNE

17 A/B LINE AS OF 1230 HRS

327 LINE
AS OF 0530 HRS

17 A/B 513

101 A/B 327

"A"

0815 HRS 17 A/B
DIVISION·LAUNCHES
ATTACK

ENEMY ATTACKS CHAMPS

4 JANUARY 1945

YARDS

0   500   1000

Map 92.

their cannon directly into the individual positions. They were followed by the German infantry. This force quickly overran and killed or captured most of the 327th men in the line; when daylight came the dead lay along the patch of ground they had never seen.

The tanks continued on into the village proper. At about 0600 Company C, the battalion reserve, consisting of a mixed platoon of riflemen and men from the Weapons Platoon and the company head-quarters command group, were committed in support of Company A which was on the right flank of the battalion. Company C was pinned down by tank fire as it moved forward, and the tank fire knocked out a 37mm antitank gun from Regimental Headquarters Company. "These tanks seem to be able to see in the dark," said the Company C commander, Capt. Walter L. Miller, as a cannon-firing tank tracked him and some of his men through the dark from a house to a haystack. Captain Miller put his men into position along the road in Champs. Two Panther tanks advancing onto the road ran over antitank mines set out the night before. The tanks caught fire and the crews bailed out "like flyers out of burning planes." A few, dropping down on the far side of the tanks, may have got away, but most were cut down by rifle fire.

The sight of the burning tanks gave pause to the following crews and they withdrew to a small drop-off on their side of the road. (The road ran along the crest of a little ridge which gave the Americans on their side of the road some protection from direct fire from the tanks' cannon and machine guns.) Then the German infantry moved forward.

The Company C men met them with rifle, carbine and machine-gun fire. A member of a 60mm mortar squad fired his weapon without using the bipod, the shells going almost straight up and down. (After the ground was regained eight dead Germans, victims of his fire, were found grouped around a machine gun.) One squad of Germans got within fifty yards of the battalion CP. The battalion sergeant-major, T/Sgt. George Gifford, opened the door: "A tank started firing .50-caliber bullets through the open door so I closed it in a hurry." The Germans were killed by fire from Company C and from that of some men from battalion Headquarters Company under Capt. Clifford J. Kjell.

The 1st Battalion of the 327th never had a fiercer fight than during the first fifteen minutes of that night. Other acts of bravery occurred in the dark, unseen by anyone. A forward observer kept calling in reports on the enemy and when a nearby machine-gun crew was knocked out he grabbed the gun and manned it against the enemy. When the ground was recovered an American was found alongside a German, blue bruises on each man's throat the only evidence of the cause of death.

The losses of the 327th on the 4th were like those of the 502d on the 3d. Company A had 41 casualties. Company C lost 30 men, many of them replacements who had joined the company four days before; two officers and 1st Sgt. Kenneth J. Whalen were among the wounded. That afternoon Company A of the 327th's 3d Battalion reinforced the depleted 1st Battalion.

The force that broke through the lines of the 327th managed to get four tanks and almost a battalion of infantry within one hundred yards of the 1st Battalion command post in Champs. Thrown in in a counterattack to turn back this attack was the 1st Battalion of the 502d, returning to the sector from which it had been relieved only a few hours before. After tough fighting in the streets of Champs two of the tanks were knocked out (though at some expense, one company, B of the 502d, losing three officers and three men in the fight). One of the tanks was stopped by Pfc. Edward M. Hunt, who deliberately left his sheltered position to get a clear line of fire for his bazooka.

The battalion accomplished its mission; Champs was safe and the paratroopers were ordered back into the 502d regimental reserve.

Though the heaviest attack hit the 327th sector it is quite probable that only the telling artillery bombardment, based on the information gained from the German runner, kept large-scale attacks from hitting other parts of the line in General Higgins' territory. During the day the enemy seemed to be constantly shifting his troops and .tanks. At one time twelve to fifteen tanks were seen approaching Longchamps but accurate artillery fire turned them away. During the early morning an attack, reinforced with tanks, was thrown against the left flank of the 2d Battalion, 502d and was turned back with artillery and long-range small-arms fire though the paratroopers took losses from the German tank cannon fire.

During the two days the Germans had finally got around to doing what they had never done during the siege—attacking simultaneously in strength at separate points of the perimeter. The airborne troops were grateful for the delay. "If they had hit us all at once like that before Christmas—we might have had it."

That afternoon additional tank destroyers were sent up to the 502d and the 327th so that the 502d had a total of twenty TDs at its command and the 327th had eight. Five hundred mines were also sent up to General Higgins' force. Relative peace settled over the sector that night. On the morning of the 6th Task Force Higgins was dissolved. Quiet set in.

THE "QUIET" PERIOD: JANUARY 5-8

The quiet lasted four days, until January 9. During these days the enemy's activity was, as expressed in the G-2 periodic reports, "confined to licking of wounds" received in his unhappy two days of attack. The 101st and the neighboring American divisions also had wounds to lick. The 101st's G-3 periodic report, which concerned itself with the Division's activity each day (the G-2 report giving the enemy counterpart), ran for four straight days under the heading "Results of Operations" an identical "Maintained defensive positions and contact with flanking units." The Division's tactical goal, the high ground around Noville, continued to dangle within sight but out of reach. More reserves than were then available would be required to take and hold it.

During this lull the major fighting was going on on the northern side of the Bulge above Bastogne. There on January 3 the First

Army had begun a two-corps counterattack aiming at Houffalize, ten miles north-northeast of Bastogne. The VII, the right-hand corps of this attack, after making some early gains on a twelve-mile front ran into stiff resistance from the Germans who were determined to keep open the escape routes for their troops and vehicles in the still salient to the west. To the left of the VII Corps the XVIII Airborne Corps attacked simultaneously and the 82d Airborne Division sparked the drive with a steady advance along a five-mile front.

By the 6th the First Army's corps had driven to and across the La-roche–St. Vith road, one of the two main east-west supply routes in the German salient. The enemy attacked bitterly and repeatedly in an effort to clear this important line of communications but without success. The next day indications of a German withdrawal from the salient were noted.

Major Schramm of the Operations Staff of the German Armed Forces Headquarters described the situation as viewed in the highest German circles:

The next few days brought with them a further worsening of conditions in the breakthrough area. The counterattack made against Bastogne led to no success of great proportion; on the contrary the enemy succeeded in so broadening the original pipelike entrance to the road crossing that our chances of once again closing it off finally disappeared. The front thus originating in the south and southwest of Bastogne was exposed to strong attacks and had to be withdrawn more and more. Consequently the situation on the south front was not only unsatisfactory but gave rise now to serious concern. At the same time the enemy attacked from the north and the northwest; he attained slow but steady successes against Sixth Panzer Army so that the situation at the point of the attack wedge was untenable in the long run. From this a new Führer directive released on 8 January drew the conclusions: it approved the withdrawal of the front to the line Dochamps (northwest of La Roche)–Longchamps (northwest of Bastogne).

By the 9th, the First Army had a firm grip on about ten miles of the Laroche–St. Vith road and stood within seven miles of Houffalize. On that day the Third Army, having regrouped, launched an attack from the south on a two-corps front with the VIII Corps on the left and the III Corps on the right. That was to be the day that peace and quiet—relative—ended for the 101st.

In the 101st sector, during the night of January 4 and the next day, there was some shuffling of units. On the extreme right of the 101st's front the 2d Battalion of the 501st relieved the 2d Battalion of the 506th. At 1500 on the 5th, near where the Foy–Bizory road crosses the railroad, the 501st's battalion received a German attack by an estimated company supported by artillery and mortars. This attack was turned back.

Company D took the most losses with ten casualties, all wounded. But the heaviest blow suffered by the 501st that day occurred when a truck loaded with two hundred land mines blew up in the courtyard of the Normal School of the Sisters of Notre Dame de Namur near regimental headquarters. The headquarters area was under constant shelling but whether a round hit the truck is not known. The twelve men from Regimental Headquarters Company on or about the truck simply disappeared; not a single particle of any of the bodies was ever found.

On the 5th, 1st Battalion of the 506th, in Division reserve, took over the 502d's 3d Battalion sector, the rightmost of the 502d position. The effect of these two moves was to shift the 506th sector one battalion to the left, giving them a front from a point a few hundred yards west of the Bastogne–Houffalize highway below Foy to a point just north of Monaville. The units on the Division line, from left to right, were, as of January 5: 1st Battalion of the 327th, 2d Battalion of the 502d, 1st Battalion of the 506th, 3d Battalion of the 506th, and 2d Battalion of the 501st.

Known to be facing, or in the vicinity of, the 101st were elements of the 19th and 20th SS Panzergrenadier Regiments, 9th SS Panzer Division; the 25th and 26th SS Panzer Regiments, 12th SS Panzer Division; the 104th Panzergrenadier Regiment and the 115th Panzer Battalion of the 15th Panzergrenadier Division; the 340th Reconnaissance Battalion; the 694th, 695th, and 696th Volksgrenadier Regiments of the 340th Volksgrenadier Division; Battle Group 304; and remnants of the 26th Volksgrenadier Division.

Prisoners taken from the beginning of the Bastogne fight through the 4th totalled 905. The 26th Volksgrenadier Division had been the biggest contributor with 419 officers and men, 224 being from the 77th Regiment of the 26th. The 15th Panzergrenadier Division accounted for 152 prisoners; the 2d Panzer Division, 143; and Panzer Lehr, 89. (The 2d Panzer Division was trapped and almost wiped out at the tip of the Bulge, near the Meuse; Panzer Lehr, after its losses at Bastogne and on to the west, was to get back to the Westwall with 10 tanks, 6 assault guns, and 400 combat troops.) Forty others were from the 3d Panzergrenadier Division, 5th Parachute Division, 2d SS Panzer Division, 12th SS Division, 9th SS Division, 340th Volksgrenadier Division, and 273d Army GHQ AA Battalion. Sixty-two prisoners were not identified as to unit. An estimated seven thousand Germans had been killed.

At least twenty German armored vehicles were knocked out on the

3d and 4th of January and by the end of January 6 the total number of such armored vehicles put out of action in the Bastogne fight totalled 196.

January 6, 7 and 8 were quiet days for the 101st. The weather which, on the 6th was marked by a heavy ground fog, on the 7th and 8th turned into occasional snow flurries; the sky was always dull. The poor visibility hampered patrolling, the chief activity of the period, though several highly successful missions were carried out. On the 6th a patrol from the 2d Battalion of the 502d under Lt. Robert M. Banker penetrated approximately five hundred yards to a point along the Longchamps–Bertogne road and captured and brought back fifteen prisoners. On the 8th S/Sgt. Ernest J. Cummings led an eight-man patrol from Company C of the 327th's 1st Battalion to spy out Rovette. The patrol returned well pleased with their snow suits which had allowed them to come close enough to a fifteen-man enemy patrol to effectively use their submachine guns; they reported they had killed about half the Germans.

On the 7th word reached the Division that General McAuliffe had been rewarded with a command of his own—the 103d Infantry Division. The General came down to say goodbye to the officers and men who backed him when he tied his name inseparably to the word "Nuts!" His brother officers gave him a farewell dinner and, to symbolize his departure from the division of booted jumpers and gliderists, a parting gift of a pair of canvas leggings.

On the 7th Division Headquarters left the military *caserne* in Bastogne and moved a mile and a half southwest to the village of Isle-le-Pré. It had become obvious that the Germans had the CP in Bastogne ranged in with their artillery; the shelling had been increasing all during the first week of January. The move was clinched when the Corps Commander, General Middleton, came to pay a call at the CP and was caught in a shelling which killed several men and wounded others. The General was unhurt. The problem of maintaining communication in Bastogne, always difficult, had become progressively worse. A week before, in an effort to avoid the heavy night shelling and bombing which were constantly knocking out the command lines, the Division's night CP was set up at Isle-la-Hesse, a mile and a half west of Bastogne. Here, in a small château belonging to the Baroness Greindl and within three hundred yards—easy mortar range—of the front lines the night command functioned peacefully and efficiently. (Baroness Greindl later wrote a book describing the war which she saw about her château.)

When the Division CP moved to Isle-le-Pré the rear echelon headquarters moved a couple of miles farther to the southwest to the larger village of Sibret, where there was space enough to accommodate such units as the Quartermaster Company with its trucks and supplies.

The everyday life of a division went on. During January 6, 2d Battalion of the 327th relieved 3d Battalion on the line, and in the 501st sector 1st Battalion of that regiment relieved 2d Battalion. On the same day a portable shower unit was set up in Bastogne and the dirty airborne and armored soldiers began, a company at a time, to take baths. Dirty clothes were collected and sent back to a laundry near Reims, returning clean on the 11th. Distribution of a newly arrived load of field ranges, sleeping bags and blankets was made. By the 8th the snow was deep enough to keep the 326th Engineers busy clearing it from the roads. Back in the artillery area that day a gun crew of the 377th Battalion found time to write a letter to a girl whose name and address they found in a cloverleaf holding three of the 659 rounds fired by the battalion that day.

Meanwhile, there had been some action on the 101st's left flank. On January 3 the 17th Airborne Division, which on Christmas Day had entered combat for the first time, came up alongside the 101st, replacing the 11th Armored as the 101st's left-flank neighbor. On the 7th the 17th Airborne and the division on its left flank, the 87th Infantry, had been committed in an attack northward. (Both divisions were, along with the 101st, part of VIII Corps.) The 17th's attack had carried across the front of the 327th who had supported it by mortar and machine-gun fire. The 101st's artillery fired in support; from its central position the Division's artillery was able to prepare and execute supporting and reinforcing fire for neighboring units on call. The forward movement of the 17th had the effect of slowly straightening the left arm of the 101st semicircle about Bastogne.

The limited attack by these two divisions of VIII Corps bogged down after some initial gains and Corps began making plans for a more ambitious attack which would drive toward Houffalize and a juncture with the First Army divisions fighting southward toward the town. Early on the morning of the 8th the message came down from Corps: "Prepare to attack on ninth January on Corps orders to capture Noville and maintain contact with the 6th Armored Division and the 17th Airborne Division." On the 8th also, in Berlin, Adolf Hitler ordered the withdrawal of the western tip of his salient to a line just west of the Bastogne–Houffalize highway. His dream of panzers across the Meuse, at Antwerp, on the Channel, was dead.

JANUARY 9 AND 10: ATTACK AND WITHDRAWAL

The attack of January 9 was to be part of an assault launched along a two-corps front by General Patton's Third Army. At the time Third Army consisted of three corps; XII on the right, III in the center, and VIII on the left. Only III and VIII Corps were to participate in the attack; XII Corps was to hold in place. The units and positions of the two attacking corps were, from right to left: III Corps with the 26th, 90th, and 35th Infantry Divisions and 6th Armored Division; VIII Corps, with the 4th Armored Division, which was to come into the line between the 101st and the 6th Armored (to which Combat Command B of the 4th Armored had been attached on the 8th), the 101st and 17th Airborne Divisions, and the 87th Infantry Division.

This drive, like the one launched the week before on the northern shoulder of the Bulge by First Army, was aimed at Houffalize. Meanwhile First Army was continuing its slow way south toward that town. When the two armies met, the Bulge would be liquidated and whatever enemy troops were west of the juncture point would be trapped. General Patton counted on this new attack, by eight divisions, to regain the initiative which had petered out in the bogged-down attack of the 87th Infantry and 17th Airborne Divisions.

The immediate assignment of the 101st, as specified by VIII Corps, was to stage a strong demonstration in the direction of Recogne at H-Hour on the 9th. The attack on past Recogne to seize Noville—a prime objective of the 101st since December—was to be on Corps orders. Both the 6th Armored on the right and the 17th Airborne on the left were to advance and the 101st was to keep its own flanks abreast of these two divisions. Attached to the 101st was Combat Command B of the 10th Armored Division, the 755th and 969th Field Artillery Battalions with their 155mm howitzers, the 705th Tank Destroyer Battalion, and Company B of the 611th Tank Destroyer Battalion.

The plan of attack worked out by the Division staff was as follows:

The 506th with Team Cherry; Battery A of the 81st AA Battalion; Companies B and C, 326th Engineers; and the 1st and 2d Platoons of Company C, 705th Tank Destroyer Battalion, was to jump off on the 9th at 1100 and, in three phases (1) clear the woods within its sector, (2) seize the high ground northwest of Noville, and (3) occupy Noville itself, accomplishing the Division's corps-assigned mission.

At the same time the 502d with Battery C of the 81st; 1st Platoon of Company A, 326th Engineers; Company C, 609th Tank Destroyer Battalion; Company A, 704th Tank Destroyer Battalion; Company B,

811th Tank Destroyer Battalion; and the Reconnaissance Platoon and 3d Platoon of Company C, 705th Tank Destroyer Battalion attached, was (1) to clear the woods within its sector, (2) to protect the left flank of the 506th and maintain contact at a crossroads in the Fazone Woods, and (3) on the withdrawal of the 327th to Division reserve to establish contact with the 17th Airborne in the vicinity of Champs.

The 501st was to jump off an hour after the 506th and 502d and, with its attachments, Battery B of the 81st AAA Battalion; 3d Platoon of Company A, 326th Engineers; Company B of the 704th TD Battalion, and Company A of the 705th TD Battalion, was (1) to seize Recogne, (2) to protect the right flank of the 506th and maintain contact at a road junction due east of Recogne, and (3) to maintain contact with the 6th Armored Division on the Bastogne–Houffalize railroad, boundary between the VIII and III Corps.

The 327th, with Company B of the 705th Tank Destroyer Battalion attached, was to maintain contact on the right with the 17th Airborne until withdrawn as Division Reserve. The artillery preparation and support was to be quite elaborate, laying down preparatory and harassing fire, smoke, and supporting fire on call.

The 9th was a dull, cloudy day and by the time of attack snow was falling thickly. Tanks and self-propelled guns slipped and slid as they came forward; for wheeled vehicles the roads were almost impassable. Though weather prevented any support from the air the attack was launched as scheduled.

At 1100 the 506th and Task Force Cherry attacked northeast through the Fazone Woods toward Noville. The regimental front had been contracted early that morning by the relief of the 3d Battalion, the rightmost battalion, by 3d Battalion of the 501st. The 3d Battalion, relieved, had moved to a forward assembly area in the woods south of Sonne Fontaine. The 2d Battalion, base battalion in the attack, pushed off after a thorough artillery battering of the woods ahead, and was followed ten minutes later by the 3d Battalion, which moved to the left and took up a position on the left flank of the advance. The 3d Battalion, 502d that afternoon passed through the 1st Battalion, which was holding the left side of the 506th sector. The relieved battalion then assembled in Regimental reserve to the rear of 3d Battalion, 506th.

To reach its first phase line, the regiment had first to clean out a section of the Fazone Woods, about 2,500 yards by 1,000 yards.

The woods were defended by the 2d Battalion of the 78th Volksgrenadier Regiment, 26th Volksgrenadier Division. Along the south edge of the woods the battalion had set up a string of strongpoints, about twelve in all, each manned by ten to fifteen men with two machine guns. All the prisoners taken by the 506th and 502d that day were from this battalion.

The woods which the troops passed through during the first part of the advance were lightly held; almost as soon as the 506th's 2d Battalion started into the woods they took prisoner an enemy platoon. However, few other Germans turned up until the 3d Battalion knocked out four outposts two hours later. At 1445 the 506th had bagged 41 prisoners. By 1630 the regiment had taken the objective for the day. It cost the regiment 69 casualties, seven of them fatalities. Hardest hit was 3d Battalion Headquarters Company, which had twenty men wounded, including the company commander, Capt. James G. Morton. The 1st Battalion lost its commanding officer, Maj. Robert F. Harwick, who had taken over the battalion when Lt. Col. James L. LaPrade was killed on the first day of the Bastogne fight. Major Harwick and his executive officer, Capt. Knut H. Raudstein, were wounded when a German SP gun scored a direct hit on the battalion CP. Maj. Charles G. Shettle, executive officer of the 2d Battalion, took command of the 1st Battalion. The next morning he too was wounded by artillery fire and the command passed temporarily to Capt. Roy M. Kessler, commander of A Company, then to Maj. Clarence Hester, regimental S-3.

The 501st had the assignment of capturing the village of Recogne. Recogne was within five hundred yards of the front lines of the 501st and opposite the point where the 2d Battalion's sector joined the 3d Battalion's (the 3d Battalion had that morning relieved the 3d Battalion of the 506th; so up to that day Recogne had been opposite the boundary between the two regiments).

The attack was made by the 501st's 2d Battalion with F as the assault company. The advance began at 1225, an hour and twenty-five minutes after the 506th jumped off. Company F reached the center of Recogne by 1335. The attached tank destroyers chased two tanks out of the village toward Noville. Company E was later committed to aid F, and the two companies, at a cost of 25 enlisted and three officer casualties mopped up the remnants of the Germans by 1700. The enemy casualties were heavy, the attackers taking almost sixty prisoners. After dark the 3d Battalion assumed defense of the town and the weary 2d Battalion reverted to regimental reserve. On the other side of the Bastogne–Noville highway, along the Foy–Bizory road the 1st Battalion remained in position preparing for the next day's attack.

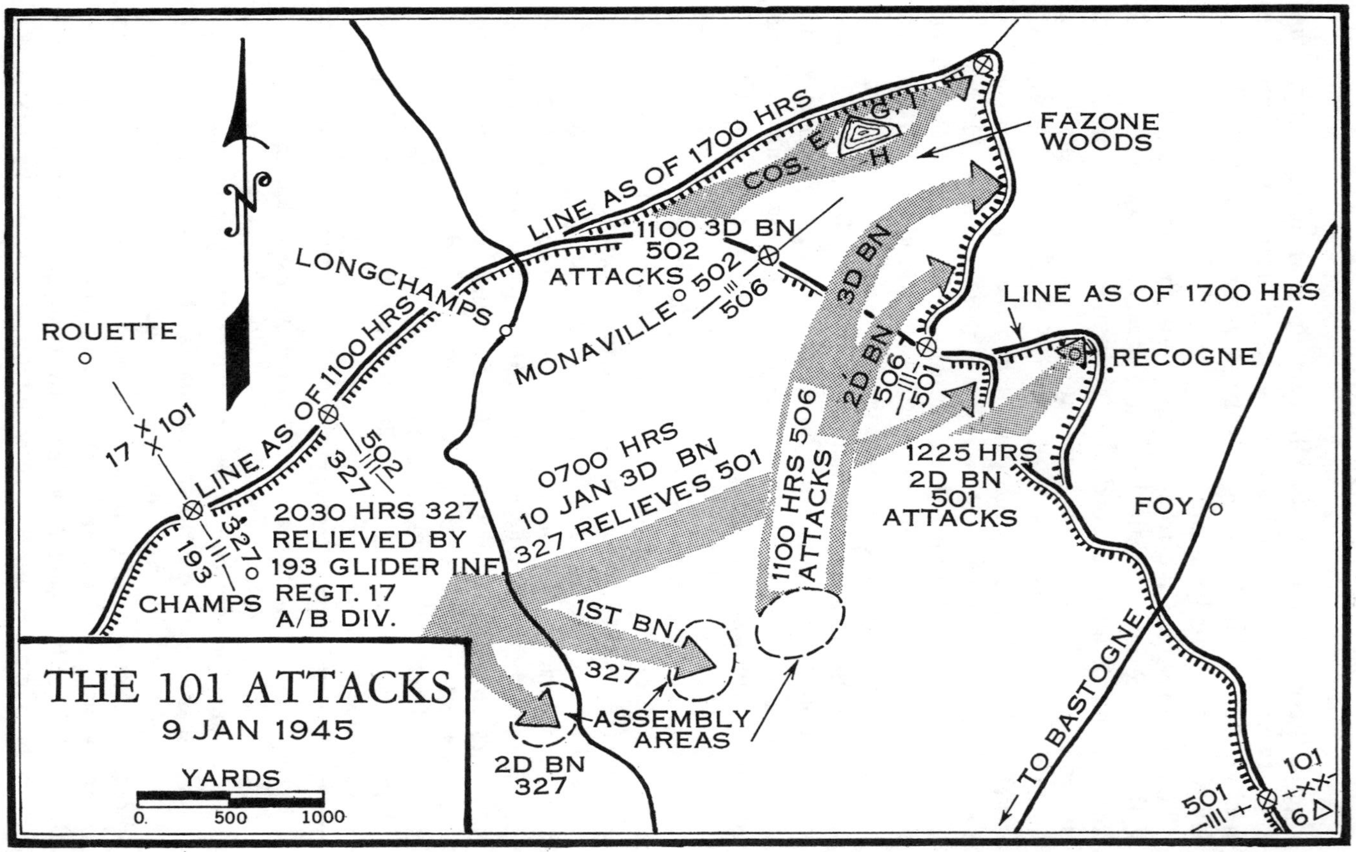

FAZONE
WOODS

LINE AS OF 1700 HRS

RECOGNE

FOY

TO BASTOGNE

101
6

501

1225 HRS
2D BN
501
ATTACKS

506 2D BN
501 2D BN

3D BN

1100 HRS 506
ATTACKS

1100 3D BN
502

ATTACKS 502
MONAVILLE

3D BN
506

0700 HRS
10 JAN 3D BN 501
RELIEVES BY 327

ASSEMBLY
AREAS

1ST BN
327

2D BN
327

LINE AS OF 1700 HRS
COSTA

LONGCHAMPS

LINE AS OF 1100 HRS

502
327

2030 HRS 327
RELIEVED BY
193 GLIDER INF
REGT. 17
A/B DIV.

327
193

CHAMPS

ROUETTE

17
101

N

THE 101 ATTACKS
9 JAN 1945

YARDS

0   500   1000

Map 93.

One of the major losses of the day was the wounding of Lt. Col. Julian J. Ewell, young regimental commander of the 501st. A foot wound ended the battle career of the officer who had so distinguished himself as a battalion commander in Normandy and Holland and, after the death of Colonel Johnson, as regimental commander. The regimental executive, Lt. Col. Robert A. Ballard, assumed command, to successfully lead the regiment through the rest of the war.

On the left flank of the 506th the 502d Parachute Infantry Regiment jumped off at the same time and in coordination with the 506th. Its mission was to protect the 506th's left flank in its advance and to clean out the Les Assins Woods just west of the Fazone Woods where the 506th was fighting. The attacking force of the 502d was the 3d Battalion with Companies G and I on line and with Company E attached. The main force moved around the north side of the Etang de Fazone, a small lake in the Fazone Woods; Company H moved around to the south of the lake. Initially the advance met little resistance but as it penetrated deeper into the snowy woods heavy small-arms, mortar and artillery fire—tree bursts—slowed down the attackers. During the attack the paratroopers encountered their first tactical wire, both single- and double-apron fences, indicating a well planned and organized defense. The battalion had reached the last phase line before the objective when it received orders to hold up and dig in. Contact was established with the 506th on the right and the 2d Battalion of the 502d on the left. The day cost the 3d Battalion thirty enlisted men and six officers, Company G suffering the most losses, sixteen men.

The only regiment which failed to see action on the 9th was the 327th. By 2030 that night the 193d Glider Infantry of the 17th Airborne Division, which was advancing on the 101st's left, had moved in and relieved the 327th. The 2d Battalion, 327th, moved into an assembly area in the Bois de Niblamont southeast of Rolle, the 1st Battalion (less Company B which had been attached during the day to the 502d) assembled in some woods about a thousand yards to the east of the 2d Battalion, and the 3d Battalion moved out to take over the 501st's sector. Now, as the neighboring divisions moved up alongside and took over part of the 101st's defensive sector, the relieved battalions were providing General Taylor with what he had been wanting—a reserve which he could use as a striking force.

During the 9th the largest gain on the Third Army front was made southeast of Bastogne in the III Corps sector by the 90th Division. The 90th was the spearhead division in the III Corps attack and picked up about a mile and a half, but at a very heavy cost in casualties. In the VIII Corps the 101st was the most successful division. The remaining divisions of the two attacking corps made very little progress.

The 10th was a cold, cloudy day, though the weather opened enough at times to allow air support. It was miserable for those waiting in the Belgian evergreen forests to begin their second day of attack. The temperature never rose above freezing and at daylight it was down below fifteen degrees. Added to the cold were the harassing and dangerous tree bursts of German shells; the paratroopers dug in as well as they could in the frozen ground and the 326th Engineers cut logs for them to use as cover for their foxholes, some of which the engineers blew out for them with TNT.

That the suffering and difficulties were not confined to the American side of the line was brought out in a letter written by the supply sergeant of a battalion of the 696th Volksgrenadiers, a regiment facing the 501st, to his commanding officer. The captured letter (which indicated that armies—and supply sergeants—are pretty much the same) was dated January 9 and read:

> Today when I received your requisition I felt like Santa Claus because your request is much too much. I can't understand why the Headquarters does not have any blankets because each man received two blankets according to the supply record. Besides, the blankets of the wounded are supposed to be there. I also left my two blankets at the front. To help you I collected back here one blanket from each man in Battalion Headquarters Company which I'll send you. It is impossible to take away more blankets from the drivers because they sleep outside and need them very much.
>
> I am going to send again two stoves forward to the Headquarters and I ask you to let me know how many dugouts are without any. Tomorrow I will have a few stoves made from old gas cans. The train CP, the finance office and the day-room have only very large stoves which are too big for the dugouts. I ask you to consider that not only the 1st Battalion of the 696th is in this vicinity but also the entire regiment and some SS troops. If we would leave our room unguarded for ten minutes you can be certain our stove would be gone.

The 101st's chief mission for the 10th remained to seize Noville. On the right flank the 4th Armored Division was to pass through the left element of the 6th Armored and attack in conjunction with the 101st to seize the village of Bovrey and its vicinity.

For the 506th the day of fighting began at 0230 on the 10th when an enemy force estimated to be a combat patrol supported by two platoons and aided by heavy artillery fire attacked the newly won positions on the eastern edge of the Fazone Woods. The 506th turned back the attack with some loss to the enemy. The artillery was so bad, however, that at 0830 the 1st Battalion, which was in reserve

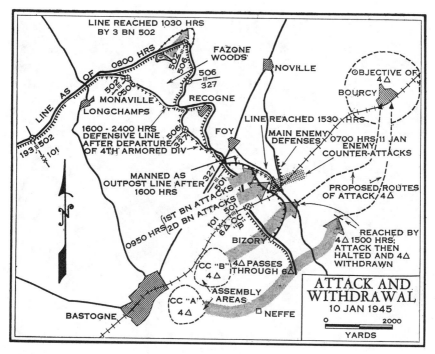

Map 94.

behind the 2d Battalion, moved about three-quarters of a mile to the southwest to get away from the shelling. Casualties from the enemy artillery during the evening and night of the 9th and early morning of the 10th totalled 126 men for the regiment. On the 10th 1st Battalion Headquarters Company suffered ten casualties, mostly from artillery, including the battalion commander, Major Shettle; other officers lost were the battalion S-3, the company commander, and a platoon leader.

The 3d Battalion of the 502d resumed its attack in the Les Assins Woods at 0825 of the morning of the 10th and by 1030 had reached its objective, some high ground in the woods. The battalion suffered 43 casualties, mostly from artillery and mortar bursts.

The most confused action of the day took place on the Division's right flank where the 501st was attacking. The 501st jumped off at 0950 with the 1st Battalion on the left, the 2d Battalion on the right and the 3d Battalion in regimental reserve. The regiment had the mission of clearing the Bois Jacques, the woods which lay in the V of territory between the highway running north from Bastogne to Noville and the railroad running northeast from Bastogne.

The first phase line, the Foy–Magéret road, about a thousand yards beyond the line of departure, was reached by 1530. During the advance

641

A paratrooper dead in the Bois Jacques during the fight of 9-10 January 1945.

the 501st had received heavy small-arms fire from along the railroad at the right. This was ominous to the 501st commanders because the 3d Battalion of the 320th Infantry Regiment, 35th Division, attached to the 6th Armored Division across the VIII-III Corps boundary of the railroad, was supposed to coordinate its advance with that of the 501st. It was beginning to look too much like the drive through the same woods on the 3d when the 50th Armored Infantry Battalion on the right had been unable to hold and the Germans had poured in on the 501st's flank. Colonel Ballard sent Capt. Elvie Roberts to reestablish contact. Captain Roberts found that the 320th's battalion had not moved at all; the battalion commander said that he had orders to hold in place. With fire hitting both the front and the uncovered right flank, Colonel Ballard did not object to the orders which reached him during the afternoon that he make the phase line he had reached his outpost line and withdraw his companies to his main line of resistance. At the same time Colonels Sink and Chappuis were notified that the attack was off and that they also were to withdraw to their original main lines of resistance, giving up the ground which they had gained during the day and a half of fighting.

Even at fairly high levels within the Division the reason for this withdrawal was not understood. It was obvious that Third Army during the 9th, while achieving nothing like a breakthrough, had been going forward satisfactorily. What had happened?

The attack was doomed when, in headquarters higher than Third Army's, concern grew that there was building up in the Saarlautern–Saarbrücken sector of the Third Army line a concentration of enemy strength capable of launching a dangerous attack. As a result General Patton was ordered, on the 10th, to withdraw an armored division and send it south as a reserve for the weak right wing of his army. The 4th Armored Division, which on the morning of the 10th had begun to attack through the 6th Armored on the 101st's right flank, was halted at noon. That night the 4th Armored began withdrawing and, with shoulder patches removed and vehicle unit insignia painted out, started south.

At the same time the 4th Armored received its order to break off the attack, the 101st got word to stop its advance and drop back to its old positions. And the same day the entire VIII Corps, now lacking the striking force of the hard-hitting armored division, went back on the defensive with operations limited to vigorous patrolling. On the Third Army front only the III Corps continued to attack.

This was all high echelon maneuvering. Down in the snowy evergreen woods the cursing soldiers knew only that they seemed to be moving aimlessly, attacking, winning, giving up without a fight the ground won, and, most personally, digging more and more foxholes in the frozen, rock-hard ground.

The withdrawal quieted the 101st's front considerably except in the 501st sector. There the outpost line established by the 501st along the farthest phase line reached that day probed the enemy in a tender spot, for his main defense position was along the Noville–Magéret road. Where the road crossed the railroad on an overpass the 501st was within a hundred yards of his position. It was an intolerable situation for the Germans, so they determinedly pushed a force across the overpass from their side of the railroad and forced the 501st back approximately 150 yards at this point.

That night, January 10, Colonel Ballard, General Higgins and Colonel Kinnard attempted to work out a plan to coordinate the 501st and the 320th; all were much concerned over the situation, a final result of the troublesome corps boundary along the railroad, but no one was ever able to establish exactly what the 320th's orders for the day had been.

A 75mm M1A1 howitzer being fired by parachute artillerymen of the 101st.

JANUARY 11 AND 12: BREATHING SPACE

On the morning of the 11th when the 11th Armored Division contacted the 101st to ask about their front line position the reply was that it was the same as it had been three days ago, before the two days of advance and falling back. It was as follows:

Beginning at the 17th Airborne Division's boundary just north of Champs the 502d held a line running along the Rouette–Longchamps road to a crossroads about half a mile west of Longchamps and from there an arc extending north of Longchamps and Monaville; from north of Monaville the 1st and 2d Battalions of the 506th held a line roughly south of the Fazone Woods to a point about a quarter of a mile southeast of Recogne (now given back to the Germans); from that point the 3d Battalion, 327th, held a sector on down to the Bastogne–Houffalize highway five hundred yards south of Foy; the Foy–Bizory highway was held from near Foy to the railroad crossing at Halt by the 1st and 2d Battalions of the 501st; the 501st was outposting in front of this position along the railroad several hundred yards toward the overpass on the Foy–Magéret road; and the remaining battalions were in Division reserve. On the right of the 501st was the 6th Armored Division.

About midnight of the 11th-12th a message arrived from VIII Corps defining the 101st's immediate mission as aggressive patrolling, seizure of key terrain features not defended by the enemy in strength, and preparation for offensive action on short notice. In spite of the promise of at least sharp local encounters implied in this directive the 12th was one of the quietest days of the entire Bastogne campaign.

644

The withdrawal which followed the cancellation of the Corps and Division attack had left an unoccupied no-man's land into which the enemy filtered only gradually and cautiously; there was no offensive action on his part all day nor any real physical contact. Front line troops of the 502d and 506th could occasionally glimpse in the snowy forests (it had snowed that morning) German reconnaissance patrols feeling out the Les Assins and Fazone Woods. Before dark the enemy had moved in several companies to reoccupy these woods.

The 12th was very cold, the official temperature at daylight being six degrees. Except in the case of the 501st the day resembled the one preceding in that there was almost no action.

Some replacements arrived during these days—among the best the 101st was ever to get. From the 1st Special Service Force, a crack U. S.–Canadian outfit trained for special combat missions, which had been inactivated on December 5 in Southern France, came about 350 enlisted men and 6 officers, all parachutists. At the time they were the only unassigned parachutists in the ETO. They were scattered throughout the parachute regiments, the 506th getting the most, and some who were trained artillerymen went to batteries of the 377th and 463d Parachute Field Artillery Battalions.

Rumors began that the Division was going to be relieved. They became an actuality for a few men and officers who were lucky enough to get five-day Paris passes; the first shipment left that day and additional groups were to leave every second day thereafter. But it was a premature hope for the Division; the last and biggest drive of the 101st's Bastogne action was to be launched the next day.

The single action of the 12th, the 501st's, was necessitated by the plans for the 13th. In order that the 327th, which was to attack through the 501st, might have a better line of departure, the 501st made a limited-objective attack at 1405 to take and stabilize a line along the Foy–Magéret road, about five hundred yards in front of their MLR. The regiment attacked with 1st Battalion on the left, 3d on the right, and 2d in regimental reserve. Ground resistance was fairly light and the objective soon fell, but artillery and mortars took their toll and the day cost the regiment forty-two casualties.

THE PAYOFF: PREPARATION

In spite of the fact that VIII Corps had had to go from the attack to the defense when the 4th Armored Division was withdrawn on the 10th, the corps had occupied St. Hubert, about thirty miles west of Bastogne, and it was apparent that the enemy was speeding up his withdrawal from the Bulge. On the 12th the 11th Armored Division was assigned to VIII Corps, replacing the withdrawn 4th Armored, and plans were made to continue the attack toward Houffalize and the consequent pinching off of the German salient.

For the 101st, H-hour was to be 0830 on the morning of the 13th. On the 12th the Division front was to be narrowed and the available reserves increased by having the newly committed 11th Armored take over the 502d Parachute Infantry Regiment's sector on the left. The 11th Armored was to jump off with the 101st and was to attack to capture the towns of Bertogne and Compogne. The 101st was to advance with regiments abreast toward its now long-standing objective, Noville, and take the town.

The attacking force, from left to right, was: 506th, 327th, and 502d, with the 501st in Division reserve. On the left the 506th, supported by Battery A (antitank) of the 81st AAA Battalion; Company C of the 609th Tank Destroyer Battalion; 3d Platoon, Company C, 326th Engineer Battalion; and the 321st Field Artillery Battalion, was to attack at 0900—H-hour plus 30 minutes—and capture the village of Foy astride the Bastogne–Noville highway. It was then to prepare to attack and clear the Fazone Woods the following day.

The 327th, with Company B of the 705th Tank Destroyer Battalion and Company A of the 326th Engineer Battalion attached, and with the 463d Parachute Field Artillery Battalion in direct support, was to pass through the 501st at 0830 and clear the northern part of the Bois Jacques.

On the right flank the 502d was to assemble after being relieved by the 11th Armored. With Battery C of the 81st; Company C of the 705th TD Battalion; Team Cherry; the 1st and 2d Platoons of Company C, 326th Engineer Battalion attached; and with the 377th Parachute Field Artillery Battalion in direct support, it was to attack toward Bourcy and seize the high ground near that village. The attack was to be made by 1st and 2d Battalions. The 3d Battalion was held in Division reserve.

Artillery preparation for the day was built up by attachment of three artillery battalions, the 687th (which, on the 9th, had replaced the 101st's comrades of the siege period, the 969th Field Artillery Battalion), the 755th, and the 420th Armored FA Battalion (the organic artillery battalion of CCB of the 10th Armored Division). At 0827—three minutes before H-hour—every gun was to fire at maximum rate for three minutes on targets in front of the 327th. Then, at 0840, the guns were to lay on the 506th sector and for twenty minutes, until the 506th's 0900 attack hour, fire on the villages of Recogne, Cobru and Foy. From 0730 to 1130 the batteries were to place harassing fires on Noville and at 0745 were to fire counterbattery on all enemy gun positions located since the previous evening. Preparatory fire for the 502d was to be laid down as the regiment directed.

Part of the 502d had been relieved by the 11th Armored during the night of the 12th-13th and the 1st and 3d Battalions moved to forward assembly areas northeast of Bastogne for the attack toward Bourcy. (Here again General Taylor was able to add to his reserves as the adjacent divisions came alongside and relieved the 101st of its defensive sectors.) The 1st Battalion was in position by 0245 and 3d Battalion by 0700 of the 13th. The 2d Battalion remained in position west of Longchamps until the next day when it was relieved by units of the 11th Armored and went into Division reserve near Savy. At 0830 on the 13th the two battalions, attacking in a northeasterly direction on the west side of the railroad, began the regiment's five-day-long attack toward Bourcy.

The placing of the 502d on the east of the railroad was General Taylor's solution of what had been one of his most persistent problems —the troublesome VIII-III Corps boundary dead along this natural entry way for infiltrating German troops. With the 502d on the east and the 327th on the west of the railroad the roadbed came entirely under the 101st. In this way General Taylor assured himself of better coordination and definite flank protection for the 101st units advancing through the Bois Jacques on the west of the railroad.

THE PAYOFF: BEGINNING ATTACK

On the 13th the 502d attacked in column of battalions, 1st in the lead, with the left flank guiding on the railroad. The open terrain and the heavy enemy small-arms and tank fire of the well-dug-in Germans made the going slow for the regiment. The regiment, like the 501st a few days earlier, had trouble keeping contact with the 320th Infantry Regiment on the right. Also, as the day progressed, the 327th, on the 502d's left, surged ahead of the paratroopers. The gap between the glidermen and the 502d widened and enemy troops slipped in behind the 327th. These troops fired on the 502d and for a time the parachutists were receiving fire from three directions. That evening the 502d had reached a line several hundred yards past the Foy–Magéret road but also a mile short of the day's objective. Here the regiment dug in, made contact by patrols with the 327th on its left, and prepared for the next day's attack.

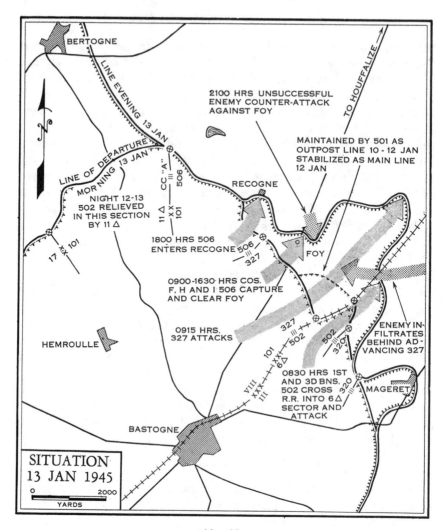

Map 95.

The losses of the 502d during the day were the largest of any of the regiments. Casualties totaled 84, including 17 dead and 4 missing. Two medics were killed while tending the casualties and S/Sgt. William N. Tucker of the regiment's Medical Detachment personally carried out five of the wounded under heavy fire and directed evacuation of twenty-five more.

On the other side of the railroad the 327th, after an intense artillery preparation, had jumped off at 0915 on the 13th, forty-five minutes after the 502d's and 327th's scheduled times. The delay was attributed to the snow, lack of coordination between regiments, and the thick woods in which even the guides got lost. At 0845 General Taylor reached the 327th CP to find out the reason for the delay. He passed the word that if the units did not reach their objectives by 1630 each commander would be fined one hundred dollars. (Actually, the regiment reached its objective ahead of schedule and each battalion received a case of cognac from the general.)

The first obstacle was the open ground just beyond the Foy–Magéret road. The ground was tenaciously defended by the Germans but was finally crossed. Once under way the glidermen went forward steadily, overrunning *Nebelwerfer* positions and sometimes coming onto dugouts whose occupants did not know an attack was on. In the latter cases the usual way of handling them was to drop a grenade down the chimney and capture or shoot the men who ran out.

The bazooka proved an effective weapon in clearing the way. In Company C two bazookamen, Pfcs. Perry R. Haworth and Joseph E. Johnson, held a field day with their weapons. First, on the open terrain that morning, they had raced across open ground to take positions within fifty yards of a tank which was holding up the advance of their company. They put three rounds into the tank and left it blazing, its crew all killed or wounded. Later, in the woods, another tank opened up on their company. Given covering fire by Pfc. Joseph Satalin who operated his Browning automatic rifle to keep down the tank's supporting infantry, the two bazookamen got within fifteen yards of the tank and with their two remaining rounds stopped it, killing two of the crew and wounding another. Still later, resupplied with ammunition by returning prisoner guards Haworth and Johnson knocked the track off a third tank, disabling it.

Because of their low strength, Companies A and C were operating in the attack as one, being combined into "Ace" Company. Capt. Walter L. Miller of Company C was the Ace Company commander and Capt. J. B. Johnson of Company A acted as executive. Ace Company had a total strength of 5 officers and 114 enlisted men, of whom only 24 were riflemen. These last were formed into a platoon under Lt. Clifford J. Bolander. During the day's fighting the large surplus of weapons and supply and administrative men were used to good advantage. They took to the rear the many prisoners uncovered in the woods and, of more importance, they carried up ammunition to the rapidly moving riflemen. There were no roads through the woods and though a halftrack which Company C had picked up brought the cases of ammunition up to within mortar range, the last eight hundred yards were straight hand-carrying.

By 1600 the northern edge of the Bois Jacques had been reached. Ace Company took a patch of woods between the Bois Jacques and Bourcy, but all afternoon the attackers were bothered by Germans who had infiltrated on the right where contact with the 502d had been lost. At least a company of Germans got in behind the 327th before the 3d Battalion was committed at 1800 between the 327th and the 502d. The battalion found the woods full of Germans and Colonel Allen had to assign the majority of his troops to cleaning up the by-passed enemy. The next morning 87 of the Germans were rounded up and sent to the prisoner-of-war inclosure.

Meanwhile, no relief got through to Ace Company, which had been cut off in its patch of woods. The glidermen dug in and with small-arms fire and artillery concentrations held off the Germans all that night and the following day, January 14. Their most precious possessions were the hoarded batteries for the SCR-300 and artillery liaison radios, for through them they were able to keep up their only contact with friendly troops and the artillery. Lt. Everett D. Eliassen of Company C with a small patrol attempted to get through to main forces on the 14th but was captured.

The 506th had begun its attack on the 13th at 0900 when Company E attacked along the western edge of the Bastogne–Houffalize highway toward the nearby village of Foy astride the road. The company fought into the edge of Foy, meeting increasing resistance, and at 1015 Company I was sent up the road to help. By 1100 both companies were well into the village and had taken 23 prisoners. At 1115 the two companies were joined by Company H; by 1630 Foy was completely cleared. Shortly after dark a combat patrol entered and seized Recogne. At 2100 a weak German counterattack against Foy failed. Sixty-nine prisoners were netted by the regiment for the day. The 6th Company of the 10th Panzergrenadier Regiment of the 9th Panzer Division was wiped out of existence in Foy.

In addition to the 502d's 84 casualties for the day the 327th lost 77 men and the 506th 47.

During the 13th the 101st captured 235 prisoners. The morale of these prisoners was different from that of those picked up during the early days of Bastogne when the German tide was flowing west. In general the spirit of the Germans ebbing east reminded the veterans in the Division of the confused and dispirited prisoners taken during the first days in Normandy and Holland. Or, more recently, of the confused and beaten Americans who had straggled back through them during the first hours at Bastogne. However, like the retreating Americans the majority of the Germans were still in no mind to give up and the organized troops facing the 101st made the days of the last attack one of bitter memory.

On the 13th General Patton said, "The attitude of the troops is completely changed. They now have full confidence that they are pursuing a defeated enemy; this in spite of the fact that the Germans north and northeast of Bastogne are resisting viciously in order to preserve their escape routes." The 101st as a division had never, even in the darkest days, lost confidence; and they took renewed hope from the obvious turn of the tide. But their last days at Bastogne were not exuberant ones. The companies had come to Bastogne under-strength. The losses had been heavy during the siege, and became even heavier in the last week of December and during January. Pfc. David Kenyon Webster, who had been wounded in Holland had, after months in hospitals and wandering through repple-depples, rejoined Company E of the 506th in Alsace. He wrote:

> When I saw what remained of the 1st Platoon, I could have cried; eleven men were left out of forty. Nine of them were old soldiers who had jumped in either Holland or Normandy or both; McCreary, Liebgott, Marsh, Cobb, Wiseman, Lyall, Martin, Rader, and Sholty. Although the other two platoons were more heavily stocked than the 1st, they were so understrength that, added to the 1st, they wouldn't have made a normal platoon, much less a company . . .
>
> I asked what had happened to Hoobler. Killed at Bastogne. Poor Hoobler, who got such a kick out of war, dead in the snow. And the others? Muck and his buddy Penkala, who had the deepest hole in one position, had been killed by a direct hit. Sawosko was shot through the head attacking Foy. And so on. Some replacements who had come in after Holland had also died. A lot of men had been evacuated for trench foot, too many, McCreary thought. The platoon wasn't what it used to be.
>
> It was good to be back with fellows I knew and could trust. Listening to the chatter in the truck, I felt warm and relaxed inside, like a lost child who has returned to a bright home full of love after wandering in a cold black forest.

However, Webster's company's losses were not remarkable in the Division or even in the 506th's 2d Battalion. Company D lost 22 men and 2 officers through the 12th, and 19 men and 4 officers after that day; Company F's losses were 35 men and an officer through the 12th, and 8 men and 2 officers thereafter; 2d Battalion Headquarters Company lost 21 men and 4 officers through the 12th and 8 men and an officer thereafter. (The entire battalion had lost 32 men, including 5 dead, from the beginning of Bastogne to the lifting of the siege on December 26.)

Heavier losses had been taken by other companies in the 506th. In the 3d Battalion Company I had lost 58 men and 4 officers through the 12th and 38 men and 2 officers after that date. Company H had lost 72 men and 5 officers through the 12th and 9 men and 3 officers thereafter. In the 1st Battalion Companies A and C had each lost over 90 officers and men. In the 502d Company A lost 42 men and 3 officers before the 13th and 30 men and 2 officers after. Company E of the 501st lost 69 enlisted men and 6 officers before the final drive in which, however, it did not lose a man. Company A of the 327th lost 78 enlisted men and officers before the 13th and 13 enlisted men during the next few days; in the 3d Battalion Company C lost 78 enlisted men and 4 officers during Bastogne, 24 men and an officer after the 12th. These losses were from rifle companies whose total strength was a normal 160 men, and which had come to Bastogne understrength from losses in Holland.

Much of the lift afforded by the knowledge that the Germans were on the retreat was offset by the added and very obvious knowledge that in order for the retreat to be successful the American troops along the withdrawal route had to be held off. The Germans tenaciously, skillfully, and without panic fought to keep back the enemy on both sides of his escape route. VIII Corps, in its G-2 estimate of the period, recognized that the 101st's pressure was on a tender spot and that there was a strong reaction: "The enemy is trading space for time: time to get as much of his force as possible through the Houffalize bottleneck. In so doing he is exacting the highest possible price for the terrain we now take. Testimony to this is the present savage and tenacious defense at Foy and Bertogne." And to the veteran in the line there was the depressing fact that most of the men who were alongside him before Christmas were no longer on their feet. Nor could he see an end to the fighting for himself. The accounts of his division being "rescued" or "relieved" on December 26 were grimly humorous.

And there was the cold. The temperature most of the time varied from zero to about twenty degrees. There was almost daily snow, the drifts piled up, the roads were difficult to bring supplies over, there was a lack of roads running into the woods northeast of Bastogne, and for many men during the last week of fighting in these woods the food situation was almost as bad as during the siege. There were still not enough overshoes, blankets, or sleeping bags; bed sacks were sent up and used for snow suits.

The terrain was also difficult. There was open ground to cross, dense woods to clear out, commanding heights to take, and solid Belgian buildings to blast. The Germans, masters of defense, dug in their men and weapons and made the attackers pay all the way. The constant frontal attack against a well dug-in enemy in bitter cold weather, for days at a time with little rest or food and inadequate equipment, made the days of the siege seem rather pleasant. Many men who went to sleep at one or two o'clock in the morning and then had to be ready to attack again at eight found themselves, after three or four days, sleepwalking.

THE PAYOFF: SECOND DAY

Action got under way on the 14th at 0415 when six enemy tanks and about 75 infantry attacked the village of Foy. The 506th companies holding the town, aided by four tank destroyers, two in the village and two on a ridge west of Foy, felt confident of their own defense. The regimental reserve, 2d Battalion, was moved up behind Foy but was not committed. Though this first attack was repulsed another attempt by the Germans with fourteen tanks and an estimated battalion of infantry had by 0600 forced the defenders out of Foy. The 2d Battalion was alerted and moved into position in the rear of the 3d Battalion. At 0900 an artillery barrage fell on Foy and by 0930 I Company was back in the village, the German tanks having withdrawn. (Though both sides at different times held Foy, both realized that the village, surrounded on all sides by high ground, was indefensible against a determined attack. When either side decided it wanted Foy it could generally go in and take it.)

At 1220 2d Battalion assembled near Recogne and moved past that village to Cobru which they took by 1800. Meanwhile 1st and 3d Battalions were moving around the left flank, 1st Battalion going forward about a mile and a half through Fazone Woods to some high ground overlooking Cobru. The 3d Battalion followed and took up a position to the south and near a small lake in the Fazone Woods. Both battalions were in position by 1500. Casualties for the day totalled 37.

On the 506th's right the 327th spent much of the morning fighting forward to relieve surrounded Ace Company and clearing its sector of Germans who had slipped in behind the regiment. All during the previous night patrols from the 327th and the 506th had felt for each other but it was 0600 before a 506th patrol finally contacted the 327th. The situation on the 327th's right flank, toward the 502d, was just as unsatisfactory and during much of the 14th there was little or no contact between the two regiments.

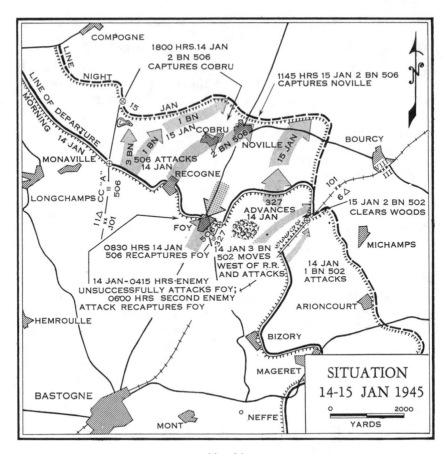

Map 96.

An estimated company of Germans had attacked at 0800 in the 327th sector; the attack had been repulsed but medium range small-arms fire and supporting fire from tanks had taken toll all day. At the end of the day the regiment had lost 53 men, including 8 killed. Lt. Col. Hartford F. Salee, who had led the 1st Battalion since before Normandy, was wounded and was succeeded as commanding officer by Maj. George P. Nichols.

On the right flank, across the railroad, the 502d proceeded slowly toward Bourcy during the 14th. Because of the gap between itself and the 327th on the west of the railroad the 3d Battalion was moved over to that side of the tracks and the 1st Battalion pulled in closer to the east side of the railroad. The 3d Battalion found that the 1st Battalion of the 327th had missed some of the Germans in the woods, and moved in to clear out the infiltrated enemy. In their drive up the rail line the two battalions found the going very tough; prisoners told them that new German battalions had been committed against them with the mission of restoring their own line of resistance. At 1800 the 502d was halted, still short of the objective, and told to hold its ground. It made contact with the 327th on the left and the 320th Infantry Regiment on the right and settled down for the night. The day had cost 37 men, 12 of these killed in action. Among them was Lt. Col. John P. Stopka, who was killed when American planes had bombed the 3d Battalion by mistake. Colonel Stopka had helped Colonel Cole lead the bayonet charge on the Carentan Causeway (just a few days before his death he had received the Distinguished Service Cross for his part in the feat), and he had succeeded to the command of the battalion when Cole was killed in Holland. Maj. Cecil L. Simmons took over command of the battalion.

During the day of fighting the 502d's medical detachment suffered three casualties; it had had two men killed the day before. The medical detachments of each regiment lost men during the two days, and the courage and sacrifice of these men during the freezing days and nights remained in keeping with what the airborne had always expected and received of them.

THE PAYOFF: THIRD DAY

On the morning of the 15th, a cold, cloudy day, the 101st resumed its drive northeast of Bastogne. On the west of the Bastogne–Houffalize highway the attacking force was the 506th with the 1st Battalion of the 501st attached. At 1030 the 1st and 2d Battalions, 506th, attacked simultaneously. The 1st Battalion, 506th, struck east out of Fazone Woods and advanced over almost a mile of open fields to take the high ground north of Cobru. At the same time the 2d Battalion, attacking from south of Noville, moved in and took the village, being in position with a perimeter defense set up by 1145. The little village and its surrounding hills, so long an objective of the 101st, passed into the Division's possession almost as an incident of the day's action.

The 3d Battalion moved into and took over the 1st Battalion's old positions in the Fazone Woods; their own position in the vicinity of the Fazone Lake was taken over by the 3d Battalion of the 501st. Colonel Sink followed his advancing battalions, moving his CP to Recogne.

On the east side of the Bastogne–Houffalize highway the 327th advanced against the high ground east of Bastogne, moving just before noon and seizing their objective before dark. They met only moderate resistance though artillery and mortar fire dogged them all the way. Contact was regained with the surrounded Ace Company, ending that

101st officers confer in battered Noville on 16 January, one day
after the capture by the 506th of this long-time Division objective.

group's day and a half of isolation. The combined company was in good shape though suffering somewhat from shortages of ammunition, food and water.

On the right flank the only aggressive action was carried out by the 2d Battalion of the 502d. The 2d Battalion, which the night before had reverted from division to regimental reserve, had moved into position in the northeast sector of the Bois Jacques about midnight of the 14th, and at 0830 of the 15th passed through the 3d Battalion and succeeded in clearing the northeast sector of the Bois Jacques.

The Battle of Bastogne was drawing to an end. The commitment of their strongest forces and the stubborn resistance of the Germans north and northeast of the town against the right flank of VIII Corps was at the expense of their lines farther to the west; and the center and left of the Corps was swinging north and east against the skillful delaying action of the last of the Germans retreating out of the Bulge. At 0945 of the 16th in Houffalize the 11th Armored Division of Third Army's VIII Corps, heading north, contacted the 2d Armored Division of First Army's VII Corps heading south—and the Bulge was pinched off. In effect the main battle of the Ardennes was ended. Though his lines were still considerably advanced over what they had been in the middle of December the enemy was now in retreat, anxious only to get out what he could of his forces, get them behind the Siegfried Line, and there stabilize a defense which would free the maximum force possible for transfer to the Eastern Front to try to turn the Russians' mid-January offensive along the Vistula River. All roads, for the German, led home now and all roads led to final defeat. In the month that ended on this day it was estimated that the Germans in their Ardennes offensive had suffered 120,000 casualties and had lost six hundred tanks and assault guns. (The German High Command estimates of their losses through December 31st varied between 81,834 and 98,024 casualties, and 324 tanks and assault guns.)   Bastogne had accounted for its share of these.

THE PAYOFF: LAST DAY

The 101st's field order for the attack of the 16th called for the 502d to move out at 0830 and to seize Bourcy and the high ground overlooking it. The 327th was to assist the 502d in capturing Bourcy. The 506th was to advance in the Vaux area in conjunction with Combat Command B of the 11th Armored Division. The 501st, less the 3d Battalion with the 506th, was to remain in Division reserve.

On the right flank the 502d got off on time, 0830, with the 2d and 3d Battalions as the attacking echelon. The battalions gained ground

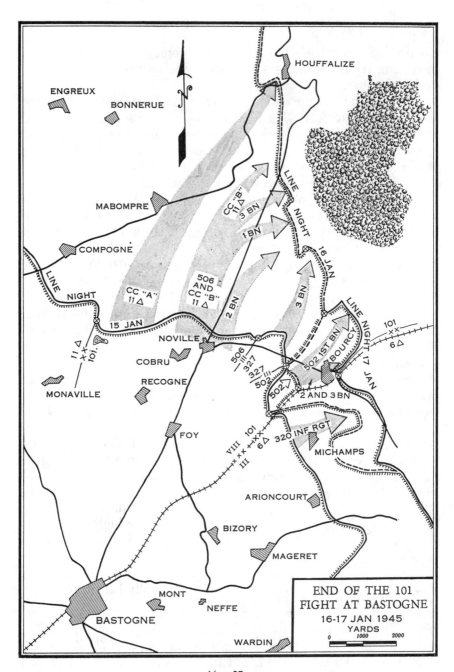

ENGREUX

BONNERUE

HOUFFALIZE

MABOMPRE

CC "B"
11
3 BN

LINE NIGHT

1 BN

16 JAN

COMPOGNE

LINE

NIGHT

15 JAN

11
101

506
AND
CC "B"
11

CC "A"
11

2 BN

3 BN

LINE NIGHT 17 JAN

101
6

NOVILLE

506
327

327
502

502

502 1ST BN

BOURCY

COBRU

RECOGNE

MONAVILLE

502

2 AND 3 BN

FOY

VIII 101

6

320 INF RGT

MICHAMPS

III

ARIONCOURT

BIZORY

MAGERET

END OF THE 101
FIGHT AT BASTOGNE
16-17 JAN 1945
YARDS

MONT

NEFFE

0   1000   2000

BASTOGNE

WARDIN

Map 97.

initially and the 1st and 3d Battalions took the high ground southwest of Bourcy; but when they attempted to move into the town they ran into intense fire from artillery and at least six dug-in tanks. The troops were ordered to hold up and dig in.

Tying in with the 502d's attack on Bourcy the 327th struck at the high ground north of Bourcy, between Bourcy and Hardigny, and at the village of Hardigny itself. At 1230 the 2d and 3d Battalions jumped off, with the 1st in reserve. The terrain was tough to attack over. The snow-covered fields were wide open, without vegetation of any kind. Just as the battalions started forward a *Nebelwerfer* concentration was fired against them, but fortunately fell two hundred yards short. It turned out that the enemy's position was a small wooded hill about half a mile southeast of the village of Rachamps. The 2d Battalion apparently hit this woods as a relief was being effected and found the machine-gun positions and other installations not manned; thirty Germans who had just reached the position were taken prisoner. The woods fell almost without a fight. By 1500 the 3d Battalion had captured Hardigny, which was not heavily defended. The 2d Battalion had taken part of the high ground north of Bourcy an hour before but heavy artillery and small-arms fire prevented the battalion from pushing on across the open ground to take the high ground just south of Hardigny.

During the night 2d Battalion patrols managed to get onto this high ground and found the Germans had withdrawn, leaving a large amount of artillery ammunition.

On the left of the 327th the 506th, working with Combat Command B of the 11th Armored, plunged ahead and as their armored neighbors fought into Houffalize to close off the German salient the three battalions abreast made up for weeks of frustration and of measuring ground gained in yards by driving two miles forward. The 2d Battalion moved up the east side of the Bastogne–Houffalize highway from Noville to Rachamps and captured the latter village by 1400. To the west of the highway the 1st and 3d Battalions advanced northeast to Wicourt. Overrunning that village, the two battalions continued east across the highway where the 3d Battalion finally halted in the Neuf Moulin area a little more than two miles from Houffalize, and the 1st Battalion took a position on the high ground between the 3d Battalion and the 2d Battalion in Rachamps. Wicourt was occupied by the 3d Battalion of the 501st, which had followed the 3d Battalion of the 506th in the advance. The 506th's losses for the day amounted to 49 casualties, including 6 officers and 11 enlisted men killed in action. The regi-

Foy, shortly after its recapture by the 506th on 17 January. Livestock are still wandering about the streets.

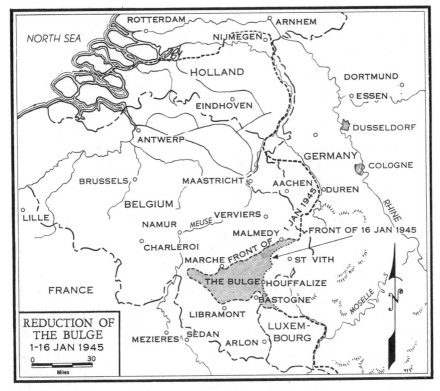

Map 98.

ment took 88 prisoners during the day. During the day the 327th had 54 casualties and the 502d 15. Although the 501st was not committed to action the regiment lost three officers and an enlisted man—all wounded—when two U.S. P-47s from a formation of twelve or fifteen pulled out and bombed and strafed two 501st jeeps on the Bastogne-Noville highway.

On the evening of the 15th and on the 16th the 101st's artillery battalions displaced forward to the vicinity of Foy on the Bastogne–Noville highway. In the village which had proven easier to take than to hold the frozen 506th and German dead of the two days of attack and counterattack still lay about. The 377th Battalion occupied the village; their After-Action Report reads: "Foy is a scene of utter desolation and ruin. No building has escaped the savage artillery fire. Scores of American and German dead attest to the bitter fighting in this vicinity. Many dead horses and cattle litter the streets. Living stock walks aimlessly through the town, foraging for food. As yet no civilians have been seen." In keeping with the death-like surroundings Battery C emplaced in a tomb.

661

On the 16th Combat Command B of the 10th Armored Division was relieved from attachment to the 101st and the next day started on the road south to Château-Salins, near Nancy. In the cafés and dancehalls of Columbus and Phenix City paratroopers of the 101st and tankers of the 10th Armored had fought bloody brawls; that now seemed a hundred years and a million miles away. A month ago in the opening days of the fight the feeling between the airborne and the armored had been something less than one of wholehearted trust. Now the names of Teams Cherry, Desobry and O'Hara were part of 101st history. The 101st could reciprocate the feelings expressed for the Combat Command by its commander, Colonel Roberts in his farewell message:

> For nearly a month CCB, 10th Armored Division, has been associated with your fine division in an action which may become historic. After the first two days this unit was attached to your division. In behalf of the officers and men of CCB, I wish to inform you that it has been a pleasure to serve with the splendid corps of officers and with the fine fighting men of the 101st, and if ever in the future there is a choice of divisions to fight with, we choose the 101st and in turn we hope that CCB may be again associated with you and your division.
>
> Your General Staff and your Special Staff have been generous, fair and solicitous in all matters. They have made my troops feel as if they belonged to the 101st instead of being the usual attached orphans. Your regimental and battalion commanders and my team commanders have worked together with a singleness of purpose that is seldom attained and is only possible where there is wholehearted cooperation on both sides. Many of our enlisted men have expressed the highest admiration of your soldiers and a willingness to go along with them anywhere the going is tough.

The Battered Bastards Depart From Their Bastion

The Battle of Bastogne was ending; the 101st had little time left in its bloody bastion. On the 16th VIII Corps had sent down word that the Division was to be relieved by the neighboring 11th Armored who would themselves be relieved in their sector by the 17th Airborne. The 101st would then assemble in corps reserve and await further orders.

There was to be one more day of fighting; time for a few more men to die, a few more to be wounded and many more to be cold and miserable, for on the 17th there was snow and rain most of the day.

The 501st had opened the fight for Bastogne at Neffe on the morning of December 19; almost a month later the 502d closed it five miles to the northeast at Bourcy. On the morning of the 17th the 502d started the final attack on the village which had been a Division objective for the better part of a week. At 0830 1st Battalion moved to the northwest of the town, clearing the high ground and the woods in that sector, while 2d and 3d Battalions attacked the village frontally a half-hour

```
     MEMORANDUM RECEIPT
              VIII CORPS
                          DATE 18 JAN 1945


        RECEIVED FROM THE 101 ST AIRBORNE DIVISION

THE TOWN OF BASTOGNE, LUXEMBOURG PROVINCE. BELGIUM.

   CONDITION: USED BUT SERVICEABLE, KRAUT DISINFECTED

                  SIGNED

                          TROY H. MIDDLETON
                          MAJ GENERAL  USA
                             COMMANDING
```

Memorandum receipt given by General Middleton during the ceremony in Bastogne, 18 January.

later. At 1030 against light opposition the village was taken. Eighty-four Germans were sent back to the prisoner-of-war inclosure, bringing to 1,728 the number captured during the month at Bastogne.

At the close of the day VIII Corps had established a defensive line from Houffalize through Hardigny and Bourcy. By 1700 the reserve regiment, the 501st, had begun entrucking and at 0315 of the 18th the 11th Armored Division had completed the relief of the 101st. Division Artillery stayed in position a few hours longer, but they too moved out during the day. The troops were quartered southwest of Bastogne, from the vicinity of Sibret, three miles down the Bastogne–Neufchâteau highway, to Bercheux, twelve miles down the highway. The 501st was near Remichampagne, the 327th around Sibret, the 502d near Nives, the 506th near Vaux-le-Rosières. The 326th Engineers were at Sure, the 81st AA Battalion was at Clochimont, and Division Artillery at Vaux-le-Rosières.

During the morning of the 18th, five hundred representative troops from all the Division units assembled in the square of the battered town whose name was now linked with that of the Division. Standing on a parachute-draped platform, the VIII Corps commander, General Middleton, presented the Silver Star Medal to Maj. John D. Hanlon, commander of the 1st Battalion of the 502d, Lt. Frank R. Stanfield of the 506th, and S/Sgt. Lawrence F. Casper, and Pvt. William J. Wolfe of the 327th.

General Taylor shakes hands with General Middleton, VIII Corps
commander, after receiving the memorandum receipt for Bastogne.

Following the awards the Mayor of Bastogne, M. Léon Jacqmin, turned to General Taylor and said, "For their gallant stand, I, as Mayor, present to your division the flag of Bastogne." Taylor accepted on behalf of the Division. General Middleton then thanked the 101st for taking over after his Corps left Bastogne a month before: "From personal acquaintance with your gallant fight at Carentan, knowledge of your deeds in Holland, and now, here in Bastogne, I think you're the best bunch of fighting men in the United States or any other army in the world!" (A few days later he wrote General Taylor: "I have been permitted to serve with or have personal contact with some thirty divisions in the U. S. Army. Of these divisions I am pleased to say I place your division at the top of the list.") He was interrupted by General Taylor who demanded a receipt for the return of Bastogne. A ready-made "memorandum receipt" was handed to the corps commander, which he signed. "Received from the 101st Airborne Division the town of Bastogne, Luxembourg Province, Belgium. Condition: Used but serviceable, Kraut disinfected." The generals then made their way through the snow and past the debris to the street corner to review the troops present at the ceremony. As the marching men turned their eyes right they saw above the reviewing officers' heads a sign, "Bastogne—Bastion of the Battered Bastards of the 101st."

That afternoon, in the midst of the rumors which were sending the 101st everywhere from Mourmelon to the Far East and home, word came of the real destination—the Seventh Army front in the Province of Alsace, France, 160 miles to the South.

The advance parties left the next day and on the 20th the main body of the Division began entrucking in the 112 10-ton and 98 2½-ton trucks furnished by VIII Corps and Third Army. The Division CP officially closed at Sibret at 1400 and opened that night at 2300 in Drulingen, Lorraine.

The trip was to be long—about thirty-six hours—and the weather as cold and miserable as any encountered during the fighting. The 326th Engineers worked day and night clearing roads in the bivouac areas and assisting the trucks in getting onto the main highways. All the way to Alsace the roads were slippery and dangerous, and falling snow kept speeds down. The men settled down in the trucks, bundled as well as they could, and saw the Bastogne countryside fall behind them.

In the 1920s and '30s thousands of Americans had toured the World War I battlefields, following the popular *Muirhead's Guide to Belgium and the Western Front*. Muirhead had described Bastogne only as "an ancient town in the dreariest part of the Ardennes." The dreariness none of the departing soldiers would dispute or deny; but Bastogne, in the books to come, they knew would be more than the name of an ancient town. They and their dead had seen to that.

Alsace

At the time the 101st left Bastogne the Western Front was divided, from the Allied military viewpoint, into three sectors. The sector in the north was manned by the Northern Group of Armies, known also as the 21st Army Group, commanded by Field Marshal Sir Bernard L. Montgomery. In the center was the Central Group of Armies or 12th Army Group under Gen. Omar N. Bradley. And to the south was the Southern Group of Armies or 6th Army Group commanded by Gen. Jacob L. Devers.

The line held by the 21st Army Group extended from the North Sea upstream along the Rhine to a point between Arnhem and Nijmegen, then swung southeast, generally following the Dutch-German border on the west bank of the Maas River, to a point where the Roer River enters the Maas. The line followed the west bank of the Roer into Germany to the vicinity of Linnich. The northern and longest section of this front was held by the Canadian First Army under Gen. H. D. G. Crerar. The southern section was held by Lt. Gen. Sir Miles Dempsey's British Second Army. Following the Roer on into Germany and around the east side of the Hürtgen Forest to the vicinity of Schleiden the line was held by the United States Ninth Army. Since the German breakthrough in December the Ninth Army had been included with the Canadian First and British Second Armies in General Montgomery's Northern Group of Armies.

Adjoining the Ninth Army and continuing south along the German border was the sector of General Bradley's Central Group of Armies. At the time of the 101st's departure from this sector General Bradley had two armies on the line; the United States First Army under Gen. Courtney H. Hodges, holding a narrow twenty-mile sector covering the northern part of what had been the Bulge, and Gen. George S. Patton's Third Army covering the southern part of the Bulge in Belgium, Luxembourg and a sector inside Germany along the Saar River to Saarlautern.

Holding the Western Front from Saarlautern to Switzerland, Gen. Jacob L. Devers had in the Southern Group of Armies two armies, the United States Seventh and the French First. The United States Seventh Army, commanded by Lt. Gen. Alexander M. Patch, held a line from Saarlautern to Gambsheim, France, almost on the Rhine. From Gambsheim, along the Rhine, through the Vosges Mountains, and around the Colmar Pocket was Gen. Jean J. de Lattre de Tassigny's French First Army.

It was the unique experience of the 101st Airborne Division to have been committed within two months' time with all three army groups:

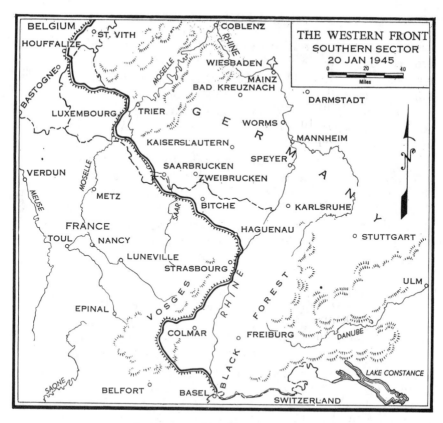

Map 99.

in Holland under Montgomery, in Belgium under Bradley, and now in Alsace, France, under Devers. Here the Division was to be attached to General Patch's Seventh Army.

The Seventh Army, veteran of Sicily and Italy, had invaded Southern France on August 15, 1944, and with the French First Army on its right had driven through to Alsace by November. The two armies were pushing slowly forward against Germans, terrain and weather when, in mid-December the enemy struck in the Ardennes. Up to that time it had been General Eisenhower's plan to establish in the south an easily defensible line along the Rhine and turn over most of the defense of Alsace-Lorraine to the French First Army, freeing the American Seventh Army for use farther north. But with the German attack in Belgium, Patton's Third Army moved north and the Seventh Army had to shift to take over part of the Third's sector. The Southern Group then went on the defensive. With the thinning out of the troops and a good defensive line not yet reached General

Eisenhower took a realistic view of General Devers' situation and ordered reserve battle positions prepared about twelve miles to the rear of the main front. During Christmas week over seventeen thousand tons of ammunition were moved to safer locations in the rear.

A few minutes after the new year the Germans began an attack in Alsace. This was Operation *Nordwind* (North Wind), ordered by Hitler as part of a plan of attack which was to hit the Allied armies with a series of blows, keeping them off balance and destroying them army by army. *Nordwind* was to pinch off the city of Strasbourg and the surrounding territory by a pincers attack, one arm coming from the north and the other from the Colmar Pocket to the south. Rundstedt didn't think very much of the Führer's masterminding, but Hitler had placed his trusted Heinrich Himmler in charge of this southern sector of the Western Front with orders to report directly to his Berlin staff instead of to Rundstedt.

The attack, shifting from point to point along the front of the two southern armies, went on during most of January. Though it gained some ground and came within ten miles of the city of Strasbourg (it was reported that Himmler had promised Hitler Strasbourg by January 30, the anniversary of the Führer's assumption of power) the Germans were never able to regain either Alsace-Lorraine or the prestige lost in the Bulge.

Alsace, the province which was to be the home of the 101st for the next month, was a long, broad trough between the Vosges Mountains of France and the Black Forest across the Rhine in Germany. The province had been incorporated into Germany as part of the spoils of the Franco-Prussian War of 1870-71, had been reincorporated into the French Republic in 1918, and had been made part of Germany again after the fall of France in 1940. In the sections where the 101st was to take up positions the architecture resembled that of the Black Forest section of Germany across the border and the spoken language and many of the customs were predominantly German. Even before the Division reached Alsace the G-2 Periodic Report passed along the word that "personnel are to be reminded of the fact that although this is friendly territory it has been subject to German rule for a long period of time and contains many German sympathizers. Although the inhabitants speak both German and French the predominant language is German. The necessity for taking proper security measures cannot be overemphasized." INTO THE LINES

Seventh Army had been notified on January 18 that the 101st was to be attached and accordingly had made plans to have the airborne troops, short-handed and tired from Bastogne, take over a quiet sector in the XV Corps area near Drulingen. The Division was bivouacked in the area between that town and Sarrebourg after having come up from Bastogne by way of Neufchâteau, Bellefontaine, Virton, Étain, Toul and Nancy. Plans were made to relieve the 141st Regimental Combat Team of the 36th Division in the line. The 36th's area was reconnoitered by officers of the 101st. Some of the artillery battalions went into position in the mountainous terrain; the 907th Glider Field Artillery Battalion on January 22 emplaced its guns near St. Louis-le-Bitche to reinforce the fire of the 100th Infantry Division's artillery. On the 24th both the 463d and the 377th Parachute Field Artillery Battalions dragged their guns into position near St. Louis only to close stations and drag them back again later in the day; the only battalion actually to fire was the 907th.

The artillerymen were not too pleased at having to haul their guns up hills where it took two jeeps to move one 75mm howitzer, dig them in in the frozen ground, and then get "close stations, march order." But if they were griped, so were the people in Division Headquarters who were ordering them around. During the 24th the Division had received orders to move, had had them countermanded, and then had had the destination changed. Finally, that evening orders came for the 101st to leave the XV Corps area and move twenty-five miles southeast to the vicinity of Hochfelden in the VI Corps area. There the 101st was to take over another "quiet" sector.

101st Joins the VI Corps

Maj. Leo H. Schweiter, who was acting as Division G-2 while Colonel Danahy was in the hospital, went down to VI Corps a day or two in advance of the Division to get the situation. He found the corps much concerned about the possibility of a German breakthrough. A glance at the situation map showed that the Germans had parts of seven or eight depleted divisions while the Americans had something more than half as many divisions. Major Schweiter had just spent a month looking at more alarming situation maps.

"What the hell are you so worried about?" he asked. "The 101st alone can lick five German divisions simultaneously; we just did." The corps staff who, like everyone else in the ETO, had followed in *Stars and Stripes* the 101's stand at Bastogne, wondered if the whole Division were that cocky; they asked Capt. Perry South, the Division's liaison officer. Though he didn't, Captain South could have told them that they hadn't heard anything from the quiet, studious major; they should have had a chance to listen to the more uninhibited Colonel Danahy. Or they should have called over a parachute regiment's network to the platoon CP of one of the Division's more fabulous characters who habitually answered his phone, "Tom Downey, Rock of Bastogne." (Outside his door was posted a sign with those words, preceded by a formal "Lt." and followed by an informal "Holds Anything." Depleted in strength though it was, there was no question but the confident Division would be a great morale booster on any front to which it might be sent.

Just before the 101st reached the new front the Germans began disturbing the quiet. On the night of January 24-25 along the Moder River held by the 222d Infantry Regiment of the 42d Division (the 42d had just arrived on the Continent and its regiments were fighting as combat teams in the 79th Division sector), the Germans struck; it was the sector for which the 101st was heading. It looked like the 101st was in for some hard fighting. The enemy succeeded in crossing the river between Haguenau and Kaltenhausen and between Neubourg and Schweighausen and surrounded and cut up a company of the 222d; but in two days of fighting the 42d Division's task force managed to regain the river bank. By the 26th, when the 101st moved by trucks into the area, the fighting was dying down. Actually, it turned out to be the last German effort in Alsace. According to captured documents Hitler on the 25th had ordered attempts to crash the Moder line halted because the forces being used were "needed as a reserve behind future defensive efforts." This coincided with General Devers' plans, for he had decided to maintain a static front in the Seventh Army sector while using his assault forces to reduce the Colmar Pocket in the French First Army sector to the south. The unconflicting aims of the two opposing armies on this local front resulted in what was to be (until the Ruhr) the 101st's most comfortable and least expensive month of warfare.

On the night of the 26th-27th the 501st and the 327th took over the 42d Division task force's sector along the south bank of the Moder River, from a point about a half-mile upstream from the town of Haguenau west to a point about a quarter of a mile from the village of Neubourg, a front of about four miles. The parachutists held a sector upstream from the glidermen. The 502d and the 506th were bivouacked in reserve, the former in the vicinity of Alteckendorf, the latter near Wickersheim. On the 101st's right was the 79th Division; on the left was the 103d (Cactus) Division under General McAuliffe.

The 463d Parachute Field Artillery Battalion moved into Keffendorf and fired in direct support of the 327th, its fire being reinforced by that of the 321st Glider Field Artillery Battalion until January 31, when the 321st moved from Huttendorf to Davendorf to support the 506th. Firing in support of the 501st was the 907th Glider Field Artillery Battalion located at Niederaltdorf and reinforced by the 377th Parachute Field Artillery Battalion located at Morschwiller. Division Artillery Headquarters was in Alteckendorf. Some of the batteries, in order to give close-up support, were located within mortar range of the enemy.

In Hochfelden was Division Headquarters, the 101st Signal Company, and the 326th Medical Company; the 326th Engineer Battalion was in Waltenheim; the 101st Quartermaster Company was in Monswiller; the 801st Ordnance Company in Steinbourg; and the 81st AA Battalion settled in Bossendorf after spending a few days in Wingersheim.

As of January 29 the following units were attached to the 101st: the 807th Tank Destroyer Battalion; Company C of the 781st Tank Battalion (a medium tank outfit); and a platoon of light tanks—3d Platoon, Company D, of the 781st Tank Battalion. Supporting the Division was the 242d Field Artillery Battalion with 105mm howitzers, and the 499th Armored Field Artillery Battalion, armed with self-propelled 105mm howitzers.

The 326th Medical Company, still not completely reorganized after the capture of most of its personnel at Bastogne, consisted of a collecting unit of 4 officers and 48 men; additional medical care was furnished by the 606th Clearing Company and the 473d and 393d Collecting Companies.

Troops in the line along the river managed wherever possible to set up their CPs and OPs in houses and cellars; most of these positions had been made relatively comfortable by the troops whom the 101st relieved. Troops in reserve and service and artillery units were billeted in schools, buildings, and bedrooms of the homes of the villagers.

Looking across the Moder River almost anywhere opposite the entire 101st front the paratroopers and glidermen could see a dense evergreen forest, the Forêt de Haguenau. This enemy-held woods was about fifteen miles long and in places five miles deep. Between the forest's edge and the river was a cleared strip, usually about a quarter of a mile wide. On the right flank of the 101st, opposite the river-bank town of Haguenau, this quarter-mile clearing widened to about a mile. On the south bank, held by the 101st, similar evergreen woods, though

Aerial view of a typical sector of the 101st's front in Alsace.

not as deep or as extensive as the Forêt de Haguenau, furnished concealment to the Americans. Snow lay on the ground and in the forests. Patrolling in snow capes was fashionable for both sides. A type of security, first met with in Holland, was furnished the troops in the line by searchlight batteries operating several miles in the rear. Their beams were thrown skyward and, reflected by particles in the air, furnished artificial moonlight over any specified sector.

LIFE IN ALSACE

The effective strength of the 101st at the end of January 1945 was 8,968 enlisted men and 674 officers. Fortunately, the enemy's inability and disinclination to launch any sort of attack in the area enabled the understrength Division not only to hold its sector with ease but also to embellish its day-to-day existence with some of the comforts of garrison life. The dirty clothes, blankets, and sleeping bags from Bastogne were picked up by the Quartermaster Company and sent to

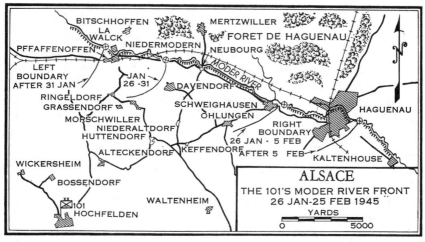

Map 100.

a GI laundry. Portable showers capable of handling 215 men an hour visited the battalions, and companies of men moved through them. A few men got leaves and furloughs; a very few got trips back to the States. On February 1 the Division Finance Office got around to paying the November payroll (of which almost two-thirds was turned back in the form of bonds, spearhead deposits, soldiers' deposits, or personal transfer accounts). Seven movie units circulated among the companies and batteries, showing such movies as "Rhapsody in Blue," "Buffalo Bill," "Mrs. Parkington," "Saboteur," and "Our Hearts Were Young and Gay." "The Muddy Engineers' Revue," a stage show, gave fourteen performances for the Division. The 502d's band played two and three jobs a day, giving concerts, playing for drill, playing for award ceremonies, and furnishing jive for dances. The daily *Stars and Stripes,* the Division's mimeographed news sheet, *Kangaroo Khronicle,* and *Yank* kept the troops up on the news. There was even a film-developing service for those men who had been able to get cameras and film, and some American beer—the first in a year and a half—trickled through.

Back in Hochfelden where Division Headquarters was located things were sufficiently settled for the local power system to furnish electricity erratically and for trains to run occasionally. Alsace Annie, believed to be a 15-inch railroad gun hidden in the German lines, usually worked on Saverne, but sometimes threw over a few rounds in the general vicinity of the Hochfelden, and once almost got the 426th Quartermaster Company kitchen. Three of the Division's Red Cross girls were operating a club where men out of the line might mingle with the headquarters and service troops and eat doughnuts, drink coffee, read, write, or dance on a floor under the unfailing decoration of any airborne social function—draped parachutes. After a week in Alsace the shoulder insignia, which had been removed on the ride from Bastogne, was again authorized and the Screaming Eagle became a familiar sight on the streets of Hochfelden, Haguenau and other Alsatian towns.

The Division succeeded in getting certain items which, while appreciated (for occasionally during the first few days the temperature dropped even lower than at Bastogne), would have been a great deal more welcome in the open fighting of six weeks before—6,100 pairs of shoepacs, arctic socks, felt insoles, and 6,000 yards of white cloth with which to make 2,000 snow suits. Trench foot and exposure losses dropped off considerably due to the warmer weather, better shelter, clothing, and cold-weather experience. Two other reminders of Bastogne came in late January: delayed messages from the mayors of English towns which had been home to part of the Division until September. "The townspeople of Newbury, England salute the 101st Airborne Division for their great stand at Bastogne which has made history." And "Inhabitants of Reading read in the newspapers and heard on the wireless of the great exploit of the 101st Airborne Division in Rundstedt's salient, and on their behalf and my own I tender to all units of the Division thanks and gratitude for a tenacious contribution to the Allied efforts."

Action in Alsace during January was almost zero. The outstanding incident either regiment on the line could report was a brush the 327th had with an eight-man enemy patrol on their first night. The patrol, in snow capes, had come out of the woods in front of Company G; the glidermen allowed it to come within close range before firing, and killed four Germans. The Germans took a measure of revenge by bringing up some 120mm mortars and making life in Schweighausen, where the 327th's 1st Battalion was, very uncomfortable.

The largest single action of Alsace—small though it was compared to any one of a number of actions at Bastogne—came on the night of January 31-February 1. It was called Operation Oscar.

OPERATION OSCAR

Oscar was planned as part of a corps operation. Five or six miles down the Moder, in the neighboring 36th Division's sector, the Germans held a stretch of territory on the American side of the river. VI Corps was interested in rectifying this situation and had planned a limited offensive action against the Germans on the south (American) side of the Moder, using the 36th Division with some armor attached. Meanwhile, in order to pin down the Germans along the rest of the Corps front, the other divisions in the Corps had been ordered to prepare limited attacks. Operation Oscar was the 101st's contribution to the evening's effort. It was to be a three-company reconnaissance in force across the Moder with no attempt being made to take or hold territory. The raid was to go to the railroad lines, which ran parallel to the river and a few hundred yards inside the German-held forest, where the companies were to grab prisoners for interrogation, shoot up the German positions, do what damage they could, and get back.

Oscar was the largest and also the most carefully prepared raid the 101st ever attempted. Once the schedule was made up an elaborate artillery timetable was mimeographed and distributed to the batteries. It called for closely timed fire preceding and during the entire raid. (A tally after the raid showed that Division Artillery fired 4,100 rounds.)

At 1100 on the morning of January 31 the commanders of the two raiding regiments, Colonel Harper and Lt. Colonel Ballard, the G-2, Lt. Colonel Danahy, and the Division Artillery commander, Colonel Sherburne, met with the Division G-3, Lt. Colonel Kinnard. Transcript notes of the meeting follow:

Colonel Ballard: Operation we have planned needs to be on a large scale to be successful. It is a good diversionary attack. Must take out the position at crossroads. There can be no halfway, either take it or not. It is flat open country with no routes of withdrawal.

Colonel Kinnard: Go over and find out what is there and shoot the thing up. The whole thing is just a raid. We feel we are in close enough contact that we must go out in force and pick a spot in the line and penetrate it. It was 501st proposal to use two companies.

Colonel Ballard: We learned from three prisoners of war that there is a battalion CP along the woods' right. Main Line of Resistance is in from road south of the edge of the woods. It is a weak MLR, strength of companies running 40 to 50 men.

Colonel Harper: We have an outpost line and MLR along edge of the stream. Feel this is an ideal thing for a diversion. If we must have this information we can get it. I want to save the whole thing and make a later push right to Berlin. Save the good men till then.

Colonel Ballard: For the raid to be successful take out the enemy and bring them back or kill them. We have to put on a good show to do it. When we pull back across we will have to do the same thing again when we do go forward. Think it will make the second go a little harder, inasmuch as the Germans will have an idea what we are going to do. Feel that they will try to reestablish.

Colonel Harper: Save what we have now. Put enough fire there and shoot enough into them to draw their fire. That should be done shortly before we put on this diversion. Think it will materially reduce casualties. They must have fifty batteries that can reach our area. I want to put company commanders and platoon leaders over the area in a Cub plane this afternoon. Will personally brief all, down to squad leaders. Everything must be registered along the line. If we do it tomorrow night the heavy mortars, machine guns, and TDs are to create a diversion all along the front. The whole thing on a division front will split the German artillery. We should have 155s to blow out German lines of communication.

Colonel Kinnard: At the meeting yesterday it was made clear that this was a raid which was in lieu of sending out numerous patrols.

Colonel Kinnard: How do you feel about the question the general raised about staying over on the other side, presuming we get the place?

Colonel Ballard: Believe it would be better not to unless the whole Division does so.

Colonel Harper: Their tanks could counterattack. We have two small spots. The Germans will notify their artillery where we are and then start shooting us up. Our artillery can give us protecting fire when we come back. We should get a few more casualties the next time we try it.

Colonel Kinnard: If we do not make this raid the Germans can continue to hold this front and send their reserves to another front. A good raid will make them jittery about releasing their reserves. The 506 will be in position by 8:00 P.M. Can lay down any sort of preparation fire we want.

Colonel Ballard: Want to start at 0100. Plan that raid should be by stealth. First artillery to be at 0255. Lift fire about 0315 or sooner if the FO calls for it. Plan is to move across the area of the mill with one company. Advance party to be about a ten-man combat patrol, the company will follow into a forward assembly area. On the right there is a foot log which the right company will go across. In the same manner the patrol will advance and the company move in. These two patrols will start into the woods to clear a path for the company. If they can get through without being detected, OK, but we will fire the artillery anyway. Companies will go in behind the combat patrol advance elements, then will turn and move toward the crossroad north of the track and fan out. About the same plan for the left. Would like to have fire on the town where we think the enemy regimental CP is. All wounded and prisoners will be evacuated as soon as this is cleared out. Right back through the mill. There is a dam that locks up the water. It is just north of Neubourg. It would be a help if a foot bridge could be put in where the log is.

Colonel Kinnard: You would need three or four foot bridges.

Colonel Ballard: Think we should wait until shooting dies down. Think it will take about an hour to come back. Will start back about 0500.

Colonel Kinnard: Suppose they do not make contact for some reason?

Colonel Ballard: They both plan to go to the north-south road. Both company commanders will be across stream in the woods. Battalion commander will have advance CP at Neubourg. Do not think there will be any difficulty between them. Suggest we take a few mines along as withdrawal protection against tanks. Put them across the road near the bend. TDs can cover to the crossroads. They will shoot enemy CP at 0255 and will be on call against any unforeseen thing that may happen on the flanks. TDs will have about 100 rounds. Will not take engineers unless they want them to take mines over. No mines, minefields, or booby traps are expected to be encountered. 501 control will be at Neubourg where Red CP is. Want the artillery control by the FOs and battalion liaison officer. Regiment will have to control only the fire of 3d and 2d battalion mortars. Artillery fire time will be set up for 0255 but may have to be fired a little sooner, depending on the situation.

Colonel Kinnard: For evacuation will take along normal company aid men.

Colonel Ballard: Germans have mill well zeroed in and I do not see how we can avoid it.

Colonel Kinnard: Suggest alternate route.

Colonel Ballard: Company on left is going to go out as wide as the company on the right. Flanks are blocked by six concentrations they have on call.

Colonel Danahy: In case they hit a company, battalion, or any type of command post grab whatever maps are available.

Colonel Kinnard: That would make a very good objective.

Colonel Ballard: Their battalion CP is in house and is moving to a dugout southwest of trail junction 945279.

Colonel Kinnard: That is a possible alternate. Think they will have some kind of CP near the railroad station.

Colonel Ballard: From the photo the ammunition dump is pretty well gutted from hits and may be a possible location of a CP as it would be a good dugout.

Colonel Kinnard: You do not think the men will be back between six and seven? We can make the whole thing contingent on the weather.

Colonel Ballard: Must have a certain amount of light. Moon will come up at 2100.

Colonel Harper: Is going to tie a black band on each man's arm or leg to distinguish friend from enemy. What 327th wants initially is a big concentration of artillery. Believes he can go in in a minimum of two hours and a maximum of three hours. Wants some smoke in the initial preparation.

Colonel Ballard: Thinks he can get along with mortar smoke.

Colonel Sherburne: Will bring plan of fire around to each one of you this afternoon.

Colonel Harper: Our problem is to neutralize two machine guns covering the clearing. Other place where they can see is from a factory in the woods. Think they are using nearby town to switch men around. We have plenty of machine guns along our line. We will put in four bridges. 463 to set up with one battery and fire on factory and keep firing as long as we are in there. Another battery to fire across the railroad bridge. Wants smoke mixed in. Another battery to fire along trail with HE—no smoke. Want five minute preparation along trail between two roads and with everything you can give. We are going to go across while you are firing. Heavy mortars will fire white phosphorus. Germans are registered on old mill. Company, less its mortars, will cross four bridges. During the time men are withdrawing there will be one or two guns firing all the time. All during this period one battery of 463d is firing. Another battery is keeping smoke. Another battery is firing in the town. And, another battery is firing in the road.

Colonel Kinnard: What is the actual objective?

Colonel Harper: To take out everything in there and bring it back. There is indication that enemy's MLR is along the trail. TDs will shoot into the side of town and will create a diversion. All men will have something black around each arm, and if there is enough, around each leg. My control point will be in a house where I can see almost the whole area of the advance. Men are instructed not to leave any wounded or dead. Strength will be about a hundred men with the platoon mortar squads. Battalion commander and TD commander, and artillery liaison officer will be with Colonel Harper who is going to oversee the whole operation. Does not want any shift of fire during the battle.

Colonel Sherburne: 463 will give 501 two batteries and 327 two batteries. Suggest we hit some of the nearby towns with 155's to cut enemy communications.

Colonel Harper: Have arranged with the engineers to set up four bridges.

Colonel Kinnard: What do you think about flares to make the enemy think that this is no patrol, no activity night?

Colonel Ballard: Think it is a good idea. 501 has asked for pyrotechnics. 501 has worked some in combat and had good luck with them. About twenty green stars are available. Cannot use red or yellow. 501 wanted these primarily for signals.

Colonel Kinnard: Be sure none of the men have their patches on.

Colonel Danahy: Recommend that men be warned on security measures. They must not carry any personal things with them.

Colonel Harper: Think we could get a better diversionary distribution of artillery fire if we wait until tomorrow night.

Colonel Kinnard: The way things stand now the raid is on for tonight.

The raid went off that night pretty much as planned. Companies A and B of the 501st and E of the 327th were the raiders. In the 501st area Company B of the 326th Engineers, at a cost of two men seriously wounded, by 0230 had installed two footbridges, one about five hundred yards upstream, the other six hundred yards downstream, from the village of Neubourg. Crossing the upstream bridge was Company B, the downstream bridge, Company A. At 0300 both companies started toward the north-south Neubourg–Mertzwiller road, Company A attacking east, B, west. Company A had the objective of driving through the woods, clearing them, and coming out on the road several hundred yards from where the road entered the lower edge of the woods. Company B was to attack closer to the river and move west along the railroad which paralleled the river on the enemy side: it was to attack the Neubourg station (Neubourg village was on the south or American side of the Moder; Neubourg station was across the river on the German side) and also clear the woods in the vicinity.

Company A, commanded by 23-year-old Capt. Hugo Sims, Jr., who had received the DSC for his leadership of the "Incredible Patrol" in Holland, advanced east through the woods, running into stiff opposition from dug-in positions, until it came to the road leading away from Neubourg station. There it set up a roadblock. There also it ran

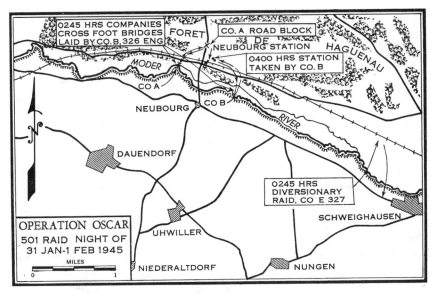

Map 101.

into a real opportunity for killing; heading down the road in a closed column were an estimated two platoons of Germans, possibly moving to relieve the Neubourg station area or to counterattack the raiders. Company A raked them with flanking fire and the enemy suffered high casualties. The company was on the objective at 0415. Every German trying to use the road was cut down. Messengers and patrols were intercepted and an antitank gun was destroyed.

Meanwhile, Company B, led by Lt. John H. Sallin, who had won the Silver Star at Bastogne, had been fighting through what appeared to be a factory area toward the station. The paratroopers overran house after house, building after building. In one they killed twelve Germans, in another seven gave up without a fight. At another point a solitary German came wandering out of the woods and joined the main body of the company without its realizing he was with them. Finally the company fought up to the station which it found occupied by Germans. The building fell at 0400.

At 0500 both companies started withdrawing by infiltrating a platoon at a time southward toward the river. Company B, closer to the Moder, had no trouble, but A found that the Germans had infiltrated back into the woods which they had earlier cleared and the company had to fight its way through them. The company's lead scout was killed by automatic-weapons fire. The 3d Platoon, under Lt. Harry J. (Monk) Mier, Jr., was deployed behind an elevated road. Onto the

German lines, not twenty-five yards away, the platoon heaved a volume of grenades; then they charged. The aggressiveness of the group cleared the woods. Meanwhile, a platoon of Germans, stumbling around in the dark, had run into the company's rear. They were taken care of by some tommy-gunners on the lookout for just such.

The 501st brought back an officer and twenty enlisted prisoners. The 501st losses were five killed, eight wounded and three missing; accompanying medics lost an officer killed and two enlisted men missing. Company B took most of the losses when it ran into mortar fire during the withdrawal. Among the dead was the company's first sergeant, Joseph A. Henderson.

In the 327th area the 3d Platoon of Company A, 326th Engineers, threw three 35-foot bridges across the Moder just west of Schweighausen and while other 327th companies along the river feinted with fire power and smoke to deceive the enemy, Capt. Robert H. Lemmon led Company E across. Its mission was to clear a section of the woods of Germans. The crossing was made between 0245 and 0345 and the company was back on the south bank by 0600. With them they brought an officer and fifteen enlisted Germans and estimated the dead left behind at fifty. Almost all the prisoners taken by either regiment were from the 47th Volksgrenadier Division. Company E lost one man killed, one missing and thirteen wounded, including two officers. Lt. John M. Kiellor personally killed two Germans and, though wounded in the head, refused to be evacuated until the raid was completed. Among the 327th enlisted men who distinguished themselves were Pvts. Philip A. Nichols and Joe Seny, both of whom made several trips back into the enemy-held woods to bring out wounded comrades. Seny had also been instrumental in helping knock out, with his bazooka, a concrete pillbox in which eight Germans were killed.

Reports of the night's success were forwarded, as they came in, to General Taylor. Shortly after daybreak the general hurried down to Company E of the 327th to pin the Silver Star on Captain Lemmon and some of his men. He was too late; the captain and his men had already taken off by truck on pass to Paris.

The night's reconnaissance in force had netted the 101st more prisoners than the entire Seventh Army had taken during the time the 101st had been a part of it.

On the evening during which the raids were carried out the 101st sector was extended about two miles upstream, when the 506th, with Batteries A and F of the 81st AAA Battalion and part of Company C of the 807th TD Battalion, relieved the neighboring 409th Infantry

Regiment of the 103d Infantry Division. The new sector included two villages, Niedermodern and Pfaffenoffen. The 506th took over this sector with 1st Battalion on the left, or upstream, side, 3d Battalion on the right, and 2d Battalion in regimental reserve in Grassendorf. The battalions on the line set up their defense with one rifle company of each battalion on the outpost line of resistance. The 57mm AT guns and .50-caliber machine guns of the 81st Battalion were used throughout Alsace in front-line support.

February in Alsace

February thus began with the 101st facing the Germans along a six-mile front on the Moder River, the 506th on the left, 501st in the center, 327th on the right, and the 502d in reserve. The first three days of the month saw little activity on any part of the front. The quiet was broken at 0245 on the 4th by the 506th, which attempted to send a platoon-strength patrol across the river. The patrol was turned back by heavy German machine-gun and mortar fire. At noon the 506th was notified that it was to be relieved by the 409th Infantry of the 103d Division and was to move from the left to the right end of the 101st sector, extending the line on that end down stream to include the large town of Haguenau. The relief began that night, the regimental CP was set up at Walck Château, and by 2200 of the 5th the 506th had relieved the units of the 313th Infantry, 79th Division, which had been holding Haguenau. The regiment went into the line with 1st Battalion on the left, 2d on the right, and 3d in regimental reserve in the outskirts of town.

Another relief took place on the 4th, the 502d taking over the 501st's sector; the 501st replaced the 502d in Division reserve.

For the next week the front was very quiet. The little Moder River, because of melting snows, had early in the month begun to rise and in places was now a hundred yards wide. The width and swiftness of the current made it difficult for either side to put patrols across. The thaw caused dug-outs and artillery gun pits to cave in and partly fill with water so that the positions had to be rebuilt above ground and sandbagged. Roads became almost impassable. The Division engineers were reinforced by two companies from Corps and some of the roads were made one-way and closed to heavy vehicles. For the troops along the river it was a week of pulling guard shifts and, eventually, of being relieved. The troops in reserve areas went in for a limited training program, firing weapons, watching films, and critiquing previous operations.

The Moder River, normally thirty or forty feet wide, floods and covers a German minefield at Rohrwiller. The picture was made on 4 February 1945.

The training was especially called for because new and green troops were received to fill in the gaps from Bastogne and even from Holland.

Many of the new men were welcomed into the Division by General Taylor; others received a mimeographed copy of the following speech:

As Division Commander, I welcome you to the 101st Airborne Division. We are proud of having you in this Division which, of all the Allied forces, was the first to land on the shores of Normandy. It is the Division which cleared the road for the British Army in its rapid advance into Holland last September. Above all, it is the Division of Bastogne which broke the back of the German counteroffensive and thus changed the course of the entire war.

To belong to this Division is an honor to me and is an honor to you. It is also a responsibility which must be met in proportion to our respective jobs. Your immediate job is to make yourself into as fine a fighting soldier as the veteran who became a casualty and created the vacancy which you are to fill. I want you often to think of this man whom you will never meet. He was a friend of ours whom we knew well and regarded highly. He fell in battle while fighting gallantly at our side in Holland or in Belgium. It is up to you to be as good a man as he was, and that is not an easy order . . .

This Division is a great Division because every man has confidence in the other fellow. This confidence is born of the knowledge gained on many a hard-fought field that men of the 101st Airborne stand together no matter how hot the fight. The men on your right and left are battle-tested. You will not have to worry about them. Don't let them have to worry about you. Reliability is the first requirement of an airborne soldier.

Your future in this Division is what you make it. There are unlimited opportunities for advancement here to the grade of noncommissioned officer and officer. Many of the finest junior officers of this Division have won their bars from the ranks by gallantry on the battlefield.

After your travels as a reinforcement, you now have a home. That home is the Division. Set about proving that it has gained something by your arrival.

Welcome to the 101st Airborne Division.

In January the 327th received from Seventh Army 487 infantry replacements and later in the month more replacements joined the regiment. Although there were at first doubts about the performance of the new troops, untrained in airborne operations and not eligible for glider or jump pay, they made such a good impression that when an attempt was made to withdraw them from the 101st General Taylor sent a message which read in part: "Men are desirable type. Most anxious to retain." These troops, after the Division's return to Mourmelon, were given glider flights and qualified as gliderists.

At about the same time unofficial word came that an entire battalion might be withdrawn from the 101st. The report was that the 463d Parachute Field Artillery Battalion, which had been attached to the 101st at Mourmelon just in time to make the Bastogne trip was to be replaced by another parachute field artillery battalion. General Taylor protested to General Brereton, Commanding General of the First Allied Airborne Army, saying "I am strongly opposed to such a substitution. The 463d is firmly united with this Division and any change will result in a serious loss of morale and efficiency both to the Division and to the Battalion." The 101st remembered Christmas Day when the German tanks broke through the infantry and the 463d threw out a last-ditch skirmish line and depressed the muzzles of their 75mm howitzers; their present to the Division was three tanks and sixteen Germans. From that day on they had a home in the 101st; and APO 472 was to be their address for the rest of the war.

About six hundred parachute replacements came up from Mourmelon in February. Since the number was not enough to fill the gaps in the companies the question of whether to use the replacements to bring one regiment up to full strength or to divide them among the three parachute regiments was put up to the parachute regiment commanders; they decided to divide them up.

The new men, when they went into the line, were assigned one new man to one veteran, and the old-timer (some of whom had rather quickly attained that status during the concentrated month's course at Bastogne) taught the rookie the methods of staying alive within rifle-range of the enemy. Schooling didn't stop at the enlisted level; there was a battalion commander's course in the Division and lieutenant colonels, majors, and captains in evening classes worked out command problems.

Shifts in the line began on February 7 when the 327th's 3d Battalion came up and replaced the 1st Battalion. On the 6th Company G of the 327th had had three men of a BAR team instantly killed when an 88 round hit directly in their foxhole. On the 8th the 327th broadened its front by extending the 1st Battalion sector five hundred yards downstream, taking over the river front held by the 1st Battalion of the 506th. On the 9th the 502d's 3d Battalion relieved its 1st Battalion on the line.

On the 10th there were two changes in Division-level staff and command positions. On that date Col. William N. Gillmore of the 1st Armored Division reported for duty and was assigned as artillery commander, relieving Colonel Sherburne, the assistant division artillery commander, who had taken over command of the Artillery when General McAuliffe had temporarily replaced General Taylor just before Bastogne. And Lt. Col. Ned Moore, who had acted as chief of staff of the Division during the siege of Bastogne, succeeded Colonel Michaelis who left the Division. Colonel Michaelis had led the 502d in Normandy and Holland, being slightly wounded on September 19 and seriously wounded three days later. He returned from the hospital on December 28 and was Division chief of staff until his old wounds forced him to leave the 101st for further hospitalization and eventual evacuation to the United States.

On the night of February 12 the 502d was ordered to send a patrol in company strength across the river and through the woods toward Hertzwiller on the German side. Company B was selected for the mission and that night forty-six men started out. But because of the swiftness, depth, and width of the almost flood-stage river all attempts at crossing by boats or swimming were failures and the mission had to be called off.

A 21-man patrol from Company C of the 327th led by Lt. Benjamin Luhring managed to cross the river that night and was more successful, capturing a prisoner, who turned out to be recently transferred from the German Navy. During the patrol T/Sgt. Ernest R. Cummings and Pfc. Milton I. Erlick traced enemy wire to an entrenchment from which their group was receiving fire. There they shot and killed a German who jumped up with a machine pistol. Later both men were wounded but managed to get back across the river. Altogether the patrol killed an estimated six to eight Germans.

A new method of manning the Division front was put into effect

on the 12th. The front was divided into four regimental sectors, each
to be held by one battalion reinforced with a company. Each regiment
held one battalion in regimental reserve, and one battalion of each
regiment reverted to Division reserve. This resulted in the 501st's
return to the line, its 3d Battalion being inserted between the 502d
and the 327th and taking over part of the front of both regiments.
The 501st kept the 2d Battalion at Minnversheim in Division reserve
and brought up the 1st Battalion to Uhlwiller as regimental reserve.

The Division front, after the new system was completely put into
effect during the 13th, was, from left to right, as follows: 502d's 3d
Battalion with Company C on line, 1st Battalion less Company C in
regimental reserve, and 2d Battalion in Division reserve; the 501st;
327th's 3d Battalion with Company A of the 1st Battalion on line,
1st Battalion less Company A in regimental reserve, and 2d Battalion
in Division reserve; and 506th's 2d Battalion with Company H on line,
3d Battalion less Company H in regimental reserve, and 1st Battalion
in Division reserve.

For the next four or five days the situation remained unchanged.
Each regiment sent out patrols, usually small, and the Germans occasionally returned the visits. Most of the 101st patrols were to check
enemy positions and usually managed to make the round trip without
becoming engaged in a fight. A more ambitious patrol was carried
out during the early hours of the 18th by 2d Battalion of the 506th.
Nine men crossed the river, attacked a house used as an OP, and
captured three Germans, one of whom was so badly wounded that
he was left to die on the far bank of the river. The patrol itself
suffered four casualties from mortar fire and *Schü* mines. The largest
enemy patrol came across the Moder in the 327th sector on the night
of the 14th under an artillery and mortar barrage; an estimated 500-
600 rounds of artillery, predominantly 150mm, and mortar, mostly
120mm, landed in the Schweighausen–Neubourg area occupied by the
327th and 501st. The group attacked the 327th positions at a point
about a quarter-mile upstream from Schweighausen but was turned
back by fire from the glidermen and artillery, and pulled back across
the river, leaving one dead and two prisoners. Four days later, under
a similar barrage, another enemy patrol of thirteen men crossed on
the downstream edge of Schweighausen and was turned back by the
3d Battalion of the 327th, Company B of that battalion capturing four
of the party. The prisoners reported that their mission was to capture
prisoners, and claimed that they did not yet know what American

unit was opposing them. They also said that the other members of the patrol had all been killed or wounded.

On the 17th and 18th there was a general change-about in battalion commitments. The 502d's 1st Battalion relieved the 3d Battalion on the line, the 501st's 1st Battalion with Company E relieved the 3d Battalion; the 327th's 2d Battalion relieved the 3d Battalion, and the 506th's 3d Battalion with Company B relieved the 2d Battalion. From then until the Division was relieved between February 22-25, the pattern of watchful waiting and occasional patrolling along the river continued to be followed.

How It Looked to Danahy and Webster

How the situation looked to the 101st G-2, Lt. Col. Paul Danahy, on an average day, February 18, is reflected in his routine G-2 Periodic Report:

1. ENEMY SITUATION AT END OF PERIOD

a. Enemy Front Lines: No change.

b. Units in Contact: No change. 3 PWs taken vicinity 034244 at 0400 hours. Unit identifications 2 Co, 103 Volksgrenadier Division, 47 Volksgrenadier Division, and 1 Co, 257 Engr Bn, 257 Volksgrenadier Division.

2. ENEMY OPERATIONS DURING PERIOD

a. General Summary: At 2300 vicinity 005243 strong enemy patrol, exact strength unknown, attempted a supported raid against 327 Glider Infantry. At close of period fire fight continues with isolated small groups of enemy attempting to fight their way back to Moder River.

b. Operation of Component Elements:

(1) Infantry: Harassing machine-gun fire received in Haguenau sector intermittently throughout period. Six enemy reported digging vicinity 028245 at 2045 hours. Fifteen enemy observed entering OP dugout vicinity 998252 at 1800 hours. Some small-arms fire received during afternoon from vicinity 015248.

(2) Artillery (including mortar): Flash of enemy gun firing from 99272850 observed at 2250 hours. Approximately 300 rounds artillery and mortar fire fell into area during period, of which the majority was 120mm mortar supporting enemy patrol activity vicinity 005243 now in progress at close of period.

(3) Armor: Occasional use as mobile artillery pieces.

(4) Engineer: Friendly combat patrol surprised and engaged an enemy mine-laying party vicinity 034244. Three PWs taken. PWs state that no mines had been laid by party at time of capture, but they further added that that area had been previously mined.

c. Adjacent Units:

(1) Corps Intelligence Summary (181800): Enemy inactivity continues. Small groups of enemy moving from Q787383 to Q783386. Enemy small-arms ammo dump vicinity R08192140 set on fire by our artillery. Only artillery re-

ported was on E flank consisting of 4-6 round concentrations of light cal and some mortar fire. Identifications: 9th Co. 11 SS Mtn Rgt vicinity Q755414.

3. MISCELLANEOUS

a. Estimated Enemy Casualties: Three PWs evacuated to PW enclosure during period. Total to date 70.

b. Weather Forecast: Overcast and fog in the morning. Probable rain in early afternoon. Visibility 1 mile in morning, 3-4 miles in later afternoon. Wind SW 3-5 miles. Minimum temperature 33 degrees F.

c. Morale: No change.

4. ENEMY CAPABILITIES: No change.

How the situation looked to a line soldier somewhat closer to the details of the patrols, machine-gun fire, and mortar bursts is described by David Kenyon Webster who, at this time, was occupying one of the 506th's outpost houses along the river front in Haguenau:

Now we were at peace with the world and could telephone at our leisure. We would lift the phone and whisper, "CP, CP, calling the CP." When we were answered, sometimes not for five minutes, if Rader or Martin were asleep, we said, "OP 2 checking in with the CP. This is Marsh," or "McCreary," or "Winn," or "Cobb," or "Sholty"—whoever was on duty. We'd ask what was new in the way of rumors and they'd inquire about events and personalities in our area. If they wanted a flare shot, they'd call back or OP would cut in. We might request the latter to check on a close shell, tell us where that machine gun was firing and why, watch the field and houses to our left as we shot a flare or keep their eyes on the stream above us—the guard upstairs thought there was somebody in wading there. Most of the hour passed very slowly, though, because there was nothing to do but hold the phone to your ear and relax half asleep in the chair and try to stay awake. If the night were unusually active, we could always eavesdrop on the party line and delight in the frantic reports of Lyall ["Hey, a shell landed 500 yards to our right! What'll I do?" "Relax," says Martin] or Liebgott ["Krauts, Krauts, they're up here behind me!" BAM! He shoots in the darkness. There are no Krauts], both of whom were getting very excitable. Even Morganti and Small, over in OP 3, who were beginning to show the cumulative strain of Normandy, Holland, and Bastogne, gave forth wild alarms. Without rest or withdrawal, the Regiment had now been on the line two months: From the middle of December to the middle of February. Some of the boys were getting nervous.

On the 18th the 2d Battalion, 506th patrol, already mentioned, crossed the Moder in Webster's sector.

The rumor that E Company was going to make a patrol crystallized into fact. Captain Winters, operating out of battalion, visited our outpost with Lieutenant Speirs one sunny day and stood in our front yard near the creek, gesturing with his hands and waving a map, while we inside cursed heartily, fearing that an

German artillery rounds start landing in Haguenau, sending civilians scurrying for shelter. In the foreground is a deserted baby carriage.

observer would spot him and call down artillery fire on our cozy home. Then Lieutenant Foley officially announced the patrol and nominated Cobb, Winn, and McCreary to represent OP 2 thereupon. I thanked God he didn't know me well enough to send me along too. A while later, together with the luckless souls from the 2d and 3d Platoons, that trio withdrew ten miles to a point on the Marne and Rhine Canal where they practiced handling the German black rubber boats with which they planned to cross our creek. For two days they were briefed and for two days the artillery and the mortars zeroed in on the key crossroads, known enemy houses and strongpoints, and all streets leading to the patrol's objectives. The night before they left, we noncombatants walked to the company CP and fetched the three collapsible boats. From OP 1 the patrol was shown the houses it was to assault.

Cocky Lieutenant Jones, a clean-cut, likable West Pointer fresh from the States who had just been put in charge of the 2d Platoon, had volunteered to lead the show. Sergeant Mann was supposed to assist him. The 3d Platoon's MacClung, who could smell Kraut, would do the scouting. Noisy McGuire from company headquarters would carry an SCR-300 for radio communication with the company CP. Mercier of the 3d Platoon, an excellent soldier, would shoot the rifle grenades. An officer from battalion and several enlisted men from regimental S-2 would travel as observers and German linguists. Assorted riflemen and BAR lads would also participate. It was planned that they should rendezvous at a D Company house, where they would drink coffee and eat sandwiches until 10:00 at night. They would then slip through our backyard and cross the stream at the edge of the woods. A rope was to be fastened to a telephone pole on the enemy side and a tree on ours by which the boys could pull their rubber boats across. Once in the field, the patrol would split in half, one section going away from us into town, the other surrounding a house right above us on the edge of the stream. Rifle grenades, followed by white phosphorus and fragmentation grenades, would be shot in the cellar windows, prisoners would be taken, and any Germans who tried to escape would be killed. The leader of the first posse to get a prisoner was to blow a whistle and bring his men back to the stream

The rifle is in the hands of Sgt. Walter H. Lyle Company G, 506th, who waits to observe the effect of a rifle grenade he has fired at the German-held house across the Moder River in Haguenau. Pfc. David Kenyon Webster was in a similar house nearby when he witnessed the 506th patrol across the Moder.

crossing as fast as possible. Upon hearing the whistle, the other group was supposed to follow immediately.

There would be plenty of support. As soon as he heard the whistle, the artillery observer, who was temporarily installed in OP 1, was alerted to call down fire on all points upon which the guns were zeroed. The 81mm mortar platoon back at battalion had similar orders. Even the company 60s were to fire. A 57mm antitank gun was smuggled in from Division and emplaced in the darkness to shoot into the basement of a house which, because of its proximity to the platoon CP building, could not be hit by indirect artillery fire. Overhead fire up the stream toward town was to be provided by a D Company .50-caliber machine gun (stolen from the 10th Armored at Bastogne, I believe) set up near the well in the woods. Our local machine gun was to be mounted and half-cocked on the front balcony of our house, ready to spray the nearest German dwelling a hundred yards away, if the enemy shot at the patrol from that point. After the patrol had passed by, we were to transfer the gun outside to the stream crossing and await its return. The officer who had planned that patrol had thought of everything.

Early in the afternoon of the appointed day McCreary, Cobb, and Winn left the house. We didn't slap their backs or shake their hands, but we wished them all the luck in the world ("We'll need it," Winn said) and secretly thanked God we were not going ourselves. To patrol an unknown front is bad enough; to go into a strongly held enemy city is the worst fate a soldier can imagine. We tested the rubber boats stacked up in the garage to see if they needed more air. A hush seemed to fall on the outpost. Twilight swept down and was swallowed up by darkness, the way a clear mountain stream is absorbed by a polluted river. Marsh lit the lamp. Lucky Sholty, on a pass to Paris. Our most convivial members were gone now. We hoped they would be back. In the next room, Hickman and Kohler were talking about the time they had in Baltimore on pass from Fort Meade. I could hear subdued laughter. Marsh tapped a cigarette on the table. "Pore Mick," he said, "I'd hate to think of losing that little guy. Winn can't swim, ya know."

At 9:00 we moved the machine gun from its table near the guard post to a porch over the front door facing the creek, set it up quietly on a wide stone railing, and adjusted the elevating and traversing mechanism until the muzzle aimed towards the basement windows of the nearest German house. It was so dark—no searchlights glowed tonight—we had to work by feel. Marsh pulled back the bolt handle and eased it forward. She was half-cocked: one more yank on the bolt handle, a touch on the trigger, and she would fire. A flare burst. We froze. We were in an open position where, if we ever shot the machine gun, the SP would spot us without the aid of observers. If the patrol were fired upon, however, we would pour every bullet we had into that house, SP or no SP. Because the lives of some twenty men might depend on us, this was one of those cases where I could see following orders even if it meant our death. Marsh went downstairs and told the phone guard to inform us when the patrol left.

The front was very still and dark that night. The SP seemed to have fallen asleep. The German mortars shot one or two flares and practically no HE at all. Our own artillery, warned of the patrol, rested on its guns, waiting for the whistle. The searchlights were out. We shot no flares. There was no small-arms firing. There was no moon, there were no stars. Silent and tense, the outposts on both sides of the creek waited for something to break.

I heard a scraping shuffle behind me and turned to see Marsh coming back. The patrol had just left the house, he said. We agreed to carry the machine gun down to the woods when we heard Lieutenant Jones' Myrmidons paddling along the stream opposite our balcony. Suddenly there was a loud *Eeyah!* . . . *Glug!*

and a gurgle down by the crossing spot. I started. Winn, the BAR man who couldn't swim, must have been dragged under the water by the weight of his ammunition belt. What a horrible way to die. We waited and waited, but we failed to hear any movement across from us. Had the patrol given up in the water? Then we heard the crash of a rifle grenade, the peculiar thumps of fragmentation grenades, the *puttutut* of a submachine gun off to our left. Having slipped past us with expert silence, the patrol had arrived at and was assaulting one of its objectives. A sound of firing rose from farther in town; the other house was also undergoing treatment. Marsh unloaded the gun and swung it on his shoulder, tripod and all. "Let's go," he whispered.

Heedless of noise, we rushed through the basement and out the garage door, followed by Kohler and Hudson, the ammunition bearers, stumbled through the woods to the bank of the creek, and set up the gun, this time pointing toward the farmhouse strongpoint, lest the Germans send a counterattack from there. In town, rifle fire mixed with the tommy-gun stutter and the grenade explosions, but no enemy shot back. The boys must have caught them asleep in their cellars; for good soldiers, those Germans could make some very strange mistakes. A piercing *bleep*—the whistle signal—surprised me so much I jumped. Then hell itself broke loose.

All the artillery massed behind us fired a terrible barrage that shook the ground and rang in our ears. The 81s shot from their tubes in a steady, drumlike cough. There was a harsh, crashing report up by platoon; the 57 had commenced firing. We saw a sheet of flame, then a red ball shoot into the basement of a dwelling across the creek. The artillery shells flashed orange on the German roads and strongpoints. Half a mile away to our direct front a house started to burn. D Company's .50 caliber opened up behind us in a steady bark. A solid stream of tracers shot up the creek, provoking a duel with a German burp gun which hosed just as steady a stream of tracers back at D Company from the protection of an undamaged cellar. On our left we heard loud, frantic shouting: the patrol was returning. We put the machine gun back in the house.

McCreary, Cobb, and Winn were sitting in the basement, calmly waiting to greet us. They were very happy. They had started to cross the creek when their boat capsized. All of them had lost their weapons. Winn, who had given the shriek we had heard, had drifted downstream a hundred yards, but he had emerged unscathed. The boat was lost. They hurried back to the house, borrowed dry clothes, and tried again, with the same negative results. Since they were delaying the patrol, Lieutenant Jones ordered them to stay inside. They didn't argue with him. The S-2 officer had also tried in vain.

Now the patrol was returning. Down at the crossing, exposed by an enemy flare, the remaining members scrambled across the creek on the rope or pulled themselves over in the boat. Vest, the likable company mail clerk, drew his pistol to kill a prisoner wounded so badly he wasn't worth ferrying across. Mann ordered him to hold his fire. They left the dying German on the other bank. The patrol ran into our house. They were just in time.

As fast as they could be loaded and fired, shells from the SP screamed into our backyard and exploded with a deadly ringing sound. In our room all was chaos. Their drawn, blackened faces lit by the flickering lamp, the patrol members crowded around two small, very calm German prisoners in a savage mood.

"Lemme kill 'em, lemme kill 'em!" shouted Vest, rushing towards them with his pistol drawn. Somebody stopped him.

"Get outta here, Vest. They want these bastards back at battalion," another guy yelled.

A little fellow I didn't know who had been wounded in the head by a German hand grenade started screaming as the shells landed outside, "Kill me! Kill me! Somebody kill me! I can't stand it, Christ I can't stand it. Kill me, for God's sake kill me!" His face was red with blood. The pain was too much for him. He broke into tears. The Germans' lives hung in the balance.

Marsh telephoned for a medic with a stretcher, quick. Roe and another aid man started down from the company CP.

"Kill me! Kill me! I want Mercier! Where's Mercier?" the little guy sobbed like a dream-frightened child crying for its mother.

Mercier stepped over to him and held his hand. "That's OK, buddy, that's OK, you'll be all right."

It was like a scene from a movie.

An intelligent soldier opened a first-aid packet and stuck a morphine syrette in the arm of the little guy, who was by now so crazed with pain he had to be held down on the bunk. A grenade fragment had apparently pierced his skull and lodged in his brain.

The Germans, who were both wearing *Kommen-Sie-hier* hats with the long visors, were a pair of very self-possessed noncoms, an *Unteroffizier* (buck sergeant) and a *Feldwebel* (staff sergeant). They stood calm, like rocks, in a hot, smelly room full of men who wanted to kill them, and they never moved a finger or twisted their expressions. They were the most poised individuals I've ever seen.

The screaming got so bad I couldn't stand it any more. I stepped to the garage door and listened to the shells zip into the yard. During a lull, the medics ran in with a stretcher. They emerged a minute or two afterwards, carrying the wounded man. Mercier walked beside the stretcher. The little guy died that night in the hospital.

When the SP ceased firing, the rest of the patrol slipped into the darkness and went home. The S-2 enlisted men ran the Germans back to battalion headquarters, where, it was rumored, the buck sergeant talked a lot and the staff remained silent, even after persuasion. We never heard whether they lived to regiment or not. Meanwhile, the S-2 officer, who had gone to sleep after the second dunking and had awakened when the raiders returned, fell asleep again and stayed with us until morning.

The night was no longer peaceful. Excited by the patrol and disturbed by the artillery, the enemy filled the darkness with flares and the sky with shells. The SP put a projectile ten feet in front of the D Company machine-gun position, almost scaring the Brooklyn accent out of Eddie Weeks and giving his companions an anxious moment. Mortar shells, exploding near Platoon, in the field, and between us and OP 3, searched the area for stragglers. In the distance, the burning house stood out like an angel in hell.

I'll always associate a , house on fire with a dramatic night in Europe. A flaming butter factory had smoldered and glowed ominously for the duration of the fantastic cross-country march we made to outflank Carentan, Normandy, the night of June 11, and when the Luftwaffe had bombed Eindhoven, Holland, the second evening after we had jumped, they had created sizable fires that crackled and flamed and lit up the countryside as we marched in from our abortive excursion toward Helmond. There's something eerie about a' fire in combat: the huge, bold flames seem so alien and strident in a situation where neither side dares show the tiniest match flame.

As the upstairs guard watched the blazing building, spellbound, he became aware of a weird noise by the stream crossing. It sounded like a person wheezing, choking, and gargling all at the same time. Apparently the wounded German abandoned by the patrol hadn't died yet. He must have been shot in the lungs or throat. What should we do? Should we let him die in peace or should we kill him? I favored the latter choice, because, if we left him alone, the Germans might send a patrol to his rescue and learn from him of the activity in and around our house. Then they would shell us. From the way they had laid them in our yard, I had no doubt they could hit our cellar. So it was him or us.

I resolved to swim the creek and knife him. I changed into a pair of wet fatigues, put my trench knife in my pocket, and sneaked out the garage. Just when I was halfway to the crossing, the Germans laid a mortar barrage on the other bank. I changed my mind. Back in the cellar, McCreary, who thought of all the angles, said it was wiser not to go anyway; the enemy might use that man as bait for a trap, a possibility which had never entered my mind. Hand grenades would be more appropriate.

Marsh and I tiptoed to a point opposite the German. We could hear him gasping and slobbering, he could hear us walking. He was so terrified that, weak as he was, he held his breath and stifled his groans, thinking, perhaps that by so doing he would be unnoticed. But he couldn't suppress his breathing very long and the ghastly wheezes commenced as strong as ever. I pitied him, dying all alone in a country far from home, dying slowly without hope or love on the bank of a dirty little creek, helpless against the killers he heard walking toward him. But if he got back alive, I might be dead. Marsh and I pulled the pins on the grenades, threw them beside the German, and flopped down behind an earthen mound. One of the grenades exploded, the other was a dud. There was no change in the sound of the breathing. We returned to the house, got two more grenades, and tried again. No luck; he continued moaning. We gave up and went to bed.

Just before sunrise, Cobb, who had also considered swimming—until he heard the mortars—threw one grenade and killed the helpless, dying German.

Dawn came. The cold yellow sun shone through the grey mist on the dead German, a monument to war and to the achievements of man.

BACK TO MOURMELON

At times a public-address system was brought around to front-line positions and surrender appeals in German were aimed across the river; as a result a few Germans would slip across at night to give themselves up. The 101st artillery units sometimes substituted propaganda leaflet rounds for high explosive and the Germans made a half-hearted attempt to lay down counterbarrages. Morale among the Germans was reported as very low but food and ammunition were sufficient. Altogether, seventy-seven prisoners were taken by the 101st in Alsace.

The general strategy on the Seventh Army front had been to maintain a static front in the VI Corps area where the 101st was, while on
the right flank Gen. Jean J. de Lattre de Tassigny's French First Army,
assisted by American divisions, made the main effort—the elimination
of the Colmar pocket. This pocket was wiped out on February 9 at a
cost of 18,000 casualties, 8,000 of which were suffered by Seventh Army
troops. With this threat to the Seventh Army's flank removed SHAEF
on February 15 ordered the withdrawal of the 101st from the Seventh
Army. The Division was to revert to control of the First Allied Airborne Army. As a result a series of reliefs was begun on the VI Corps
front. On the 19th the 14th Armored Division was put into the line
and the section from Bischwiller to the Rhine was taken over by the
French First Army. The 36th Division on the 101st's right began moving over to relieve the airborne regiments.

The month-long Alsatian campaign had been, in terms of dead and
wounded, the least costly the Division up to that time had experienced.
The January casualties in Alsace had been confined to the 501st and
the 327th, each listing a total of fourteen in all categories. For the
month of February casualties totalled 187 enlisted men and 12 officers,
of whom 29 enlisted men and 2 officers were fatalities. The heaviest
loser was the 327th, with 68 total casualties, including 12 dead. The
hardest hit companies were E, which suffered 15 of its 17 casualties
during the company raid across the Moder on the early morning of
February 1, and Company G with 13 casualties, including 5 of the
Regiment's KIAs. Four of the five were killed on February 6 when
a German mortar round dropped directly into a dugout.

The 506th had 44 casualties during February. Company D had eight,
and F and G seven each. The regiment had three enlisted men and an
officer killed. The 501st had 41 casualties, including 6 men killed. A
large part of the month's loss was suffered on the two-company raid
across the Moder on the morning of February 1 when 16 casualties were
incurred. Fourteen of the 16, including four dead, were from Company B. The lightest losses of the campaign were those of the 502d
which had 22 casualties, including four killed. Company C was the
heaviest loser with six enlisted men and an officer on the casualty list.
Among the other units of the Division the largest losses were those of
the 81st AA Battalion with six men wounded, and the 326th Engineers
with three enlisted men and two officers wounded. On the night of
the 22d the 502d was relieved and during the next several days all battalions of the regiment were moved to Buhl.

On the 23rd the 506th was relieved and moved to the vicinity of

Saverne, a large town twenty-five miles west of Haguenau. On the following day and on the 25th the 327th was relieved. The 501st was relieved on the 25th.

The bulk of the 101st returned to Mourmelon by rail, riding in straw-filled 40-and-8 boxcars; this was a type of travel which the Division had not yet tried but it was an immediate hit with the veterans of the trek by truck from Holland and to and from Bastogne. The 506th left from Saverne on the 25th, accompanied by the 321st Field Artillery Battalion, part of the 81st AA Battalion and Company A of the 326th Engineers. On the 27th the 327th and the 502d left from Reding, a station just outside of Sarrebourg and twenty miles west of Saverne. With them went the 463d Artillery Battalion and Headquarters Batteries of Division Artillery and of the 377th Battalion. On the 28th the 501st, 377th, and 907th Artillery Battalions and the 81st AA Battalion left from Reding. Other units of the Division returned in truck convoys via Sarrebourg, Nancy, Toul, and Châlons, the last units clearing Alsace on March 1.

The trip took about eighteen hours and each trainload as it rolled into the village of Mourmelon-le-Petit was greeted by the music of the 502d band.

Mourmelon: March

The 101st had heard while still in Alsace that the buildings at Mourmelon in which they had lived before going up to Bastogne had been taken over by some army hospitals, and word had got out that this time it was to be pyramidal tents. When the 40-and-8s pulled into the station at Mourmelon-le-Petit the passengers were driven to their new homes which each unit's advance detail had got into shape a few days before. Their first days were given over to making these tents comfortable. A typical improvement program was carried out by Pfc. David Kenyon Webster's squad of Company E, 506th Parachute Infantry:

With Matthews and Masseoni around, our tent was amply furnished with personalities, but of physical comforts—benches, tables, etc.—there was a great lack. For those two and the rest of us—Marsh, Collette, Hudson, Hickman, Kohler, Sholty, Winn, and myself—there were only sagging wooden bunks, a squat stove, and two tall, rickety board lockers. We soon remedied this equipment shortage. In the night, we infiltrated the Air Corps' bailiwick and carried off kindling and wooden planks for our floor. If we wandered in that area in the daytime, we were apt to be told to keep our hands in our pockets and move out—too many paratroopers had been there already. Collette and I lifted a good table from the future noncoms' club, and somebody else made off with several benches which a careless KP had thoughtfully left outside the Air Corps officers' mess. Lighting was a more difficult problem, because, although the company had a captured gasoline generator and the requisite wire, neither they nor the Air Corps owned bulbs or sockets. Matthews took me down on his motorcycle one day to the old regimental area, where, after much searching, we found a small chandelier, which we promptly ripped from the ceiling. With its forest of imitation candles, it would make a splendid lighting fixture for our tent. Clutching Matthews' belt and holding the chandelier out at arm's length, I bounced back to the company, an object of amusement. My prize was so heavy, however, that we had to tie it to a tentpole. It came down after the first regimental inspection and Collette installed a regular socket he had found. Winn built himself a locker to match the others. We stole coke from the Air Corps and chopped logs provided by regiment, thus keeping our home warm day and night. Gradually this tent became livable.

Usually six or eight men occupied a tent (though there were some 12-men tents); officers had their own tent rows with two officers to a small wall tent. Latrines were pit-style, surrounded by canvas walls. Water was hauled in and was available in Lyster bags. Washing was done in helmets. Two shower units served the entire Division and companies went up on schedule. Messes were set up in tents and most units built tables and benches; the chow was generally considered good and the PX ration with which it could be supplemented was somewhat larger than it had been in the combat zones.

Most of the first week was given over to sleep, getting the tents in order, and exploring the two Mourmelons and Reims. The first ceremony held was that of March 1 when the 1st Battalion of the 401st Glider Infantry Regiment officially became what in actuality it had been for a year, the 3d Battalion of the 327th. This was a part of a broad reorganization of the Division which also saw the 506th, which had hitherto been, like the 501st, attached to the 101st, become an assigned regiment of the Division. After that the Division settled down to preparing for two things—further combat and the ceremony at which General Eisenhower was to present the Division with the Distinguished Unit Citation.

For Gallantry in Action

Notifications that the 101st was to be awarded the Distinguished Unit Citation, the first time in the history of the United States Army that an entire division was to be so cited, had been received in Alsace and a little marching-to-music had begun there. But it was upon return to Mourmelon and after the initial rest period that the practice for the parade and decoration ceremony went into high gear. There was a great to-do and a washing of cartridge belts, pressing of uniforms, issuing of ribbons and insignia, linseed-oiling of stocks, and mirror-shining of boots. It was the 101st's most sweated-out ceremony (except for those members who remained long enough to come back with the 82d Airborne Division; they spent ten days in Camp Shanks, New York, preparing for the biggest parade of the war, that of January 12, 1946, when the 82d marched down Fifth Avenue, New York City).

The presentation took place on Thursday, March 15, on a broad field near the main camp. General Eisenhower, who had been furnished with an honor guard of about 100 officers and men whose home state, Kansas, was the same as his, inspected the Division front. Then from the parachute-decorated reviewing platform, where stood General Taylor; Lt. Gen. Sir Frederick Morgan; Lt. Gen. Lewis H. Brereton; President Roosevelt's secretary, Stephen Early; Maj. Gen. Paul Williams; Maj. Gen. Lowell Rooks; Maj. Gen. Matthew B. Ridgway, and other prominent military personalities of the ETO, General Eisenhower spoke:

It is a great personal honor for me to be here today to take part in a ceremony that is unique in American history. Never before has a full division been cited by the War Department in the name of the President for gallantry in action. This day marks the beginning of a new tradition in the American Army. With that tradition, therefore, will always be associated the name of the 101st Airborne Division and of Bastogne.

Yet you men, because you are soldiers of proved valor and of experience, would be the last to claim that you are the bravest and the best. All the way from where the Marines are fighting on Iwo Jima, through the Philippines and

The 101st Airborne Division receives the Distinguished
It was the first time in the history of the United

southeast Asia, on through the Mediterranean and along this great front, and on the Russian frontiers, are going forward day by day those battles sustained by the valor of you and the other Allied units that are beating this enemy to his knees. They are proving once and for all that dictatorship cannot produce better soldiers than can aroused democracy. In many of those actions are units that have performed with unexcelled brilliance.

So far as I know there may be many among you that would not rate Bastogne as your bitterest battle. Yet it is entirely fitting and appropriate that you should be cited for that particular battle. It happened to be one of those occasions when the position itself was of the utmost importance to the Allied forces. You, in reserve, were hurried forward and told to hold that position. All the elements of drama, of battle drama, were there. You were cut off, you were surrounded. Only valor, complete self-confidence in yourselves and in your leaders, a knowledge that you were well trained, only the determination to win, could sustain soldiers under those conditions. You were given a marvelous opportunity, and you met every test.

Therefore, you become a fitting symbol on which the United Nations, all the citizens of the United Nations, can say to their soldiers today, "We are proud of you," as it is my great privilege to say to you here today, to the 101st Division and all its attached units, "I am awfully proud of you."

With this great honor goes also a certain responsibility. Just as you are the beginning of a new tradition, you must realize, each of you, that from now on,

Unit Citation at Mourmelon, France, 15 March 1945.
States Army that an entire division was so honored.

the spotlight will beat on you with particular brilliance. Whenever you say you are a soldier of the 101st Division, everybody, whether it's on the street in the city or in the front line, will expect unusual conduct of you. I know that you will meet every test of the future like you met it at Bastogne.

Good luck and God be with each of you.

TRAINING

Training preceded ánd followed the month's highlight of the review and presentation. An increasingly large percentage of the men had seen no combat or only that of Alsace. Hikes, range firing, basic subjects, and problems were on the training schedule as well as the specialized work on dummy troop-carrier-plane mockups and gliders. The Division set up its own parachute training course to qualify non-jumping members of the Division as jumpers (the class made its qualifying jump the day the Division received notice of its Ruhr mission), and during the month glider flights were flown to qualify as gliderists the infantry replacements received after Bastogne. Units such as the engineers, medics, and ordnance followed out their own specialized schedules of training.

Generals Eisenhower, Taylor, Brereton, and Ridgway, and Presidential
Secretary Stephen T. Early review the 101st at the presentation ceremony.

The broad training program for the Division was based on a six-
weeks schedule which, at the end of that time, was to result in a state
of readiness for a daylight airborne or air-landing mission under Operation Eclipse, the final crackdown on Germany. Under Eclipse the 101st,
with the 82d Airborne Division and a British airborne division, was to
drop and airland in the Berlin area, contact the Russians, and join with
them in wiping out the German resistance in the Nazi capital.

The training began on March 5; it was broken off by the move to the Ruhr Pocket at the end of the month, and the airborne phase of Eclipse was never carried out. The 501st, after the Division left for the Ruhr and South Germany, remained at Mourmelon ready to carry out a mission of jumping on Nazi prisoner-of-war camps. This mission likewise was never carried out and the regiment later rejoined the Division at Berchtesgaden after VE-day.

The training at Mourmelon progressed through squad and platoon to company and then to battalion level before the move to the Ruhr. One of the battalion problems was twice marred by accidents; on the morning of March 22 while the 2d Battalion of the 502d was going through the problem a round from an 81mm mortar fell short, killed a lieutenant and wounded six men. Two days later, while the 3d Battalion of the 502d was going through the same problem, another 81mm mortar round fell short; a lieutenant was killed and three men were wounded.

Another bad accident had occurred earlier in the month, on March 7, when a new type of hand grenade being demonstrated went off and injured eleven persons including General Higgins, Colonel Kinnard and Lieutenant Austin, the last two seriously. Lt. Col. Charles H. Chase, able executive of the 506th since activation, became acting G-3 until Colonel Kinnard returned to duty in Berchtesgaden on May 12.

But the days were not all training. The winter was ending, the war was ending, the race across Germany was under way, and victory was in the air. There was still fighting going on and fighting to be done, and the transport planes came in on the fields adjacent to the airborne camp, bringing back wounded to the hospitals at Mourmelon. Some of the planes brought in German prisoners of war and there was a stockade of them nearby, guarded partly by Russians, Poles and other freed or displaced persons; the prisoners were used for work about the hospitals and the camp.

And that there was still fighting to be done was recalled forcibly to paratroopers and glidermen of the 101st on the morning of March 24 when they looked up from whatever they were doing to wave and shout at great Vs of transport planes which were taking off and forming overhead; of all the watchers only they could know the feelings of the occupants of those planes, parachutists of the 17th Airborne Division, now on their way to their first combat jump across the Rhine.

The 17th had been at Mourmelon when the 101st got back there. A little matter of looted barracks bags had aroused bitter suspicions among the Eagle men who had come back from seventy days of combat to find their jump suits, souvenir pistols, personal articles, and prized jump boots missing. Whether their suspicions were right or wrong (much of the bitterness was directed at the 101st's own rear echelon personnel who had been left to take care of the bags) there were only good wishes and prayers for the men going out on the mission; and the high count of returning planes later in the day was a cause for cheering.

There were more furloughs, leaves and passes than the Division had ever known; to England, the Riviera, Paris and Brussels. At the camp were several movie theaters for those who cared to sweat out the long lines. A number of Camp Shows performed for the Division and some big-name performers such as Marlene Dietrich. There were evening passes to Reims. Along with these relaxations were some of the other things which went with garrison life: a summary court was set up in the Division area and a man found in improper uniform found himself quickly relieved of five dollars; carrying a Luger in one's pocket was worth a twenty-five dollar fine; speeding a jeep or truck cost ten to twenty dollars; and disorderly conduct was a twenty-five dollar offense. The relaxation after the weeks of fighting filled the stockade and by the time the Division had been back two weeks 139 men were in confinement.

March ended. The first promise of spring was in the air. April began. And again the 101st was alerted for a combat mission. This time it was to be Germany, the Ruhr Pocket.

The Ruhr

When the 101st pulled into Mourmelon Camp at the beginning of March for what was to turn out to be a month's stay the battle lines on the Western Front were still west of the Rhine; the Germans had so far been successful in keeping their watch on that ancient barrier. When the month was up and the Division returned to the war the east bank of the river was held by the Germans only on the lower course in Holland, the upper course between Kaiserslautern and Switzerland, and along a 65-mile sector in the center from Bonn to Duisburg.

The Rhine had been bridged first on the 7th of March when a patrol of the 9th Armored Division pushed up to the river at Remagen, crossed the 1,300-foot Ludendorff Bridge, removed the demolition charges, and established a bridgehead. This bridgehead had been rapidly expanded. Later in the month the Rhine was crossed in two other sectors; on the 22d-23d General Patton's Third Army had crossed near Oppenheim and on the 24th, in history's greatest river-crossing, the 21st Army Group, made up of the Canadian First, British Second, U. S. Ninth, and part of the First Allied Airborne Armies (the last including the 17th Airborne Division, whose takeoff had been watched by the 101st in Mourmelon) had crossed in the Wesel sector.

By the end of March the German armies in the west were facing defeat. They had chosen to fight it out with the Allies west of the Rhine and they had been beaten. Now their river barrier no longer existed. A new general, Field Marshal Albert Kesselring, who had been successful on the defensive Italian front, was brought in to replace Von Rundstedt, but the hour was late.

A sideshow to the races across Germany—though at any other time it might have been the main feature—was the mop-up of the Ruhr Pocket. The Pocket was a legacy of the German policy which had proven so disastrous at Stalingrad and elsewhere of stubbornly holding instead of dropping back to more defensible positions. But the order to give up the Ruhr would have been a heart-breaking one for any German commander. Here was the very heart of Germany's industrial might, the most densely populated section of the Reich, containing such manufacturing cities as Düsseldorf, Essen and Dortmund, all of more than half a million pre-war population, Duisburg with 457,000 and Gelsenkirchen with 322,000; it was a military prize which had figured in the Allied plans as far back as Operation Overlord. On Easter Sunday, April 1, Combat Command B of the 2d Armored Division, breaking out from the down-river bridgeheads established by the ground-airborne assault of March 24, and the 3d Armored Division from the up-river Remagen bridgehead, met at Lippstadt; and their meeting completed the greatest encirclement of all time.

The 4,000-square mile pocket lay entirely east of the Rhine, with that river as a west boundary, the Lippe River roughly the north boundary, and the Sieg River the southern boundary. From north to south the pocket measured about 55 miles, from east to west about 70. Enclosed in this area, about half the size of New Jersey and considerably more industrialized, were almost a third of a million German troops, chiefly of Field Marshal Walter Model's Army Group B. In general the encircled troops were well supplied, much matériel having been trapped with them and some being manufactured in the area. There were a large number of 88mm and other caliber guns which had been concentrated for the antiaircraft defense of the Ruhr factories and which now were being depressed for ground-level use.

The cleaning out of this sizable and still-dangerous pocket became the job of a number of divisions of the First, Ninth and Fifteenth Armies; the number varied as divisions or parts of divisions fought for awhile and then, as the size and danger of the Pocket steadily decreased, went east to get in on the kill of the main German forces.

The plan of attack was for the Ninth Army on the north along the Lippe River to attack south; the First Army, south and east of the pocket, was to attack north and west; and along the Rhine, which formed the west boundary, the Fifteenth Army was to hold fast, tie up German troops by poising a continuous threat, and prevent nuisance raids. Of the three armies the Fifteenth seemed to have the most to offer anyone who wanted to spend a few weeks in contact—but not too close contact—with unfriendly German troops. It was to this quiet and relatively safe side of the Pocket that the 101st was sent. That the front bore out its promise is testified to by the Division casualty figures for the month of April: 9 enlisted men and an officer killed in action; total casualties for the month, 45 enlisted men and 3 officers, including 15 men missing in action. Half of the casualties—5 of the dead and 25 of the total 48—were from one regiment, the 506th. A few of these casualties occurred in Southern Germany after the removal of the Division to that sector.

To the Banks of the Rhine

On the 30th of March, Good Friday, came this message: "All units of this Division with the exception of the 501st Parachute Infantry are hereby alerted to be in readiness to depart from this station on a combat mission at 0800, 1 April 1945." Those men who, months before, had planned to attend Christmas services in the Reims Cathedral and had wound up in Bastogne and now were hoping to get there for Easter services (April 1 was Easter Sunday) found themselves instead packing and drawing ammunition. The Division was to go up to the Ruhr Pocket.

The advance party left Mourmelon on Saturday night, March 31, and on Monday, April 2, the convoys of 10-ton trailer-trucks began pulling out. The advance party had set up a headquarters at Glehn, seven miles west of the Rhine and about midway between the cities of München-Gladbach to the west and Düsseldorf, across the Rhine, to the east. The CP was officially opened at 1800 on April 1. The Division became part of XXII Corps of Fifteenth Army, the corps commander being Maj. Gen. Ernest N. Harmon and the army commander Lt. Gen. Leonard T. Gerow.

The Division bivouacked around Glehn. Headquarters was in that town, Division Artillery Headquarters was in Norf. The 327th settled near Büttgen, the 506th near Gohr, the 321st Glider FA Battalion near Nievenheim, the 463d Parachute Field Artillery Battalion near Busch-hausen, the 377th Parachute FA Battalion and the 907th Glider FA Battalion around Neuss, the 326th Medical Company in Luttenglehn, the 326th Engineer Battalion in Horster-Schelsen, the 801st Ordnance Company near Korschenbroich, and the 81st AA Battalion near Dycker-Scheisen. On the 4th the 101st completed the relief of the 386th and 387th Regiments of the 97th (Trident) Infantry Division and the 33d Cavalry Squadron.

The 101st's area was about thirteen miles from north to south and about twenty miles deep from east to west. Actually, the Rhine, which was the front line, was so crooked in this sector that there were about twenty-four miles of river front. The front extended from the town of Nieder-Cassel on the north (just across from the northern suburbs of the east-bank city of Düsseldorf, the most important industrial city of the Rhine valley) south to the vicinity of Worringen. The 101st's neighbor on the north was the 302d Infantry Regiment of the 94th Division; the boundary was obligingly drawn along the bottom edge of the 1:100,000 map of the area. The division to the south was a more familiar one—the 101st's airborne comrades of Normandy and Holland, the 82d Airborne Division.

The sector occupied by the 101st was a flat plain, partly farming, partly manufacturing, with a number of neat, small villages, a few towns, and, after the Division area was extended on April 10, München-Gladbach, Rheydt and Rheydt-Odenkirchen (actually, since all three adjoined, a tri-city of about 200,000 population).

Düsseldorf, across the Rhine, as seen from Neuss, held by the 327th.

Crossing the 300-500-yard wide Rhine on the Division front were five bridges, all wrecked. The bridges had crossed from Düsseldorf to Nieder-Cassel and nearby Neuss except for one, a wrecked ponton bridge a mile or so to the north.

On the east bank of the Rhine facing the 101st were two German divisions of an estimated 2,500 men each. They were the 176th and 338th Volksgrenadier Divisions. Their maximum offensive capability during the entire time was the dispatching of an occasional reconnaissance patrol to the west bank. Later, as the situation on the other side of the Pocket became desperate, the two divisions, with the exception of a battalion of the 183d held in mobile reserve, were shifted across the Pocket. Left holding the Rhine opposite the 101st were the 3d Police Battalion, the Walther Battalion composed of firemen and hastily trained *Volkssturm,* and several ragtag units, supported by the fire of three antiaircraft battalions.

The Division front was divided between the 327th and the 506th, the glider-riders taking the northern portion from just north of Nieder-Cassel down to the Erft, a stream running northeast into the Rhine, and the parachutists holding the longer sector from the Erft down to Worringen. The 327th divided its front between the 1st and 2d Battalions, with the 2d Battalion holding the northern and the 1st Battalion the southern half of the sector. The 3d Battalion was in Neuss, a town of about 55,000, where it was guarding food supplies, taking care of factories, patrolling the streets, and supervising some displaced persons camps. The 506th divided its sector between the 2d and 3d Battalions with the 3d Battalion taking the northern half adjoining the 327th, and the 2d Battalion the southern half next to the 504th Parachute Infantry Regiment of the 82d Airborne Division. The 1st Battalion was in regimental reserve at Nievenheim. The Division artillery and engineers assumed their normal supporting roles with the 463d and

706

377th Battalions in direct support of the 327th, the 321st supporting the
506th, and the 907th in general support. The 502d and the 81st AA
Battalion were the Division reserve.

"Never Had It So Good"

Living in the Ruhr surpassed the Division's previous high, Alsace.
The houses, even along the front, were modern and relatively undamaged. Unlike in Alsace, which was part of France, the men
had no inhibitions about requisitioning whatever living quarters were
needed. The 502d, back in reserve and administering the military
government setup in the rear areas, often had billets which brought out
all the overtones of the Army saying, "They never had it so good,"
especially when an undamaged wine cellar went along with the house.

Mail for the Division came by C-47 or truck and more promptly and
abundantly than it ever had before in combat. The Division Special
Service Section arranged for improvised theaters throughout the area
and movies were shown regularly; it was not Special Service's fault
that the XXII Corps' film library was limited and contained mostly
films which the 101st had seen a year before. Several USO and GI
shows got around to the units. A daily delivery was made of the Liège
edition of *Stars and Stripes*. German breweries were located and their
product apportioned to the various units. Once a ration of three cans
per man of American beer was issued; another time Coca-Cola enough
for the Division was given out and stern warnings passed down about
turning in the bottles. Before the troops had been in the Ruhr a week
both the 502d and 506th had formed boxing teams, and the boxers
moved in together and began training. Baseball, softball, and volleyball equipment was issued to the companies and batteries.

For those men who could find something to spend money on, the
Division Finance Officer brought up the February and March enlisted
and the March officers' payrolls. Excluding what was due men absent
and the rear echelon back at Mourmeloh almost two million dollars
were paid out, with more than half being turned back in in the form
of PTAs, War Bonds, and other forms of soldiers' savings. This was
the first distribution to the 101st of Allied military mark notes, and all
French, English and American money was ordered turned in in exchange for marks.

The situation was considered quiet enough to allow the men who had
not qualified as glider riders to return to Mourmelon for their qualifying rides. From the 327th alone about four hundred went back.
Planes weekly took 10 officers and 85 enlisted men to the Riviera and

the same number to England. Other leave groups went to Paris and Brussels.

Though the chow situation wasn't good at first—Fifteenth Army was brand new, having been activated on March 30, and its bakeries and depots hadn't come up when the 101st arrived—the shortages in bread and fresh meat were sometimes alleviated in individual cases by stealthy exchanges of cigarettes and soap for German *Pumpernickel* and eggs. The Division Quartermaster Company scrounged bread from Army bakeries as far back as Aachen and Liège. After a week Fifteenth Army began baking and solved the bread shortage.

PATROLS ACROSS THE RHINE

What fighting there was occurred when the patrols from the line regiments slipped across the river at night—the once-thought impregnable Rhine, now vulnerable to any squad with a boat—and bumped into the still-dangerous defenders. Not that all the losses were on raids; the Germans still threw over artillery. The first and one of the most severe blows suffered in the Ruhr occurred on the morning of the 5th when a round from a large-caliber gun, believed to have been a railroad piece, landed across the street from the 327th's 3d Battalion CP. Two members of the Regimental Antitank Company were killed and four were wounded. A fragment which penetrated the Battalion CP hit Lt. Col. Ray C. Allen, who lost a leg. Colonel Allen, although he had been in Neuss all day, had been busy inspecting the DP camps, factories and other installations his battalion was to guard, and he did not get to the building in which his staff had set up the CP until almost midnight. When he saw the old wire leading into the building he realized that it had been the CP of the unit his battalion had relieved; and only the fact that he would have to wake and re-billet his sleeping men kept him from moving that night. He figured that the Germans on the other side of the river knew that the building was being used as a headquarters, and he determined to get out the first thing in the morning. Ironically, Colonel Allen, who had led the battalion with distinction from Normandy through Holland, Bastogne, Alsace and into the Ruhr, was the only casualty the battalion had in the Pocket and was the last loss it suffered from enemy action in the war. He was succeeded by his battalion S-3, Capt. Robert J. McDonald.

Another veteran officer of the Division was lost a week later when Maj. William Leach, who had been S-2 of the 506th throughout combat, accompanied a regimental patrol across the Rhine. The patrol was detected in midstream by the Germans, who opened fire; this fire was then taken up from the American side. The boat Major Leach was in was hit and he and several others were wounded. Two days later his body was recovered several hundred yards downstream.

Almost nightly patrolling across the Rhine by the 506th and the 327th began on the night of the 5th when all the battalions on the line sent patrols across the river. These patrols were usually of squad size or less. Whenever possible the leaders, prior to the mission, were flown in Cub planes over the area they were to patrol. Two patrols of company size crossed the Rhine during the campaign; these two raids furnished most of the action seen by the Division in the Ruhr.

The first of these company-size patrols crossed the Rhine to carry out a corps mission on the night of April 8-9. It was made up of Company A of the 327th, less the 60mm mortar crews, and was accompanied by ten men from the 326th Engineers and four from the 463d Parachute FA Battalion, a total of 118 soldiers. The original mission was to seize the east end of the destroyed Neuss–Düsseldorf railroad bridge, hold the position for twenty-four hours, using it as a base from which to send out patrols and place demolitions and booby traps, and to return on the following night. To hold this position the company was given two of the new 57mm recoilless guns, mines, booby traps, and some of the captured German *Panzerfausts,* one-shot bazooka affairs which were very effective against armor. However, a few hours before jump-off time the mission was changed on corps orders so that the company was to return that same night. This decision may have been influenced by the unfortunate experience of Company A of the adjoining 504th Parachute Infantry Regiment of the 82d. Company A had crossed on a somewhat similar mission on the early morning of the 6th, and had been heavily attacked during the day. Only 70 of the 140 participants had managed to return.

The 327th's crossing was made east of Neuss, not far from the regiment's southern flank. The strong current scattered the fifteen assault boats but by midnight Capt. Philip G. Walker had reassembled his command. The company moved north, downstream, killing two Germans and taking three prisoners along the river dike. At 0300 a pillbox and a machine-gun nest were encountered; two Germans were killed in the former and the entire crew of the latter was killed. Several more machine guns were met and knocked out, six more enemy killed and two more prisoners taken. By this time the glidermen were fighting on the outskirts of the village of Hamm, just across the river from Neuss. In the houses and factories in this area they killed or wounded a number of enemy, knocked out several guns and strongpoints, took a few more

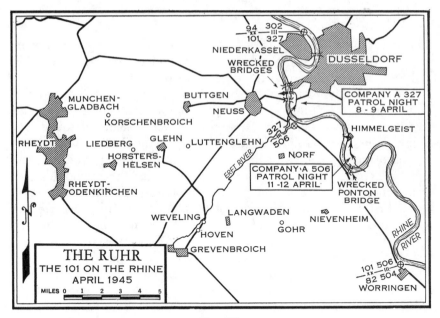

Map 102.

prisoners. During all this action the Division's artillery was laying down fire on call.

It was now getting late; so the withdrawal was begun. The return crossing was to be made opposite Neuss. First the prisoners and engineers were evacuated; then the platoons covered each other as they fell back. The crossing itself was uneventful except for the capsizing of one of the boats which resulted in the drowning of one man. By 0515 the party was back on the friendly bank. Three other men were missing during the rear-guard fighting on the far bank.

The troops had taken sixteen prisoners, including three civilians. The prisoners were not élite, but had fought hard; most were former policemen, firemen and the like, had had little training, and were glad to get their part of the war over with.

The other large raid of the campaign was carried out on the night of April 11-12 by Company A of the 506th. One hundred twenty-six members of the company and four from the 321st Artillery Battalion crossed the Rhine in sixteen assault boats just after midnight and attacked the river-bank village of Himmelgeist. They ran into a scattering of small-arms fire, killed two defenders, and entered the town. In Himmelgeist they captured seven civilians suspected of having taken part in the defense of the place and then withdrew, getting back to the far shore by 0415. The raid cost the company three killed and four

710

wounded, mostly from small-arms fire, though there was some flat-trajectory shelling during the withdrawal. Two boats capsized in mid-stream under enemy artillery fire and eight men were missing, believed drowned.

These two patrols accounted for the greater part of the Division's activities and, incidentally, a good part of the losses in the Ruhr. The two regiments on the line spent the rest of the time watching the river flow between them and the enemy and in sending over the nightly small patrols. A typical small patrol was that carried out on the night of April 5-6 by an officer and six men of Company A of the 327th.

The leader was Lt. Clifford J. Myer who was handicapped by a broken arm in a plaster cast. (Lieutenant Myer also helped lead the full company raid three nights later, for which he received the Silver Star Medal.) With him were Sgt. Don Ellenberger and five volunteers from the company's jump platoon (so called because all the members were either qualified parachutists or were waiting to take parachute training). These men were Pfc. J. B. Eason, Pfc. Jack Damsky, Pfc. Woodrow Bauer, Pvt. William Lamb and Pvt. Bob Landers.

Along the waterfront in Neuss Lieutenant Myer and Sergeant Ellenberger had located a former German boat club with a boathouse full of kayaks, racing shells, rowboats, scows, sailboats, motor boats, and whatnot. For several days before the patrol, on a lagoon protected from enemy observation by a dyke, the two men had tested the various boats and decided on an outboard-motor boat with paddles.

The night before the raid the lieutenant and the sergeant had taken out the kayak and had gone over the selected route for the crossing. They decided that it was going to be a real job; not only was the river three hundred yards wide at the spot but the current was swift.

The next night it was raining and very dark. Just before 2300 the patrol went down to the lagoon in which the boat was hidden and pushed off. Their mission was to reconnoiter the hostile shore and locate the enemy defenses ˑin that sector. For armament the patrol relied on .45-caliber ammunition, taking six Thompson submachine guns and eight automatic pistols; they also carried hand grenades. They had a signal lamp with which to call for support, if necessary.

The motorless outboard, once launched, immediately caused trouble. Water began seeping through holes in the boat's sides and it settled in the river. They banked it, looked around, and finally chose an engineer assault boat.

The new boat was watertight and the party pulled away from the friendly shore along which lay their buddies of the jump platoon, ready

One of the three wrecked Neuss–Düsseldorf bridges across the Rhine. It was across this bridge that Lt. Clifford J. Myer's Company H, 327th, patrol returned on the night of 5-6 May after their boats had been sunk.

to give protective fire if needed, and at 2325 they beached just where they had planned. In the rain and darkness Lieutenant Myer looked over his men to pick a boat guard; it was then he found he had an extra man. Along for the ride and to see how his men made out was the company commander, Captain Walker. The patrol leader left Captain Walker and a man at the boat and took off into the dark.

Along the river the patrol found trenches six feet deep and two feet wide and, at 100-yard intervals, concrete pillboxes. None of these installations was manned, but the group came finally to a small shack which turned out to be a sentry box. The German on guard opened fire; the patrol rushed the shack and with grenades and submachine-gun fire quieted him.

By now it was 0300 and time to start back. The group returned to the boat and pushed off. But the return trip turned out to be rougher than the ride over. The first attempt found the current bringing the boat back to shore only a few yards from the starting point. A second try got them as far as midstream, where the current carried the boat toward one of the destroyed bridges which had crossed the Rhine from Neuss to Düsseldorf. Suddenly they smacked against a submerged part of the wrecked bridge and, as the last man crawled out and onto the nearby girders, the boat sank.

The bridge had been buckled and dropped into the river. Between the points where the Düsseldorf side sloped down to the water and the Neuss side rose again was a gap of running water. The patrol was on the Düsseldorf side.

The night was ending and something had to be done. Feeling around the men found some pieces of timber. Working with these they started to bridge the gap. The last open section was closed by a two-by-four which was nudged out into the darkness until it hit something solid on the other side.

Sergeant Ellenberger stripped and, straddling the board with his legs dangling in the water, inched across. The timber bent dangerously as he reached the middle but he finally made it. From the other side, out of sight of his comrades, he called for all the belts and clothes to be tied into a rope and for the next man to bring one end across. After the makeshift rope was across and tied above the bridge the crossing was easier. Finally, everybody was across except Lieutenant Myer, who was handicapped by his broken arm, and Damsky.

Sergeant Ellenberger, who had gone ashore, got some signal wire and returned, recrossing to where Lieutenant Myer and Damsky were. He tied all the weapons in a bundle, fastened them to one piece of wire, and had the men on the friendly side drag them over. Then Damsky started over; he had been held back purposely because he was the heaviest man on the patrol. Halfway across the plank broke under him but, hanging onto the wire which Ellenberger had strung in place of the makeshift rope, he worked his way to the 101st half of the bridge.

Now only Myer and Ellenberger were left. For the lieutenant there was no choice. He hooked his injured arm across the wire and, with his good hand, laboriously pulled himself across the gap. Sergeant Ellenberger followed. The cold, wet, naked men climbed in the only transportation available, an ambulance, and rode back to their platoon area. It was listed as a routine patrol, "without casualties."

MILITARY GOVERNMENT AND DPs

One other job of the line regiments was the maintenance of military government in their sector—duty which was to become increasingly more important and familiar during the next months in Germany and Austria. All of the units, whether in the line or to the rear, were made responsible for the maintenance of their civilian sectors. The Division's reserve regiment, the 502d, though called upon to send several small patrols across the Rhine, undertook the biggest part of the military government.

BILL MAULDIN Copr. 1945 by United Feature Syndicate, Inc.   3-27

"It's best not to speak to paratroopers about saluting. They always ask where you got your boots."

This Mauldin cartoon appeared in Stars and Stripes during the spring of 1945. It was probably the all-time favorite of the paratroopers of the 101st. (Reproduced by courtesy of the copyright owner.)

General Taylor was appointed Military Governor of the district occupied by the 101st and a military government office was set up under the Civil Affairs Officer, Maj. Robert S. Smith. Major Smith and his staff of officers and enlisted men visited the various units and instructed the military government officers who had been appointed by each unit commander to handle affairs within the area for which the unit commander was responsible. The immediate problems were in connection with the camps of displaced people—Poles, Russians, Czechs, Dutch, Italians, French, Belgians, Yugoslavs—people of all countries of Europe who had come, chiefly against their will, to work in Germany. Now they were being held in camps until arrangements could be made to get them back home. The 101st inherited the camps, the people and their problems. As soon as possible the military government officials segregated the DPs according to nationality, registered them, and placed them in former labor camps, monasteries and factories. Food was a problem as well as sanitary arrangements and heat and shelter. As soon as possible these people were sent on back to the rear.

Most of the DPs caused no trouble; they merely took it easy and rejoiced that the years of work for the Germans were over. Their happiness, singing, and willingness to do favors for the soldiers endeared them to the airborne troops. With few exceptions all KP and heavy work outside of punishment and training ended; GI chow alone was enough to command for the rest of the stay in Europe more workers than there was work available. Poles, Russians and Yugoslavs joined companies and batteries in the Ruhr, picked up American phrases, uniforms, friends, profanity, and customs, and some of them parted with the Division only upon the return to France in July. In fact, though strict orders were given that no DPs were to be taken along, some of the personnel unloading from the 40-and-8s in Auxerre spoke very broken English, never appeared in formations, and seemed to do a great deal of kitchen police.

For each DP camp a detail of one airborne officer and at least two enlisted men, one of whom spoke the language of the people in the camp, was provided. Among the DPs one responsible person was chosen to head the camp and he in turn selected a staff to help him; these officials cooperated with and carried out the orders of the American staff. Food was provided by the *Bürgermeisters* of the nearby German communities, though occasionally and for short periods this food had to be supplemented by army rations. Later, UNRRA supplemented special items such as food for babies and clothing. The battalion surgeons were responsible for the health of the camps. In general the

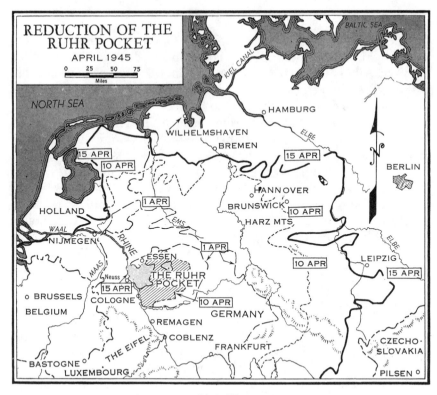

Map. 103.

camps ran not unlike army installations, with work and mess details, daily sick call and curfew.

What trouble there was in the rear areas was generally caused by DPs, sometimes under the influence of liquor and wanting something to eat or wear or deciding to collect from the German population at least a part of the pay due them for two, three, or four years of slave labor. The German civilian population gave little trouble. The Nazi *Bürgermeisters* and officials were replaced by non-Nazis. Those Germans jailed were usually Nazi bigshots, picked up by the Counter-intelligence Corps or turned in by their non-Nazi neighbors, or were people found out after curfew or violating some other military decree. The only incidents which might have had serious results were an explosion in a school just evacuated by 101st troops, an act traced to members of the *Hitler-Jugend,* or youth movement; and the discovery in a town in the Division area of two tons of dynamite. This explosive was believed intended for the use of the German underground Werewolf movement.

The 502d, which was responsible for maintaining military government in the rear area, had the job of operating jeep patrols and enforcing the curfew, guarding power plants, factories and other buildings and installations and maintaining on a continuous alert one motorized rifle company ready to move out at once in case of disturbances. The assignment also allowed, to the disgust of the men, the carrying on of small-unit training. But on the 10th the Division's area of responsibility was considerably enlarged to take in the tri-city of München-Gladbach–Rheydt-Odenkirchen, with the pick of fine billets and five DP camps. The 1st Battalion of the 502d moved into the city. The camps were always a welcome addition during the period of strict enforcement of the non-fraternization rule. Those troopers who could speak Polish, Italian, French or any of the other languages of the camp were in demand as social go-betweens.

The 502d had no monopoly on these camps; there were now thirteen large camps in the Division area. Battery C of the 81st AA Battalion had two of the largest, in Hulchrath and Langwaden; the 326th Engineers had two, in Glehn and near Leidberg; the 327th administered one in Neuss, while the 506th had charge of the camp in Ober-Cassel.

As mid-April came and the Ruhr Pocket was being compressed and liquidated with increasing speed, the shocking news of the death of President Roosevelt was announced. On the 14th memorial services were held in all units. The impact of the President's death was probably greater in the airborne divisions than in any others because of the youthfulness of the men; a majority could hardly remember another President.

Collapse of the Pocket

About this time both the artillery and the line companies began getting limiting lines beyond which artillery and mortar fire were not to be laid; the American forces compressing the Pocket were coming within range. On the afternoon of the 16th, the 303d Infantry Regiment of the 97th Infantry Division, driving north on the far side of the Rhine, reached the town of Baumberg across from the 506th. Two days later the 327th received from the 13th Armored (Black Cat) Division Lt. William J. Manning and two enlisted men of Company E who had been captured while on patrol on the 14th-15th and recaptured by the armored division. The 13th Armored Artillery Headquarters took over control of the 101st's artillery firing except for observed targets and all missions were cleared through them.

The resistance in the Ruhr Pocket ceased even sooner, probably, than General Eisenhower had expected. It had been his plan, if the encircled troops had put up a stout resistance, to hold them with a relatively few divisions and to starve them out. But the German attempts to attack had been beaten back, the ammunition factories one by one quit producing, shortages mounted, and by the 13th it was apparent to the American High Command that the end was near. On the 14th the Pocket was cut in two by the meeting at Hagen of the First and Ninth Armies; and on that day the 101st received a warning order to be prepared to move by rail and truck to the Seventh Army in South Germany. On the 16th the eastern half collapsed and on the 18th all resistance in the Pocket ended. Immense stores of supplies and equipment fell into American hands as well as 325,000 prisoners.

With the end of resistance across the river the 101st began preparing for its next mission. The 94th Division, on the 101st's left, took over the now peaceful river front, the 302d Regiment relieving both the 506th and 327th on the 17th. On the 18th the 94th took over all military government functions in the 101st area. The battalions gathered in their respective areas and waited for movement orders.

The Ruhr Pocket fight and the 101st's contribution was summed up in a commendation addressed by the XXII Corps commander, General Harmon, to General Taylor:

Upon relief of the 101st Airborne Division from attachment to XXII Corps, I wish to express to you and through you to the officers and men of your command my personal thanks and appreciation for the splendid service rendered while under my command.

During the battle of the Ruhr, the Corps, and in particular its frontline divisions, had an unwritten mission of holding the maximum number of troops on the east bank of the Rhine while the Ninth and First Armies completed their encircling maneuvers. That this mission was successfully accomplished is attested by the tremendous prisoner total taken from the Ruhr. All credit for this achievement goes to the gallant men of the 101st and adjacent divisions for their skillful and aggressive patrolling across a most difficult water barrier.

Of equal importance from the Corps standpoint was the Division's complete cooperation in the tasks peculiar to our occupational role. The efficient and painstaking combing of the division area for contraband and the establishment of the basic framework of Military Government contributed greatly to the stabilization of the Corps area.

Your Division has again proved that it is a great fighting machine. Though initially foreseen, I accept its loss to this command with regret. In parting, my headquarters and I wish you Godspeed and continuing success in your next action.

THE 501st's OPERATION JUBILANT

While the rest of the 101st was in the Ruhr and later in South Germany and Austria, one regiment, the 501st, had been left behind at

Mourmelon to prepare for an airborne mission. The mission, Operation Jubilant, was a part of the final mop-up plan, Eclipse. Being similarly held in marshalling areas for other missions under Eclipse were the 13th Airborne Division and the 508th Parachute Infantry Regiment. None of their missions was to come off, and VE-day found the airborne units still waiting at the marshalling areas.

The mission of the 501st was to prepare for and carry out parachute landings on Allied prisoner-of-war camps in Germany. As soon as the 101st pulled out for the Ruhr the 501st began intensive training for its mission. During the first week in April the regimental staff was briefed on the operation. Plans for the regiment were completed by the 501st S-3, Maj. Elvie Roberts, on April 14 and the battalion commanders were briefed the next day.

The regiment was to drop in teams onto eleven prisoner-of-war camps. These drops were to be made only when the German will to fight was so near to collapse that only token resistance would be met. When it was decided that this time had come, advance forces were to drop inside or in the vicinity of the camps with high-powered radios. They would be followed by the main body of the parachutists dropping into the stockades. Following them would come ten gliders per battalion, bringing in supplies, including medicines and food. An additional medical company had been assigned to the regiment as well as a pool of linguists and prisoner-of-war interrogators. Personnel from the 877th and 878th Airborne Aviation Engineer Battalions were also to come in with the 501st.

The No. 1 priority was Offlag (Officers' Camp) IV-C at Saalhaus, Germany, where there were believed to be interned 5 U. S. and 364 British prisoners, many of high diplomatic or political rank. The other camps, all in Germany, were Stalag VII-A at Moosburg with 9,812 U. S. and 7,600 British prisoners; Stalag XI-B, Fallingbostel, 1,500 U. S. and 4,355 British; Stalag IV-B, Muhlberg, 4,500 U. S. and 10,019 British; Stalag Luft I, Barth-Vogelsang, 5,391 U. S. and 7,300 British; Stalag 383, Hohenfels, 5,929 U. S. and 5,366 British; Stalag III-A, Luckenwald, 6,000 U. S. and 4,666 British; Stalag XIII-D, Langwasser, 5,000 U. S. and British; Stalag XI-A, Altengrabow, 12 U. S. and 4,069 British; Stalag II-A, Neubrandenburg, 2,965 U. S. and 200 British; and three camps west of Westertimke, Marlag, Milag and Dulag with a total of 6,000 U. S. and 9,272 British.

The operation posed some unique problems, especially of administration. The drop would have had the one regiment scattered over a 500-mile area and the regimental command group would necessarily have to be with one of the battalions. Control would be by radio and each battalion would bring in by glider a high-powered 199 set. Morning and strength reports, it was tentatively decided, were to be picked up daily by fast photo-reconnaissance planes. Another point of interest was that when the regiment was detached from the 101st it was attached for operational control to the First Allied Airborne Army and for administration to Oise Base Section. Thus it was a regiment working directly with two large and separate headquarters, bypassing the usual division and corps channels.

South Germany and Austria

When the Ruhr Pocket collapsed the American armies had already pushed the nearest German forces more than a hundred miles east of it. Now the Central Group of Armies, General Bradley's 12th Army Group, was a few miles from the Elbe River and almost in contact with the westward driving Russians; and the U. S. Third Army of this group had penetrated into Czechoslovakia. On the left Field Marshal Montgomery's 21st Army Group had cut through to the North Sea, isolating the German forces in Holland, and was driving for Bremen, Hamburg, the German coast, and Denmark. On the right General Devers' 6th Army Group was closing in on the German "National Redoubt."

It was in this National Redoubt that the Nazis would, it was generally believed, try to make their last stand. Even when Hitler and his closest henchmen, after the cutting in two of the Reich, stayed in Berlin in the northern segment it was still believed that the area around Berchtesgaden would be the scene of the Third Reich's *Götterdämmerung*. General Eisenhower in his report on the war described the situation and the Redoubt:

Although the Redoubt was not, therefore, to be the last seat of the Nazi government, the possibility remained that it would still be the scene of a desperate stand by the fanatical elements of the armies south of the dividing line, together with those which might retreat northward out of Italy. These armies, totaling about 100 nominal divisions, included the bulk of the remaining German armored and SS formations and up to 30 panzer divisions, and might conceivably be concentrated behind the mountain barriers. In addition, most of the surviving German jet fighter plane strength was located in the south . . .

Extending some 240 miles in length and 80 miles in depth, the Redoubt comprised the western half of Austria, with small portions of Germany to the north and Italy to the south. It was bounded on the north by the Bavarian Plains, on the south by the Dolomites and Carnic Alps, on the west by the Swiss frontier and the Rhine Valley, and on the east by the Lageneurt Basin and the eastern extremity of the Niedere Tauern. Within it lay Berchtesgaden and Hitler's "Eagle's Nest."

The whole area was extremely mountainous and thus unsuitable for large-scale airborne operations, while the roads into it followed narrow valleys which could easily be held by determined defenders.

After the fall of the Redoubt an examination of the country and interrogation of the German generals revealed little evidence that any real planning or preparation had been made for a last stand there. But the attacking troops didn't know this at the time; they were only amazed at the lack of resistance and wondered when the much advertised positions on which the Germans were to stand would be reached.

Attacking this area were the two armies making up General Devers'

721

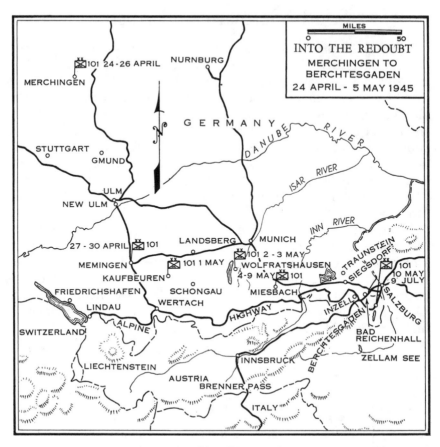

Map 104.

6th Army Group, the U. S. Seventh and the French First. When the orders came which sent the 101st from the Fifteenth Army of General Bradley's 12th Army Group to the Seventh Army it was a repetition of the move made exactly three months before when the Division had gone from Bastogne in General Bradley's sector south to General Devers.'

When the 101st was relieved along the Rhine, General Taylor sent for his commanders. The day before he had flown to the new front. Now he briefed them on what he had seen and learned. The following notes were taken on his briefings:

Seventh Army front is generally a little bit south of east. XV Corps is its left boundary, and then XXI Corps and VI Corps. The going is very difficult, generally strong on the right flank and gradually easier on the left. There are large numbers of German divisions on the front of the Army—an estimated 18,000 men. The previous day they took 6,000 prisoners so actually it cut down the

plane, from the Germans, anywhere it could, just so it could keep moving. Sometimes the tanks were able to use the excellent *Autobahn*, the broad highway Hitler had built for his own military movements. Occasionally they ran onto German fighter planes using these long lanes for flight strips.

An estimate of the German strength, issued at this time by VI Corps, reads as follows:

The VI Corps zone is at present being defended by an estimated 6,500 enemy and includes the following major formations: Elements of the 559th Division (100 men), elements of the 246th Volksgrenadier Division (500 men), the 198th Volksgrenadier Division with an estimated strength of 1,600, the 553d Volksgrenadier Division with 1,500 men, elements of the 9th Volksgrenadier Division (800 men), and a battle group of the 719th Volksgrenadier Division (300 men). There is also the usual array of replacement, alarm and heterogeneous abortions—the 380th Replacement Battalion with 100 men, the 151st Alarm Battalion with 300 men, the Battle Group Mockross, which was formerly attached to the 212th Volksgrenadier Division and has an estimated 300 men, and the Battle Group Rossenheim with 300 men.

It should be kept in mind that all of these larger formations are in a pitiful state of deterioration and disorganized to the point where they function as a division in name only. In his present precarious situation the enemy is not believed to have any reserves in the VI Corps sector. On the other hand reinforcements or replacements will probably dribble in and continue to diminish. . . . To what extent the OKW [Wehrmacht High Command] will be able to cope with this situation remains to be observed. The amazing elasticity and ability of German commanders to muster critical replacements, as shown in the past, is no longer extant. However, they probably will gather together all possible manpower and fight until crushing and final defeat.

The enemy in his present situation can only hope to preserve his existence, maintain a cohesive line and put off the indubitable end.

For the most part, the 101st's war was over. No matter how often the units moved the Germans had generally moved faster and there was no contact. On the 26th the advance echelon of Division Headquarters moved out of Merchingen and the next day the Division began following south to the vicinity of Memmingen in Bavaria. Memmingen had been captured on the 26th by the 44th Division and 3,336 Allied prisoners of war, including 504 Americans, held near there had been freed. In the distance the snow-topped Alps were visible. In the unbombed towns—as the fighting drew into the mountains the traces of war damage became increasingly less—the troops moved into clean, often modern, houses and took hot showers. Every house seemed to have a white sheet flying as a surrender token. The comfortable German kitchens with their stainless steel and porcelain stoves became the social centers and most of the platoon life centered about the stove, adorned with boiling coffee and frying eggs, and with a radio, borrowed from the living room, on a nearby shelf.

As the Division CP moved into Memmingen the 506th moved out toward Landsberg, about forty miles east of Memmingen and halfway to Munich with the mission of securing the roads in that area and of protecting the VI Corps left, or east, flank. Here on the 28th the 506th relieved the 411th Infantry Regiment of General McAuliffe's 103d (Cactus) Division. The 10th Armored Division had captured Landsberg the day before. The town contained the fortress prison in which Hitler had been imprisoned after his unsuccessful Munich *Putsch* of 1923. His cell had become a shrine and over the door was a bronze plaque (which quickly disappeared to souvenir hunters):

Here a dishonorable system imprisoned Germany's greatest son from November 11, 1923, to December 20, 1924. During this time Adolf Hitler wrote the book of the National Socialist Revolution, *Mein Kampf*.

But even more impressive remembrances of Hitler and the National Socialist Revolution were in the town. Six concentration camps showed the paratroopers that the things they had heard for years but perhaps only half-believed were true. Here were the skeletonized bodies, not in pictures but lying on the ground behind the barbed wire—of Jews, Russians, Poles, French, non-Nazi Germans—three hundred dead in one camp and six hundred more near-dead wandering aimlessly around. There were terrible-smelling remains of people who had been burned alive. Maj. Leo Schweiter, an unusually cool observer, whose job as Assistant G-2 and later G-2 had taken him to many scenes of violence and death between Normandy and Berchtesgaden, became for the first time physically sick at what he saw. Those men who saw the camps would never forget them.

As the kill drew nearer the tasks assigned the Division changed almost from day to day, and often the pace of the war made them meaningless as the Germans retreated faster than the troops could move forward to carry them out. Within the Seventh Army, VI Corps, to which the 101st was attached, was the right or westernmost corps, being bounded on the left by XXI Corps and on the right by the French First Army. Besides the 101st, VI Corps had the 44th and 103d Divisions. The Corps was driving south toward Innsbruck and the famous passageway from Germany into Italy, the Brenner Pass.

When the month ended the 506th was in the Landsberg area protecting the VI Corps left flank, the 502d was en route from Memmingen to the vicinity of Wertach, about forty miles south of Memmingen,

Landsberg concentration camp taken over by the 506th on 28 April. Shown here are inmates starved or burned to death.

and the 327th was still closing in from the Merchingen area to the vicinity of Schongau, twenty miles south of Landsberg. For a division which had once fought ringed about a single Belgian town the distances —more than two hundred miles between the foremost and rearmost echelons—were breath-taking.

On May Day the Division CP moved again, this time from Memmingen thirty miles west to the town of Kaufbeuren. On this day also the 502d took over the protection of VI Corps' right flank, relieving the 324th Infantry Regiment of the 44th Division of the sector from Wertach to Kempten, about fifteen miles north toward Memmingen. The 506th began policing the Corps' rear areas for by-passed enemy groups, and the 327th finished closing into the Schongau area. The rest of the Division was scattered all the way back to Merchingen.

Now along the highways, marked here and there by charred vehicles and abandoned guns, the airborne troops saw again the signs of confusion they had witnessed in the first days of the Bulge in Belgium, but this time the disaster threatening was even more terrible and directed toward the enemy. The Division and the units of the Division were closing in on new CPs only to send out advance parties immediately to set up even farther ahead. Sometimes the main body came up to their new area only to find it already abandoned and word left to keep coming. As the trucks, DUKWs and every other sort of vehicle carried the 101st onward an even more numerous stream of soldiers passed going the other way. The *Wehrmacht* was moving back to the prison cages, in small groups, in long streams of men, in trucks, on foot, sometimes unguarded or under watch of armed DPs.

727

German prisoners move back to the 101st POW stockade at Miesbach.

The DPs were also on the move and walked or hitched rides until they were finally shunted to collecting camps. Some of them were released prisoners of war wearing old pieces of their French, Polish, Belgian or Russian uniforms; and some of them were badly starved and were terrible to see.

On the German side there was chaos. Divisions and regiments lost their identities. Resistance came from battle groups made up of from ten to five hundred men collected from all kinds of units and led by the highest-ranking officer or noncom. The resistance they offered was usually token, consisting of firing a few shots, blowing bridges and then dropping back until they finally surrendered. The increasingly high mountains and the few roads which channeled through narrow valleys could have made even this resistance tough if they had not realized that there was little point in further fighting. Both sides, in the houses in which they were living out the last of the war, listened to the radio news which hour after hour, day and night, told in a half-dozen languages the story of the disintegration of one of the most feared armies of history.

During the 2d the 101st, the corps' reserve division, continued to police the rear areas, beating woods and the barns for *Wehrmacht* stragglers and deserters and waiting for their meager transportation to haul them on forward. The assumption that an airborne division would be used for special missions and therefore could get along with less transportation than regular infantry divisions had always been a sore point whenever the 101st had been committed as ground troops. The transportation shortage never was more apparent than now during the rat race through the Alps. What trucks there were were shuttling back and forth but were still unable to keep the entire Division up near the fighting. There was an increasing amount of unofficial transportation ranging from bicycles to *Wehrmacht* trucks and civilian touring cars but these means were not reliable for large-scale movements. Sergeant Koskimaki made these notes covering the period.

May 1: Moved southeast to Kaufbeuren. Passed long lines of liberated Czech, Russian and Polish prisoners. Radio says Hitler is dead. Almost a blizzard out today. *May 2:* More snow falling. The last fighting and the last Germans in Italy surrendered today. The Company moved forward again today but Walker, Kennedy, Goosson and I stayed behind. *May 3:* Kennedy and I went out "scrounging" on his motor bike. Germans surrendering by regiments and divisions now.

Meanwhile, on the 2d the 101st was ordered from the VI Corps to the neighboring XXI Corps, commanded by Maj. Gen. Frank W.

Milburn. The move was ordered completed by the 4th; however, because of lack of transportation the war was to be over several days before the last of the 101st could come into the XXI Corps area. The Division CP moved from Kaufbeuren to Wolfratshausen, a town in the XXI Corps area twenty miles south of Munich. The nearest Division troops to the XXI Corps, the 506th, also began moving into the new Corps area that day, assembling in the vicinity of Miesbach, east and south of Wolfratshausen. It was at this time and from this area that the 506th received and carried out the 101st's last combat mission of the war.

THE LAST COMBAT MISSION

The mission, as assigned, was for the 506th to capture Berchtesgaden. What Berlin was to the troops in North Germany, Berchtesgaden had become to those in the south—a city tied up with Hitler and the Nazi rulers. For weeks the rumors had named it the last-stand capital of the Reich. (Actually, Goering had sent Hitler, trapped by his own stubbornness in Berlin, a message suggesting that Der Führer turn over the rule to him, Goering, in Berchtesgaden. This infuriated Hitler and he had ordered Goering's arrest.) It was believed to be full of big-shot Nazis, souvenirs, and not too well defended. Therefore there was more than the usual expectancy among Colonel Sink's paratroopers when, on the night of the 3d, the orders came to take on extra ammunition and rations and move out by truck at 0600 the next morning along the Salzburg *Autobahn* to the town containing Hitler's home and Eagle's Nest.

Early on the 4th the 506th, accompanied by Battery A of the 321st FA Battalion and the 1st Platoon of Battery A, 81st AA Battalion, and with four of the new recoilless 75mm rifles from the 377th Battalion took off east over the splendid Munich–Salzburg *Autobahn*. They crossed the Inn River near Rosenheim, skirted the beautiful Chiem-See, and finally reached the crossroads at Siegsdorf, fifty miles from Miesbach. Here they turned right on the most direct route to Berchtesgaden. About eight or nine miles down this road at the village of Inzell they ran into the tail of a column of stalled tanks from Combat Command V of the French 2d Armored Division, the first division to enter Paris. With the tanks was the Division's famed commander, Gen. Jacques Philippe Leclerc. A look up the road told the story— the Germans had blown a bridge over one of the deep ravines and the French had no bridging material. Fortunately, the 506th had plenty of Bailey bridge units and began constructing a crossing. This was

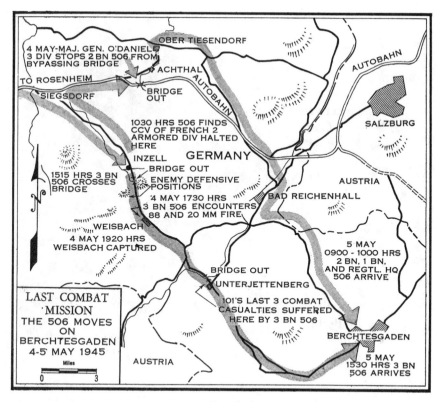

Map 105.

not as simple a process as it might have been, for on the far side and high up in the snow the Germans had set up .50-caliber and possibly 20mm guns and were laying plunging fire on the bridge builders. So the paratroopers had to climb down the steep sides of the ravine, cross the mountain creek, and climb hundreds of feet upward to take care of die-hard defenders.

Since it was going to take some time to get across the gap and there was reason to believe that other bridges farther along the road were also out Colonel Sink decided to divide his regiment and send one battalion, the 2d, back up to the *Autobahn,* east on that highway to the turnoff to Bad Reichenhall, and then through Bad Reichenhall and by that back way into Berchtesgaden. Colonel Strayer about-faced his battalion, headed back to the *Autobahn,* and was proceeding uneventfully down it until he came to a blown bridge. This was not a serious roadblock because there was a by-pass along a dirt road through the 3d Division area. At the head of this road, though, was a block in the person of the 3d Division's commander, Maj. Gen. John W.

731

The 1st Battalion, 506th, enters Berchtesgaden on the morning of 5 May 1945.

O'Daniel, which no bridging material could cross. There just weren't enough roads that day; a message received by XXI Corps offered the explanation: "Everybody and his brother are trying to get into the town."

At 1558 that day a motorized column entered Berchtesgaden; and that evening the 7th Infantry Regiment of the 3d Division entered. When General O'Daniel received the message of his regiment's entrance he lifted his ban, allowed the 101st to come over his road, and Colonel Strayer followed the 7th Regiment's route. The 1st Battalion of the 506th, still at the Inzell bridge, turned about and followed the 2d Battalion down the *Autobahn* and through Bad Reichenhall to Berchtesgaden. This left Colonel Patch's 3d Battalion to finish the bridge and move on to Berchtesgaden by the Regiment's original route. There were other bridges out and altogether the battalion had to construct three large bridges. They got into Berchtesgaden on the afternoon of the 5th. On the way the Battalion lost three men, Pvt. Nick Kozovosky of Headquarters Company and Pfc. Claude E. Rankin of Company H, killed in action, and Pfc. William C. Knox of Company I, wounded. These were the last combat casualties of the Division. Battery A of the 321st FA Battalion, which came into Berchtesgaden with the 506th's

732

Berchtesgaden. The high mountain in the background is the Watzmann.

3d Battalion, had at 1800 on the 4th fired three white phosphorus rounds to neutralize a German 88mm firing on the advancing paratroopers; these were the last combat rounds fired by the Division's artillery.

It was in Berchtesgaden, on May 6, while preparing to move south to the Bruck–Zell-am-See area that the 506th received the following message:

Effective immediately all troops will stand fast on present positions. German Army Group G in this sector has surrendered. No firing on Germans unless fired upon. Notify French units in vicinity. Full details, to be broadcast, will be issued by SHAEF.

Alles Kaput

During this time the 502d in the Kempten area was marking time, comfortably established in the best houses in the occupied villages, and waiting word to move up. On the 3d there was a flurry of excitement and some of the companies prepared to move on Berchtesgaden the next morning. At daylight DUKWs and trucks were spotted in the village streets and the troops were packed and ready; but the order to move out never came, the news of Berchtesgaden's fall was later announced, and the DUKWs and trucks moved out empty.

The most the 502d saw of the war at this time was prisoners coming down into the villages. The regimental after-action report for the period runs: "*May 1*, 1,400 prisoners taken; *May 2*, 1,510 prisoners; *May 3*, 1,400 prisoners; *May 4*, 900 prisoners; *May 5*, number of prisoners unknown; *May 6*, lost count of prisoners." Actually, these prisoners represented no effort on the part of the 502d, most of them streaming down from the 44th Division front. The long lines would trudge from village to village, stopping upon command and patiently spreading out their possessions for the inspection of the souvenir hunters. Some of the very young and very old of the *Volkssturm* were unofficially told to go on home; the rest went on to the PW cages. When the war was officially over on the 7th the Division had counted 14,935 prisoners for the week.

Sergeant Koskimaki recorded his view of the last days of the war from his vantage point in the Division CP:

May 4: Once more we moved. We are south of Munich at Miesbach [the CP having moved there that day from Wolfratshausen], only eighteen miles from Austria and about forty-five miles from Hitler's hideout. *May 5:* We are living in a large German hotel that originally housed some of the Wehrmacht. Most of the boys have either a car or a motorcycle. *May 6:* The German Army Group in front of our Division has surrendered. I sent the 506th a message to stop their advance. *May 7:* German radio announced that the Armistice was signed at 0241 this morning. No reports have come out at Supreme Allied Headquarters. Sorrells and Neils piled up a motorcycle. *May 8:* Today the official announcement came out saying the war is over in Europe. It didn't have any effect on our boys because the war is only half over.

It did have this effect on the soldiers on both sides and on the civilians. For the first time in years the Germans could leave their shades up at night and let the light shine out; and so could the troops. So ingrained had become the blackout that it took all concerned several days to overcome the instinct to hide any light. For the troops it marked, though this was gradual on the conqueror's side, a successive turning in and no longer having to carry or wear the gas mask, the steel helmet and, finally, the rifle or carbine.

The surrender of German Army Group G—the Group mentioned by Sergeant Koskimaki—ended the fighting in the XXI Corps area. There were still back in the mountains armed forces who wanted to do their own parleying about terms. The negotiations with the largest group to surrender to the 101st—the XIII SS Corps—is recorded in the Division Diary. A verbatim account of the discussion held in Miesbach on the afternoon of May 7 between General Taylor and his interpreter, Lieutenant Peter Frank, and the German General Hans Berger and his interpreter, a German colonel, follows:

General Taylor: Tell the general I am General Taylor, commanding the 101st Airborne Division.

[The colonel's interpreter conveyed the message to General Berger.]

General Taylor: I have just received a telegram from higher authority which reads as follows:

"A representative of the German High Command signed the unconditional surrender of all German land, sea, and air forces in Europe to the Allied Expeditionary Forces and simultaneously to the Soviet High Command at 0141 hours central European time, 7 May, under which all forces will cease active operations at 0001B hours 9 May. Effective immediately all offensive operations by all Expeditionary Army forces will cease and troops will remain in present positions. Moves involved in occupational duties will continue. Due to difficulties of communication there may be some delay in similar orders reaching enemy troops so full defensive precautions will be taken. All informed down to and including divisions, tactical air commands and groups, base sections, and equivalent. No repeat no release will be made to the press pending announcement to the heads of the three government. Signed: EISENHOWER."

In other words as of today representatives have surrendered simultaneously all air, sea and land forces of the German Army, with the hour to take place at 0001 on the 9th of May. In other words the general can be assured that complete surrender has been agreed upon at that time.

That is the advance text of the terms of surrender. [*Hands it to the German general.*]

I am prepared to receive the general's surrender under those conditions.

German colonel: The general is coming to tell you that he was not charged with the running of the prisoners in this camp. That the high officers fled from the camp and are in Switzerland now.

General Taylor: Does he have a list of the officers? [*List of prisoners in camp given to General Taylor.*] They are safe in Switzerland now?

German colonel: Yes. The safety of those officers was not possible to take, however.

General Taylor: There are the terms. What does he propose to do about them?

German colonel: We are assembling our men.

General Taylor: Is he prepared to work out the details with them of the surrender?

German colonel: The general asked if it is possible to fix a point to make up his staff to assist.

General Taylor: I am prepared to do so now. The time is up at 0001 on the 9th and if it is not met with, he is responsible for the consequences. Does the general wish to discuss the details of the surrender of his troops?

German colonel: Yes. He says that the details of the surrender itself are not possible by him alone as he is a representative of the SS Replacement Army, and he came with details of the prisoners and other details.

General Taylor: I want it understood that he is to make it known to his troops that if they don't surrender by that time, we will resume the offensive.

German colonel: He says that is no trouble.

General Taylor: Can his staff officers, who are prepared to discuss the details, come to my headquarters tomorrow to discuss them?

German colonel: Yes.

General Taylor: We will arrange for Cólonel McClellan, CO, 101st Cavalry Group, to bring your staff back to this headquarters after meeting at an appointed spot in Colonel McClellan's area. What else would the general like to discuss?

German colonel: The general seems to be worried about the pay problem of the prisoners in this area. He suggests a small staff of German-Americans to work out the last details of administration.

General Taylor: We will take care of that and all details after we have come to surrender terms.

German colonel: He says the papers are very scattered and the problem is connected with his job. He says it is a question of everything connected with war prisoners. He was charged with sums that have not been disbursed or distributed to people who have earned them.

General Taylor: Tell him when he surrenders we will turn it over to proper people who will work together with him on these details of which I have no authority.

German colonel: In the Linz area there are approximately 48,000 soldiers. In the St. Polten–Semmering–Linz area there is a Corps of 44,000 Cossacks, and 8,000 men in Czechoslovakia. These men were willing to fight with the German Army.

General Taylor: What is the force in our immediate area?

German colonel: The last remains of divisions. The 17th SS Panzer and two others.

General Taylor: And numerically how many is that?

German colonel: Not more than 3,000. He wants us to note the 44,000 Cossacks. He says that he feels it his duty to make known the whereabouts of these troops because if they fall into the Russian hands they will be eradicated and much blood shed. Roughly there are 16,000 Serbs, 20,000 Ukrainians, 9,000 civilian women and children.

General Taylor: Where is that exactly? [*Colonel Charles Chase left to obtain a map of the whole continent.*]

Lieutenant Frank: Is Marshal Kesselring still alive?

German colonel: We saw him three days ago.

General Taylor: We had just heard that he was captured. The report just came in.

German colonel: Four days ago the general spoke with Field Marshal Kesselring.

General Taylor: Tell the general I am concerned if the troops know of the surrender. Does he have means of notifying them, such as radio, messenger, etc.?

German colonel: Ninety-nine per cent is done. Within the Corps it will be done without fail; most of them have already been told.

General Taylor: Tell the general that today we are sending out patrols under white flags and that they are to get through; otherwise we are going to send in tactical units.

German colonel: That is understood. All our troops know they are not to make resistance any more.

[*Colonel Chase returned with the map and the German general pointed out the area referred to before where the 44,000 people are.*]

General Taylor: Tell the general I will inform higher authority of the location.

German colonel: He will be very obliged if you will mention that to the high command because there will be very much blood shed if not.

General Taylor: Tomorrow we will work out the details of the surrender of the troops in our own area. Colonel McClellan will arrange for an appointed spot for the general and his staff to meet at eight o'clock in the morning and from there will be escorted up here to make the arrangements. Meanwhile the troops should be billeted in villages; their arms taken away from them and placed in a designated place. He will establish which troops are under his command and if he is not the actual physical commander of others, to have staff officers of those units down here with him. In other words he will have down here a representative of all three divisions.

German colonel: He will have the chief in command of all three.

General Taylor: Ask the general what his personal intentions are. When the time comes I will have him escorted to Army Headquarters.

Three paratroopers and a fire engine figured in another surrender. The paratroopers, S/Sgt. William H. Bowen, Jr. and Pvts. Harry A. Barker and McFarlan Barnson, late in the evening of May 6 found a big oil-burning fire engine, "with all the gadgets ever invented for fighting fires." They thought the big truck would be just the thing for their transportation-shy platoon. They began to throw off the unnecessary gadgets; then they found the oil supply was low. Starting out—they were several miles southwest of Berchtesgaden—they drove down the highway hunting diesel oil. Finally, seventeen miles from Berchtesgaden and just over the Austrian border near the settlement of Hirschbichl they came to a blown bridge. Sergeant Bowen started on foot across the foundations; in the dark he felt something poke him in the ribs and heard a German command to put his hands up. In a moment all three paratroopers were facing the burp gun and trying, unsuccessfully, to convince its holder that the war was over.

The German prodded the Americans toward a farmhouse. Inside they found a houseful of SS troops, including several officers. From the rank there they guessed they were in something higher than a company or battalion CP.

The paratroopers were able to half-convince the Germans that the war was over. They asked if they could be taken to a higher-ranking German officer; they could. While Sergeant Bowen and Private Barker were held in the room, Barnson, who could speak some German, was taken to the ranking officer, Lt. Gen. Theodor Tolsdorf, commander of the German LXXXII Corps.

General Tolsdorf, whose corps had shrunk to about 1,200 men from the 36th, 416th and 256th Volksgrenadier Divisions with a few scattered *Wehrmacht, Luftwaffe* and SS units, was an interesting character.

At this wrecked bridge Staff Sgt. William H. Bowen, Jr., and Pvts. Harry A. Barker and McFarlan Barnson were captured on the night of 6 May. The jeeps belong to the 101st party which came up on 7 May to arrange surrender terms with General Tolsdorf.

Thirty-five years old, a Prussian, he had in his eleven years in the army almost set a record for advancement. He had been wounded eleven times, had most of the German awards for bravery, and had earned among his troops the nickname of "Tolsdorf the Mad" because of his recklessness with their lives and his own. He was said to go on patrols for prisoners and to drive his own motorcycle. The ranks of his division were supposed to have been refilled and destroyed three times since the Ardennes. At the time of the Ardennes he had commanded the 340th Volksgrenadier Division which on January 3, to the east of Bastogne, had come up against the 101st. The 340th had been one of the 101st's chief opponents in the bitter fighting in the Bois Jacques and around Foy and Noville, and the 101st had helped empty the

General Tolsdorf, second from left, surrenders his LXXXII Corps to Colonel Sink.

Volksgrenadiers ranks. Tolsdorf himself at the time had had a foot badly injured by an artillery round.

In the roomful of SS troops Sergeant Bowen and Private Barker carried on an all-night conversation with an English-speaking lieutenant. It was mostly a brag session, the German talking up the 88 while the paratroopers extolled the 75, the Germans pointing out the quality of the *Luftwaffe* while the Americans did the same for the AAF, and so on, until 0600 came, along with Private Barnson and General Tolsdorf.

Tolsdorf sent Barnson and Barker back to Berchtesgaden to bring out a surrender party; the ranking man, Sergeant Bowen, was kept as a hostage. The two privates crossed the bridge and tried to start the fire engine; it wouldn't. So they hit the road at double-time and double-time they went all the way to Berchtesgaden. At 1040 a jeep came up to the bridge. In it were Barnson and Barker, the 506th 3d Battalion S-3, Capt. Joseph B. Doughty, Lt. Perrin Walker of Company G, and an interpreter from Division. As they came in sight a German colonel standing with Sergeant Bowen said in English: "Looks like we can all go home now."

The initial negotiations were entered into without formality between General Tolsdorf (who thought he deserved somebody higher than a captain) and Captain Doughty. Later in the morning Colonel Sink

739

arrived and accepted the corps surrender, to be effective at 1200 the 8th of May. He ordered Tolsdorf to collect his weapons and ammunition and leave them at designated spots. Tolsdorf was then to form his troops and, with whatever transportation, kitchens and food supplies· he had, march them to Melleck, a German border town to the north.

Meanwhile the three 506th firemen climbed into a jeep and went back to Berchtesgaden.

The style in which the Germans expected to surrender was made clear when Tolsdorf and his staff came down in thirty-one vehicles, loaded with personal baggage, liquor, cigars and cigarettes. There were also plenty of accompanying girl friends. One officer even tried to trade his own pistol for an American .45. That day began what must have been a series of disillusioning days for these troops.

The period during which these surrenders were being negotiated and carried out was rather weird, especially to the combat veterans. The only German soldiers they had ever seen had either been armed and therefore prime targets, or prisoners. Now they found themselves walking guard beside armed Germans, possibly black-uniformed SS troops. For higher headquarters had set up the highway which ran north and south through Rosenheim as a surrender line: all German soldiers found west of that line were to be called prisoners of war and were to be sent on back to the PW cages; all troops east of the highway were to be formed into groups with the senior officer in charge, acting more or less as camp commander and being responsible for the feeding of the group. The local surrender terms allowed each German division to keep one hundred rifles and thirty rounds of ammunition per rifle until all personnel, arms and equipment were gathered. There was much elaborate ignoring of each other as the airborne troops moved into the same towns and villages (a signal for the German troops to move out of the houses and into the barns or schools). When squads and details passed each other there were, along with sidewise stares of interest, attempts to maintain step and rhythm which pleased the more drill-minded officers on both side.

BAGGING THE BIGWIGS

Though individual troops for weeks continued to come down out of the mountains and even straggle over the Alps from Italy the bulk of the Germans was collected in the first few days of the peace. But not so the individual German military and political big-shots. The Berchtesgaden area had been a place of final refuge and for weeks the hunting remained good. Any GI might make a name for himself by turning up Hitler or Himmler and there was no lack of amateur detecting. The 101st picked up its share of disguised Nazi leaders, including two of the twenty-four who went on trial at Nürnberg.

The roundup started on a note of comedy. Field Marshal Albert Kesselring, Commander-in-Chief of the German Armies, a first-rate prize for anybody, was sitting in his private nine-car train, *The Brunswick,* at Saalfelden, north of Zell am See. Camped around the train were his own armed troops, paratroopers from the 506th (who, directed by a message from General Taylor to Colonel Sink had got to Kesselring first), troops from the 116th Cavalry Reconnaissance Squadron of the 101st Cavalry Group, and a captain from the 3d Division who was trying very hard but unsuccessfully to get the general. There were also rumors that some die-hard SS were trying to get in on grabbing the general. German MPs tried to keep the jeep traffic straight, a colonel from XXI Corps tried to keep the captors straight, and two helmeted and armed Germans at the door of the railroad car snapped to attention whenever a newspaper correspondent entered to interview the unsurrendered general.

On the 10th, after two days of negotiations, Kesselring surrendered to General Taylor. He and his staff were brought to Berchtesgaden and at first installed in the Berchtesgaden Hof, the hotel later used as a rest center for the Division officers. These captives were identified by white arm bands and were allowed to carry pistols; several of them ran into airborne troops who were more souvenir- than protocol-conscious and a notice had to be put out that these officers, as well as certain civilian police, were entitled to carry sidearms.

Though the biggest prizes of whom the 101st could say "we seen him first" were taken by the 502d, an even greater prize, the second most important Nazi, Hermann Goering, had been assigned to Colonel Sink in the same message that sent him after Kesselring; but it turned out to be a false lead and the 36th Infantry Division got Hermann. And the glory of finding the No. 1 Nazi, Adolf Hitler himself, for half a day hovered over Company C of the 502d after they found his body in the woods above Hutte; then the battalion surgeon went up, took a look at the two-weeks corpse and declared it a woman.

The second fish caught by the 101st was Doctor Robert Ley, leader of the Nazi Labor Front and the Strength Through Joy movement. On the morning of May 16 a priest from Schleching, Germany, brought Capt. Neil J. Sweeney, commanding officer of Company B of the 502d, a note stating that Ley had been seen going into a house in that village. Captain Sweeney, his first sergeant, William

Nazi Minister of Labor Robert Ley on his way to Division Headquarters between Pfc. Robert Guggenheim and Lt. Walter Rice, both of the 1st Battalion, 502d.

Odum, his interpreter, Pfc. Peter Rosenfelder, and Pvt. Aloysius P. Meenan drove the five miles from the company CP in Marquartstein, found the house, a shoemaker's, and entered. On the third floor they found Ley asleep. As they pulled him out of the bed he grabbed a small bottle and tried to drink from it; they took it away and threw it out of the window. When told to get dressed the prisoner stalled and denied that he was Ley, though Rosenfelder, who was a native of Germany, told him to quit stalling, that he had seen him many times in Munich. His hemming and hawing became too much for the paratroopers who said, "To· hell with you; if you don't want to get dressed, come as you are." Because it was cool outside they threw him a coat, hat and a pair of shoes. Besides the clothes there was nothing else in the room except a pistol and a few rings.

In Marquartstein the local *Bürgermeister* identified Ley who became very angry and called the *Bürgermeister* a traitor to Germany; the *Bürgermeister* in turn blew his stack and told the Nazi it was the likes of him who had got the country into the shape it was in. Captain Sweeney then sent his prisoner to regimental headquarters at Kossen, Austria, where he was turned over to the 502d's prisoner-of-war interrogator, Capt. Joseph Pangerl, Jr.

The individual was brought into my office for interrogation [wrote Captain

Franz Xavier Schwarz (seated), *Treasurer of the Nazi Party, and his son Franz, shortly after they were captured by the 506th.*

Pangerl]. His appearance—he wore only a pair of pajamas with an old overcoat thrown over them, German Army shoes and a soft grey hat pulled low over his eyes. He had a several days' growth of stubble beard and looked very morose and haggard. His expression was one of contempt and disdain not unmixed with some fear, but he kept aloof and remained silent for the most part. Upon being questioned by myself as to his identity he at first remained silent, merely shrugging his shoulders. This I later believed meant that he thought he had not been definitely identified as Dr. Ley and as such would refuse to speak to anyone unless they were of sufficient rank to warrant his answer. As I did not pointedly address him as Dr. Ley he evidently thought that he might not yet be identified and would be released. He now began to talk and told me in a sullen tone that he was a certain Dr. Distelmeyer, a research chemist on dehydrated foods. He claimed glumly to have escaped from the Russian lines around Vienna and was now trying to make his way back to his home in Düsseldorf. When I questioned him regarding his lack of identification he claimed to have destroyed this to avoid recognition by the Russians. His German and manner of speaking and action indicated, however, that he might very easily be Dr. Ley so I called in a German Army colonel, who was then stationed in Kossen, to

743

Julius Streicher, notorious anti-Semite, listens to Lt. Col. Paul Danahy, 101st's G-2. Streicher, caught by the 502d, was later hung at Nürnberg. At the right is Lt. Peter Frank, member of the "Incredible Patrol" in Holland.

identify Dr. Ley. The colonel looked at him carefully and then said he did not recognize the man. (Later, however, upon my return from Berchtesgaden, I called him in and asked him why he had refused to acknowledge Ley; he replied that his sense of duty forbade him at the time from doing so in front of Ley.)

Lieutenant Walter Rice and one enlisted man were given me by Colonel Chappuis to aid in guarding Dr. Ley while he was being driven to Berchtesgaden. Ley's only comment during the entire hour and a half trip was a request to drive more slowly because of a claimed weak heart.

Upon arriving in Berchtesgaden I left Lt. Rice on guard and went into the G-2 offices. Telling Major Schweiter of the capture I asked if he had a book on German war criminals. Major Schweiter produced a book and opened it to Dr. Ley's picture which, though taken under much different circumstances, had all the facial characteristics of the captured individual. Major Schweiter and I walked out to the jeep around which a crowd had by now gathered and pictures were being taken of the captive. The photograph in the war criminals book definitely identified him as Dr. Ley.

In the CP Ley was recognized by two prisoners taken by the 506th, Franz Xavier Schwarz, Treasurer of the Nazi Party, and Schwarz's son, Franz. Later, while being questioned, Ley tried to swallow poison which he had hidden on him. After two more unsuccessful attempts at suicide he finally managed, during the trials at Nürnberg, to hang himself while sitting on the toilet in his cell.

A week after Ley's capture an anonymous phone call sent the 502d S-2, Maj. Henry Plitt, Capt. Hugh Roberts, Cpl. Victor R. Nelson and Pfc. Howard Hartley to a farmhouse near Waldring. There they found

744

a painter by the name of Sailor enthusiastically applying paint to canvas and disclaiming any interest in or knowledge of politics. When Major Plitt accused him of being Julius Streicher, high-ranking Nazi, owner of one of the world's greatest pornographic libraries, and Germany's most virulent Jew-baiter, he acknowledged his identity. His capture was a particular satisfaction to Major Plitt, one of the most decorated Jewish officers of the Division. Later, at Nürnberg, the other defendants protested against having to eat with Streicher, and Ley was the only one who would talk to him. Streicher was one of the thirteen who were finally hanged.

There were other captures, some of people whose military or political significance was less than their sensational value. One of the more *bona fide* hauls, made by the "Capturing" 502d, was *Obergruppenführer* Karl Albrecht Oberg, whose rank was the equivalent of that of a lieutenant general. He had been chief of the German SS in occupied France and had had charge of all police activities—duties which had earned him the nickname of "The Butcher of Paris." The 3d Battalion of the 506th in Stuhlfelden picked up the Nazi tank expert, General Heinz Guderian. An interesting captive was Eric Kempke, Hitler's chauffeur. He had been in the Reich Chancellery in Berlin during the last days of that city, had witnessed the burning of the bodies of Hitler and Eva Braun, and had escaped through the Russian lines to Berchtesgaden where the 101st had picked him up. Another person connected with Hitler, his sister, Paula Hitler Wolf, was found living in Berchtesgaden in the home of Dietrich Eckart, Nazi poet and Hitler favorite. She was put under house arrest but later released.

"We Got It Made"

The Berchtesgaden area was a final refuge for more than fleeing Nazis. While the Division with one hand was uncovering important persons, with the other it was turning up treasures. The town of Berchtesgaden, because of its close association with Hitler, Goering, and the Nazi movement, was a prize in itself. Few places in Germany held the attraction of this resort town with mountain homes of Hitler and Goering topped by the Eagle's Nest mountain-top retreat. Hitler's establishment had not been in the town of Berchtesgaden itself but on the side of the Ober Salzburg which lies just across a small river running through the town. No matter what the local chamber of commerce had originally thought when the Führer had chosen that location instead of the town proper the choice was a happy one at the end; for the RAF had concentrated on the mountain to the virtual neglect of the town.

Hitler's Eagle's Nest retreat above Berchtesgaden. This picture, made in June, shows the ever-present snow.

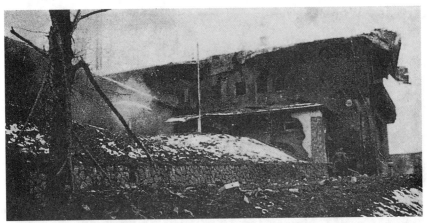

Hitler's home at Ober Salzburg, just outside of Berchtesgaden. The house is still smouldering.

On a ledge on the mountainside Hitler had his house, the Berghof; Goering had been a neighbor, and so had Martin Bormann, the Nazi Party Secretary. Nearby was the Platterhof Hotel, where visiting dignitaries stayed, the SS barracks and more than a dozen other buildings. Here, in years past, Hitler had summoned and bulldozed Chamberlain, Daladier, Mussolini, Schuschnigg and other European leaders. Now most of the buildings were wrecked from the bombings and the souvenir hunters.

In better shape was the Adlershorst, the Eagle's Nest, Hitler's stone retreat on the snow-covered Kehlstein, more than eight thousand feet above sea level. One of the world's remarkable road-building jobs enabled cars to drive to a parking place within a few hundred feet of the house. Here a shaft ran into the center of the mountain to an elevator (for field-grade officers and higher) which lifted into the Eagle's Nest itself. Most of the visitors climbed the zigzag trail from this last parking lot to the house.

And the visitors came—in trucks, weapons-carriers, jeeps, motorcycles, sedans, ambulances. By the first of June they were averaging three thousand daily and as many as ten thousand on Sundays. The airborne troops acted as guides and guards and signs warned against taking souvenirs in Hitler's houses, but everything removable, from bed springs to doorknobs and light fixtures, went. The weather was good for sightseeing, the roads to Berchtesgaden were excellent, and apparently everybody in South Germany eventually turned up, usually with a camera or a pair of binoculars around his neck. On the mountain a man might run into anybody; his senator, the Queen of the Belgians, Gertrude Stein, Field Marshal Alexander, or the buddy he last saw in the IRTC at Camp Croft, South Carolina.

747

Members of the 327th unloading Hermann Goering's looted art treasures at Unterstein, just outside of Berchtesgaden.

There were other attractions for the Berchtesgaden tourist in the summer of 1945. Almost within walking distance of the town was Germany's most beautiful lake, the König-See, six miles long, with shores which were often sheer cliffs. The best accommodations were not for the visiting GIs but for the enlisted men of the 101st. The shore hotels had been taken over as rest camps and extra beds had been placed in the high-priced bedrooms. Germans had been hired to cook, clean, and wait on tables and men from all units of the 101st were eligible to come here on 72-hour passes. The swimming beach and electric motor launches on the lake, however, were open to the touring GIs. In Berchtesgaden the luxurious Berchtesgaden Hof, once Kesselring and his staff had been moved out, was taken over as a rest center for the Division's officers.

In an inn at Unterstein, about halfway between Berchtesgaden and the lake, was another tourist attraction. A sign hanging outside, "The Hermann Goering Art Collection—Through Courtesy of the 101st Airborne Division," explained the contents. Those who could get in (at first admittance was general but after some of the smaller pictures dis-

748

appeared, a pass was necessary) could see, and for a while pick up, examine, and rub to make sure they were genuine, five Rembrandts, including "An Elderly Amsterdam Gentleman" and a portrait of the artist's first wife; Rubens' "Crucifixion," "The Bath of Diana" and others; Van Gogh's "Sunflower" and "Bridge at Arles"; and works of other ancients and moderns such as Andrea del Sarto, Giovanni Bellini, Hans Meling, Van Dyck, and Renoir. Jan van de Meer's famous "Christ and the Adulteress" was there, having been found wrapped inside a stovepipe, in the possession of Goering's wife's nurse. There was a roomful of wrought-gold pieces such as vases, candelabra and tureens. There were stacks of solid gold tableware, tapestries, carpets, drawerfuls of Goering's medals—in all a treasure trove valued at anywhere from two to five hundred million dollars. The collection was put in charge of Capt. Harry V. Anderson of the Division's Military Government Section, and he located Goering's curator and buyer, Walter Andreas Hofer, to help catalog the pieces. The bored glidermen detailed there were always wishing they were guarding something more interesting like the electric boats on the König-See.

The art treasures had been found in a sealed tunnel near Berchtesgaden. Nearby had also been Goering's private train with its luxurious double-bed sleeping rooms, tiled bathrooms, and lounge cars. The train was pulled out on a siding and became an attraction in its own right. Hitler's four-ton armored Mercedes-Benz touring car was picked up and replaced General Taylor's jeep. Colonel Sink got from place to place in Goering's roadster, another mammoth armored affair.

Among the other outstanding finds was a cache of approximately $4,080,000 in twenty-six different currencies. This was dug up on May 23 in a barn near St. Johann and was supposed to have been a private fund buried for Heinrich Himmler. Another fund of 900,000 Reichsmarks was dug up on May 30 at Ruhpolding–Zell. In the Bad Reichenhall home of Dr. Morell, a personal physician to Hitler, was found what was believed to be the largest microscope in the world. Working on electronic principles and weighing 22 tons, the instrument was said to have a magnification of 100,000 power.

All of these large and valuable finds, while interesting to the line soldier, did not have the personal appeal that certain other more humble but also more tangible treasures had. The more or less legitimate loot which a man had a chance of finding and keeping for himself included cameras and binoculars (both of which, during hostilities and for a short time after, Germans were not allowed to have), pistols, shotguns, hunting rifles, telescopic sights, and the like. These items were supposed to be turned in by civilians to their *Bürgermeisters* and those officials were to hold them for the military authorities. But there were many slips between the home and the *Bügermeister's* office and enterprising Americans often saved the villages and farmers a trip by taking over the contraband themselves. Liquor was another choice find and many a thirsty man probed for bottles more thoroughly than he had ever probed for mines.

Some of the happiest hunting took place in the matériel assembly areas, where the German Army units brought together their weapons and supplies. A rifle company in a far mountain village might find itself heir to and overseer of a pastureful of everything a German division had in its possession at the end of the war: a couple of batteries of 150mm guns; fifty or a hundred vehicles of every nationality, description and condition; a hundred or so horses; several thousand rifles (the rifles which went home represented the choice of the lot); a miscellany of machine guns, military radios, ordnance tools, tents, telescopic sights, helmets, gas masks, and pistols; perhaps cases of brand new P-38s, Berettas, or Walthers. Sometimes some of these things just disappeared, sometimes the German soldiers bringing them in were saved having to carry them all the way to the dump. Some Germans refused to turn in their pistols and hid them (woodpiles were favorite places, apparently on the theory that next winter, when the Americans were gone, the users of the wood would find them) or threw them into the streams. Hundreds were taken from streams within a few yards of bridges and many a woodpile was torn down. Some were hidden in the attics of schools or buried. The net result was a sharp break in the price of pistols within the Division itself although a more united front was presented to the thousands of visitors. The shrewder traders would take their pistols to Berchtesgaden or König-See, discreetly drop a few hints to the less fortunate GI tourists, and return to their companies richer in schillings, marks, francs, cameras or whatever the visitors may have had. There were even some *Luftwaffe* planes in flying condition; after a couple of experimental flights and the crash-death of a 506th officer Division put out a strict notice grounding its airborne personnel.

The horses picked up in these assembly grounds were generally either draft horses which had been worn out during the retreat or cavalry horses which were often in good shape. Sometimes almost every man in a company had his own horse and great were the protests when a farmer looked out to see a hundred or so head corraled in his pasture. The 506th organized a parachute cavalry. After the initial enthusiasm wore off most of the horses were disposed of, each organization keeping a few for riding purposes and giving the rest back to the German troops, to DPs, or to friendly native farmers.

A number of dogs also appeared. Some were bought and others were just acquired.

What effect did living in this wartime wonderland have on the troops themselves? David Kenyon Webster, who gave the period the name of "The Golden Age," says:

It was the only time I enjoyed military life.

It all began the first night after we arrived in Berchtesgaden. I stepped out the door and there was Luz in a *Volkswagen*. He had just made a trip to Hitler's hideout, he said, for a couple of cases of champagne for the platoon CP. Was he returning there? He was. I fetched a large wooden packing case, joined him and O'Keefe, who was also thirsty, and drove off in the dripping darkness. We went down the hill through Berchtesgaden, crossed the stream in the valley, and started on the steep, winding road that led up to the Nazis' Valhalla. German trucks, 6-by-6s, and even armored cars raced toward the cellar. One or two 3d Division lads, somewhat the worse for carbonated grape juice, zigzagged down the hill. When we reached the end of the trail, Hitler's halfway house (the road to the mountain-top home, or Eagle's Nest, was blocked by bomb damage), we were greeted with the sight of GIs and Frenchmen dashing madly in and out of a battered chalet lit by headlights. Although the British had bombed the grounds and ruined some SS barracks nearby, this building seemed to have sustained no direct hits, for, despite shattered windows and a gaping roof, the house and cellar were still intact. Prevented by the darkness from making a thorough exploration, we hastily examined a roomful of radios and proceeded through rubble and broken glass to the wine cellar, a cool cavern, about thirty feet by fifty and ten high, filled with metal bottle racks and excited, scrambling GIs. O'Keefe held a flashlight, while Luz and I, working against time and the arrival of more soldiers, stuffed my wooden box with bottles. I was shocked to find that most of the champagne down here was new and mediocre. Here was no Napoleon brandy, here were no fine liqueurs; all the champagne had been bottled in the late 1930s. I was disappointed in Hitler—a man that powerful drinking such cheap liquor. Maybe he kept this home and cellar for the small fry, the nickel Nazis and bargain-counter traitors, and saved the superior drinks in the Eagle's Nest for people like Goering, Ribbentrop, and Quisling. . . .

We slept between sheets. We ate off china plates (mess kits were definitely *passé*). We took hot baths in real bathtubs; we lived in new, Alpine-style SS buildings. Each squad had an apartment complete with modern bath, up-to-the-minute kitchen, and four or five bedrooms . . .

We found a cognac cache down the road, so we celebrated VE-day and many another day in appropriate style. Indeed, it was a social error to be caught without a corkscrew in Berchtesgaden. We killed cows for steaks and roasts and ate the SS food hidden under coal piles in the cellar, while German prisoners did our KP. We had our pick of vehicles. Our captain got a black, bullet-proof Mercedes-Benz, rumored to have been Goering's, while the rest of us raced about the countryside in *Volkswagens, Wehrmacht* staff cars, command cars, trucks, and ambulances. My platoon sergeant had a fire engine complete with siren. If we needed gas we helped ourselves at the nearest filling station. Guard duty was light and we spent our leisure time swimming, mountain climbing and rubbernecking.

Non-fraternization, an unwise policy with an effect on the GI analogous to that of King Canute on the waves, was in force but it didn't prevent some of us from meeting the local *Fräuleins*. For souvenirs, we had our pick of pistols, knives, rifles, bayonets and enemy uniforms; also a few watches, turned in or abandoned by the German soldiers in our PW inclosures. We were in the beautiful Alps in May; the war was over, and we were having the time of our lives.

The Division Settles Down

Most of the units of the Division, after an average of two or three moves during the days immediately following the surrender, managed to settle down in one area and to remain there with a possible single additional move, until leaving Austria or Germany (for Berchtesgaden was a finger of Germany sticking into the Austrian mountains, and sometimes a battalion would have companies in both countries). By the middle of June in or very close to Berchtesgaden itself was Division Headquarters with such units as the MP Platoon, the Reconnaissance Platoon, the Band, the Signal Company, and two regiments, the 327th and the 501st, the latter having come up from Mourmelon in late May. Twelve miles away, in the health and sports resort town of Bad Reichenhall, and occupying the big mural-covered barracks formerly used by the *Wehrmacht*, were the Division Quartermaster, Medical, and Ordnance Companies. This used up the large towns in the Division area; the rest of the 101st scattered out through the villages and small towns. The 502d had the responsibility for the western part of the area with regimental headquarters at Kossen. The 506th had the southern sector with headquarters in Zell am See, an attractive resort on the Zeller See, a 2½-mile-long lake. (Many of the hotels here were German military hospitals, filled with wounded soldiers.) At Bayer were Division Artillery Headquarters and the 463d Parachute Field Artillery Battalion; the 907th was at Karlstein, and the 321st at Gmain. The 81st AA Battalion was in and about Inzell, and the 326th Engineers at Lofer.

By the middle of July many of the units had moved to other villages. The most important move was that of Division Headquarters to Badgastein, well to the south of Berchtesgaden, only forty airline miles from Italy. Here was a resort town as luxurious as any in Austria. Though many of its hotels were hospitals and still occupied by wounded Germans, enough were vacant or vacated to allow the troops to live in unsoldierly luxury. All the units which had been in Berchtesgaden

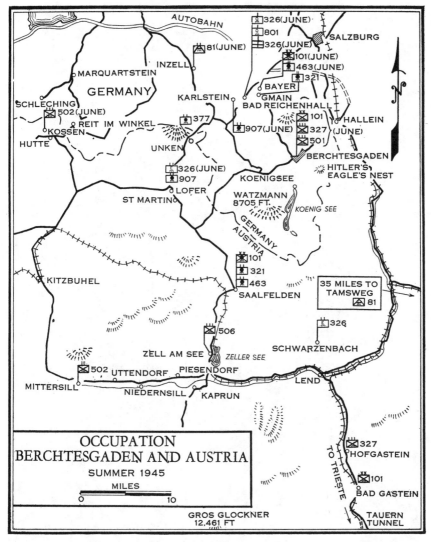

Map 106.

moved here except the 327th which moved to Hofgastein, five miles from Badgastein, and Headquarters, Special Troops and the Division Signal Company, both of which went to Bad Reichenhall. Meanwhile the 326th Medical and the 426th Quartermaster Companies moved from Bad Reichenhall, the former to Badgastein and the latter to Bischofshofen, between Berchtesgaden and Bad Reichenhall. In June the 502d had moved from its area in the west down into the villages along the valley of the Salzach River in the south adjoining the 506th area. Regi-

Two DPs—displaced persons—at Zell am See, Austria

mental headquarters was in Mittersill, twenty miles west of Zell am See; twenty miles southwest of Mittersill, over the 12,000-foot snow-topped Gross Venediger, lay Italy. Division Artillery Headquarters and the 321st and 463d Battalions, moved to Saalfelden, a dozen miles north of Zell am See. The 907th Battalion moved from Karlstein to Lofer,

the 81st from Inzell to Tamsweg, and the 326th Engineers left Lofer
for Schwarzach.

In Badgastein the 101st found not only hotels full of wounded Germans but also hotels and houses filled with diplomats, enemy and
neutral, who were representing their countries in Germany when the
war ended. They ranged from pro-Nazi Arab refugees (the Grand
Mufti of Jerusalem had been there until he "escaped" from the 3d Division) to the delegation from Afghanistan. The Japanese, numbering
over a hundred, were still installed in the best hotel, a situation General
Higgins immediately corrected. All diplomats from enemy countries
were rounded up and put under guard.

Life during the summer months was in many ways as pleasant as a
soldier could ask. Being in tourist country the towns and most of the
villages contained hotels or inns which would comfortably accommodate from a squad to a company; most had modern plumbing. The
same things which had attracted the tourists, the beautiful mountains,
the scenery, the lakes and waterfalls, the natural hot baths at the various
Bads, the suspended cable cars up the mountain at Bad Reichenhall,
the hiking trails, the ski runs (if you went high enough, even in July),
the hunting and fishing (plenty of high-powered rifles and ammunition, courtesy the *Wehrmacht*)—all these were available to the airborne trooper spending the summer in one of the many *Gasthäuser.*
There were plenty of DPs and Germans anxious to do KP or any other
work for food, cigarettes, and soap; it was a rare man who washed his
own clothes. Passes—to France, England, the Riviera, the König-See—
were plentiful; a system was worked out whereby even companies and
batteries set up rest camps to which a platoon at a time went.

There did develop a shortage of food, for the 101st was at the very
end of the Seventh Army supply line; and in late May Seventh Army
made a general ten per cent cut; but this was a relative matter and it
was a rare German or Austrian whose diet approached that of the
American soldiers. During these times the company messes were some
times supplemented by hunting expeditions, for there were plenty of
deer in the woods, and no one asked the game wardens whether or not
there was a closed season. In the more remote villages other interested persons organized after-dark expeditions and went out and
rustled and butchered a cow. When the helpless farmers themselves
were unable to protect their stock (said one ex-cowpuncher mess
sergeant who had been caught in the act and had had to scare off the
owner, "First time I ever shot at a man before I shot at his cow"), they
protested to the Division's military government officers; a stiff direc-

tive came down to the companies which ended most of the cow-killing.

Cows weren't the only things that got shot. The casualties from the numerous pistols and vehicles created losses within the Division about as great as those of some of the Division's quieter campaigns. Strenuous efforts were made to get all pistols out of the hands of the troops and each company provided a strong box in which pistols, tagged with their owner's name, were to be kept. But pistols kept popping up and popping off and cars and jeeps kept going off the mountain roads; between May 11 and June 2 the Division had seventy wrecks, and in a six-week period of June and July in one way or another eleven enlisted men and two officers were killed.

Not that life was entirely a matter of passes, eating, killing cows, getting shot or running a jeep off a mountainside. There was always guard to be pulled—you couldn't hire Germans, Austrians or DPs to do that. The guard duty itself was routine, for the beaten Austrians gave almost no trouble and the threatened Werewolf underground never openly developed. Almost the only cases of trouble were a few cut telephone lines and, on the 21st of July, the partial destruction of a bridge near Unken by a charge of explosive. There was military government to maintain, roadblocks to be manned, forests to be searched for *Wehrmacht* equipment, reports of SS troops in the mountains—in the reports they were always SS—to be investigated; any number of duties some new and some interesting. For example, the 326th Engineers, whose jobs in the past were more likely to have been tough and tedious than glamorous, were, a week after the German surrender, reporting a single day's activities: Company A, guarding Bailey bridges, German signal, ordnance and ration dumps (any of which might turn up interesting finds for curious guards), a hotel and wine cellar (ditto), and a German laboratory. Company B was guarding the electric boats at König-See, opening safes at Division Headquarters, and repairing the elevator to the Eagle's Nest. Company C was guarding a detention camp at Lofer. A month later Company A had been relieved of guarding bridges and was constructing a rifle range. Company B was now not only guarding but was operating the electric boats. Company C was putting up bleachers in the Berchtesgaden stadium for a track meet, and was clearing snow from the Glockner Pass with a tractor.

This pass, at 7,518 feet, the highest over the Alps, separates the provinces of Salzburg and Carinthia. It was opened to civilian traffic on June 26 for the first time since 1939. General Taylor made the formal opening before an honor guard of the 506th to the accompaniment of an Austrian band, dressed in native leather knee breeches.

REDEPLOYMENT

There were changes in the duties of the other units of the Division as the summer drew on. The German soldiers were gradually shipped out to the Munich area, sometimes in trains, sometimes in long convoys of dissimilar vehicles burning gasoline, charcoal or diesel oil, and sometimes in lines of horse-drawn vehicles which the airborne troops watched with amazement as they went slowly up and down the mountains and camped along the roads at night.

Many took their girl friends along. It had surprised the Americans to see the large number of young and pretty girls who had been following and living with the German soldiers at the war's end. A walk through the barns or the little shacks thrown up by the camped German troops almost always revealed German privates and noncoms apparently happily set up at housekeeping with a field *Frau*. These girls were not to be confused with the several companies of uniformed German Army nurses and WAC-like detachments captured and handled through regular military channels.

The 101st settled down to governing its territory with a lot of time for athletics and care and cleaning of equipment. Then in mid-June came word of what was to be the 101st's future in the Pacific War. The Division was in category II—to be redeployed to the Southwest Pacific. At the same time the 501st Parachute Infantry Regiment, a regiment which had never known another Division, which had fought attached to the 101st in every action from Normandy through Alsace, was to be inactivated and was to serve as a vehicle to transport all high-point men from the Division back to the U. S. for discharge or redeployment.

After this definite commitment as to the future of the 101st training and discipline stiffened all down the line. Retreat ceremonies and inspections became more regular. Even in the most isolated company messes officers were required to wear their blouses to the evening meal. A regular program of training in ground tactics went into effect in the companies and plans for airborne training were in the making. The 502d's newspaper, the *Screamer,* ran an article on Formosa "just in case," and the various company commanders reminded themselves that much of Japan was mountainous and started their troops out on climbs instead of the usual morning runs.

In late June more definite word on the status of the 101st was brought by General Taylor, who had made a trip to the U. S. with Gen. Omar Bradley and had talked with high officers in the War Department. General Taylor passed the information on to the troops himself, travelling throughout the Division area and talking to the assembled units.

After stressing how impressed he had been by the reputation the 101st had among both soldiers and civilians in the States, he gave the troops the latest. The Division was to go, not directly to the Pacific, but to the U. S., probably around the first of the year. It was to be one of ten or twelve divisions which would constitute a general reserve in the U. S. Fort Bragg or nearby Camp Mackall was to be the 101st's Stateside home. Of immediate importance was the War Department's insistence that the Division, like the others which were to return to the general reserve, reach the U. S. trained and prepared for its primary mission.

The training entered into in Austria was chiefly basic, such as firing of weapons and elementary military subjects. The general had also brought back the information that the Division would shortly return to France. This set at rest the anxieties of the training officers who could picture no airborne and very little other training in the mountain-locked, snowed-in villages during an Alpine winter.

The last month in Austria was not, however, a training grind. There were as many passes and furloughs as ever. Athletics were organized and teams played baseball, boxed, and competed in track and field events on company, regimental and Division basis. In the Berchtes-gaden stadium where in 1936 Hitler had watched his favorite athletes train for the Olympics the 101st won a track meet from the 94th Division, beat the 17th Airborne Division, and later won the II Corps championship. Of the 38 members on the II Corps team which took part in the Third Army meet in Nürnberg, 33 were from the 101st. Later, these airborne track men, by placing eight men and taking two relay seconds, helped Third Army win the ETO championship. The Division's swimmers were almost as helpful when II Corps won second place in the Third Army swimming meet; 48 of the Corps' 75 points were scored by 101st swimmers. The baseball and soft-ball teams had less successful seasons though both nines got to the finals of the II Corps tournaments. The boxing team fought one match, which it won, 6-1, from the 11th Armored Division.

Actually, it is doubtful whether much effective training could have been done during the first weeks after the end of the fighting in Europe. There had been too much excitement, too much restlessness, too many new places and things to be looked into. And the companies still had men with 85 points, waiting for shipment home. These men felt that they were through with the Army and the war and they impatiently sweated out the vast machinery which was trying to haul them back to the United States. But eventually the highest numbers began to be called up, one or two at a time, and they packed, said their goodbyes, and were gone. Then they began to go in larger groups, their places filled by low-point men from the 501st, the 82d and the 17th Airborne Divisions. By the middle of July, 1,819 of the 11,339 enlisted men and 500 of the 800 officers on duty with the 101st when the war in Europe ended had left on their way home. There was also a large shipment of very low-point ment which went to the 17th Airborne Division for reshipment direct to the Pacific. Eventually when the last of the high-pointers left there were few of their old buddies with whom to shake hands and say "So long!"

Extracts from Sergeant Koskimaki's diary (he was a 74-pointer) for a month reveal how frequent were these departures within one company:

Jun 30: Item: Schmidt, Caggiano, Zimmerman, Lewis, Byrd and Sheppard left radio platoon on their first step toward home. Lucky boys! *July 14:* Degrace left for discharge yesterday—another ole guy gone! *July 22:* Pyle and a couple other guys leave tomorrow for home. *July 23:* We are losing a hundred men tomorrow. All of them are low-point men. Our platoon is losing twenty-nine men, including Sorrells, Lenzing, Younger and Zeleniak. *July 24:* It is a very strange place around here with so many buddies gone. *July 26:* It looks like we'll be losing ten more men this week-end on points. We are not gonna have many men left when it is all over. *July 27:* Tom Austin, Young, Swain, Hershman, Fedorchak and Bill Austin left for 501 today. They have enough points to get out of the Army. *July 29:* Lucker, Lindgren, Stark and Ditoma left for Berchtesgaden and the 501.

On July 23 the Division got two new recruits. Reporting for duty were Capt. Ann D. Neal and 2d Lt. Kathryn Martin, WAC. The two troopers were assigned to Division Headquarters and became the only women to wear—officially—the Screaming Eagle insignia.

LAST DAYS IN THE ALPS

One of the first symptoms that the Golden Age was losing some of its glitter was the drying up of the liquor supply. Not that there was ever a drought, and the officers' supply, due to the fortunate discovery of several thousand bottles of *Wehrmacht* liquor cached away in the officers' rest center, remained adequate throughout the period. But for the rank and file the easily discovered bottles of the first days in the Alps were drunk up and the remaining supply was apparently better hidden so that it had to be bargained or bartered for. The initial flood of pistols and other legitimate booty dried up. The obtaining of cameras and binoculars for the asking ended when the natives were granted the right again to own these things. It became a great time of trading, with Lugers, Leicas and Zeiss binoculars going from man to man within a company as the swappers wandered from billet to billet.

Pressure very early had been applied to get vehicles out of the hands of the troops. Everything from Mercedes-Benzes to bicycles, except for a few kept by units for official purposes, was protestingly turned back. Roadblocks became more rigid; no longer could a man, as at least one don't-give-a-damn paratrooper had done during the first confused days of peace, steal a German car, load it with loot, and drive unmolested across Germany and France to Paris where the car and contents were sold and the proceeds used to finance a prolonged AWOL spree. The regimental and Division stockades began slowly taking on more guests as the enforcement of regulations tightened all down the line.

Thus life settled down to a routine of a lot of physical exercise, mostly organized athletics, a few hours daily of basic military training, occasional details and guard, and plenty of time to intensively explore all the possibilities of the now well worked over Alpine country. Sometimes a few men got a trip accompanying some of the DPs back to their homeland. One such detail from the 502d, which took a trainload of Hungarians back to their country disappeared entirely for several weeks. About the time the rumors of their deaths and dire fate had reached a peak they returned with remarkable stories of what it was like to spend a week in inflation-ridden Budapest; the only other Americans there had been members of a small mission and the paymaster had made them temporary millionaires by paying the detail a partial payment in American greenbacks. Only too soon had their Russian hosts found them a train back to Austria.

The DPs had mostly left except for some eastern Europeans who for one reason or another did not want to return to homes in countries under Russian influence. The effect of these departures was mostly felt in a social way and Austrian girls began, secretly or openly, to take the place occupied by the armband-wearing DPs. But there remained more than enough DPs willing and anxious to work in return for the privilege of eating army chow and there were always plenty of Austrians anxious for any work.

There developed in the Division an increasing interest in preparing for the return to civilian life. A few United States Armed Forces Institute correspondence and self-teaching courses came down to the companies and batteries and were eagerly grabbed up by the men, sometimes two or more men sharing a single textbook. Many more signed up for courses and forwarded their orders for textbooks and assignments. The Information and Education Section of the Division began expanding a program which had begun running at an increasing tempo before the end of the war. Classes in a number of subjects ranging from photography (for many a man found that his box-camera experience was not adequate to cope with a suddenly acquired Contax or Rolleiflex) to mathematics.

The return to France was preceded by the usual guessing contest as to what would be the Division's new home grounds. The question was settled when an advance detail left in the latter part of July for Auxerre, an old town 140 miles southeast of Paris. In that town the 13th Airborne Division had waited out the last months of the war in Europe, ready to jump and glide into Germany on missions which never materialized. Now the 13th had gone back to the U. S. and the 101st was to occupy the 13th's old quarters and use the level plains around the town for training until its own turn came to ship back to the U. S. and later, possibly, on west to the Pacific.

The movement from Austria was by truck convoy and train with most of the men going in the usual 40-and-8 boxcars. The jeeps left in convoys daily from July 30 until August 2. The trains left from Bischofswiesen, between Berchtesgaden and Bad Reichenhall, from Bruck, just below Zell am See, and from Badgastein. The trains left on July 30, 31 and August 1. At least one passenger from the 502d, writing in that regiment's paper, the *Screamer*, thought the service could be improved:

Once everyone was boarded and all the cars attached to the locomotive the procession was off. Traveling through Austria was fine. An electric engine pulled the freight along at great speed and efficiency. Great speed is a little faster than slow. Slow is faster than stopped.

Then all of a sudden it happened. The border of France was crossed and things began to go from slow to stopping. The electric engine was changed to a steam-powered one invented and built before James Watt was born. Every so often it had to stop and take on water. On close inspection of this locomotive one could understand the reason. It seemed every connection of pipe, every seam riveted together, every nut and bolt leaked steam and water. The popular name for this pile of junk should be "The Clinging Cloud"; it certainly looked like one.

The trip was not uneventful. At one place the weary travelers were held up for some time while officials released themselves from the obligation of explaining what happened to some freight taken by someone of the 502 Meteor. Why, every one knows that no one in this outfit would dare or even think of taking anything that did not belong to them. The nerve of some people!

Shortly afterwards the train was again stopped by MPs puffing out of Nancy. (The train was puffing.) This time they accused one of the Deuce's members of picking up more loot. More time wasted. This stopping for water and other inconveniences slowed down the trip considerably.

The carnival was once stopped because some careless traveler fell off and was lying on the road bed a few miles back. This caused some concern to the conductor when he was ordered to put the affair in reverse and pick up the fallen man. That was something too much for the engineer who jumped from his

cab and yelled things in French which meant it was impossible to put this locomotive in reverse. It could go forward but not reverse.

After a period of time and still not going backwards another locomotive came
along side with the fallen comrade. Luckily he was not dead, just beat up a
little. The reason why the engineer could not back up was obvious. In order
to do this feat he had to crawl into the works of his engine and overhaul a
few gears before it could even budge in the other direction. It was too hot
inside the boiler for that.

After producing a huge key and winding up the engine once more the convoy
was on the way again. Banging along at the top notch speed of a little faster
than double-time we arrived in Auxerre some five days after leaving Austria.
This broke all records for speed and put M. Piquet's record of five and a half
days on roller skates in second place.

Possibly other passengers viewed the trip with more tolerance. The
weather was warm, there were points of interest such as bombed Munich, there were frequent feeding points along the way where the
Army, with the help of German prisoners, served hot meals at all
hours, and there were sometimes apple trees along the right-of-way
when the train went slow enough. It was a three-to-four-day trip and
many thousands of games of poker and gin rummy were run.

At noon on August 1 the 101st officially turned over its Austrian territory to the 42d Infantry Division and at that hour officially opened
its CP in Auxerre, France. It was to be the 101's last CP.

France: The Last Chapter

After months spent as conquerors in the tourist hotels, inns and homes of Germany and Austria, France was a rude change for the 101st. In Auxerre and the neighboring towns of Joigny and Sens the airborne troopers found the French, one of the victor nations of the war, wearing poorer clothes, possessed of fewer luxuries and living in worse houses whose plumbing—yardstick of Americans abroad—was inferior to that of the conquered Germans and Austrians. The latter in their unbombed Alps, were still relatively prosperous from years of living off the fat of conquered and looted Europe. Now the Division was in walled and wired military *casernes,* "caserntration" camps, groups of old French Army barracks, none too comfortable at best and in bad shape from the hard usage of the war years. Some of the troops were moved into tents. Instead of an Austrian's most comfortable bed, mattress, sheets and pillows, the trooper found his bed a homemade wooden double decker, his mattress possibly a straw-filled bed sack.

The three towns occupied by the 101st—and before it by the 13th Airborne Division—were, in order of size, Auxerre, Sens and Joigny. Auxerre, a town of about 25,000, was the capital of the Department of Yonne; Sens with about 18,000 and Joigny with about 7,000 were both in this Department. The three towns lay along the banks of the Yonne River with Auxerre upstream, Sens about forty miles downstream and Joigny middleway between the two. In Auxerre were Division Headquarters, the 502d, the 326th Engineers, and the smaller Division units. In nearby St. Georges was the 81st AAA Battalion. The 377th FA Battalion was in Seignelay, north of Auxerre; and north of Seignelay, in Brienon, was the 426th Quartermaster Company. The 327th Regiment and the 321st FA Battalion were in Sens, and the 506th and the Division's remaining artillery units were in Joigny.

All three towns were ancient, dating back to Roman times. Auxerre had been an important outpost of the Roman Empire and Sens had been the capital of a Gallic people who, in 390 B.C., had besieged and captured Rome. The streets in these old towns were narrow, cobblestoned and steep, running up from the river. In Auxerre were several notable old cathedrals including the Cathedral of St. Étienne, a fine specimen of thirteenth-century Gothic architecture. A cathedral of the same name in Sens was equally noted, being one of the earliest Gothic buildings in France. Joigny had churches almost as old, and the Porte du Bois, a gateway with two flanking towers, once formed part of a tenth-century castle in that town.

But the paratroopers and gliderists were not interested in architecture, art or history—they, like the millions of other Americans in Europe in

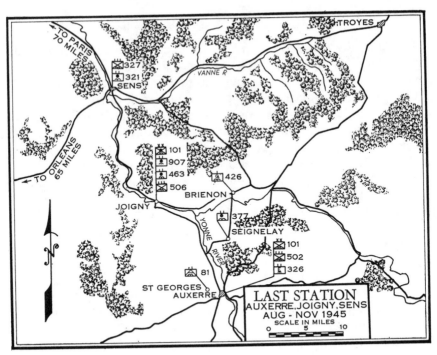

Map 107.

the fall of 1945, wanted to go home. When the war in the Pacific ended that urge became overwhelming and it was aided by strong clamor from the States that the boys be brought back immediately. The physical limitations of shipping space made little impression on anybody concerned. Everybody in every theater of war wanted to get home right then, and for each soldier wanting to go home there were at home several people wanting him back immediately. Patience was not one of the characteristics of the last half of 1945.

It was that impatience, coupled with the experience of having lived as conquerors all summer and returning to poverty-stricken and uncomfortable France, which set up in the Americans a state of mind that was bound to lead to trouble. That this trouble was headed off before it reached a serious stage was a credit to the troops themselves as well as to the commanders of the Division. Cooperation was obtained from the troops by direct appeals from the unit commanders, by limiting the number of men allowed in town on evening passes and by putting on the streets almost as many MPs and officers and noncoms on "chute patrol" as there was pass-holders.

The troubles in France had started almost as soon as the 101st had unpacked, and before a week was out the Auxerre newspaper had printed an editorial commenting on the conduct of the troops quartered in the towns. It was a bad situation on both sides. The Americans, wanting to get home, resented the shabby, dilapidated, broken-windowed barracks with their promise of being even worse when the weather turned cold, resented also the apparent lack of response of the local girls after a season of "chocolate bar" success in Austria, and the drought of drinkable liquor. Their resentment was not eased by a few characters among the local population who sold them, at black market prices, some of the vilest so-called cognac ever distilled. Though relations constantly improved during the fall as the troops and the populace got to know each other better the basic situation could only be improved by what everybody was devoutly hoping for—redeployment.

Training for Japan

The country along the Yonne was ideal for airborne training; level, with broad fields for parachute and glider landings. The 13th Airborne had left some training installations such as firing ranges, and the 101st began construction of more. Training started within a few days after arrival and took up where it had left off in Austria. Requisitions were put in for planes and gliders and the G-3 and S-3 officers began writing up airborne training problems.

On August 6 President Truman announced the dropping, sixteen hours earlier, of the first atomic bomb on Hiroshima. On the 8th Russia entered the war against Japan and the next day the second atomic bomb landed on Nagasaki. On the 14th Japan accepted the terms of the Allies and on September 2 aboard the battleship *Missouri* in Tokyo Bay the Japanese signed the official instrument of surrender.

During this climactic month training went on under Corps orders and to the accompaniment of a chorus of gripes from the trainees. The chorus hit its peak when it was announced that all parachutists would make a jump or go off jump status and forfeit future jump pay.

To jump or not to jump replaced home as the leading topic in the parachute barracks. Jumping began on September 10 and ended on October 16. Probably never had so large a group—more than five thousand parachutists—jumped under such ideal conditions. The jumps were from a 1,200-foot altitude, the planes throttled down to minimum speed, the jumpers carried no equipment and there was no assembly problem. Instead, the Division's Red Cross girls were at the jump field with coffee, iced tea and doughnuts. But Operation Money or Mission Greenback, as the jump was unofficially called, was never popular and in some companies a quarter or more of the men failed

The clock tower in Auxerre.

Joigny, from across the Yonne.

to jump. A few men reached the jump field so well fortified that their recollections of the experience were at best very hazy. A few others persuaded some of their more jump-happy buddies to take their place in the stick, which worked if the jumpmaster failed to recognize the jumper. The operation was climaxed by a volunteer stick of sixteen men who set what was believed to be a new record for a mass jump. The stick went out at 12,600 feet and landed in a fairly compact group in the designated drop zone. The heaviest man travelled the two and a third miles down in less than ten minutes, the lightest man hit after thirteen and a half minutes.

Even before the jumps began the Division had practically abandoned military training. The goal now was to keep the troops reasonably healthy and happy until their shipping date. This was accomplished chiefly through the I & E program, athletics and planned recreation.

I & E, ATHLETICS AND RECREATION

Versatility had always been one of the qualities attributed to an airborne division. As a glider- and parachute-borne shock force the 101st had proved itself in Normandy and Holland, and it had further proved itself as a superb, even though lightly armed and equipped, infantry division in the latter phases of those two operations and at Bastogne, Alsace and the Ruhr. In the Ruhr and in South Germany and Austria it had demonstrated that a division commander could govern a province and that a company commander or a platoon leader

767

Parading in Auxerre, 7 November 1945. Following the band is a special honor company.

could handle the civil affairs of a village. Now it was to show that it could on a few days' notice turn an entire division into a school, a school in which almost every man was enrolled in one or more courses. Attendance was not compulsory but a large majority of the men in the Division had a real interest in the classes; for those who did not sign up, a schedule of military training and details was prescribed and this threw a few uninterested persons into the classes. Dean of this 101st University was the head of the Division's I & E program, Maj. Floyd Eldridge.

The teachers in the program were volunteers, ranging from privates to field-grade officers; and a few French civilians also taught. The classrooms were in the *casernes,* in tents set up in nearby fields, in schoolrooms borrowed from the local communities, even in an Auxerre dancehall. The Army furnished textbooks and teaching aids, but these were generally in short supply; it was up to the teachers and students to improvise and this they did ingeniously. Classes were set up in any subject in which enough students were interested and for which a teacher could be found. A typical curriculum was that with which the 502d opened its "tent university" on the outskirts of Auxerre on September 10; economic geography, French, arithmetic, elementary reading and writing, retail salesmanship, plane trigonometry, blueprint reading, business English, algebra, poultry raising, livestock production, business law, psychology, basic mathematics, auto mechanics, English grammar, plane geometry and ballroom dancing. Later, other courses were added. The auto mechanics worked on the regimental vehicles, the animal husbandry classes visited nearby model stock farms and dairies, and the ballroom dancing classes were never able to find a place large enough to accommodate the number of men wanting to take this popular subject.

There were other opportunities for students. At Shrivenham, England, the Army was running a university with eight-week courses. A similar university (but on the luxurious side) was in operation at Biarritz on the Riviera. There were technical schools open, a limited number of soldiers were being accepted in the civilian universities of France and England, there was an On-the-Job Training program and a Training-Within-Civilian-Agencies program. The 101st sent men to all of these. And for men who wanted to stay in the Army the Division set up noncom schools where a soldier could prepare himself for the openings which were coming up fast as the redeployment went into high gear.

While the I & E schools were generally filling a man's morning,

The 426th Airborne QM Company distributed hoarded jump boots for the Division's Fifth Avenue parade—a rendezvous the 101st failed to keep.

athletics took up most of his afternoon. Swimming, baseball, volleyball, tennis, tag football, boxing, basketball—each had a following. Until the weather got cold the Yonne River attracted the swimmers in all three towns. One of the first to try it was Sergeant Koskimaki who has the following entry:

August 4: J. Tucker, Hix, Nesbitt, McCoy and I went swimming in a large river near here. We dove off a fifteen foot board into four and a half feet of water. Result—six stitches for Nesbitt's noggin.

Volleyball was a popular mass sport, as was softball, tag football, and basketball.

Athletic teams were organized on company, regiment and Division levels. The more talented athletes had discovered in Austria that getting on the regimental or Division team meant moving into a training camp with good chow and no details; in Austria the camp was likely to be a hotel or a *Bad,* in France, a château. These training conditions were almost ideal and the athletes were among the most satisfied of the soldiers sweating out redeployment. They also turned out good teams though a coach never knew from week to week which of his stars would still be available and which would be on their way to the U.S. or another division; he could only hope that among the new men

770

Colonel Kinnard and General Taylor team up to represent the 101st at Wimbledon. The pair survived several rounds in the ETO tournament before they were eliminated.

coming into his organization would be some capable replacements.

The largest training camp was that of the Division football squad. The coach, Capt. Robert Dickson, turned out a team which beat the 89th, 9th and 71st Infantry Divisions, the 1st Armored Division and Army Air Forces and lost close games to Oise Base and the 84th Infantry Division. In the regimental football league Special Troops won the championship. The game which was to have been played between the 502d and the 506th in the "Champagne Bowl" at Reims on Christmas Day, 1944—a date which failed to take into account Hitler's plans for a winter offensive—was finally, though inconclusively, played off in a two-game series in which each team won a game.

The Division boxing team fought two matches and won both, one victim being the 508th Parachute Regiment of the 82d Airborne Division. Pfc. Jim McHale won the ETO amateur golfing championship and set a new course record on the famous Fontainebleau course.

771

Brigadier General William N. Gillmore, CG of
the 101st from 22 August to 25 September 1945.

McHale ran a golf clinic at Fontainebleau for 101st men who wanted
to improve their game.

A team unique in the ETO or any other theater of the war was that
which represented the 101st in tennis. General Taylor and his G-3,
Col. Harry W. O. Kinnard, both outstanding tennis players in their

Brigadier General Gerald St. Clair Mickle, who commanded the 101st from 25 September to 9 October 1945.

day at West Point, met and defeated all opposition and won for the Division the XVI Corps doubles championship. They then went on to Wimbledon, England where they represented the Corps in the ETO championship play. There the Seventh Army champions, a sergeant and a private first class, eliminated them.

There were other means of absorbing the soldier's time: increased pass and furlough quotas, movies shown in theaters and, as long as the weather was good, in the *caserne* courtyards, and shows—some USO, some brought in from Paris, some put on by the men themselves. The outstanding productions were the 506th's three-act musical comedy, "Out of This World," the 502d's "Malfunctions of 1945" and the 327th's "A Waste of Time." A 45-voice glee club was organized under the direction of Pfc. Keith P. Brown. The singers, mostly from the 506th, moved into special billets in Auxerre and after several weeks of rehearsals sang not only throughout the Division but broadcast over the Armed Forces Network station in Paris and the BBC and made a six-day tour of England, singing in theaters and hospitals. The Red Cross, with its clubs, girls and doughnuts helped the men pass the time. The program of the Red Cross in Sens for the month of September is fairly typical of the programs carried out in the other towns. During the month the girls conducted twenty dancing classes, fourteen dances, four pinochle parties, and three ping-pong tournaments as well as classes in French and sketching. They made available equipment for croquet, horseshoe pitching, badminton, ping-pong, tennis, chess and card games. Each day they served an average of five thousand dough-

Brigadier General Stuart Cutler, last commander of the 101st Airborne Division.

nuts and one hundred gallons of coffee; and they sold 1,464 cases of Coca-Cola. Even the French barkeepers made some effort to cooperate. The 327th newspaper, *Skyrider,* reported that 104 bars in the Sens area had agreed to stabilize their prices to GIs at the following rates: Cognac, 20 francs per glass; *vin blanc* 12 to 15 francs; champagne, 200 to 300 francs a bottle; schnapps-kirsch, 15 francs; and beer—very weak—5 francs. These prices were posted in each bar.

REDEPLOYMENT

During these months there was an endless stream of men coming into and going out of the 101st. When the Japanese signed the surrender document the Army recomputed the critical scores as of VJ instead of VE-day, giving each man who had been in the ETO over the summer at least eight more points. Then the scores for return and discharge were lowered from 85 to 80, to 70 for October redeployment, to 60 for November and on down month by month. As the higher-point men left, low-point men from other divisions took their places. By the end of October the Division magazine, the *Screaming Eagle,* reported that

The outfit seemed more like a repple-depple than a combat division. On parade the companies looked like the Screaming Eagle Division—from the left side. From the right side one could spot the patches of the 13th, 17th, and the 82d Airborne and the 75th and 89th Infantry Divisions, and XVI Corps.

There were troopers who had been shifted as the situation and the missions of the various airborne divisions had been changed until, when they landed in the 101st, they could lay claim to having been in all four of the airborne divisions in Europe.

As the personnel changed so did the command. On August 11 Gen. Gerald Higgins, Assistant Division Commander, left for the U.S. to take command of the Parachute School at Fort Benning. He was succeeded by Colonel Sink and the command of the 506th passed to Lt. Col. Charles H. Chase. Eleven days later the commander who had led the 101st through combat, Maj. Gen. Maxwell D. Taylor, told the Division goodbye and flew back to the U.S. to become Superintendent of the United States Military Academy at West Point. Eventually so many of his 101st officers joined him there—General Higgins, Colonels Sink, Sherburne, and Moore, Lt. Colonel Ginder, Majors Legere and Hoffman—that the Academy got the nickname of "101 Ranch." Command of the Division went to Brig. Gen. William Nelson Gillmore.

General Gillmore, a graduate of West Point, class of 1925, had come to the 101st in February 1945 as Division Artillery Commander after having held that position with the 34th Infantry Division and the 1st Armored Division in Italy. He was promoted from colonel to brigadier general in May.

General Gillmore was succeeded on September 25 by Brig. Gen. Gerald St. Clair Mickle, formerly the division commander of the 75th Infantry Division, which had been a part of XVI Corps and was now being redeployed to the U.S. General Mickle, a graduate of the U.S. Military Academy in the class of 1918, had fought with his division in the Rhineland, Ardennes and Central Germany campaigns. General Mickle served as Division Commander for two weeks and was succeeded on October 9 by Brig. Gen. Stuart Cutler.

General Cutler, a veteran of the 1916 Mexican Border campaign and of World War I, had earned four battle stars in World War II. He had served in the U.S. as Assistant Division Commander of the 13th Airborne Division and in the ETO as Chief of the Airborne Section,

Headquarters, First U.S. Army Group. During Normandy he had been on temporary duty with the 101st. Later he was Deputy Chief of Staff of the First Allied Airborne Army. He was to be the 101st's last commander.

A Division Passes

In the busy days of 1942 in Louisiana and North Carolina when the 101st was being shaped into a fighting division it isn't likely that anybody gave much thought to what would happen to the Division when the war was over. If they thought about it the vision was probably of triumphant columns of men marching in victory through the streets of some great American city and then going on to become an airborne division of the regular U.S. Army; or possibly of a final impressive ceremony on some broad parade ground, with flags, music, a last casing of the colors, and dissolution. Probably no one foresaw the end as it actually was to be.

Shortly after the finish of the war with Japan the War Department plans for the 101st were announced. The Division was to be the Regular Army airborne division. The 101st and the 82d Airborne Divisions were to make an exchange of personnel, the 82d to take all high-point personnel and the 101st the low-pointers. The 82d would precede the 101st to the U.S., discharge its people and then be inactivated. The 101st was given a sailing date of December 5, was to land in New York, parade there and then go to Fort Bragg where it would be permanently stationed. Awaiting the Division at Fort Bragg was an old friend, for the new post commander was General McAuliffe.

By the 25th of September plans called for about three thousand men to go to the 75th Division during the first week in October for immediate redeployment. After these men left all others with more than 70 points were to go to the 82d in exchange for that division's low-point men.

The Division proceeded with plans for what was to be the big parade of the war—down Fifth Avenue in New York City. The new jump boots, which for a year everybody had talked about and nobody had seen, turned up and were issued along with a parachute silk scarf to each man. Two members of the Division Parachute Maintenance Company spent almost a month on a fifty-foot square banner to drape over the side of the ship as she sailed into New York Harbor. The higher commanders were worried about how the men on the boat would be able to keep their overcoats clean enough to parade in. There was considerable discussion about the parade itself and how to reward the men afterward (Said Colonel Sink, as recorded in the Division Diary:

"Have a helluva big dance at the Madison Square Garden with, say, about 5,000 wenches.").

So the planning went, through September and October. The Division got a taste of what its victory march might be like when on September 3 approximately one thousand members represented the United States Army in a parade in Brussels celebrating the first anniversary of the liberation of that city. Led by Lt. Col. Raymond V. Bottomly, Jr.— he had led the battalion which had made first contact with the Germans outside another Belgian town, Bastogne—the 101st veterans passed through cheers which drowned out the sound of the music, through thrown flowers and kissing *mademoiselles*. Another Belgian honor came in November, on the afternoon of the 7th, when representatives of that government in the marketplace building in Auxerre awarded to the 101st the Belgian *fourragère*. Then a few hours after the ceremony the phone rang and from Corps came the news: the 101st was to trade places with the 82d.

The first announcement called for the 101st to prepare to return immediately to the U.S. as a carrier for high-point personnel and there be inactivated. Later, even this was changed. The 101st was to die in France.

During the grey winter days the work of inactivating a division went on; the paperwork, the turning in of equipment and vehicles, the closing out of the quarters, the departure of the men. Those who had been replacements at Bastogne and in Alsace and who were now the high-pointers left, man after man, and finally the low-pointers and those who had chosen to stay until the end loaded up and went to Camp Philip Morris to join the 82d. Three years and three months before the 82d Infantry Division had divided its officers and men to form the 82d and 101st Airborne Divisions. Now the men who made up the 101st became part of the division which carried on the tradition and wore the "All American" patch of the parent organization. The 101st Airborne Division was history and a memory.

Last Rendezvous

In Auxerre on November 30 Col. Harry W. O. Kinnard, G-3, wrote the Division's last daily bulletin. Kinnard had joined the 501st when it was activated as a regiment in November, 1942. On the morning of June 6 he, along with six other members of his West Point class of '39, had parachuted into Normandy. One, Carl Buechner, after Normandy had gone to the First Allied Airborne Army. Of the remaining six, three were dead before Christmas. Bill Turner, killed

This banner, made by the 101st Parachute Maintenance Company, to be hung over the side of the Queen Mary when the Division docked in New York. This display in Auxerre was the only one held.

going up to St. Come-du-Mont. Bob Cole, with the Medal of Honor on the Carentan Causeway and a bullet in the head in Holland. Jim LaPrade, dead the first day of Bastogne. Pinky Ginder, crippled in Holland. Julian Ewell, wounded in January at Bastogne and evacuated, never to return. All had been lieutenant colonels; and the two who were with the 101st into 1945, Ewell and Kinnard, before they were 30 were wearing eagles. Kinnard wrote:

> To those of you left to read this last daily bulletin—do not dwell on the disintegration of our great unit, but rather be proud that you are of the "old guard" of the greatest division ever to fight for our country. Carry with you the memory of its greatness wherever you may go, being always assured of respect when you say, "I served with the 101st."

Of the men who had organized the 101st's parachute regiments only Sink was still around, and he was in a Division job; the Curahee regiment was going out under command of the man who had been his steady right hand throughout the war, Charles Chase. Steve Chappuis,

778

who had come to the 502d as a company commander when the Deuce was a battalion and Pearl Harbor had not yet happened, still commanded the regiment he had taken over in Holland. Death had taken Johnson, wounds Moseley, Michaelis and Ewell. Ballard had seen the 501st inactivated and had gone back to the U.S.

That day the last entry was made in the Division diary:

Div inactivated 30 Nov. 45
NM
C/S

NM was Col. Ned Moore, last chief of staff of the Division. In August 1942, a major, he had been sent to Camp Claiborne to serve as personnel officer of the new airborne division. He had gotten there two days before the 101st was activated; so he had seen it come into existence. Now he initialled it out.

Over in Sens Col. Joseph H. Harper, called "Bud" by his fellow officers, watched the regiment he had commanded since Normandy leave. Long before the last days it was rare for him to see a man who had landed on the Normandy beach; there were not too many left who less than a year before had helped the regiment hold almost half the circle around Bastogne. Colonel Harper had been in the 82d Infantry Division, had been an original member of the 101st at Claiborne. After his regiment had closed out he found it lonesome in Sens; so he moved over to Auxerre.

And thus there gathered in the last days the remaining colonels of the Division. Each of them represented a major element of the 101st; Moore of Division, Harper of the 327th, Kinnard of the 501st, Chappuis of the 502d, and Sink of the 506th.

The last of the field desks and boxes and crates were hauled out of the school which had housed Division Headquarters and the building was hollow and cold. The *casernes* were empty, the fields where the tents had stood bore only the beaten outlines on the ground, the football goalposts stood on the deserted playing fields, there were no pairs of airborne soldiers strolling along the banks of the Yonne. It got the better of the colonels. They packed their stuff and sent it on to the redeployment area. Then early one rainy morning they took off for Paris.

Cold War Years To 1965

Following World War II the fluctuating fortunes of the 101st Airborne Division followed an erratic pattern. For several months during the next eleven years the outfit lived only in the hearts of its veterans, for it was inactivated and reactivated no less than three times during that period. And its active duty was as a training division. The proud eagle appeared minus "Airborne" strip with clipped wings and muffled scream.

The first post war activation took place at Camp Breckinridge, Kentucky, in July, 1948. Inactivated in May, 1949, the division was called back for Korean War duty, again at Breckinridge, in August, 1950. It retired again in December, 1953, but five months later appeared once more at Fort Jackson, South Carolina, where it drew its cadre personnel from the 8th Infantry Division. Here it was to remain until March, 1956, when it was transferred to Fort Campbell, Kentucky. But this time it flew. The "Airborne" was back, and the Screaming Eagle in full feather and voice donned combat gear to return to his rightful place in the ranks of the airborne legions.

Even during its training duties, however, the 101st maintained its reputation of being commanded by top-notch generals, many of whom went on to add more stars to their shoulders in succeeding years. In order of appearance were: Major General William R. Schmidt, Major General Cornelius E. Ryan, Major General Ray E. Porter, Major General Paul DeWitt Adams, Major General Riley F. Ennis and Major General Frank S. Bowen.

With the reactivation order came a special assignment. The 101st had been chosen to pioneer a brand new concept in Infantry division organization: The "Pentomic Division." Five-sided ("penta") and cellular in structure, the new division was designed to survive and fight on the atomic battlefield. Hence, "Pentomic." Eventually all Infantry divisions adopted the structure which was unlike anything that had ever appeared before on American organization charts.

The battle group became the basic fighting unit of the division, and there were five of them. Each contained a headquarters company, five rifle companies, an organic battery of 4.2 mortars, and necessary reconnaissance, anti-tank, and logistic units to make it an independent, self-sustaining fighting force. Supporting units of the division were similarly organized in cellular multiples of five to facilitate function. The artillery was grouped

THE SCREAMING EAGLE FLIES AGAIN . . . September 21, 1956, at Fort Campbell, Ky., the colors of the 101st Airborne Division were presented to Major General T. L. Sherburne, by Secretary of the Army Wilbur M. Brucker and Chief of Staff of the Army General Maxwell Taylor.

into five batteries of howitzers and a battery of Little-John rockets. The 501st Signal Battalion and the 326th Engineers were back.

The Command and Control Battalion contained a five-platoon cavalry troop and military police, intelligence, and chemical detachments, as well as headquarters and administrative units. Here too was the Band which soon became widely known for its ability to jump, march, and play at the double-time. In the Support Group were a Quartermaster parachute supply and maintenance company, the 326th Medical Company, the 426th Supply and Transportation Company and the 801st Maintenance Battalion.

Total personnel strength of the Pentomic Airborne Division was 11,500, some 5000 less than the conventional airborne division. However, the introduction of new, powerful weapons had more than made up for the loss of personnel. Equipment glimpsed only in wishful dreams during World War II was now on hand to make the new division the most potent instrument of destructive might ever to don airborne wings.

781

ORGANIZATION DAY . . . 21 September 1956
Colors Mass—Commanders Pray at Organization
Day for the 101st Airborne Division

The atomic-armed Little John rocket battery gave the 101st the distinction of being the first division to have an organic nuclear capability. There was also the SPAT (Self Propelled Anti-Tank), that 17-ton off-spring of an anti-tank gun and a tank. Nicknamed the "Scorpion" its 90mm stinger on a full-tracked chassis was soon "jumping" right along with the battle group. Present at reorganization, or joining within the next few years, were jeep-mounted 106mm recoiless rifles, the Davy Crockett (also jeep mounted) which gave the infantryman his own atomic punch, new radios, new fixed-wing aircraft, new helicopters capable of performing a multitude of tasks ranging from transporting vertical assault echelons of riflemen to delivering cascades of aerial rockets. There was the new M-60 machine gun. And there was the "mule," the motorized platform capable of carrying a thousand-pound load. The driver could ride it, walk behind it, or gear it down and steer it while crawling in its wake.

BATTLE GROUP FORMATION . . . 327th Airborne Battle Group.
A PENTOMIC BATTLE GROUP

The individual rifleman was not neglected either. He maintained his pre-eminent position with a new combat pack and a new rifle, the M-14, which he turned in for the still newer, lighter-weight, higher-velocity M-16 early in 1965. But it is important to note that there is still a bayonet on the end of that rifle, and the doughboy today is just as capable of using that bayonet as were his forefathers back there in the days when his heritage was being forged on distant battlefields.

Airborne weapons and equipment had grown in size and weight; and, of course, the means of delivering them into combat had grown too. A new generation of aircraft was on hand: the twin-boomed C-119 "Boxcar", the ponderous C-123 "Provider", the giant "Globemaster" C-124, and the mighty turbo-powered "Hercules" C-130.

New aircraft configuration and bigger parachutes permitted the aerial delivery of loads heavier and bulkier than ever before. Artillery came down in one piece; 2-1/2 ton trucks were dropped intact; bulldozers and SPAT's were parachuted with early echelons. And the individual soldier also got a new parachute, the

783

THE TRIUMVERATE OF COMMAND
Summer 1958

Major General W. C. Westmoreland   Brigadier General Andrew McAnsh   Brigadier General C. W. G. Rich
Commander   Assistant Commander   Assistant Commander
April 1958 - June 1960   Operations and Training   Personnel and Logistics

T-10 with a 28-foot canopy. With a more gradual deployment, from apex down, the T-10 not only lessened the opening shock but provided a more positive opening than did the T-7. Its rate of descent was slightly less too, but it was more difficult to control, and its stubborn reluctance to collapse in a ground wind provided occasional ugly climaxes to beautiful PLF's. This latter characteristic was later counteracted by the addition of "canopy releases" on harness shoulder straps which allow a dragged jumper to free himself from a billowing chute while in a full tail-down skid. However, lest the T-7 veteran scoff, it should be noted that reserve parachutes are still worn and frequently deployed. Jumpers still land in trees, rivers, and power lines; and troopers still get dragged across jump zones. Hospital records and aching muscles attest to the fact that the "exit from aircraft in flight" is still worth every bit of that exra $55 per month the airborne soldier earns.

SKY DIVING . . . a member of the Fort Campbell Sports Parachute Club floats gently to earth during a free-fall parachute demonstration at Fort Campbell.

The Spring and Summer of 1956 were busy seasons at Fort Campbell as the division collected, formed, trained, developed strength and flexed its new muscles. Activation Day was September 21, 1956. It was a proud and glorious day for the 101st Airborne Division.

Secretary of the Army Wilber M. Brucker journeyed from Washington to present the division colors to the commanding general, Major General Thomas L. Sherburne. "The glorious

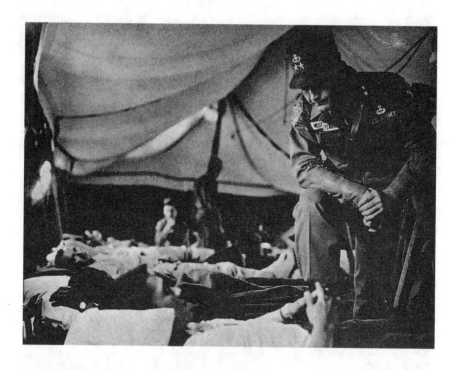

A COMMANDER VISITS HIS TROOPS . . . EAGLE WING . . . April 1958. Major General William C. Westmoreland visits a Field Hospital where injured are treated after jump on Exercise Eagle Wing. 5 were killed and 155 injured.

record of the 101st Airborne should be a source of pride and satisfaction," said Secretary Brucker, "to all its present members, many of whom helped to write that record. We have every reason to be proud of the part it is destined to play in the future . . ."

Army Chief of Staff and former Division Commander, Maxwell D. Taylor, was also on hand to welcome back his old command and to charge the young eagles "to carry forward the magnificent record of this division into the future, bearing in mind your obligation to your forebearers to maintain the reputation of the 101st established in World War II."

The 101st Airborne stood tall, indeed, that September afternoon as long-cased battle flags tossed in the breeze and the Screaming Eagle frowned out his pugnacious challenge from ten thousand airborne shoulders. Drums rolled, trumpets sounded and the helmeted troopers swung by the reviewing stand in a full division parade.

It was a mingling of the old and the new: new organizations, old guidons; new equipment, old battle streamers. There were

LITTLE JOHN
Mighty Mite
Divarty's Pride and Joy

stalwart veterans stiffening the ranks that day, men who had jumped into Normandy, fought in Holland, and endured the frozen hell that was Bastogne. But mostly it was new faces, young faces, that snapped to "eyes right" when they passed the assemblage of honored guests. By and large it was a new generation, a noble generation carrying on the traditions of a noble family. The esprit, the determination, the jaunty step, all were there, just as before. Rebirth of the Division? Ridiculous! The 101st had never died. S.L.A. Marshall spotted the fact and said so as military editor of *The Detroit News:*

With the re-activation of the 101st Division the Screaming Eagles will again take wing. I trust, as one informed observer, that no nonsense will be written about the rebirth of an immortal outfit. The word wouldn't fit. Rebirth is a matter of the spirit, not of the flesh. That spirit has flamed ever higher in the years that men who knew it have been able to look back at the old Division, pondering what it did for them and for the flag. Nothing more is needed than clear memory if the new is lovingly to treasure the tradition of the old. No more inspiring example may be held high before the eyes of fighting men than the flaming spirit of the 101st of World War II. This was the best; in years to come there will be none better. Why was it so? Wherein lay the difference which set the 101st part, so

787

ROCKET FIRING
at
FORT CAMPBELL, Ky.

that one who had reason to compare its performance and attitude with those of many others was conscious of its superiority? Many times along the trail which started inshore from Utah Beach and led finally to Auxerre I was asked this question, by leaders of the Division, including General Taylor, and by ranks no less interested in the answer.

My own conclusions stressed three principles:

First, officers and men were closer together in the 101st than in others. Regimental and Battalion officers not only knew Company NCO's by name: they knew their qualities, experience, and often, their family background. It was literally true that in the Division every man was treated as a potential leader until his substance was proved one way or the other beyond doubt. There is no surer road to uniting comradeship.

Second, the Division was physically fit, and if men didn't have leg-push, they weren't fit for the club. In this machine age, we tend to forget the supreme value of the march over distance—that there is no better way, short of battle to separate the men from the boys. The Division did not put an inordinate physical demand on man: it insisted on a training which kept them battle sound.

Last, the Division maximized the value of surprise. No other Division compares with it in that particular. There was respect for other principles; but the emphasis was on the main one. Wherein lay the key to success? Again it was a matter of the spirit. Screaming Eagles believed that in combat, whatever the

HOOKED-UP AND READY TO GO...

High over a Drop Zone at Fort Campbell, Kentucky troopers of the 101st Airborne Division Stand-up—and Hook-up ready for that command to GO!!!

enemy situation, if only a few men who wore the patch were around, it was time to attack. Go back and search the record: the great victories of the Division were the cumulative effects of astonishing acts of boldness by small groups against seemingly impossible odds. The pivotal parts played by minor outposts, picket squads and misdropped fragments run through the story like a golden thread. No change in warfare or weapons lessens the importance of these three values. The 101st was always tuned to the new age: the job is to carry on.

Following formal reactivation, the 101st Airborne Division entered a four-month test period. The series of shakedown exercises, called JUMP LIGHT, culminated with a full combat team jump at Fort Bragg. Platoon, company, battalion and division-sized problems filled the days and nights as concepts were tested, developed, perfected. Check, modify, recheck. New ideas came to light, were tried, changed, retried, accepted, discarded. How? When? Where? What . . . a thousand questions . . . a thousand answers.

It was not until the test period was completed in January 1957 that the Pentomic Division, described previously, emerged in its final form. The fact that the pentomic organization was

789

One thousand . . . two thousand . . . three thousand . . . and into space goes another trooper of the 101st Airborne Division, waiting for that opening of the canopy.

adopted by Infantry divisions Army wide attests to the soundness of the basic concept and the excellence of the 101st effort.

In succeeding months and years the 101st Airborne Division settled down to the never-ending task of building, improving, and perfecting its posture of readiness—readiness to go anywhere, anytime and come down fighting. As it developed into front-line, cold war veterans the division traveled far and wide. Screaming

TROOPERS OF THE 101st Airborne Division still attached to static lines wait for the opening shock of their parachute.

Eagle patches appeared from Alaska to Puerto Rico, from the Philippines to Iran in scores of alerts, exercises and maneuvers.

In the fall of 1957 elements of the 101st Airborne Division were called upon to perform civil disturbance duty in Little Rock, Arkansas. With the eyes of the world upon them, they did the difficult and unpleasant task with a disciplined dignity which earned them praise from all quarters.

Major General William C. Westmoreland assumed command of the division in April 1958, and that same month the 101st conducted Exercise EAGLE WING. This was, in a sense, the division's commencement exercise where it received its graduate degree as a full-fledged, combat-ready division. Deployed on the Fort Campbell reservation, the 101st simulated a withdrawal from action and within five days, refitted, packed, and took off to a series of six departure airfields spread from Ohio to Arkansas. There it marshalled, rigged for heavy drop, and mounted a division-size airborne assault on Fort Campbell drop zones. The exercise took a disastrous turn when the 502d Battle Group encountered freak ground winds on the DZ. Five troopers were

791

BILLOWING CHUTES . . . ANOTHER SAFE LANDING
for troopers of the 101st Airborne Division.

killed; 155 others injured. Despite the disaster, however, EAGLE
WING proved most valuable.

The following month STRAC (Strategic Army Corps) was
established and the division became one of the foremost fighting elements. Many of the techniques pioneered by the 101st
were eventually adopted by all STRAC units, and the Screaming Eagles managed to conduct the first STRAC alert a full
week before the public announcement was made of STRAC's
existence.

One of the first real tests of the division's ability to respond
came when the safety of Vice President Nixon was threatened
during his South American tour in May 1958. Two rifle companies of the 506th Battle Group were given the no-notice nod
to GO and were in Puerto Rico in record time. Two companies
of marines provided stimulating competition in the race to
Puerto Rico. Needless to say the Screaming Eagles won the race—
although to this very day there are marines who will dispute this.

In March 1960, the division participated in PUERTO PINE,
a mass airlift exercise during which 8000 troops and 40,000 tons

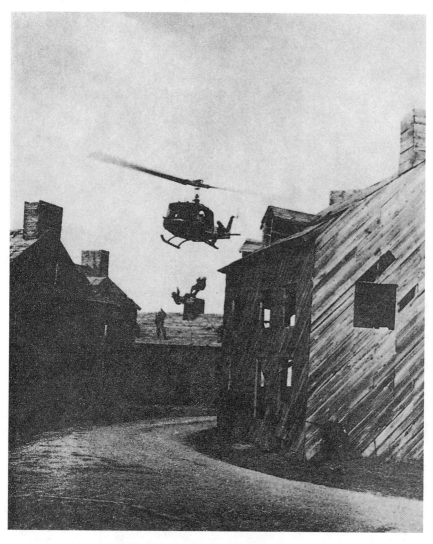

COMBAT IN CITIES—Surprise attack by helicopter . . .
Fort Campbell, Ky.

of equipment were airlifted to Puerto Rico; and the following month Exercise QUICK STRIKE—an operation conducted in a simulated nuclear-chemical warfare environment—was held at Fort Campbell and Camp Breckinridge.

It was also during General Westmoreland's command that the RECONDO School was established at Fort Campbell. RECONDO (a word derived from "reconnaissance" and "doughboy") became a finishing school for the small unit leader. The

RED HILLS
Fort Campbell, Ky.
Winter 1962
"The Kentucky-Tennessee hills ran red—with mud!"

gruelling three-week course features concentrated airborne-ranger training ranging from hand-to-hand combat and survival practice to the planning and performance of long-range patrols. Brawn, brains, stamina and plain old-fashioned guts in generous portion, are required for the successful completion of the school and the right to wear the arrowhead patch of the recondo graduate.

794

CALLING THE SHOTS . . . *Moving Out: A forward observer, covered.*

In June 1960, Major General Ben Harrell took command of the 101st Airborne Division and two months later the division conducted what was described as the "biggest U.S. airdrop since World War II," at Fort Bragg, North Carolina. Over 7000 troops and 409 tons of equipment were delivered from the air in Exercise BRIGHT STAR. Two hundred troops jumped at Fort Riley, Kansas, in October and promptly named the DZ "Geronimo Drop Zone" simply because it needed a name and they happened to be members of the 501st. Exercise SOUTH WIND, the 10,000 man maneuver at Elgin AFB, Florida, was the big event in October.

Major General C.W.G. Rich assumed command of the division in July 1961. In August the division joined the 82d Airborne in SWIFT STRIKE I, the first of a series of joint Swift Strike exercises held over wide areas of North and South Carolina. The two-week, 35,000 man maneuver was one of the largest war games held in the United States since World War II. A year laetr there was SWIFT STRIKE II, 60,000 men, and the next year a 100,000 man-strong SWIFT STRIKE III. In each of these major maneuvers the 101st Airborne Division played a major

795

role and added a major chapter to its growing reputation as one of the finest—if, indeed, not the finest—of the Army's combat divisions.

In September, 1961, the Airborne Battle Group of the 327th Infantry tested its readiness by hopping over to Turkey to take part in the multi-nation exercies CHECK MATE II. Five months later the 506th Battle group went a bit further in the opposite direction to jump in the Philippines as a participant in GREAT SHELF.

In January-February 1962, weather-plagued RED HILLS was held on, and in the vicinity of, the Fort Campbell reservation; and in May it was Joint Exercise QUICK KICK at Camp Lejeune, N.C., where 40,000 soldiers, sailors, airmen and marines waged a "war" involving forces from all the services.

October 1962 brought the Cuban Crisis and the world held its breath, waited, and wondered what would be done if the missiles were not withdrawn. The men of the 101st waited too, but they had a pretty good idea what would be done, and they were all set to take part in the doing. Grim-faced men sitting in marshalling areas, coiled, cocked, ready. The missiles came out. The world relaxed. And the 101st Airborne Division slowed to its normal pace—a headlong gallop.

Relaxation is an ill-afforded luxury as far as the 101st is concerned, crisis or no crisis. The parachute and long-range air transport have combined to thrust the 101st Airborne Division onto the very ramparts of the Cold War. War drums of brewing troubles the world over throb loud at Fort Campbell. A government falls in South America; a friend is threatened in Africa; a saber rattles in the Middle East . . . Each event triggers a small reaction in the 101st, a quiet coil, a silent alertness, a subtle shift of balance. The Screaming Eagle may be perched in Kentucky, but his distance from almost any point in the world is measured in hours.

An important element of the division's alert posture is the DRF, the Division Ready Force. Composed of a reinforced infantry battalion, complete with a battery of artillery and necessary supporting elements, the DRF stands 24 hours a day prepared to board aircraft ready to fight twelve hours from the moment of alert. Personnel are restricted to the post; vehicles and equipment are ready for rigging; ammunition and supplies to sustain the 1000-man force are packaged and pre-positioned. One reinforced rifle company of this battalion, known as the Immediate

MAJOR GENERAL BEVERLEY E. POWELL
20th Commander of the 101st Airborne
Division
Fires the XM-161 Rifle

Ready Force (IRF) is restricted to barracks, equipment rigged for heavy drop, just three hours from load-out. Units perform the duty on a weekly rotational basis, and the division is never without a DRF. When the force is alerted, a stand-by battalion takes its place, and as the standby moves out another unit automatically moves into position. So on, until the full division is committed. The story of the 101st trooper's wife who turns on her radio to find out why her husband is late coming home from work is not really so far-fetched as it may seem.

In February 1963 Major General Harry H. Critz arrived to command the division and lead the continuing parade of command post exercises, field maneuvers, training tests, and practice alerts that filled the balance of the year.

In early 1964 the division underwent another reorganization and almost overnight, with hardly a break in its stride, shook off its Pentomic garb and donned the new look of ROAD (Reorganization Objective Army Division). It wasn't an easy task, for the changes were radical and far reaching.

The new organization further increased divison firepower, improved ground mobility, provided greater flexibility, and facilitated command and control. Key features of the present ROAD organization are three brigade headquarters, capable of controlling a varying number of combat elements, and a support command which contains and coordinates supporting echelons. The combat building blocks of the airborne ROAD division are nine infantry battalions, a cavalry squadron, and three artillery battalions. Other combat elements include an engineer battalion, an aviation battalion, and the Little John rocket battery. The 1st and 2d Battalions of the historic 501st, 502d, 506th and 327th Infantry now make up eight of the nine Infantry battalions, while the 3d Battalion, 187th Infantry completes the list. The 2d Squadron, 17th Cavalry (the Army's first airborne cavalry squadron) provides the division with long range eyes and ears. The Division Artillery battalions come from the 319, 321, and the 320th Artillery Regiments. The Rocket Battery is still with the division and so is the 326th Engineer Battalion. Falling under Support Command are the 801st Maintenance Battalion, 426th Supply and Transportation Battalion, 326th Medical Battalion and the 101st Administration Company.

The ROAD reorganization was completed in February—a month ahead of original schedule—and the following month Major General Beverley E. Powell, assumed command. In April the 1st Brigade flew half way around the world and made a parachute jump in Iran to join Iranian forces in Exercise DELAWAR.

The whole division traveled to California, in May, for Exercise DESERT STRIKE, the vast desert maneuver encompassing a sizable portion of the Mojave Desert and involving some 100,000 troops. The Air Force flew 619 missions to transport the 101st contingent of 11,500 men and 7,840 tons of equipment. Entering the "battle area" via parachute and air assault landing, the troopers of the 101st grappled mightily with armored units, in armor country. It was a maneuver of movement, with wide frontages, great depths, and supply lines that stretched up to a hundred miles—hardly the best setting for a light, infantry unit. But they did well, these troopers of the 101st, and they returned home with new knowledge and a new cockiness.

The rest of 1964 was devoted to local field exercises, practice alerts, and the all important maintenance of readiness. Division resources, both personnel and equipment, were heavily tapped

A 3.5 rocket launcher goes into action . . . *ONE SHOT DORA* . . .

for support of the 11th Air Assault Division Tests during the late summer and fall.

In September, a delegation of twenty-six troopers journeyed to Holland to join in commemorative ceremonies marking the 20th anniversary of MARKET GARDEN. There, by the city of Veghel, on the very fields where jump boots pounded in 1944, they conducted a parachute jump led by the Division Commander, Major General Beverley E. Powell. They returned home with warm memories and mementos symbolizing the strong ties of friendship that span an ocean and a couple of decades to bind the 101st Airborne and the Dutch people.

The division entered 1965 amidst plans for busy and profitable months ahead.

A skeleton outline of major maneuvers, such as this, cannot possibly tell the full story of the 101st Airborne Division since World War II. That story is the sum total of all the experiences of the thousands of troopers who have worn the Screaming Eagle patch since the war—millions of experiences, large and small. Quite beyond the scope of these few pages are the countless cold nights, wet days, exhausting marches, good jumps, bad jumps, selfless deeds, courageous acts, hard decisions, triumphs, disappointments, and achievements that fill the halls of memory and

799

OBSERVANCE OF MASS IN THE FIELD
*Under field conditions—Mass is observed by
troopers of the 101st Airborne Division.*

form the story of the 101st. Above all, there were achievements—numerous and far-reaching. In competitions of every kind the 101st has stood high. In the field of sports, for example, the division has captured far more than her fair share of trophies, and two of her sons have come home with Olympic medals. When it comes to soldiering, the Screaming Eagle proves second to none.

At the root of all achievement over the years has been a hard-driving, inexhaustible esprit de corps. This elusive quality that makes good outfits great has been abundantly present all during the division's proud march through history. It is precious quality both rugged and fragile. It overcomes odds and wins battles; yet it must be ever nourished. Confidence is its father, Heritage its mother.

It was only fitting that the 101st Airborne Division Association held its 1965 Reunion at Fort Campbell. There, in August, former members of this great outfit saw in full bloom the fruits of yesteryear effort and experienced once more that surge of esprit that sets the division apart from all others. Unseen, but also present amidst the muffled sound of ghostly trumpets were the thousands of others who once wore the patch of the Screaming Eagle. Thus assembled, the former Sons of Destiny joined the troopers of today to honor the 101st Airborne Division——past, present, and future.

Division Hq. & Hq. Co.

Alexander, Winston L, Tec 5
Claypool, George E, Pfc
Cross, Herbert B, Capt
Doyle, Thomas J, Sgt
Henry, Emerson M, Pvt
Hill, Farrell E, Tec 4
Lucas, Henry D, Pfc
Nelson, Ellsworth F, Pfc
Parkinson, Roger W, Lt Col
Pratt, Don F, Brig Gen
Rusch, Elmer A, Capt

326th Airborne Engineer Bn.

Aper, Henry J, Sgt
Barnes, Roy E, 2 Lt
Bauman, LeRoy C, Jr, Pvt
Blastic, Clarence J, Sgt
Blickhahn, Earl W, Pvt
Blumeier, Richard J, Sgt
Blunt, Greydon H, Cpl
Bopp, William R, Sgt
Cali, Dominick D, Pvt
Carlson, Clayton W, Pvt
Carson, Raymond L, Pvt
Christiano, Rocco, Pvt
Connor, Merll C, Pvt
Crismon, Clifford R, Pvt
Cunningham, Robert D, Pvt
DiSalle, Tony, Jr, Pfc
Dieckman, Douglas G, Pvt
DiGaetano, Louis, Sgt
Dopjera, Rudolph J, Pvt
Ellzey, Ceyril M, Sgt
Englehardt, Albert J, Sgt
Esposito, Angelo J, Tec 5
Ferra, Mariano S, S Sgt
Froemke, Donald H, Capt
Garcia, Alberto, Pfc
Garrard, Clarence S, Tec 5
Geiger, Elmer J, Cpl
Hanford, Theodore, Cpl
Hayes, Thomas H, S Sgt
Hielscher, Paul H, Tec 5
Hightower, Mack W, Pvt
Hiltunen, Ray J, 1 Lt
Holin, Julius A, Pvt
Hovi, Lauri W, Pvt

Hoyt, Paul R, Pvt
Hruby, Anton F, Pvt
Hunter, John J, Pvt
Huss, Clarence W, Cpl
Jabin, Bruce R, 1 Lt
Jones, Calbert M, Cpl
Jones, Theodore T, Jr, 1 Lt
Jordon, Millard C, Pvt
Kendziorski, Adam Z, Pfc
Kiddy, Cecil T, Pfc
Kwilasz, Stanley I, Pvt
LeMay, Robert J, Tec 5
Legg, Paul K, Pvt
Loebe, Henry J, Jr, Pfc
Maranto, Salvatore, Pvt
Mason, John M, 2 Lt
McGinnis, Daniel P, Pvt
McGuire, William J, Pfc
Miller, Burman R, Pvt
Montgomery, Eldon L, Pvt
Mullen, Ancel D, Tec 5
Myrick, Willis G, Pvt
Northrup, Jacob R, Pfc
Norwood, Thomas A, Capt
O'Laughlin, James F, Sgt
Pappas, John C, Lt Col
Pena, Fernando A, Jr, Pvt
Plummer, William H, 1 Lt
Pontiggia, Joseph, Pfc
Portugal, Walter C, S Sgt
Prato, Nick, Pvt
Prussman, Quentin H, Pfc
Ravencraft, Henry R, Pvt
Reich, Barnett, Pfc
Rogers, Jack L, Capt
Rogers, James H, Pfc
Smith, Bruce C, Pvt
Sorrels, Odis T, Pfc
Spielvogel, Bernard, Pfc
Stackhouse, Wendell L, Pvt
Stockstill, Raymond F, Pvt
Turin, Peter V, Pfc
Varone, Anthony M, Pvt
Watson, James R, 2 Lt
Werner, Richard W, Pvt

326th Airborne Medical Co.

Bennett, Harry K, Pfc
Fox, William E, Tec 5

Frank, Melvin, S Sgt
Holoubek, Francis J, Tec 5
Landon, Thomas G, Pvt
Lewis, Charles T, 2 Lt
Miller, Jacob M, Pfc
Muoio, Frank D, Pvt
Petropol, James E, Pvt
Place, Robert M, Pvt
Roach, Robert E, Pfc
Schadegg, Louis G, 1 Lt
Sewall, Homer, Pvt
Smith, Russell, F, 1 Sgt
Stewart, Earl, Sgt
Sullivan, Henry G, Pfc
Tallman, Charles W, Pfc
Vestal, Charles S, Cpl
Vogt, Everett C, 1 Lt

101st Airborne Signal Co.

Demonge, Raymond E, Pfc
Dottavanio, Joseph, Pvt
Gerwig, Gustave O, Pvt
Johnson, Teddy T, Pvt
Jugan, Michael, Pvt
McCollum, Robert W, Tec 5
Mihalko, Peter, Cpl
Millican, Roy G, Pvt
Minshall, Olen, Pvt
Robbins, Lawrence, Cpl
Russell, Conrad E, M Sgt
Vella, Thomas F, Pvt
Weber, William G, Tec 5
Zajelka, Stanley M, Pvt

426th Airborne QM Co.

Britt, Robert F, Pvt
East, Robert C, Pvt
Mathis, Perry, Cpl
Norton, Sammie C, Tec 5
Ouellette, Raymond W, Pvt
Van Laningham, Donald, Pfc

101st Airborne MP Platoon

Brown, John W, Pfc
Konter, Ambrose F, Pvt
Paris, Joseph P, Sgt
Smith, William H, Pfc

327th Glider Infantry (Including 1st Battalion 401 Glider Inpantry and 101st Airborne Division Reconnaissance Platoon)

Abraham, Lester L, Pfc
Acquisto, Peter A, Pfc
Adams, Willis E, Sgt
Adkins, Elwood, Pfc
Adkison, Thomas C, Pfc
Aiello, Michael, S Sgt
Alamovich, Frank, Pfc
Alberico, Ernest, Pfc
Alhadeff, David P, Pfc
Alle, Ivan S, Pvt
Allen, Robert K, S Sgt
Allison, Leighton O, Pvt
Alvarez, Antonio R, S Sgt
Amburgey, John J, Pfc
Amino, Frank E, 2 Lt
Anderson, Luke S, Pfc
Anderson, William J, Pfc
Andrews, James J, Pvt
Aspinwall, John E, 2 Lt
Atherton, James A, Pfc
Austerman, Myron W, T Sgt
Bacco, Donald E, Pvt
Bacus, Earl, Pfc
Bader, Frederick W, Pfc
Baker, Carl R, Pvt
Baker, Harold A, Pfc
Baker, Leslie R, Pfc
Baker, Louis E, Pvt
Banister, J D, Pfc
Barrett, Henry J, Sgt
Barski, Alphonse S, Pfc
Bassetti, Alfonso P, Pfc
Bates, Forrest H, Pfc
Beck, Edgar G, Pfc
Bedford, Edward N, Pvt
Bella, Renzo C, Pfc
Bennett, Carl E, Pfc
Bertella, Dominick P, Pfc
Bever, Nelson B, Sgt
Bischoff, Robert G, Pvt
Blackwell, Harold W, Pfc
Blake, Woodrow, Pfc
Blankenship, Delbert, Pfc
Bliss, Harry W, Pfc
Blondin, Leo J, Pfc
Bobek, Henry W, Pfc
Bobic, Walter C, Pfc
Bock, John S, Sgt
Boettcher, Robert O, Pfc
Bond, Frank E, Jr., Pfc
Bonner, George W, T Sgt
Booker, Bruce H, 1 Lt
Booth, Linwood E, Pvt
Borovkoff, Walter J, Pfc
Bosh, Leonard E, Pfc
Bovenschen, Willis J, Pfc
Boyle, Robert J, Pfc
Bragg, Walter J, Pfc
Brandon, James B, Pfc
Braun, William L, Sgt
Brazier, Charles B, Pfc
Brechko, John, Sgt
Brickell, Ernest B, Pvt
Broadley, William H, 1 Lt
Brockway, Carroll W, Cpl
Brown, Early A, Pfc
Brunner, Emanuel, S Sgt
Bullian, Albert W, Pvt
Bumpus, Julian, Pfc
Burdiss, Cornelius F, Pfc
Burke, John J, S Sgt
Burns, Clifton W, Pfc
Cadena, Jesus G, Pvt
Cady, Otis B, Pfc
Cammarata, Joseph, Pvt

Campbell, Lemuel R, Pfc
Campbell, Raymond E, Pfc
Carder, Glen, T Sgt
Carpenter, Joe E, 1 Lt
Carpenter, Joseph L, Pfc
Carr, Joseph C, 1 Sgt
Cartwright, John O, Pvt
Case, Jack A, Cpl
Castleman, Bennie E, Sgt
Cermak, John R, Pvt
Cerullo, Anthony L, Pvt
Charbonneau, A J, Pfc
Chasse, Leo F, Pfc
Cherr, Joseph, Pvt
Chestnut, Freddie L, Pfc
Chinn, Gilbert M, S Sgt
Chriscoe, Gurnie, Pfc
Clappes, Homer H, Pvt
Clark, Allerton M, Pfc
Clark, Stanley V, Pfc
Clever, Paul B, Pvt
Clodfelter, Charles D, Pfc
Cody, Paul M, Pfc
Cohen, Reuben B, 2 Lt
Coker, Thomas J, Pvt
Davis, James H, Pvt
Davis, Jesse W, Pfc
Davis, Raymond N, Pfc
De la Rosa, Frank L, Pfc
DeMarco, Frank J, S Sgt
DeRenne, Arnold D, Pfc
DeVivo, Sebastian, Pfc
Deal, Harold K, Pfc
Dees, Arnold G, Pfc
Delaney, John G, Pvt
Dennison, Noah R, Pfc
Deubel, Frederick J, Pvt
Dever, Harold W, Pfc
DiAmbrosia, Louis C, Pvt
DiLeo, Anthony S, Pvt
DiNucci, Ralph J, Pvt
Dicken, Will E, Pfc
Dickerson, Leslie D, Pfc
Dierkis, Edward S, Pfc
Dietzsch, Maroy C, S Sgt
Cole, Roger V, Pfc
Collins, Douglas E, Pfc
Combs, James G, Pvt
Comer, James F, Pfc
Conrow, Raymond J, Pvt
Cowan, Olen D, Sgt
Cowell, Gordon H, M Sgt
Craig, John K, Pfc
Crawford, Seeber, S Sgt
Crooks, Stiles D, Sgt
Crossley, Fred, Jr, Pfc
Crump, Charles C, S Sgt
Cunningham, Chester C, Pfc
Curley, Gerald F, Pfc
Dade, Elmer W, Sgt
Damato, George, Pfc
Damron, Amos, Pvt
Danalds, Russell H, Pfc
Datwyler, Amos F, S Sgt
Diuble, Paul G, Pfc
Dodd, Beryl E, Pfc
Dome, Alvin L, Pvt
Donals, Robert L, Sgt
Donoho, Larry M, T Sgt
Dorman, Daniel F, 1 Lt
Duffy, Allan W, Pvt
Dugan, Richard L, Pvt
Duke, Howard M, Pfc
Dunn, Odie, Cpl
Dyer, Marc P, Tec 5
Dziedziak, Stanley J, Cpl
Eastmer, Earl W, Cpl
Edgell, Ernest R, Pfc
Eilermann, Alphonse H, Pfc
Elliott, Virgil K, Pvt
Ellis, Allen M, 1 Lt

Engman, Olaf W, Sgt
Epsom, William J, Pfc
Erler, LeRoy F, Pfc
Esco, John B, Pvt
Esparza, Antonio B, Pvt
Eubank, Gilbert G, Sgt
Evans, Frank, T Sgt
Ewing, Clarence T, Pfc
Fahey, Neil J, 1 Lt
Fahrner, Neil A, Pvt
Faith, Luther C, Pfc
Feathers, Eugene H, Pvt
Felder, Ed A, 1 Lt
Fields, Ralph A, Pfc
Finco, Andrew V, Pvt
Finder, Edward R, Pvt
Finicle, Ralph A, Jr, Pfc
Fitzgerald, Joseph R, Pfc
Fitzhenry, Joseph F, Pfc
Flemming, Emmett J, T Sgt
Forbes, Harley, Pvt
Franklin, Benjamin S, Pvt
Franklin, Sherman, Pfc
Fristik, Henry E, Pfc
Gacek, John R, S Sgt
Garlak, Walter J, S Sgt
Garrett, Daniel W, Pfc
Garrett, Warren H, Pfc
Gauntt, Edward E, S Sgt
Gebhardt, Charles H, Tec 5
Gentile, Dominic J, Pfc
Geraci, Anthony J, Pfc
Gere, Ernest J, Pvt
Gierlak, John H, Pfc
Gilbertson, Neil L, Pfc
Givens, Marion L, Pfc
Goad, Floyd B, Pfc
Goble, Everett L, Pfc
Goedkoop, Gerald J, Pvt
Gonnella, Alphonso R, Pfc
Gonyer, John D, Pfc
Goodson, Thomas E, Jr, 1 Lt
Goonan, Edward S, Pfc
Gordon, Lynwood B, Pvt
Gordon, Robert E, Pvt
Graef, Robert S, 2 Lt
Grapentine, Edward J, Jr, S Sgt
Green, Howard H, Jr., Pvt
Green, J. B. Pfc
Green, Leonard F, Pfc
Greggs, Robert E, Pfc
Gregory, Howard, Pfc
Gregory, Willie B, Pvt
Gresh, John H, Jr, Pvt
Grethel, Frederick W, Sgt
Griffiths, LeRoy E, Pvt.
Gunnoe, Marion L, Pfc
Haake, Frank G, Pfc
Haberer, Martin, Pvt
Hamblin, Ira E, Capt
Hamby, Charles L, Pfc
Hamm, James A, Pfc
Hammer, William D, Pfc
Handlin, Arthur A, Sgt
Hannon, John Joseph, Pfc
Harden, Max J, Pvt
Harmon, Russell C, Pvt
Harris, William G, Pfc
Harrison, Joseph E, Jr, Pfc
Harrison, Willard C, 1 Lt
Harrold, Ira O, Jr, Pvt
Harter, Ralph W, Pvt
Hatchel, Gordon A, Sgt
Hayes, Richard D, Pvt
Hayward, Gordon H, Pvt
Heatherley, Robert V, Pfc
Hefner, Andy E, Pfc
Helmar, James R, Pfc
Henn, Richard G, Pvt
Henry, Hugh F, Tec 4
Hernandez, Jesus G, Pvt

Herren, Joseph G, Sgt
Hill, Howard B, Pfc
Hill, Howard C, Pvt
Hill, Wilho K, S Sgt
Hinan, James H, Pvt
Hodge, James R, Pvt
Hoffman, Charles M, Cpl
Hojnacki, Stanley, S Sgt
Hollis, Eugene T, Pfc
Holmes, Oliver W, Pfc
Honeycutt, Ray A, Pvt
Horan, Edward W, Pvt
Horton, N A, Pfc
Howard, Ernest P, Pfc
Howell John C, Pfc
Hull, Dwight A, Pfc
Hull, Myron L, Pvt
Humbrock, Austin F, Pfc
Hunter, George, S Sgt
Idaszak, Stanley, Pfc
Insolo, John A, Pfc
Isenhart, Carl H, Pfc
Isermann, Edward A, Pvt
Iski, John S, Pfc
Jacobs, Ellis C, Sgt
Jaeger, Albert R, Pvt
Janis, Beverly A, Pfc
Jensen, Lawrence J, Pfc
Johnson, Harold R, Pvt
Johnson, Homer R, Pfc
Johnson, Melvin L, Pvt
Jones, Paul D, Pvt
Judd, Cale E, Pfc
Justus, Raymond D, Pfc
Kacerik, Stephen F, Pvt
Kaldenberg, Robert L, Pfc
Kamp, Lyman G, Sgt
Karcy, Ray A, 2 Lt
Karickhoff, Kyle D, Pfc
Kassan, Joseph F, Pvt
Keane, Patrick B, Pfc
Kelley, Vivian C, Pfc
Kelly, Daniel P, Pfc
Kelso, John D, Sgt
Kempt, Charles W, Pfc
Kervin, James B, Sgt
Kilby, James L, Pfc
Kincaid, Bert L, Pfc
King, Edmund E, Pvt
King, Robert A, Pvt
Kirby, Roy W, Pfc
Kish, Ernest, Sgt
Klughart, Frank R, Pvt
Kohl, Howard F, 1 Lt
Konarski, John S, Pfc
Kosterno, Edward, Pfc
Kraus, Leonard M, T Sgt
Kubinski, John J, Sgt
Kuchinskas, Joseph G, Pfc
Kuhn, Robert C, Pvt
Kulczycki, Joseph, Pfc
Kulp, Louis J, S Sgt
Lacey, John F, Pvt
Lachut, Louis, Pfc
Landrum, James T, Pvt
Lasky, Paul N, Pfc
Lavelett, James M, Sgt
LeBlanc, Louis P, Jr, Pvt
Lee, Jack, Pfc
Lee, John N, Pfc
Lee, William F, T Sgt
Leigh, Olen L, Sgt
Lemaster, William H, Pfc
Lesakowski, Albin A, Pfc
Lesh, John J, Pvt
Levy, Philip M, Pvt
Lewis, Chad B, Cpl
Likens, Fred, Pfc
Linthicum, Howard A, Pfc
Lombardino, Frank V, Pfc
Long, Harold W, Sgt

Loo, Jack, D, Sgt
Lovett, John M, 2 Lt
Lynn, Vernon E, Pfc
Lyons, John W, Pvt
Macejak, John, Pfc
Mackiewicz, Peter S, Sgt
Madonia, Philip F, Pfc
Majoros, Paul, Pfc
Malachowski, Francis, Sgt
Marine, Frank A, Pfc
Martin, Harold D, Sgt
Mayeux, Hubert J, Pfc
Maynor, Harry O, Sgt
Mazur, Chester N, Pfc
McAbée, Porter B, Pvt
McBride, James, Jr, Pfc
McClure, Leonard, Pfc
McCrary, Alfred L, Pfc
McCreary, Silas W, Pfc
McCurry, Willard R, Pfc
McDevitt, James P, Pfc
McGlothlin, J C, Pfc
McLaughlin, Basil G, Sgt
McMinn, James A, Pfc
McNeil, Harold M, Pvt
Meadows, John, Pfc
Meling, Truman A, Pfc
Mentlik, Lewis S, Capt
Mentz, Arthur G, Pvt
Metz, Carl E, S Sgt
Metzler, John J, Pvt
Mieloszyk, Frank E, Pvt
Migliore, Sam J, Sgt
Miller, Archie H, Pvt
Miller, Ernest J, Pfc
Miller, Grover L, Pfc
Miller, Philip T, Pfc
Miller, Raymond L, Tec 5
Mills, Warren U, Pfc
Moats, Glenn E, Sgt
Monson, Ernest L, Sgt
Moore, Ellis A, Pfc
Mora, Mateo P, Pfc
Moran, Eugene M, Pvt
Morehead, Russel A, Tec 5
Mraunac, Peter, Pfc
Murrah, J D, Pvt
Murray, Williams F, Pvt
Myers, Oswald J, Pvt
Myers, Robert F, Pvt
Naugher, Eldridge, Capt
Nestroy, Emil R, Pvt
Newbern, John C, Jr, Pfc
Newberry, George W, Pfc
Newman, Louis G, Pfc
Newton, Robert G, S Sgt
Nichols, Clyde L, Pvt
Niedzialek, Joseph J, Pfc
Nielsen, William R, Pvt
Nolan, Albert D, Pfc
Nycz, Henry J, Sgt
O'Brian, Joseph M, 1 Lt
Odom, Samuel E, Pfc
O'Melia, James L, Pfc
Ondo, Frank, Pfc
Onstott, William W, Jr, Pfc
Ori, John, Pfc
Orr, Lloyd R, Sgt
Ozoroff, David, Pvt
Pabst, George H, Jr, S Sgt
Pacheco, Frank S, Pfc
Padgett, Everett G, Pvt
Padgett, Ordway H, Pfc
Palermo, Raymond Sam, Pfc
Palzer, James D, Pvt
Parent, Harold A, Sgt
Parker, Millard L, T Sgt
Parsons, James S, Pfc
Patey, Randol, 1 Lt
Paulsen, Walter J, S Sgt
Payne, Romie, Pfc

Perry, Harold D, Pvt
Pert, Clifford H, Pvt
Perusek, Frank M, Pfc
Pethtel, Charles, Pfc
Phillips, Earl, Pvt
Phillips, Joseph L, 1 Lt
Pierce, Delburt L, Pfc
Pike, Russell M, Pfc
Piledggi, Andrew P, Pfc
Pinneke, Edward G, Pfc
Podraza, Lee M, Pfc
Poling, Frederick D, Sgt
Pollard, Patrick G, Pvt
Poloian, Ralph M, Pfc
Porter, Frank L, Sgt
Potter, John R, Pfc
Powell, Donald L, Pfc
Proppe, Henry C, Pfc
Pugh, Thomas E, Cpl
Purcell, John A, Pfc
Putney, Wilburn C, Pfc
Quam, Raymond O, S Sgt
Rau, Fred J, 1 Lt
Reed, Burnham E, Pvt
Reeves, John Pfc
Rehler, Robert W, Sgt
Rhodes, William L, Pfc
Richgels, Anthony B, Pfc
Riley, LeRoy E, Pfc
Ritchie, William H, Pfc
Roberts, Bruce, S Sgt
Roberts, Joseph B, Pfc
Robertson, Bennie G, Pfc
Rockhold, Floyd W, Pfc
Rucker, Ray M, S Sgt
Rutherford, Arthur E, Pvt
Sadoff, Louis, S Sgt
Sandercock, T G, Sgt
Santos, Arnold F, Pfc
Sarnikowski, Frank, Sgt
Sarvas, Dave, Pfc
Scherrer, Henry P, Pfc
Schlueter, Roy H, Sgt
Schmidt, Louis F, Pfc
Schoening, Roland F, Pfc
Scott, Howard M, Pfc
Scott, John L, Sgt
Seles, John J, Pfc
Selmer, John S, S Sgt
Shadix, Charlie M, Pvt
Shanko, Lewis J, Pvt
Sherer, Walter G, Pvt
Sherman, Claude L, Pfc
Shevetz, Joe, Pfc
Shields, Thomas S, Cpl
Shipley, William C, Pvt
Shook, Claude E, Pfc
Short, Alfred E, Pfc
Shutack, Charles P, T Sgt
Sieffert, Regis C, Pfc
Silver, Melvin J, Pvt
Silverman, Harold, Pfc
Simon, John M, Jr, Pfc
Sims, Harold W, S Sgt
Sindad, Joseph, Sgt
Sines, Arthur J, Pfc
Single, James C, T Sgt
Slish, Joseph, Sgt
Small, Austin J, Sgt
Smith, Elbert R, Pvt
Smith, Elmo D, Pvt
Smith, Ernest, Pfc
Smith, Freddie R, S Sgt
Smith, Robert A, Jr, Pfc
Snavely, Donald O, Pfc
Snyder, Carl R, Sgt
Sokolowski, Edward S, Pfc
Somers, Howard L, Pvt
Sopczyk, Joseph L, S Sgt
Spear, Bud S, Sgt
Spevacek, Frank E, T Sgt

Spikula, Edward M, Pfc
Spraguer, Harold J, Pvt
Sprister, Roy W, Sgt
Stady, Kenneth C, Tec 5
Star, William R, Pfc
Steel, John R, Capt
Steinmetz, Harry L, S Sgt
Sternot, Edmund J, S Sgt
Stone, Willie C, S Sgt
Strakis, George E, S Sgt
Stringer, John E, Sgt
Stubblefield, Warren D, Jr, Maj
Studant, Frank C, S Sgt
Swanson, Richard M, Sgt
Sweigart, Orvil E, S Sgt
Swiger, Carl V, Cpl
Syfan, Rollins C, Jr, 1 Lt
Taylor, Marion W, Pvt
Tedford, Samuel B, Pvt
Teeter, Arthur H, Sgt
Teixeira, Joseph A, Pvt
Thomasson, Rethel M, Tec 5
Thurston, Frank, Pfc
Tishaw, Floyd J, Pvt
Toepker, Charles C, Pfc
Torrence, Lorne J, Pvt
Towns, Preston E, Capt
Trappasse, Joseph R, Pvt
Trenner, Robert B, Capt
Tritsch, Fred A, Pfc
Troy, Francis E, S Sgt
Trudeau, Frank V, S Sgt
Twedt, Curtis E, Pfc
Tyson, Harry L, Pvt
Updyke, Lee E, S Sgt
Urschel, Herbert P, T Sgt
Utegg, Carl H, Pfc
Veronesi, Zeno B, Pfc
Walitalo, Carl R, Pfc
Wallace, Homer L, Sgt
Wallace, Milo H, S Sgt
Walloch, Gilbert W, Pfc
Wane, William J, T Sgt
Ward, Benny J, Pvt
Ward, Edward S, Pfc
Ward, Harold J, S Sgt
Warren, George L, S Sgt
Wason, Donald B, 2 Lt
Waterman, Frank W, Pfc
Waters, Walter L, Pfc
Watkins, Jarvis B, Pfc
Weakland, Robert E, Pfc
Weaver, Harold S, 1 Sgt
Weeden, Russell, Pvt
Welsh, Charles P, Pfc
Werner, Carlton G, 1 Lt
Wernert, Bernard E, Pfc
Whetzel, John W, Sgt
Whiteman, Charles P, Pvt
Whitfield, Alonza R, Tec 5
Wiblitzhouser, K F, Jr, Pvt
Willadsen, Hans C, Pfc
Williams, Herman C, Pvt
Williamson, Wade W, Pvt
Wilson, Frank C, Pfc
Wilson, Harmon C, Pvt
Winters, Kenneth E, Sgt
Wisniewski, Walter M, Pfc
Wofford, Louie O, Pfc
Wolfe, Charles W, S Sgt
Wong, Bing P, Pvt
Woodbury, Joseph W, Pvt
Word, Arnold A, Pfc
Yahtin, Gilbert, Pvt
Yianitsas, John, Pvt
Young, Howard O, Pfc
Youngberg, Thor A, Pfc
Zamazal, Frank F, S Sgt
Zimmerman, Kenneth O, Pvt
Zingale, Louis T, Pvt
Zirn, Richard H, Tec 5

Zukosky, John C, Pfc

501st Parachute Infantry

Adams, George H, Jr, S Sgt
Adomitis, George, Sgt
Alberico, Joe, Pvt
Aldrich, Francis M, Pvt
Alexander, John A, Cpl
Allwein, Joseph R, Pfc
Altich, John F, Cpl
Ammons, Wilburn, 1 Sgt
Amos, Harry L, Sgt
Anderson, Daniel T, Pvt
Anderson, Oskar, Pvt
Anderson, Paul P, Tec 5
Angus, David G, Pvt
Anuszewski, Fred J, Pvt
Ardrey, Lawrence W, S Sgt
Arnold, Harold J, Pfc
Artinger, Harry R, Pfc
Atkinson, John W, Jr, 1 Lt
Austin, Richard C, Pvt
Baer, Frank, Pvt
Bahel, Robert C, Pvt
Bailey, Herman F, Pfc
Baird, Ellis L, Pfc
Balducci, Michael, Pvt
Balek, Joseph J, Pfc
Ballassis, Angelo G, Pfc
Banko, Alex, Pfc
Barbour, Sheldon E, 2 Lt
Barrett, John K, Pvt
Bartrope, Walter D, Pvt
Bay, John O, Pvt
Bazan, Joseph C, Pvt
Beall, Henry V, Sgt
Beals, Leo L, Pvt
Bedsworth, William E, Pvt
Beechinor, Donald C, 2 Lt
Beisser, Chester, Pvt
Bennett, Walter W, Pvt
Bennett, Thurman L, Pvt
Berlin, John C, Tec 5
Billman, LeRoy H, Tec.5
Blanchette, Normand D, Pfc
Blessing, Albert I, Pvt
Blodgett, Maurice F, Pvt
Bobbitt, Jesse T, Sgt
Bodah, Henry F, Pvt
Bogart, Loyal K, Capt
Bohn, John W, Pvt
Bosworth, Chester I J, Pfc
Bourland, Dale E, Cpl
Bowie, James W, Pvt
Boxell, Billy S, Tec 5
Boyajian, Edward M, Pvt
Bradley, Edward V, Pfc
Bradybaugh, Ralph E, Cpl
Bragg, Thomas, Cpl
Braml, Joseph J, Pfc
Brannon, Freddie, Pvt
Brazzle, Delbert S, Cpl
Brice, Ray E, Pvt
Bright, LeRoy, S Sgt
Brisco, Harold J, Pvt
Brown, Leon W, S Sgt
Brown, Harry B, Pfc
Brown, Ernest, Pvt
Brown, Leonard L, Pvt
Brumley, Rudolph C, Sgt
Burd, William G, Capt
Burk, Forest G, Sgt
Burnett, Tony A, Jr, Pfc
Burns, William D, Sgt
Burtis, Charles W, Pvt
Busby, Martin, Pfc
Butch, Robert E, Pvt
Butcher, Thomas W, Sgt
Byrd, James E, Pfc
Callahan, Roy M, Tee 4

Calloway, Wayne A, Pvt
Camarena, Frank C, Pvt
Cambray, Francis L, Pvt
Candee, John J, Pvt
Canei, Angelo, Pvt
Canteau, Albert, Pfc
Caroon, Bonnie G, Cpl
Carroll, Robert C, Lt Col
Cerra, Joseph J, Pvt
Cessarini, Elio, Pvt
Chastant, Thomas A, Capt
Chavez, San J, Pfc
Chavous, Samuel J, Cpl
Chellin, Erland W, Pvt
Cherney, Joseph A, S Sgt
Chilton, Charles D, Sgt
Choate, Patrick H, Sgt
Chorzempa, Edward M, S Sgt
Clapper, John A, Cpl
Clark, William T, Pfc
Clifford, William F, Pvt
Colangelo, Donald G, Pvt
Comeau, Joseph R, Pfc
Condon, John W, Pvt
Coney, Letcher H, Pvt
Conn, John W, Pfc
Conway, James R, Pfc
Cook, Kenneth E, Pvt
Cooper, Walter D, Pvt
Cooper, Cleo T, Pvt
Cooter, Walter E, Pfc
Cormier, Lawrence T, Pvt
Cote, Paul M, Capt
Couch, Alston P, Sgt
Couger, Quincy M, 2 Lt
Craft, Orlin L D, Pfc
Craighill, Edley, Jr, 1 Lt
Craley, Walter, Pvt
Creig, Edward W, Pvt
Criswell, Thomas D, Sgt
Cross, William D, Pvt
Crotts, Eldon L, Jr, Cpl
Crouch, Everett G, 2 Lt
Culbreth, James E, Pfc
Culler, Irvin W, Pvt
Cunningham, Paul J, Pfc
Curitti, John L, Pvt
Curran, John E, 1 Lt
Daley, Alvin, Pvt
Danielson, Frank W, 1 Lt
Dashner, James W, Pfc
Davidson, Charles K, 2 Lt
Davis, William H, Pvt
Davis, John D, III, Pfc
Davis, William F, Pvt
Davis, Stirling G, Pvt
Davis, Leonard A, Sgt
Dawson, Richard P, Sgt
DeHaven, Ollie J, Pfc
DeLay, Jack W, Pvt
Delgadillo, Richard, Pvt
Dellapenta, William J, Pvt
Delsanto, Stanley W, Pvt
Dermer, Clayton H, Cpl
Dick, Norman L, Tec 5
Diefenbach, Wallace E, Pvt
Dipietro, Fred J, Pvt
Dirmitt, Charles E, Pvt
Docteur, Clarence J, Pvt
Doebert, Arthur E, Pvt
Dorman, Malcom W, S Sgt
Dornick, Alfred C, Jr, Sgt
Doucet, Wilfred P, Pvt
Dougherty, Lee A, Pfc
Dubiel, Michael B, Tec 4
Duffy, William R. Pfc
Durbin, Anthony G, Pfc
Durkee, Lawrence L, Cpl
Dziedzic, Edward, Pvt
Eady, Caley J, Tec 4
Eakin, Eugene C, Pfc

Earl, Arthur J, Pvt
Edgell, Raymond R, S Sgt
Edwards, Melvin D, Cpl
Elbert, Bernard J, S Sgt
Ell, John W, 1 Lt
Eller, William J, Sgt
Emerson, Charles S, Pfc
Engasser, Norman A, S Sgt
Evans, Leon F, S Sgt
Fair, Donald J, Pvt
Falick, Larry, Pvt
Fernan, Francis T, Cpl
Fiato, Vincent J, Pvt
Ficarotta, Frank G, Pfc
Fleishman, Ward D, Pfc
Flora, Aubrin E, Pvt
Fontana, Edoardo F, S Sgt
Forese, Joseph J, Pvt
Forte, Peter L, Pvt
Foster, Walter S, Tec 5
Foust, Robert J, Pvt
Franklin, Herman, Pvt
Frase, Robert J, 1 Lt
French, Frank A, Tec 5
Frisby, Orven E, Pvt
Fulk, Paul H, Pfc
Fulton, James E, Jr, Pvt
Fuquay, Cecil O, 2 Lt
Furr, Henry E, Pfc
Galiotto, James A, Pfc
Gallagher, Charles E, S Sgt
Garcia, Joe C, Cpl
Garretson, Chester R, Pvt
Garrity, Joseph W, Pvt
Garver, William B, Pfc
Gauthier, Wilbrod A, Pfc
Gawron, Michael, Cpl
Gaxiola, Gus J, Sgt
Gazia, Tony S, Pfc
Gehrken, Willard W, Pvt
Geiger, Alvin O, Pfc
Giles, Clifford H, Sgt
Gilmore, William R, Pvt
Glasser, Elmer J, Cpl
Gober, Wilbur F, Pvt
Gonzales, Joe B, Pfc
Goodall, Frank N, Pfc
Gotchall, John H, Pvt
Graham, John J, Pvt
Gray, Harry F, Pfc
Gray, Warren E, Sgt
Greene, Robert T, Cpl
Griffith, Alvie K, Pfc
Grimaldi, Alfonso, 1 Lt
Groy, William R, Sgt
Gulick, Edward T, Pfc
Gullick, Henry L, Tec 5
Gullo, Thomas, Tec 4
Hall, George E, Pvt
Hall, Francis R, Cpl
Hamm, Ira J, Pvt
Harkiewicz, Joseph T, Pvt
Harman, Joseph R, 1 Lt
Harris, Thomas, Cpl
Harrison, Robert R, 1 Lt
Haugh, Nelson L, Pvt
Haun, Edmond E, S Sgt
Hayden, Edward C, Pfc
Hayes, George L, Cpl
Hayes, Spencer R, S Sgt
Head, Marvel A, Pvt
Hegstrom, Everett T, Pvt
Heitsman, Melvin A, Cpl
Hellinger, Paul, Pfc
Henderson, Charles S, Pfc
Henderson, Joseph A, 1 Sgt
Herman, Charles W, Pfc
Hernandez, Arthur, Pvt
Hetrick, Everett L, Cpl
Hibbard, Harold E, Pvt
Hill, Gussie, Pvt

Hixon, Willard H, Sgt
Hoffman, Richard J, Pfc
Holleran, John M, Pvt
Holloman, Wallace S, Cpl
Holstein, Charles E, Tec 4
Hoobing, Carl D, 2 Lt
Hope, Claude E, Pvt
Hopper, Walter E, Pfc
Hosie, Donald, Pvt
Hoskinson, Ruell O, Pfc
Hotchkiss, Alvin J, Pvt
Hotchkiss, Richard E, Capt
Houlihan, John A, Pfc
Howell, Russell, Pvt
Hudson, Charles R, Cpl
Hughes, Homer G, Sgt
Hunt, Robert I, Cpl
Hurt, George F, S Sgt
Huston, Robert T, Pfc
Hutchison, Edwin B, Jr, 1 Lt
Huttner, Arthur, S Sgt
Hylton, Roy J, Pvt
Jackson, Harold R, Pvt
Jacobs, William T, Pvt
Jacobs, Garrel A, Pfc
Jacobs, Royal A, Pfc
Janelle, Laurence P, Pfc
Jean, Maurice A, Pvt
Jeffery, Robert B, Pvt
Johnson, John H, Tec 5
Johnson, Howard R, Col
Johnson, Robert M, Pfc
Johnson, Charles R, Pfc
Johnston, Lloyd R, Cpl
Jones, Claude P, Jr, 1 Lt
Jones, Edward L, Pvt
Jordan, George R, Cpl
Joseph, John A, Pvt
Kaczmarski, John, Pfc
Kahoun, Robert J, Pfc
Kaminski, Stanley J, Cpl
Kane, Joseph J, Pvt
Kasinski, Thaddeus S, Pvt
Keating, Arthur N, Cpl
Keel, James A, Pvt
Kelleher, Cyril T, Pvt
Kelley, Edgar L, Pvt
Kelly, George M, Pvt
Kemble, Glen H, Cpl
Kennel, Robert A, Sgt
Kester, Robert, Pvt
Ketchum, Loren H, Pvt
Kinney, Gene S, Pvt
Kinsella, Stephen P, Pvt
Kirby, Lawrence W, Jr, Pfc
Kirkpatrick, Roy D, Pvt
Kiselka, Clifford E, Pvt
Kizer, Clark L, Pvt
Klopp, Clarence R, Jr, Pfc
Klores, Daniel N, Pfc
Knight, Dale C, Tec 5
Koches, Michael R, Pvt
Koffel, Francis H, Pvt
Kos, George A, Pvt
Kowalski, Norbert H, Cpl
Kraeger, Vernon, Capt
Kraimer, Harold J, Pfc
Kraska, Bronislaw, Pvt
Kreider, Charles D, Pfc
Kribs, Robert A, Pvt
Krill, Michael, Pvt
Krombholtz, Arnold E, Sgt
Kunkel, Richard, Pfc
LaClave, Andy E, Pvt
Ladner, Carman S, Cpl
Langlinais, Euel J, S Sgt
Langston, Merle, Pvt
Lantow, Norman D, Cpl
Lapin, Sam P, Pfc
Leach, Bobby E, Pfc
Leasure, Carl D, Pvt

Leck, Stanislaw, Pfc
Lee, Charles W, Pvt
Lee, George E, Pfc
Lee, Robert E, Pvt
Leeking, Paul B, Sgt
Lenz, Frederick J, Pvt
Leonard, Maurice J, Pfc
Lewis, Kendall C, Tec 5
Lierly, William F, Pvt
Lindsay, Robert A, Cpl
Lloreda, Joseph, Jr, Tec 4
Lochridge, Harold D, Pfc
Lopachin, Felix J, Pvt
Lorance, Robert W, Pfc
Loudermilk, Oris O, Jr, Sgt
Love, William H, Pvt
Luce, James J, Pvt
Ludy, Milo W, Pfc
Luther, Larry R, Pvt
Lyon, Robert A, Pfc
MacMillin, Donald J, Pfc
MacNew, Dewey L, Pfc
Madden, Denver R, Pfc
Maese, Floyd A, Pvt
Magney, Ray A, Cpl
Mahoney, Andrew W, Jr, Pvt
Mangano, Carl M, Pvt
Maria, Carmine A, Pvt
Markos, John T, Jr, Pvt
Marks, Nathan M, 1 Lt
Marlow, Jack L, Pvt
Marnye, John C, Pvt
Marrs, Guy R, Cpl
Marshall, Thomas I, Pfc
Martin, Harry C, Pvt
Marzlin, Leighton W, Sgt
Mason, Harry C, Pfc
Mastandrea, Michael, Pvt
Matthews, Edward A, 2 Lt
Maue, William B, Cpl
McClain, William C, Pvt
McClung, Wayne A, Pvt
McCormick, John G, Pvt
McDonough, Thomas F, Pvt
McDougall, Donald J, Pvt
McDowell, Jack D, Pfc
McElwain, Glenn H, Pvt
McFadden, Hugh J, Pfc
McFarland, Richard R, Sgt
McGregor, Joseph C, 1 Lt
McKeen, Dennis M, Pvt
McKenney, Kent H, S Sgt
McKeown, Francis J, Pvt
McKinnon, Stuart A, Pfc
McMichael, Laurance, Pfc
McNabb, Thomas G, Cpl
McNally, John F, Tec 5
McReynolds, Altus F, Capt
Meek, Darrell M, Pfc
Mero, Joseph E, Tec 4
Merritts, Charles J, Pfc
Meyer, Albert, Pfc
Michuax, Harold L, Pvt
Miller, Orville J, Pvt
Millican, Jimmie S, Pfc
Milonas, John C, S Sgt
Mitchell, Albert W, Capt
Mizerak, Joseph W, Pfc
Morris, Eugene A, Pfc
Morris, George D, Pvt
Morrison, Eugene W, Cpl
Mueller, Fred, 1 Sgt
Mullikin, William H, Pvt
Munoz, Rubon R, Pvt
Munsee, Delbert C, Pvt
Murphy, Dennis W, Jr, Pfc
Murray, George R, Tec 4
Murray, Ronald I, 1 Lt
Mythaler, David L, Pvt
Nadeau, Armand E, Pvt
Nash, Arthur P, Tec 5

Needham, Edward L, Pvt
Nelson, Milton F, Cpl
Nennich, John J, Jr, Pvt
Neumann, Elmer A, Pvt
Newson, Alfred J, Pfc
Newton, Ralph A, Pfc
Nicholson, Joel A, Pvt
Nicholson, Ian D, 1 Lt
Noland, William B, Pfc
Norwood, Lowell E, Sgt
Odle, Edward, Pfc
Oehler, Raymond A, 2 Lt
Ohms, Wilbur R, Pvt
O'Keefe, Robert J, Tec 4
O'Keefe, William T, Pfc
Olender, Walter V, Pvt
Olevsky, Louis E, Cpl
Onger, Ellsworth H, Pvt
Ostrowski, Henry W, Pfc
Overholt, Amos E, Sgt
Owens, Fred' A, Capt
Pacheco, Isaac, Pfc
Packham, Leo P, Tec 5
Paine, Everett S, Pvt
Palmer, King R, Pvt
Paquin, Edward H, Pvt
Parks, Herschel, 1 Sgt
Parks, Edward L, Pfc
Patterson, Floyd T, Pvt
Paulson, Lyle M, Pfc·
Pavalescu, John, Jr, Pvt
Pegg, John S, Pvt
Peluso, John, Pvt
Peninger, Robert L, Pfc
Pennington, Jessie L, Pvt
Penrod, John K, 2 Lt
Penta, John J, Pvt
Perry, Buford H, Cpl
Petersen, James H, 1 Lt
Petrow, George J, Pvt
Petty, Paul H, Pfc
Petzolt, Edward E, Pfc
Phillips, Charles H, Pvt
Phillips, Pete T, Pvt
Phillips, George W, Pvt
Phillips, Gerald S, Pfc
Phinney, Reandall W, Tec 5
Picotte, Emery O, Pvt
Pierce, John T, Pvt
Pierce, Lenory L, S Sgt
Pitts, Mallie D, Pvt
Platt, James F, Pvt
Plotz, Edwin A, Jr, Pvt
Plourde, Donat M, Pvt
Poe, Alton D, Cpl
Poziemski, Frank E, Cpl
Prahm, LeRoy W, Pfc
Price, Hasel H, Pvt
Price, William A, Tec 5
Puhalski, Henry J, 2 Lt
Purdy, William, Tec 5
Pushcare, Michael L, Pvt
Quinlan, James T, Pfc
Quinlan, John M, Pfc
Radel, Walter J, Cpl
Raffety, Louis E, 1 Lt
Randolph, Lester R, Pvt
Randt, Corwin J, Pvt
Rebic, John, Sgt
Rector, Norbert H, Cpl
Reiller, Kenneth P, Pfc
Reno, Joseph, Pvt
Reynolds, James, Pvt
Richardson, Albert R, Pvt
Richards, Robert P, Pfc
Riemenschneider, C H, Pvt
Rion, Aubrey H, 1 Lt
Rippy, Joseph G, Pfc
Ritchie, Andrew J, Cpl
Ritchie, Robert A, Tec 4
Roark, William B, S Sgt

Roberts, Harry, Jr, Pfc
Robinson, William J, Pvt
Robison, William S, 1 Lt
Roble, William C, Cpl
Roby, Irving, 2 Lt
Rofar, Michael, Pvt
Rollyson, Charles C, Pfc
Rozman, Joseph, Pfc
Rubio, Trinidad M, Pvt
Ruggiero, Thomas J, Pfc
Rupp, Arnold F, Pvt
Rutherford, Robert I, Pvt
Sabuda, Emil P, Pfc
Sakovics, Stephen, Tec 5
Salazar, David R, Pfc
Salemi, Anthony, Pfc
Sandy, Vaughn D, Pvt
Sanzone, Leo, Pvt
Sargis, Carl L, 1 Sgt
Sarlas, George L, Pvt
Sass, Peter, Pvt
Scanlan, Martin J, Sgt
Schadt, John A, Sgt
Scheffert, Ernest R, Pvt
Schill, Albert W L, Sgt
Schinkoeth, Donald E, Cpl
Schmidt, George E, 2 Lt
Schneider, John H, Sgt
Schooley, Myron L, Tec 5
Schorsch, Robert S, 1 Lt
Schuler, Harry F, Pvt
Schwabe, Henry M, Pfc
Sciortino, George A, Pvt
Seale, Charles H, Capt
Sears, Ernest E, Pvt
Sellers, Harold E, Pfc
Sheen, James B, Pfc
Sheets, Hermas E, Pvt
Shirley, John H, Pfc
Shoemaker, William S, 2 Lt
Shumate, William W, Pvt
Simmons, Walter A, Pfc
Simpson, Jack M, Pvt
Siriani, Joseph C, Pvt
Slatton, Robert W, Pvt
Smith, Earl F, Pvt
Smith, George H, Pvt
Smith, Thomas J, Pvt
Smith, Charles L, Pfc
Smith, Clifford K, Pvt
Smith, Francis B, Pfc
Smortz, John E, Pfc
Smythe, Edward S, Pfc
Sobieralski, William, Cpl
Sorace, Louis, Pvt
Spangler, Clarence E, 1 Sgt·
Spirz, Irwin A, Cpl
Spitz, Matthew J, Pvt
Spruell, Doyce F, Pfc
Stallings, James F, Pvt
Steets, Theodore P, Tec 4
Stemp, Elmer L, Pvt
Stephens, Roscoe W, Pfc
Stepko, Francis P, Pvt
Stroupe, Jessie H, Pvt
Struneski, Stanley S, Pvt
Style, Robert G, Pvt
Suder, Stephen, Pfc
Sullivan, John J, Pfc
Sutliffe, Thomas, Lt Col
Suwarsky, Stanley, Pvt
Tantalo, Bartholomew, Pvt
Tapley, Edward, Sgt
Taylor, Richard E, Pfc
Tedder, Jack L, Pvt
Teichman, Arthur R, Pfc
Thomas, Walter E, Pfc
Thompson, Allan L, Pfc
Thompson, Stacy W, Jr, Cpl
Trabue, Lonnie B, Pvt
Trevino, Jimmie, Pvt

Tryon, Edgar L, Pvt
Turner, Billy A, Jr, 1 Lt
Turner, John A, Pvt
Tyrrell, Clarence J, S Sgt
Vahaly, Michael, Pvt
Vail, Robert W, Pvt
Vallejos, Elmer E, Pvt
Vandersee, Albert L, Cpl
Vandeveer, Richard C, Pfc
Vasques, Manuel R, Pvt
Vathis, George T, Pvt
Via, Stephen, Jr, Pfc
Vickery, Ralph D, Pvt
Volango, Alfred J, 2 Lt
Waldrep, Richard H, Pvt
Wallace, Claude D, Jr, Capt
Wallace, Robert H, Pfc
Waller, Russell G, Cpl
Walsh, Bernard T, Pvt
Walsh, Raymond J, Pfc
Warrener, Charles F, 1 Lt
Weaver, Benjamin S, Pfc
Webb, John C, Pfc
Weir, William W, Sgt
Weiss, Herbert, Pvt
Wells, Zale, Pvt
Westcoat, Louis, Sgt
White, Richard F, Pvt
White, John L, 1 Lt
Wicker, William D, Pvt
Wilcombe, Douglas L, 1 Lt
Williams, Buster E, Cpl
Williams, Miller, Pvt
Williams, Earle F, Jr, Pvt
Wilson, Wayne E, Pvt
Wilson, Ruel H, Pfc
Wingard, Jacob H, Sgt
Witt, Kenneth A, Pvt
Woodall, Otto, Pvt
Wright, Samuel W, Pvt
Wright, Maurice, Pvt
Yaquinto, Mathew J, Sgt
Yeager, Elbert F, Cpl
Young, William F, Pfc
Young, James M, Cpl
Young, Milburn H, Pvt
Zanakos, Peter, Jr, Pfc

502d Parachute Infantry

Adams, George R, Cpl
Adams, Rodney B, 1 Lt
Addleson, Herman, Pvt
Alexander, Donald C, 1 Lt
Allen, David G, 1 Lt
Amann, Charles L, Pvt
Ambrose, Edmund P, Pfc
Anderson, William A, Pvt
Apsega, Walter F, Pvt
Armentrout, Forrest W, Pfc
Atchison, Woodrow W, Pfc
Auman, Pershing D, Pvt
Auten, Myron L, Pvt
Axelrod, Abraham I, Pvt
Baas, John, Jr, Pvt
Babich, Michael, Pfc
Bachulak, Joseph G, Pfc
Bacon, Lewis C, Pvt
Baker, Clarence M, 1 Lt
Baker, Foy E, 2 Lt
Baker, William E, Pvt
Ballard, George W, Pvt
Ballard, John C, Jr, Pvt
Barba, James N, Cpl
Bauer, Ivan A, S Sgt
Beard, Philip L, Pvt
Belanger, Joseph C, Pfc
Berry, John W, S Sgt
Bibry, Hugo P, Pvt
Bilodeau, Henry F, Tec 5
Bilque, John J, Cpl

Birchell, Harold R, Pvt
Bircher, Warren G H, Pvt
Bisbee, Jessie W, Pfc
Black, Clarence E, Jr, Pvt
Blanchard, George A, Pvt
Blazina, Theodore C, Sgt
Blohm, Ralph J, Pfc
Bobb, Joseph, Pfc
Boffo, Jerry A, Sgt
Bogan, Roy, Cpl
Bone, LeRoy F, 1 Lt
Botzis, Archie P, Pvt
Bowman, Jay C, Pvt
Bradley, Edward J, Jr, Pvt
Breen, Raymond M, Pvt
Briant, Edward L, 2 Lt
Brigham, Robert W, Cpl
Brining, Elmer G, 1 Lt
Brison, William B, Pvt
Brodie, James W, Sgt
Brookins, Ira L, Pvt
Bruce, Leonard E, Pfc
Brune, James O, Tec 5
Brungard, Winfield F, 1 Lt
Bruno, Ernest F, Pvt
Bucior, Bernard C, 1 Lt
Burciaga, Ernesto G, Tec 4
Burgert, Howard R, Pfc
Burke, Joseph M, Pvt
Burriss, Aubrey F, Pfc
Burt, William J, Cpl
Burton, Durward L, Pfc
Butz, Earl H, Cpl
Byers, Glenn E, Cpl
Cage, Lamar E, Pvt
Campbell, Billy C, Pvt
Campbell, Wilbur E, Cpl
Carberry, William F, Sgt
Cary, Donald E, Pfc
Cassel, Robert D, Pfc
Caughran, Willard B, Pfc
Cavalier, Ralph, Pfc
Cheatham, Floyd D, Jr, Pfc
Cherub, Michael P, Pfc
Chesney, Lawrence B, Pfc
Chirico, Domenick, Pvt
Chisholm, Quinn L, Pvt
Cid, Fred, Pvt
Clark, John H, Tec 5
Clark, John R, Pvt
Clark, Laymon D, 1 Lt
Clements, Joe L, S Sgt
Clute, Daniel H, Pvt
Cobb, Albert L, Jr, Pvt
Cole, Abner R, Pvt
Cole, Robert G, Lt Col
Cole, Warren F, Pvt
Cole, William K, Pvt
Colon, James A, Sgt
Combs, Homer J, 1 Lt
Cook, Raymond F, Pfc
Cooper, William A, Pvt
Cordell, Charles W, Pvt
Corder, Lloyd A, Pfc
Cotten, Henry W, Pvt
Cournoyer, Norman, Pfc
Courson, Simpson P, Pvt
Craig, Willie F, Sgt
Craine, John C, Sgt
Creager, Kenneth L, Pfc
Crouch, Sewell W, Pfc
Crouse, Jack L, Pvt
Cumming, Norwood A, Sgt
Curtis, Calvin W, Tec 5
DaCunzi, Antonio, Pvt
DaSilva, Ernesto, Pvt
Dagostino, Pasquale J, Pfc
Dagres, George C, Cpl
Dalto, James V, Cpl
Daly, Richard A, 1 Lt
Dandorf, Harry T, Pfc

Darcy, William J, Jr, Pvt
Davenport, Charles R, Pvt
Davidson, George L, 2 Lt
Davidson, Richard L, Capt
Davis, John L, Cpl
Davis, Joseph B, Sgt
Davis, Lester J, Pfc
Davis, Luther W, Pvt
Dawson, Robert L, Tec 5
DeRose, Charles J, Sgt
Deckard, Robert L, Pvt
Delulio, Alex, Jr, Pfc
Deyak, Carl A, Pvt
Dodson, James A, Pvt
Doran, Robert E, Tec 5
Drapeau, Aime H, 1 Sgt
Drennan, Fred O, Capt
Driskill, Donald R B, Pfc
Drummond, James W, Pvt
Dulabon, William C, Pfc
Duncan, Jack W, S Sgt
Durham, Garson W, Sgt
Durka, John P, S Sgt
Dwyer, William O, Jr, 1 Lt
Dye, Everett D, Sgt
Eaton, Hobart J, Pvt
Eberle, George M, 1 Lt
Eckert, Clarence C, Pvt
Edmondson, Paul S, Pfc
Eisenberger, James G, Pvt
Emberlin, George H, Pvt
Engelhardt, Herman A, Pvt
Erickson, Glenn V W, Pvt
Ervin, J C, Pvt
Estes, Albert R, Pvt
Etling, Smith J, Pvt
Evans, William B, Cpl
Everding, William F, 1 Lt
Evers, Lloyd M, 2 Lt
Eversole, Billie S, Pfc
Fatzer, George M, Pfc
Featherston, Clyde E, Sgt
Fenimore, Joseph A, Pvt
Fenker, George F, Pfc
Fern, Ira G, Sgt
Fiero, Archie F, Pfc
Firor, George W, Pfc
Fischer, Arthur W, Pvt
Fisher, John W, Pfc
Floerchinger, Fay R, Pvt
Flores, Johnny R, Sgt
Foglia, Anthony, Pvt
Foley, William E, Pvt
Frankenfield, C H, Pvt
Frulla, Armando J, Pfc
Fryear, Robert F, Pvt
Fuller, Emerson, Pfc
Fulmer, Edward L, Pvt
Funk, Edwin E, Pfc
Funk, John H, Pvt
Gallagher, Gerard C, Pfc
Gaukel, Eugene O, Pvt
Gentle, Paul B, Pfc
Gifford, David C, Pfc
Ginsburg, David, Pvt
Girouard, Normand V, Pfc
Gist, Calvin C, Pvt
Gjersten, Alton W, Pvt
Goldberg, Joseph, Pvt
Gomez, Carrol F, Pvt
Goodman, Harry N, Pfc
Goodmanson, Vernon A, Tec 4
Gore, Lloyd A, Pvt
Gorecki, Edward, Pvt
Gorman, Douglas H, Pvt
Gray, Dean W, Jr, Pfc
Gray, Frank W, Jr, Pfc
Green, Arylis W, Pvt
Greeninger, Clarence, Cpl
Grosvenor, Francis V, Pfc
Grunert, Warren P, Pfc

Guisti, Frank, Sgt
Gupp, Chester B, Pvt
Haddick, William F, Jr, Pfc
Hagan, John W, Cpl
Hamon, Orville E, Pfc
Harris, DeWitt, Pvt
Harris, Ernest O, 1 Lt
Harrison, Bailey, Sgt
Harry, Cecil E, Pvt
Haseltine, Robert I J, Pvt
Hatcher, Alfred C, Pfc
Hatton, Danny D, Pfc
Hatton, Thomas F, Jr, Pfc
Hayes, Timothy J, Sgt
Heacock, James W, Pvt
Heather, William J, Pfc
Hester, Robert G, Pvt
Hicks, R C, Jr, Pvt
Hickson, Charles A, Pvt
Hickson, Robert W, Pvt
Hill, Joseph D, Pvt
Hill, Joseph F, Pfc
Hill, Roy A, Pfc
Hoffman, Matt J, Pvt
Hoffman, Raymond T, Pfc
Hogue, James D, Pvt
Hoover, Edwin H, S Sgt
Hoppe, Walter F, Tec 4
House, Raymond L, Pfc
Howard, Sidney L, Pfc
Hroma, Andrew T, Pvt
Hudak, Joseph B, Pvt
Hugi, Charles W, Pfc
Huntington, Howard T, S Sgt
Hyde, Willard C, Pvt
Inglin, Carl H, Cpl
Irven, Sidney W, Pvt
Irving, Albert V, Tec 5
Jackson, Henry L, Pvt
Jantosik, Frank, Pfc
Jennings, Elbon, S Sgt
Jesper, Robert E, Pvt
Johnson, Allan L, Pfc
Johnson, Charles C, Pvt
Johnson, Donald G, Pvt
Johnson, Herman L, Cpl
Jones, Fred S, Jr, Pfc
Jones, Herman C, Pvt
Jones, Robert W, Pvt
Jones, Royce, Pfc
Jourdan, Robert E, Sgt
Kalasausky, Peter J, Pfc
Kalinowski, Chester, Cpl
Kalonsky, Andrew, Tec 4
Kaufman, John H, Pfc
Kell, Clarence J, Tec 4
Kennick, Louis J, Pfc
Kent, Thomas W, Jr, Sgt
Kern, John A, Jr, Pfc
Kessler, Frank T, Jr, Pvt
Kilgore, Johnnie B, Pfc
Killian, David R, Pfc
Kish, John, Jr, Pvt
Kitcheos, Alexander J, Pfc
Klader, George P, Pvt
Kleinfelder, John D, Pvt
Klemantovich, Benny J, 2 Lt
Kocyon, Frank J, Pfc
Koller, Lawrence J, Jr, Pvt
Korocinski, Sigmund, Pvt
Krainovich, Nicholas, Pvt
Krause, Alfred L, Pvt
Kubsch, Clarence J, Pvt
Kushmerick, Albert J, Cpl
LaFrance, Charles J, Pvt
LaVallee, Napoleon T, 2 Lt
Lake, Robert W, 2 Lt
Lambert, Eugene O, Pvt
Land, Roy R, Tec 5
Lang, William J, S Sgt
Lansdale, Morris, Pvt

Lantow, Robert A, Pfc
Lapikas, John M, Cpl
Lappin, Joseph J, Pvt
Larish, George A, 1 Lt
Larkins, Virgil L, Pvt
Laster, Clarence E, Pvt
Laubach, Melvin E, Pfc
Lawhorn, Cecil B, Pvt
LeClerc, Leon F, Pvt
LeFort, William I, Pfc
Leafty, Junior E, Pvt
Lee, Lawrence P, Jr
Lee, Wilson L, Pfc
Lehman, Jay E, Pfc
Leisner, Frederick E, Pvt
Lenz, Donald J, Pfc
Lesko, John P, Pfc
Leviski, John A, Pfc
Lewis, Duane M, Pfc
Lewis, Max W, Pvt
Lillard, Thomas J, 2 Lt
Linaburg, Delmer D, Pvt
Lineberry, George, Pfc
Lischin, Solomon J, Pfc
Little, Porter C, 1 Lt
Loniewski, Joseph, Pfc
Lotakis, Stephen G, Pfc
Loveless, Robert D, Cpl
Loving, Nathan E, Pfc
Lowry, Milton S, Jr, Cpl
Luna, J D, Pvt
Luther, Onroe H, Pvt
Lyell, John T, Jr, Pfc
Lynch, Peter W, Jr, Pfc
Mabb, Floyd M, Pfc
MacDonald, Robert L, Cpl
Mackall, J John, Pvt
Magri, Ralph S, 2 Lt
Majure, Gordon N, Tec 4
Malone, Gerald B, Pvt
Manhardt, George W, 2 Lt
Mann, Joe E, Pfc
Marcotte, Robert R, Pvt
Marcozzi, Anthony F, Pfc
Markowitz, John R, Pvt
Marois, Robert J, Tec 5
Marquart, Floyd P, Pfc
Martinez, Louis J, Pfc
Marvin, Richard R, Pvt
Massucco, Raymond R, Pvt
Matesich, Stephen L, Cpl
Matey, John, Pvt
Matkovich, Charlie P, Pfc
Mattes, Robert L, Pvt
Maughan, Vern W, Pfc
Mazzeo, Albert, Cpl
McClelland, Richard, Tec 4
McClimate, William J, Pfc
McDaniel, Arthur L, Cpl
McGroarty, John W, Pvt
McLane, Frank G, Pvt
McLaughlin, Frank A, Pfc
Meadows, William D, Pfc
Menchaca, Isaac R, Pvt
Mentzer, Daniel A, Pvt
Merritt, Earl, Pvt
Mershonne, Jack H, Pfc
Middleton, James A, Tec 5
Migacz, Thaddeus, Pfc
Migliarese, Louis P, Pfc
Milewski, Thomas J, Pfc
Miller, Cecil F, Sgt
Miller, Cyrus W, Cpl
Miller, Joseph A, Sgt
Mills, Garland E, Pfc
Monroe, William H, S Sgt
Morgan, John M, Pfc
Morris, J T, Pvt
Morss, Willard, Tec 5
Mottola, Nicholas, 1 Lt
Mowson, William F, Pvt

Mueller, Arthur D, Pvt
Mullane, Daniel, Pvt
Mullis, Shelley H, Pfc
Murphy, James A, Pvt
Myers, Patrick, Pvt
Nardo, Anthony C, 2 Lt
Neises, Nicholas J, Tec 5
Nemeth, James J, Sgt
Nesbit, William A, Pfc
Newbury, David S, Tec 5
Niles, Reo K, Pvt
Nilo, James R, Pvt
Nix, Emmitt T, Pfc
Nordberg, George F, Pvt
Norris, Troy W, S Sgt
Norton, John C, Pvt
Novak, James, Pvt
Nowak, Jerome T, Pvt
Nowakowski, Frank, Jr, Pfc
Nuanes, Edgar N, Pvt
Nussbaum, Leslie B, Pvt
O'Brien, John J, Jr, Pvt
Ofchinick, Richard P, Pvt
O'Neill, Joseph P, Pvt
O'Quinn, William S, Jr, Pvt
Orsonne, Paul A, Pfc
Osborne, Floyd E, Pvt
Outlaw, William L, 1 Sgt
Owen, Owen, Jr, 2 Lt
Owens, Cornelius W, Cpl
Pace, James R, Pvt
Painschab, John P, 1 Lt
Peden, William K, Jr, Pfc
Pelletier, Adrian J, Pvt
Penn, Billy J, Pvt
Perko, Louis P, Tec 4
Peterson, Sterling, Sgt
Peyton, Virgil E, Pfc
Pichler, Leo E, Cpl
Pilwallis, Frank J, Cpl
Pineda, Manuel M, Pfc
Pinson, Jack A, Sgt
Pitts, Hubert G, Pvt
Plumb, Jack R, Pvt
Podkulski, William F, Pvt
Pontecorvo, Albert A, Pfc
Porter, Gordon, S Sgt
Pottorff, Irven P, Pfc
Powless, Randall A, Pfc
Pyle, Klaty A, Tec 4
Rakas, Joseph S, Pfc
Ramirez, Rosalio E, Pvt
Raupach, Paul P, Pfc
Reeves, Harry D, Pvt
Reid, Eugene L E, Pfc
Reidy, John F, Pfc
Rentz, Paul G, Pvt
Repko, George J, Sgt
Rice, Leonard M, Pvt
Richard, Everett C, Pfc
Rigsby, Louis H, Pfc
Riley, Lawrence T, Pfc
Rivera, Domingo, Tec 5
Robbins, Herbert A, Jr, Pvt
Rodriquez, Julio T, Pvt
Rosenberger, Edward F, Pvt
Rosick, William S, Pvt
Ruby, David P, Pvt
Ruffin, Roy E, Pvt
Runkel, Jack W, Pvt
Rushton, Rufus G, Pfc
Ruurs, Henry H, Cpl
Ryan, James A, Jr, Pvt
Salazar, Benigno G, Pvt
Sanderlin, Millard T, Pvt
Sanders, Ray E, Pfc
Sanderson, Walter H, Pvt
Scheier, Gerald J, S Sgt
Schein, Elmer F, Pvt
Schell, Frank, 2 Lt
Schiltz, Nicholas C, 1 Lt

Schlensker, Oswald G, S Sgt
Schmollinger, Charles, Pvt
Schwarting, Howard H, Pvt
Seaman, Jack R, Pvt
See, Louis C, Sgt
Senger, Joseph, Tec 5
Setlock, Edward J, 2 Lt
Sevier, Jerry A, Cpl
Shaffer, Elmer E, Pfc
Shaub, Benjamin C, Sgt
Shealy, Carroll F, Sgt
Sheppard, George W, Jr, Sgt
Sherman, Nick F, Cpl
Sherrod, Roy J, Pvt
Short, Alton F, Pfc
Sickles, Robert W, 2 Lt
Sikora, Fleury W, Cpl
Silva, Lawrence J, Sgt
Simomns, Clarence P, S Sgt
Skipton, Harold C, Pfc
Smith, Halcott L, Pvt
Smith, R, V, Pvt
Smith, Thomas E, Pvt
Smolarsky, Julius, 2 Lt
Snead, Robert Z, Pfc
Sommer, Herbert, Pfc
Sovak, Julius J, S Sgt
Sowder, Edward R, Pvt
Sparks, Carl J, Sgt
Spaulding, Frank L, Cpl
Spear, George E, Cpl
Spiriti, Gaetano F, Pfc
Sprenkle, Wilbert E, Cpl
St Clair, Joe R, Pfc
Stalzer, Rudolph, Pfc
Stands, Philip P, Pvt
Starzyski, Peter J, Sgt
Steele, Birchard G, Pfc
Stein, Raymond F, Cpl
Steinbach, Daniel A, Sgt
Steincamp, Harlan G, Pvt
Stephens, Roy L, Pvt
Stopka, John P, Lt Col
Storino, William, Sgt
Stovall, Clarence W, Pfc
Streifel, Thomas P, Tec 4
Stuart, Roland J, Pfc
Sullivan, Edward J, Pfc
Sullivan, Paul T, Pvt
Suski, John E, Pfc
Sutliffe, Thomas H, Lt Col
Sykes, Byron T, Pvt
Takacs, Alex G, Pvt
Tanguay, Emile W, S Sgt
Taylor, Lester A, Cpl
Taylor, William H, Tec 5
Taylor, Wilfred H, Pfc
Teal, Baxter M, Pfc
Tedeschi, Frank J, Cpl
Tedford, Donald C, Sgt
Tetrick, Melvin L, Pvt
Theall, Bartow R, Sgt
Thompson, Robert D, Pvt
Thompson, Sylvester J, Pvt
Thurston, William C, S Sgt
Tkaczyk, Stanley W, Pfc
Torchetti, Guy A, Sgt
Toscano, Joseph D, Pfc
Toy, James F, III, 1 Lt
Treloar, Glenn E, Pvt
Trisler, James R, S Sgt
Troutman, Delbert L, Pfc
Tutterow, Marvin E, Pvt
Tuttle, Lenwood E, Sgt
Tyree, Edward G, 1 Lt
Valencia, Pete G, Pvt
Vanzandt, James W, Pvt
Vaughan, Davis H, S Sgt
Vaughan, J W, Maj
Volland, Paul F, Pfc
Von Dreau, Harry K, Cpl

Waller, Harold E, S Sgt
Ward, Ivie A, Jr, Pvt
Ward, Kenneth R, Cpl
Webb, John F, Pfc
Weber, Donald L, Pfc
Weeks, Edward J, Pvt
Wells, Bulkeley L, Jr, Pvt
Wells, Redmond D, Pvt
Westenhaver, Lorain O, Pvt
Westphal, Louis C, Pfc
White, Elwin G, Pvt
White, John T, S Sgt
Whitlock, John E, Cpl
Whitlock, William W, Tec 4
Willard, Frank A, Tec 5
Willburn, Richard A, Sgt
Willey, LeRoy, Sgt
Williamson, Jack K, Pfc
Wilson, Claude A, Pfc
Winzek, Walter J, Pvt
Wolcoff, Nick, Pvt
Wolfe, Robert M, 1 Lt
Wollen, John, 1 Sgt
Wood, Edwin B, Tec 5
Works, Charles W, Pvt
Wright, Willie A, Pvt
Yonce, Eugene J, Pvt
Young, John Q, Cpl
Zembrycki, Peter N, Sgt
Zerbe, Ralph J, Pfc

506th Parachute Infantry

Abbey, Philip D, Pvt
Abercrombie, Alex M, Tec 5
Adams, Charles H, Sgt
Adams, Robert E, Tec 5
Allen, Robert G, Pvt
Allison, Charles F, Tec 4
Allred, Jesse T, Pvt
Almeraz, Jose S, Pfc
Alvarado, Salome G, Pvt
Alvarez, Secundino, Pvt
Amabisco, Gilbert, Pfc
Andrako, Andrew, Pvt
Andres, Anthony F, Pvt
Androsky, John P, Pvt
Anthony, Milton G, Pfc
Arico, Anthony, Pvt
Arledge, William H, Pfc
Arhold, Aubrey W, Pvt
Ash, William E, Pvt
Atlee, William H, Tec 5
Atwood, Dale H, Pvt
Auseon, Edward L, Pvt
Austill, Ulysses E, Pvt
Austin, Roy H, S Sgt
Bahus, David, Pvt
Bailey, Bert J, Jr, Pvt
Bailey, George R, Cpl
Baker, Joseph S, Pvt
Baranski, Leonard, Pvt
Baribeau, Roland R, Pvt
Barkey, Raymond O, Pvt
Barling, Lintno A, 1 Lt
Barr, Jay F, Pvt
Barrington, Ollie E J, Cpl
Bateman, Raymond L, Pfc
Beatty, Kenneth A, 1 Lt
Beauchamp, Armand R, Pfc
Beazley, Donald D, Cpl
Bielski, John A, Pvt
Bignall, Donald E, Cpl
Bjorness, George H, Pfc
Blackwelder, Hubert L, Pvt
Blankenship, Robert R, Pfc
Blaum, Paul E, 2 Lt
Bloser, Robert J, Pvt
Bochm, Robert A, Pvt
Boggs, John, Pfc
Bolte, Rudolph E, 1 Lt

Bonilla, Nicholas L, Pfc
Bonitz, Herman C, Pfc
Bottacin, Angelo A, Pvt
Boye, Harold C, Pvt
Bray, John E, Jr, Tec 4
Brewer, Daniel, Sgt
Brewer, Jack R, Tec 5
Bright, Russel J, T Sgt
Broadhead, John W, Pfc
Brogan, Harold J, S Sgt
Broncheau, Phillip, Pvt
Brown, James L, Jr, Cpl
Brown, Martin I, Pfc
Brown, William J, Pvt
Brownley, Arlo L, Jr, Pvt
Brucker, Harold L, Tec 4
Bryan, Andrew T, Jr, Cpl
Bryan, Keith K, Pvt
Buchter, Richard K, Pfc
Buffington, Edward K, Pvt
Bugeler, Walter J, Pvt
Buren, Clifford L, Sgt
Burg, Harry L, Jr, Pfc
Burke, John J, Pfc
Busone, Anthony D, Pfc
Butler, Jack R, Pvt
Buxton, Harry W, Jr, Cpl
Bye, Roy F, Pvt
Byrnes, William J, S Sgt
Caccese, John J, Pvt
Caivano, Joseph A, Sgt
Calhoon, Richard L, Pfc
Call, Thomas W, Tec 5
Callihan, Laurel M, Pvt
Campas, James G, Pfc
Campbell, Colin, Pfc
Campbell, James D, Cpl
Cappelletti, Guido, Pfc
Carlton, Thayer U, Sgt
Carney, Warren K, Pfc
Carpenter, Woodrow W, Pvt
Carpenter, Lloyd M, Pfc
Carter, Donald W, Pfc
Carter, Harold B, 1 Lt
Carter, Paul R, Pvt
Casto, James A, Jr, Pfc
Cato, Franklin A, Pvt
Ceniceros, Salvador G, Pfc
Cervo, Joseph, Pvt
Chambliss, T M, Jr, 1 Lt
Cheel, Jay E, Pfc
Cheetham, Charles J, Pfc
Cheever, Robert L, Tec 4
Christain, Billy G, Pvt
Christensen, Dean F, Sgt
Ciano, Cosmo, Pvt
Clawson, Harry A, S Sgt
Clements, William H, Sgt
Clifton, Mainard D, Tec 4
Cline, Garland W,
Closson, Norman E, Pvt
Cole, Scott L, S Sgt
Collier, Garland W, Sgt
Collins, Herman F, Tec 5
Collins, Martin P, Pfc
Colt, Freeling T, 1 Lt
Conley, Sidney, Pfc
Cook, James P, Pfc
Coon, Raymond J, Pfc
Corder, John L, Pvt
Cordes, Herman J, Pvt
Corgan, Alfred G, Pfc
Corrington, Floyd J, Sgt
Cosner, Glen H, Pfc
Coyle, Clarence A, Pvt
Cramer, Harold F, 2 Lt
Cress, Frank A, Pfc
Cressey, Robert H, Pvt
Crolly, Anthony P, Pvt
Cronin, Raymond E, Pvt
Cross, Harvey A, Pfc

Croteau, Wilbur D, Pfc
Crowder, John P, Pvt
Cureton, Malcolm E, Pvt
Cutting, Raymond, Pvt
Cyran, Andrew P, Pfc
Daudt, Ralph G, Pvt
Davidson, James L, Pvt
Davis, Don P, Pfc
Davis, John L, Tec 5
Davis, William A, Pvt
Davison, Fred E, Pfc
Dawson, Robert A, Tec 5
Day, John K, Pvt
DeLuca, Victor J, Pvt
Devoe, Paul K, Pfc
Dean, Dale, Sgt
Deem, Charles R, Jr, Pfc
Defatta, Anthony S, Cpl
Demaio, Arthur, Pvt
Demetri, David A, Pvt
Demkowicz, Nick, Sgt
Derencin, Marijan P, Pfc
Descant, Marvin J, Pvt
Devaney, Ralph B, Pvt
Dickey, Charles, Jr, Pvt
Dickey, Lyman, Pvt
Diel, James L, 2 Lt
Diener, David, Pfc
Dodge, Martin J, Pvt
Dominic, Ralph J, Pfc
Doss, Joel H, Pvt
Downing, Chester M, Pvt
Doyle, Lawrence R, Pvt
Doyle, Wilson J, Pvt
Dukeman, William H, Jr, Cpl
Dziura, Henry A, Pvt
Easter, Charles L, Sgt
Eckels, Donald D, Pfc
Edmonds, Preston F, Pvt
Egan, Joseph P, Pfc
Eliuk, Michael, Pvt
Elliott, George L, Pvt
Elsner, Henry, Pvt
Ely, Franklin K, Pvt
Ervin, Simmie C, Sgt
Evans, Robert Y, Pvt
Evans, Williams S, 1 Sgt
Farrell, James J, Pvt
Farrow, Leonard L, Pfc
Fell, Emanuel, Pvt
Feneran, Frederick J, Pfc
Fenton, Lyle C, 1 Lt
Finder, Edwin, Pvt
Findley, Joseph A, Cpl
Fischer, Ralph D, Cpl
Fitzpatrick, L M, 1 Lt
Forshee, Harold S, Cpl
Foster, Berttran J, Jr, Pvt
Fountain, Bryce L, Pfc
Francis, Donald B, Cpl
Frazier, Harold M, Pfc
French, Scott S, Pvt
Fritz, Ralph H, Pvt
Fruge, Charles C, Pvt
Frye, Warren H, 2 Lt
Garland, Dennis D, Pvt
Gendreau, Joseph N, Pfc
Gensler, Finis G, Pvt
German, Lee O, Pvt
Germer, Philip, Pvt
Gibbs, Fred A, 1 Lt
Gibson, Harry, Pfc
Goetz, George L, Pvt
Goldbacher, Robert H, Pvt
Gonzales, Augustine, Pvt
Gonzales, Eli, Pvt
Goodman, John B, Tec 4
Goodrich, Arthur M J, Tec 5
Goodson, Frank J, Pvt
Gordon, William W, Tec 5
Gos, Francis E, Tec 5

Grant, George S, Maj
Gray, Albert C, Pvt
Gray, Everett J, Pfc
Green, William D, Tec 4
Grennan, James P, Pfc
Griese, Norman J, Pfc
Griffin, Rufus R, Pvt
Gromnicki, Edwin, Pfc
Gross, Jerre S, Capt
Guckenberger, George, Pfc
Gunther, Walter J, 1 Lt
Gurdak, Joe B, Pfc
Hackman, Don G, Pfc
Hagen, Bernard H, Pvt
Hagenbuch, James H, Pvt
Hahn, John W, Cpl
Hale, John R, Cpl
Hale, William C, Pfc
Hall, John D, Tec 5
Hall, Russell E, 2 Lt
Hall, Soini A, Pvt
Halls, John D, Pfc
Halstead, Clifford M, Sgt
Hamlin, Glenn E, Pfc
Haney, Maning G, Pvt
Hannah, Carl, Pvt
Hanson, Godfrey J, Pfc
Harmon, Clark M, Pvt
Harms, Donald R G, Pfc
Harris, Terrence C, Pfc
Harrison, Jack W, Tec 5
Harvey, James A, Pvt
Hattenbach, John A, Pfc
Hawkins, Jesse M, Pvt
Hayes, Harold G, Pvt
Hedl, Alfred T, Pvt
Hensel, Robert J, Pfc
Hernandez, Joaquin, Pvt
Hernandez, Jose, Jr, Pfc
Herron, A P, Pfc
Hester, Robert G, Pfc
Hibbitt, Roland M, Pfc
Hickman, Chester L R, Pvt
Hill, Andrew F, WO JG
Hill, Marion G, Jr, Pfc
Hinson, Bryant L, Pfc
Hobbs, Andrew J, Sgt
Hodge, Howard P, Pvt
Hodgkin, Charles F, Pvt
Holand, Orval B, Tec 5
Holstun, James D, 1 Lt
Hoobler, Donald B, Cpl
Hopkins, Joseph R, Sgt
Horn, Charles D, Pvt
Horton, Oliver M, Maj
Houck, Julius A, Sgt
Houk, John J, Pfc
Howard, Gerald V, Jr, 1 Lt
Howard, Harold E, Pvt
Howe, Donn S, Pvt
Hughes, Richard J, Pvt
Huie, Lilburn V, Pvt
Hull, Kenneth A, Pfc
Hult, Walter J, Pvt
Hundley, Prentice E, Pfc
Hunt, Charles L, Pvt
Hunton, Charles R, Pvt
Husband, Elmer W, Pvt
Irwin, Lewis, Pvt
Isler, Clarence E, Pvt
Ivey, John E, Pvt
Jackson, Eugene E, Pvt
Jackson, Thomas E, Sgt
James, Russell A, Sgt
Japhet, James H, S Sgt
Johns, Leland L, Pvt
Johnson, John W, Jr, Pvt
Jordan, Joseph M, Pfc
Joseph, Joseph L, Cpl
Julian, John T, Pfc
Justice, John E, Pvt

Justus, Hubert W, Pvt
Kajack, Joseph J, Pfc
Kane, Robert L, Sgt
Kangas, Robert W, Pvt
Karalunas, George J, Pvt
Katz, Abraham W, Tec 4
Kautz, Henry, Pvt
Kenfield, George E, Pfc
Kermode, Raymond F, Pvt
Kessler, Roy M, Capt
Keter, John J, Pvt
Keyes, Orin F, Jr, Pfc
Kiefer, Charles H, Jr., Pfc
Kiehn, William F, Sgt
Kilby, Lawrence J, Pvt
Kiley, John W, Capt
Kincaid, John Jr, Pvt
King, James D, Pvt
Kinzy, Robert C, Pvt
Kirkpatrick, James E, Pfc
Kissee, Earl K, Pvt
Kittia, John J, Pfc
Knapp, Thomas A, Pvt
Knerr, Glenn L, Pvt
Knight, Jerome C, 1 Lt
Knight, Leo, Pfc
Knott, Eugene P, Jr, 1 Lt
Koenig, Thomas C, Cpl
Korrow, Walter J, Pvt
Koval, Michael B, Pfc
Kozorsky, Nick, Pvt
Kribbs, Elden M, Pfc
Krom, Irving, Pfc
LaCount, Victor F, Pfc
LaCour, John M, Pvt
LaPrade, James L, Lt Col
Lacy, Melvin C, Pvt
Laferrera, Salvatore, Pvt
Laingo, Joseph, Cpl
Lambrecht, Harold W, Cpl
Lance Ralph E, Pvt
Langschultz, Philip W, Pvt
Lanocha, Walter S, Pfc
LaRose, Oliver L, Pvt
Laudick, Gordon J, Cpl
LaViolette, Joseph M, Pvt
Lawrence, Lester P, Pfc
LeCursi, Nicholas A, Pvt
Leach, William, Maj
Lecuyer, Leo J H, Pfc
Lee, Charles H, Pvt
Lee, Thomas J, Jr, Pvt
Lev, Orel H, Pfc
Levebvre, Hector A, Pvt
Lewsey, Joseph H, Pvt
Liccardo, Joseph, Pvt
Lilly, George M, Pfc
Lipp, Louis J, Cpl
Littell, Howard D, 1 Lt
Loika, Grover C, Pvt
Louis, Charles K, Pvt
Lovell, George E, Pfc
Lovett, James M, Sr, Pvt
Lukoskie, Joseph C, Pvt
Lundquist, Leonard E, Pfc
Lynn, Andrew A, Cpl
MacDowell, Carll B, 1 Lt
Macauley, Walter S, Jr, Pfc
Machen, Robert C, 1 Lt
Maczuga, Frank J, Pvt
Madona, Joseph P, S Sgt
Magie, Owen D, Pfc
Magyari, George M, Pvt
Manlove, Beverly J, Sgt
Manry, Thomas W, Sgt
Marquardt, Addison H, Sgt
Martinez, Oziel T, Pvt
Martinez, Guillermo, Pfc
Martinez, Victor P,
Massey, Laymon H, Jr, Pvt
Materewicz, Frank R, Pvt

Mather, Gordon E, Sgt
Mathews, Robert L, 2 Lt
Mattz, Jack E, Cpl
McAndrew, Martin J, Pfc
McCarson, Roy M, Pvt
McCarthy, Albert J J, Cpl
McCarthy, John J, Pvt
McClelland, Ralph W, Pfc
McClernan, C J, Pvt
McCrea, Donald H, Pvt
McCrory, William E, Pvt
McConigal, W T, Jr, Pfc
McGrath, Earl F, Pfc
McMahan, Rue D, Pvt
Medina, Manuel T, Pvt
Meehan, Thomas, 1 Lt
Melendez, Timoteo G, Pvt
Mellen, Charles W, 2 Lt
Mellett, Francis J, Cpl
Mendez, Trino, Pfc
Menze, Vernon J, Pfc
Mero, Richard M, Sgt
Mershon, George L, Pvt
Metzler, William S, Pfc
Mick, Donald K, Pfc
Middleton, Eugene E, Cpl
Millard, Vester B, Pvt
Miller, Halbert L, Jr
Miller, James W, Pfc
Miller, John N, Pfc
Miller, William T, Pfc
Millican, James E, Tec 5
Million, Fred A, Pfc
Mize, Martin E, Tec 5
Mock, James D, Pvt
Modracek, Robert J, Pfc
Monson, Carl T, Sgt
Montgomery, James E, Pvt
Montilio, George, Sgt
Moore, James H, 1 Lt
Morneweck, Robert E, Pfc
Morris, Willie A, Sgt
Morrison, Luther F, Pvt
Morse, Melvin R, Pvt
Mosser, Harold C, Pvt
Moya, Sergio G, Pfc
Muck, Warren H, Sgt
Mueller, William W, Cpl
Mull, Vernon H, Pvt
Muller, Bernard D, Pfc
Mullins, Robert A, S Sgt
Murray, Elmer L, Jr, Sgt
Murray, Edward J, Pvt
Myers, William R, Sgt
Naimola, Robert M, Pfc
Nakelski, Chester J, Pfc
Napier, Carl, Pfc
Neely, Harrison E, Pfc
Neill, Fred C, Pfc
Neill, Patrick H, Pvt
Nelson, Warren E, Tec 5
Newport, George B, Pvt
Noble, Robert R, Pvt
Norton, Shelby C, Pfc
Norvell, Robert A, Pfc
Oats, Earnest L, Pvt
Oleskiewicz, Joseph J, Cpl
Olson, William E, Pfc
Opferkuch, Anton W, Pvt
Orsag, Andrew D, Pfc
Osborne, John R, Pvt
Owen, Richard E, Sgt
Padlovsky, Leo, Cpl
Parros, Manuel W, S Sgt
Payne, Earnest O, Pvt
Pease, Carl E, Pvt
Pein, Carl E, Pfc
Pellechia, Frank, Pfc
Penkala, Alex M, Jr, Pfc
Pennell, Robert M, Jr, 1 Lt
Perkins, Warren W, Pvt

Peternel, Dominick J, S Sgt
Peters, Edward A, Capt
Peterson, Claire M, Pvt
Peterson, Leland, S Sgt
Petrowski, Edward F, Pfc
Pettinella, Sam A, Cpl
Pettis, Randal, Pvt
Pfaff, Marvin E, Pvt
Phillips, Howard, Pvt
Phillips, Willis, Sgt
Pinchot, John, Pfc
Plyler, Sam D, Pfc
Pobieglo, Ignacy S, Pfc
Politis, James, Pfc
Ponte, Albert J, Pvt
Porter, Howard R, Tec 5
Poynter, Alvin, Pfc
Prawdzik, Herman W, Pvt
Prezikowski, Edwin J, Pvt
Proper, Francis E, Pvt
Psar, Thomas G, Pfc
Purcell, William J, Pvt
Purdie, John B, Pfc
Radeka, George, Pvt
Radovich, Steve, Pvt
Ramirez, Willie, Pvt
Rankin, Claud W, Pfc
Rapino, Alexander, Pfc
Reasor, Hubert, Cpl
Reeder, Foster P,
Reichel, Harry G, Pvt
Reid, Robert L, Pfc
Repine, Robert L, Tec 4
Retan, George O, 2 Lt
Rick, Frank E, S Sgt
Rigaux, George J, Pvt
Riggs, Carl N, Sgt
Rigsby, Louis H, Pfc
Riley, Leslie B, Tec 5
Rinehart, John A, Pvt
Rinne, Bernard J, Pvt
Risner, Charles T, Pvt
Rizzo, Rosario P, Pvt
Robbins, Orris V, Pfc
Roberts, Murray B, S Sgt
Roberts, Floyd J, Pfc
Rogers, Charles J, S Sgt
Rogers, Robert M, S Sgt
Rogers, William B, Pvt
Rogoshewski, John, Pfc
Rohr, David W, Pvt
Roman, Eugene C, Pfc
Ronzani, Francis, Pvt
Roper, Amory S, Pfc
Russo, Daniel H, Pvt
Rybinski, Bruno W, Pvt
Rylah, Benjamin H, Tec 4
Sanchez, Mariano, Sgt
Sanders, George D, Pvt
Santillan, Marcos S, Pfc
Satterfield, Lars L, Pvt
Sawosko, Carl C, Pfc
Schmitz, Raymond G, 1 Lt
Seibel, Thomas J, 2 Lt
Semon, Charles H, 2 Lt
Shade, Earl V, Pvt
Sharp, Eliza L, Pvt
Sharp, James P, Pvt
Shea, Jack, Sgt
Shears, James R, Pvt
Shepherd, Othis C, S Sgt
Sherbon, John, Pfc
Shindoll, Johnnie E, Pvt
Shirley, James P, 1 Sgt
Shrout, Clarence L, Pvt
Siegwarth, George J, Pfc
Simco, Leonard J, Pvt
Simioni, Dino Ciprano, Tec 4
Simrell, Paul L, S Sgt
Skoglund, Donald I, Cpl
Skoglund, Donald L, Sgt

Slakanich, George, Pvt
Slosarczyk, Joseph F, Tec 5
Smith, Albert C, Sgt
Smith, Cleadith C, Cpl
Smith, Eugene A, Pfc
Smith, Frederick P, Pfc
Smith, Homer R, Pvt
Smith, Howard A, Pvt
Smith, James E, Pvt
Smith, Joseph E, Tec 4
Smith, Lloyd R, Pfc
Smith, William C, Pvt
Smutek, Frank J, Pvt
Snelling, Forrest L, Sgt
Snider, Gerald R, Pfc
Sobol, Michael J, Pvt
Sorrell, Thomas H, Pvt
Souther, Delmar M, Pvt
Sowards, James R, Jr, Pvt
Speake, Roy H, Sgt
Speer, Siber E, Pfc
Spisak, John J, Pfc
Stallings, Marvin M, Cpl
Stanley, Robert I, Jr, 2 Lt
Stephens, John H, Jr, Pfc
Stewart, Robert L, Pvt
Stewart, Harry D, Pvt
Stewart, William G, Pvt
Stidham, Jack, Pvt
Stockins, Stanley E, Tec 4
Stoney, Benjamin J, Tec 4
Stroble, Franklin F, Cpl
Stuart, Roy F, Pvt
Sumner, Carl E, Cpl
Supco, John, Pvt
Sutherland, Sherman N, 2 Lt
Swanson, Francis L, Pfc
Sweigart, Glenn E, Pfc
Swinney, Jack, Pvt
Syer, Charles A, Pfc
Talhelm, Roy U, Pvt
Tasker, Joseph W, Pfc
Tellez, Ruben R, Pvt
Telstad, Elmer L, Pfc
Terziu, Francis X, Pfc
Thirlkeld, C M, Jr, 2 Lt
Thomas, Morris L, Pvt
Tindall, Leslie F, Pfc
Tinsley, Roger L, 2 Lt
Todd, Robert L, Sgt
Tom, Bernard B, Pfc
Trotman, George A, Pvt
Trpelka, Joseph J, Jr, Pvt
Truett, Edgar J, Pvt
Tucker, Robert C, Sgt
Turkovich, Victor A, Sgt
Turner, William L, Lt Col
Tyra, Charlie L, Pfc
Utilla, Angelo, Pvt
Valenzuela, F R, Pvt
Van Antwerp, Harold E, Capt
Van Erdewyk, Leo J, 1 Sgt
Van Thiel, James C, Pvt
Vanderpool, Orville, Tec 5
Vanklinken, Robert, Pvt
Vece, William T, Pvt
Vendelis, John A, Pvt
Vernatter, Ardean D, Pvt
Villalobos, Victor S, Pfc
Waggoner, Gus A, Pvt
Walker, James W, Pfc
Walling, Garrett A, Pfc
Walsh, Jack J, Cpl
Ward, Raymond, Pvt
Warren, Thomas W, Pfc
Waterman, Elwood L, Jr, Pfc
Waters, James F, Pfc
Watkins, Joseph M, Pfc
Watkins, Harold E, 2 Lt
Watts, Robert M, Pfc
Weathersby, Newton P, Pfc

Webb, Harold D, Pfc
Webb, Kenneth J, Pfc
Weber, George L, Pfc
Weber, Paul J, Pvt
Weirich, Glen L, Pvt
Weisenberger, John F, 1 Lt
Wentzel, Jerry A, Tec 5
Wesp, Robert E, Pvt
West, Henry, Pvt
West, James W, S Sgt
Wetherell, Donald W, Sgt
Wheeldon, Earl F, Tec 5
Whitaker, Frederick W, Pvt
White, Harvey N, Cpl
Whitesel, William H, Pvt
Wiley, Archie C, Tec 5
Williams, Hugh F, Pvt
Williams, Leslie E, Pvt
Wimer, Ralph H, Tec 5
Winans, Wayne E, 1 Lt
Wincenciak, A M, Jr, Pvt
Winn, Benjamin F, Pvt
Winner, Dean E, Pfc
Wisniewski, John C, Pvt
Withers, James D, Pfc
Wolford, Thomas B, Cpl
Wolverton, Robert L, Lt Col
Wright, Clarence M, Pvt
Wright, John A, Pvt
Wright, Robert, Pvt
Yodis, Anthony J, Pvt
York, John R, Sgt
Yorko, William J, Pvt
Young, Melvin L, Pvt
Zavacki, Harry A, Cpl
Zebrosky, Stanley, Cpl
Zettwich, Joseph P, Pvt
Zoltz, Edward P, Pfc

101st Airborne Division Artillery Hq. & Hq. Battery

Davis, Paul F, 1 Lt
Hebert, Howard H, Pvt
Radde, Jackson E, Pvt
Rose, Herschel A, Pvt
Sherry, John M, 1 Lt

321st Glider FA Bn.

Calabro, James J, Pvt
Canham, Francis A, 1 Lt
Dillard, Carl F, 1 Lt
Falcon, Rudolph C, Pvt
Fuller, John M, Capt
Hutchins, Arthur A, Pvt
Kanspik, Frank J, Pfc
Kowalczyk, Henry, 2 Lt
Patterson, John H, Pvt
Reidman, Samuel, Pvt
Robinson, Pervey S, Pfc
Ruhling, Raymond P, S Sgt
Shefler, Manuel C, Pvt
Simmons, Carroll D, Cpl
Smith, Earnest H, Pvt
Sowell, William A, Jr, Pvt
Szur, James J, Cpl
Vetter, John J, Pfc
Weidle, Joseph, Pfc

907th Glider FA Bn.

Benson, James W, Pvt
Crews, William M, Pvt
Cynkar, Stanley A, Cpl
Dickman, Robert A, Sgt
Foytack, John J, Jr, Pvt
Harper, Dana H, Tec 4
Hilton, George W, Pfc
Hollis, Paul, Tec 4
Kiesel, Frank P, Tec 4

Kuehn, Gordon H, Pvt
Lodge, Charles A, Pvt
Marcelle, Charles E, Cpl
Marucas, Nickolas A, Pvt
McFarland, Dan, Pfc
McMurtry, Ernest H J, Pvt
Minich, John G, Sgt
Moore, Thomas D, 1 Lt
Pickens, Walter L, Pfc
Potaski, Jacob S, Pvt
Riggs, Jess L, Pvt
Riley, Jack O, 1 Lt
Robinson, H C, Pvt
Shebel, Edward, Cpl
Tousignant, Leo A, Pvt
Walls, James E, Pvt
Williamson, Jack L, 2 Lt

377th Parachute FA Bn.

Allard, Wilfrid A, Tec 5
Ball, Edward, Pfc
Barr, Charles E, Pvt
Baur, Frank X, Pfc
Bettis, Willis W, Pfc
Bolek, Matthew J, Cpl
Brinkley, James L, Pvt
Brooks, Russell C, Sgt
Brown, Hugh M, Pvt
Brown, William C, Tec 4
Bryant, Harry, Pvt
Burdge, Myron M, Cpl
Burri, Herman A, Sgt
Casto, David E, S Sgt
Cerny, Otaker, Pvt
Clayton, William E, Pvt
Conover, John J, Tec 4
Coutu, Herman G, Pvt
Crowe, Roscoe O, Tec 5
Cynar, Joseph J, Pfc
Davis, Lawrence J, Pfc
Dereta, Samuel, Pfc
Dotzler, Dennis, Pvt
Duncan, Kenneth, Tec 5
Engle, Robert E, Pfc
Feathers, Curtis C, Pfc
Field, William M, Cpl
Fletcher, Cleget M, Cpl
Fossum, Karsten A, Tec 5
Fultz, Joseph F, Jr, Pvt
Fultz, Raymond F, Pvt
Garrity, Harry R, Pvt
Gerken, Wilbur G, Pfc
Gibson, Benton L, Pfc
Gores, Melvin N, Pfc
Hann, Joseph M, Pfc
Hannon, Gerald P, Tec 4
Hebert, Lawrence R, Pfc
Hensley, Lawrence G J, 2 Lt
Hersh, Frederic H, Pvt
Hicke, Emil J, Pfc
Hicks, Ernest W, Tec 5
Holstege, Bernard, Pfc
Humphrey, Wellington, Cpl
Johnson, Earl G, Sgt

Jones, George R, 1 Lt
Justice, Joe, Pvt
Kalinowski, Theodore, Pfc
Kruvant, Arnold B, 1 Lt
Labrack, Louis E, Pvt
Landrau, Charles, Pvt
Legg, Joseph H, Tec 5
Lester, Richard W, Pvt
Liberator, John, Tec 4
Lindenmuth, Thomas R, Pfc
Lines, Harold F, Pvt
Lutz, Peter, S Sgt
Lyle, Lester E, Cpl
Mack, William R, Tec 5
Meyer, Edward, Pvt
Michalak, Marion, Pvt
Mitchell, Edward A, Jr, 1 Lt
Moriarity, Michael F, Pvt
Murphy, John T, Tec 5
Nasatka, William E, Tec 5
Neilson, Courtney B, Maj
Neubert, Robert C, Pfc
O'Bryan, Charles E, Pvt
Pappas, Gus A, Cpl
Pearson, James G, 1 Lt
Perry, William H, Sgt
Phillips, Fred F, Sgt
Phillips, John R, Pvt
Pinkosky, John, Pvt
Purdue, John E, Pvt
Reamsma, Henry, Cpl
Reeves, Rudolph R, Cpl
Rogers, David, 2 Lt
Rose, Carl B, Pvt
Sanwald, Walter L, Pfc
Sauers, Harold J, Pfc
Schaefer, Warren W, 1 Lt
Schroeder, Herbert M, Pvt
Shaw, Kenneth R, 1 Lt
Sims, Broadway, Tec 5
Sluzevich, John M, 1 Lt
Smith, Verlin C, Cpl
Spruiell, Melvin M, 1 Lt
Stajkowski, Sigmond F, Pvt
Stewart, Melvin V, T Sgt
Sullivan, Joseph H, Pfc
Tart, Howard, Pvt
Tertychny, Paul, Pvt
Underwood, Mitchel A, Cpl
Upchurch, Howard B, Capt
White, Melvin G, S Sgt
Williams, Newton A, Tec 5
Winebrener, Raymond L, Pvt
Wooster, Royal J, Pfc

463d Parachute FA Bn.*

Adler, Frisbie M, Pvt
Bryan, Rester W, Cpl
Connolly, Raymond J, Pfc
Gill, John C, 2 Lt
Hickenlooper, Howard, Pvt
Ouelette, Leo A, Pvt
Pearo, Dale A, Pvt
Ragsdale, James G, Pvt

Schoeneck, George W, 1 Lt
Terry, Jack S, 2 Lt
Whisman, Cyril J, Tec 5

——————
This battalion had the following
fatalities before joining the 101st
in December 1944:

Butts, Ollie F, Pvt
Hall, John T, Pfc
Harris, Joseph D, Capt
Hay, John J, Pvt
Higdon, John B, 1 Lt
Hulshizer, Allen H, Pvt
Jozefski, Chester B, Pvt
Langfeld, Robert D, Pvt
Legg, Theodore N, Pfc
Ruell, George P, Pfc
Sparkes, William N, 1 Lt

81st Airborne AA Bn.

Alexander, Edward L, Pvt
Beasley, Richard F, 1 Sgt
Berdine, Kenneth, Pvt
Briere, Walter B, 1 Lt
Brown, George A, Pfc
Burns, Cecil H, Pfc
Chambers, James O, Sgt
Clarke, William G, S Sgt
Claus, Arthur H, Jr, T Sgt
Cullen, Clifford E, Sgt
Deaton, Rodger J, Pfc
DeGraff, James W, Pvt
Destefano, Emilio L, Pfc
DiLazzero, Frank L, Pvt
Dindinger, John H, Pvt
Disbennett, Donald W, Cpl
Eldridge, Claude F, Pvt
Freda, Dan S, Pvt
Hanawalt, Edward L, Tec 5
Haney, Chester B, Cpl
Haralson, Charles R, Pvt
Harness, Harold L, Cpl
Hibbs, Richard R, Cpl
Hilton, Robert G, Pvt
Kurtz, Arthur C, Pvt
Lively, Claude H, Pvt
Maligian, Stanley W, Cwo
McAllister, Donald E, Cpl
McIntosh, Clarence C, Tec 5
Mitchell, Richard J, Pfc
Nestich, Stephen G, Pfc
Novak, Adam, Pvt
Pate, James R, Cpl
Rogers, William B, Pvt
Rugg, Harlan E, 2 Lt
Shapiro, Robert, Pvt
Sicurella, John F, Pfc
Slade, Melvin H, Pvt
Spaulding, Russell L, Sgt
Taylor, Ralph L, Jr, Pvt
Wafer, Guy R, Tec 5
Webb, George M, Pvt
Whisenhunt, Charles E, Pvt
Zax, Nathan, Pvt

Individual Decorations[1]

Aadland, Wallace L., SS
Abeene, Marell V., SS
Acheson, George S., SS
Adams, George H., SS
Adams, John L., Jr., SS★
Adkins, Floyd, SS
Alexander, Donald C., SS
Alexander, Winston L., SS
Allen, Ray C., SS★★
Allen, Richard J., SS
Amerman, Walter, DSC
Amman, Richard V., SS
Anderson, Marvin W., SS
Andrews, Robert E., SS
Archie, Edwin P., SS
Atkins, Floyd, SS
Austin, Roy H., SS
Axelrod, Louis, SS

Bahlau, Fredrick A., SS★
Baker, Champ L., SS
Baker, Donald G., SS
Baker, Leslie R., SS
Balduc, Timothy R., SS
Ballard, Robert A., SS
Banker, Robert M., SS
Barker, Harry A., SM
Barton, Raymond F., DSC, SS
Bauer, Ivan A., SS
Beams, Kenneth L., SS
Beard, David L., SS
Beasley, Richard F., SS
Becker, Fredrick J., SS
Beishline, Theodore E., SS
Bennett, Ralph S., SS
Bernay, David W., SS
Bieber, John P., SS
Birch, Wallace H., SM
Blackburn, George W., SS
Blackmon, Sumpter, SS
Blair, Ancle F., SS
Blake, George B., SS
Blasingame, Franklin R., SS
Blaufuss, Cecil E., SS
Blombaum, Carl, SS
Bobuck, Alex, SS
Boehlke, Otto A., AM★★
Boitano, John N., SS
Bolander, Clifford J., Jr., SS
Bolduc, Timothy P., SS
Borden, Hugh G., SS
Borrelli, Anthony N., SS
Bottomly, Raymond V., Jr., SS
Bowen, Alvie F., SS
Bowles, Howard G., Jr., SS
Boye, Harold C., SS
Bradley, Robert O., SS
Brandenberger, Elmer F., SS
Branley, Edward, SS
Brennan, Fred O., SS
Brininstool, Donald W., SS
Broadway, Ealsby E., SS

Brock, Raymond I., SS
Brooks, Elton E., DSC
Brown, Early A., SS
Brown, Frank L., SS
Brown, Nathan W., SS
Browning, James C., SS
Bunn, Thomas G., SS
Burdette, William K., SS
Burkett, George I., AM
Butler, Marlin L., SS
Buxton, Harry W., Jr., SS
Bynell, Wallin D., AM★
Byrnes, James F., SS

Cahill, Thomas F., SS
Campbell, Arthur L., SS
Campbell, Richard A., SS
Canestra, Dominic J., SS
Canfield, William R., SS
Caraker, Cecil C., SS
Carlock, Robert H., SS
Carmichael, Edward L., SS
Carpenter, Frank J., SS
Carpenter, Joe E., SS
Carrel, Francis E., SS
Carrier, Clifford C., SS
Carroll, Robert C., SS
Cases, Ralph D., SS
Casper, Lawrence F., SS
Cassidy, Patrick F., DSC, SS
Caumartin, Hugh T., SS
Chalfin, Harold L., SS
Chamberlain, Lyle B., SS
Chandler, Carlton P., SS
Chappuis, Steve A., DSC, SS
Charpentier, Leo P., SS
Chase, Charles H., SS, LM
Cherry, Henry T., Jr., SS★
Chovan, Robert N., SM
Christian, Howard C., SS
Clawson, Harry A., SS
Clements, Robert L., SS
Cline, Charles F., SS
Cole, Robert G., MH
Cole, Scott L., SS
Combs, Homer J., SS
Compton, Lynn D., SS
Cooney, Paul O., SS, AM
Cooper, John T., SS
Corcoran, Robert L., SS
Cordes, Herman J., DSC
Corley, Laurence J., LM
Corr, James J., SS
Cortez, Jesus A., SS
Cote, Paul M., SS
Coulson, Okra G., SS
Coyle, Paul B., SS
Craft, George H., SS
Craighill, Edley, Jr., SS
Crossley, Fred, Jr., SS
Crotts, Eldon L., Jr., SS
Crusan, Earl W., SS

Cullen, Clifford E., SS
Culpepper, Willie E., SS
Cummings, Ernest R., SS★
Curran, John E., SS

Dale, Doyle A., SS
Danahy, Paul A., SS, LM
Danforth, Vergial E., DSC
Daniels, Leonard A., SS
Davidson, Douglas T., Jr., SS
Davies, Reginald E., SS
Davis, Grayson A., SS
Decker, Ted R., SS
Dekle, Zelmah Q., SS
DeLaughter, Philip V., SS
DePinquertaine, Robert L., SS
Desobry, William R., SS
Devereaux, John D., SS
Dickson, Robert S., III, SS
Dimmerling, William G., SS
Dingman, Harley S., SS
Dobbyn, Elden C., SS
Dobson, Joseph R., AM★★★
Doiel, Robert S., SS
Dopjera, Rudolph J., SS
Drennan, Fred O., DSC, SS
Duc, Jules, Jr., SS
Dulaney, Jack F., SS
Dunn, Lawrence R., SS
Durka, John P., SS
Dworsky, Otto F., SS

Earnest, Charles F., SM
Easter, Charles L., SS
Everle, George M., DSC
Edmondson, Paul S., SS
Elkins, Harry W., SS
Ellenberger, Don M., SS
Ellerman, Glenn H., AM★★★
Ellis, Nathaniel F., SS
Emary, Robert J., SS
Embry, Lige, SS
Emerson, Charles S., SS
Emery, Allen T., SS
Erlick, Milton I., SS
Eubank, Gilbert G., SS
Evans, Clarence, SS
Evans, James L., SS
Everding, William F., SS
Every, Gilbert, DSC
Ewell, Julian J., DSC, SS★

Farley, Gerald F., SS
Feeney, William H., SS
Findley, Joseph A., SS
Flaherty, John J., SS
Fleming, Francis, SM
Fletcher, Ira L., SS
Ford, Edward E., DSC
Ford, Francis, SS
Forester, William R., SS
Fort, Richard A., AM★

Forte, Nicholas, SS
Fowler, Willis H., SS
Frank, Gerald W., SS
Frank, Peter R., SS
Fraundorfer, Edward A., SS
Fuquay, Cecil O., SS

Gage, Philip S., Jr., SS
Galayda, Andy, SS
Galvin, Charles C., SS
Garrett, Daniel W., SS
Gehauf, Ralph B., SS
Gifford, David C., SS
Goodall, Robert G., SM
Goodman, John B., SS
Goolsby, William V., SS
Gott, Carroll F., SS
Graham, S. L., SS
Granche, Robert F., SS
Gregg, Frank A., SS
Greggs, Robert E., SS
Griffith, Gordon G., SS
Grigg, Emmett H., SS
Griswold, George M., SS
Grosvenor, Francis V., SS
Guarnere, William J., SS
Gulick, Edward T., SS
Gunn, George C., SS

Haddick, William F., SS
Hagens, David K., SS
Hahn, John W., SS
Hall, Robert P., SS
Hammersla, Warren H., SS
Hammond, George J., SS
Hancock, Fred A., SS
Hanford, Theodore J., SS
Hanlon, John D., SS
Hansford, Orville, SS
Harbaugh, Francis L., DSC
Hardie, William D., SS
Harding, Forrest G., SS
Harmon, David, SS
Harms, Donald G., SS
Harper, Joseph H., SS, LM
Harrell, Edward M., SS
Harris, Ernest O., DSC
Harrison, Bailey, DSC
Hartmann, William F., SS
Harwick, Robert F., SS
Haskell, Warren B., SS
Hassenzahl, Albert M., SS
Haworth, Perry R., SS
Hayes, Joe W., SS
Heaton, William P., SS
Heatwole, Jacob A., AM★★
Hebenstreit, William P., AM★★★
Herman, David C., SS
Hettel, Charles M., SS
Higgins, Gerald J., LM, SS
Hiner, Ben M., SS
Hohl, Edwin S., SS
Hollis, Eugene T., SS
Holt, Newt P., SS
Honaker, Milton B., SS
Horton, Oliver M., SS
Houston, Robert J., DSC
Howenstine, Don R., SS
Hughes, Lawrence T., SS
Hunt, Edward M., SS
Hunter, John J., SS
Huntley, Taze R., SS
Hustead, Charles L., Jr., SS
Hutto, Albert D., SS

Inman, Roy L., SS

Jackson, Schuyler W., SS
Johnson, Arthur L., SS
Johnson, Howard R., SS

Johnson, Homer R., SS
Johnson, LeGrand K., SS★
Jones, Allan, SS
Jones, Claude, SS
Jourdan, Robert E., SS

Karin, Ahzez, SS
Karshner, Thomas W., SS
Keester, John F., AM★
Kellner, Robert C., SS
Kennedy, LM
Kent, Edward F., SS
Kessler, Donald J., SS
Kessler, Frank T., Jr., SS
Keter, John J., SS
Kidder, Alvin W., SS
Kiellor, John M., SS
King, Bernard C., SS
King, James P., SS
King, William J., SS
Kinnard, Harry W. O., Jr.,
                     DSC, SS, LM
Kloth, Frederick S., DFC, AM
Knight, Bernardo H., Jr., AM★
Knight, Elton L., SS
Knight, Leo, SS
Kohls, Cary W., LM
Kraeger, Vernon, SS

Lage, George H., SS
LaGrave, Maurice G., SS
Laino, Vincent, SS
Lanci, Joseph V., LM
Landry, John J., SS
Langen, Robert E., DSC
Langston, Merle, SS
LaPrade, James L., SS★
Larson, Harry H., SS
Leach, Edison, SS
Leach, William, SS
Lecuyer, Leo J., SS
Ledford, Alvin, SS
Lee, William C., DSM
Leffel, Emmett F., SS
Legere, Lawrence J., Jr., SS
Leino, Loyd J., DSC
Lemmon, Robert H., SS
Lengoza, Walter A., SS
Lenz, William F., SS
Lesniak, Michael, SS
Lev, Ovel H., DSC
Levin, Abe, SS
Leviski, John A., SS
Lillyman, Frank L., DSC
Lindsay, Robert A., SS
Loftsgard, Ollard O., SS
Long, Edwin, SS
Long, James V., SS
Long, Robert, SS
Loraine, Gerald J., SS★
Ludlow, David A., SS
Lufkin, Arthur R., SS
Luhring, Benjamin J., SS
Lina, J. D., SS
Lunin, Arthur P., SS
Lynch, James R., SS

MacDonald, Robert J., SS★
MacGregor, Joseph C., SS
Madden, Denver R., SS
Madona, Joseph P., SS
Maloney, John S., DSC
Mann, Joe E., MH
Marquart, Floyd P., SS
Marrs, Guy R., SS
Marshall, Clifton W., SS
Martin, Michael J., SS
Martin, Thomas E., DSC
Martino, Harold S., SS
Massucco, Raymond R., SS

Maurer, Robert O., AM
Mayer, Arthur C., DSC
McAuliffe, Anthony C.,
                  DSC, DSM, SS
McClure, Franklin E., SS
McConnell, Charles D., Jr., SS
McDonald, Robert J., SS★
McEwan, C. C., SS
McGee, Tildon S., DSC
McGirr, John P., SS
McGrath, John, SS
McIntosh, Ben C., SS
McKearney, Bernard J., SS
McLaughlin, Forrest L., SS
McLean, David, Jr., AM★
McMahon, Edward J., SS
McRae, William M., Jr., AM★
McReynolds, Altus F., SS
Metheny, Fred R., DSC
Michaelis, John H., SS, LM
Mier, Harry J., SS
Millener, Raymond D., DSC
Miller, Cyrus W., SS
Miller, Lester E., SS
Miller, Raymond L., SS
Miller, Robert W., SS
Miller, Ronald L., SS
Miller, Walter L., Jr., SS★
Minikus, Donald F., SS
Mishler, John D., SS
Mitchell, Jachin, DSC
Mize, Paul H., LM
Montgomery, James E., SS
Montilio, George, DSC
Moore, Kenneth J., SS
Moore, Ned D., SS, LM
Moore, Thomas D., SS
Morrison, Stanley A., SS
Moseley, G. Van Horn, Jr., LM
Moyer, Bert J., SS
Mroczkowski, Stanley J., SS
Mulleniz, Austin E., SS
Mullins, Robert A., SS
Murn, George C., SS
Murphy, Dennis M., Jr., SS
Murphy, James C., SS
Myer, Clifford L., SS

Navarro, Arcadio, SS
Nelson, Clarence F., SS
Nelson, Clifford E., SS
Nesbitt, James C., SM
Nichols, George P., SS
Nichols, Phillip A., SS
Nickrent, Roy W., SS
Niland, Thomas J., Jr., SS
Nordall, Robert, SS
Nygren, Burdette J., AM

O'Brien, John J., Jr., SS
Odom, Hubert, DSC
O'Halloran, John T., SS
O'Hara, James, SS
Oleson, Gilbert E., SS
Olson, Donald R., SS
O'Shaughnessy, John P., SS
Osterberg, Norman A., DSC
O'Toole, Joseph P., SS
Owen, Roy W., AM
Owens, Fred A., SS
Owens, Paul B., AM★★★

Pakisak, Frank J., SS
Parker, Herschel C., SS
Parlaman, Thomas E., SM
Passanisi, Robert, SS
Patch, Lloyd E., DSC, SS
Patching, Frederick E., SS
Patterson, Floyd T., SS
Payne, Ralph L., SS

Pelham, Wm. E., SS
Pendzinski, John, SS
Pentz, Chester C., SS
Pernusch, Edward S., SS
Perreault, Albert R., SS
Peters, Edward A., SS
Phillips, Curtis L., SS
Phillips, Ivan G., SS
Phillips, Robert H., SS
Pick, Robert G., DSC
Plitt, Henry G., SS★
Podulski, William F., SS
Porter, Hubert C., SS
Powers, Joseph E., SS
Powers, Shannon C., AM★★
Price, Jack J., AM
Prichard, Conrad, SS
Puflett, George R., SM
Puhalski, Henry J., SS

Ragland, Eugene, SS
Rainey, Francis F., SS
Raudstein, Knut H., DSC
Reed, Ronald E., SS
Renfro, Curtis D., SS★
Rice, Ben J., SS
Rice, J. F., SS
Richardson, Marvin R., SS
Riewe, Karl R., SS
Riggins, Jack F., SS
Riley, Harry T., AM
Rivera, Domingo, Jr., SS
Rizzo, Rosario, SS
Robbins, Woodrow W., SS
Roberts, Dorsey R., SS
Roberts, Gleason F., SS
Roberts, Rogie, SS
Roberts, William L., SS
Roberts, William T. S., SS
Robinson, James A., SS
Roderick, Charles L., SS
Rogan, Joseph F., SS
Rogers, Lee N., DSC
Rosemond, St. Julian F., DSC
Roughneen, James P., SS
Rouzie, Thomas J., SS★
Rowe, Frank A., SS
Rudd, Jack L., DSC
Ruelf, Jerry, DFC
Runge, Leo F., SS
Rusin, Bronislaus T., SS
Russell, Conrad E., SS
Russo, William J., SS
Ryan, Bernard J., SS★
Ryan, Clarence J., SS

Saber, Eugene, SS
Salee, Hartford F., SS★★
Sallin, John J., SS★
Sanchez, Mariano, SS
Sanderson, Walter H., SS
Santasiero, Charles J., DSC
Satterfield, James L., SS
Savage, Schuyler L., Jr., SS
Saver, Eugene W., SS
Schiltz, Nicholas C., SS
Schmicke, William, SS
Schmidt, George N., SS

Schneider, Clyde C., SS
Schoeneck, George W., AM★
Schorsch, Robert S., SS
Schroeder, Bruno E., SS
Scofield, Hampton B., SS
Seny, Joe, SS
Serwatka, Frank, SS
Shaab, Benjamin C., SS
Shell, Robert E., SS
Sheller, Ronald F., SS
Sherburne, Thomas L., Jr., LM
Sherry, John M., AM
Shrader, William E., SS
Sims, Hugo S., Jr., SS
Sims, Virgil T., SS
Single, James C., DSC
Sink, Robert F., SS★, LM
Skaggs, Wallace, SS
Slabinski, Joseph J., SS
Slatton, Robert W., SS
Smith, Fred T., SS
Smith, John M., SS
Smith, Lloyd R., SS
Sosnack, Andrew, DSC
Speirs, Ronald C., SS
Sprecher, Kenneth N., DSC
Spurr, Alexander, SS
Stach, Stanfield A., SS
Stanfield, Frank R., SS
Stanley, Cecil D., SS
Steele, Birchard G., SS
Stephens, Ben F., SS
Stephens, Roscoe W., SS
Stephens, Thomas W., SS
Stephenson, Clyde M., SS
Sternot, Edmund J., SS
Stevens, Gerald W., SS
Stevens, Weld M., AM★
Stevenson, Lincoln L., AM
Stewart, William F., AM
Stopka, John P., SS
Strauss, John L., SS
Strayer, Robert L., SS
Stubblefield, Warren D., SS
Stumpus, Achilles, AM
Summers, Harrison C., DSC
Surgalski, Alfred J., AM
Sutfin, Lewis R., SS
Sutliffe, Thomas H.
Swanson, Wallace A., SS
Swart, Robert N., SS

Tarquini, James V., SS
Taylor, Allen S., SS
Taylor, Frank, SS
Taylor, John H., SS
Taylor, Maxwell D.,
          DSC, LM, DSM, SS
Teeter, Arthur H., SS
Templeton, Clifford, SS
Terrell, Thomas W., SS
Terry, Jack S., AM
Tertychny, Paul, SS
Theall, Bartow R., SS
Thomas, Edward G., SS
Thompson, Stacy W., Jr., SS
Thornton, Evans C., SS
Timmes, Charles J., DSC, SS

Tipton, Virgil, SS
Tobinas, George R., SS
Toms, Tom E., SS
Towns, Preston E., SS★
Tripp, Robert C., SS
Tritt, Howard C., AM★
Tubbs, Herbert A., DSC
Tucker, Robert C., SS
Turner, William L., DSC
Turvey, Irvin, Jr., SS
Tyler, Charles H., SS
Tyrrell, Clarence J., SS

Ulrich, Lester T., SS
Utz, Vincent P., SS

Varner, Dock J., SS
Varone, Anthony M., SS
Vaught, William R., SS
Veselka, Rudolph F., SS
Vetland, Theodore, SS

Waggoner, Lowell O., SS
Waldman, Thomas A., AM★★★
Waldmann, William J., SS
Walker, Perrin, SS
Walker, Philip G., SS★
Wallace, Jack E., SS
Walsh, Edward J., Jr., AM
Warren, Joseph E., SS
Washichek, Jack N., AM★
Watson, Ralph A., Jr., SS
Webb, William J., SS
Webster, Willie H., SS
Weeks, Edward J., SS
Werner, Carlton, DSC
West, James W., SS
Westphal, Allen L., SS
Whalen, Kenneth J., SS
Whipple, Raymond M., SS
White, Thomas J., SS
Whitfield, Alonza R., SS
Whitfield, George A., DSC
Wilbur, Roland J., SS
Wilder, Thomas P., SS
Willis, Joseph A., SS
Wilson, Glenn L., SS
Winters, Richard D., DSC
Wisely, Martin R., SS, LM
Wiskemann, Frederick, SS
Wolf, William J., SS
Wollen, John, SS
Wolverton, Robert L., LM
Wood, Graham, Jr., SS
Wray, Clayton R., SS
Wright, Benjamin F., AM★★★
Wright, Lynn C., SS
Wright, Robert E., SS
Wynne, Talfourd T., SS

Yates, Gordon W., SS
Youre, Joseph, AM

Zahn, Donald E., DSC
Zajac, Henry, SS
Zax, Nathan, SS
Zeppenfeld, Bernard M., AM

Distinguished Unit Citations

BATTLE HONORS. As authorized by Executive Order No. 9396 (sec I, Bul. 22, WD, 1943), superseding Executive Order No. 9075 (sec. III, Bul. 11, WD, 1942), the following unit is cited by the War Department under the provisions of section IV, Circular No. 333, War Department, 1943, in the name of the President of the United States as public evidence of deserved honor and distinction. The citation reads as follows:

101st Airborne Division (less 2d Battalion, 401st Glider Infantry Regiment[1]) with the following attached units:

501st Parachute Infantry Regiment
506th Parachute Infantry Regiment
463d Parachute Field Artillery Battalion
Counterintelligence Detachment, 101st Airborne Division
Order of Battle Detachment Number 5
Military Intelligence Interpreter Team Number 410
Photo Interpreter Teams Number 9 and 81
Prisoner of War Interrogation Teams Number 1, 9 and 87
Third Auxiliary Surgical Group, Team Number 3
969th Field Artillery Battalion
755th Field Artillery Battalion
705th Tank Destroyer Battalion

Combat Command B, 10th Armored Division, including:

   Headquarters and Headquarters Company, Combat Command B, 10th Armored Division
   3d Tank Battalion (less Company C)
   20th Armored Infantry Battalion (less Company A)
   54th Armored Infantry Battalion (less Companies A and C)
   420th Armored Field Artillery Battalion
   Troop D, 90th Cavalry Reconnaissance Squadron (Mechanized)
   Company C, 609th Tank Destroyer Battalion (less 1st Platoon; with 2d Platoon Reconnaissance Company attached)
   Battery B, 796th Antiaircraft Artillery Automatic Weapons Battalion
   Company C, 55th Armored Engineer Battalion
   Company C, 21st Tank Battalion

Reserve Command, 9th Armored Division, including:

   Headquarters Reserve Command, 9th Armored Division
   Headquarters and Headquarters Company, 12th Armored Group
   2d Tank Battalion
   52d Armored Infantry Battalion
   73d Armored Field Artillery Battalion
   Company C, 9th Armored Engineer Battalion
   Company C, 811th Tank Destroyer Battalion
   Battery C, 482d Antiaircraft Artillery Automatic Weapons Battalion (Self-Propelled)

---

[1]2d Battalion, 401st Glider Infantry Regiment, was attached to the 82d Airborne Division in the spring of 1944 and never rejoined the 101st Airborne Division.

These units distinguished themselves in combat against powerful and aggressive enemy forces composed of elements of 8 German divisions during the period from 18 December to 27 December 1944, by extraordinary heroism and gallantry in defense of the key communications center of Bastogne, Belgium. Essential to a large scale exploitation of his break-through into Belgium and northern Luxembourg, the enemy attempted to seize Bastogne by attacking constantly and savagely with the best of his armor and infantry. Without benefit of prepared defenses, facing almost overwhelming odds and with very limited and fast dwindling supplies, these units maintained a high combat morale and an impenetrable defense, despite extremely heavy bombing, intense artillery fire, and constant attacks from infantry and armor on all sides of their completely cut off and encircled position. This masterful and grimly determined defense denied the enemy even momentary success in an operation for which he paid dearly in men, material, and eventually morale. The outstanding courage and resourcefulness and undaunted determination of this gallant force is in keeping with the highest traditions of the service. [*General Orders No. 17, War Department, 13 March 1945.*]

The following units received the Distinguished Unit Citation for action in Normandy:

101st Airborne Division Headquarters and Headquarters Company
101st Airborne Division Military Police Platoon
326th Airborne Engineer Battalion
326th Airborne Medical Company
101st Airborne Signal Company
501st Parachute Infantry Regiment
502d Parachute Infantry Regiment
506th Parachute Infantry Regiment
377th Parachute Field Artillery Battalion
Batteries A and B, 81st Airborne AA Battalion

The following unit received the Meritorious Service Unit Plaque for service in Holland:

801st Airborne Ordnance Company

Foreign Citations

French Croix de Guerre with Palm. Awarded under Decision No. 367, 22 July 1946, by the President of the Provisional Government of the French Republic, with the following citation:

A splendid airborne unit which gave proof of extraordinary heroism in the course of the Normandy landing operations on 6 to 8 June 1944. It parachuted before dawn on the assault beach on 6 June and in spite of all sorts of difficulties, succeeded in regrouping. Attacked by important forces with violent fire, it nevertheless occupied positions of strategic importance for the landing of friendly troops. This action opened the way to La Douve and the Carentan road for the assault troops. In this way, it greatly contributed to the first phase of the liberation of France.

Belgian Croix de Guerre. Awarded under Decree No. 828, dated 30 July 1945, as amended by Decree No. 1196, 22 October 1945, by Charles, Prince of Belgium, Regent of the Kingdom, with the following citation:

By its glorious resistance from 22 to 27 December 1944, in the hardest time of the Battle of the Ardennes, it kept, completely isolated, the key position Bastogne. The 101st Airborne Division, with its attached units, caused the failure of the enemy's plan. This required a deep penetration into Belgium and this division served as a pivot to the operations of the counteroffensive which liberated the invaded territories. During these operations, because of its courage, endurance, discipline and experience in fighting, the 101st Airborne Division pushed back the unceasing attacks of the elements belonging to eight German divisions, in spite of scarce supplies. These troops and their chiefs wrote one of the most beautiful pages of military history and earned the admiration of the world and the everlasting gratitude of Belgium.

Belgian Croix de Guerre. Awarded under Decree No. 1196, 22 October 1945, by Charles, Prince of Belgium, Regent of the Kingdom, with the following citation:

The 101st Airborne Division, U. S. Army, landing by parachute, glider and assault craft on the coast of France, 6 June 1944, was one of the first units to attack the enemy in the campaign that was to liberate Europe from German domination. It was necessary for small groups to battle fiercely in many places in order that they might reach and unite at the assembly point. Many casualties were inflicted upon the enemy and many casualties were sustained by the division while it subdued enemy strongpoints, attacked and held vital communication centers, bridges and observation posts. The success with which these missions were accomplished hindered the enemy from using reinforcements which could have caused the failure of the U. S. VII Corps, which later participated in the liberation of Belgium.

Belgian Fourragère of 1940. Awarded under Decree No. 1196, 22 October 1945, by Charles, Prince of Belgium, Regent of the Kingdom.

Under the Belgian custom two awards of the *Croix de Guerre* entitles a unit to the *Fourragère*.

Netherlands Orange Lanyard. Awarded under Ministerial Decree No. P-203, 20 September 1945, by the Netherlands Minister of War, with the following citation:

Considering that the outstanding performance of duty of the 101st Airborne Division, United States Army, during the airborne operations and the ensuing fighting actions in the southern part of the Netherlands in the period from 17 September to 28 November 1944, has greatly contributed to the liberation of that part of the country; considering also, that it is desirable for each member of the division, who took part in the aforesaid operations, to possess a lasting memento of this glorious struggle; Decrees: That each member of the personnel of the 101st Airborne Division, United States Army, who took part in the operations in the southern part of the Netherlands in the period from 17 September to 28 November 1944, is authorized to wear the Orange Lanyard of the Royal Netherlands Army.

Battle Credits

The 101st Airborne Division earned the following battle credits:

Normandy
Rhineland
Ardennes-Alsace
Central Europe

The 101st Airborne Division earned Bronze Service Arrowheads for the following amphibious or airborne assault landings:

Normandy
Holland

ESTIMATED CASUALTIES: NORMANDY, HOLLAND,

	Normandy[1]					
	Killed and Died of Wounds	Wounded and Injured	Missing and Captured	Total	Killed and Died of Wounds
Division Headquarters and Headquarters Company	7	12	13	32	1
Military Police Platoon . . .	4	9	0	13	0
326th Airborne Engineer Battalion	16	27	25	68	21
326th Airborne Medical Company	13	31	14	58	3
101st Airborne Signal Company	4	20	8	32	1
426th Airborne Quartermaster Company .	1	0	0	1	3
801st Airborne Ordnance Maintenance Company . .	0	3	0	3	1
327th Glider Infantry Regiment (Including 1st Battalion 401st Glider Infantry Regiment and the Division Reconnaissance Platoon)	103	406	15	524	158
501st Parachute Infantry Regiment	213	490	195	898	172
502d Parachute Infantry Regiment	200	600	50	850	162
506th Parachute Infantry Regiment	231	569	183	983	176
101st Airborne Division Artillery Headquarters and Headquarters Battery .	1	2	0	3	1
321st Glider Field Artillery Battalion	0	18	1	19	13
907th Glider Field Artillery Battalion	3	12	1	16	12
377th Parachute Field Artillery Battalion	59	70	152	281	12
463d Parachute Field Artillery Battalion[2]					
81st Airborne Antiaircraft Battalion	13	34	8	55	16
	868	2303	665	3836	752

[1]The casualties for Normandy and Holland are as estimated by the 101st G-1 on 12 December, 1944. (Additional information would increase these estimates, especially in the number of deaths.)

The casualty figures for Bastogne are as estimated by the 101st G-1 on 14 January, 1945. The next several days of fighting added a number of casualties not included in this estimate.

Statistics

BASTOGNE (Before 14 January 1945)

Holland[1]			Bastogne (as of 14 January)			
Wounded and Injured	Missing and Captured	Total	Killed and Died of Wounds	Wounded and Injured	Missing and Captured	Total
9	8	18	5	6	5	16
1	0	1	1	5	0	6
66	11	98	27	92	23	142
12	4	19	1	1	140	142
2	8	11	3	10	0	13
1	0	4	0	1	0	1
0	0	1	0	0	0	0
402	102	662	84	405	91	580
505	44	721	132	644	89	865
467	54	683	103	523	107	733
565	63	804	102	601	59	762
6	5	12	0	3	2	5
21	11	45	2	27	1	30
26	69	107	3	25	0	28
54	4	70	5	23	0	28
			6	18	8	32
14	15	45	8	65	2	75
2151	398	3301	482	2449	527	3458

[1]The 463d Parachute Field Artillery Battalion was attached to the 101st Airborne Division in December 1944, just before Bastogne.

821

Estimated Casualties of Major Units Attached to 101st Airborne Division at Bastogne

(As of 14 January 1945)

	Killed and Died of Wounds	Wounded	Missing and Captured	Total
Combat Command B, 10th Armored Division	73	279	116	468
705th Tank Destroyer Battalion	34	107	14	155
755th Field Artillery Battalion	0	21	0	21
969th Field Artillery Battalion	10	15	4	29

Infantry Battalion Strength as of 13 January 1945

327th Glider Infantry Regiment

	O	EM
1st Battalion	22	468
2d Battalion	20	489
3d Battalion	24	520
Special Units	22	204
	88	1681

502d Parachute Infantry Regiment

	O	EM
1st Battalion	29	413
2d Battalion	30	392
3d Battalion	26	308
Special Units	26	238
	111	1351

501st Parachute Infantry Regiment

	O	EM
1st Battalion	24	314
2d Battalion	24	277
3d Battalion	22	275
Special Units	37	267
	107	1133

506th Parachute Infantry Regiment

	O	EM
1st Battalion	28	362
2d Battalion	30	373
3d Battalion	22	285
Special Units	32	236
	112	1256

Strength by Units[1]

	4 June 1944 O	4 June 1944 EM	16 Sept. 1944 O	16 Sept. 1944 EM	23 Dec. 1944[5] O	23 Dec. 1944 EM	14 Jan. 1945 O	14 Jan. 1945 EM
Division Headquarters and Headquarters Company	53	188	50	233	20	85	39	132
Military Police Platoon . . .	2	49	3	61	2	54	2	58
326th Airborne Engineer Battalion	35	498	39	611	39	454	36	378
326th Airborne Medical Company	21	212	23	231	8	72	4	47
101st Airborne Signal Company	9	185	10	194	7	165	7	170
426th Airborne Quartermaster Company . .	6	125	7	173	2	12	5	121
801st Airborne Ordnance Maintenance Company . . .	8	77	7	82	4	27	6	62
327th Glider Infantry Regiment (including 1st Bn. 401st Glider Infantry Regiment)	152	3027	141	2936	83	1743	83	1635
501st Parachute Infantry Regiment[2]	168	2175	172	2409	147	1903	107	1133
502d Parachute Infantry Regiment	172	2205	174	2464	135	1825	109	1290
506th Parachute Infantry Regiment[3]	173	2190	181	2429	129	1589	108	1203
101st Airborne Division Artillery Headquarters and Headquarters Battery	18	129	21	171	15	130	21	118
321st Glider Field Artillery Battalion	28	516	37	490	24	383	25	384
907th Glider Field Artillery Battalion	27	527	36	489	25	368	24	359
377th Parachute Field Artillery Battalion	45	612	50	732	34	553	36	569
463d Parachute Field Artillery Battalion[4] . . .					41	549	35	520
81st Airborne Antiaircraft Battalion	34	535	31	561	32	484	30	359
	951	13250	982	14266	747	10396	677	8538
Attachments	32	313[6]	28	103	276	3781[7]	194	3127[8]

[1]G-1 Estimates.

[2]The 501st Parachute Infantry Regiment was attached, not assigned, to the 101st Airborne Division throughout combat.

[3]The 506th Parachute Infantry Regiment was attached to the 101st Airborne Division until March 1945, then assigned.

[4]The 463d Parachute Field Artillery Battalion was attached to the 101st Airborne Division in December 1944, just before Bastogne; assigned in March 1945.

[5]These figures cover only troops at Bastogne; they do not include troops at Mourmelon or elsewhere outside the encirclement.

[6]Includes 10 officers and 254 enlisted men of the 3807 and 3808 Quartermaster Truck Companies.

[7]Includes 182 officers and 2648 enlisted men of Combat Command B, 10th Armored Division, 15 officers and 295 enlisted men of the 705th Tank Destroyer Battalion, 41 officers and 439 enlisted men of the 333d Field Artillery Group (mostly from the 969th Field Artillery Battalion), and 20 officers and 369 enlisted men of the 755th Field Artillery Battalion.

[8]Includes 141 officers and 2118 enlisted men of Combat Command B, 10th Armored Division, 23 officers and 535 enlisted men of the 705th Tank Destroyer Battalion, and 30 officers and 474 enlisted men of the 755th Field Artillery Battalion.

Airborne Songs and Poems

GORY, GORY

(Tune of "Battle Hymn of the Republic")

He was just a rookie trooper and he surely
    shook with fright
As he checked all his equipment and made
    sure his pack was tight;
He had to sit and listen to those awful
    engines roar,
    "You ain't gonna jump no more!"

Chorus

Gory, Gory, what a helluva way to die!
Gory, Gory, what a helluva way to die!
Gory, Gory, what a helluva way to die!
    And he ain't gonna jump no more.

II

"Is everybody happy?" cried the sergeant,
    looking up.
Our hero feebly answered "yes," and then
    they stood him up;
He jumped right out into the blast, his
    static line unhooked,
    And he ain't gonna jump no more.

III

He counted long, he counted loud, he
    waited for the shock,
He felt the wind, he felt the cold, he felt
    the awful drop;
He pulled reserve, the silk spilled out and
    wrapped around his sock.
    And he ain't gonna jump no more.

IV

The days he'd lived and loved and laughed
    kept running through his mind,
He thought about the girl back home, the
    one he'd left behind,
He thought about the medics and won-
    dered what they'd find,
    And he ain't gonna jump no more.

V

The ambulance was on the spot, the jeeps
    were running wild,
The medics jumped and howled with glee,
    rolled up their sleeves and smiled,
For it had been a week or more since last
    a 'chute had failed.
    And he ain't gonna jump no more.

VI

The lines were twisted round his neck, the
    connectors broke his dome,
The risers tied themselves in knots around
    each skinny bone;
The canopy became his shroud as he hurtled
    to the ground.
    And he ain't gonna jump no more.

VII

He hit the ground, the sound was "splatt,"
    the blood it spurted high.
His comrades, they were heard to say:
    "What a pretty way to die!"
He lay there rolling around in the welter of
    his gore,
    And he ain't gonna jump no more.

VIII

There was blood upon the risers, there was
    brains upon the 'chute,
Intestines were a-danglin' from his para-
    trooper suit;
They picked him up still in his 'chute and
    poured him from his boots.
    And he ain't gonna jump no more.

IX

They operated all night through but it was
    in despair,
For every bone that he possessed was ruined
    beyond repair;
And so he was buried then, his silken 'chute
    his shroud,
    And he ain't gonna jump no more.

X

They say he went to heaven and arriving
    there I'm told
He got a pair of silver boots and a para-
    chute of gold;
He may be very happy there but I'll stick
    here below,
    Cause he ain't gonna jump no more.

AUTHOR UNKNOWN.

BEAUTIFUL STREAMER

(Tune of "Beautiful Dreamer")

Beautiful streamer, open for me,
Blue skies above me and no canopy;
Counted nine thousand, waited too long,
Reached for my rip cord, the darn thing
    was gone.

Beautiful streamer, why must it be?
White silk above me is what I should see
Just like my mother that looks over me;
To hell with the rip cord, 'twas not made
    for me.

Beautiful streamer, follow me down,
Time is elapsing and here is the ground;
Six hundred feet and then I can tell
If I'll go to heaven or end up in hell.

Beautiful streamer, this is the end,
Gabriel is blowing, my body won't mend;
All you jump-happy sons of a gun,
Take this last warning as jumping's no fun.

AUTHOR UNKNOWN.

OH, HOW I HATE TO JUMP OUT OF A TRANSPORT

(Tune of "Oh, How I Hate to Get Up in the Morning").

Oh, how I hate to jump out of a transport!
Oh, how I'd love to remain on the ground!
For the hardest thing I know
Is to hear that man yell "GO!"
You gotta jump out; you gotta jump out;
You gotta jump out of the transport.

Someday I'm going to murder the jump-
master,
Someday they're going to find him dead;
And then I'll get the other pup,
The guy that takes the transport up,
And spend the rest of my life in bed.

AUTHOR UNKNOWN.

GLIDER FLIGHT

(Tune of "The Marine Corps Hymn")

We work and strain and load the plane,
We pray it's loaded right.
The ache and pain come back again,
To plague us through the night.

The bugle blows; it's dark, God knows,
Too dark to find our stuff.
The men in rows are on their toes,
But they know it's another bluff.

We eat our meal and take, not steal,
What we can find around.
We do not feel that this is real,
We doubt we'll leave the ground.

We jam aboard and praise the Lord
And pass the ammunition;
We load the cord and holler "Gawd,
Another dry-run mission."

The planes go high into the sky,
We'll glide real smooth we hope,
The channel's nigh, we hear a cry,
"It's no dry run, you dope."

PFC. TOM DUNNE.

THE GLIDER RIDERS[1]

(Tune of "Daring Young Man on the Flying Trapeze")

One day I answered the popular call,
And got in the Army to be on the ball,
An Infantry outfit, foot-soldiers and all,
Is where they put me to train.

II

They gave me my basic at Camp Claiborne,
There I was happy and never forlorn,
Till one day they split us and made us
Airborne,
But the pay was exactly the same.

Chorus

Oh! Once I was happy, but now I'm
Airborne
Riding in gliders all tattered and torn,
The pilots are daring, all caution they scorn,
And the pay is exactly the same.

III

We glide through the air in our flying
caboose,
Its actions are graceful just like a fat goose,
We hike on the pavement till our joints
come loose,
And the pay is exactly the same.

IV

Once I was infantry, now I'm a dope,
Riding gliders attached to a rope,
Safety in landing is only a hope,
And the pay is exactly the same.

V

We glide through the air in a tactical state,
Jumping is useless, it's always too late,
No 'chute for the soldier who rides in a
crate,
And the pay is exactly the same.

VI

We fight in fatigues, no fancy jump-suits,
No bright leather jackets, no polished jump
boots,
We crash-land by glider without parachutes,
And the pay is exactly the same.

---

[1]The words for this song were composed in England. . . . I had a hand in writing the song and,
as I remember it, Lt. Col. Edward Schmitt,
Division AG, Captain Noonan, Division Postal
Officer, and others I do not recall. It was almost
in the nature of a true ballad because so many
participated in its writing. The song was first
sung in the large reception room of Greenham
Lodge. As may be guessed from the tone of the
song, it was written at a time when glidermen
and parachutists wore different insignia and only
parachutists wore boots and jump suits. The
principal complaint, however, among the glidermen was that they drew no flight pay. This was
corrected later by act of Congress. After the
song was written and published copies were sent,
to my knowledge, to various Members of Congress. The song may have had a very important
part in obtaining congressional action because it
was not many months afterward that flight pay
became effective for glidermen.—TRUEMAN E.
O'QUINN

VII

We glide through the air with "Jennie" the
    jeep
Held on our laps, unable to leap,
If she breaks loose, our widows will weep,
And the pay is exactly the same.

VIII

We work in headquarters, we sit on a chair,
We figure out tactics and take to the air,
We fly over Jerry and drop in his lair,
And the pay is exactly the same.

IX

We hike and we sweat, and we load and we
    lash,
We tie it down well just in case of a crash,
We take off and land and climb out like a
    flash,
And the pay is exactly the same.

X

We glide through the air with the greatest
    of ease,
We do a good job and we try hard to please,
The Finance Department we pester and
    tease,
But the pay is exactly the same.

PURPLE HEART LANE

We drink to the men so bronzed and tan,
Who marched down the road to Carentan.
They were the ones who so long had to
    train,
To fight this battle of Purple Heart Lane.
Yes, this is that road stretched 'cross the
    plain,
This piece of macadam called Purple Heart
    Lane.

Why was it called this you want to know?
Well, Jerry was there to give us his show.
He had mortars, machine-guns and 88s too,
With plenty of armor to back up this crew.
Then there were snipers whom we could
    not see,
They kept firing at us, my buddies and me.

We had laughed at crawling, keeping close
    to the ground,
But we did it and liked it, right up into
    town.
Then came the charge that led to their guns,
Invincible, they said, and they weren't far
    wrong,
But we made them sing another sort of a
    song.

The long battle over, we trudged up the
    hill,
There we paused to look back at our
    comrades so still.
We think of the boys, who died not in vain,
Our pals, yes, the heroes of Purple Heart
    Lane.

R. D. CREAD and
R. H. BYRANT, 502d PIR.

SAGA OF HELL'S HIGHWAY

Ole Trotter[2] jumped down from his jeep
    with a bound,
    Having beaten Hell's Highway from
        Uden to Zon,
And told all the men in his words most
    profound
    That devilish road to be free—safe and
        sound.
So onto that Highway the Service men
    rolled,
    Their twenty-two trucks whining shrilly
        in gear,
And shoved and then swore at the mud and
    the cold
    As the convoy contrived to take definite
        mould.
From Zon on to Oedenrode, all is too well—
    The trucks are all here, Limey traffic's
        not bad.
From Oedenrode on, (it is needless to tell)
    To Halo's dark corridor rolling like hell.

But the leader swerves o'er at the shock of
    blast.
    Trucks scream to a halt, and skilled
        drivers dismount.
All vault into holes as Hun bullets zing
    past,
    And Jerry siegs, "Heil, we have got 'em
        at last!"

Now they're giving the Limeys a bit of a
    shell
    Just ahead of the Yanks, but they're
        working south fast,
The mortars are coughing and eighty-eights
    yell
    As Schmeissers start burping the Kid-
        nappers' knell.

The question which tears through the
    fevered Yank brain
    As he sits in his hole at the side of the
        road,
Is whether to let the Hun seize the whole
    train
    Or try to get out from his bulleting rain.

---

[2] Warrant Officer (later Lt.) Stanley E. Trotter,
Service Co., 506th PIR.

The answer is easy, so up out of holes
  Come twenty-two drivers, (the sharpest
    connivers
Who ever slip out from the Jerry's square
    nose),
  And up to the cabs of their trucks they
    arose.

Their trailers are dropped mid a deafening
    roar,
  As trucks faced south with a clashing of
    gears,
Dropt trailers re-hooked, and then off as
    before
  Leaving Jerry, no doubt, plenty god-awful
    sore.

But Jerry, made angry, forced tanks to the
    fray
  And caught two Kidnappers before they
    could scram
With the rest of the men on that hellish
    macadam
  But completed the turn to Heinies'
    dismay.

For Trotter (the b———) who came down
    to tell
  That roads all were open along that hot
    line,
Those drivers have chosen a place close
    to hell—
  With friends of that sort they decline
    long to dwell.

  GEORGE L. BARTON III, 506th PIR.

COMMENDATION

The following named officers and enlisted
men of the 506th Parachute Infantry are
commended for meritorious service in action. On 26 September 1944, in Holland,
their supply convoy of twenty-two vehicles
was halted by enemy fire from both flanks,
forcing all personnel to seek cover by the
roadside. All movement was restricted by
enemy small arms fire. Enemy artillery fire
began destroying vehicles forward of the
convoy. Immediate appraisal of the situation
prompted these men to leave their protective cover, return to their vehicles, turn
them around, and take them to safety. As
a result of these actions, twenty of the
twenty-two vehicles were saved. The remaining two were cut off by enemy tanks
and destroyed.

Captain George L. Barton III, 2d Lieut.
John C. Garvey, T/5 Paul A. Metz, PFCs
Foster M. Bateman, Max R. Bulger, Marijan
Derencin, John I. Fadrosh, Joseph A. Gorick,
Ephraim E. Kreitzer, George Reppert, Jr.,

Howard E. Rogers, Michael Scaprino, Wil-
mer C. Strahl, William Turberville. Pvts.
Webster P. Bailey, Steve J. Barney, James
D. Deist, Edward De Palma, Frank Harin,
Howard Heaberling, Warren E. Henry,
Donald Lancaster, William D. Sherron,
Edward Southworth, and Luther Turner.

  By Command of
  Major General TAYLOR.

GERONIMO IS DEAD

This is the beautiful land he played a lead-
    ing role in liberating,
The once quiet, peaceful land of Holland.
Its orchards are scarred and injured;
Most of its neat little homes lie as only
    crumpled brick;
The smooth farmland over which his little
    Geronimos moved on toward Arnhem
Lies flooded.

His body lies far below the heights he
    lived in;
For Geronimo was king of the paratroopers;
None hit the silk as he.

This was not his first invasion, but it was
    his last.
He could have stayed in some other place,
    but it's more peaceful where he now
    lies.

One hundred and thirty odd times he'd felt
    the cold chill of the prop—
Never again for him.
Colonel Johnson's parachute days are
    through.

Lean, tough paratroopers of his Geronimo
    band stand at attention amid the cold
    grey crosses.
Death to them was no stranger—
Yet burial was.
So that's what they do with the ones that
    fall, we thought they just lay where
    they fell.
Farther in the field grey soldiers of another
    army stand as ghosts to mock the dead.
They are the PWs, the grave-diggers,
Who must love their job.

He shouldn't be lonesome here.
He has so much company, acres and acres,
    beneath the damp cold earth.
They should understand his faint whispers,
    men of the '101st and 82d Airborne.
Yet somehow he looks lonesome.

The Chaplain has said his word, the volley
    is fired, the generals file past his grave.
Now the three ranks file off slowly.

They pass among the rows, careful not to
· disturb the sleeping:
Case, Baldwin, Serawatka, Kane, Parrish,
McMorries;
Each pauses at his grave, gazes in at the
camouflaged parachute the king sleeps
in.
It looks cold down there, wonder if he'll
keep warm.
Slowly the moving-picture camera clicks
away, recording the procedure;
But never could it record the feelings of
the tough men who pass the grave.
No pity, no tears.
They had lived too long for that, saw death
too often,
Three of the men who pass that way, their
guns have killed over thirty in one day.

Somehow it's wrong.
Maybe a year ago it would have been easy
to figure;
But now it's too late, you only know that
as soon as the last man of the honor
guard files past you will go back to the
line and the only life you do under-
stand, war.
No, he is not going back.
Propeller blasts have died away.
His parachute days are through.
Yes, there will be a telegram;
Oh! but if she only knew.
The sun is getting lower, the words they
speak are few,
Yet each trooper's thought lingers on
Geronimo,
King of the parachute crew.

"TEX," Co. G, 501st PIR².

TONY McAULIFFE'S ANSWER

You can have your famous backtalk—
All those famous cries of yore,
Which a nation's toughest scrappers
Hurled to any foe in war;
But for "cracks" enshrined in story
By our men most famed for "guts,"
Gimme Tony C. McAuliffe's
Classic, candid answer, "Nuts!"

From the fighting men of Breeds Hill,
Mystic town or Concord Bridge,
Gettysburg, Atlanta, Shiloh,
To the World War's Bloody Ridge
Have come phrases with the wallop
Of a blow from rifle butts;
As for me I'll make the payoff
On McAuliffe's one word: "Nuts!"

²"You are welcome to it, sign it Tex or something."

"Fight it on this line all summer" . . .
"Damn torpedoes! Speed ahead!" . . .
"I have just begun to fight!" . . . How
These have glorified our dead!
"Till you see the whites of eyes" once
Rang out with scorn that sears and cuts,
But I like that guy McAuliffe
And his snappy answer "Nuts."

"You may fire when you're ready" . . .
"Up and at 'em!" . . . "Give 'em hell!"
"Stand or die" and "Give no quarter!" . . .
These were cries that rang the bell;
But for answers clear and final,
Like an iron door that shuts,
I will string with T. McAuliffe's
Simple, all-out slogan—"NUTS!"

H. I. PHILLIPS.

NUTS! OF McAULIFFE AND HIS PARATROOPERS

*(This is a translation of the poem
on page 588)*

Followed by his bands of killers,
The Boche has returned to the heart of the
Ardennes.
Villages are aflame. The snow of the plains
Is stained by the sinister glimmer of burn-
ing towns.

His face is contorted with an idiot grin
Of the brute who slobbers for the next feast.
He encircles Bastogne, and full of an ob-
scene pride
Thinks that she will fall without fighting,
without honor.

For his order calls upon the besieged
soldiers
Who, outnumbered ten to one, are fighting
like madmen, to surrender or to die.
McAuliffe says "Nuts!" Von Rundstedt
pales under the affront.
In his flight he leaves behind him only
ruins.
The one will enter History; the other goes
to Oblivion.

POEM

We have only died in vain if you believe so;
You must decide the wisdom of our
choice
By the world which you shall build upon
our headstones
And the everlasting truths which have
your voice.

Though dead, we are not heroes yet, nor
can be,
Till the living by their lives which are
the tools,
Carve us the epitaphs of wise men
And give us not the epitaphs of fools.

DAVID J. PHILLIPS, 506th PIR.

THE HILLS OF BASTOGNE

The crops should be full in Belgium next
year,
The soil should be fertile, but the price
has been dear.
The wheat should be red on the hills of
Bastogne
For its roots have been drenched by the
blood of our own.

Battered and reeling we stand in their way,
Embittered, wrathful, we watch our pals
fall,
God where's the end, the end of it all?

Confident and powerful they strike at our
lines,
But we beat them back—fighting for
time.
Berserk with fury they are hitting us now
. Flesh against steel. We'll hold—but how?
For each day that we stay more mothers
will grieve
For each hill that we hold more men
must we leave.
Yes, honor the men who will some day
come home,
But pray for the men 'neath the hills of
Bastogne.

BERNARD J. MCKEARNEY, 502d PIR.

Abbreviations

AAA	Antiaircraft artillery
AA–AT	Antiaircraft-antitank
AP	Armor-piercing
APO	Army post office (the 101st had APO 472)
BAR	Browning automatic rifle
Bn	Battalion
CO, CG	Commanding officer, commanding general
CP	Command post
CT, RCT	Combat team, regimental combat team
DP	Displaced person
DZ	Drop zone (parachute)
FO	Forward observer (artillery)
G–1, S–1	Personnel officer or adjutant
G–2, S–2	Intelligence officer
G–3, S–3	Operations officer
G–4, S–4	Supply officer
GIR	Glider infantry regiment
HE	High-explosive (artillery ammunition)
KIA	Killed in action
LD	Line of departure
LCI	Landing craft, infantry
LSI	Landing ship, infantry
LST	Landing ship, tank
LZ	Landing zone (glider)
MG	Machine gun
ML, MLR	Main line, main line of resistance
mm	Millimeter
OP, OPL, OPLR	Outpost, outpost line, outpost line of resistance
PIR	Parachute infantry regiment
POW, PW	Prisoner of war
PZ, PZG	Panzer, panzergrenadier
SCR	Signal corps radio
SP	Self-propelled (gun)
SS, SA	German storm troops
TD	Tank destroyer (self-propelled antitank gun)
TO	Table of organization
VG	Volksgrenadier

Times in this history are given in the 24-hour system used by the armed forces during World War II. One minute after midnight (12.01 A. M.) is 0001, and one minute before midnight (11:59 P.M.) is 2359. Noon is 1200.